Tobias George Smollett

**History of England from the revolution to the death of George the Second**

Tobias George Smollett

**History of England from the revolution to the death of George the Second**

ISBN/EAN: 9783742839039

Manufactured in Europe, USA, Canada, Australia, Japa

Cover: Foto ©ninafisch / pixelio.de

Manufactured and distributed by brebook publishing software (www.brebook.com)

Tobias George Smollett

# History of England from the revolution to the death of George the Second

# THE HISTORY OF ENGLAND,

FROM

THE REVOLUTION

TO THE

DEATH OF GEORGE THE SECOND.

DESIGNED AS

A CONTINUATION OF MR. HUME'S HISTORY.

BY T. SMOLLETT, M.D.

A NEW EDITION,

WITH THE AUTHOR'S LAST CORRECTIONS AND IMPROVEMENTS.

IN THREE VOLUMES.
VOL. II.

LONDON:

LONGMAN, GREEN, LONGMAN, ROBERTS, AND GREEN; HATCHARD AND CO.; S. BAGSTER AND SONS; J. AND F. H. RIVINGTON; HAMILTON AND CO.; SIMPKIN, MARSHALL, AND CO.; W. H. ALLEN AND CO.; WHITTAKER AND CO.; E. HODGSON; E. BUMPUS; J. BAIN; SMITH, ELDER, AND CO.; A. C. CAPES; J. HEARNE; W. MORRISH AND SON; T. AND W. BOONE; BICKERS AND SON; WILLIS AND SOTHERAN; J. SNOW; L. BOOTH; J. WALLER; M. COOMBS; TEGG AND CO.; VIRTUE BROTHERS AND CO.; ARTHUR HALL AND CO.; J. CORNISH; E. F. WILLIAMS; AND BRIGHTON, BELL, AND CO.; AND MACMILLAN AND CO., CAMBRIDGE: AND J. H. PARKER, OXFORD.

1864.

# CONTENTS OF VOL. II.

## CHAPTER XIII.

### GEORGE I.

Difference between King George and the Czar of Muscovy. — The King of Sweden is killed at Frederickstadt. — Negotiation for a quadruple Alliance. — Proceedings in Parliament. — James Shepherd executed for a Design against the King's Life. — Parliament prorogued. — Nature of the quadruple Alliance. — Admiral Byng sails to the Mediterranean. — He destroys the Spanish Fleet off Cape Passaro. — Remonstrances of the Spanish Ministry. — Disputes in Parliament touching the Admiral's attacking the Spanish Fleet. — Act for strengthening the Protestant Interest. — War declared against Spain. — Conspiracy against the Regent of France. — Intended Invasion by the Duke of Ormond. — Three Hundred Spaniards land and are taken in Scotland. — Account of the Peerage Bill. — Count Merci assumes the Command of the Imperial Army in Sicily. — Activity of Admiral Byng. — The Spanish Troops evacuate Sicily. — Philip obliged to accede to the quadruple Alliance. — Bill for securing the Dependency of Ireland upon the Crown of Great Britain. — South-Sea Act. — Charters granted to the Royal and London Assurance Offices. — Treaty of Alliance with Sweden. — The Prince of Hesse elected King of Sweden. — Effects of the South-Sea Scheme. — The Bubble breaks. — A Secret Committee appointed by the House of Commons. — Inquiry carried on by both Houses. — Death of Earl Stanhope and Mr. Craggs, both Secretaries of State. — The Estates of the Directors of the South-Sea Company are confiscated. — Proceedings of the Commons with respect to the Stock of the South-Sea Company .. .. .. .. .. .. .. .. .. .. .. Page 1

## CHAPTER XIV.

Bill against Atheism and Immorality postponed. — Session closed. — Alliance between Great Britain, France, and Spain. — Plague at Marseilles. — Debates in the House of Lords about Mr. Law, the Projector. — Sentiments of some Lords touching the War with Spain. — Petition of the Quakers. — The Parliament dissolved. — Rumours of a Conspiracy. — The Bishop of Rochester is committed to the Tower. — New Parliament. — Declaration of the Pretender. — Report of the Secret Committee. — Bill of Pains and Penalties against the Bishop of Rochester — Who is deprived, and driven into perpetual Exile. — Proceedings against those concerned in the Lottery at Harburgh. — Affairs of the Continent. — Clamour in Ireland on Account of Wood's Coinage. — Death of the Duke of Orleans. — An Act for lessening the Public Debts. — Philip, King of Spain, abdicates the Throne. — Abuses in Chancery. — Trial of the Earl of Macclesfield. — Debates about the Debts of the Civil List. — A Bill in Favour of the late Lord Bolingbroke. — Treaty of Alliance between the Courts of Vienna and Madrid. — Treaty of Hanover. —

Approved in Parliament. — Riots in Scotland on account of the Malt-Tax. — A small Squadron sent to the Baltic. — Admiral Hosier's Expedition to the West Indies. — Disgrace of the Duke de Ripperda. — Substance of the King's Speech to Parliament. — Debate in the House of Lords upon the approaching Rupture with the Emperor and Spain. — Memorial of Mr. Palms, the Imperial Resident at London. — Conventions with Sweden and Hesse-Cassel. — Vote of Credit. — Siege of Gibraltar by the Spaniards. — Preliminaries of Peace. — Death and Character of George I., King of Great Britain .. .. .. .. .. .. .. .. Page 42

## CHAPTER XV.

### GEORGE II.

George II. ascends the Throne of Great Britain. — Characters of the principal Persons concerned in the Ministry. — Debates in Parliament concerning the Civil List. — Changes and Promotions. — New Parliament. — Violent Dispute concerning the national Debt. — Vote of Credit. — A double Marriage between the Houses of Spain and Portugal. — Liberality of the Commons. — Debates on the subsidies of Hesse-Cassel and Wolfenbuttel. — Committee for inspecting the Gaols. — Address touching the Spanish Depredations. — A Sum voted to the King on account of Arrears due on the Civil-List Revenue. — Proceedings in the House of Lords. — Wise Conduct of the Irish Parliament. — Abdication of the King of Sardinia. — Death of Pope Benedict XIII. — Substance of the King's Speech to both Houses. — Objections to the Treaty of Sevillo in the House of Lords. — Opposition in the Lower House to a standing Army. — Bill prohibiting Loans to foreign Princes or States. — Charter of the East India Company prolonged. — The Emperor resents the Treaty of Sevillo. — Seven Indian Chiefs arrive in England. — Revolution at Constantinople. — England infested with Robbers, Assassins, and Incendiaries. — Bill against Pensioners sitting as Members in the House of Commons. — Treaty of Vienna. — Death of the Duke of Parma. — Don Carlos takes possession of his Territories. — France distracted by religious Disputes. — The Ministry violently opposed in Parliament. — Debate on a standing Army. — Account of the Charitable Corporation. — Revival of the Salt-Tax. — Mr. Pulteney's Name struck out of the List of Privy-Councillors. — The King sets out for Hanover .. .. 81

## CHAPTER XVI.

Remarkable instance of Suicide. — Affairs of the Continent. — Meeting of the Parliament. — Address to the King touching the Spanish Depredations. — The Excise Scheme proposed by Sir Robert Walpole. — Opposition to the Scheme. — Bill for a Dower to the Princess Royal. — Debates in the House of Lords concerning the Estates of the late Directors of the South-Sea Company. — Double Election of a King in Poland. — The Kings of France, Spain, and Sardinia join against the Emperor. — The Prince of Orange arrives in England. — Altercation in the House of Commons. — Debate about the Removal of the Duke of Bolton and Lord Viscount Cobham from their respective Regiments. — Motion for the Repeal of the Septennial Act. — Conclusion of a remarkable Speech by Sir W. Wyndham. — Message from the King for Powers to augment the Forces in the Intervals between the two Parliaments. — Opposition in the House of Peers. — Parliament dissolved. — Dantzic besieged by the Russians. — Philipsburgh taken by the French. — Don Carlos takes Possession of Naples. — Battle of Parma. — The Imperialists are again worsted at Guastalla. — An Edict in France compelling the

# CONTENTS OF VOL. II.

British Subjects in that Kingdom to enlist in the French Army. — New Parliament in Great Britain. — Debate on a Subsidy to Denmark. — Petition of some Scottish Noblemen to the House of Peers. — Bill explaining an Act of the Scottish Parliament touching wrongous Imprisonment. — Misunderstanding between the Courts of Spain and Portugal. — Sir John Norris sails with a strong Squadron to Lisbon. — Preliminaries signed by the Emperor and the King of France. — Proceedings in Parliament. — Bill for preventing the Retail of Spirituous Liquors. — Another for the Relief of Quakers in the Article of Tithes. — Mortmain Act. — Remarkable Riot at Edinburgh. — Rupture between the Czarina and the Ottoman Porte. — The Session of Parliament opened by Commission. — Motion in both Houses for a Settlement on the Prince of Wales. — Fierce Debate on this Subject. — Scheme by Sir John Barnard for reducing the Interest of the National Debt. — Bill against the City of Edinburgh. — Playhouse Bill .. .. .. .. .. .. Page 123

## CHAPTER XVII.

The Russians take Oczakow. — Death of Gaston de Medicis, Duke of Tuscany. — Death of Caroline, Queen Consort of England. — Dispute in Parliament about the standing Army. — Spanish Depredations. — Motives of the Minister for avoiding a War. — Address to the King on the Subject of the Depredations. — Bill for securing the Trade of his Majesty's Subjects in America. — Debates in the House of Lords. — Birth of Prince George. — Admiral Haddock sails with a Squadron to the Mediterranean. — Progress of the War against the Turks. — Disputes and Rupture between Hanover and Denmark. — Sir Robert Walpole extols the Convention in the House of Commons. — Motion for an Address, that the Representations, Letters, &c., relating to the Spanish Depredations should be laid before the House. — Petitions against the Convention. — Substance of that Agreement. — Debate in the House of Commons on the Convention. — Secession of the chief Members in the Opposition. — Debate in the House of Lords upon an Address to his Majesty touching the Convention. — Message from the Throne touching a Subsidy to Denmark, and a Power to augment the Forces of the Kingdom. — Parliament prorogued. — The King of Spain publishes a Manifesto. — The Emperor and Czarina conclude a Peace with the Turks. — Preparations for War in England. — Apology in the House of Commons for the seceding Members. — Pension Bill revived and lost. — Portobello taken by Admiral Vernon. — Hard Frost. — Marriage of the Princess Mary to the Prince of Hesse. — Strong Armament sent to the West Indies. — Death of the Emperor and Czarina. — Proceedings in Parliament. — Seamen's Bill. — Discontents against the Ministry. — Motion for removing Sir Robert Walpole from his Majesty's Councils and Presence for ever. — Debate on the Mutiny Bill. — Proceedings in the House of Lords. — Close of the last Session of this Parliament .. .. .. .. .. .. .. .. .. .. .. 170

## CHAPTER XVIII.

The Army under Lord Cathcart and Sir Chaloner Ogle proceeds to the West Indies. — Nature of the Climate on the Spanish Main. — Admiral Vernon sails to Carthagena. — Attack of Fort Lazar. — Expedition to Cuba. — Rupture between the Queen of Hungary and the King of Prussia. — Battle of Molwitz. — The King of Great Britain concludes a Treaty of Neutrality with France for the Electorate of Hanover. — A body of French Forces joins the Elector of Bavaria. — He is crowned King of Bohemia at Prague. — Fidelity of the Hungarians. — War between Russia and Sweden. — Revolution in Russia. — The Spanish and French

Squadrons pass unmolested by the English Admiral in the Mediterranean.—Inactivity of the naval Power of Great Britain.—Obstinate Struggle in electing Members in the new Parliament.—Remarkable Motion in the House of Commons by Lord Noel Somerset.—The Country Party obtain a Majority in the House of Commons.—Sir Robert Walpole created Earl of Orford.—Change in the Ministry.—Inquiry into the Administration of Sir Robert Walpole.—Obstructed by the new Ministry.—Reports of the Secret Committee.—The Elector of Bavaria chosen Emperor.—The King of Prussia gains the Battle of Czaslau.—Treaty at Breslau.—The French Troops retire under the Cannon of Prague.—A fresh Body sent with the Mareschal de Maillebois to bring them off.—Extraordinary Retreat of M. de Belleisle.—The King of Great Britain forms an Army in Flanders.—Progress of the War between Russia and Sweden.—The King of Sardinia declares for the House of Austria.—Motions of the Spaniards in Italy and Savoy.—Conduct of Admiral Matthews in the Mediterranean.—Operations in the West Indies.—The Attention of the Ministry turned chiefly on the Affairs of the Continent.—Extraordinary Motion in the House of Lords by Earl Stanhope.—Warm and obstinate Debate on the Repeal of the Gin Act.—Bill for quieting Corporations.—Convention between the Emperor and the Queen of Hungary.—Difference between the King of Prussia and the Elector of Hanover.—The King of Great Britain obtains a Victory over the French at Dettingen.—Treaty of Worms.—Conclusion of the Campaign.—Affairs in the North.—Battle of Campo-Santo.—Transactions of the British Fleet in the Mediterranean.—Unsuccessful Attempts upon the Spanish Settlements in the West Indies .. .. .. .. Page 211

## CHAPTER XIX.

Debate in Parliament against the Hanoverian Troops.—Supplies granted.—Projected Invasion of Great Britain.—A French Squadron sails up the English Channel.—The Kingdom is put in a Posture of Defence.—The Design of the French defeated.—War between France and England.—Bill against those who should correspond with the Sons of the Pretender.—Naval Engagement off Toulon.—Advances towards Peace made by the Emperor.—Treaty of Frankfort.—Progress of the French King in the Netherlands.—Prince Charles of Lorraine passes the Rhine.—The King of Prussia makes an Irruption into Bohemia.—Campaign in Bavaria and Flanders.—The King of Naples joins Count Gages in Italy.—Battle of Coni.—Return of Commodore Anson.—Sir John Balchen perishes at Sea.—Revolution in the British Ministry.—Session of Parliament.—Death of the Emperor Charles VII.—Accommodation between the Queen of Hungary and the young Elector of Bavaria.—The King of Prussia gains two successive Battles at Friedberg and Sohr, over the Austrian and Saxon Forces.—Treaty of Dresden.—The Grand Duke of Tuscany elected Emperor of Germany.—The Allies are defeated at Fontenoy.—The King of Sardinia is almost stripped of his Dominions.—The English Forces take Cape Breton.—The importance of this Conquest.—Project of an Insurrection in Great Britain.—The eldest Son of the Chevalier de St. George lands in Scotland.—Takes Possession of Edinburgh.—Defeats Sir John Cope at Preston Pans.—Efforts of the Friends of Government in Scotland.—Precautions taken in England.—The Prince Pretender reduces Carlisle, and penetrates as far as Derby.—Consternation of the Londoners.—The Rebels retreat into Scotland.—They invest the Castle of Stirling.—The King's Troops under Hawley are worsted at Falkirk.—The Duke of Cumberland assumes the command of the Forces in Scotland.—The Rebels undertake the Siege of Fort William .. .. .. .. .. .. 261

## CHAPTER XX.

The Rebels are totally defeated at Culloden. — The Duke of Cumberland takes Possession of Inverness, and afterwards encamps at Fort Augustus. — The Prince Pretender escapes to France. — Convulsion in the Ministry. — Liberality of the Commons. — Trial of the Rebels. — Kilmarnock, Balmerino, Lovat, and Mr. Ratcliffe, are beheaded on Tower-Hill. — The States-General alarmed at the progress of the French in the Netherlands. — Count Saxe subdues all Flanders, Brabant, and Hainault. — Reduces the strong Fortress of Namur, and defeats the allied Army at Roucoux. — The French and Spaniards are compelled to abandon Piedmont and the Milanese. — Don Philip is worsted at Codogno, and afterwards at Porto Freddo. — The Austrians take possession of Genoa. — Count Brown penetrates into Provence. — The Genoese expel the Austrians from their City. — Madras in the East Indies taken by the French. — Expedition to the coast of Bretagne, and Attempt upon Port L'Orient. — Naval Transactions in the West Indies. — Conferences at Breda. — Vast Supplies granted by the Commons of England. — Parliament dissolved. — The French and Allies take the Field in Flanders. — The Prince of Orange elected Stadtholder, Captain-General, and Admiral of the United Provinces. — The Confederates defeated at Laffeldt. — Siege of Bergen-op-Zoom. — The Austrians undertake the Siege of Genoa, which, however, they abandon. — The Chevalier de Belleisle slain in the Attack of Exiles. — A French Squadron defeated and taken by the Admirals Anson and Warren. — Admiral Hawke obtains another Victory over the French at Sea. — Other naval Transactions. — Congress at Aix-la-Chapelle. — Compliant Temper of the new Parliament. — Preliminaries signed. — Preparations for the Campaign in the Netherlands. — Siege of Maestricht. — Cessation of Arms. — Transactions in the East and West Indies. — Conclusion of the definitive Treaty at Aix-la-Chapelle .. .. .. .. .. .. .. .. .. .. .. .. .. Page 309

## CHAPTER XXI.

Reflections on the Peace. — The Prince of Wales's Adherents join the Opposition. — Character of the Ministry. — Session opened. — Debate on the Address. — Supplies granted. — Exorbitant Demand of the Empress-Queen opposed. — Violent Contest concerning the Seamen's Bill. — Objections to the Mutiny Bill. — Bill for limiting the Term of a Soldier's Service. — Measures taken with respect to the African Trade. — Scheme for improving the British Fishery. — Attempt to open the Commerce to Hudson's Bay. — Plan for manning the Navy. — Fruitless Motions made by the Opposition. — Severities exercised upon some Students at Oxford. — Duke of Newcastle chosen Chancellor of the University of Cambridge. — Tumults in different Parts of the Kingdom. — Scheme for a Settlement in Nova Scotia. — Town of Halifax founded. — French Attempt to settle the Island of Tobago. — Rejoicings for the Peace of Aix-la-Chapelle. — Pretender's eldest Son arrested at Paris. — Appearance of a Rupture between Russia and Sweden. — Interposition of the King of Prussia. — Measures taken by the French Ministry. — Conduct of the different European Powers. — Insolence of the Barbary Corsairs. — Disturbances in England. — Session opened. — Subjects of Debate. — Scheme for reducing the Interest of the National Debt. — Act passed for that Purpose. — New Mutiny Bill. — Bill for encouraging the Importation of Iron from America. — Erection of the British Herring Fishery. — New African Company. — Westminster Election. —

Earthquakes in London. — Pestilential Fever at the Session in the Old Bailey. — Disputes between Russia and Sweden. — Plan for electing the Archduke Joseph King of the Romans. — Opposition of the King of Prussia. — Disputes with the French about the Limits of Nova Scotia. — Treaty with Spain. — Session opened. — Debate on the Address. — Supplies granted. — Death and Character of the Prince of Wales. — Settlement of a Regency, in Case of a minor Sovereign. — General Naturalization Bill. — Censure passed upon a Paper entitled Constitutional Queries. — Proceedings of the Commons on the Westminster Election. — Mr. Murray sent Prisoner to Newgate. — Session closed. — Style altered .. Page 353

## CHAPTER XXII.

Death of the Queen of Denmark and Prince of Orange. — Misunderstanding between the Czarina and King of Prussia. — Measures for electing a King of the Romans. — Death of the King of Sweden. — Session opened. — Animosity of the Commons towards Mr. Murray. — Proceedings upon a Pamphlet entitled the Case of Mr. Murray. — Supplies granted. — Civil Regulations. — Law relating to the forfeited Estates in Scotland. — New Consolidations of Funds. — Two Ports opened for the Importation of Irish Wool. — The King sets out for Hanover. — Affairs of the Continent. — Dispute between Hanover and Prussia, concerning East Friezeland. — Misunderstanding between the Courts of London and Berlin. — Improvement of Pomerania. — Treaty with the Elector Palatine. — Session opened. — Supplies granted. — Game Act. — Act for performing Quarantine — and for preventing the plundering of shipwrecked Vessels. — Bill relating to the Bounty on Corn exported. — Turkey Trade laid open. — Naturalization of the Jews. — Marriage Act. — Deliberations concerning the Sugar Colonies. — Fate of the Register Bill. — Sir Hans Sloane's Museum purchased by Parliament. — Story of Elizabeth Canning. — Execution of Dr. Cameron. — Tumults in different Parts of the Kingdom. — Disturbances in France. — Proceedings of the Diet relative to East Friezeland. — Treaty between the Court of Vienna and the Duke of Modena. — Conferences with respect to Nova Scotia broken up. — Description of Nova Scotia. — Disputes concerning its Limits .. 419

## CHAPTER XXIII.

Ambitious Schemes of the French in North America. — Rise and Conduct of the Ohio Company. — Letter from the Governor of Virginia to the French Commander at Rivière-au-Bœuf. — Perfidious Practices of the French in Nova Scotia. — Major Laurence defeats the French Neutrals. — British Ambassador at Paris amused with general Promises. — Session opened. — Supplies granted. — Repeal of the Act for naturalizing Jews. — Motion for repealing a former Act favourable to the Jews. — East India Mutiny-Bill. — Case of Le ——. — Session closed. — Death of Mr. Pelham. — Change in the Ministry. — New Parliament assembled and prorogued. — Disputes in the Irish Parliament. — Transactions in the East Indies. — Account of the English Settlements on the Malabar and Coromandel Coasts. — Dispute about the Government of Arcot. — Mahommed Ali Khan supported by the English. — Mr. Clive takes Arcot — And defeats the Enemy in the plains of Arani, and at Koveripauk. — He reduces three Forts, and takes M. d'Anteuil. — Chunda Saib taken and put to Death, and his Army routed. — Convention between the East India Companies of England and France. — General View of the British Colonies

in North America. — New England and New York. — New Jersey. — Pennsylvania. — Maryland. — Virginia. — The two Carolinas. — Georgia. — The French surprise Logs Town, on the Ohio. — Conference with the Indians at Albany. — Colonel Washington defeated and taken by the French on the Ohio. — Divisions among the British Colonies. — The hereditary Prince of Hesse-Cassel professes the Roman Catholic Religion. — Parliament of Paris recalled from Exile. — Affairs of Spain and Portugal. — Session opened. — Supplies granted. — Bill in behalf of Chelsea Pensioners. — Oxfordshire Election. — Message from the King to the House of Commons. — Court of Versailles amuses the English Ministry. — Session closed.
Page 462

## CHAPTER XXIV.

Preparations for War. — Earl Paulet's Motion against the King's going to Hanover. — Regency appointed during his Majesty's Absence. — Boscawen's Expedition. — The Alcide and Lys taken. — French Ambassador recalled. — Their Trade greatly distressed. — Affairs of the English in America. — Colonel Monckton takes Beausejour. — General Braddock's unfortunate Expedition. — He falls into an Ambuscade; is defeated and killed. — Disagreement between the Governor and Assembly of Pennsylvania. — Expedition against Crown-Point and Niagara resolved on. — General Johnson encamps at Lake George — Where he is attacked by the French, who are entirely defeated. — Bravery of Captain M'Ginnes. — General Johnson created a Baronet. — Description of Fort Oswego and Lake Ontario. — Neglect of the English in not fortifying it. — Expedition against Niagara. — General Shirley returns to Albany. — End of the Campaign in America. — Fruitless Intrigues of the French in Spain and Germany. — Treaty of the King of Great Britain with the Landgrave of Hesse-Cassel. — News of the Capture of the Alcide and Lys reaches England. — The King returns from Hanover, and concludes a Treaty with Russia. — Declaration of the French Ministry at the Court of Vienna. — Spirited Declaration of the King of Prussia. — The French make another unsuccessful Attempt upon the Court of Spain. — The Imperial Court refuses Auxiliaries to England. — The French take the Blandford Man of War, but return it. — State of the English and French Navies. — Session opened. — Remarkable Addresses of the Lords and Commons. — His Majesty's Answer. — Alterations in the Ministry. — Mr. Fox made Secretary of State. — Supplies voted. — Earthquake at Lisbon. — Relief voted by Parliament to the Portuguese. — Troops, &c., voted. — Mutiny Bill, Marine, and Mariners' Acts continued. — Act for raising a Regiment of Foot in North America. — Maritime Laws of England extended to America. — Quiet of Ireland restored. — Treaty concluded with Prussia. — New Militia Bill passed by the Commons, but rejected by the Lords. — Session closed .. .. .. .. 511

## CHAPTER XXV.

Letter from M. Rouillé to the Secretary of State. — The two Nations recriminate on each other. — The French threaten Great Britain with an invasion. — Requisition of Six Thousand Dutch Troops according to Treaty. — Message from the King to the Parliament. — A Body of Hessians and Hanoverians transported into England. — French Preparations at Toulon. — Admiral Byng sails for the Mediterranean. — He arrives at Gibraltar. — Engages M. de la Galissonnière off Minorca — and returns to Gibraltar. — Ferment of the People at Home. — Admiral Byng superseded, and sent Home Prisoner. — Account of the Siege of St. Philip's Fort, in Minorca. — Precautions taken by General Blakeney. — Siege commenced. —

English Squadron appears. — General Attack of the Works. — The Garrison capitulates. — Sir Edward Hawke sails to Minorca. — Rejoicings in France, and Clamours in England. — Gallantry of Fortunatus Wright. — General Blakeney created a Baron. — Measures taken for the Defence of Great Britain. — Proclamation. — Earl of Loudoun appointed Commander-in-Chief in America. — His Britannic Majesty's Declaration of War. — Substance of the French King's Declaration. — Address of the City of London. — Trial of General Fowke. — Affairs of America. — Colonel Bradstreet defeats a Body of French on the River Onondaga. — Earl of Loudoun arrives at New York. — Oswego reduced by the Enemy. — Further proceedings in America. — Naval Operations in that Country. — Transactions in the East Indies. — Calcutta besieged by the Viceroy of Bengal. — Deplorable Fate of those who perished in the Dungeon there. — Additional Cruelties exercised on Mr. Holwell. — Resolution against Angria. — Fort of Geria taken by Admiral Watson and Mr. Clive. — Their subsequent Proceedings in the River Ganges .. .. .. .. .. .. .. .. .. .. .. .. Page 551

## CHAPTER XXVI.

Motives of the War in Germany. — Conspiracy in Sweden. — Measures taken by the King of Prussia and Elector of Hanover. — Endeavours of the Court of Vienna to frustrate them. — His Prussian Majesty demands an Explanation from the Empress-Queen. — Her Answer. — The Prussian Army enters Saxony, and publishes a Manifesto. — Prince Ferdinand takes Leipsic. — King of Prussia takes possession of Dresden, and blocks up the King of Poland at Pirna. — Prussian Army penetrates into Bohemia, and fights the Battle of Lowoschntz. — Saxon Army surrenders. — King of Poland's Memorial to the States-General. — Imperial Decrees published against the King of Prussia. — Declarations of different Powers. — His Prussian Majesty's Answer to the Saxon Memorial — And Justification of his Conduct. — Remarks on both those Pieces. — Disputes between the Parliament of Paris and the Clergy. — Dearth of Corn in England. — Hanoverian Auxiliaries sent back. — Session opened. — Debates on the Address. — Bill passed for prohibiting the Exportation of Corn. — Message to the House concerning Admiral Byng. — Supplies granted. — Reflections on the continental War. — Messages from the King to the Parliament. — Measures taken to remove the Scarcity of Corn. — Militia Bill. — Petitions for and against it. — Altered by the Lords. — Bill for quartering the foreign Troops, and for regulating the Marines while on Shore. — Bill for the more speedy recruiting the Land Forces and Marines. — Act relating to Pawnbrokers and Gaming-houses. — Laws relating to the Wages of Weavers, and to the Improvement of the British Fishery. — Act for importing American Iron, Duty free. — Regulations with respect to the Importation of Silk. — Smugglers encouraged to enter into his Majesty's Service. — Inquiry into the Scarcity of Corn. — Investigation of the Loss of Minorca. — Examination of the American Contract. — Inquiry into the Conduct of Admiral Knowles, as Governor of Jamaica. — Resolutions concerning Milford-Haven. — Session closed. — Trial of Admiral Byng. — Recommended to Mercy. — Message from the King to the Parliament respecting the Sentence. — Bill to release the Members of the Court Martial from their Oath of Secrecy. — Execution of Admiral Byng. — Paper delivered by him to the Marshal of the Admiralty. — Remarks on his Fate .. .. .. .. .. 600

# THE HISTORY OF ENGLAND.

## CHAPTER XIII.

### GEORGE I.

DIFFERENCE BETWEEN KING GEORGE AND THE CZAR OF MUSCOVY. — THE KING OF SWEDEN IS KILLED AT FREDERICKSTADT. — NEGOTIATION FOR THE QUADRUPLE ALLIANCE. — PROCEEDINGS IN PARLIAMENT. — JAMES SHEPHERD EXECUTED FOR A DESIGN AGAINST THE KING'S LIFE. — PARLIAMENT PROROGUED. — NATURE OF THE QUADRUPLE ALLIANCE. — ADMIRAL BYNG SAILS TO THE MEDITERRANEAN. — HE DESTROYS THE SPANISH FLEET OFF CAPE PASSARO. — REMONSTRANCES OF THE SPANISH MINISTRY. — DISPUTES IN PARLIAMENT TOUCHING THE ADMIRAL'S ATTACKING THE SPANISH FLEET. — ACT FOR STRENGTHENING THE PROTESTANT INTEREST. — WAR DECLARED AGAINST SPAIN — CONSPIRACY AGAINST THE REGENT OF FRANCE. — INTENDED INVASION BY THE DUKE OF ORMOND. — THREE HUNDRED SPANIARDS LAND AND ARE TAKEN IN SCOTLAND. — ACCOUNT OF THE PEERAGE BILL. — COUNT MERCI ASSUMES THE COMMAND OF THE IMPERIAL ARMY IN SICILY. — ACTIVITY OF ADMIRAL BYNG. — THE SPANISH TROOPS EVACUATE SICILY. — PHILIP OBLIGED TO ACCEDE TO THE QUADRUPLE ALLIANCE. — BILL FOR SECURING THE DEPENDENCY OF IRELAND UPON THE CROWN OF GREAT BRITAIN. — SOUTH-SEA ACT. — CHARTERS GRANTED TO THE ROYAL AND LONDON ASSURANCE OFFICES. — TREATY OF ALLIANCE WITH SWEDEN. — THE PRINCE OF HESSE ELECTED KING OF SWEDEN. — EFFECTS OF THE SOUTH-SEA SCHEME. — THE BUBBLE BREAKS. — A SECRET COMMITTEE APPOINTED BY THE HOUSE OF COMMONS. — INQUIRY CARRIED ON BY BOTH HOUSES. — DEATH OF EARL STANHOPE AND MR. CRAGGS, BOTH SECRETARIES OF STATE. — THE ESTATES OF THE DIRECTORS OF THE SOUTH-SEA COMPANY ARE CONFISCATED. — PROCEEDINGS OF THE COMMONS WITH RESPECT TO THE STOCK OF THE SOUTH-SEA COMPANY.

DURING these transactions, the negotiations of the North were continued against the King of Sweden, who had penetrated into Norway, and advanced towards Christianstadt, the capital of that kingdom. The czar had sent five-and-twenty thousand Russians to assist the allies in the reduction of Wismar, which he intended to bestow upon his niece, lately married to the Duke of Mecklenburgh-Schwerin; but, before his troops arrived, the place had surrendered, and the Russians were not admitted into the garrison; a circumstance which increased the misunderstanding between him and the King

1717. Difference between King George and the Czar of Muscovy.

of Great Britain. Nevertheless, he consented to a project for making a descent upon Schonen, and actually took upon him the command of the allied fleet; though he was not at all pleased to see Sir John Norris in the Baltic, because he had formed designs against Denmark, which he knew the English squadron would protect. He suddenly desisted from the expedition against Schonen, on pretence that the season was too far advanced; and the King of Denmark published a manifesto, remonstrating against his conduct on this occasion. By this time Baron Gortz had planned a pacification between his master and the czar, who was discontented with all his German allies, because they opposed his having any footing in the empire. This monarch arrived at Amsterdam in December, whither he was followed by the czarina; and he actually resided at the Hague when King George passed through it, in returning to his British dominions; but he declined an interview with the King of England. When Gyllenburgh's letters were published in London, some passages seemed to favour the supposition of the czar's being privy to the conspiracy. His minister at the English court presented a long memorial, complaining that the king had caused to be printed the malicious insinuations of his enemies. He denied his having the least concern in the design of the Swedish king. He charged the court of England with having privately treated of a separate peace with Charles, and even with having promised to assist him against the czar, on condition that he would relinquish his pretensions to Bremen and Verden. Nevertheless he expressed an inclination to re-establish the ancient good understanding, and to engage in vigorous measures for prosecuting the war against the common enemy. The memorial was answered by the King of Great Britain, who assured the czar he should have reason to be fully satisfied, if he would remove the only obstacle to their mutual good understanding; in other words, withdraw the Russian troops from the empire. Notwithstanding these professions, the two monarchs were never perfectly reconciled.

The czar made an excursion to the court of France, where he concluded a treaty of friendship with the regent, at whose earnest desire he promised to recall his troops from Mecklenburgh. At his return to Amsterdam, he had a private interview with Gortz, who, as well as Gyllenburgh, had been set at

*The King of Sweden is killed at Frederickstadt.*

liberty. Gortz undertook to adjust all difference between the czar and the King of Sweden within three months; and Peter engaged to suspend all operations against Sweden until that term should be expired. A congress was opened at Abo, between the Swedish and Russian ministers; but the conferences were afterwards removed to Aland. By this convention, the czar obliged himself to assist Charles in the conquest of Norway; and they promised to unite all their forces against the King of Great Britain, should he presume to interpose. Both were incensed against that prince; and one part of their design was to raise the pretender to the throne of England. Baron Gortz set out from Aland for Frederickstadt in Norway, with the plan of peace, but, before he arrived, Charles was killed by a cannon-ball from the town, as he visited the trenches, on the thirteenth of November. Baron Gortz was immediately arrested, and brought to the scaffold by the nobles of Sweden, whose hatred he had incurred by his insolence of behaviour. The death of Charles was fortunate for King George. Sweden was now obliged to submit: while the czar, the King of Denmark, and the Elector of Hanover, kept possession of what they had acquired in the course of the war.

Thus Bremen and Verden were secured to the house of Hanover: an acquisition towards which the English nation contributed by her money, as well as by her arms; an acquisition made in contradiction to the engagements into which England entered when King William became guarantee for the treaty of Travendahl; an acquisition that may be considered as the first link of a political chain by which the English nation was dragged back into expensive connexions with the continent. The king had not yet received the investiture of the duchies; and until that should be procured, it was necessary to espouse with warmth the interest of the emperor. This was another source of misunderstanding between Great Britain and Spain. Prince Eugene gained another complete victory over a prodigious army of the Turks at Belgrade, which was surrendered to him after the battle. The emperor had engaged in this war as an ally of the Venetians, whom the Turks had attacked and driven from the Morea. The pope considered it as a religious war against the infidels; and obtained repeated assur-

*Negotiation for the quadruple alliance.*

ances from the King of Spain, that he would not undertake any thing against the emperor, while he was engaged in such a laudable quarrel. Philip had even sent a squadron of ships and galleys to the assistance of the Venetians. In the course of this year, however, he equipped a strong armament, the command of which he bestowed on the Marquis de Lede, who sailed from Barcelona in July, and landing at Cagliari in Sardinia, which belonged to the emperor, made a conquest of the whole island. At the same time, the King of Spain endeavoured to justify these proceedings by a manifesto, in which he alleged that the archduke, contrary to the faith of treaties, encouraged and supported the rebellion of his subjects in Catalonia, by frequent succours from Naples, and other places; and that the Great-Inquisitor of Spain had been seized, though furnished with a passport from his holiness. He promised, however, to proceed no further, and suspend all operations, that the powers of Europe might have time and opportunity to contrive expedients for reconciling all differences, and securing the peace and balance of power in Italy: nay, he consented that this important affair should be left to the arbitration of King George and the States-General. These powers undertook the office. Conferences were begun between the ministers of the emperor, France, England, and Holland; and these produced, in the course of the following year, the famous quadruple alliance. In this treaty it was stipulated that the emperor should renounce all pretensions to the crown of Spain, and exchange Sardinia for Sicily, with the Duke of Savoy; that the succession to the Duchies of Tuscany, Parma, and Placentia, which the Queen of Spain claimed by inheritance, as Princess of the house of Farnese, should be settled on her eldest son, in case the present possessors should die without male issue. Philip, dissatisfied with this partition, continued to make formidable preparations by sea and land. The King of England and the Regent of France interposed their admonitions to no purpose. At length his Britannic majesty had recourse to more substantial arguments, and ordered a strong squadron to be equipped with all possible expedition.*

* The pretender, who resided at Urbino, having received intelligence from Paris, that there was a design formed against his life, Pope Clement XI. gave directions that all foreigners in that neighbourhood, especially English, should be arrested. The Earl of Peterborough, arriving at Bologna, with a few armed followers, was seized with all his papers. Being interrogated, he said he came to pass some time in Italy for the benefit of

On the third day of November, the Princess of Wales was delivered of a prince, the ceremony of whose baptism was productive of a difference between the grandfather and the father. The Prince of Wales intended that his uncle, the Duke of York, should stand godfather. The king ordered the Duke of Newcastle to stand for himself. After the ceremony, the prince expressed his resentment against this nobleman in very warm terms. The king ordered the prince to confine himself within his own apartments; and afterwards signified his pleasure that he should quit the palace of St. James's. He retired with the princess to a house belonging to the Earl of Grantham; but the children were detained at the palace. All peers and peeresses, and all privy-counsellors and their wives, were given to understand, that in case they visited the prince and princess, they should have no access to his majesty's presence; and all who enjoyed posts and places under both king and prince were obliged to quit the service of one or other, at their option. When the Parliament met on the twenty-first day of November, the king, in his speech, told both Houses that he had reduced the army to very near one half, since the beginning of the last session: he expressed his desire that all those who were friends to the present happy establishment might unanimously concur in some proper method for the greater strengthening the Protestant interest, of which, as the church of England was unquestionably the main support and bulwark, so would she reap the principal benefit of every advantage accruing from the union and mutual charity of all Protestants. After the addresses of thanks, which were couched in the usual style, the Commons proceeded to take into consideration the estimates and accounts, in order to settle the establishment of the army, navy, and ordnance. Ten thousand men were voted for the sea-service. When the supply for the army fell under deliberation, a very warm debate ensued, upon the number of troops necessary to be maintained. Sir William

*Proceedings in Parliament.*

the air. He was close confined for a whole month in Fort Urbino, and his attendants were sent to prison. Nothing appearing to justify the suspicion, he was dismissed with uncommon civility. The king demanding reparation for this insult, the pope wrote with his own hand a letter to an ally of Great Britain, declaring that the legate of Bologna had violently and unjustly, without the knowledge of his holiness, caused the Earl of Peterborough to be seized upon suspicions which proved to be ill-grounded. The cardinal legate sent a declaration to the English admiral in the Mediterranean, that he had asked forgiveness of his holiness, and now begged pardon of his Britannic majesty, for having unadvisedly arrested a peer of Great Britain on his travels.

Wyndham, Mr. Shippen, and Mr. Walpole, in a long elaborate harangue, insisted upon its being reduced to twelve thousand. They were answered by Mr. Craggs, secretary at war, and Sir David Dalrymple. Mr. Shippen, in the course of the debate, said the second paragraph of the king's speech seemed rather to be calculated for the meridian of Germany than for Great Britain; and it was a great misfortune that the king was a stranger to our language and constitution. Mr. Lechmere affirmed this was a scandalous invective against the king's person and government; and moved that he who uttered it should be sent to the Tower. Mr. Shippen, refusing to retract or excuse what he had said, was voted to the Tower by a great majority; and the number of standing forces was fixed at sixteen thousand three hundred and forty-seven effective men.

*James Shepherd executed for a design against the king's life. The Parliament prorogued.*

On account of the great scarcity of silver coin, occasioned by the exportation of silver, and the importation of gold, a motion was made to put a stop to this growing evil by lowering the value of gold specie. The Commons examined a representation which had been made to the treasury by Sir Isaac Newton, master of the mint, on this subject. Mr. Caswell explained the nature of a clandestine trade carried on by the Dutch and Hamburghers, in concert with the Jews of England and other traders, for exporting the silver coin and importing gold, which, being coined at the mint, yielded a profit of fifteen pence upon every guinea. The House, in an address to the king, desired that a proclamation might be issued, forbidding all persons to utter or receive guineas at a higher rate than one-and-twenty shillings each. His majesty complied with their request; but people hoarding up their silver, in hopes that the price of it would be raised, or in apprehension that the gold would be lowered still farther, the two Houses resolved that the standard of the gold and silver coins of the kingdoms should not be altered in fineness, weight, or denomination; and they ordered a bill to be brought in, to prevent the melting down of the silver coin. At this period, one James Shepherd, a youth of eighteen, apprentice to a coach-maker, and an enthusiast in jacobitism, sent a letter to a nonjuring clergyman proposing a scheme for assassinating King George. He was immediately apprehended, owned the design, was tried, condemned, and executed at Tyburn. This was likewise the fate of the Marquis de Palleotti, an Italian nobleman, brother to the Duchess of Shrewsbury. He had, in a transport of passion, killed his own servant, and seemed indeed to be disordered in his brain. After he had received sentence of death, the king's pardon was earnestly solicited by his sister the duchess, and many other persons of the first distinction; but the common people became so clamorous, that it was thought dangerous to rescue him from the penalties of the law, which he accordingly underwent in the most ignominious manner. No subject produced so much heat and altercation in Parliament during this session as did the bill for regulating the land-forces, and punishing mutiny and desertion: a bill which was looked upon as an encroachment upon the liberties and constitution of England, inasmuch as it established martial law, which wrested from the civil magistrate the cognizance of crimes and misdemeanours committed by the soldiers and officers of the army: a jurisdiction inconsistent with the genius and disposition of the people. The dangers that might accrue from such a power were explained in the Lower House by Mr. Hutchinson, Mr. Harley, and Mr. Robert Walpole, which last, however, voted afterwards for the bill. In the House of Lords, it was strenuously opposed by the Earls of Oxford, Strafford, and Lord Harcourt. Their objections were answered by Lord Carteret. The bill passed by a great majority; but divers lords entered a protest. This affair being discussed, a bill was brought in for vesting in trustees the forfeited estates in Britain and Ireland, to be sold for the use of the public; for giving relief to lawful creditors, by determining the claims, and for the more effectual bringing into the respective exchequers the rents and profits of the estates till sold. The time of claiming was prolonged: the sum of twenty thousand pounds was reserved out of the sale of the estates in Scotland for erecting schools; and eight thousand pounds for building barracks in that kingdom. The king having signified, by a message to the House of Commons, that he had lately received such information from abroad as gave reason to believe that a naval force, employed where it should be necessary, would give weight to his endeavours; he therefore thought fit to acquaint the House with this circumstance, not doubting

Oldmixon.
Annals.
Lamberty.
Burchet.
Hist. Reg.
Tindal.
St. Trials.
Parlia.
Bolingbr.
Lives of the Admirals.

but that in case he should be obliged, at this critical juncture, to exceed the number of men granted this year for the sea-service, the House would provide for such exceeding. The Commons immediately drew up and presented an address, assuring his majesty that they would make good such exceedings of seamen as he should find necessary to preserve the tranquillity of Europe. On the twenty-first day of March, the king went to the House of Peers, and having passed the bills that were ready for the royal assent, ordered the Parliament to be prorogued.[b]

<small>1718.
Nature of the quadruple alliance.</small>
The King of Spain, by the care and indefatigable diligence of his prime minister, Cardinal Alberoni, equipped a very formidable armament, which, in the beginning of June, set sail from Barcelona towards Italy; but the destination of it was not known. A strong squadron having been fitted out in England, the Marquis de Montcleone, ambassador from Spain, presented a memorial to the British ministry, importing that so powerful an armament in time of peace could not but give umbrage to the king his master, and alter the good intelligence that subsisted between the two crowns. In answer to this representation, the ministers declared that the king intended to send Admiral Byng with a powerful squadron into the Mediterranean, to maintain the neutrality in Italy. Meanwhile, the negotiations between the English and French ministers produced the quadruple alliance, by which King George and the regent prescribed a peace between the emperor, the King of Spain, and the King of Sicily, and undertook to compel Philip and the Savoyard to submit to such conditions as they had concerted with his imperial majesty. These powers were allowed only three months to consider the articles, and declare whether they would reject them, or acquiesce in the partition. Nothing could be more contradictory to the true interest of Great Britain than this treaty, which destroyed the balance in Italy, by throwing such an accession of power into the hands of the house of Austria. It interrupted the commerce with Spain, involved the kingdom in an immediate war with that monarchy, and gave rise to all

<small>[b] Earl Cowper, lord chancellor, resigned the great seal, which was at first put in commission, but afterwards given to Lord Parker, as high chancellor. The Earl of Sunderland was made president of the council, and first commissioner of the treasury; Lord Stanhope and Mr. Craggs were appointed secretaries of state; Lord Stanhope and Lord Cadogan were afterwards created earls.</small>

the quarrels and disputes which have arisen between England and Spain in the sequel. The States-General did not approve of such violent measures, and for some time kept aloof; but at length they acceded to the quadruple alliance, which indeed was no other than a very expensive compliment to the emperor, who was desirous of adding Sicily to his other Italian dominions.

The King of England had used some endeavours to compromise the difference between his imperial majesty and the Spanish branch of the house of Bourbon. Lord Stanhope had been sent to Madrid with a plan of pacification, which being rejected by Philip as partial and iniquitous, the king determined to support his mediation by force of arms. Sir George Byng sailed from Spithead on the fourth day of June, with twenty ships of the line, two fire-ships, two bomb-vessels, and ample instructions how to act on all emergencies. He arrived off Cape St. Vincent on the thirtieth day of the month, and despatched his secretary to Cadiz, with a letter to Colonel Stanhope, the British minister at Madrid, desiring him to inform his Most Catholic Majesty of the admiral's arrival in those parts, and lay before him this article of his instructions: "You are to make instances with both parties to cease from using any farther acts of hostility; but in case the Spaniards do still insist, with their ships of war and forces, to attack the kingdom of Naples, or other the territories of the emperor in Italy, or to land in any part of Italy, which can only be with a design to invade the emperor's dominions, against whom only they have declared war by invading Sardinia; or if they should endeavour to make themselves masters of the kingdom of Sicily, which must be with a design to invade the kingdom of Naples; in which case you are, with all your power, to hinder and obstruct the same. If it should so happen, that at your arrival, with our fleet under your command, in the Mediterranean, the Spaniards should already have landed any troops in Italy in order to invade the emperor's territories, you shall endeavour amicably to dissuade them from persevering in such an attempt, and offer them your assistance, to help them to withdraw their troops, and put an end to all farther acts of hostility. But in case these your friendly endeavours should prove ineffectual, you shall, by keeping company with, or intercepting their ships or convoy, or, if

*Admiral Byng sails to the Mediterranean.*

it be necessary, by openly opposing them, defend the emperor's territories from any farther attempt." When Cardinal Alberoni perused these instructions, he told Colonel Stanhope with some warmth, that his master would run all hazards, and even suffer himself to be driven out of Spain, rather than recall his troops, or consent to a suspension of arms. He said the Spaniards were not to be frightened; and he was so well convinced that the fleet would do their duty, that in case of their being attacked by Admiral Byng, he should be in no pain for the success. Mr. Stanhope presenting him with a list of the British squadron, he threw it upon the ground with great emotion. He promised, however, to lay the admiral's letter before the king, and to let the envoy know his majesty's resolution. Such an interposition could not but be very provoking to the Spanish minister, who had laid his account with the conquest of Sicily, and for that purpose prepared an armament, which was altogether surprising, considering the late shattered condition of the Spanish affairs. But he seems to have put too much confidence in the strength of the Spanish fleet. In a few days he sent back the admiral's letter to Mr. Stanhope, with a note under it, importing, that the Chevalier Byng might execute the orders he had received from the king his master.

*He destroys the Spanish fleet off Cape Passaro.* The admiral, in passing by Gibraltar, was joined by Vice-Admiral Cornwall, with two ships. He proceeded to Minorca, where he relieved the garrison of Port-Mahon. Then he sailed for Naples, where he arrived on the first day of August, and was received as a deliverer; for the Neapolitans had been under the utmost terror of an invasion from the Spaniards. Sir George Byng received intelligence from the viceroy, Count Daun, who treated him with the most distinguishing marks of respect, that the Spanish army, amounting to thirty thousand men, commanded by the Marquis de Lede, had landed in Sicily, reduced Palermo and Messina, and were then employed in the siege of the citadel belonging to this last city; that the Piedmontese garrison would be obliged to surrender, if not speedily relieved; that an alliance was upon the carpet between the emperor and the King of Sicily, which last had desired the assistance of the imperial troops, and agreed to receive them into the citadel of Messina. The admiral immediately resolved to sail thither, and took under his convoy a reinforcement of two thousand Germans for the citadel, under the command of General Wetzel. He forthwith sailed from Naples, and on the ninth day of August was in sight of the Faro of Messina. He despatched his own captain, with a polite message to the Marquis de Lede, proposing a cessation of arms in Sicily for two months, that the powers of Europe might have time to concert measures for restoring a lasting peace; and declaring, that should this proposal be rejected, he would, in pursuance of his directions, use all his force to prevent further attempts to disturb the dominions his master had engaged to defend. The Spanish general answered, that he had no power to treat, and consequently could not agree to an armistice, but should obey his orders, which directed him to reduce Sicily for his master the King of Spain. The Spanish fleet had sailed from the harbour of Messina on the day before the English squadron appeared. Admiral Byng supposed they had retired to Malta, and directed his course towards Messina, in order to encourage and support the garrison in the citadel. But, in doubling the point of Faro, he descried two Spanish scouts, and learned from the people of a felucca from the Calabrian shore, that they had seen from the hills the Spanish fleet lying-to in order of battle. The admiral immediately detached the German troops to Reggio, under convoy of two ships of war. Then he stood through the Faro after the Spanish scouts that led him to their main fleet, which before noon he descried in a line of battle, amounting to seven-and-twenty sail, large and small, besides two fire-ships, four bomb-vessels, and seven galleys. They were commanded in chief by Don Antonio de Castanita, under whom were the four Rear-Admirals Chacon, Mari, Guevara, and Cammock. At sight of the English squadron, they stood away at large, and Byng gave chase all the rest of the day. In the morning, which was the eleventh of August, Rear-Admiral de Mari, with six ships of war, the galleys, fire-ships, and bomb-ketches, separated from the main fleet, and stood in for the Sicilian shore. The English admiral detached Captain Walton with five ships in pursuit of them: and they were soon engaged. He himself continued to chase their main fleet; and about ten o'clock the battle began. The Spaniards seemed to be distracted in their councils, and acted in confusion. They made a running fight: yet the admirals behaved with courage and activity, in spite of which they were all taken, except Cammock, who made his escape with three ships of war and three frigates. In this engagement, which happened off Cape Passaro, Captain Haddock, of the Grafton, signalized his courage in an extraordinary manner. On the eighteenth the admiral received a letter from Captain Walton, dated off Syracuse, intimating that he had taken four Spanish ships of war, together with a bomb-ketch, and a vessel laden with arms; and that he had burned four ships of the line, a fire-ship, and a bomb-vessel.ᵉ Had the Spaniards followed the advice of Rear-Admiral Cammock, who was a native of Ireland, Sir George Byng would not have obtained such an easy victory. That officer proposed that they should remain at anchor in the road of Paradise, with their broadsides to the sea; in which case the English admiral would have found it a very difficult task to attack them; for the coast is so bold, that the largest ships could ride with a cable ashore; whereas farther out the currents are so various and rapid, that the English squadron could not have come to anchor, or lie near them in order of battle; besides, the Spaniards might have been reinforced from the army on shore, which would have raised batteries to annoy the assailants. Before King George had received an account of this engagement from the admiral, he wrote him a letter with his own hand, approving his conduct. When Sir George's eldest son arrived in England, with a circumstantial account of the action, he was graciously received, and sent back with plenipotentiary powers to his father, that he might negotiate with the several princes and states of Italy as he should see occasion. The son likewise carried the king's royal grant to the officers and seamen of all the prizes they had taken from the Spaniards. Notwithstanding this victory, the Spanish army carried on the siege of the citadel of Messina with such vigour, that the governor surrendered the place by capitulation on the twenty-ninth day of September. A treaty was now concluded at Vienna between the emperor and the Duke of Savoy. They agreed to form an army for the conquest of Sardinia in behalf of the duke; and in the mean time this prince engaged to evacuate

---

ᵉ This letter is justly deemed a curious specimen of the laconic style.
"Sir,
"We have taken and destroyed all the Spanish ships and vessels which were upon the coast; the number as per margin. I am, &c.
"G. WALTON."

Sicily; but until his troops could be conveyed from that island, he consented that they should co-operate with the Germans against the common enemy. Admiral Byng continued to assist the imperialists in Sicily during the best part of the winter, by scouring the seas of the Spaniards, and keeping the communication open between the German forces and the Calabrian shore, from whence they were supplied with provisions. He acted in this service with equal conduct, resolution, and activity. He conferred with the Viceroy of Naples and the other imperial generals about the operations of the ensuing campaign, and Count Hamilton was despatched to Vienna, to lay before the emperor the result of their deliberations; then the admiral set sail for Mahon, where his ships might be refitted, and put in a condition to take the sea in the spring.

The destruction of the Spanish fleet was a subject that employed the deliberations and conjectures of all the politicians in Europe. Spain exclaimed against the conduct of England, as inconsistent with the rules of good faith, for the observation of which she had always been so famous. The Marquis de Monteleone wrote a letter to Mr. Secretary Craggs, in which he expostulated with him upon such an unprecedented outrage. Cardinal Alberoni, in a letter to that minister, inveighed against it as a base unworthy action. He said the neutrality of Italy was a weak pretence, since every body knew that neutrality had long been at an end; and that the prince's guarantees of the treaty of Utrecht were entirely discharged from their engagements, not only by the scandalous infringements committed by the Austrians in the evacuation of Catalonia and Majorca; but also because the guarantee was no longer binding than till a peace was concluded with France. He taxed the British ministry with having revived and supported this neutrality, not by an amicable mediation, but by open violence, and artfully abusing the confidence and security of the Spaniards. This was the language of disappointed ambition. Nevertheless it must be owned, that the conduct of England, on this occasion, was irregular, partial, and precipitate.

*Remonstrances of the Spanish ministry.*

The Parliament meeting on the eleventh day of November, the king, in his speech, declared that the court of Spain had rejected all his amicable proposals, and broke through their most solemn engagements, for the security of the

British commerce. To vindicate, therefore, the faith of his former treaties, as well as to maintain those he had lately made, and to protect and defend the trade of his subjects, which had in every branch been violently and unjustly oppressed, it became necessary for his naval forces to check their progress: that notwithstanding the success of his arms, that court had lately given orders at all the ports of Spain and of the West Indies to fit out privateers against the English. He said he was persuaded that a British Parliament would enable him to resent such treatment; and he assured them that his good brother, the Regent of France, was ready to concur with him in the most vigorous measures. A strong opposition was made in both Houses to the motion for an address of thanks and congratulation proposed by Lord Carteret. Several peers observed, that such an address was, in effect, to approve a sea-fight which might be attended with dangerous consequences, and to give the sanction of that august assembly to measures which, upon examination, might appear either to clash with the law of nations, or former treaties, or to be prejudicial to the trade of Great Britain: that they ought to proceed with the utmost caution and maturest deliberation, in an affair wherein the honour as well as the interest of the nation were so highly concerned. Lord Strafford moved for an address, that Sir George Byng's instructions might be laid before the House. Earl Stanhope replied, that there was no occasion for such an address, since by his majesty's command he had already laid before the House the treaties, of which the late sea-fight was a consequence; particularly the treaty for a defensive alliance between the emperor and his majesty, concluded at Westminster on the twenty-fifth day of May, in the year one thousand seven hundred and sixteen; and the treaty of alliance for restoring and settling the public peace, signed at London on the twenty-second day of July. He affirmed, that the court of Spain had violated the treaty of Utrecht, and acted against the public faith in attacking the emperor's dominions, while he was engaged in a war against the enemies of Christendom; that they had rejected his majesty's friendly offices and offers for mediating an accommodation. He explained the cause of his journey to Spain, and his negotiations at Madrid. He added, it was high time to check the growth of the naval power of Spain, in order to protect and secure the trade of the British subjects, which had been violently oppressed by the Spaniards. After a long debate, the motion was carried by a considerable majority. The same subject excited disputes of the same nature in the House of Commons, where Lord Hinchingbroke moved, that in their address of thanks they should declare their entire satisfaction in those measures which the king had already taken for strengthening the Protestant succession, and establishing a lasting tranquillity in Europe. The members in the opposition urged, that it was unparliamentary and unprecedented, on the first day of the session, to enter upon particulars: that the business in question was of the highest importance, and deserved the most mature deliberation: that before they approved the measures which had been taken, they ought to examine the reasons on which those measures were founded. Mr. Robert Walpole affirmed, that the giving sanction, in the manner proposed, to the late measures, could have no other view than that of screening ministers, who were conscious of having begun a war against Spain, and now wanted to make it the Parliament's war. He observed, that instead of an entire satisfaction, they ought to express their entire dissatisfaction, with such conduct as was contrary to the law of nations, and a breach of the most solemn treaties. Mr. Secretary Craggs, in a long speech, explained the nature of the quadruple alliance, and justified all the measures which had been taken. The address, as moved by Lord Hinchingbroke, was at length carried, and presented to his majesty. Then the Commons proceeded to consider the supply. They voted thirteen thousand five hundred sailors; and twelve thousand four hundred and thirty-five men for the land-service. The whole estimate amounted to two millions two hundred and fifty-seven thousand five hundred eighty-one pounds, nineteen shillings. The money was raised by a land-tax, malt-tax, and lottery.

On the thirteenth day of December, Earl Stanhope declared, in the House of Lords, that, in order to unite the hearts of the well-affected to the present establishment, he had a bill to offer under the title of "An act for strengthening the Protestant interest in these kingdoms." It was accordingly read, and appeared to be a bill repealing the acts against occasional conformity, the growth of schism, and some clauses in the corporation and test acts. This had been concerted by the ministry in

*Act for strengthening the Protestant interest.*

private meetings with the most eminent dissenters. The tory lords were astonished at this motion, for which they were altogether unprepared. Nevertheless, they were strenuous in their opposition. They alleged that the bill, instead of strengthening, would certainly weaken the church of England, by plucking off her best feathers, investing her enemies with power, and sharing with churchmen the civil and military employments of which they were then wholly possessed. Earl Cowper declared himself against that part of the bill by which some clauses of the test and corporation acts were repealed; because he looked upon those acts as the main bulwark of our excellent constitution in church and state, which ought to be inviolably preserved. The Earl of Ilay opposed the bill, because in his opinion it infringed the *pacta conventa* of the treaty of union, by which the bounds both of the church of England and of the church of Scotland were fixed and settled; and he was apprehensive, if the articles of the union were broken with respect to one church, it might afterwards be a precedent to break them with respect to the other. The Archbishop of Canterbury said the acts which by this bill would be repealed were the main bulwark and supporters of the English Church: he expressed all imaginable tenderness for well-meaning conscientious dissenters; but he could not forbear saying, some among that sect made a wrong use of the favour and indulgence shown to them at the Revolution, though they had the least share in that happy event: it was, therefore, thought necessary for the legislature to interpose, and put a stop to the scandalous practice of occasional conformity. He added, that it would be needless to repeal the act against schism, since no advantage had been taken of it to the prejudice of the dissenters. Dr. Hoadley, Bishop of Bangor, endeavoured to prove, that the occasional and schism acts were in effect persecuting laws; and that by admitting the principle of self-defence and self-preservation in matters of religion, all the persecutions maintained by the heathens against the professors of Christianity, and even the popish inquisition, might be justified. With respect to the power of which many clergymen appeared so fond and so zealous, he owned the desire of power and riches was natural to all men; but that he had learned, both from reason and from the gospel, that this desire must be kept within due bounds, and not intrench upon the rights and liberties of their fellow-creatures and countrymen. After a long debate, the House agreed to leave out some clauses concerning the test and corporation acts : then the bill was committed, and afterwards passed. In the Lower House it met with violent opposition, in spite of which it was carried by the majority.

The king, on the seventeenth day of December, sent a message to the Commons, importing, that all his endeavours to procure redress for the injuries done to his subjects by the King of Spain having proved ineffectual, he had found it necessary to declare war against that monarch. When a motion was made for an address, to assure the king they would cheerfully support him in the prosecution of the war, Mr. Shippen and some other members said, they did not see the necessity of involving the nation in a war on account of some grievances of which the merchants complained, as these might be amicably redressed. Mr. Stanhope assured the House, that he had presented five-and-twenty memorials to the ministry of Spain on that subject, without success. Mr. Methuen accounted for the dilatory proceedings of the Spanish court in commercial affairs, by explaining the great variety of regulations in the several provinces and ports of that kingdom. It was suggested, that the ministry paid very little regard to the trade and interest of the nation; inasmuch as it appeared by the answers from a secretary of state to the letter of the Marquis de Monteleone, that they would have overlooked the violation of the treaties of commerce, provided Spain had accepted the conditions stipulated in the quadruple alliance; for it was there expressly said, that his majesty, the King of Great Britain, did not seek to aggrandize himself by any new acquisitions, but was rather inclined to sacrifice something of his own to procure the general quiet and tranquillity of Europe. A member observed, that nobody could tell how far that sacrifice would have extended; but certainly it was a very uncommon stretch of condescension. This sacrifice was said to be the cession of Gibraltar and Port-Mahon, which the Regent of France had offered to the King of Spain, provided he would accede to the quadruple alliance. Horatio Walpole observed, that the disposition of Sicily in favour of the emperor was an infraction of the treaty of Utrecht; and his brother exclaimed against the injustice of attacking the Spanish fleet before a declaration

*War declared against Spain.*

of war. Notwithstanding all these arguments and objections, the majority agreed to the address; and such another was carried in the Upper House without a division. The declaration of war against Spain was published with the usual solemnities; but this war was not a favourite of the people, and therefore did not produce those acclamations that were usual on such occasions.

Meanwhile Cardinal Alberoni employed all his intrigues, Conspiracy against the Regent of France. power, and industry, for the gratification of his revenge. He caused new ships to be built, the seaports to be put in a posture of defence, succours to be sent to Sicily, and the proper measures to be taken for the security of Sardinia. He, by means of the Prince de Cellamare, the Spanish ambassador at Paris, caballed with the malecontents of that kingdom, who were numerous and powerful. A scheme was actually formed for seizing the regent, and securing the person of the king. The Duke of Orleans owed the first intimation of this plot to King George, who gave him to understand, that a conspiracy was formed against his person and government. The regent immediately took measures for watching the conduct of all suspected persons; but the whole intrigue was discovered by accident. The Prince de Cellamare entrusted his despatches to the Abbé Portocarrero, and to a son of the Marquis de Monteleone. These emissaries set out from Paris in a postchaise, and were overturned. The postilion overheard Portocarrero say, he would not have lost his portmanteau for a hundred thousand pistoles. The man, at his return to Paris, gave notice to the government of what he had observed. The Spaniards, being pursued, were overtaken and seized at Poitiers, with the portmanteau, in which the regent found two letters that made him acquainted with the particulars of the conspiracy. The Prince de Cellamare was immediately conducted to the frontiers; the Duke of Maine, the Marquis de Pompadour, the Cardinal de Polignac, and many other persons of distinction, were committed to different prisons. The regent declared war against Spain on the twenty-ninth day of December; and an army of six-and-thirty thousand men began its march towards that kingdom in January, under the command of the Duke of Berwick.

Cardinal Alberoni had likewise formed a scheme in favour of the pretender. The Duke of Ormond, repairing to Madrid, held conferences with his eminence; and measures were concerted for exciting another insurrection in Great Britain. The Chevalier de St. George quitted Urbino by stealth; and embarking at Netteno, landed at Cagliari in March. From thence he took his passage to Roses in Catalonia, and proceeded to Madrid, where he was received with great cordiality, and treated as King of Great Britain. An armament had been equipped of ten ships of war and transports, having on board six thousand regular troops, with arms for twelve thousand men. The command of this fleet was bestowed on the Duke of Ormond, with the title of captain-general of his Most Catholic Majesty. He was provided with declarations in the name of that king, importing, that for many good reasons he had sent part of his land and sea forces into England and Scotland, to act as auxiliaries to King James. His Britannic majesty, having received from the Regent of France timely notice of this intended invasion, offered, by proclamation, rewards to those that should apprehend the Duke of Ormond, or any gentleman embarked in that expedition. Troops were ordered to assemble in the north, and in the west of England: two thousand men were demanded of the States-General: a strong squadron was equipped to oppose the Spanish armament; and the Duke of Orleans made a proffer to King George of twenty battalions for his service. *Intended invasion the Duke by of Ormond.*

His majesty having communicated to both Houses of Parliament the repeated advices he had received touching this projected descent, they promised to support him against all his enemies. They desired he would augment his forces by sea and land; and assured him they would make good the extraordinary expense. Two thousand men were landed from Holland, and six battalions of imperialists from the Austrian Netherlands. The Duke of Ormond sailed from Cadiz, and proceeded as far as Cape Finisterre, where his fleet was dispersed and disabled by a violent storm, which entirely defeated the purposed expedition. Two frigates, however, arrived in Scotland, with the Earls Marischal and Seaforth, the Marquis of Tullibardine, some field officers, three hundred Spaniards, and arms for two thousand men. They were joined by a small body of Highlanders, and possessed themselves of Donan Castle. Against these adventurers General Wightman marched with a body of regular troops from Inverness. They had taken possession of the pass at Glenshiel; but, at *Three hundred Spaniards land and are taken in Scotland.*

the approach of the king's forces, retired to the pass at Strachell, which they resolved to defend. They were attacked and driven from one eminence to another till night, when the Highlanders dispersed, and next day the Spaniards surrendered themselves prisoners of war. Marischal, Seaforth, and Tullibardine, with some officers, retired to one of the western isles, in order to wait an opportunity of being conveyed to the continent.

<small>Account of the peerage bill.</small> On the last day of February the Duke of Somerset represented in the House of Lords, that the number of peers being very much increased, especially since the union of the two kingdoms, it seemed absolutely necessary to take effectual measures for preventing the inconveniences that might attend the creation of a great number of peers, to serve a present purpose; an expedient which had been actually taken in the late reign. He therefore moved that a bill should be brought in, to settle and limit the peerage, in such a manner, that the number of English peers should not be enlarged beyond six above the present number, which, upon failure of male issue, might be supplied by new creations: that instead of the sixteen elective peers from Scotland, twenty-five should be made hereditary on the part of that kingdom; and that this number, upon failure of heirs male, should be supplied from the other members of the Scottish peerage. This bill was intended as a restraint upon the Prince of Wales, who happened to be at variance with the present ministry. The motion was supported by the Duke of Argyle, now lord steward of the household, the Earls of Sunderland and Carlisle. It was opposed by the Earl of Oxford, who said that, although he expected nothing from the crown, he would never give his vote for lopping off so valuable a branch of the prerogative, which enabled the king to reward merit and virtuous actions. The debate was adjourned to the second day of March, when Earl Stanhope delivered a message from the king, intimating, that as they had under consideration the state of the British peerage, he had so much at heart the settling it upon such a foundation as might secure the freedom and constitution of Parliaments in all future ages, that he was willing his prerogative should not stand in the way of so great and necessary a work. Another violent debate ensued between the two factions. The question here, as in almost every other dispute, was not, Whether the measure proposed

was advantageous to the nation? but, Whether the tory or the whig interest should predominate in Parliament? Earl Cowper affirmed, that the part of the bill relating to the Scottish peerage was a manifest violation of the treaty of union, as well as a flagrant piece of injustice, as it would deprive persons of their right without being heard, and without any pretence of forfeiture on their part. He observed that the Scottish peers excluded from the number of the twenty-five would be in a worse condition than any other subjects in the kingdom; for they would be neither electing nor elected, neither respresenting nor represented. These objections were overruled: several resolutions were taken agreeably to the motion; and the judges were ordered to prepare and bring in the bill. This measure alarmed the generality of Scottish peers, as well as many English commoners, who saw in the bill the avenues of dignity and title shut up against them; and they did not fail to exclaim against it, as an encroachment upon the fundamental maxims of the constitution. Treatises were written and published on both sides of the question; and a national clamour began to arise, when Earl Stanhope observed, in the House, that as the bill had raised strange apprehensions, he thought it advisable to postpone the further consideration of it till a more proper opportunity. It was accordingly dropped, and the Parliament prorogued on the eighteenth day of April, on which occasion his majesty told both Houses that the Spanish king had acknowledged the pretender. Annals. Corbet. Tindal. Hist. Reg. Deb. in Parliament. Lives of the Admirals.

The king, having appointed lords justices to rule the kingdom in his absence, embarked in May for Holland, from whence he proceeded to Hanover, where he concluded a peace with Ulrica, the new Queen of Sweden. By this treaty Sweden yielded for ever to the royal and electoral house of Brunswick, the duchies of Bremen and Verden, with all their dependencies: King George obliged himself to pay a million of rix-dollars to the Queen of Sweden; and to renew, as King of Great Britain and Elector of Hanover, the alliances formerly subsisting between his predecessors and that kingdom. He likewise mediated a peace between Sweden and his former allies, the Danes, the Prussians, and the Poles. The czar, however, refused to give up his schemes of conquest. He sent his fleet to the Scheuron or Batses of 1719. Count Merci assumes the command of the Imperial army in Sicily.

Sweden, where his troops landing, to the number of fifteen thousand, committed dreadful outrages; but Sir John Norris, who commanded an English squadron in those seas, having orders to support the negotiations, and oppose any hostilities that might be committed, the czar, dreading the fate of the Spanish navy, thought proper to recall his fleet. In the Mediterranean, Admiral Byng acted with unwearied vigour in assisting the imperialists to finish the conquest of Sicily. The court of Vienna had agreed to send a strong body of forces to finish the reduction of that island; and the command in this expedition was bestowed upon the Count de Merci, with whom Sir George Byng conferred at Naples. This admiral supplied them with ammunition and artillery from the Spanish prizes. He took the whole reinforcement under his convoy, and saw them safely landed in the Bay of Patti, to the number of three thousand five hundred horse, and ten thousand infantry. Count Merci, thinking himself more than a match for the Spanish forces commanded by the Marquis de Lede, attacked him in a strong camp at Franca-Villa, and was repulsed with the loss of five thousand men, himself being dangerously wounded in the action. Here his army must have perished for want of provision, had they not been supplied by the English navy.

Admiral Byng no sooner learned the bad success of the attack at Franca-Villa than he embarked two battalions from the garrison of Melazzo, and about a thousand recruits, whom he sent under a convoy through the Faro to Scheso-bay, in order to reinforce the imperial army. He afterwards assisted at a council of war with the German generals, who, in consequence of his advice, undertook the siege of Messina. Then he repaired to Naples, where he proposed to Count Gallas, the new viceroy, that the troops destined for the conquest of Sardinia should be first landed in Sicily, and co-operate towards the conquest of that island. The proposal was immediately despatched to the court of Vienna. In the mean time the admiral returned to Sicily, and assisted at the siege of Messina. The town surrendered; the garrison retired into the citadel; and the remains of the Spanish navy, which had escaped at Passaro, were now destroyed in the Mole. The emperor approved of the scheme proposed by the English admiral, to whom he wrote a very gracious letter, intimating that he had despatched orders to the governor of Milan, to detach the

*Activity of Admiral Byng.*

troops designed for Sardinia to Vado, in order to be transported into Italy. The admiral charged himself with the performance of this service. Having furnished the imperial army before Messina with another supply of cannon, powder, and shot, upon his own credit, he set sail for Vado, where he surmounted numberless difficulties, started by the jealousy of Count Bonneval, who was unwilling to see his troops, destined for Sardinia, now diverted to another expedition, in which he could not enjoy the chief command. At length Admiral Byng saw the forces embarked, and convoyed them to Messina, the citadel of which surrendered in a few days after their arrival. By this time the Marquis de Lede had fortified a strong post at Castro-Giovanne, in the centre of the island; and cantoned his troops about Aderno, Palermo, and Catanea. The imperialists could not pretend to attack him in this situation, nor could they remain in the neighbourhood of Messina, on account of the scarcity of provisions. They would, therefore, have been obliged to quit the island during the winter, had not the admiral undertaken to transport them by sea to Trapani, where they could extend themselves in a plentiful country. He not only executed this enterprise, but even supplied them with corn from Tunis, as the harvest of Sicily had been gathered into the Spanish magazines. It was the second day of March before the last embarkation of the imperial troops were landed at Trapani.

The Marquis de Lede immediately retired with his army to Alcamo, from whence he sent his mareschal de camp to Count Merci and the English admiral, with overtures for evacuating Sicily. The proposals were not disagreeable to the Germans; but Sir George Byng declared that the Spaniards should not quit the island while the war continued, as he foresaw that these troops would be employed against France or England. He agreed, however, with Count Merci, in proposing, that if the marquis would surrender Palermo, and retire into the middle part of the island, they would consent to an armistice for six weeks, until the sentiments of their different courts should be known. The marquis offered to surrender Palermo, in consideration of a suspension of arms for three months; but while this negotiation was depending, he received advice from Madrid that a general peace was concluded. Nevertheless, he broke off the treaty in obedience to a secret order for that purpose. The King of Spain hoped to obtain the restitution of St. Sebastian's, Fontarabia, and other places taken in the course of the war, in exchange for the evacuation of Sicily. Hostilities were continued until the admiral received advice from the Earl of Stair at Paris that the Spanish ambassador at the Hague had signed the quadruple alliance. By the same courier packets were delivered to the Count de Merci and the Marquis de Lede, which at last gave the admiral and imperial general to understand that he looked upon the peace as a thing concluded; and was ready to treat for a cessation of hostilities. They insisted upon his delivering up Palermo: on the other hand, he urged that, as their masters were in treaty for settling the terms of evacuating Sicily and Sardinia, he did not think himself authorized to agree to a cessation, except on condition that each party should remain on the ground they occupied, and expect further orders from their principals. After a fruitless interview between the three chiefs at the Cassine de Rossignola, the imperial general resolved to undertake the siege of Palermo: with this view he decamped from Alcamo on the eighteenth day of April, and followed the Marquis de Lede, who retreated before him, and took possession of the advantageous posts that commanded the passes into the plain of Palermo; but Count Merci, with indefatigable diligence, marched over the mountains, while the admiral coasted along shore, attending the motions of the army. The Spanish general, perceiving the Germans advancing into the plain, retired under the cannon of Palermo, and fortified his camp with strong intrenchments. On the second day of May the Germans took one of the enemy's redoubts by surprise, and the Marquis de Lede ordered all his forces to be drawn out to retake this fortification: both armies were on the point of engaging, when a courier arrived in a felucca, with a packet for the marquis, containing full powers to treat and agree about the evacuation of the island, and the transportation of the army to Spain. He forthwith drew off his army, and sent a trumpet to the general and admiral, with letters informing them of the orders he had received. Commissioners were appointed on each side, the negotiations begun, and the convention signed in a very few days. The Germans were put in possession of Palermo, and the Spanish army marched to Tauromini, from whence they were transported to Barcelona.

The admiral continued in the Mediterranean until he had seen the islands of Sicily and Sardinia evacuated by the Spaniards, and the mutual cessions executed between the emperor and the Duke of Savoy; in consequence of which, four battalions of Piedmontese troops were transported from Palermo to Sardinia, and took possession of Cagliari in the name of their master. In a word, Admiral Byng bore such a considerable share in this war of Sicily, that the fate of the island depended wholly on his courage, vigilance, and conduct. When he waited on his majesty at Hanover, he met with a very gracious reception. The king told him he had found out the secret of obliging his enemies as well as his friends; for the court of Spain had mentioned him in the most honourable terms, with respect to his candid and friendly deportment, in providing transports and other necessaries for the embarkation of their troops, and in protecting them from oppression. He was appointed treasurer of the navy, and rear-admiral of Great Britain: in a little time the king ennobled him, by the title of Viscount Torrington: he was declared a privy-counsellor; and afterwards made knight of the bath, at the revival of that order. During these occurrences in the Mediterranean, the Duke of Berwick advanced with the French army to the frontiers of Spain, where he took Fort Passage, and destroyed six ships of war that were on the stocks: then he reduced Fontarabia and St. Sebastian's, together with Port Antonio in the bottom of the bay of Biscay. In this last exploit the French were assisted by a detachment of English seamen, who burnt two large ships unfinished, and a great quantity of naval stores. The King of England, with a view to indemnify himself for the expense of the war, projected the conquest of Corunna in Biscay, and of Peru in South America. Four thousand men, commanded by Lord Cobham, were embarked at the Isle of Wight, and sailed on the twenty-first day of September, under convoy of five ships of war, conducted by Admiral Mighels. Instead of making an attempt upon Corunna, they reduced Vigo with very little difficulty; and Pont-a-Vedra submitted without resistance: here they found some brass artillery, small arms, and military stores, with which they returned to England. In the mean time, Captain Johnson, with two English ships of war, destroyed the same number of Spanish ships in the

*Philip obliged to accede to the quadruple alliance.*

port of Ribadeo, to the eastward of Cape Ortegas; so that the naval power of Spain was totally ruined. The expedition to the West Indies was prevented by the peace. Spain being oppressed on all sides, and utterly exhausted, Philip saw the necessity of a speedy pacification. He now perceived the madness of Alberoni's ambitious projects. That minister was personally disagreeable to the emperor, the King of England, and the Regent of France, who had declared they would hearken to no proposals while he should continue in office: the Spanish monarch, therefore, divested him of his employment, and ordered him to quit the kingdom in three weeks. The Marquis de Beretti Landi, minister from the court of Madrid at the Hague, delivered a plan of pacification to the states; but it was rejected by the allies; and Philip was obliged at last to accede to the quadruple alliance.

On the fourteenth day of November, King George returned to England, and on the twenty-third opened the session of Parliament with a speech, in which he told them that all Europe, as well as Great Britain, was on the point of being delivered from the calamities of war, by the influence of British arms and councils. He exhorted the Commons to concert proper means for lessening the debts of the nation; and concluded with a panegyric upon his own government. It must be owned he had acted with equal vigour and deliberation in all the troubles he had encountered since his accession to the throne. The addresses of both Houses were as warm as he could desire. They in particular extolled him for having interposed in behalf of the Protestants of Hungary, Poland, and Germany, who had been oppressed by the practices of the popish clergy, and presented to him memorials, containing a detail of their grievances. He and all the other Protestant powers warmly interceded in their favour; but the grievances were not redressed. The peerage bill was now revived by the Duke of Buckingham; and, in spite of all opposition, passed through the House of Lords. It had been projected by Earl Stanhope, and eagerly supported by the Earl of Sunderland; therefore, Mr. Robert Walpole attacked it in the House of Commons with extraordinary vehemence. Here too it was opposed by a considerable number of whig members; and, after warm debates, rejected by a large

*Bill for securing the dependency of Ireland upon the crown of Great Britain.*

majority. The next object that engrossed the attention of the Parliament was a bill for better securing the dependency of Ireland upon the crown of Great Britain. Maurice Annesley had appealed to the House of Peers in England from a decree of the House of Peers in Ireland, which was reversed. The British Peers ordered the barons of the exchequer in Ireland to put Mr. Annesley in possession of the lands he had lost by the decree in that kingdom. The barons obeyed this order; and the Irish House of Peers passed a vote against them, as having acted in derogation to the king's prerogative in his high court of Parliament in Ireland, as also of the rights and privileges of that kingdom, and of the Parliament thereof; they likewise ordered them to be taken into custody of the usher of the black rod; they transmitted a long representation to the king, demonstrating their right to the final judicature of causes; and the Duke of Leeds, in the Upper House, urged fifteen reasons to support the claim of the Irish Peers. Notwithstanding these arguments, the House of Lords in England resolved that the barons of the exchequer in Ireland had acted with courage, according to law in support of his majesty's prerogative, and with fidelity to the crown of Great Britain. They addressed the king to confer on them some marks of his royal favour as a recompense for the ill usage they had undergone. Finally, they prepared the bill, by which the Irish House of Lords was deprived of all right to pass sentence, affirm or reverse any judgment or decree, given or made, in any court within that kingdom. In the House of Commons it was opposed by Mr. Pitt, Mr. Hungerford, Lords Molesworth and Tyrconnel; but was carried by the majority, and received the royal assent.

The king having recommended to the Commons the consideration of proper means for lessening the national debt, was a prelude to the famous South-Sea act, which became productive of so much mischief and infatuation. The scheme was projected by Sir John Blunt, who had been bred a scrivener, and was possessed of all the cunning, plausibility, and boldness requisite for such an undertaking. He communicated his plan to Mr. Aislabie, the chancellor of the exchequer, as well as to one of the secretaries of state. He answered all their objections; and the project was adopted. They foresaw their own private advantage in the execution of the design, which was imparted in the name of the South-Sea Company, of which Blunt was a director, who influenced all their proceedings. The pretence for the scheme was to discharge the national debt, by reducing all the funds into one. The bank and South-Sea Company outbid each other. The South-Sea Company altered their original plan, and offered such high terms to government, that the proposals of the bank were rejected; and a bill was ordered to be brought into the House of Commons, formed on the plan presented by the South-Sea Company. While this affair was in agitation, the stock of that company rose from one hundred and thirty to near four hundred, in consequence of the conduct of the Commons, who had rejected a motion for a clause in the bill, to fix what share in the capital stock of the company should be vested in those proprietors of the annuities who might voluntarily subscribe; or how many years' purchase in money they should receive in subscribing, at the choice of the proprietors. In the House of Lords, the bill was opposed by Lord North and Grey, Earl Cowper, the Dukes of Wharton, Buckingham, and other peers. They affirmed it was calculated for enriching a few and impoverishing a great number: that it countenanced the fraudulent and pernicious practice of stock-jobbing, which diverted the genius of the people from trade and industry: that it would give foreigners the opportunity to double and treble the vast sums they had in the public funds; and they would be tempted to realize and withdraw their capital and immense gains to other countries; so that Great Britain would be drained of all its gold and silver: that the artificial and prodigious rise of the South-Sea stock was a dangerous bait, which might decoy many unwary people to their ruin, alluring them by a false prospect of gain to part with the fruits of their industry, to purchase imaginary riches: that the addition of above thirty millions capital would give such power to the South-Sea Company as might endanger the liberties of the nation; for by their extensive interest they would be able to influence most if not all the elections of the members; and consequently overrule the resolutions of the House of Commons. Earl Cowper urged, that in all public bargains the individuals in the administration ought to take care that they should be more advantageous to the state than to private persons; but that a contrary method

*Annals. Corbet. Hist. Reg. Tindal. Lives of the Admirals.*

1720.

had been followed in the contract made with the South-Sea Company; for, should the stocks be kept at the advanced price to which they had been raised by the oblique arts of stock-jobbing, either that company or its principal members, would gain above thirty millions, of which no more than one-fourth part would be given towards the discharge of the national debts. He apprehended that the repurchase of annuities would meet with insuperable difficulties; and, in such case, none but a few persons who were in the secret, who had bought stocks at a low rate, and afterwards sold them at a high price, would in the end be gainers by the project. The Earl of Sunderland answered their objections. He declared that those who countenanced the scheme of the South-Sea Company had nothing in view but the advantage of the nation. He owned that the managers for that company had undoubtedly a prospect of private gain, either to themselves or to their corporation; but, he said, when the scheme was accepted, neither the one nor the other could foresee that the stocks would have risen to such a height; that if they had continued as they were, the public would have had the far greater share of the advantage accruing from the scheme; and should they be kept up to the present high price, it was but reasonable that the South-Sea Company should enjoy the profits procured to it by the wise management and industry of the directors, which would enable it to make large dividends, and thereby accomplish the purpose of the scheme. The bill passed without amendment or division; and on the seventh day of April received the royal assent. By this act the South-Sea Company was authorized to take in, by purchase or subscription, the irredeemable debts of the nation, stated at sixteen millions five hundred forty-six thousand four hundred eighty-two pounds, seven shillings, one penny farthing, at such times as they should find it convenient before the first day of March of the ensuing year, and without any compulsion on any of the proprietors, at such rates and prices as should be agreed upon between the company and the respective proprietors. They were likewise authorized to take in all the redeemable debts, amounting to the same sum as that of the irredeemables, either by purchase, by taking subscriptions, or by paying off the creditors. For the liberty of taking in the national debts, and increasing their capital stock accordingly, the company consented that their present and to be increased annuity should be continued at five per cent. till Midsummer, in the year one thousand seven hundred and twenty-seven; from thence to be reduced to four per cent. and be redeemable by Parliament. In consideration of this and other advantages expressed in the act, the company declared themselves willing to make such payments into the receipt of the exchequer as were specified for the use of the public, to be applied to the discharge of the public debts incurred before Christmas, in the year one thousand seven hundred and sixteen. The sums they were obliged to pay for the liberty of taking in the redeemable debts, four years and a half's purchase for all long and short annuities that should be subscribed, and one year's purchase for such long annuities as should not be subscribed, amounted on the execution of the act to about seven millions. For enabling the company to raise this sum, they were empowered to make calls for money from their members; to open books of subscription; to grant annuities redeemable by the company; to borrow money upon any contract or bill under their common seal, or on the credit of their capital stock; to convert the money demanded of their members into additional stock, without, however, making any addition to the company's annuities, payable out of the public duties. It was enacted, that out of the first monies arising from the sums paid by the company into the exchequer, such public debts, carrying interest at five per cent., incurred before the twenty-fifth day of December, in the year one thousand seven hundred and sixteen, founded upon any former act of Parliament, as were now redeemable, or might be redeemed before the twenty-fifth day of December, in the year one thousand seven hundred and twenty-two, should be discharged in the first place: that then all the remainder should be applied towards paying off so much of the capital stock of the company as should then carry an interest of five per cent. It was likewise provided that after Midsummer, in the year one thousand seven hundred and twenty-seven, the company should not be paid off in any sums being less than one million at a time.

The heads of the Royal Assurance and London Assurance Companies, understanding that the civil list was considerably in arrears, offered to the ministry six hundred thousand pounds towards the discharge of that debt, on condition of their obtaining the king's charter, with a parliamentary sanction, for the establishment of their respective companies. The proposal was embraced; and the king communicated it in a message to the House of Commons, desiring their concurrence. A bill was immediately passed, enabling his majesty to grant letters of incorporation to the two companies. It soon obtained the royal assent; and on the eleventh day of June, an end was put to the session. This was the age of interested projects, inspired by a venal spirit of adventure, the natural consequence of that avarice, fraud, and profligacy which the monied corporations had introduced. This of all others is the most unfavourable era for an historian. A reader of sentiment and imagination cannot be entertained or interested by a dry detail of such transactions as admit of no warmth, no colouring, no embellishment; a detail which serves only to exhibit an inanimate picture of tasteless vice and mean degeneracy.

*Charters granted to the Royal and London Assurance offices.*

By this time an alliance offensive and defensive was concluded at Stockholm between King George and the Queen of Sweden, by which his majesty engaged to send a fleet into the Baltic, to act against the Czar of Muscovy, in case that monarch should reject reasonable proposals of peace. Peter loudly complained of the insolent interposition of King George, alleging that he had failed in his engagements, both as Elector of Hanover and King of Great Britain. His resident at London presented a long memorial on this subject, which was answered by the British and Hanoverian ministry. These recriminations served only to inflame the difference. The czar continued to prosecute the war, and at length concluded a peace without a mediator. At the instances, however, of King George and the Regent of France, a treaty of peace was signed between the Queen of Sweden and the King of Prussia, to whom that princess ceded the city of Stetin, the district between the rivers Oder and Pehnne, with the isles of Wollin and Usedom. On the other hand, he engaged to join the King of Great Britain in his endeavours to effect a peace between Sweden and Denmark, on condition that the Danish king should restore to Queen Ulrica that part of Pomerania which he had seized; he likewise promised to pay to that queen two millions of rix-dollars, in consideration of the cessions she had made. The treaty be-

*Treaty of alliance with Sweden.*

tween Sweden and Denmark was signed at Frederickstadt in the month of June, through the mediation of the King of Great Britain, who became guarantee for the Dane's keeping possession of Sleswick. He consented, however, to restore the Upper Pomerania, the Isle of Rugen, the city of Wismar, and whatever he had taken from Sweden during the war, in consideration of Sweden's renouncing the exemption from toll in the Sound, and the two Belts, and paying to Denmark six hundred thousand rix-dollars.

Sir John Norris had again sailed to the Baltic with a strong squadron, to give weight to the king's mediation. When he arrived at Copenhagen he wrote a letter to Prince Dolgorouki, the czar's ambassador at the court of Denmark, signifying that he and the king's envoy at Stockholm were vested with full powers to act jointly or separately in quality of plenipotentiaries, in order to effect a peace between Sweden and Muscovy, in the way of mediation. The prince answered that the czar had nothing more at heart than peace and tranquillity; and in case his Britannic majesty had any proposals to make to that prince, he hoped the admiral would excuse him from receiving them, as they might be delivered in a much more compendious way. The English fleet immediately joined that of Sweden as auxiliaries; but they had no opportunity of acting against the Russian squadron, which secured itself in Revel. Ulrica, Queen of Sweden and sister to Charles XII., had married the Prince of Hesse, and was extremely desirous that he should be joined with her in the administration of the regal power. She wrote a separate letter to each of the four states, desiring they would confer on him the sovereignty; and after some opposition from the nobles, he was actually elected king of Sweden. He sent one of his general officers to notify his elevation to the czar, who congratulated him upon his accession to the throne: this was the beginning of a negotiation which ended in peace, and established the tranquillity of the north. In the midst of these transactions, King George set out from England for his Hanoverian dominions; but, before he departed from Great Britain, he was reconciled to the Prince of Wales, through the endeavours of the Duke of Devonshire and Mr. Walpole, who, with Earl Cowper, Lord Townshend, Mr. Methuen, and Mr. Pulteney, were received into favour, and reunited with the ministry. The Earls of Dorset and

Bridgewater were promoted to the title of dukes; Lord Viscount Castleton was made an earl; Hugh Boscawen was created a baron, and Viscount Falmouth; and John Wallop, baron, and Viscount of Lymington.

While the king was involved at Hanover in a labyrinth of negotiations, the South-Sea scheme produced a kind of national delirium in his English dominions. Blunt, the projector, had taken the hint of his plan from the famous Mississippi scheme formed by Law, which in the preceding year had raised such a ferment in France, and entailed ruin upon many thousand families of that kingdom. In the scheme of Law, there was something substantial. An exclusive trade to Louisiana promised some advantage; though the design was defeated by the frantic eagerness of the people. Law himself became the dupe of the regent, who transferred the burden of fifteen hundred millions of the king's debts to the shoulders of the subjects: while the projector was sacrificed as the scapegoat of political iniquity. The South-Sea scheme promised no commercial advantage of any consequence. It was buoyed up by nothing but the folly and rapaciousness of individuals, which became so blind and extravagant, that Blunt, with moderate talents, was able to impose upon the whole nation, and make tools of the other directors, to serve his own purposes, and those of a few associates. When this projector found that the South-Sea stock did not rise according to his expectation upon the bills being passed, he circulated a report that Gibraltar and Port-Mahon would be exchanged for some places in Peru; by which means the English trade to the South-Sea would be protected and enlarged. This rumour, diffused by his emissaries, acted like a contagion. In five days the directors opened their books for a subscription of one million, at the rate of three hundred pounds for every hundred pounds capital. Persons of all ranks crowded to the house in such a manner, that the first subscription exceeded two millions of original stock. In a few days this stock advanced to three hundred and forty pounds; and the subscriptions were sold for double the price of the first payment. Without entering into a detail of the proceedings, or explaining the scandalous arts that were practised to enhance the value of the stock, and decoy the unwary, we shall only observe that, by the promise of prodigious dividends, and other infamous arts, the stock was raised to one thousand; and the whole nation infected with the spirit of stock-jobbing to an astonishing degree. All distinctions of party, religion, sex, character, and circumstances, were swallowed up in this universal concern, or in some such pecuniary project. Exchange-alley was filled with a strange concourse of statesmen and clergymen, churchmen and dissenters, whigs and tories, physicians, lawyers, tradesmen, and even with multitudes of females. All other professions and employments were utterly neglected; and the people's attention wholly engrossed by this and other chimerical schemes, which were known by the denomination of bubbles. New companies started up every day, under the countenance of the prime nobility. The Prince of Wales was constituted governor of the Welsh Copper Company: the Duke of Chandos appeared at the head of the York-buildings Company: the Duke of Bridgewater formed a third, for building houses in London and Westminster. About a hundred such schemes were projected and put in execution, to the ruin of many thousands. The sums proposed to be raised by these expedients amounted to three hundred millions sterling, which exceeded the value of all the lands in England. The nation was so intoxicated with the spirit of adventure, that people became a prey to the grossest delusion. An obscure projector, pretending to have formed a very advantageous scheme, which, however, he did not explain, published proposals for a subscription, in which he promised, that in one month the particulars of his project should be disclosed. In the mean time he declared that every person paying two guineas should be entitled to a subscription for one hundred pounds, which would produce that sum yearly. In one forenoon this adventurer received a thousand of these subscriptions; and in the evening set out for another kingdom. The king, before his departure, had issued a proclamation against these unlawful projects; the lords justices afterwards dismissed all the petitions that had been presented for charters and patents; and the Prince of Wales renounced the company of which he had been elected governor. The South-Sea scheme raised such a flood of eager avidity and extravagant hope, that the majority of the directors were swept along with it even contrary to their own sense and inclination; but Blunt and his accomplices still directed the stream.

The infatuation prevailed till the eighth day of September,

when the stock began to fall. Then did some of the adventurers awake from their delirium. The number of the sellers daily increased. On the twenty-ninth day of the month the stock had sunk to one hundred and fifty: several eminent goldsmiths and bankers, who had lent great sums upon it, were obliged to stop payment and abscond. The ebb of this portentous tide was so violent that it bore down every thing in its way; and an infinite number of families were overwhelmed with ruin. Public credit sustained a terrible shock: the nation was thrown into a dangerous ferment; and nothing was heard but the ravings of grief, diappointment, and despair. Some principal members of the ministry were deeply concerned in these fraudulent transactions: when they saw the price of stock sinking daily, they employed all their influence with the bank to support the credit of the South-Sea Company. That corporation agreed, though with reluctance, to subscribe into the stock of the South-Sea Company, valued at four hundred per cent., three millions five hundred thousand pounds, which the company was to repay to the bank on Lady-day and Michaelmas of the ensuing year. This transaction was managed by Mr. Robert Walpole, who, with his own hand, wrote the minute of agreement, afterwards known by the name of the bank contract. Books were opened at the bank to take in a subscription for the support of public credit; and considerable sums of money were brought in. By this expedient the stock was raised at first, and those who contrived it seized the opportunity to realize. But the bankruptcy of goldsmiths and the Sword-blade Company, from the fall of South-Sea stock, occasioned such a run upon the bank, that the money was paid away faster than it could be received from the subscription. Then the South-Sea stock sunk again; and the directors of the bank, finding themselves in danger of being involved in that company's ruin, renounced the agreement, which, indeed, they were under no obligation to perform, for it was drawn up in such a manner as to be no more than the rough draft of a subsequent agreement, without due form, penalty, or clause of obligation. All expedients having failed, and the clamours of the people daily increasing, expresses were despatched to Hanover, representing the state of the nation, and pressing the king to return. He accordingly shortened his intended stay in Germany, and arrived in England on the eleventh day of November.

*A secret committee appointed by the House of Commons.*

The Parliament being assembled on the eighth day of December, his majesty expressed his concern for the unhappy turn of affairs, which had so deeply affected the public credit at home : he earnestly desired the Commons to consider of the most effectual and speedy methods to restore the national credit, and fix it upon a lasting establishment. The Lower House was too much interested in the calamity to postpone the consideration of that subject. The members seemed to lay aside all party distinctions, and vie with each other in promoting an inquiry, by which justice might be done to the injured nation. They ordered the directors to produce an account of all their proceedings. Sir Joseph Jekyll moved, that a select committee might be appointed, to examine the particulars of this transaction. Mr. Walpole, now paymaster of the forces, observed, that such a method would protract the inquiry, while the public credit lay in a bleeding condition. He told the House he had formed a scheme for restoring public credit; but before he would communicate this plan, desired to know whether the subscriptions of public debts and incumbrances, money subscriptions, and other contracts made with the South-Sea Company, should remain in the present state. After a warm debate, the question was carried in the affirmative, with this addition, " Unless altered for the ease and relief of the proprietors, by a general court of the South-Sea Company, or set aside in due course of law." Next day Walpole produced his scheme, to engraft nine millions of South-Sea stock into the bank of England, and the like sum into the East India Company, on certain conditions. The House voted, that proposals should be received from the bank, and those two companies, on this subject. These being delivered, the Commons resolved, that an engrossment of nine millions of the capital stock of the South-Sea Company, into the capital stock of the bank and East India Company, as proposed by these companies, would contribute very much to the restoring public credit. A bill upon this resolution was brought in, passed through both Houses, and received the royal assent. Another bill was enacted into a law, for restraining the sub-governor, deputy-governor, directors, treasurer, under-treasurer, cashier, secretary, and accountants, of the South-Sea Company, from quitting the kingdom, till the end of the next session of Parliament; and for discovering their estates and effects, so as to prevent them from being transported or alienated. A committee of secrecy was chosen by ballot, to examine all the books, papers, and proceedings, relating to the execution of the South-Sea act.

The Lords were not less eager than the Commons to prosecute this inquiry, though divers members in both Houses were deeply involved in the guilt and infamy of the transaction. Earl Stanhope said the estates of the criminals, whether directors or not directors, ought to be confiscated, to repair the public losses. He was seconded by Lord Carteret, and even by the Earl of Sunderland. The Duke of Wharton declared he would give up the best friend he had, should he be found guilty. He observed, that the nation had been plundered in a most flagrant and notorious manner; therefore, they ought to find out and punish the offenders severely without respect to persons. The sub and deputy-governors, the directors and officers of the South-Sea Company, were examined at the bar of the House. Then a bill was brought in, disabling them to enjoy any office in that company, or in the East India Company, or in the bank of England. Three brokers were likewise examined, and made great discoveries. Knight, the treasurer of the South-Sea Company, who had been entrusted with the secrets of the whole affair, thought proper to withdraw himself from the kingdom. A proclamation was issued to apprehend him; and another for preventing any of the directors from escaping out of the kingdom. At this period the secret committee informed the House of Commons, that they had already discovered a train of the deepest villany and fraud that hell ever contrived to ruin a nation, which in due time they would lay before the House: in the mean while they thought it highly necessary to secure the persons of some of the directors and principal officers of the South-Sea Company, as well as to seize their papers. An order was made to secure the books and papers of Knight, Surman, and Turner. The persons of Sir George Caswell, Sir John Blunt, Sir John Lambert, Sir John Fellowes, and Mr. Grigsby, were taken into custody. Sir Theodore Jansen, Mr. Sawbridge, Sir Robert Chaplain, and Mr. Eyles, were expelled the House, and apprehended. Mr. Aislabie resigned his employments of chancellor of the exchequer and lord of the treasury; and orders were given to remove all directors of the South-Sea Company from the places they possessed under the government.

The Lords, in the course of their examination, discovered that large portions of South-Sea stock had been given to several persons in the administration and House of Commons, for promoting the passing of the South-Sea act. The House immediately resolved, that this practice was a notorious and most dangerous species of corruption; that the directors of the South-Sea Company having ordered great quantities of their stock to be bought for the service of the company, when it was at a very high price, and on pretence of keeping up the price of stock; and at the same time several of the directors, and other officers belonging to the company, having, in a clandestine manner, sold their own stock to the company, such directors and officers were guilty of a notorious fraud and breach of trust, and their so doing was one great cause of the unhappy turn of affairs, that had so much affected public credit. Many other resolutions were taken against that infamous confederacy, in which, however, the innocent were confounded with the guilty. Sir John Blunt refusing to answer certain interrogations, a violent debate arose about the manner in which he should be treated. The Duke of Wharton observed, that the government of the best princes was sometimes rendered intolerable to their subjects by bad ministers: he mentioned the example of Sejanus, who had made a division in the imperial family, and rendered the reign of Claudius hateful to the Romans. Earl Stanhope, conceiving this reflection was aimed at him, was seized with a transport of anger. He undertook to vindicate the ministry; and spoke with such vehemence as produced a violent headache, which obliged him to retire. He underwent proper evacuations, and seemed to recover; but next day, in the evening, he became lethargic, and being seized with a suffocation, instantly expired. The king deeply regretted the loss of this favourite minister, which was the more unfortunate as it happened at such a critical conjuncture; and he appointed Lord Townshend to fill his place of secretary. Earl Stanhope was survived but a few days by the other secretary, Mr. Craggs, who died of the small-pox on the sixteenth day of February. Knight, the cashier of the South-Sea Company, being seized at Tirlemont, by the vigilance of Mr. Gandot, secretary to Mr. Leathes, the British resident at Brussels, was confined in the citadel of Antwerp. Application was made to the court of Vienna, that he should be delivered to such persons as might be appointed to receive him; but he had found means to interest the states of Brabant in his behalf. They insisted upon their privilege granted by charter, that no person apprehended for any crime in Brabant should be tried in any other country. The House of Commons expressed their indignation at this frivolous pretence: instances were renewed to the emperor: and in the mean time Knight escaped from the citadel of Antwerp.

The committee of secrecy found that, before any subscription could be made, a fictitious stock of five hundred and seventy-four thousand pounds had been disposed of by the directors, to facilitate the passing the bill. Great part of this was distributed among the Earl of Sunderland, Mr. Craggs, senior, the Duchess of Kendal, the Countess of Platen and her two nieces, Mr. Secretary Craggs, and Mr. Aislabie, chancellor of the exchequer. *The estates of the directors of the South-Sea Company are confiscated.* In consequence of the committee's report, the House came to several severe though just resolutions against the directors and officers of the South-Sea Company; and a bill was prepared for the relief of the unhappy sufferers. Mr. Stanhope, one of the secretaries of the treasury, charged in the report with having large quantities of stock and subscriptions, desired that he might have an opportunity to clear himself. His request was granted; and the affair being discussed, he was cleared by a majority of three voices. Fifty thousand pounds in stock had been taken by Knight for the use of the Earl of Sunderland. Great part of the House entered eagerly into this inquiry; and a violent dispute ensued. The whole strength of the ministry was mustered in his defence. The majority declared him innocent; the nation in general was of another opinion. He resigned his place of first commissioner in the treasury, which was bestowed upon Mr. Robert Walpole; but he still retained the confidence of his master. With respect to Mr. Aislabie, the evidence appeared so strong against him, that the Commons resolved, he had promoted the destructive execution of the South-Sea scheme, with a view to his own exorbitant profit, and combined with the directors in their pernicious practices, to the ruin of public credit. He was expelled the House, and committed to the Tower. Mr. Craggs, senior, died of the small-pox, before he underwent the censure of the House. Nevertheless, they resolved that he was a notorious accomplice with Robert Knight, and some of the directors, in carrying on their scandalous practices; and, therefore, that all the estate of which he was possessed, from the first day of December in the preceding year, should be applied towards the relief of the unhappy sufferers in the South-Sea Company. The directors, in obedience to the order of the House, delivered inventories of their estates, which were confiscated by act of Parliament, towards making good the damages sustained by the Company, after a certain allowance was deducted for each, according to his conduct and circumstances.

*Oldmixon. Annals. Hist. Reg. Polit. State. Deb. in Parliam. Tindal.*

The delinquents being thus punished by the forfeiture of their fortunes, the House converted their attention to means for repairing the mischiefs which the scheme had produced. This was a very difficult task, on account of the contending interests of those engaged in the South-Sea Company, which rendered it impossible to relieve some but at the expense of others. Several wholesome resolutions were taken, and presented with an address to the king, explaining the motives of their proceedings. On the twenty-ninth day of July, the Parliament was prorogued for two days only. Then his majesty, going to the House of Peers, declared that he had called them together again so suddenly, that they might resume the consideration of the state of public credit. The Commons immediately prepared a bill upon the resolutions they had taken. The whole capital stock, at the end of the year one thousand seven hundred and twenty, amounted to about thirty-seven millions eight hundred thousand pounds. The stock allotted to all the proprietors did not exceed twenty-four millions five hundred thousand pounds; the remaining capital stock belonged to the company in their corporate capacity. It was the profit arising from the execution of the South-Sea scheme; and out of this the bill enacted, that seven millions should be paid to the public. The present act likewise directed several additions to be made to the stock of the proprietors, out of that possessed by the company in their own right; it made a particular distribution of stock, amounting to two millions two hundred thousand pounds; and upon remitting five millions of the seven to be paid to the public, annihilated two millions of their capital. It was enacted that, after these distributions, the remaining capital

*1721. Proceedings of the Commons with respect to the stock of the South-Sea Company.*

stock should be divided among all the proprietors. This dividend amounted to thirty-three pounds six shillings and eight-pence per cent., and deprived the company of eight millions nine hundred thousand pounds. They had lent above eleven millions on stock unredeemed; of which the Parliament discharged all the debtors, upon their paying ten per cent. Upon this article the company's loss exceeded six millions nine hundred thousand pounds; for many debtors refused to make any payment. The proprietors of the stock loudly complained of their being deprived of two millions; and the Parliament in the sequel revived that sum which had been annihilated. While this affair was in agitation, petitions from counties, cities, and boroughs, in all parts of the kingdom, were presented to the House, crying for justice against the villany of the directors. Pamphlets and papers were daily published on the same subject; so that the whole nation was exasperated to the highest pitch of resentment. Nevertheless, by the wise and vigorous resolutions of the Parliament, the South-Sea Company was soon in a condition to fulfil their engagements with the public; the ferment of the people subsided; and the credit of the nation was restored.

## CHAPTER XIV.

BILL AGAINST ATHEISM AND IMMORALITY POSTPONED. — SESSION CLOSED. — ALLIANCE BETWEEN GREAT BRITAIN, FRANCE, AND SPAIN. — PLAGUE AT MARSEILLES. — DEBATES IN THE HOUSE OF LORDS ABOUT MR. LAW THE PROJECTOR. — SENTIMENTS OF SOME LORDS TOUCHING THE WAR WITH SPAIN. — PETITION OF THE QUAKERS. — THE PARLIAMENT DISSOLVED. — RUMOURS OF A CONSPIRACY. — THE BISHOP OF ROCHESTER IS COMMITTED TO THE TOWER. — NEW PARLIAMENT. — DECLARATION OF THE PRETENDER. — REPORT OF THE SECRET COMMITTEE. — BILL OF PAINS AND PENALTIES AGAINST THE BISHOP OF ROCHESTER — WHO IS DEPRIVED, AND DRIVEN INTO PERPETUAL EXILE. — PROCEEDINGS AGAINST THOSE CONCERNED IN THE LOTTERY AT HARBURGH. — AFFAIRS OF THE CONTINENT. — CLAMOUR IN IRELAND ON ACCOUNT OF WOOD'S COINAGE. — DEATH OF THE DUKE OF ORLEANS. — AN ACT FOR LESSENING THE PUBLIC DEBTS. — PHILIP, KING OF SPAIN, ABDICATES THE THRONE. — ABUSES IN CHANCERY. — TRIAL OF THE EARL OF MACCLESFIELD. — DEBATES ABOUT THE DEBTS OF THE CIVIL LIST. — A BILL IN FAVOUR OF THE LATE LORD BOLINGBROKE. — TREATY OF ALLIANCE BETWEEN THE COURTS OF VIENNA AND MADRID. — TREATY OF HANOVER — APPROVED IN PARLIAMENT. — RIOTS IN SCOTLAND ON ACCOUNT OF THE MALT-TAX. — A SMALL SQUADRON SENT TO THE BALTIC. — ADMIRAL HOSIER'S EXPEDITION TO THE WEST INDIES. — DISGRACE OF THE DUKE DE RIPPERDA. — SUBSTANCE OF THE KING'S SPEECH TO PARLIAMENT. — DEBATE IN THE HOUSE OF LORDS UPON THE APPROACHING RUPTURE WITH THE EMPEROR AND SPAIN. — MEMORIAL OF MR. PALME, THE IMPERIAL RESIDENT AT LONDON. — CONVENTIONS WITH SWEDEN AND HESSE-CASSEL. — VOTE OF CREDIT. — SIEGE OF GIBRALTAR BY THE SPANIARDS. — PRELIMINARIES OF PEACE. — DEATH AND CHARACTER OF GEORGE I. KING OF GREAT BRITAIN.

*1721. Bill against atheism and immorality postponed.*

DURING the infatuation produced by this infamous scheme, luxury, vice, and profligacy increased to a shocking degree of extravagance. The adventurers, intoxicated by their imaginary wealth, pampered themselves with the rarest dainties, and the most expensive wines that could be imported: they purchased the most sumptuous furniture, equipage, and apparel, though without taste or discernment: they indulged their criminal passions to the most scandalous excess: their discourse was the language of pride, insolence, and the most ridiculous ostentation: they affected to scoff at religion and morality; and even to set Heaven at defiance. The Earl of Nottingham complained in the House of Lords of the growth of atheism, profaneness, and immorality; and a bill was brought in for suppressing blasphemy and profaneness. It contained several articles seemingly calculated to restrain the liberty granted to nonconformists by the laws of the last session; for that reason it met with violent opposition. It was supported by the Archbishop of Canterbury, the Earl of Nottingham, Lords Bathurst and Trevor, the Bishops of London, Winchester, and Lichfield and Coventry. One of these said, he verily believed the present calamity occasioned by the South-Sea project was a judgment of God on the blasphemy and profaneness of the nation. Lord Onslow replied, "That noble peer must then be a great sinner, for he has lost considerably by the South-Sea scheme." The Duke of Wharton, who had rendered himself famous by his wit and profligacy, said he was not insensible of the common opinion of the town concerning himself, and gladly seized this opportunity of vindicating his character, by declaring he was far from being a patron of blasphemy, or an enemy to religion. On the other hand, he could not but oppose the bill, because he conceived it to be repugnant to the holy scripture. Then pulling an old family Bible from his pocket, he quoted several passages from the epistles of St. Peter and St. Paul; concluding with a desire that the bill might be thrown out. The Earl of Peterborough declared, that though he was for a parliamentary king, yet he did not desire to have a parliamentary God, or a parliamentary religion; and should the House declare for one of this kind, he would go to Rome, and endeavour to be chosen a cardinal; for he had rather sit in the conclave than with their lordships upon those terms. After a vehement debate, the bill was postponed to a long day, by a considerable majority.

The season was far advanced before the supplies were granted; and at length they were not voted with Session that cheerfulness and good humour which the closed. majority had hitherto manifested on such occasions. On the sixteenth day of June, the king sent a message to the House of 'Commons, importing that he had agreed to pay a subsidy to the crown of Sweden, and he hoped they would enable him to make good his engagements. The leaders of the opposition took fire at this intimation. They desired to know whether this subsidy, amounting to seventy-two thousand pounds, was to be paid to Sweden over and above the expense of maintaining a strong squadron in the Baltic. Lord Molesworth observed that, by our late conduct, we were become the allies of the whole world, and the bubbles of all our allies; for we were obliged to pay them well for their assistance. He affirmed that the treaties which had been made with Sweden, at different times, were inconsistent and contradictory: that our late engagements with that crown were contrary to the treaties subsisting with Denmark, and directly opposite to the measures formerly concerted with the Czar of Muscovy. He said, that in order to engage the czar to yield what he had gained in the course of the war, the King of Prussia ought to give up Stetin, and the Elector of Hanover restore Bremen and Verden: that, after all, England had no business to intermeddle with the affairs of the empire: that we reaped little or no advantage by our trade to the Baltic, but that of procuring naval stores: he owned that hemp was a very necessary commodity, particularly at this juncture; but he insisted, that if due encouragement were given to some of our plantations in America, we might be supplied from thence at a much cheaper rate than from Sweden and Norway. Notwithstanding these arguments, the Swedish supply was granted; and in about three weeks, their complaisance was put to another proof. They were given to understand, by a second message, that the debts of the civil list amounted to five hundred and fifty thousand pounds; and his majesty hoped they would empower him to raise that sum upon the revenue, as he proposed it should be replaced in the civil list, and reimbursed by a deduction from the salaries and wages of all officers, as well as from the pensions and other payments from the crown. A bill was prepared for this purpose, though not without warm opposition; and, at the same time, an act passed for a general pardon. On the tenth day of August, the king closed the session with a speech, in which he expressed his concern for the sufferings of the innocent, and a just indignation against the guilty, with respect to the South-Sea scheme. These professions were judged necessary to clear his own character, which had incurred the suspicion of some people, who whispered, that he was not altogether free from connexions with the projectors of that design; that the emperor had, at his desire, refused to deliver up Knight; and that he favoured the directors and their accomplices.

Lords Townshend and Carteret were now appointed secretaries of state; and the Earl of Ilay was vested with the office of lord privy-seal of Scotland. In June the treaty of peace between Great Britain and Spain was signed at Madrid. The contracting parties engaged to restore mutually all the effects

*Alliance between Great Britain, France, and Spain.*

seized and confiscated on both sides. In particular, the King of England promised to restore all the ships of the Spanish fleet which had been taken in the Mediterranean, or the value of them, if they were sold. He likewise promised, in a secret article, that he would no longer interfere in the affairs of Italy; and the King of Spain made an absolute cession of Gibraltar and Port-Mahon. At the same time, a defensive alliance was concluded between Great Britain, France, and Spain. All remaining difficulties were referred to a congress at Cambray, where they hoped to consolidate a general peace, by determining all differences between the emperor and his Catholic majesty. In the mean time, the powers of Great Britain, France, and Spain, engaged, by virtue of the present treaty, to grant to the Duke of Parma a particular protection for the preservation of his territories and rights, and for the support of his dignity. It was also stipulated, that the States-General should be invited to accede to this alliance. The congress at Cambray was opened; but the demands on both sides were so high that it proved ineffectual. In the mean time, the peace between Russia and Sweden was concluded, on condition that the czar should retain Livonia, Ingria, Estonia, part of Carelia, and of the territory of Wyburg, Riga, Revel, and Nerva, in consideration of his restoring part of Finland, and paying two millions of rix-dollars to the King of Sweden. The personal animosity subsisting between King George and the czar seemed to increase. Bastigif, the Russian resident at London, having presented a memorial that contained some unguarded expressions, was ordered to quit the kingdom in a fortnight. The czar published a declaration at Petersburgh, complaining of this outrage, which, he said, ought naturally to have engaged him to use reprisals; but, as he perceived it was done without any regard to the concerns of England, and only in favour of the Hanoverian interest, he was unwilling that the English nation should suffer for a piece of injustice in which they had no share. He, therefore, granted to them all manner of security, and free liberty to trade in all his dominions. To finish this strange tissue of negotiations, King George concluded a treaty with the Moors of Africa, against which the Spaniards loudly exclaimed.

In the course of this year, Pope Clement XI. died; and the Princess of Wales was delivered of a prince, baptized by the name of William Augustus, the late Duke of Cumberland. A dreadful plague raging at Marseilles, a proclamation was published, forbidding any person to come into England, from any part of France between the Bay of Biscay and Dunkirk, without certificates of health. Other precautions were taken to guard against contagion. An act of Parliament had passed in the preceding session, for the prevention of infection, by building pest-houses, to which all infected persons, and all persons of an infected family, should be conveyed ; and, by drawing trenches and lines round any city, town, or place infected. The king, in his speech at opening the session of Parliament, on the nineteenth day of October, intimated the pacification of the north, by the conclusion of the treaty between Muscovy and Sweden. He desired the House of Commons to consider of means for easing the duties upon the imported commodities used in the manufactures of the kingdom. He observed, that the nation might be supplied with naval stores from our own colonies in North America ; and that their being employed in this useful and advantageous branch of commerce would divert them from setting up manufactures which directly interfered with those of Great Britain. He expressed a desire that, with respect to the supplies, his people might reap some immediate benefit from the present circumstances of affairs abroad ; and he earnestly recommended to their consideration means for preventing the plague, particularly by providing against the practice of smuggling.

*Plague at Marseilles.*

One of the first objects that attracted the attention of the Upper House was the case of John Law, the famous projector. The resentment of the people on account of his Mississippi scheme had obliged him to leave France. He retired to Italy, and was said to have visited the pretender at Rome. From thence he repaired to Hanover, and returned to England from the Baltic, in the fleet commanded by Sir John Norris. The king favoured him with a private audience : he kept open house, and was visited by great numbers of persons of the first quality. Earl Coningsby represented in the House of Lords, that he could not but entertain some jealousy of a person who had done so much mischief in a neighbouring kingdom, who, being immensely rich, might do a great deal more hurt here, by tampering with those who were grown desperate,

*Debates in the House of Lords about Mr. Law the projector.*

in consequence of being involved in the calamity occasioned by the fatal imitation of his pernicious projects. He observed, that this person was the more dangerous, as he had renounced his natural affection to his country, his allegiance to his lawful sovereign, and his religion, by turning Roman Catholic. Lord Carteret replied, that Mr. Law had, many years ago, the misfortune to kill a gentleman in a duel; but, having at last received the benefit of the king's clemency, and the appeal lodged by the relations of the deceased being taken off, he was come over to plead his majesty's pardon. He said there was no law to keep an Englishman out of his country; and, as Mr. Law was a subject of Great Britain, it was not even in the king's power to hinder him from coming over. After some dispute, the subject was dropped, and this great projector pleaded his pardon in the King's Bench, according to the usual form.

The ministry had by this time secured such a majority in both Houses, as enabled them to carry any point without the least difficulty. Some chiefs of the opposition they had brought over to their measures, and amongst the rest Lord Harcourt, who was created a viscount, and gratified with a pension of four thousand pounds. Nevertheless they could not shut the mouths of the minority, who still preserved the privilege of complaining. Great debates were occasioned by the navy-debt, which was increased to one million seven hundred thousand pounds. Some members in both Houses affirmed that such extraordinary expense could not be for the immediate service of Great Britain; but in all probability, for the preservation of foreign acquisitions. The ministers answered, that near two-thirds of the navy-debts were contracted in the late reign; and the Parliament acquiesced in this declaration; but in reality, the navy-debt had been unnecessarily increased, by keeping seamen in pay during the winter, and sending fleets to the Mediterranean and Baltic, in order to support the interests of Germany. The Duke of Wharton moved that the treaty with Spain might be laid before the House. The Earl of Sunderland said it contained a secret article which the King of Spain desired might not be made public, until after the treaty of Cambray should be discussed. The question was put, and the duke's motion rejected. The Earl of Strafford asserted, that as the war with Spain had been undertaken without necessity or just provocation, so the peace was concluded without any benefit or advantage: that, contrary to the law of nations, the Spanish fleet had been attacked without any declaration of war; even while a British minister and a secretary of state were treating amicably at Madrid: that the war was neither just nor politic, since it interrupted one of the most valuable branches of the English commerce, at a time when the nation groaned under the pressure of heavy debts, incurred by the former long expensive war. He, therefore, moved for an address to his majesty, desiring that the instructions given to Sir George Byng, now Lord Torrington, should be laid before the House. This motion being likewise, upon the question, rejected, a protest was entered. They voted an address, however, to know in what manner the king had disposed of the ships taken from the Spaniards. Disputes arose also from the bill to prevent infection. Earl Cowper represented, that the removal of persons to a lazaret, or pest-house, by order of the government, and the drawing lines and trenches round places infected, were powers unknown to the British constitution; inconsistent with the lenity of a free government, such as could never be wisely or usefully put in practice; the more odious, because copied from the arbitrary government of France; and impracticable, except by military compulsion. These obnoxious clauses were accordingly repealed, though not without great opposition. Indeed, nothing can be more absurd than a constitution that will not admit of just and necessary laws and regulations to prevent the dire consequences of the worst of all calamities. Such restrictions, instead of favouring the lenity of a free government, would be the most cruel imposition that could be laid on a free people, as it would act in diametrical opposition to the great principle of society, which is the preservation of the individual.

The quakers having presented a petition to the House of
*Petition of the quakers. The Parliament dissolved.* Commons, praying that a bill might be brought in for omitting, in their solemn affirmation, the words " in the presence of Almighty God," the House complied with their request; but the bill gave rise to a very warm debate among the Peers. Dr. Atterbury, Bishop of Rochester, said he did not know why such a distinguished mark of indulgence should be allowed to a set of people who were hardly Christians. He was supported by the Archbishop of York, the Earl of Strafford,

and Lord North and Grey. A petition was presented against the bill by the London clergy, who expressed a serious concern lest the minds of good men should be grieved and wounded, and the enemies of Christianity triumph, when they should see such condescensions made by a Christian legislature, to a set of men who renounce the divine institutions of Christ, particularly that by which the faithful are initiated into his religion, and denominated Christians. The petition, though presented by the Archbishop of York, was branded by the ministry as a seditious libel, and rejected by the majority. Then, upon a motion by the Earl of Sunderland, the House resolved that such lords as might enter protestations with reasons should do it before two o'clock on the next sitting day, and sign them before the House rises. The supplies being granted, and the business of the session despatched as the court was pleased to dictate, on the seventh day of March the Parliament was prorogued. In a few days it was dissolved, and another convoked by proclamation. In the election of members for the new Parliament, the ministry exerted itself with such success, as returned a great majority in the House of Commons, extremely well adapted for all the purposes of their administration.* Annals. Hist. Reg. Debates in Parliament. Pol. State. Tindal.

In the beginning of May, the king is said to have received from the Duke of Orleans full and certain information of a fresh conspiracy formed against his person and government. A camp was immediately formed in Hyde-park. All military officers were ordered to repair to their respective commands. Lieutenant-General Macartney was despatched to Ireland to bring over some troops from that kingdom. Some suspected persons were apprehended in Scotland: the states of Holland were desired to have their auxiliary or guarantee troops in readiness to be embarked; and Colonel Churchill was sent to the court of France with a private commission. The apprehension raised by this supposed plot affected the public credit. South-Sea stock began to fall; and crowds 1722. Rumours of a conspiracy. The Bishop of Rochester is committed to the Tower.

---

* The Earl of Sunderland died in April, having incurred a great load of popular odium, from his supposed connexions with the directors of the South-Sea Company. He was a minister of abilities, but violent, impetuous, and headstrong. His death was soon followed by that of his father-in-law, the great Duke of Marlborough, whose faculties had been for some time greatly impaired. He was interred in Westminster Abbey with such profusion of funeral pomp, as evinced the pride and ostentation, much more than the taste and concern, of those who directed his obsequies. He was succeeded as master of the ordnance, and colonel of the first regiment of foot guards, by Earl Cadogan.

of people called in their money from the bank. Lord Townshend wrote a letter to the mayor of London, by the king's command, signifying his majesty's having received unquestionable advices, that several of his subjects had entered into a wicked conspiracy, in concert with traitors abroad, for raising a rebellion in favour of a popish pretender: but that he was firmly assured the authors of it neither were nor would be supported by any foreign power. This letter was immediately answered by an affectionate address from the court of aldermen; and the example of London was followed by many other cities and boroughs. The king had determined to visit Hanover, and actually settled a regency, in which the Prince of Wales was not included; but now this intended journey was laid aside: the court was removed to Kensington, and the prince retired to Richmond. The Bishop of Rochester having been seized, with his papers, was examined before a committee of the council, who committed him to the Tower for high-treason. The Earl of Orrery, Lord North and Grey, Mr. Cochran, and Mr. Smith, from Scotland, and Mr. Christopher Layer, a young gentleman of the Temple, were confined in the same place. Mr. George Kelly, an Irish clergyman, Mr. Robert Cotton, of Huntingdonshire, Mr. Bingley, Mr. Fleetwood, Neynoe, an Irish priest, and several persons, were taken into custody; and Mr. Shippen's house was searched. After Bishop Atterbury had remained a fortnight in the Tower, Sir Constantine Phipps presented a petition to the court at the Old Bailey, in the name of Mrs. Morris, that prelate's daughter, praying that, in consideration of the bishop's ill state of health, he might be either brought to a speedy trial, bailed, or discharged; but this was overruled. The churchmen through the whole kingdom were filled with indignation at the confinement of a bishop, which they said was an outrage upon the church of England and the episcopal order. Far from concealing their sentiments on this subject, the clergy ventured to offer up public prayers for his health, in almost all the churches and chapels of London and Westminster. In the mean time the king, attended by the Prince of Wales, made a summer progress through the western counties.

New Parliament. The new Parliament being assembled on the ninth day of October, his majesty made them acquainted with the nature of the conspiracy. He said the conspirators had, by their emissaries, made the strongest instances for succours from foreign powers; but were disappointed in their expectations. That, nevertheless, confiding in their numbers, they had resolved once more upon their own strength to attempt the subversion of his government. He said they had provided considerable sums of money; engaged great numbers of officers from abroad; secured large quantities of arms and ammunition; and had not the plot been timely discovered, the whole nation, and particularly the city of London, would have been involved in blood and confusion. He expatiated upon the mildness and integrity of his own government; and inveighed against the ingratitude, the implacability, and madness of the disaffected, concluding with an assurance, that he would steadily adhere to the constitution in church and state, and continue to make the laws of the realm the rule and measure of all his actions. Such addresses were presented by both Houses as the fears and attachments of the majority may be supposed to have dictated on such an occasion. A bill was brought into the House of Lords for suspending the habeas corpus act for a whole year; but they were far from being unanimous in agreeing to such an unusual length of time. By this suspension they, in effect, vested the ministry with a dictatorial power over the liberties of the people.

The opposition in the House of Commons was so violent, that Mr. Robert Walpole found it necessary to alarm their apprehensions by a dreadful story of a design to seize the bank and exchequer, and to proclaim the pretender on the Royal Exchange. Their passions being inflamed by this ridiculous artifice, they passed the bill, which immediately received the royal assent. The Duke of Norfolk, being brought from Bath, was examined before the council, and committed to the Tower, on suspicion of high treason. On the sixteenth day of November, the king sent to the House of Peers the original and printed copy of a declaration signed by the pretender. It was dated at Lucca, on the twentieth day of September, in the present year, and appeared to be a proposal addressed to the subjects of Great Britain and Ireland, as well as to all foreign princes and states. In this paper, the Chevalier de St. George, having mentioned the late violation of the freedom of elections, conspiracies invented to give a colour to new oppressions, infamous informers, and the state of proscription in which

*Declaration of the pretender.*

he supposed every honest man to be, very gravely proposed, that if King George would relinquish to him the throne of Great Britain, he would, in return, bestow upon him the title of king in his native dominions, and invite all other states to confirm it; he likewise promised to leave to King George his succession to the British dominions secure, whenever, in due course, his natural right should take place. The Lords unanimously resolved, that this declaration was a false, insolent, and traitorous libel; and ordered it to be burned at the Royal Exchange. The Commons concurred in these resolutions. Both Houses joined in an address, expressing their utmost astonishment and indignation at the surprising insolence of the pretender; and assuring his majesty, they were determined to support his title to the crown with their lives and fortunes. The Commons prepared a bill for raising one hundred thousand pounds upon the real and personal estates of all Papists, or persons educated in the popish religion, towards defraying the expenses occasioned by the late rebellion and disorders. This bill, though strenuously opposed by some moderate members as a species of persecution, was sent up to the House of Lords, together with another, obliging all persons, being Papists, in Scotland, and all persons in Great Britain refusing or neglecting to take the oaths appointed for the security of the king's person and government, to register their names and real estates. Both these bills passed through the Upper House without amendments, and received the royal sanction.

Mr. Layer, being brought to his trial at the King's Bench, on the twenty-first day of November, was convicted of having enlisted men for the pretender's service, in order to stir up a rebellion, and received sentence of death. He was reprieved for some time, and examined by a committee of the House of Commons; but he either could not, or would not, discover the particulars of the conspiracy, so that he suffered death at Tyburn, and his head was fixed up at Temple Bar. Mr. Pulteney, chairman of the committee, reported to the House, that from the examination of Layer and others, a design had been formed by persons of figure and distinction at home, in conjunction with traitors abroad, for placing the pretender on the throne of these realms: that their first intention was to procure a body of foreign troops to invade the kingdom

*Report of the secret committee.*

at the time of the late elections; but that the conspirators, being disappointed in this expectation, resolved to make an attempt at the time that it was generally believed the king intended to go to Hanover, by the help of such officers and soldiers as could pass into England unobserved from abroad, under the command of the late Duke of Ormond, who was to have landed in the river with a great quantity of arms, provided in Spain for that purpose; at which time the Tower was to have been seized. That this scheme being also defeated by the vigilance of the government, they deferred their enterprise till the breaking up of the camp; and, in the mean time, employed their agents to corrupt and seduce the officers and soldiers of the army: that it appeared from several letters and circumstances, that the late Duke of Ormond, the Duke of Norfolk, the Earl of Orrery, Lord North and Grey, and the Bishop of Rochester, were concerned in this conspiracy: that their acting agents were Christopher Layer and John Plunket, who travelled together to Rome; Dennis Kelly, George Kelly, and Thomas Carte, nonjuring clergymen; Neynoe, the Irish priest, who by this time was drowned in the river Thames, in attempting to make his escape from the messenger's house; Mrs. Spilman, alias Yallop, and John Sample.

This pretended conspiracy, in all likelihood, extended no farther than the first rudiments of a design that was never digested into any regular form; otherwise the persons said to be concerned in it must have been infatuated to a degree of frenzy; for they were charged with having made application to the Regent of France, who was well known to be intimately connected with the King of Great Britain. The House of Commons, however, resolved, that it was a detestable and horrid conspiracy for raising a rebellion, seizing the Tower and the city of London, laying violent hands upon the persons of his most sacred majesty and the Prince of Wales, in order to subvert our present happy establishment in church and state, by placing a popish pretender upon the throne; that it was formed and carried on by persons of figure and distinction, and their agents and instruments, in conjunction with traitors abroad. Bills were brought in, and passed, for inflicting pains and penalties against John Plunket and George Kelly, who were by these acts to be kept in close custody during his majesty's pleasure, in any

*Bill of pains and penalties against the Bishop of Rochester.*

prison in Great Britain; and that they should not attempt to escape on pain of death, to be inflicted upon them and their assistants. Mr. Yonge made a motion for a bill of the same nature against the Bishop of Rochester. This was immediately brought into the House, though Sir William Wyndham affirmed there was no evidence against him but conjectures and hearsay. The bishop wrote a letter to the speaker, importing, that though conscious of his own innocence, he should decline giving the House any trouble that day, contenting himself with the opportunity of making his defence before another, of which he had the honour to be a member. Counsel being heard for the bill, it was committed to a grand committee on the sixth day of April, when the majority of the tory members quitted the House. It was then moved, that the bishop should be deprived of his office and benefice, and banished the kingdom for ever. Mr. Lawson and Mr. Oglethorpe spoke in his favour.

*Annals. Tindal. Debates in Parliament. Pol. State.*

The bill being passed and sent up to the Lords, the bishop was brought to his trial before them on the ninth of May. Himself and his counsel having been heard, the Lords proceeded to consider the articles of the bill. When they read it a third time, a motion was made to pass it, and then a long and warm debate ensued. Earl Paulet demonstrated the danger and injustice of swerving in such an extraordinary manner from the fixed rules of evidence. The Duke of Wharton, having summed up the depositions, and proved the insufficiency of them, concluded with saying, that, let the consequences be what they would, he hoped such a hellish stain would never sully the lustre and glory of that illustrious House, as to condemn a man without the least evidence. Lord Bathurst spoke against the bill with equal strength and eloquence. He said, if such extraordinary proceedings were countenanced, he saw nothing remaining for him and others to do, but to retire to their country-houses, and there, if possible, quietly enjoy their estates within their own families, since the least correspondence, the least intercepted letter, might be made criminal. He observed, that Cardinal Mazarin boasted, that if he had but two lines of any man's writing, he could, by means of a few circumstances, attested by witnesses, deprive him of his life at his pleasure. Turning to the bench of bishops,

*1723. Who is deprived, and driven into perpetual exile.*

who had been generally unfavourable to Dr. Atterbury, he said he could hardly account for the inveterate hatred and malice some persons bore the learned and ingenious Bishop of Rochester, unless they were intoxicated with the infatuation of some savage Indians, who believed they inherited not only the spoils, but even the abilities, of any great enemy whom they had killed in battle. The bill was supported by the Duke of Argyle, the Earl of Seafield, and Lord Lechmere, which last was answered by Earl Cowper. This nobleman observed, that the strongest argument urged in behalf of the bill was necessity: but that, for his part, he saw no necessity that could justify such unprecedented and such dangerous proceedings, as the conspiracy had above twelve months before been happily discovered, and the effects of it prevented: that besides the intrinsic weight and strength of the government, the hands of those at the helm had been still further fortified by the suspension of the habeas corpus act, and the additional troops which had been raised. He said the known rules of evidence, as laid down at first, and established by the law of the land, were the birthright of every subject in the nation, and ought to be constantly observed, not only in the inferior courts of judicature, but also in both Houses of Parliament, till altered by the legislature; that the admitting of the precarious and uncertain evidence of the clerks of the post-office was a very dangerous precedent. In former times (said he) it was thought very grievous that in capital cases a man should be affected by similitude of hands; but here the case is much worse, since it is allowed that the clerks of the post-office should carry the similitude of hands four months in their minds. He applauded the bishop's noble deportment, in declining to answer before the House of Commons, whose proceeding in this unprecedented manner, against a lord of Parliament, was such an encroachment on the prerogative of the peerage, that if they submitted to it, by passing the bill, they might be termed the last of British peers, for giving up their ancient privileges. The other party were not so solicitous about answering reasons, as eager to put the question, when the bill passed, and a protest was entered. By this act the bishop was deprived of all offices, benefices, and dignities, and rendered incapable of enjoying any for the future: he was banished the realm, and subjected to the pains of death in case he should return, as were all persons who should correspond with him during his exile. Dr. Friend, the celebrated physician, who was a member of the House of Commons, and had exerted himself strenuously in behalf of the bishop, was now taken into custody, on suspicion of treasonable practices.

<small>Proceedings against those concerned in the lottery at Harburgh.</small> The next object that excited the resentment of the Commons was the scheme of a lottery, to be drawn at Harburgh, in the king's German dominions. The House appointed a committee to inquire into this and other lotteries at that time on foot in London. The scheme was published, on pretence of raising a subscription for maintaining a trade between Great Britain and the king's territories on the Elbe; but it was a mysterious scene of iniquity, which the committee, with all their penetration, could not fully discover. They reported, however, that it was an infamous, fraudulent undertaking, whereby many unwary persons had been drawn in, to their great loss: that the manner of carrying it on had been a manifest violation of the laws of the kingdom: that the managers and agents of this lottery had, without any authority for so doing, made use of his majesty's royal name, thereby to give countenance to the infamous project, and induce his majesty's subjects to engage or be concerned therein. A bill was brought in to suppress this lottery, and to oblige the managers of it to make restitution of the money they had received from the contributors. At the same time the House resolved, that John Lord Viscount Barrington had been notoriously guilty of promoting, abetting, and carrying on that fraudulent undertaking; for which offence he should be expelled the House. The court of Vienna having erected an East India Company at Ostend, upon a scheme formed by one Colebrook, an English merchant, Sir Nathaniel Gould represented to the House of Commons the great detriment which the English East India Company had already received, and were likely further to sustain, by this Ostend company. The House immediately resolved, that for the subjects of this kingdom to subscribe, or be concerned in encouraging any subscription, to promote an East India Company now erecting in the Austrian Netherlands, was a high crime and misdemeanour; and a law was enacted for preventing British subjects from engaging in that enterprise. By another act, relating to the South-Sea Company, the two millions of

stock which had been annihilated were revived, added to the capital, and divided among the proprietors. A third law passed, for the more effectual execution of justice in a part of Southwark, called the Mint, where a great number of debtors had taken sanctuary, on the supposition that it was a privileged place. On the twenty-seventh day of May the session was closed, with a speech that breathed nothing but panegyric, acknowledgment, and affection to a Parliament which had complied with all his majesty's wishes.

His majesty, having ennobled the son of Mr. Robert Walpole, in consideration of the father's services, made a good number of church promotions. He admitted the imprisoned lords and gentlemen to bail; granted a pardon to Lord Bolingbroke; and ordered the Bishop of Rochester to be conveyed to the continent. Then he himself set out for Hanover, leaving the administration of his kingdoms in the hands of a regency, Lord Harcourt being one of the justices. The king was attended by the two secretaries, Lords Townshend and Carteret, who were counted able negotiators. The affairs of the continent had begun to take a new turn. The interests and connexions of the different princes were become perplexed and embarrassed; and King George resolved to unravel them by dint of negotiation. Understanding that a treaty was on the carpet between the czar and the King of Sweden, favourable to the Duke of Holstein's pretensions to Sleswick, the possession of which the Elector of Hanover had guaranteed to Denmark, his majesty began to be in pain for Bremen and Verden. The Regent of France and the King of Spain had now compromised all differences; and their reconciliation was cemented by a double marriage between Philip's sons and the regent's daughters. The former proposed new treaties to England; but insisted upon the restitution of Gibraltar and Port-Mahon, as well as upon the king's openly declaring against the Ostend company. His Britannic majesty was apprehensive that, should the emperor be hard pressed on that subject, he might join the czar and the King of Sweden, and promote their designs in favour of the Duke of Holstein. On the other hand, all the Italian powers exclaimed against the treaty of London. The pope had protested against any thing that might have been decided at Cambray to the prejudice of his right. Memorials to the same effect had been presented by the

King of Sardinia, the Dukes of Tuscany, Parma, and Modena. France and Spain were inclined to support these potentates against the house of Austria. Europe seemed to be on the eve of a new war. King George was entangled in such a variety of treaties and interests that he knew not well how to extricate himself from the troublesome engagements he had contracted. By declaring for the emperor he must have countenanced the new establishment at Ostend, which was so prejudicial to his British subjects, and incurred the resentment of France, Spain, and their allies of Italy. In renouncing the interest of the emperor he would have exposed his German dominions. In vain he exhorted the emperor to relax in his disputes with Spain, and give up the Ostend company, which was so detrimental and disagreeable to his faithful allies: the court of Vienna promised in general to observe the treaties which it had concluded, but declined entering into any particular discussion; so that all his majesty's endeavours issued in contracting closer connexions with Prussia and Denmark. All those negotiations carried on, all those treaties concluded by King George, with almost every prince and state in Christendom, which succeeded one another so fast, and appear, at first view, so intricate and unaccountable, were founded upon two simple and natural principles, namely, the desire of ascertaining his acquisitions as Elector of Hanover, and his resolution to secure himself against the disaffection of his British subjects, as well as the efforts of the pretender.

Great Britain at this period enjoyed profound tranquillity. Ireland was a little ruffled by an incident which seemed to have been misrepresented to the people of that kingdom. William Wood had obtained a patent for furnishing Ireland with copper currency, in which it was deficient. A great clamour was raised against this coin. The Parliament of that kingdom, which met in September, resolved, that it would be prejudicial to the revenue, destructive of trade, and of dangerous consequence to the rights of the subject: that the patent had been obtained by misrepresentation: that the halfpence wanted weight: that, even if the terms of the patent had been complied with, there would have been a great loss to the nation: that granting the power of coinage to a private person had ever been highly prejudicial to the kingdom, and would at

*Clamour in Ireland on account of Wood's coinage.*

all times be of dangerous consequence. Addresses from both Houses were presented to the king on this subject. The affair was referred to the lords of the privy-council of England. They justified the conduct of the patentee, upon the report of Sir Isaac Newton and other officers of the Mint, who had made an assay and trial of Wood's halfpence, and found he had complied with the terms of the patent. They declared that this currency exceeded in goodness, fineness, and value of metal, all the copper money which had been coined for Ireland, in the reigns of King Charles II., King James II., King William and Queen Mary. The privy-council likewise demonstrated, that his majesty's predecessors had always exercised the undoubted prerogative of granting patents for copper coinage in Ireland to private persons: that none of these patents had been so beneficial to the kingdom as this granted to William Wood, who had not obtained it in an unprecedented manner, but after a reference to the attorney and solicitor-general, and after Sir Isaac Newton had been consulted in every particular: finally, they proved, by a great number of witnesses, that there was a real want of such money in Ireland. Notwithstanding this decision, the ferment of the Irish nation was industriously kept up by clamour, pamphlets, papers, and lampoons, written by Dean Swift and other authors; so that Wood voluntarily reduced his coinage from the value of one hundred thousand to forty thousand pounds. Thus the noise was silenced. The Commons of Ireland passed an act for accepting the affirmation of the quakers instead of an oath; and voted three hundred and forty thousand pounds towards discharging the debt of the nation, which amounted to about double that sum.

In the month of October, England lost a worthy nobleman in the death of Earl Cowper, who had twice discharged the office of lord chancellor, with equal discernment and integrity. He was profoundly skilled in the laws of his country; in his apprehension quick and penetrating; in his judgment clear and determinate. He possessed a manly eloquence; his manner was agreeable, and his deportment graceful. This year was likewise remarkable for the death of the Duke of Orleans, Regent of France, who, since the decease of Louis XIV., had ruled that nation with the most absolute authority. He was a prince of taste and spirit, endowed with shining

*Death of the Duke of Orleans.*

talents for empire, which he did not fail to display, even in the midst of effeminate pursuits and idle debauchery. From the infirm constitution of the infant king, he had conceived hopes of ascending the throne, and taken his measures accordingly; but the young monarch's health began to be established, and all the duke's schemes were defeated by an apoplexy, of which he died, in the fiftieth year of his age, after having nominated the Duke of Bourbon as prime minister. King George immediately received assurances of the good disposition of the French court to cultivate and even improve the good understanding so happily established between France and Great Britain. The king arrived in England on the eighteenth day of December; and on the ninth day of January the Parliament was assembled. His majesty, in his speech, recommended to the Commons the care of the public debts; and he expressed his satisfaction at seeing the sinking fund improved and augmented, so as to put the debt of the nation into a method of being speedily and gradually discharged.

1724.

This was the repeated theory of patriotism, which, unhappily for the subjects, was never reduced to practice: not but that a beginning of such a laudable work was made in this very session, by an act for lessening the public debts. This law provided that the annuities at five per cent. charged on the general fund by a former act, except such as had been subscribed into the South-Sea, together with the unsubscribed blanks of the lottery in the year one thousand seven hundred and fourteen, should be paid off at Lady-day of the year next ensuing, with the money arising from the sinking fund. The ministry, however, did not persevere in this path of prudent economy. The Commons granted all the supplies that were demanded. They voted ten thousand seamen; and the majority, though not without violent opposition, agreed to maintain four thousand additional troops, which had been raised in the preceding year; so that the establishment of the land-forces amounted to eighteen thousand two hundred and sixty-four. The expense of the year was defrayed by a land-tax and malt-tax. The Commons, having despatched the supply, took into consideration a grievance arising from protections granted by foreign ministers, peers, and members of Parliament, under which profligate persons used to screen

*An act for lessening the public debts.*

Oldmixon.
Pol. State.
Hist. Reg.
Annals of K. George.
Mem. Hist.
Tindal.

themselves from the prosecution of their just creditors. The Commons resolved, that all protections granted by members of that House should be declared void, and immediately withdrawn. The Lords made a declaration to the same purpose, with an exception of menial servants, and those necessarily employed about the estates of peers.[b] On the twenty-fourth day of April, his majesty closed the session in the usual manner, made some alterations in the disposition of the great offices of state, and sent Mr. Horatio Walpole as ambassador-extraordinary to the court of France.

In the beginning of this year, Philip, King of Spain, retiring with his queen to the monastery of St. Idlefonso, sent the Marquis of Grimaldi, his principal secretary of state, to his son Louis, Prince of Asturias, with a solemn renunciation of the crown, and a letter of advice, in which he exhorted him to cultivate the Blessed Virgin with the warmest devotion; and put himself and his kingdoms under her protection. The renunciation was published through the whole monarchy of Spain; and the council of Castile resolved, that Louis might assume the reins of government without assembling the Cortez. The English minister at Paris was instructed to interpose in behalf of the French Protestants, against whom a severe edict had been lately published; but his remonstrances produced no effect. England, in the mean time, was quite barren of such events as deserve a place in history. The government was now firmly established on the neck of opposition, and commerce flourished even under the load of grievous impositions. *Philip, King of Spain, abdicates the throne.*

The next Parliament, which met on the twelfth day of November, seemed to be assembled for no other purpose than that of establishing funds for the expense of the ensuing year: yet the session was distinguished by a remarkable incident; namely, the trial of the Earl of Macclesfield, lord chancellor of England. This noble- *Abuses in chancery.*

---

[b] The Duke of Newcastle was now appointed secretary of state; the Duke of Grafton, lord chamberlain; and Lord Carteret, lord lieutenant of Ireland.

The king instituted a professorship for the modern languages in each university.

In the month of May died Robert Harley, Earl of Oxford and Earl Mortimer, who had been a munificent patron of genius and literature; and completed a very valuable collection of manuscripts.

The practice of inoculation for the small-pox was by this time introduced into England from Turkey. Prince Frederick, the two Princesses Amelia and Carolina, the Duke of Bedford and his sister, with many other persons of distinction, underwent this operation with success.

Dr. Henry Sacheverel died in June, after having bequeathed five hundred pounds to the late Bishop of Rochester.

man had connived at certain venal practices touching the sale of places, and the money of suitors deposited with the masters of chancery, so as to incur the general reproach of the nation. He found it necessary to resign the great seal in the beginning of January. On the ninth day of the ensuing month, the king sent a message to the Commons, importing, that his majesty, having reason to apprehend that the suitors in the court of chancery were in danger of losing a considerable sum of money, from the insufficiency of some of the masters, thought himself obliged, in justice and compassion to the said sufferers, to take the most speedy and proper method the law would allow for inquiring into the state of the masters' accounts, and securing their effects for the benefit of the suitors; and his majesty, having had several reports laid before him in pursuance of the directions he had given, had ordered the reports to be communicated to the House, that they might have as full and as perfect a view of this important affair as the shortness of the time, and the circumstances and nature of the proceedings, would admit.

<small>1725.</small>

<small>Trial of the Earl of Macclesfield.</small> These papers being taken into consideration, Sir George Oxenden observed, that enormous abuses had crept into the high court of chancery: that the crimes and misdemeanours of the late lord chancellor were many and various, but might be reduced to the following heads: that he had embezzled the estates and effects of many widows, orphans, and lunatics: that he had raised the offices of masters in chancery to an exorbitant price; trusting in their hands large sums of money belonging to suitors, that they might be enabled to comply with his exorbitant demands: and that in several cases he had made divers irregular orders. He therefore moved, that Thomas Earl of Macclesfield should be impeached of high crimes and misdemeanours. Mr. Pulteney moved, that this affair might be left to the consideration of a select committee. Sir William Wyndham asserted, that in proceeding by way of impeachment upon reports from above, they would make a dangerous precedent; and seem to give up the most valuable of their privileges, the inquest after state criminals. The question being put, it was carried for the impeachment. The earl was accordingly impeached at the bar of the Upper House: a committee was appointed to prepare articles; and a bill was brought in, to indemnify

<small>Annals. Hist. Mem. Deb. in Parliam. Tindal.</small>

the masters in chancery from the penalties of the law, upon discovering what considerations they had paid for their admission to their respective offices. The trial lasted twenty days: the earl was convicted of fraudulent practices, and condemned in a fine of thirty thousand pounds, with imprisonment until that sum should be paid. He was immediately committed to the Tower, where he continued about six weeks; but upon producing the money he was discharged; and Sir Peter King, now created Baron of Oakham, succeeded him in the office of chancellor.

His majesty, on the 8th day of April, gave the House of Commons to understand, that having been engaged in some extraordinary expenses, he hoped he should be enabled to raise a sum of money, by making use of the funds lately established for the payment of the civil list annuities, in order to discharge the debts contracted in the civil government. Mr. Pulteney, cofferer of the household, moved for an address, that an account should be laid before the House of all moneys paid for secret service, pensions, and bounties, from the twenty-fifth day of March, in the year one thousand seven hundred and one, to the twenty-fifth of the same month in the present year. This address being voted, a motion was made to consider the king's message. Mr. Pulteney urged that this consideration should be postponed until the House should have examined the papers that were the subject of the address. He expressed his surprise, that a debt amounting to above five hundred thousand pounds should be contracted in three years; he said, he did not wonder that some persons should be so eager to make good the deficiencies of the civil list, since they and their friends enjoyed such a share of that revenue; and he desired to know whether this was all that was due, or whether they should expect another reckoning? This gentleman began to be dissatisfied with the measures of the ministry; and his sarcasms were aimed at Mr. Walpole, who undertook to answer his objections. The Commons took the message into consideration, and passed a bill enabling his majesty to raise a sum, not exceeding one million, by exchequer bills, loans, or otherwise, on the credit of the deductions of sixpence per pound, directed by an act of Parliament of the seventh year of his majesty, and of the civil list revenues, at an interest not exceeding three pounds per cent. till repayment of the principal.

*Debates about the debts of the civil list.*

On the twentieth day of April, a petition was presented to the House by Lord Finch, in behalf of Henry St. John, late Viscount Bolingbroke, praying that the execution of the law with respect to his forfeitures might be suspended, as a pardon had suspended it with respect to his life. Mr. Walpole signified to the House, by his majesty's command, that, seven years before, the petitioner had made his humble application and submission to the king, with assurances of duty, allegiance, and fidelity: that, from his behaviour since that time, his majesty was convinced of his being a fit object of his mercy; and consented to his petitioning the House. The petition being read, Mr. Walpole declared himself fully satisfied that the petitioner had sufficiently atoned for his past offences; and therefore deserved the favour of that House, so far as to enable him to enjoy the family inheritance that was settled upon him, which he could not do by virtue of his majesty's pardon, without an act of Parliament. Lord Finch moved that a bill might be brought in for this purpose, and was warmly opposed by Mr. Methuen, comptroller of the household, who represented Bolingbroke as a monster of iniquity. His remonstrance was supported by Lord William Paulet, and Mr. Onslow; nevertheless, the bill was prepared, passed through both Houses, and received the royal assent. An act being passed for disarming the Highlanders of Scotland; another for regulating elections within the city of London; a third for reducing the interest of several bank annuities, together with some bills of a private nature, the Parliament was prorogued in May, after the king had, in the warmest terms of acknowledgment, expressed his approbation of their conduct. Then he appointed lords-justices to govern the nation in his absence; and set out in June for his German dominions.[b]

The tide of political interests on the continent had begun to flow in a new channel, so as to render ineffectual the mounds which his Britannic majesty had raised by his multiplicity of negotiations. Louis, the Spanish monarch, dying

---

[b] On the fifth day of December the Princess of Wales was delivered of a princess, christened by the name of Louisa, and afterwards married to the King of Denmark. She died December the nineteenth, one thousand seven hundred and fifty-one.

Immediately after the session of Parliament, the king revived the order of the Bath, thirty-eight in number, including the sovereign.

William Bateman was created Baron of Calmore in Ireland, and Viscount Bateman; and Sir Robert Walpole, who had been one of the revived knights of the Bath, was now honoured with the order of the Garter.

soon after his elevation to the throne, his father Philip resumed the crown which he had resigned; and gave himself up implicitly to the conduct of his queen, who was a princess of indefatigable intrigue and insatiate ambition. The infanta, who had been married to Louis XV. of France, was so disagreeable to her husband, that the whole French nation began to be apprehensive of a civil war in consequence of his dying without male issue; he therefore determined, with the advice of his council, to send back the infanta, as the nuptials had not been consummated; and she was attended to Madrid by the Marquis de Monteleone. The Queen of Spain resented this insult offered to her daughter; and in revenge dismissed Mademoiselle de Beaujolois, one of the regent's daughters, who had been betrothed to her son Don Carlos. As the congress at Cambray had proved ineffectual, she offered to adjust her differences with the emperor, under the sole mediation of Great Britain. This was an honour which King George declined. He was averse to any undertaking that might interrupt the harmony subsisting between him and the court of Versailles; and he had taken umbrage at the emperor's refusing to grant the investiture of Bremen and Verden, except upon terms which he did not choose to embrace. The peace between the courts of Vienna and Madrid which he refused to mediate was effected by a private negotiation, under the management of the Duke de Ripperda, a native of the States-General, who had renounced the Protestant religion, and entered into the service of his Catholic Majesty. By two treaties, signed at Vienna in the month of April, the emperor acknowledged Philip as King of Spain and the Indies, and promised that he would not molest him in the possession of those dominions that were secured to him by the treaty of Utrecht. Philip renounced all pretensions to the dominions in Italy and the Netherlands, adjudged to the emperor by the treaty of London: Charles granted the investiture of the dukedoms of Tuscany, Parma, and Placentia, to the eldest son of the Queen of Spain, in default of heirs in the present possessors, as masculine fiefs of the empire. Spain became guarantee of the Austrian succession, according to the pragmatic sanction, by which the dominions of that house were settled on the emperor's heirs general, and declared to be a perpetual, indivisible, and inseparable

*Treaty of alliance between the courts of Vienna and Madrid.*

feoffment to the primogeniture. By the commercial treaty of Vienna, the Austrian subjects were entitled to advantages in trade with Spain, which no other nation enjoyed. His Catholic Majesty guaranteed the Ostend East India company, and agreed to pay an annual subsidy of four millions of piastres to the emperor. Great sums were remitted to Vienna: the imperial forces were augmented to a formidable number; and other powers were solicited to engage in this alliance, to which the court of Petersburgh actually acceded.

<small>Treaty of Hanover.</small> The King of Great Britain took the alarm. The emperor and he had for some time treated each other with manifest coolness. He had reason to fear some attempts upon his German dominions, and projected a defensive treaty with France and Prussia. This alliance, limited to the term of fifteen years, was negotiated and concluded at Hanover in the month of September. It implied a mutual guarantee of the dominions possessed by the contracting parties, their rights and privileges, those of commerce in particular, and an engagement to procure satisfaction to the Protestants of Thorn, who had lately been oppressed by the Catholics, contrary to the treaty of Oliva. The king, having taken these precautions at Hanover, set out on his return for England; embarked at Helvoetsluys in the middle of December; and, after having been exposed to the fury of a dreadful storm, was landed with great difficulty at Rye, from whence he proceeded by land to London. The Parliament meeting on the twentieth day of the next month, he gave them to understand that the distressed condition of some of their Protestant brethren abroad, and the negotiations and engagements contracted by some foreign powers, which seemed to have laid the foundation of new troubles and disturbances in Europe, and to threaten his subjects with the loss of several of the most advantageous branches of their trade, had obliged him to concert with other powers such measures as might give a check to the ambitious views of those who were endeavouring to render themselves formidable, and put a stop to the further progress of such dangerous designs. He told them, that the enemies of his government were already very busy, by their instruments and emissaries in those courts whose measures seemed most to favour their purposes, in soliciting and promoting the cause of the pretender. One sees at first

sight, that the interests of Germany dictated the treaty of Hanover; but, in order to secure the approbation of Great Britain, upon which the support of this alliance chiefly depended, it was judged necessary to insert the articles relating to commerce and the Protestant religion, as if the engagement had been contracted purely for the advantage and glory of England. In a word, the ministry began now to ring the changes upon a few words that have been repeated ever since, like cabalistical sounds, by which the nation has been enchanted into a very dangerous connexion with the concerns of the continent. They harangued, they insisted upon the machinations of the disaffected, the designs of a popish pretender, the Protestant interest, and the balance of power, until these expressions became absolutely terms of ridicule with every person of common sense and reflection. The people were told that the emperor and the King of Spain, exclusive of the public treaties concluded at Vienna, had entered into private engagements, importing, that the imperialists should join the Spaniards in recovering Gibraltar and Port-Mahon by force of arms, in case the King of England should refuse to restore them amicably, according to a solemn promise he had made; that a double marriage should take place between the two infants of Spain and the two archduchesses of Austria; and that means should be taken to place the pretender on the throne of Great Britain.

When the treaties of Vienna and Hanover fell under consideration of the House of Commons, Horatio Walpole, afterwards termed, in derision, "the balance master," opened the debate with a long unanimated oration, giving a detail of the affairs of Europe since the treaty of Utrecht. He enumerated the barrier treaty, the convention for executing that treaty, the defensive alliance with the emperor, the other with the most Christian king and the States-General, another convention, the quadruple alliance, the congress at Cambray, the treaty of Hanover, and that of Vienna. He explained the nature of each engagement. He said, the main design of the treaty of commerce concluded between the emperor and Spain was to countenance and support the East India Company established at Ostend, which interfered so essentially with the East India Companies of England and Holland, and was directly contrary to several solemn treaties still in force.

*Approved in Parliament.*

He enlarged upon the danger to which the balance of power would be exposed, should the issue male of this projected marriage between the houses of Austria and Spain ever possess the imperial dignity and the kingdom of Spain together. The reader will take notice, that this very man was one of those who exclaimed against that article of the treaty of Utrecht, which prevented the power of those two houses from being immediately united in the person of the emperor. He did not forget to expatiate upon the pretended secret engagement concerning Gibraltar and Minorca, and the king's pious concern for the distressed Protestants of Thorn in Poland. In vain did Mr. Shippen urge, that the treaty of Hanover would engage the British nation in a war for the defence of the king's German dominions, contrary to an express provision made in the act of limitation. These arguments had lost all weight. The opposition was so inconsiderable, that the ministry had no reason to be in pain about any measure they should propose. An address was voted and delivered to his majesty, approving the alliance he had concluded at Hanover, in order to obviate and disappoint the dangerous views and consequences of the treaty of peace betwixt the emperor and the King of Spain; and promising to support his majesty against all insults and attacks that should be made upon any of his territories, though not belonging to the crown of Great Britain. An address of the same kind was presented by the House of Lords in a body. A bill was brought in, empowering the commissioners of the treasury to compound with Mr. Richard Hampden, late treasurer of the navy, for a debt he owed to the crown, amounting to eight-and-forty thousand pounds. This deficiency was occasioned by his embarking in the South-Sea scheme. The king recommended his petition; and the House complied with his request, in consideration of his great-grandfather, the famous John Hampden, who made such a noble stand against the arbitrary measures of the first Charles.

Riots in Scotland on account of the malt-tax.
The malt-tax was found so grievous to Scotland, that the people refused to pay it, and riots were excited in different parts of the kingdom. At Glasgow, the populace, armed with clubs and staves, rifled the house of Daniel Campbell, their representative in Parliament, who had voted for the bill: and maltreated

some excisemen who attempted to take an account of the malt. General Wade, who commanded the forces in Scotland, had sent two companies of soldiers, under the command of Captain Bushel, to prevent or appease any disturbance of this nature. That officer drew up his men in the street, where they were pelted with stones by the multitude, which he endeavoured to disperse by firing among them without shot. This expedient failing, he ordered his men to load their pieces with ball; and at a time when the magistrates were advancing towards him in a body to assist him with their advice and influence, he commanded the soldiers to fire four different ways, without the sanction of the civil authority. About twenty persons were killed or wounded on this occasion. The people, seeing so many victims fall, were exasperated beyond all sense of danger. They began to procure arms, and breathed nothing but defiance and revenge. Bushel thought proper to retreat to the castle of Dunbarton, and was pursued above five miles by the enraged multitude. General Wade, being informed of this transaction, assembled a body of forces; and being accompanied by Duncan Forbes, lord advocate, took possession of Glasgow. The magistrates were apprehended, and conveyed prisoners to Edinburgh, where the lords justiciary, having taken cognizance of the affair, declared them innocent; so that they were immediately discharged. Bushel was tried for murder, convicted, and condemned; but instead of undergoing the penalties of the law, he was indulged with a pardon, and promoted in the service. Daniel Campbell having petitioned the House of Commons that he might be indemnified for the damage he had sustained from the rioters, a bill was passed in his favour, granting him a certain sum to be raised from an imposition laid upon all the beer and ale brewed in the city of Glasgow. The malt-tax was so sensibly felt in Scotland, that the convention of the royal burghs presented a remonstrance against it, as a grievous burden, which their country could not bear: petitions to the same purpose were delivered to the Commons from different shires of that kingdom.[d] On the twenty-fourth day of March the king sent

*marginal notes:* Oldmixon. Annals. Debates in Parliament. Historical Memoirs. Tindal.

[d] The Duke of Wharton, having consumed his fortune in riot and extravagance, repaired to the court of Vienna, from whence he proceeded to Rome, and offered his service to the pretender. There he received the order of the garter, and the title of Duke of Northumberland. He was sent by the Chevalier de St. George with credentials to the court of

a message to the House by Sir Paul Methuen, desiring an extraordinary supply, that he might be able to augment his maritime force, and concert such other measures as should be necessary in the present conjuncture. A debate ensued; but the majority complied with the demand. Some members in the Upper House complained that the message was not sent to both Houses of Parliament, and this suggestion gave rise to another debate, in which Lord Bathurst and others made some melancholy reflections upon the state of insignificance to which the peers of England were reduced. Such remarks, however, were very little minded by the ministry, who had obtained a complete victory over all opposition. The supplies, ordinary and extraordinary, being granted, with every thing else which the court thought proper to ask, and several bills passed for the regulation of civil economy, the king dismissed the Parliament on the twenty-fourth day of May.

By this time Peter the Czar of Muscovy was dead, and his Empress Catharine had succeeded him on the Russian throne. This princess had begun to assemble forces in the neighbourhood of Petersburgh; and to prepare a formidable armament for a naval expedition. King George, concluding that her design was against Sweden, sent a strong squadron into the Baltic, under the command of Sir Charles Wager, in order to anticipate her views upon his allies. The English fleet being joined at Copenhagen by a Danish squadron, alarmed the court of Russia, which immediately issued orders for reinforcing the garrisons of Wibourg, Cronstadt, Revel, and Riga. The English admiral, having had an audience of his Swedish majesty, steered towards Revel, and sent thither a lieutenant, with a letter from the King of Great Britain to the czarina. This was an expostulation, in which his majesty observed, that he and his allies could not fail of being alarmed at her great preparations by sea and land. He complained that measures had been taken at her court in favour of the pretender: that his repeated instances for establishing a lasting friendship with the crown of Russia had been treated with neglect; and he gave her to understand, that he had ordered his admiral to prevent her ships

*A small squadron sent to the Baltic.*

Madrid, where he abjured the Protestant religion, married a lady of the Queen of Spain's bedchamber, and obtained the rank and appointment of a lieutenant-colonel in the Spanish service.

from coming out of her harbours, should she persist in her
resolution to execute the designs she had projected. The
czarina, in her answer to the king, expressed her surprise
that she had not received his majesty's letter until his fleet
was at anchor before Revel, since it would have been more
agreeable to the custom established among sovereigns, and
to the amity which had so long subsisted between her kingdoms and the crown of Great Britain, to expostulate with
her on her armament, and expect her answer, before he had
proceeded to such an offensive measure. She assured him
that nothing was farther from her thoughts than any design
to disturb the peace of the North; and with regard to the
pretender, it was a frivolous and stale accusation, which had
been frequently used as a pretext to cover all the unkind
steps lately taken against the Russian empire. Sir Charles
Wager continued in his station until he received certain
intelligence that the Russian galleys were laid up in their
winter harbour: then he set sail for the coast of Denmark, from whence he returned to England in the month
of November.

King George, that he might not seem to convert all his
attention to the affairs of the North, had equipped *Admiral
two other squadrons, one of which was destined for Hosier's
the West Indies, under the command of Admiral to the West
Hosier; the other, conducted by Sir John Jennings, Indies.*
having on board a body of land-forces, sailed from St.
Helen's on the twentieth day of July, entered the bay of
St. Antonio, then visited Lisbon, from whence he directed
his course to the Bay of Bulls, near Cadiz, and cruized off
Cape St. Mary's, so as to alarm the coast of Spain, and fill
Madrid with consternation. Yet he committed no act of
hostility; but was treated with great civility by the Spanish
governor of Cadiz, who supplied him with refreshments.
Rear-Admiral Hosier, with seven ships of war, had sailed
in April for the Spanish West Indies, with instructions to
block up the galleons in the ports of that country; or
should they presume to come out, to seize and bring them
to England. Before his arrival at the Bastimentos, near
Porto-Bello, the treasure, consisting of above six millions
sterling, had been unloaded, and carried back to Panama,
in pursuance of an order sent by an advice-boat which had
the start of Hosier. This admiral lay inactive on that
station, until he became the jest of the Spaniards. He

returned to Jamaica, where he found means to reinforce his crews; then he stood over to Carthagena. The Spaniards had by this time seized the English South-Sea ship at La Vera Cruz, together with all the vessels and effects belonging to that company. Hosier in vain demanded restitution; he took some Spanish ships by way of reprisal, and continued cruizing in those seas until the greater part of his men perished deplorably by the diseases of that unhealthy climate, and his ships were totally ruined by the worms. This brave officer, being restricted by his orders from obeying the dictates of his courage, seeing his best officers and men daily swept off by an outrageous distemper, and his ships exposed to inevitable destruction, is said to have died of a broken heart; while the people of England loudly clamoured against this unfortunate expedition, in which so many lives were thrown away, and so much money expended, without the least advantage to the nation. It seems to have been a mean piratical scheme to rob the court of Spain of its expected treasure, even while a peace subsisted between the two nations. The ministry of Great Britain, indeed, alleged, that the Spanish king had entered into engagements in favour of the pretender.

The Dukes of Ormond and Wharton, and the Earl Marischal, were certainly at Madrid; and the Duke de Ripperda, now prime minister of Spain, dropped some expressions to the English envoy that implied some such design, which, however, the court of Madrid positively denied. Ripperda, as a foreigner, fell a sacrifice to the jealousy of the Spanish ministers. He was suddenly dismissed from his employments, with a pension of three thousand pistoles. He forthwith took refuge in the house of Vandermeer, the Dutch ambassador, who was unwilling to be troubled with such a guest. He therefore conveyed the duke in his coach to the house of Colonel Stanhope, the British minister, whose protection he craved and obtained. Nevertheless, he was dragged from thence by force, and committed prisoner to the castle of Segovia. He afterwards made his escape, and sheltered himself in England from the resentment of his Catholic majesty. Colonel Stanhope complained of this violation of the law of nations, which the Spanish ministers endeavoured to excuse. Memorials and letters passed between the two courts, and every thing tended to a rupture. The King of Spain purchased ships of war;

*Disgrace of the Duke de Ripperda.*

began to make preparations for some important undertaking; and assembled an army of twenty thousand men at St. Roch, on pretence of rebuilding the old castle of Gibraltar. Meanwhile the States-General and the King of Sweden acceded to the treaty of Hanover; but the King of Prussia, though his majesty's son-in-law, was detached from the alliance by the emperor, with whom he contracted new engagements.

On the seventeenth day of January, the British Parliament was opened with a long elaborate speech, importing, that the proceedings and transactions of the emperor and King of Spain, and the secret offensive alliance concluded between them, had laid the foundation of a most exorbitant and formidable power; that they were directly levelled against the most valuable and darling interests and privileges of the English nation, which must either give up Gibraltar to Spain, and acquiesce in the emperor's usurped exercise of commerce, or resolve vigorously to defend their undoubted rights against those reciprocal engagements, contracted in defiance and violation of all national faith, and the most solemn treaties. He assured them that one of those secret articles was the placing the pretender on the throne of Great Britain; and another, the conquest of Gibraltar and Port-Mahon. He affirmed that those combinations extended themselves into Russia; and that the English fleet seasonably prevented such designs as would have opened a way to the invasion of these kingdoms. He exhorted the Commons to grant such supplies as should be necessary for the defence of their country, and for making good his engagements with the allies of Great Britain. He told them, that the King of Spain had ordered his minister residing in England to quit the kingdom; and that he had left a memorial little short of a declaration, in which he insisted upon the restitution of Gibraltar. He did not fail to touch the energetic strings which always moved their passions; the balance of power in Europe, the security of the British commerce, the designs of a popish pretender, the present happy establishment, the religion, liberties, and properties of a protestant people. Such addresses of thanks were penned in both Houses as the ministers were pleased to dictate; yet not without opposition from a minority, which was far from being formidable, though headed by chiefs of uncommon talents and resolution. The Commons voted twenty thousand seamen, besides six-and-twenty thousand three hundred and eighty-three men for the land service; and, to defray the extraordinary expense, a land-tax of four shillings in the pound was granted.

<small>Debate in the House of Lords upon the approaching rupture with the emperor and Spain.</small>

The House of Lords having taken into consideration the letters and memorials between the ministers of Great Britain, France, and Spain, and the papers relating to the accession of the States-General in the treaty of Hanover, a warm debate ensued. Lord Bathurst took notice, that the accession of the States-General to the treaty was upon condition that this their act should be approved and ratified by the King of Great Britain, the most Christian king, and the King of Prussia; but that the minister of his Prussian majesty had refused to sign the act of accession, which was therefore of no effect: that if the court of France should, for the same reason, think itself disengaged from the Hanover alliance, Britain alone would be obliged to bear the burden of an expensive war against two of the greatest potentates of Europe. He said he could not see any just reason for a rupture with Spain: that, indeed, the Duke de Ripperda might have dropped some indiscreet expressions; he was known to be a man of violent temper; and he had been solemnly disavowed by his Catholic majesty; that, in the memorial left by the Spanish ambassador, he imputed the violent state of affairs between the two crowns to the ministers of England; and mentioned a positive promise made by the King of Great Britain for the restitution of Gibraltar: that methods of accommodation might be tried before the kingdom engaged in a war, which must be attended with dangerous consequences: that the nation was loaded with a debt of fifty millions; and, in order to maintain such a war, would be obliged to raise seven millions yearly; an annual sum by which the people would soon be exhausted. He observed, that in some papers laid before the House, mention was made of great sums distributed in divers places, to bring certain measures to bear. He declared, that for his own part, he had touched neither Spanish nor English gold: he was neither a Spaniard nor a Frenchman, but a true Englishman, and so long as he had the honour to sit in that House, he would speak and act for the good of his country. He, therefore, desired their lordships seriously to consider the matter before them, which was of the last consequence and importance to the whole nation. He said nothing could be gained by the war, should it prove successful; and every thing would be lost should it prove unprosperous. He was answered by Lord Townshend, who affirmed that his majesty had received positive and certain information with respect to the secret article of alliance between the Courts of Vienna and Madrid, in favour of the pretender, though the safety of the state did not permit him to lay these advices before the Parliament. After much altercation, the majority resolved, that the measures his majesty had thought fit to take were honourable, just, and necessary for preventing the execution of the dangerous engagements entered into in favour of the pretender; for preserving the dominions belonging to the crown of Great Britain, by solemn treaties, and particularly those of Gibraltar and the isle of Minorca; and for maintaining to his people their most valuable rights and privileges of commerce, and the peace and tranquillity of Europe. Seventeen lords entered a protest against this resolution. Disputes of the same nature arose from the same subject in the Lower House. Lord Townshend had affirmed in the House of Peers, that no promise of restoring Gibraltar had been made; Sir Robert Walpole owned such a promise in the House of Commons; a motion was made for an address, desiring these engagements might be laid before the House: another member moved for a copy of the memorial presented by Mr. Pointz to the King of Sweden, and for the secret offensive article between the courts of Vienna and Madrid; a third motion was made to address the king for such memorials and representations from the courts of Sweden and Denmark, as induced him, in the course of the preceding year, to send a squadron to the Baltic. In the account of the money granted for the service of the last year, there was an article of one hundred and twenty-five thousand pounds charged in general terms, as issued out for other engagements and expenses, over and above such as were specified. Mr. Pulteney moved for an address on this subject; but each of these motions was rejected on a division; and the majority concurred in an address of thanks to his majesty, for the great wisdom of his conduct. They expressed the most implicit confidence in his goodness and discretion; they promised to support him in all such further measures as he should find necessary and expedient for preventing a rupture, as well as for consulting the honour and advantage of these kingdoms.

His majesty's speech gave such umbrage to the court of Vienna, that Mr. Palms, the imperial resident at London, was ordered to present a warm memorial to the king, and afterwards to publish it to the whole nation. In this bold remonstrance, the king was charged with having declared from the throne, as certain and undoubted facts, several things that were either wrested, misrepresented, or void of all foundation. The memorialist affirmed, that the treaty of Vienna was built on the quadruple alliance; that the treaty of commerce was calculated to promote the mutual and lawful advantages of the subjects of both parties, agreeably to the law of nations, and in no respect prejudicial to the British nation. He declared that there was no offensive alliance concluded between the two crowns; that the supposed article relating to the pretender was an absolute falsehood: that the insinuation with respect to the siege of Gibraltar was equally untrue, his master having made no engagements with the King of Spain but such as were specified in the treaty communicated to his Britannic majesty. He said, however, the hostilities notoriously committed in the West Indies and elsewhere against the King of Spain, in violation of treaties, seemed to justify that prince's undertaking the siege of Gibraltar. Finally, he demanded, in the name of his imperial majesty, suitable reparation for the injury his honour had sustained from such calumnious imputations. Both Houses of Parliament expressed their indignation at the insolence of this memorial in an address to his majesty; and Mr. Palms was ordered to depart the kingdom. Virulent declarations were presented by the ministers of the emperor and the King of Great Britain to the diet of the empire at Ratisbon; and such personal reflections retorted between these two potentates, that all hope of reconciliation vanished.

*Memorial of Mr. Palms, the imperial resident at London.*

King George, in order to secure himself against the impending storm, entered into more strict engagements with the French king; and agreed to pay fifty thousand pounds for three years to the King of Sweden, in consideration of that prince's holding in readiness a body of ten thousand troops for the occasions of the alliance. He concluded a fresh treaty with the King of Denmark, who promised to furnish a certain number of

*Conventions with Sweden and Hesse-Cassel.*

auxiliaries, on account of a large subsidy granted by the King of France. The proportions of troops to be sent into the field in case of a rupture were ascertained. His Britannic majesty engaged for four-and-twenty thousand men, and a strong squadron to be sent into the Baltic. He made a convention with the Prince of Hesse-Cassel, who undertook to provide eight thousand infantry and four thousand horse, in consideration of seventy-four thousand pounds, to be paid by Great Britain immediately, and fifty thousand pounds more in case the troops should be required, besides their pay and subsistence. Such was the fruit of all the alliances so industriously planned since the accession of King George to the throne of Great Britain. In the day of his trouble, the King of Prussia, who had espoused his daughter, deserted his interest; and the States-General stood aloof. For the security of his German dominions, he had recourse to the King of France, who was a precarious ally; to the Kings of Sweden and Denmark, and the Principality of Hesse Cassel: but none of these powers would contribute their assistance without being gratified with exorbitant subsidies, though the danger was common, and the efforts ought to have been equal. Instead of allies, they professed themselves mercenaries. Great Britain paid them for the defence of their own dominions: she moreover undertook to maintain a powerful fleet for their safety. Is there any Briton so weak as to think, or so foolhardy as to affirm, that this was a British quarrel? *Annals. Debates in Parliament. Tindal. Lives of the Admirals.*

For the support of those expensive treaties, Mr. Scroope, secretary of the treasury, moved in the House of Commons, that in the malt-tax bill they should insert a clause of appropriation, empowering the king to apply such sums as should be necessary for defraying the expenses and engagements which had been or should be made before the twenty-fifth day of September, in concerting such measures as he should think most conducive to the security of trade, and restoring the peace of Europe. To little purpose did the members in the opposition urge, that this method of asking and granting supplies was unparliamentary: that such a clause would render ineffectual that appropriation of the public money, which the wisdom of all Parliaments had thought a necessary security against misapplication, which was the more to be feared, as no *1727. Vote of credit.*

provision was made to call any person to account for the money that should be disposed of by virtue of this clause: that great sums had already been granted: that such an unlimited power ought never to be given in a free government; that such confidence in the crown might, through the influence of evil ministers, be attended with the most dangerous consequences: that the constitution could not be preserved but by a strict adherence to those essential parliamentary forms of granting supplies upon estimates, and of appropriating these supplies to services and occasions publicly avowed and judged necessary: that such clauses, if not seasonably checked, would become so frequent, as in time to lodge in the crown and in the ministers an absolute and uncontrollable power of raising money upon the people, which by the constitution is, and with safety can only be, lodged in the whole legislature. The motion was carried, the clause added, and the bill passed through the other House without amendment, though not without opposition. Notwithstanding this vote of credit, Sir William Yonge moved, that towards the supply granted to the king, the sum of three hundred and seventy thousand pounds should be raised by loans on exchequer bills, to be charged on the surplus of the duties on coal and culm, which was reserved for the Parliament's disposal. Though this motion was vigorously opposed by Sir Joseph Jekyll and Mr. Pulteney, as a dangerous deviation from several votes and acts of Parliament, by which the exceedings of the public funds were appropriated to the discharge of the national debt, or to the increase of the sinking fund, it was carried by the majority.

On the fifteenth day of May the Parliament was prorogued, after the king had acknowledged their zeal, liberality, and despatch; and given them to understand that the siege of Gibraltar was actually begun.

*Siege of Gibraltar by the Spaniards.*

The trenches were opened before this fortress on the eleventh day of February, by the Condé de las Torres, at the head of twenty thousand men. The place was well provided for a defence; and the old Earl of Portmore, who was governor, embarked with a reinforcement from England, under convoy of a fleet commanded by Sir Charles Wager. He arrived at Gibraltar in the beginning of April, where he landed the troops, with a great quantity of ammunition, warlike stores, and four-and-twenty pieces of cannon. At the same time, five hundred men arrived from Minorca ; so that the garrison amounted to six thousand, plentifully supplied with fresh provisions from the coasts of Barbary, and treated the efforts of the besiegers with great contempt. The States-General, being apprehensive of an attempt upon their barrier in the Netherlands, desired the king would hold in readiness the ten thousand auxiliaries stipulated in the treaty. These were immediately prepared for embarkation, and the forces of England were augmented with thirty new raised companies. Sir John Norris set sail with a powerful fleet for the Baltic, and was joined by a Danish squadron : but the czarina dying on the seventeenth day of May, he had no occasion to commit hostilities, as the Russian armament was laid aside.

Meanwhile the powers at variance, though extremely irritated against each other, were all equally averse to a war that might again embroil all Europe. The King of France interposed his mediation, which was conducted by the Duke de Richelieu, his ambassador at Vienna. Plans and counterplans of pacification were proposed between the two crowns and the allies. At length, all parties agreed to twelve preliminary articles, which were signed in May at Paris, by the ministers of the Hanover alliance, and afterwards at Vienna, by the imperial and Spanish ambassadors. These imported, that hostilities should immediately cease : that the charter of the Ostend company should be suspended for seven years : and that a congress should in four months be opened at Aix-la-Chapelle, for adjusting all differences, and consolidating the peace of Europe. This congress was afterwards transferred to Soissons, for the conveniency of the French minister, whose presence was necessary at court. The siege of Gibraltar was raised, after it had lasted four months, during which the Spaniards lost a great number of men by sickness, while the garrison sustained very little damage. The court of Madrid, however, started some new difficulties, and for some time would not consent to the restitution of the South-Sea ship, which had been detained at La Vera Cruz, in the West Indies ; so that Sir Charles Wager continued to cruise on the coast of Spain ; but these objections were removed in the sequel.
*Preliminaries of peace.*

King George, having appointed a regency, embarked at Greenwich on the third day of June, and landing in Holland on the seventh, set out on his journey to Hanover. He was suddenly seized with a paralytic disorder on the road; he forthwith lost the faculty of speech, became lethargic, and was conveyed in a state of insensibility to Osnabruck. There he expired on Sunday, the eleventh day of June, in the sixty-eighth year of his age, and in the thirteenth of his reign.'—George I. was plain and simple in his person and address; grave and composed in his deportment, though easy, familiar, and facetious in his hours of relaxation. Before he ascended the throne of Great Britain, he had acquired the character of a circumspect general, a just and merciful prince, a wise politician, who perfectly understood, and steadily pursued, his own interest. With these qualities, it cannot be doubted but that he came to England extremely well disposed to govern his new subjects according to the maxims of the British constitution, and the genius of the people; and if ever he seemed to deviate from these principles, we may take it for granted that he was misled by the venal suggestions of a ministry whose power and influence were founded on corruption.

*Death and character of George I. King of Great Britain.*

* George I. married the Princess Sophia Dorothy, daughter and heiress of the Duke of Zell, by whom he had King George II. and the late Queen of Prussia. The king's body was conveyed to Hanover, and interred among his ancestors. From the death of Charles II. to this period, England had made a considerable figure in every branch of literature. Dr. Atterbury and Dr. Clarke distinguished themselves in Divinity; Mr. Whiston wrote in defence of Arianism; John Locke shone forth the great restorer of human reason; the Earl of Shaftesbury raised an elegant, though feeble system of moral philosophy; Berkley, afterwards Bishop of Cloyne in Ireland, surpassed all his contemporaries in subtilty and variety in metaphysical arguments, as well as in the art of deduction; Lord Bolingbroke's talents as a metaphysician have been questioned since his posthumous works appeared; great progress was made in mathematics and astronomy, by Wallis, Halley, and Flamsteed; the art of medicine owed some valuable improvement to the classical Dr. Friend, and the elegant Dr. Mead. Among the poets of this era we number John Phillips, author of a didactic poem called Cyder, a performance of real merit; he lived and died in obscurity; William Congreve, celebrated for his comedies, which are not so famous for strength of character and power of humour, as for wit, elegance, and regularity; Vanbrugh, who wrote with more nature and fire, though with far less art and precision; Steele, who in his comedies successfully engrafted modern characters on the ancient drama; Farquhar, who drew his pictures from fancy rather than from nature, and whose chief merit consists in the agreeable pertness and vivacity of his dialogue; Addison, whose fame as a poet greatly exceeded his genius, which was cold and enervate, though he yielded to none in the character of an essayist, either for style or matter; Swift, whose muse seems to have been mere misanthropy; he was a cynic rather than a poet, and his natural dryness and sarcastic severity would have been unpleasing, had not he qualified them by adopting the extravagant humour of Lucian and Rabelais; Prior, lively, familiar, and amusing; Rowe, solemn, florid, and declamatory; Pope, the prince of lyric poetry, unrivalled in satire, ethics, and polished versification; the agreeable Parnell; the wild, the witty, and the whimsical Garth; Gay, whose fables may vie with those of La Fontaine, in native humour, ease, and simplicity, and whose genius for pastoral was truly original. Dr. Bentley stood foremost in the list of critics and commentators. Sir Christopher Wren raised some noble monuments of architecture. The most remarkable political writers were Davenant, Hare, Swift, Steele, Addison, Bolingbroke, and Trenchard.

## CHAPTER XV.

### GEORGE II.

George II. ascends the Throne of Great Britain. — Characters of the principal Persons concerned in the Ministry. — Debates in Parliament concerning the Civil-List. — Changes and Promotions. — New Parliament. — Violent Dispute concerning the National Debt. — Vote of Credit. — A double Marriage between the Houses of Spain and Portugal. — Liberality of the Commons. — Debates on the Subsidies of Hesse-Cassel and Wolfenbuttel. — Committee for inspecting the Gaols. — Address touching the Spanish Depredations. — A Sum voted to the King on Account of Arrears due on the Civil-List Revenue. — Proceedings in the House of Lords. — Wise Conduct of the Irish Parliament. — Abdication of the King of Sardinia. — Death of Pope Benedict XIII. — Substance of the King's Speech to both Houses. — Objections to the Treaty of Seville in the House of Lords. — Opposition in the Lower House to a Standing Army. — Bill prohibiting Loans to Foreign Princes or States. — Charter of the East India Company prolonged. — The Emperor assents to the Treaty of Seville. — Seven Indian Chiefs arrive in England. — Revolution at Constantinople. — England infested with Robbers, Assassins, and Incendiaries. — Bill against Pensioners sitting as Members in the House of Commons. — Treaty of Vienna. — Death of the Duke of Parma. — Don Carlos takes Possession of his Territories. — France distracted by religious Disputes. — The Ministry violently opposed in Parliament. — Debate on a Standing Army. — Account of the Charitable Corporation.' — Revival of the Salt-Tax. — Mr. Pulteney's Name struck out of the List of Privy-Councillors. — The King sets out for Hanover.

At the accession of George II. the nation had great reason to wish for an alteration of measures. The public debt, notwithstanding the boasted economy and management of the ministers; notwithstanding the sinking fund, which had been extolled as a growing treasure sacred to the discharge of national incumbrances, was now increased to fifty millions two hundred sixty-one thousand two hundred and six pounds, nineteen shillings, eight-pence three farthings. The kingdom was bewildered in a labyrinth of treaties and conventions, by which it stood engaged in pecuniary subsidies to many powers upon the continent, with whom its real interests could never be connected. The wealth of the nation had been lavished upon those foreign connexions, upon unnecessary wars, and fruitless expeditions. Dangerous encroachments had been made upon the constitution by the repeal of the act for triennial Parliaments; by frequent suspensions of the habeas-corpus act upon frivolous occasions; by repealing clauses in the act of settlement; by votes of credit; by habituating the people to a standing army; and, above all, by establishing a system of corruption, which at all times would secure a majority in Parliament. The nature of prerogative, by which the liberties of the nation had formerly been often endangered, was now so well understood, and so securely restrained, that it could no longer be used for the same oppressive purposes: besides, an avowed extension of the prerogative required more ability, courage, and resolution, than the present ministry could exert. They understood their own strength, and had recourse to a more safe and effectual expedient. The vice, luxury, and prostitution of the age, the almost total extinction of sentiment, honour, and public spirit, had prepared the minds of men for slavery and corruption. The means were in the hands of the ministry; the public treasure was at their devotion: they multiplied places and pensions, to increase the number of their dependents: they squandered away the money of the nation without taste, discernment, decency, or remorse; they enlisted an army of the most abandoned emissaries, whom they employed to vindicate the worst measures, in the face of truth, common sense, and common honesty; and they did not fail to stigmatize as Jacobites, and enemies to the government, all those who presumed to question the merit of their administration.

*Character of the principal persons concerned in the ministry.* The supreme direction of affairs was not yet engrossed by a single minister. Lord Townshend had the reputation of conducting the external transactions relating to treaties and negotiations. He is said to have understood that province, though he did not always follow the dictates of his own understanding. He possessed an extensive fund of knowledge; and was well acquainted with the functions of his office. The Duke of N., his colleague, was not remarkable for any of these qualifications: he owed his promotion to his uncommon zeal for the illustrious house of Hanover, and to the strength of his interest in Parliament, rather than to his judgment, precision, or any other intellectual merit. Lord C., who may be counted an auxiliary, though not immediately concerned in the administration, had distinguished himself in the character of envoy at several courts in Europe. He had attained an intimate knowledge of all the different interests and connexions subsisting among the powers of the continent; and he infinitely surpassed all the ministers in learning and capacity. He was, indeed, the only man of genius employed under this government. He spoke with ease and propriety; his conceptions were just and lively; his inferences bold, his counsels vigorous and warm. Yet he depreciated his talents, by acting in a subordinate character to those whom he despised; and seemed to look upon the pernicious measures of a bad ministry with silent contempt rather than with avowed detestation. The interior government of Great Britain was chiefly managed by Sir Robert W., a man of extraordinary talents, who had from low beginnings raised himself to the head of the treasury. Having obtained a seat in the Lower House, he declared himself one of the most forward partisans of the whig faction. He was endued with a species of eloquence, which, though neither nervous nor eloquent, flowed with great facility, and was so plausible on all subjects, that even when he misrepresented the truth, whether from ignorance or design, he seldom failed to persuade that part of his audience for whose hearing his harangue was chiefly intended. He was well acquainted with the nature of the public funds, and understood the whole mystery of stock-jobbing. This knowledge produced a connexion between him and the money corporations, which served to enhance his importance. He perceived the bulk of mankind were actuated by a sordid thirst of lucre; he had sagacity enough to convert the degeneracy of the times to his own advantage; and on this, and this alone, he founded the whole superstructure of his subsequent administration. In the late reign he had, by dint of speaking decisively to every question, by boldly impeaching the conduct of the tory ministers, by his activity in elections, and engaging as a projector in the schemes of the monied interest, become a leading member in the House of Commons. By his sufferings under the tory Parliament, he attained the rank of a martyr to his party: his interest, his reputation, and his presumption daily increased: he opposed Sunderland as his rival in power, and headed a dangerous defection from the ministry, which evinced the greatness of his influence and authority. He had the glory of being principally concerned in effecting a reconciliation between the late king and the Prince of Wales: then he was re-associated in the administration with additional credit; and, from the death of the Earls of Sunderland and Stanhope, he had been making long strides towards the office of prime minister. He knew the maxims he had adopted would subject him to the hatred, the ridicule, and reproach of some individuals, who had not yet resigned all sentiments of patriotism, nor all views of opposition; but the number of these was inconsiderable, when compared to that which constituted the body of the community; and he would not suffer the consideration of such antagonists to come in competition with his schemes of power, affluence, and authority. Nevertheless, low as he had humbled anti-ministerial association, it required all his artifice to elude, all his patience and natural phlegm to bear, the powerful arguments that were urged, and the keen satire that was exercised against his measures and management, by a few members in the opposition. Sir William Wyndham possessed all the energy of elocution: Mr. Shippen was calm, intrepid, shrewd, and sarcastic: Mr. Hungerford, sly, insinuating, and ironical. Mr. W. P. inherited from nature a good understanding, which he had studiously cultivated. He was one of the most learned members in the House of Commons, extremely well qualified to judge of literary productions; well read in history and politics; deeply skilled in the British constitution, the detail of government, and the nature of the finances. He spoke with freedom, fluency, and uncommon warmth of declamation, which was said to be the effect of personal animosity to Sir R. W., with whom he had been formerly connected.

*Debates in Parliament concerning the civil-list.* An express arriving on the fourteenth day of June, with an account of the king's death, his late majesty King George II. repaired from Richmond, where he received this intelligence, to Liecester-house; and the members of the privy-council, being assembled, were sworn anew. The king declared his firm purpose to preserve the constitution in church and state, and to cultivate those alliances which his father had made with foreign princes. At the same time, he took and subscribed the oath for the security of the church of Scotland, as required by the act of union. Next day he was proclaimed King of Great Britain. The Parliament assembled in pursuance of the act made for that purpose; but was immediately prorogued by commission to the twenty-seventh day of the month. All the great officers of state continued in their places: Sir Robert Walpole kept possession of the treasury: and the system of politics which the late king had established underwent no sort of alteration. The king, in his speech to both Houses at the opening of the session, professed a fixed resolution to merit the love and affection of his people, by maintaining them in the full enjoyment of their religious and civil rights. He promised to lessen the public expense as soon as the circumstances of affairs would permit: he observed to the Commons, that the grant of the greatest part of the civil-list revenues was now determined; and that it would be necessary for them to make a new provision for the support of him and his family: lastly, he recommended it to both Houses to despatch the business that should be necessarily brought before them, as the season of the year and the circumstances of time required their presence in the country. Addresses of condolence and congratulation being drawn up and presented, the Commons, in a committee of the whole House, took into consideration a motion for a supply to his majesty. Sir Robert Walpole, having observed that the annual sum of seven hundred thousand pounds granted to and settled on the late king had fallen short every year, and that his present majesty's expenses were likely to increase, by reason of the largeness of his family, moved, that the entire revenues of the civil-list, which produced about eight hundred thousand pounds per annum, should be settled on the king during his life. Mr. Shippen opposed this motion, as inconsistent with the trust reposed in them as representatives of the people, who ought to be very frugal in exercising the right of giving away the public money. He said the sum of seven hundred thousand pounds was not obtained for his late majesty without a long and solemn debate; and every member who contended for it at that time allowed it to be an ample royal revenue: that, although his majesty's family should be enlarged, a circumstance which had been urged as one reason for the motion, he presumed the appointments of Prince Frederick would be much inferior to those settled on his present majesty when he was Prince of Wales: besides, it was to be hoped that many personal, many particular expenses in the late reign, especially those for frequent journeys to Hanover, would be discontinued and entirely cease. He observed that the civil-list branches in the queen's reign did not often exceed the sum of five hundred and fifty thousand pounds; nevertheless, she called upon her Parliament but once, in a reign of thirteen years, to pay the debts contracted in her civil government; and these were occasioned by the unparalleled instances of her piety and generosity. She gave the first-fruits and tenths, arising to nineteen thousand pounds a year, as an augmentation of the maintenance of the poor clergy. She bestowed five thousand pounds per annum out of the post-office on the Duke of Marlborough: she suffered seven hundred pounds to be charged weekly on the same office for the service of the public: she expended several hundred thousand pounds in building the castle of Blenheim: she allowed four thousand pounds annually to Prince Charles of Denmark: she sustained great losses by the tin contract: she supported the poor Palatines: she exhibited many other proofs of royal bounty: and immediately before her death she had formed a plan of retrenchment, which would have reduced her yearly expenses to four hundred and fifty-nine thousand nine hundred and forty-one pounds. He affirmed, that a million a year would not be sufficient to carry on the exorbitant expenses so often and so justly complained of in the House of Commons: that, over and above the yearly allowance of seven hundred thousand pounds, many occasional taxes, many excessive sums were raised, and all sunk in the bottomless gulf of secret service. Two hundred and fifty thousand pounds were raised in defiance of the ancient parliamentary methods, to secure the kingdom from a Swedish invasion: then the two insurance offices were erected, and paid near three hundred thousand pounds for their charters: our enmity with Sweden being changed into alliance, a subsidy of seventy-two thousand pounds was implicitly granted to fulfil some secret engagements with that crown; four-and-twenty thousand pounds were given for burning merchant ships arrived from infected places, though the goods, which ought to have been destroyed for the public safety, were afterwards privately sold: a sum of five hundred thousand pounds was demanded, and granted, for paying the debts of the civil-list; and his majesty declared, by message, he was resolved to retrench his expenses for the future. Notwithstanding this resolution, in less than four years, a new demand of the like sum was made and granted, to discharge new encumbrances: the Spanish ships of war which Admiral Byng took in the Mediterranean were sold for a considerable sum of money: one hundred and twenty-five thousand pounds were granted in the last session, to be secretly disposed of for the public utility; and there was still a debt in the civil government, amounting to above six hundred thousand pounds. He took notice, that this amazing extravagance happened under the conduct of persons pretending to surpass all their predecessors in the knowledge and care of the public revenue; that as none of these sums had been accounted for, they were, in all probability, employed in services not fit to be owned. He said, he heartily wished that time, the great discoverer of hidden truths and concealed iniquities, might produce a list of all such as had been perverted from their public duty by private pensions; who had been the hired slaves and the corrupt instruments of a profuse and vainglorious administration. He proposed, that instead of granting an addition to the civil-list, they should restrict that revenue to a certain sum, by concluding the question with these words, "in like manner as they were granted and continued to his late majesty, so as to make up the clear yearly sum of seven hundred thousand pounds." To these particulars, which were indeed unanswerable, no reply was made. Even this mark of decency was laid aside as idle and superfluous. The House agreed to the motion; and a bill was brought in for the better support of his majesty's household. The Commons, having received a message from the king, desiring they would make a further provision for the queen his consort, resolved, that in case she should survive his majesty, the sum of one hundred thousand pounds should be settled upon her for life, charged upon the revenues of the civil-list, together with his majesty's palace of Somerset-house, and Richmond Old-park. A bill was formed on this resolution, which, as well as the other, passed both Houses; and received the royal assent on the seventeenth day of July, when the king, in a speech to both Houses, expressed his satisfaction with their conduct; and congratulated them upon the wealth and glory of the nation, by which they had acquired such weight in holding the balance of Europe. Then the lord chancellor prorogued the Parliament to the twenty-ninth day of August; but on the seventh of that month a proclamation was issued for dissolving this, and convoking another.

In the interim, some changes were made in different departments of civil economy. Lord Viscount Torrington was placed at the head of the Admiralty: the Earl of Westmoreland was appointed first lord-commissioner of trade and plantations. Philip Dormer Stanhope, Earl of Chesterfield, a nobleman remarkable for his wit, eloquence, and polished manners, was nominated ambassador at the Hague. The privy-council being dissolved, another was appointed of the members then present. The Duke of Devonshire was dignified with the place of president; and the Duke of St. Alban's was appointed master of the horse. On the eleventh day of October the coronation of the king and queen was performed at Westminster-Abbey, with the usual solemnity.* By this time the courts of France and Spain were perfectly reconciled; all Europe was freed from the calamities of war: and the peace of Great Britain suffered no interruption, except from some transient tumults among the tinners of Cornwall, who, being provoked by a scarcity of corn, rose in arms and plundered the granaries of that county.

<small>New Parliament.</small> The elections in England and Scotland for the Parliament having succeeded on the new system according to the wishes of the ministry, the two Houses met on the twenty-third day of January, when the Commons unanimously chose for their speaker Arthur Onslow, esquire, knight of the shire for Surrey, a gentleman of extensive knowledge, worth, and probity; grave, eloquent, venerable, and every way qualified for the discharge of that honourable and important office. The king, in his speech to this new Parliament, declared, that by the last advices from abroad, he had reason to hope the difficulties which had hitherto retarded the execution of the preliminaries, and the opening of the congress, would soon be entirely removed: in the mean time he represented the absolute necessity of continuing the preparations which had hitherto secured the nation, and prevented an open rupture in Europe. He promised, that his first care should be to reduce, from time to time, the expense of the public, as often and as soon as the interest and safety of his people would permit such reduction. He expressed an earnest desire of seeing the foundation laid of an effectual scheme for the increase and encouragement of seamen in general, that they might be invited rather than compelled

---

* King George II. ascended the throne in the forty-fourth year of his age. On the second day of September, 1705, he espoused the Princess Wilhelmina Charlotte Carolina, daughter to John Frederick, Marquis of Brandenburgh Anspach, by whom he had two sons, Frederick Louis, Prince of Wales, born at Hanover, on the thirty-first day of January, 1707, and William Augustus, born at London, on the fifteenth day of April, 1721. She had likewise borne four princesses, namely, Anne, Amelia, Caroline, Mary, and was afterwards delivered of Louisa, married in the sequel to the King of Denmark.

into the service of their country. Finally, he recommended unanimity, zeal, and despatch of the public business. Those speeches, penned by the minister, were composed with a view to soothe the minds of the people into an immediate concurrence with the measures of the government; but without any intention of performing those promises of economy, reformation, and national advantage. The two Houses seemed to vie with each other in expressions of applause and affection to his majesty. The Lords, in their address, hailed him as the best of kings, and the true father of his country. The Commons expressed the warmest sense of gratitude for the blessings they enjoyed in his reign, though it was not yet eight months old. They approved of all his transactions; promised to support him in all his undertakings; and declared they would cheerfully grant whatever supplies should be wanted for the public service. Having considered the estimates which were laid before them by order of his majesty, they voted two-and-twenty thousand nine hundred and fifty-five men for guards and garrisons; and fifteen thousand seamen for the service of the ensuing year. They granted two hundred and thirty thousand nine hundred and twenty-three pounds for the maintenance of twelve thousand Hessian troops; a subsidy of fifty thousand pounds to the King of Sweden; and half that sum to the Duke of Brunswick Wolfenbuttel.[b] The expense of the year amounted to four millions, raised by a land-tax of three shillings in the pound, a malt-tax, and by borrowing of the bank one million seven hundred and fifty thousand pounds, for which annuities to the amount of seventy thousand pounds, to be raised by duties on coals imported into the city of London, were granted to that corporation.

All these sums, however, were not granted without question. The number of land-forces occasioned a debate; and the Hessian auxiliaries were not allowed without dispute and opposition. When they deliberated on the loan of the bank, Mr. W. Pulteney observed, that the shifting of funds was but perpetuating taxes, and putting off the evil day; that notwithstanding the great merit which some persons had built on the sinking

*Violent dispute concerning the national debt.*

---

[b] Nothing could be a greater burlesque upon negotiation than this treaty of alliance concluded with the petty Duke of Wolfenbuttel, who very gravely guarantees to his Britannic majesty the possession of his three kingdoms, and obliges himself to supply his majesty with five thousand men, in consideration of an annual subsidy of five-and-twenty thousand pounds for four years.

fund, it appeared that the national debt had been increased since the setting up that pompous project. Some warm altercation passed between him and Sir Robert Walpole on this subject. The lord-mayor, aldermen, and common-council of London, presented a petition, setting forth, that the duties already laid upon coals and culm, imported into London, affected the trade of that city only; that the inequality of the burden was a great discouragement to their manufactures, and a hardship upon all the trading inhabitants. The petition was rejected, and the tax imposed. The House having addressed the king for a particular and distinct account of the distribution of two hundred and fifty thousand pounds, charged to have been issued for securing the trade and navigation of the kingdom, and preserving and restoring the peace of Europe, he declined granting their request, but signified in general, that part of the money had been issued and disbursed by his late majesty, and the remainder by himself, for carrying on the same necessary services, which required the greatest secresy. Such a message in the reign of King William would have raised a dangerous flame in the House of Commons.

1728. Mr. W. Pulteney inveighed against such a vague and general way of accounting for the public money, as tending to render Parliaments altogether insignificant, to cover embezzlements, and to screen corrupt and rapacious ministers. The Commons, having taken into consideration the state of the national debt, examined the accounts, and interrogated the proper officers. A motion was made by a court member, that it appeared the moneys already issued, and applied towards discharging the national debts, together with a sum to be issued at Lady-day, amounted to six millions six hundred and forty-eight thousand seven hundred and sixty-two pounds, five shillings, one penny, one farthing. In vain did the leaders of the opposition expose the fallacious tendency of this motion. In vain did they demonstrate the fraudulent artifice used in drawing up the accounts: the motion was carried; and several resolutions were taken on the state of the national debts. In the particular account of these debts, upon which the House resolved to form a representation to his majesty, an article of three hundred thousand pounds relating to the duty upon wrought plate was totally omitted. This extraordinary omission being discovered, gave rise to a very warm debate, and to very severe reflections against those who superintended the public accounts. This error being rectified, a committee appointed for the purpose drew up the representation, containing a particular detail of the national debts discharged and incurred since the twenty-fifth day of December, in the year one thousand seven hundred and sixteen, with a state of the sinking fund and of the public credit. The draft, being approved by the House, was presented to the king, who received it graciously. He took this opportunity of saying, that the provision made for gradually discharging the national debts was now become so certain and considerable, that nothing but some unforeseen event could alter or diminish it: a circumstance that afforded the fairest prospect of seeing the old debts discharged without any necessity of incurring new incumbrances.

This answer, fraught with many other expressions of fatherly tenderness for his people, paved the way for a message to the House, demanding a vote of credit to fulfil certain engagements entered into, and concerted, with the advice and concurrence of the last Parliament, for securing the trade and navigation of the kingdom, and for restoring and preserving the peace of Europe. Though a debate ensued upon this message, the majority resolved, that an address should be presented to his majesty, declaring the duty and fidelity of the Commons, their entire confidence in his royal care and goodness, and their readiness to enable his majesty to fulfil his engagements. A vote of credit passed accordingly. During this session, the Peers were chiefly employed in examining copies of several treaties and alliances which the king submitted to their perusal; they likewise prepared a bill for amending the statute of limitation, which, however, did not pass into a law: they considered the state of the national debt, a subject fruitful of debates; they passed the mutiny bill, and those that were sent up from the Commons, touching the supplies; together with an act, obliging ships arriving from infected places to perform quarantine; and some others of a more private nature. These bills having received the royal assent, the king closed the session on the twenty-eighth day of May, when he thanked the Commons for the effectual supplies they had raised, and in particular, for having empowered him to borrow five hundred thousand pounds for the discharge of wages due to the seamen employed in the navy.

England was at this period quite barren of remarkable events. The king's uncle, Ernest Augustus, Prince of Brunswick, Duke of York, and Bishop of Osnabruck, died on the third day of August, and was succeeded in the bishopric by the Elector of Cologn, according to the pactum by which Osnabruck is alternately possessed by the house of Brunswick and that Elector. In the beginning of December, his majesty's eldest son, Prince Frederick, arrived in England from Hanover, where he had hitherto resided, was introduced into the privy-council, and created Prince of Wales. Signior Como, resident from the Duke of Parma, was ordered to quit the kingdom, because his master paid to the pretender the honours due to the King of Great Britain. The congress opened at Soissons, for determining all disputes among the powers of Europe, proved ineffectual. Such difficulties occurred in settling and reconciling so many different pretensions and interests, that the contracting parties in the alliance of Hanover proposed a provisional treaty, concerning which no definitive answer was given as yet by the courts of Vienna and Madrid. The fate of Europe, therefore, continued in suspense: the English fleet lay inactive and rotting in the West Indies; the sailors perished miserably, without daring to avenge their country's wrongs; while the Spanish cruisers committed depredations with impunity on the commerce of Great Britain. The court of Spain, at this juncture, seemed cold and indifferent with regard to a pacification with England. It had renewed a good understanding with France, and now strengthened its interest by a double alliance of marriage with the royal family of Portugal. The infanta of this house was betrothed to the Prince of Asturias; while the Spanish infanta, formerly affianced to the French king, was now matched with the Prince of Brazil, eldest son of his Portuguese majesty. In the month of January, the two courts met in a wooden house built over the little river Coya, that separates the two kingdoms, and there the princesses were exchanged.

*A double marriage between the houses of Spain and Portugal.*

The Parliament of Great Britain meeting according to their last prorogation on the twenty-first day of January, the king in his speech communicated the nature of the negotiation at the congress. He

*Liberality of the Commons.*

demanded such supplies as might enable him to act vigorously in concert with his allies, provided his endeavours to establish an advantageous peace should miscarry; and he hinted that the dilatory conduct of the courts of Vienna and Madrid proceeded in a great measure from the hopes that were given of creating discontents and divisions among the subjects of Great Britain. This suggestion was a ministerial artifice to inflame the zeal and resentment of the nation, and intimidate the members in the opposition. Accordingly the hint was pursued, and in the addresses from both Houses, which could not fail of being agreeable, considering the manner in which they were dictated, particular notice was taken of this article: both Peers and Commons expressed their detestation and abhorrence of those who, by such base and unnatural artifices, suggested the means of distressing their country, and clamoured at the inconveniences which they themselves had occasioned. In these addresses, likewise, the Parliament congratulated his majesty on the arrival of the Prince of Wales in his British dominions; and the Commons sent a particular compliment to his royal highness on that occasion. The estimates having been examined in the usual form, the House voted fifteen thousand seamen for the ensuing year: but the motion for continuing the same number of land-forces which had been allowed in the preceding year was not carried without dispute. All the arguments against a standing army in time of peace, as inconsistent with the British constitution, and dangerous to the liberties of the people, were repeated with great vivacity by Mr. Shippen and Mr. W. Pulteney. These, however, were answered, and represented as absurd, by Mr. Horatio Walpole and Mr. D., two staunch adherents of the minister. The first had, in despite of nature, been employed in different negotiations: he was blunt, awkward, and slovenly; an orator without eloquence, an ambassador without dignity, and a plenipotentiary without address. The other had natural parts and acquired knowledge; spoke with confidence; and in dispute was vain, sarcastic, petulant, and verbose.

The subsidies to Sweden, Hesse-Cassel, and Wolfenbuttel, were continued, notwithstanding the remonstrances of Sir Joseph Jekyll, Mr. Lutwyche, and Mr. Pulteney; which last observed, that as the Landgrave of Hesse-Cassel, and the Duke of Brunswick-Wolf-

*Debates on the subsidies of Hesse-Cassel and Wolfenbuttel.*

enbuttel, usually maintained a certain number of troops in their pay, it was but reasonable that Great Britain should defray no more than the expense of the additional forces which those powers had raised in consequence of their conventions with the King of England. Sir Robert Walpole, perceiving that this remark made an impression on the House, thought it necessary to vindicate his measure. He expatiated upon the wisdom of the late king, in concluding the Hanover alliance. He affirmed, that the convention with Hesse-Cassel had prevented a war in the empire, for which the court of Vienna had made great preparations: that the emperor had not only augmented his own forces by the help of Spanish subsidies, but also retained the troops of three electors; and if he had not been overawed by the Hessians, would certainly have rejected the preliminaries, and all other advances towards a pacification: that, therefore, they ought not to grudge an expense which had already proved so beneficial to the tranquillity of Europe. Sir Joseph Jekyll replied, that whatever gloss might be put upon such measures, they were repugnant to the maxims by which England in former times had steered and squared its conduct with relation to its interest abroad: that the navy was the natural strength of Great Britain— its best defence and security; but if, in order to avoid a war, they should be so free-hearted as to buy and maintain the forces of foreign princes, they were never likely to see an end of such extravagant expenses. This gentleman, who exercised the office of master of the rolls, had approved himself a zealous defender of whig principles, was an able lawyer, a sensible speaker, and a conscientious patriot. The supplies were raised by a continuation of the land-tax, the duties upon malt, cyder, and perry, an additional imposition on unmalted corn used in distilling, and by sale of annuities to the bank not exceeding fifty thousand pounds per annum.

Petitions were delivered to the House of Commons from the merchants of London, Liverpool, and Bristol, complaining of the interruptions they had suffered in their trade for several years, by the depredations of the Spaniards in the West Indies. These being considered, the House ordered the Lords of the Admiralty to produce the other memorials of the same kind which they had received, that they might be laid before the congress at Soissons: then they addressed his majesty for

*Committee for inspecting the gaols.*

copies of all the letters and instructions which had been sent to Admiral Hosier, and those who succeeded him in the command of the West India squadron. Mr. Oglethorpe, having been informed of shocking cruelties and oppressions exercised by gaolers upon their prisoners, moved for an examination into these practices, and was chosen chairman of a committee appointed to inquire into the state of the gaols of the kingdom. They began with the Fleet-prison, which they visited in a body: there they found Sir William Rich, baronet, loaded with irons, by order of Bambridge the warden, to whom he had given some slight cause of offence. They made a discovery of many inhuman barbarities, which had been committed by that ruffian, and detected the most iniquitous scenes of fraud, villainy, and extortion. When the report was made by the committee, the House unanimously resolved, that Thomas Bambridge, acting warden of the Fleet, had wilfully permitted several debtors to escape; had been guilty of the most notorious breaches of trust, great extortions, and the highest crimes and misdemeanours, in the execution of his office; that he had arbitrarily and unlawfully loaded with irons, put into dungeons, and destroyed prisoners for debt, under his charge, treating them in the most barbarous and cruel manner, in high violation and contempt of the laws of the kingdom. John Huggins, esquire, who had been warden of the Fleet-prison, was subjected to a resolution of the same nature. The House presented an address to the king, desiring he would direct his attorney-general forthwith to prosecute these persons and their accomplices, who were committed prisoners to Newgate. A bill was brought in, disabling Bambridge to execute the office of warden; another for the better regulating the prison of the Fleet, and for more effectually preventing and punishing arbitrary and illegal practices of the warden of the said prison.<sup>c</sup>

Other merchants complained by petition of the losses sustained by the Spaniards. The House, in a grand committee, deliberated on this subject, inquired into the particulars, examined evidence, and drew up an address to the king, desiring his majesty would be graciously pleased to use his utmost endeavours for preventing such depredations; for procuring just and

*Address touching the Spanish depredations.*

* It afterwards appeared that some of the members of this inquest were actuated by other motives than those they professed; and the committee was suffered to sink into oblivion.

reasonable satisfaction; and for securing to his subjects the free exercise of commerce and navigation to and from the British colonies in America. The king assured them he would use his best endeavours to answer the desires and expectations of his people, in an affair of so much importance; and they, in another address, thanked him for his gracious answer. They did not, however, receive such a satisfactory reply to a former address, touching the sum of sixty thousand pounds that had been stated in the public account, without specification of the particular uses to which it was applied. His majesty gave them to understand that the money had been issued and disbursed for secret services; and that a distinct and particular account of the distribution of it could not be given without a manifest prejudice to the public. A bill was prepared for the more effectual preventing bribery and corruption in elections for members of Parliament; and it passed through the House without opposition; but their attention was chiefly employed upon the Spanish depredations, which had raised a great clamour through the whole kingdom, and excited very warm disputes in Parliament; for they were generally reputed the fruits of negligence, incapacity, or want of vigour in the ministers. The Commons having made further progress in the inquiry, and received fresh petitions from the merchants, passed some resolutions, in which the Spaniards were accused of having violated the treaties subsisting between the two crowns; and with having treated inhumanly the masters and crews of ships belonging to Great Britain. They justified the instructions given to Admiral Hosier, to seize and detain the flota and galleons of Spain, until justice and satisfaction should be rendered to his majesty and his allies; nay, even declared that such seizure would have been just, prudent, and necessary, tending to prevent an open rupture, and to preserve the peace and tranquillity of Europe. They again addressed the king to use his endeavours to procure satisfaction; and he promised to comply with their request.

Mr. Scroope, member for Bristol, moved for an address entreating his majesty to order an account of the produce of the civil-list revenues for one year to be laid before the House. The address was presented, the account produced, and the House, in a grand committee, took this affair into consideration. The

*A sum voted to the king on account of arrears due on the civil-list revenue.*

courtiers affirmed that they fell short of the eight hundred thousand pounds settled upon his majesty; and Mr. Scroope proposed that the sum of one hundred and fifteen thousand pounds should be granted to the king on account of those deficiencies and arrears. The motion was vigorously opposed by Mr. Pulteney and other members. They expressed their surprise that it should be made so late in the session, when no further demand of money could be reasonably expected; and they said it was the more extraordinary, because it appeared in the former session, from the examination of the accounts then before the House, that the revenues of the civil-list produced yearly a much greater sum than that for which they were given. Mr. Pulteney moved, that the accounts and papers should be referred to the examination of a select committee, properly empowered to investigate the truth. The ministers opposed this motion; and the question being put, it passed in the negative. The majority voted the sum demanded; and in a bill for settling the price of imported corn, they inserted the resolution for granting to his majesty the sum of one hundred and fifteen thousand pounds, on account of arrears due on the civil-list revenues.

The House of Lords having prepared a bill for the more effectual punishment of forgery, which was passed into a law, and ordered the judges to bring in another on the report of a committee appointed to consider the case of imprisoned debtors, at length deliberated upon the state of the nation, particularly the positive demand made by the court of Spain for the restitution of Gibraltar, grounded on a letter written by the late king to his Catholic majesty. From a copy of the letter laid before the House, it plainly appeared that King George I. had consented to this restitution. A motion being made for a resolution, importing, that for the honour of his majesty, and the preservation and security of the trade and commerce of the kingdom, effectual care should be taken in the present treaty that the King of Spain should renounce all claim and pretension to Gibraltar and Minorca, in plain and strong terms; a debate ensued, and the question, being put, passed in the negative, though not without a protest. Then the majority resolved, that the House did entirely rely upon his majesty, that he would, for maintaining the honour and securing the trade of this kingdom, take effectual care in the present treaty to preserve his undoubted right to Gibraltar and Minorca. When the House examined the papers relating to the Spanish depredations, many severe reflections were uttered against the conduct of the ministry; and the motion was made, to resolve that Hosier's expedition was an unreasonable burden on the nation: but this too was rejected, and occasioned another protest. Nor did the clause in the corn bill, for granting one hundred and fifteen thousand pounds to his majesty, pass through the House of Peers without warm opposition. Divers lords alleged, that, instead of a deficiency in the civil-list revenues, there was a considerable surplus; that this was a new grant, and a new burden on the people; that the nation was loaded, not to complete, but to augment the sum designed for the civil-list; and this at a time when the public debts were increased; when the taxes were heavily felt in all parts of the country; when the foreign trade of Britain was encumbered and diminished; when her manufactures were decayed, her poor multiplied, and she was surrounded by many other national calamities. They observed, that if the produce of the civil-list revenue should not amount to the yearly sum of eight hundred thousand pounds, the deficiency must be made good to his majesty by the public; whereas no provision was made, by which, if the produce of these revenues should exceed that sum, the surplus could accrue to the benefit of the public: that, by this precedent, not only real deficiencies were to be made good, but also supplies were to be given for arrears standing out at the end of the year, which should come on before the supplies could be granted, though the supply given to make good arrears in one year would certainly increase the surplusages in another: that the revenues of the civil-list were variable in their own nature; and even when there is a deficiency in the produce, there might be arrears in the receipt: these might be easily increased by the management of designing ministers, by private directions to receivers, and by artful methods of stating accounts. All these arguments, and other objections equally strong and plausible, against this unconscionable and unparliamentary motion, served only to evince the triumph of the ministry over shame and sentiment, their contempt of public spirit, and their defiance of national reproach.<sup>d</sup>

The king had, on the twenty-fourth day of March, given the royal assent to five bills; and on the fourteenth day of May, the same sanction was given to thirty other bills, including an act, enabling the queen to be regent in the kingdom during his majesty's absence, without taking the oaths, and another for the relief of insolvent debtors. At the same time two-and-thirty private bills were passed: then the king expressed his approbation of the Parliament, signified his intention of visiting his German dominions, and ordered the chancellor to prorogue both Houses. His majesty, having appointed the queen regent of the realm, set out for Hanover, on the seventeenth day of May, in order to remove a petty misunderstanding which had happened between that electorate and the court of Berlin. Some Hanoverian subjects had been pressed or decoyed into the service of Prussia; and the regents of Hanover had seized certain Prussian officers by way of reprisal. The whole united kingdom of Great Britain at this juncture enjoyed uninterrupted repose; and commerce continued to increase, in spite of all restriction and discouragement. The people of Ireland found themselves happy under the government of Lord Carteret; and their Parliament, assembling in the month of September, approved themselves the fathers of their country. They established funds for the discharge of their national debt, and for maintaining the expense of government; they enacted wholesome laws for the encouragement of manufactures, trade, and agriculture; and they formed wise regulations in different branches of civil economy. Some time after this session, which was conducted with so much harmony and patriotism, Lord Carteret returned to England, and was succeeded by the Duke of Dorset in the government of that kingdom. In the month of May, Charles Lord Townshend resigned the seals, which were given to Colonel Stanhope, now created Earl of Harrington; so that Sir R. W. now reigned without a rival. James Earl of Waldegrave was appointed ambassador to the court of France, which about that time was filled with joy by the birth of a dauphin.

<sup>d</sup> The peers that distinguished themselves in the opposition were, Beaufort, Strafford, Craven, Foley, Lichfield, Scarsdale, Gower, Mountjoy, Plymouth, Bathurst, Northampton, Coventry, Oxford and Mortimer, Willoughby de Broke, Boyle, and Warrington.

In the month of September, Victor Amadeus, King of Sardinia, resigned his crown to his son Charles Emanuel, Prince of Piedmont. The father reserved to himself a revenue of one hundred thousand pistoles per annum, retired to the castle of Chamberry, and espoused the Countess Dowager of St. Sebastian, who declined the title of queen, but assumed that of Marchioness of Somerive. Though the congress of Soissons proved abortive, conferences were begun at Seville between the plenipotentiaries of England, France, and Spain; and a treaty was concluded on the ninth day of November, not only without the concurrence of the emperor, but even contrary to his right, as established by the quadruple alliance. On this subject he communicated an imperial commissorial decree to the states of the empire assembled in the diet at Ratisbon, which was answered by the French minister De Chavigny. In October, Peter II., Czar of Muscovy, and grandson of Peter I., died in the fifteenth year of his age, at Moscow, and was succeeded on the Russian throne by the Princess Anne Ivanowna, second daughter of John Alexowitz, elder brother of the first Peter, and widow of Frederick William Duke of Courland. The following month was rendered remarkable by the death of Pope Benedict XIII., in whose room Cardinal Laurence Corsini was raised to the pontificate, and assumed the name of Clement XII.

The British Parliament assembling on the thirteenth day of January, the king gave them to understand, that the peace of Europe was now established by the treaty of Seville, built upon the foundation of former treaties, and tending to render more effectual what the contracting powers in the quadruple alliance were before engaged to see performed. He assured them that all former conventions made with Spain in favour of the British trade and navigation were renewed and confirmed: that the free, uninterrupted exercise of their commerce was restored: that the court of Spain had agreed to an ample restitution and reparation for unlawful seizures and depredations: that all rights, privileges, and possessions, belonging to him and his allies, were solemnly re-established, confirmed, and guaranteed; and that not one concession was made to the prejudice of his subjects. He told them he had given orders for reducing a great number of his land-forces, and for laying up great part of the fleet; and observed that there would be a considerable saving in the expense of the current year. After both Houses had presented their addresses of thanks and congratulation to the king on the peace of Seville, the Lords took that treaty into consideration, and it did not pass inquiry without severe animadversion.

The Lords in the opposition excepted to the article by which the merchants of Great Britain were obliged to make proof of their losses at the court of Spain. They said this stipulation was a hardship upon British subjects, and dishonourable to the nation: that few would care to undertake such a troublesome and expensive journey, especially as they had reason to apprehend their claims would be counterbalanced by the Spaniards; and, after all, they would have no more than the slender comfort of hoping to obtain that redress by commissaries which they had not been able to procure by plenipotentiaries. They thought it very extraordinary that Great Britain should be bound to ratify and guarantee whatever agreement should be made between the King of Spain and the Dukes of Parma and Tuscany, concerning the garrisons once established in their countries; that the English should be obliged to assist in effectuating the introduction of six thousand Spanish troops into the towns of Tuscany and Parma, without any specification of the methods to be taken, or the charge to be incurred in giving that assistance; that they should guarantee for ever, not only to Don Carlos, but even to all his successors, the possession of the estates of Tuscany and Parma; a stipulation which in all probability would involve Great Britain in endless quarrels and disputes, about a country with which they had no concern. They affirmed that the treaty of Seville, instead of confirming other treaties, was contradictory to the quadruple alliance; particularly in the article of introducing Spanish troops into Tuscany and Parma in the room of neutral forces stipulated by the former alliance; and agreeing that they should there remain until Don Carlos and his successors should be secure and exempt from all events. They complained that these alterations, from the tenor of the quadruple alliance, were made without the concurrence of the emperor, and even without inviting him to accede; an affront which might alienate his friendship from England, and hazard the loss of such an ancient, powerful, and faithful ally: they declared that throughout the whole treaty there seemed to be an artful omission of any express stipulation, to secure Great Britain in her right to Gibraltar and Minorca. Such was the substance of the objections made to the peace: then Lord Bathurst moved for a resolution, that the agreement on the treaty of Seville, to secure the succession of Don Carlos to the duchies of Tuscany, Parma, and Placentia, with Spanish troops, was a manifest violation of the fifth article of the quadruple alliance, tending to involve the nation in a dangerous and expensive war, and to destroy the balance of power in Europe. The question was put, and the motion rejected. Such too was the fate of two other motions, to resolve that Great Britain's right of sovereignty, dominion, possession, and claim to Gibraltar and Minorca were not ascertained by the treaty of Seville; and that the stipulations in that treaty for repairing the losses of the British merchants were insufficient and precarious. The majority, far from stigmatizing this transaction, resolved, that the treaty did contain all necessary stipulations for maintaining and securing the honour, dignity, rights, and possessions of the crown: that all due care was taken therein for the support of the trade of the kingdom, and for repairing the losses sustained by the British merchants. On these resolutions an address of approbation was founded; but when a motion was made for an address to his majesty, that he would order to be laid before the House a list of all pensions payable to the crown, it was immediately resolved in the negative. Divers contests of the same kind arose upon the mutiny bill, the pension bill, and the maintenance of the twelve thousand Hessians; but the ministry bore down all opposition, though their triumphs were clogged with vigorous protests, which did not fail to make impression upon the body of the people.

*Opposition in the Lower House to a standing army.*

Nor was the success of the court interest in the House of Commons altogether pure, and free from exception and dispute. When the charge of the land-forces fell under the consideration of the Commons, and Mr. Henry Pelham, secretary at war, moved that the number of effective men for the land-service of the ensuing year should be fixed at seventeen thousand seven hundred and nine, Mr. Pulteney insisted upon its being reduced to twelve thousand. Mr. Shippen affirmed, that Mr. Pelham's motion was a flat negative to the address for which he voted on the first day of the session, as it plainly implied a distrust of the validity of the late treaty, which he then assured the House would immediately produce all the blessings of an absolute peace, and deliver the kingdom from the apprehensions and inconveniences of a war. He said the motion tended directly towards the establishment of an army in Great Britain, which he hoped would never be so far Germanized, as tamely to submit to a military government. He observed, that the nation could have no occasion for all the troops that were demanded, considering the glorious scene of affairs which was now opened to all Europe. "They are not necessary (said he) to awe Spain into a firm adherence to its own treaty; they are not necessary to force the emperor into an immediate accession; nor are they in any sort necessary for the safety of his majesty's person and government. Force and violence are the resort of usurpers and tyrants only; because they are, with good reason, distrustful of the people whom they oppress; and because they have no other security for the continuance of their unlawful and unnatural dominion than what depends entirely on the strength of their armies." The motion, however, was carried in the affirmative.

Another warm debate was excited by a bill which the courtiers brought in, to prevent any subjects of Great Britain from advancing sums of money to foreign princes or states, without having obtained licence from his majesty, under his privy-seal, or some greater authority. The minister pretended that this law was proposed to disable the emperor, who wanted to borrow a great sum of the English merchants, from raising and maintaining troops to disturb the tranquillity of Europe. The bill contained a clause, empowering the king to prohibit by proclamation all such loans of money, jewels, or bullion: the attorney-general was empowered to compel, by English bill, in the court of exchequer, the effectual discovery, on oath, of any such loans; and it was enacted, that in default of an answer to any such bill the court should decree a limited sum against the person refusing to answer. Mr. Daniel Pulteney, a gentleman of uncommon talents and ability, and particularly acquainted with every branch of commerce, argued strenuously against this bill, as a restraint upon trade that would render Holland the market of Europe, and the mart of money to the nations of the continent. He

*Bill prohibiting loans to foreign princes or states.*

said that by this general prohibition, extending to all princes, states, or potentates, the English were totally disabled from assisting their best allies: that among others, the King of Portugal frequently borrowed money of the English merchants residing within his dominions: that while the licensing power remained in the crown, the licences would be issued through the hands of the minister, who by this new trade might gain twenty, thirty, or forty thousand a year: that the bill would render the exchequer a court of inquisition; and that whilst it restrained our merchants from assisting the princes and powers of Europe, it permitted our stockjobbers to trade in their funds without interruption. Other arguments of equal weight were enforced by Mr. Barnard, a merchant of London, who perfectly understood trade in all its branches, spoke with judgment and precision, and upon all occasions steadily adhered to the interests and liberties of his country. After having explained his reasons, he declared he should never consent to a bill which he deemed a violation of our fundamental laws, a breach of our dearest liberties, and a very terrible hardship on mankind. Sir William Wyndham distinguished himself on the same side of the question: the bill was vindicated by Sir Robert Walpole, Mr. Pelham, and Sir Philip York, attorney-general; and being supported by the whole weight of ministerial influence, not only passed through the House, but was afterwards enacted into a law.

*Charter of the East India Company prolonged.* The subsidies were continued to the Landgrave of Hesse-Cassel and the Duke of Brunswick-Wolfenbuttel, in spite of all that could be urged against these extraneous incumbrances; and the supply for the ensuing year was granted according to the estimates which the ministry thought proper to produce, amounting to about two millions two hundred and eighty thousand pounds. It must be owned, however, for the credit of this session, that the House appropriated one million of the surpluses arising from the sinking fund towards the discharge of the national debt; and by another act extinguished the duties upon salt, by which expedient the subject was eased of a heavy burden, not only in being freed from the duty, but also from a considerable charge of salaries given to a great number of officers employed to collect this imposition. They likewise encouraged the colony of Carolina with an act, allowing the planters and traders of that province to export rice directly to any part of Europe southward of Cape Finisterre; and they permitted salt from Europe to be imported into the colony of New York. The term of the exclusive trade granted by act of Parliament to the East India Company drawing towards a period, many considerable merchants and others made application for being incorporated and vested with the privilege of trading to those countries, proposing to lay that branch of trade open to all the subjects of Great Britain on certain conditions. In consideration of an act of Parliament for this purpose, they offered to advance three millions two hundred thousand pounds, for redeeming the fund and trade of the present East India Company. This proposal was rejected; and the exclusive privilege vested in the Company was, by act of Parliament, protracted to the year one thousand seven hundred and sixty-six, upon the following conditions: that they should pay into the exchequer the sum of two hundred thousand pounds towards the supplies of the year, without interest or addition to their capital stock: that the annuity or yearly fund of one hundred and sixty thousand pounds, payable to them from the public, should be reduced to one hundred and twenty-eight thousand: that after the year one thousand seven hundred and sixty-six, their right to the exclusive trade should be liable to be taken away by Parliament, on three years' notice, and repayment of their capital.

On the fifteenth day of May the king went to the House of Peers, and closed the session. In his speech he expressed his joy, that notwithstanding all the clamours which were raised, the Parliament had approved of those matters which fell under their consideration; a circumstance which, he said, could not fail to inspire all mankind with a just detestation of those incendiaries, who, by scandalous libels, laboured to alienate the affections of his people; to fill their minds with groundless jealousies and unjust complaints, in dishonour of him and his government, and in defiance of the sense of both Houses of Parliament.* The emperor was so much incensed at the

1730. The emperor resents the treaty of Seville.

---

* In the course of this session the Commons passed a bill for making more effectual the laws in being, for disabling persons from being chosen members of Parliament who enjoyed any pension during pleasure, or for any number of years, or any offices holden in trust for them, by obliging all persons hereafter to be chosen to serve for the Commons in Parliament, to take the oath therein mentioned. In all probability this bill would not have made its way through the House of Commons, had not the minister been well assured it would stick with the Upper House, where it was rejected at the second reading, though not without violent opposition.

insult offered to him in the treaty of Seville, with respect to the garrisons of Tuscany and Parma, that he prohibited the subjects of Great Britain from trading in his dominions: he began to make preparations for war, and actually detached bodies of troops to Italy, with such despatch as had been very seldom exerted by the house of Austria. Yet the article of which he complained was not so much a real injury as an affont put upon the head of the empire; for the eventual succession to those Italian duchies had been secured to the infant, Don Carlos, by the quadruple alliance; and all that the emperor required was that this prince should receive the investiture of them as fiefs of the empire.

In Great Britain, this year was not distinguished by any transactions of great moment. Seven chiefs of the Cherokee nations of Indians in America were brought to England by Sir Alexander Cumin. Being introduced to the king, they laid their crown and regalia at his feet; and by an authentic deed acknowledged themselves subjects to his dominion, in the name of all their compatriots, who had vested them with full powers for this purpose. They were amazed and confounded at the riches and magnificence of the British court: they compared the king and queen to the sun and moon, the princes to the stars of heaven, and themselves to nothing. They gave their assent in the most solemn manner to articles of friendship and commerce, proposed by the lords commissioners for trade and plantations; and being loaded with presents of necessaries, arms, and ammunition, were reconveyed to their own country, which borders on the province of South Carolina. In the month of September a surprising revolution was effected at Constantinople, without bloodshed or confusion. A few mean janissaries displayed a flag in the streets, exclaiming that all true Mussulmen ought to follow them, and assist in reforming the government. They soon increased to the number of one hundred thousand, marched to the seraglio, and demanded the grand vizier, the kiaja, and captain pacha. These unhappy ministers were immediately strangled. Their bodies being delivered to the insurgents were dragged through the streets, and afterwards thrown to the dogs to be devoured. Not contented with this sacifice, the revolters deposed the Grand Signior Achmet, who was confined to the same prison from whence they brought his nephew Machmut, and raised

*Seven Indian chiefs arrive in England. Revolution at Constantinople.*

this last to the throne, after he had lived seven-and-twenty years in confinement.

England was at this period infested with robbers, assassins, and incendiaries, the natural consequences of degeneracy, corruption, and the want of police in the interior government of the kingdom. This defect, in a great measure, arose from an absurd notion, that laws necessary to prevent those acts of cruelty, violence, and rapine, would be incompatible with the liberty of British subjects; a notion that confounds all distinctions between liberty and brutal licentiousness, as if that freedom was desirable, in the enjoyment of which people find no security for their lives or effects. The peculiar depravity of the times was visible even in the conduct of those who preyed upon the commonwealth. Thieves and robbers were now become more desperate and savage than ever they had appeared since mankind was civilized. In the exercise of their rapine, they wounded, maimed, and even murdered the unhappy sufferers, through a wantonness of barbarity. They circulated letters demanding sums of money from certain individuals, on pain of reducing their houses to ashes, and their families to ruin; and even set fire to the house of a rich merchant in Bristol, who had refused to comply with their demand. The same species of villany was practised in different parts of the kingdom; so that the government was obliged to interpose, and offer a considerable reward for discovering the ruffians concerned in such execrable designs.

*England infested with robbers, assassins, and incendiaries.*

In the speech with which the king opened the session of parliament on the twenty-first day of January, he told them, that the present critical conjuncture seemed in a very particular manner to deserve their attention: that as the transactions then depending in the several courts of Europe were upon the point of being determined, the great event of peace or war might be very much affected by their first resolutions, which were expected by different powers with great impatience. He said, the continuance of that zeal and vigour with which they had hitherto supported him and his engagements must at this time be of the greatest weight and importance, both with regard to his allies, and to those who might be disposed, before the season of action, to prevent, by an accommodation, the fatal consequences of a general rupture. The

*Bill against pensioners sitting as members in the House of Commons.*

former scene was repeated. Both Houses, in their addresses, promised to support his majesty in all his engagements; yet the members in the opposition demonstrated the absurdity of promising to fulfil engagements before they could possibly know whether or not they were for the service of Great Britain. Another bill was brought into the House of Commons, to prevent pensioners from sitting as members of Parliament; and after a third reading, carried up to the Lords for their concurrence. When the supply fell under consideration, the debates were renewed upon the subsidies to the Landgrave of Hesse-Cassel and the Duke of Wolfenbuttel, which, however, were continued; and every article was granted according to the estimates given in for the expense of the ensuing year. Two petitions being presented to the Commons, representing the delays of justice occasioned by the use of the Latin tongue in proceedings at law, a bill was brought in for changing this practice, and enacting that all those processes and pleadings should be entered in the English language. Though one would imagine that very little could be advanced against such a regulation, the bill met with warm opposition, on pretence that it would render useless the ancient records which were written in that language, and introduce confusion and delay of justice, by altering the established form and method of pleading: in spite of these objections, it passed through both Houses, and obtained the royal assent. A great number of merchants from different parts of the kingdom having repeated their complaints of depredations and cruelties committed by the Spaniards in the West Indies, their petitions were referred to the consideration of a grand committee. Their complaints upon examination appeared to be well founded. The House presented an address to the king desiring his majesty would be graciously pleased to continue his endeavours to prevent such depredations for the future; to procure full satisfaction for the damages already sustained; and to secure to the British subjects the full and uninterrupted exercise of their trade and navigation to and from the British colonies in America. The bill against pensions produced a warm debate in the House of Lords, where it was violently opposed by the Dukes of Newcastle and Argyle, the Earl of Ilay, and Dr. Sherlock, Bishop of Bangor. This prelate, in a remarkable speech, represented it as a scheme to enlarge the power of the House of Commons, and to break the balance between the powers essential to the constitution, so as, sooner or later, to prove the ruin of the whole. The great barrier provided against bribery and corruption by this bill consisted in an oath to be imposed on all members of the Lower House, by which they must have solemnly sworn and declared, that they had not directly, nor indirectly, any pension during pleasure, or for any number of years, or any office in part or in the whole, held for them, or for their benefit, by any persons whatsoever; and that they would not accept any such pensions or offices, without signifying the same to the House within fourteen days after they should be received or accepted. The bill was vindicated as just and necessary by the Earls of Winchelsea and Strafford, Lord Bathurst, and Lord Carteret, who had by this time joined as an auxiliary in the opposition.*

The House of Peers proceeded to consider the state of the national debt; they read a bill for the free importation of wool from Ireland into England, which was fiercely opposed and laid aside, contrary to all the rules of sound policy. They passed the bill for carrying on proceedings at law in the English language; and a fruitless motion was made by Lord Bathurst for an address, to desire his majesty would give directions for discharging the Hessian troops that were in the pay of Great Britain. On the seventh day of May the Parliament was prorogued, after the king had given them to understand, that all apprehensions of war were now happily removed by a treaty signed at Vienna between him and the emperor. He said it was communicated to the courts of France and Spain, as parties to the treaty of Seville, the execution of which it principally regarded; and that it was likewise submitted to the consideration of the States-General. He observed, that the conditions and engagements into which he had entered on this occasion were agreeable to that necessary concern which the British nation must always have for the security and pre-

1731. Treaty of Vienna.

---

* Nothing was heard within doors in Parliament but sarcastic repartee and violent declamation between the two parties, who did not confine their altercation to these debates, but took the field against each other in periodical papers and occasional pamphlets. The paper called the Craftsman had already risen into high reputation all over England, for the wit, humour, and solid reasoning it contained. Some of the best writers in the opposition, including Lord Bolingbroke and Mr. P., made use of this vehicle to convey their animadversions upon the minister, who, on his side, employed the most wretched scribblers to defend his conduct. It was in consequence of two political pamphlets, written in opposition to each other, by Lord Hervey and Mr. P., and some recrimination they produced in the House of Commons, that his lordship challenged the other to single combat, and had well nigh lost his life in the duel, which was fought in Hyde-Park.

servation of the balance of power in Europe: and that this happy turn, duly improved with a just regard to former alliances, yielded a favourable prospect of seeing the public tranquillity re-established.

In the month of January the Duke of Parma died, after having made a will in which he declared his duchess was three months advanced in her pregnancy; entreating the allied powers of Europe to have compassion upon his people, and defer the execution of their projects until his consort should be delivered. In case the child should be still-born, or die after the birth, he bequeathed his dominions and allodial estates to the infant Don Carlos of Spain, and appointed five regents to govern the duchy. Notwithstanding this disposition, a body of imperial troops immediately took possession of Parma and Placentia, under the command of General Stampa, who declared they should conduct themselves with all possible regularity and moderation, and leave the administration entirely to the regents whom the duke had appointed. They publicly proclaimed in the market-place that they took possession of these duchies for the infant Don Carlos; and that if the duchess-dowager should not be delivered of a prince, the said infant might receive the investiture from the emperor whenever he would, provided he should come without an army. Though these steps seemed to threaten an immediate war, the King of Great Britain and the States-General interposed their mediation so effectually with the Court of Vienna, that the emperor desisted from the prosecution of his design; and on the sixteenth day of March concluded at Vienna a treaty with his Britannic Majesty, by which he consented to withdraw his troops from Parma and Placentia. He agreed that the King of Spain might take possession of these places in favour of his son Don Carlos, according to the treaty of Seville. He likewise agreed, that the Ostend company, which had given such umbrage to the maritime powers, should be totally dissolved, on condition that the contracting powers concerned in the treaty of Seville should guarantee the pragmatic sanction, or succession of the Austrian hereditary dominions to the heirs female of the emperor, in case he should die without male issue. The Dutch minister residing at the imperial court did not subscribe this treaty, because, by the maxims received in that republic, and the nature of her government, he could not be vested with full powers so soon as it would have been necessary; nevertheless the States-General were, by a separate article, expressly named as a principal contracting party.

On the twenty-second day of July a new treaty was signed at Vienna between the emperor and the kings of Great Britain and Spain, tending to confirm the former. In August, a treaty of union and defensive alliance between the electorates of Saxony and Hanover was executed at Dresden. *Don Carlos takes possession of his territories.* The court of Spain expressing some doubts with regard to the pregnancy of the Duchess of Parma, she underwent a formal examination by five midwives of different nations, in presence of the elder duchess-dowager, several ladies of quality, three physicians, and a surgeon; and was declared with child: nevertheless, after having kept all Europe in suspense for six months, she owned she had been deceived; and General Stampa, with the imperial forces, took formal possession of the duchies of Parma and Placentia. Spain and the Great Duke of Tuscany having acceded to the last treaty of Vienna, the crown of Great Britain engaged to equip an armament that should convoy Don Carlos to his new dominions. Accordingly, Sir Charles Wager sailed with a strong squadron from Portsmouth on the twenty-sixth day of August; and in September arrived at Barcelona, where, being joined by the Spanish fleet and transports, they sailed together to Leghorn; from whence the Admiral returned to England. Don Carlos passed through part of France, and embarking at Antibes on board of the Spanish galleys, arrived at Leghorn in December. Then the imperial general withdrew his forces into the Milanese, and the infant took possession of his new territories.

During these transactions France was distracted by religious disputes, occasioned by the bull Unigenitus thundered against the doctrines of Jansenius; a bull which had produced a schism in the Gallican church, *France distracted by religious disputes.* and well nigh involved that country in civil war and confusion. It was opposed by the Parliaments and lay tribunals of the kingdom; but many bishops, and the Jesuits in general, were its most strenuous assertors. All the artifices of priestcraft were practised on both sides to inflame the enthusiasm, and manage the superstition, of the people. Pretended miracles were wrought at the tomb of Abbé Paris, who had died without accepting the bull, consequently was declared damned by the abettors of that constitution. On the other hand, the Jesuits exerted all their abilities and industry in preaching against the Jansenists; in establishing an opinion of their superior sanctity; and inspiring a spirit of quietism among their votaries, who were transported into the delirium of possession, illumination, and supernatural converse. These arts were often used for the most infamous purposes. Female enthusiasts were wrought up to such a violence of agitation, that nature fainted under the struggle, and the pseudo-saint seized this opportunity of violating the chastity of his penitent. Such was said to be the case of Mademoiselle la Cadière, a young gentlewoman of Toulon, abused in this manner by the lust and villany of Père Girard, a noted Jesuit, who underwent a trial before the Parliament of Aix, and very narrowly escaped the stake.

The Parliament of Great Britain meeting on the thirteenth day of January, the king in his speech declared, that the general tranquillity of Europe was restored and established by the last treaty of Vienna; and Don Carlos was actually possessed of Parma and Placentia: that six thousand Spaniards were quietly admitted and quartered in the duchy of Tuscany, to secure, by the express consent and agreement of the great duke, the reversion of his dominions; and that a family convention was made between the courts of Spain and Tuscany, for preserving mutual peace and friendship in the two houses. He told the Commons, that the estimates for the service of the current year would be considerably less than those of former years. He recommended unanimity: he observed that his government had no security but what was equally conducive to their happiness, and to the protection of his people: that their prosperity had no foundation but in the defence and support of his government. "Our safety," said he, "is mutual, and our interests are inseparable." The opposition to the court measures appears to have been uncommonly spirited during the course of this session. The minister's motions were attacked with all the artillery of elocution. His principal emissaries were obliged to task their faculties to their full exertion, to puzzle and perplex where they could not demonstrate and convince, to misrepresent what they could not vindicate, and to elude the arguments which they could not refute. In the House of Commons Lord Hervey, lately appointed vice-chamberlain

*The ministry violently opposed in Parliament.*

of his majesty's household, made a motion for an address of thanks, in which they should declare their entire approbation of the king's conduct, acknowledge the blessings they enjoy under his government, express their confidence in the wisdom of his councils, and declare their readiness to grant the necessary supplies. This member, son to the Earl of Bristol, was a nobleman of some parts, which, however, were more specious than solid. He condescended to act as a subaltern to the minister, and approved himself extremely active in forwarding all his designs, whether as a secret emissary or public orator; in which last capacity he appears to have been pert, frivolous, and frothy. His motion was seconded by Mr. Clutterbuck, and opposed by Sir Wilfred Lawson, Mr. Shippen, Mr. W. Pulteney, Sir William Wyndham, and Mr. Oglethorpe. They did not argue against a general address of thanks; but exposed the absurdity and bad tendency of expressions which implied a blind approbation of all the measures of the ministry. Sir Wilfred Lawson observed, that notwithstanding the great things we had done for the crown of Spain, and the favours we had procured for the royal family of that kingdom, little or no satisfaction had as yet been received for the injuries our merchants had sustained from that nation. Mr. Pulteney took notice, that the nation, by becoming guarantee to the pragmatic sanction, laid itself under an obligation to assist the Austrian family when attacked by any potentate whatever, except the grand signior: that they might be attacked when it would be much against the interest of the kingdom to engage itself in a war upon any foreign account: that it might one day be for the interest of the nation to join against them, in order to preserve the balance of Europe, the establishing of which had already cost England such immense sums of money. He insisted upon the absurdity of concluding such a number of inconsistent treaties; and concluded with saying, that if affairs abroad were now happily established, the ministry which conducted them might be compared to a pilot, who, though there was a clear, safe, and straight channel into port, yet took it in his head to carry the ship a great way about, through sands, rocks, and shallows; who, after having lost a great number of seamen, destroyed a great deal of tackle and rigging, and subjected the owners to an enormous expense, at last by chance hits the port and triumphs in his good conduct. Sir William Wyndham spoke to the same purpose. Mr. Oglethorpe, a gentleman of unblemished character, brave, generous, and humane, affirmed that many other things related more nearly to the honour and interest of the nation than did the guarantee of the pragmatic sanction. He said he wished to have heard that the new works at Dunkirk had been entirely razed and destroyed; that the nation had received full and complete satisfaction for the depredations committed by the natives of Spain; that more care was taken in disciplining the militia, on whose valour the nation must chiefly depend in case of invasion; and that some regard had been shown to the oppressed Protestants in Germany. He expressed his satisfaction to find that the English were not so closely united to France as formerly; for he had generally observed, that when two dogs were in a leash together, the stronger generally ran away with the weaker; and this he was afraid had been the case between France and Great Britain. The motion was vigorously defended by Mr. Pelham, paymaster of the forces, and brother to the Duke of Newcastle, a man whose greatest fault was his being concerned in supporting the measures of a corrupt ministry. In other respects he was liberal, candid, benevolent, and even attached to the interest of his country, though egregiously mistaken in his notions of government. On this occasion he asserted that it was no way inconsistent with the honour or dignity of that House to thank his majesty in the most particular terms for every thing he had been pleased to communicate in his speech from the throne: that no expressions of approbation in the address could be any way made use of to prevent an inquiry into the measures which had been pursued, when the treaties should be laid before the House. He said, at the opening of a session the eyes of all Europe were turned towards Great Britain, and from the Parliament's first resolves all the neighbouring powers judged of the unanimity that would ensue between his majesty and the representatives of his people: that their appearing jealous or diffident of his majesty's conduct would weaken his influence upon the councils of foreign states and potentates, and perhaps put it out of his power to rectify any false step that might have been made by his ministers. His arguments were reinforced by a long speech from Mr. H. Walpole. The question was put, the motion carried, and the address presented.

The next subject of debate was the number of land-forces. When the supply fell under consideration, Sir W. Strickland, secretary at war, moved that the same number which had been maintained in the preceding year should be continued in pay. On the other hand, Lord Morpeth, having demonstrated the danger to which the liberties of the nation might be exposed, by maintaining a numerous standing army in time of peace, made a motion that the number should be reduced to twelve thousand. A warm debate ensuing, was managed in favour of the first motion by Lord Hervey, Sir Robert Walpole and his brother, Mr. Pelham, and Sir Philip York, attorney-general. This gentleman was counted a better lawyer than a politician, and shone more as an advocate at the bar than as an orator in the House of Commons. The last partisan of the ministry was Sir William Yonge, one of the lords commissioners of the treasury; a man who rendered himself serviceable and necessary, by stooping to all compliances, running upon every scent, and haranguing on every subject with an even, uninterrupted, tedious flow of dull declamation, composed of assertions without veracity, conclusions from false premises, words without meaning, and language without propriety. Lord Morpeth's motion was espoused by Mr. Watkin Williams Wynne, a gentleman of an ancient family and opulent fortune in Wales, brave, open, hospitable, and warmly attached to the ancient constitution and hierarchy; he was supported by Mr. Walter Plumer, who spoke with weight, precision, and severity, by Sir W. Wyndham, Mr. Shippen, Mr. W. Pulteney, and Mr. Barnard. The courtiers argued that it was necessary to maintain such a number of land-forces as might defeat the designs of malecontents, secure the interior tranquillity of the kingdom, defend it from external assaults, overawe its neighbours, and enable it to take vigorous measures in case the peace of Europe should be re-embroiled. They affirmed, the science of war was so much altered, and required so much attention, that no dependence was to be placed upon a militia: that all nations were obliged to maintain standing armies, for their security against the encroachments of neighbouring powers: that the number of troops in Great Britain was too inconsiderable to excite the jealousy of the people even under an ambitious monarch: that his majesty never entertained the least thought of infringing the liberties of his subjects: that it could not be supposed that the officers, among whom were many gentlemen of family and fortune, would ever concur in a design to enslave their country; and that the forces now in pay could not be properly deemed a standing army, inasmuch as they were voted and maintained from year to year by the Parliament, which was the representative of the people. To these arguments the members in the opposition replied, that a standing force in time of peace was unconstitutional, and had been always thought dangerous: that a militia was as capable of discipline as a standing army, and would have more incentives to courage and preseverance: that the civil magistrate was able to preserve the peace of the country: that the number of the malecontents was altogether contemptible, though it might be considerably augmented by maintaining a standing army, and other such arbitrary measures: that other nations had been enslaved by standing armies; and howsoever they might find themselves necessitated to depend upon a military force for security against encroaching neighbours, the case was very different with regard to Great Britain, for the defence of which nature had provided in a peculiar manner: that this provision was strengthened and improved by a numerous navy, which secured her the dominion on the sea; and if properly disposed, would render all invasion impracticable, or at least ineffectual: that the land-army of Great Britain, though sufficient to endanger the liberties of an unarmed people, could not possibly secure such an extent of coast, and therefore could be of very little service in preventing an invasion: that though they had all imaginable confidence in his majesty's regard for the liberty of his subjects, they could not help apprehending, that should a standing army become part of the constitution, another prince of more dangerous talents, and more fatal designs, might arise and employ it for the worst purposes of ambition: that though many officers were gentlemen of honour and probity, these might be easily discarded, and the army gradually moulded into a quite different temper. By these means, practised in former times, an army had been new modelled to such a degree, that they turned their swords against the Parliament, for whose defence they had been raised, and destroyed the constitution both in church and state: that with respect to its being wholly dependent on the Parliament, the people of England would have reason to complain of the same hardship, whether a standing army should be declared at once indispensable, or regularly voted from year to year, according to the direction of the ministry: that the sanction of the legislature, granted to measures which in themselves are unconstitutional, burdensome, odious, and repugnant to the genius of the nation, instead of yielding consolation, would serve only to demonstrate, that the most effectual method of forging the chains of national slavery would be that of ministerial influence operating upon a venal Parliament. Such were the reasons urged against a standing army, of what number soever it might be composed: but the expediency of reducing the number from about eighteen thousand to twelve thousand was insisted upon as the natural consequence of his majesty's declaration, by which they were given to understand that the peace of Europe was established; and that he had nothing so much at heart as the ease and prosperity of his people. It was suggested, that if eighteen thousand men were sufficient on the supposed eve of a general war in Europe, it was surely reasonable to think that a less number would suffice when peace was perfectly re-established. Whatever effect these reasons had upon the body of the nation, they made no converts in the House, where the majority resolved that the standing army should be maintained without reduction. Mr. Plumer complained, that the country was oppressed by an arbitrary method of quartering soldiers, in an undue proportion, upon those publicans who refused to vote in elections according to the direction of the ministry. Mr. Pulteney asserted, that the money raised for the subsistence of eighteen thousand men in England would maintain sixty thousand French or Germans, or the same number of almost any other people on the continent. Sir William Wyndham declared, that eighteen thousand of the English troops in the late war were maintained on less than two-thirds of the sum now demanded for the like number: but no regard was paid to these allegations.

The next object of importance that attracted the notice of the House was the state of the Charitable Corporation. This company was first erected in the year one thousand seven hundred and seven. Their professed intention was to lend money at legal interest to

*Account of the Charitable Corporation.*

the poor, upon small pledges; and to persons of better rank upon an indubitable security of goods impawned. Their capital was at first limited to thirty thousand pounds; but, by licences from the crown, they increased it to six hundred thousand pounds, though their charter was never confirmed by act of Parliament. In the month of October, George Robinson, esquire, member for Marlow, the cashier, and John Thompson, warehouse-keeper of the corporation, disappeared in one day. The proprietors, alarmed at this incident, held several general courts, and appointed a committee to inspect the state of their affairs. They reported, that for a capital of above five hundred thousand pounds no equivalent was found; inasmuch as their effects did not amount to the value of thirty thousand, the remainder having been embezzled by means which they could not discover. The proprietors, in a petition to the House of Commons, represented that by the most notorious breach of trust in several persons to whom the care and management of their affairs were committed, the corporation had been defrauded of the greatest part of their capital; and that many of the petitioners were reduced to the utmost degree of misery and distress: they therefore prayed, that as they were unable to detect the combinations of those who had ruined them, or to bring the delinquents to justice, without the aid of the power and authority of Parliament, the House would vouchsafe to inquire into the state of the corporation and the conduct of their managers, and give such relief to the petitioners as to the House should seem meet. The petition was graciously received, and a secret committee appointed to proceed on the inquiry. They soon discovered a most iniquitous scene of fraud, which had been acted by Robinson and Thompson, in concert with some of the directors, for embezzling the capital and cheating the proprietors. Many persons of rank and quality were concerned in this infamous conspiracy: some of the first characters in the nation did not escape suspicion and censure. Sir Robert Sutton and Sir Archibald Grant were expelled the House of Commons, as having had a considerable share in those fraudulent practices: a bill was brought in to restrain them and other delinquents from leaving the kingdom, or alienating their effects. In the mean time, the committee received a letter from Signior John Angelo Belloni, an eminent banker at Rome, giving them to understand, that Thompson was secured in that city, with all his papers, and confined to the castle of St. Angelo; and that the papers were transmitted to his correspondent at Paris, who would deliver them up, on certain conditions stipulated in favour of the prisoner. This letter was considered as an artifice to insinuate a favourable opinion of the pretender, as if he had taken measures for securing Thompson, from his zeal for justice, and affection for the English people. On this supposition, the proposals were rejected with disdain; and both Houses concurred in an order that the letter should be burned at the Royal Exchange, by the hands of the common hangman. The Lower House resolved, that it was an insolent and audacious libel, absurd and contradictory; that the whole transaction was a scandalous artifice, calculated to delude the unhappy, and to disguise and conceal the wicked practices of the professed enemies to his majesty's person, crown, and dignity.

No motion, during this session, produced such a warm contest as did that of Sir Robert Walpole, when, after a long preamble, he proposed that the duties on salt, which about two years before had been abolished, should now be revived, and granted to his majesty, his heirs and successors, for the term of three years. In order to sweeten this proposal, he declared that the land-tax for the ensuing year should be reduced to one shilling in the pound. All the members of the country party were immediately in commotion. They expressed their surprise at the grossness of the imposition. They observed that two years had scarce elapsed since the king, in a speech from the throne, had exhorted them to abolish some of the taxes that were the most burdensome to the poor: the House was then of opinion, that the tax upon salt was the most burdensome and the most pernicious to the trade of the kingdom, of all the impositions to which the poor were subjected, and therefore it was taken off; but that no good reason could be produced for altering their opinion so suddenly, and resolving to grind the faces of the poor, in order to ease a few rich men of the landed interest. They affirmed, that the most general taxes are not always the least burdensome: that after a nation is obliged to extend their taxes farther than the luxuries of their country, those taxes that can be raised with the least charge to the public are the most convenient and easiest to the people; but they

*Revival of the salt-tax.*

ought carefully to avoid taxing those things which are necessary for the subsistence of the poor. The price of all necessaries being thus enhanced, the wages of the tradesman and manufacturer must be increased; and where these are high, the manufacturers will be undersold by those of cheaper countries. The trade must of consequence be ruined; and it is not to be supposed that the landed gentleman would choose to save a shilling in the pound from the land-tax, by means of an expedient that would ruin the manufacturers of his country, and decrease the value of his own fortune. They alleged that the salt-tax particularly affected the poor, who could not afford to eat fresh provisions; and that, as it formerly occasioned murmurs and discontents among the lower class of people, the revival of it would, in all probability, exasperate them into open sedition. They observed, that while it was exacted in England, a great number of merchants sent their ships to Ireland to be victualled for their respective voyages; that, since it had been abolished, many experiments had been successfully tried with salt for the improvement of agriculture, which would be entirely defeated by the revival of this imposition. They suggested that the land-tax was raised at a very small expense, and subject to no fraud, whereas that upon salt would employ a great number of additional officers in the revenue, wholly depending upon the ministry, whose influence in elections they would proportionably increase. They even hinted, that this consideration was one powerful motive for proposing the revival of an odious tax, which was in effect an excise, and would be deemed a step towards a general excise upon all sorts of provisions. Finally, they demonstrated that the salt-tax introduced numberless frauds and perjuries in different articles of traffic. Sir Robert Walpole endeavoured to obviate all these objections in a long speech, which was minutely answered and refuted in every article by Mr. Pulteney. Nevertheless, the question being put, the minister's motion was carried in the affirmative, and the duty revived: yet, before the bill passed, divers motions were made, and additional clauses proposed, by the members in the opposition. New debates were raised on every new objection, and the courtiers were obliged to dispute their ground by inches.

The pension bill was revived, and for the third time rejected in the House of Lords. A bill for the encouragement of the sugar colonies passed through the Lower House with great difficulty, but was lost among the Peers: another, for the better securing the freedom of Parliaments, by further qualifying members to sit in the House of Commons, was read the third time and thrown out upon the question. A committee had been appointed to inquire into a sale of the estate which had belonged to the late Earl of Derwentwater. It appeared by the report, that the sale had been fraudulent: a bill was prepared to make it void: Dennis Bond, esquire, and Serjeant Birch, commissioners for the sale of the forfeited estates, were declared guilty of notorious breach of trust, and expelled the House, of which they were members: George Robinson, esquire, underwent the same sentence, on account of the part he acted in the Charitable Corporation, as he and Thompson had neglected to surrender themselves, according to the terms of a bill which had passed for that purpose. During this session, five members of Parliament were expelled for the most sordid acts of knavery; a sure sign of national degeneracy and dishonour. All the supplies were granted, and, among other articles, the sum of two-and-twenty thousand six hundred and ninety-four pounds, seven shillings, and sixpence, for the agio or difference of the subsidies payable to the crown of Denmark, in pursuance of the treaty subsisting between the late king and that monarch; but this was not obtained without a violent dispute. Mr. Pulteney, who bore a considerable share in all these debates, became in a little time so remarkable as to be thought worthy of a very particular mark of his majesty's displeasure. The king, on the first day of July, called for the council-book, and with his own hand struck the name of William Pulteney, esquire, out of the list of privy-councillors; his majesty further ordered him to be put out of all the commissions of the peace. The several lord lieutenants, from whom he had received deputations, were commanded to revoke them; and the lord chancellor and secretaries of state were directed to give the necessary orders for that purpose.

Nor did the House of Peers tamely and unanimously submit to the measures of the ministry. The pension bill, being read, was again rejected, and a protest entered. A debate arose about the number of standing forces; and the Earl of Chesterfield argued for the court motion. The Earl of Oxford moved that they might be reduced to twelve thousand effective men. The Earl of Winchelsea observed, that a standing army rendered ministers of state more daring than otherwise they would be, in contriving and executing projects that were grievous to the people: schemes that never could enter into the heads of any but those who were drunk with excess of power. The Marquis of Tweeddale, in reasoning against such a number as the ministry proposed, took occasion to observe, that not one shilling of the forfeited estates was ever applied to the use of the public: he likewise took notice, that the eighteen thousand men, demanded as a standing force, were modelled in such a manner, that they might be speedily augmented to forty thousand men on any emergency. The Duke of Argyle endeavoured to demonstrate the danger of depending for the safety of the kingdom upon an undisciplined militia, a fleet, or an army of auxiliaries. Then he represented the necessity of having recourse to a regular army in case of invasion; and after all acknowledged, that the number proposed was no way sufficient for that purpose. All his arguments were answered and refuted in an excellent speech by Lord Carteret: nevertheless, victory declared for the minister. The Parliament having granted every branch of the supply, towards the payment of which they borrowed a sum from the sinking-fund, and passed divers other acts for the encouragement of commerce and agriculture, the king, on the first day of June, gave the royal assent to the bills that were prepared, and closed the session, after having informed both Houses that the States-General had acceded to the treaty of Vienna; that he had determined to visit his German dominions, and to leave the queen regent in his absence. He accordingly set out for Hanover in the beginning of June. By this time the pragmatic sanction was confirmed by the diet of the empire, though not without a formal protest by the Electors Palatine, Bavaria, and Saxony.

## CHAPTER XVI.

Remarkable Instance of Suicide. — Affairs of the Continent. — Meeting of the Parliament. — Address to the King touching the Spanish Depredations. — The Excise Scheme proposed by Sir Robert Walpole. — Opposition to the Scheme. — Bill for a Dower to the Princess Royal. — Debates in the House of Lords concerning the Estates of the late Directors of the South-Sea Company. — Double Election of a King in Poland. — The Kings of France, Spain, and Sardinia join against the Emperor. — The Prince of Orange arrives in England. — Altercation in the House of Commons. — Debate about the Removal of the Duke of Bolton and Lord Viscount Cobham from their respective Regiments. — Motion for the Repeal of the Septennial Act. — Conclusion of a remarkable Speech by Sir W. Wyndham. — Message from the King for Powers to augment the Forces in the Intervals between the two Parliaments. — Opposition in the House of Peers. — Parliament dissolved. — Dantzic besieged by the Russians. — Philipsburgh taken by the French. — Don Carlos takes Possession of Naples. — Battle of Parma. — The Imperialists are again worsted at Guastalla. — An Edict in France compelling the British Subjects in that Kingdom to enlist in the French Army. — New Parliament in Great Britain. — Debate on a Subsidy to Denmark. — Petition of some Scottish Noblemen to the House of Peers. — Bill explaining an Act of the Scottish Parliament touching wrongous Imprisonment. — Misunderstanding between the Courts of Spain and Portugal. — Sir John Norris sails with a strong Squadron to Lisbon. — Preliminaries signed by the Emperor and the King of France. — Proceedings in Parliament. — Bill for preventing the Retail of Spirituous Liquors. — Another for the Relief of Quakers in the Article of Tithes. — Mortmain Act. — Remarkable Riot at Edinburgh. — Rupture between the Czarina and the Ottoman Porte. — The Session of Parliament opened by Commission. — Motion in both Houses for a Settlement on the Prince of Wales. — Fierce Debate on this Subject. — Scheme by Sir John Barnard for reducing the Interest of the National Debt. — Bill against the City of Edinburgh. — Playhouse Bill.

THE most remarkable incident that distinguished this year in England was a very uncommon instance of suicide; an act of despair so frequent among the English, that in other countries it is objected to them as a national reproach. Though it may be generally termed the effect of lunacy proceeding from natural causes operating on the human body, in some few instances it seems to have been the result of cool deliberation. Richard Smith, a bookbinder, and prisoner for debt within the liberties of the King's Bench, persuaded his wife to follow his example in making away with herself, after they had murdered their little infant. This wretched pair were in the month of April found hanging in their bedchamber, at about a yard's distance from each other; and in a separate apartment the child lay dead in a cradle. They left two papers enclosed in a short letter to their landlord, whose kindness they implored in favour of their dog and cat. They even left money to pay the porter who should carry the enclosed papers to the person for whom they were addressed. In one of these the husband thanked that person for the marks of friendship he had received at his hands; and complained of the ill offices he had undergone from a different quarter. The other paper, subscribed by the husband and wife, contained the reasons which induced them to act such a tragedy on themselves and their offspring. This letter was altogether surprising for the calm resolution, the good humour, and the propriety, with which it was written. They declared, that they withdrew themselves from poverty and rags; evils that, through a train of unlucky accidents, were become inevitable. They appealed to their neighbours for the industry with which they had endeavoured to earn a livelihood. They justified the murder of their child, by saying it was less cruelty to take her with them, than to leave her friendless in the world, exposed to ignorance and misery. They professed their belief and confidence in an Almighty God, the fountain of goodness and beneficence, who could not possibly take delight in the misery of his creatures: they, therefore, resigned up their lives to him without any terrible apprehensions: submitting themselves to those ways which, in his goodness, he should appoint after death. These unfortunate suicides had been always industrious and frugal, invincibly honest, and remarkable for conjugal affection.

Trustees having been appointed by charter to superintend a new settlement in Georgia, situated to the southward of Carolina in America, Mr. Oglethorpe, as general, and governor of the province, embarked at Gravesend, with a number of poor families to plant that colony. The King of Spain having equipped a very powerful armament, the fleet sailed on the fourth day of June from the road of Alicant, under the command of the Count de Montemar, and arrived on the coast of Barbary in the neighbourhood of Oran, where a considerable body of troops was landed without much opposition. Next day, however, they were attacked by a numerous army of Moors, over whom they obtained a complete victory. The bey or governor of Oran immediately retired with his garrison, and the Spaniards took possession of the place, from which they had been driven in the year one thousand seven hundred

*Affairs of the continent.*

and eight. The strong fort of Mazalaquivir was likewise surrendered to the victors at the first summons; so that this expedition answered all the views with which it had been projected. Victor Amadeus, the abdicated King of Sardinia, having, at the instigation of his wife, engaged in some intrigues, in order to re-ascend the throne, his son, the reigning king, ordered his person to be seized at Montcalier, and conveyed to Rivoli, under a strong escort. His wife, the Marchioness de Spigno, was conducted to Seva. The old king's confessor, his physician, and eight-and-forty persons of distinction were imprisoned. The citadel of Turin was secured with a strong garrison; and new instructions were given to the governor and senate of Chamberri. The dispute which had long subsisted between the King of Prussia and the young Prince of Orange, touching the succession to the estates possessed by King William III. as head of the house of Orange, was at last accommodated by a formal treaty signed at Berlin and Dieren. The Dutch were greatly alarmed about this time with an apprehension of being overwhelmed by an inundation, occasioned by worms, which were said to have consumed the piles and timber-work that supported their dykes. They prayed and fasted with uncommon zeal, in terror of this calamity, which they did not know how to avert in any other manner. At length they were delivered from their fears by a hard frost, which effectually destroyed those dangerous animals. About this time, Mr. Dieden, plenipotentiary from the Elector of Hanover, received, in the name of his master, the investiture of Bremen and Verden from the hands of the emperor.

The history of England at this period cannot be very interesting, as it chiefly consists in an annual revolution of debates in Parliament; debates, in which the same arguments perpetually recur on the same subjects. When the session was opened on the sixteenth day of January, the king declared, that the situation of affairs, both at home and abroad, rendered it unnecessary for him to lay before the two Houses any other reasons for calling them together but the ordinary despatch of the public business, and his desire of receiving their advice in such affairs as should require the care and consideration of Parliament. The motion made in the House of Commons for an address of thanks implied, that they should express their satisfaction at the present situation of affairs both at home

*Meeting of the Parliament.*

and abroad. The motion was carried, notwithstanding the opposition of those who observed, that the nation had very little reason to be pleased with the present posture of affairs; that the French were employed in fortifying and restoring the harbour of Dunkirk, contrary to the faith of the most solemn treaties; that the British merchants had received no redress for the depredations committed by the Spaniards; that the commerce of England daily decreased; that no sort of trade throve but the traffic of 'Change-alley, where the most abominable frauds were practised; and that every session of Parliament opened a new scene of villany and imposition.

The pension bill was once more revived, and lost again in the House of Peers. All the reasons formerly advanced against a standing army were now repeated; and a reduction of the number insisted upon with such warmth, that the ministerial party were obliged to have recourse to the old phantom of the pretender. Sir Archer Croft said a continuation of the same number of forces was the more necessary, because, to his knowledge, popery was increasing very fast in the country; for, in one parish which he knew, there were seven popish priests; and that the danger from the pretender was the more to be feared, because they did not know but he was then breeding his son a Protestant. Sir Robert Walpole observed, that a reduction of the army was the chief thing wished for and desired by all the Jacobites in the kingdom: that no reduction had ever been made but what gave fresh hopes to that party, and encouraged them to raise tumults against the government; and he did not doubt but that, if they should resolve to reduce any part of the army, there would be post-horses employed that very night to carry the good news beyond sea to the pretender. His brother Horatio added, that the number of troops then proposed was absolutely necessary to support his majesty's government, and would be necessary as long as the nation enjoyed the happiness of having the present illustrious family on the throne. The futility, the self-contradiction, and ridiculous absurdity of these suggestions were properly exposed: nevertheless, the army was voted without any reduction. Sir Wilfred Lawson having made a motion for an address to the king, to know what satisfaction had been made by Spain for the depredations committed on the British merchants, it was after a violent debate approved, and the

*Address to the king touching the Spanish depredations.*

address presented. The king in answer to this remonstrance gave them to understand, that the meeting of the commissioners of the two crowns had been so long delayed by unforeseen accidents, that the conferences were not opened till the latter end of the preceding February: and that, as the courts of London and Madrid had agreed that the term of three years stipulated for finishing the commission should be computed from their first meeting, a perfect account of their proceedings could not as yet be laid before the House of Commons. A bill had been long depending for granting encouragement to the sugar colonies in the West Indies; but, as it was founded upon a prohibition that would have put a stop to all commerce between the French islands and the British settlements in North America, it met with a very warm opposition from those who had the prosperity of those northern colonies at heart. But the bill, being patronized and supported by the court interest, surmounted all objections; and afterwards passed into a law. While the Commons deliberated upon the supply, Sir Robert Walpole moved, that five hundred thousand pounds should be issued out of the sinking fund for the service of the ensuing year. Sir William Wyndham, Mr. Pulteney, and Sir John Barnard, expatiated upon the iniquity of pillaging a sacred deposit, solemnly appropriated to the discharge of the national debt. They might have demonstrated the egregious folly of a measure, by which the public, for a little temporary ease, lost the advantage of the accumulating interest which would have arisen from the sinking fund if properly managed and reserved. All objections vanished before the powers of ministerial influence, which nothing now could check but the immediate danger of popular commotion. Such hazardous interposition actually defeated a scheme which had been adopted by the minister, and even before its appearance alarmed all the trading part of the nation.

The House having resolved itself into a committee, to deliberate upon the most proper methods for the better security and improvement of the duties and revenues charged upon tobacco and wines, all the papers relating to these duties were submitted to the perusal of the members: the commissioners of the customs and excise were ordered to attend the House, the avenues of which were crowded with multitudes of people; and the members in the opposition waited impatiently for a proposal

*The excise scheme proposed by Sir Robert Walpole.*

in which they thought the liberties of their country so deeply interested. In a word, there had been a call of the House on the preceding day. The session was frequent and full: and both sides appeared ready and eager for the contest when Sir Robert Walpole broached his design. He took notice of the arts which had been used to prejudice the people against his plan before it was known. He affirmed that the clamours occasioned by these prejudices had originally risen from smugglers and fraudulent dealers, who had enriched themselves by cheating the public; and that these had been strenuously assisted and supported by another set of men, fond of every opportunity to stir up the people of Great Britain to mutiny and sedition. He expatiated on the frauds that were committed in that branch of the revenue arising from the duties on tobacco; upon the hardships to which the American planters were subjected by the heavy duties payable on importation, as well as by the ill usage they had met with from their factors and correspondents in England, who, from being their servants, were now become their masters; upon the injury done to the fair trader; and the loss sustained by the public with respect to the revenue. He asserted that the scheme he was about to propose would remove all these inconveniences, prevent numberless frauds, perjuries, and false entries, and add two or three hundred thousand pounds per annum to the public revenue. He entered into a long detail of frauds practised by the knavish dealers in those commodities; he recited the several acts of Parliament that related to the duties on wine and tobacco; he declared he had no intention to promote a general excise: he endeavoured to obviate some objections that might be made to his plan, the nature of which he at length explained. He proposed to join the laws of excise to those of the customs: that the further subsidy of three farthings per pound charged upon imported tobacco should be still levied at the custom-house, and payable to his majesty's civil-list as heretofore: that then the tobacco should be lodged in warehouses, to be appointed for that purpose by the commissioners of the excise: that the keeper of each warehouse, appointed likewise by the commissioners, should have one lock and key, and the merchant-importer have another: and that the tobacco should be thus secured until the merchant should find vent for it, either by exportation or home consumption: that the part designed for exportation should be weighed at the custom-house, discharged of the three farthings per pound which had been paid at its first importation, and then exported without further trouble: that the portion destined for home consumption should, in presence of the warehousekeeper, be delivered to the purchaser, upon his paying the inland duty of fourpence per pound weight to the proper officer appointed to receive it; by which means the merchant would be eased of the inconvenience of paying the duty upon importation, or of granting bonds and finding sureties for the payment, before he had found a market for the commodity; that all penalties and forfeitures, so far as they formerly belonged to the crown, should for the future be applied to the use of the public: that appeals in this, as well as in all other cases relating to the excise, should be heard and determined by two or three of the judges, to be named by his majesty; and in the country by the judge of assize upon the next circuit, who should hear and determine such appeals in the most summary manner, without the formality of proceedings in courts of law or equity.

Such was the substance of the famous excise scheme, in favour of which Sir Robert Walpole moved, that the duties and subsidies on tobacco should from and after the twenty-fourth day of June cease and determine. *Opposition to the scheme.* The debate which ensued was managed and maintained by all the able speakers on both sides of the question. Sir Robert Walpole was answered by Mr. Perry, member for the city of London. Sir Paul Methuen joined in the opposition. Sir John Barnard, another representative of London, distinguished himself in the same cause. He was supported by Mr. Pulteney, Sir William Wyndham, and other patriots. The scheme was espoused by Sir Philip Yorke, appointed lord chief justice of the king's bench, and ennobled in the course of the ensuing year. Sir Joseph Jekyll approved of the project, which was likewise strenuously defended by Lord Hervey, Sir Thomas Robinson, Sir William Yonge, Mr. Pelham, and Mr. Winnington, which last excelled all his contemporaries of the ministry in talents and address. Those who argued against the scheme accused the minister of having misrepresented the frauds, and made false calculations. With respect to the supposed hardships under which the planters were said to labour, they affirmed that no planter had ever dreamed of complaining, until instigated by letters and applications from London: that this scheme, far from relieving the planters, would expose the factors to such grievous oppression, that they would not be able to continue the trade, consequently the planters would be entirely ruined; and, after all, it would not prevent those frauds against which it was said to be provided: that from the examination of the commissioners of the customs, it appeared that those frauds did not exceed forty thousand pounds per annum, and might in a great measure be abolished, by a due execution of the laws in being; consequently this scheme was unnecessary, would be ineffectual in augmenting the revenue, destructive to trade, and dangerous to the liberties of the subject, as it tended to promote a general excise, which was in all countries considered as a grievous oppression. They suggested that it would produce an additional swarm of excise-officers and warehouse-keepers, appointed and paid by the treasury, so as to multiply the dependents on the crown, and enable it still further to influence the freedom of elections: that the traders would become slaves to excisemen and warehouse-keepers, as they would be debarred all access to their commodities, except at certain hours, when attended by those officers: that the merchant, for every quantity of tobacco he could sell, would be obliged to make a journey, or send a messenger, to the office for a permit, which could not be obtained without trouble, expense, and delay: and that, should a law be enacted in consequence of this motion, it would in all probability be some time or other used as a precedent for introducing excise laws into every branch of the revenue; in which case the liberty of Great Britain would be no more. In the course of this debate, Sir Robert Walpole took notice of the multitudes which had beset all the approaches to the House. He said it would be an easy task for a designing seditious person to raise a tumult and disorder among them; that gentlemen might give them what name they should think fit, and affirm they were come as humble suppliants; but he knew whom the law called sturdy beggars: and those who brought them to that place could not be certain but that they might behave in the same manner. This insinuation was resented by Sir John Barnard, who observed that merchants of character had a right to come down to the court of requests, and lobby of the House of Commons, in order to solicit their friends and acquaintance against any scheme or project which they might think prejudicial to their commerce: that when he came into the House, he saw none but such as deserved the appellation of sturdy beggars as little as the honourable gentleman himself, or any gentleman whatever. After a warm dispute the motion was carried by a majority of sixty-one voices. Several resolutions were founded on the proposal: and to these the House agreed, though not without another violent contest. The resolutions produced a bill, against which petitions were preferred by the lord mayor, aldermen, and common council of London, the city of Coventry, and Nottingham. A motion was made that counsel should be heard for the city of London; but it was rejected by the majority, and the petitions were ordered to lie upon the table. Had the minister encountered no opposition but that which appeared within doors, his project would have certainly been carried into execution: but the whole nation was alarmed, and clamoured loudly against the excise bill. The populace still crowded around Westminster-hall, blocking up all the avenues to the House of Commons. They even insulted the persons of those members who had voted for the ministry on this occasion; and Sir Robert Walpole began to be in fear of his life. He, therefore, thought proper to drop the design, by moving that the second reading of the bill might be postponed till the twelfth day of June. Then, complaint being made of the insolence of the populace, who had maltreated several members, divers resolutions were taken against those tumultuous crowds, and their abettors; these resolves were communicated to the lord mayor of London, the sheriff of Middlesex, and the high-bailiff of Westminster. Some individuals were apprehended in the court of requests, as having fomented the disturbances; but they were soon released. The miscarriage of the bill was celebrated with public rejoicings in London and Westminster; and the minister was burned in effigy by the populace. After the miscarriage of the excise scheme, the House unanimously resolved to inquire into the frauds and abuses in the customs; and a committee of twenty-one persons was chosen by ballot for this purpose.

The subsequent debates of this session were occasioned by a bill to prevent the infamous practice of stock-jobbing, which with great difficulty made its way to the House of Lords, who proposed some amendments, in consequence of which it was laid aside; and suc- *Bill for a dower to the princess royal.*

ceeded by another bill establishing a lottery, to raise five hundred thousand pounds for the relief of those who had suffered by the charitable corporation. After having undergone some alterations, it passed through both Houses, and obtained the royal assent. The king, by a message to Parliament, had signified his intention to give the princess royal in marriage to the Prince of Orange, promising himself their concurrence and assistance, that he might be enabled to bestow such a portion with his eldest daughter as should be suitable to the occasion. The Commons immediately resolved, that out of the moneys arising from the sale of lands in the island of St. Christopher's, his majesty should be empowered to apply fourscore thousand pounds, as a marriage dower for his daughter; and a clause for this purpose was inserted in the bill, for enabling his majesty to apply five hundred thousand pounds out of the sinking fund for the service of the current year.

*Debates in the House of Lords concerning the estates of the late directors of the South-Sea Company.* The opposition in the House of Lords was still more animated, though ineffectual. The debates chiefly turned upon the pension bill, the number of land-forces, and a motion made by Lord Bathurst for an account of the produce of the forfeited estates which had belonged to the directors of the South-Sea Company. The trustees for these estates had charged themselves with a great sum of money, and the lords in the opposition thought they had a right to know how it had been disposed. The ministry had reasons to stifle this inquiry; and therefore opposed it with all their vigour. Nevertheless, the motion was carried, after a warm dispute, and the directors of the South-Sea Company were ordered to lay the accounts before the House. From this it appeared that the large sums of money arising from the forfeited estates had been distributed among the proprietors by way of dividend, even before recourse was had to Parliament for directions in what manner that produce should be applied: Lord Bathurst therefore moved for a resolution of the House, that the disposal of this money by way of dividend, without any order or direction of a general court for that purpose, was a violation of the act of Parliament made for the disposal thereof, and a manifest injustice done to the proprietors of that stock. The Duke of Newcastle, in order to gain time, moved, that as the account was confused, and almost unintelligible, the present directors of the company might be ordered to lay before the House a further and more distinct account of the manner in which the money had been disposed. A violent contest ensued, in the course of which the House divided, and of fifty-seven peers who voted for the delay, forty-six were such as enjoyed preferment in the church, commissions in the army, or civil employments under the government. At length Lord Bathurst waived his motion for that time: then the House ordered that the present and former directors of the South-Sea Company, together with the late inspectors of their accounts, should attend and be examined. They were accordingly interrogated, and gave so little satisfaction, that Lord Bathurst moved for a committee of inquiry; but the question, being put, was carried in the negative: yet a very strong protest was entered by the lords in the opposition. The next subject of altercation was the bill for misapplying part of the produce of the sinking fund. It was attacked with all the force of argument, wit, and declamation, by the Earl of Strafford, Lords Bathurst and Carteret, and particularly by the Earl of Chesterfield, who had by this time resigned his staff of lord-steward of the household, and renounced all connexion with the ministry. Lord Bathurst moved for a resolution, importing that in the opinion of the House, the sinking fund ought for the future to be applied, in time of peace and public tranquillity, to the redemption of those taxes which were most prejudicial to the trade, most burdensome on the manufactures, and most oppressive on the poor of the nation. This motion was overruled, and the bill adopted by the majority. On the eleventh day of June, the king gave the royal assent to the bills that were prepared, and closed the session with a speech, in which he took notice of the wicked endeavours that had been lately used to inflame the minds of the people, by the most unjust misrepresentations.

Europe was now involved in fresh troubles by a vacancy on the throne of Poland. Augustus died at Warsaw in the end of January, and the neighbouring powers were immediately in commotion. The Elector of Saxony, son to the late king, and Stanislaus, whose daughter was married to the French monarch, declared themselves candidates for the Polish throne. The emperor, the czarina, and the King of Prussia, espoused

*Double election of a King of Poland.*

the interest of the Saxons; the King of France supported the pretensions of his father-in-law. The foreign ministers at Warsaw forthwith began to form intrigues among the electors: the Marquis de Monti, ambassador from France, exerted himself so successfully that he soon gained over the primate, and a majority of the Catholic dietines, to the interests of Stanislaus; while the imperial and Russian troops hovered on the frontiers of Poland. The French king no sooner understood that a body of the emperor's forces was encamped at Silesia, than he ordered the Duke of Berwick to assemble an army on the Rhine, and take measures for entering Germany, in case the imperialists should march into Poland. A French fleet set sail for Dantzic, while Stanislaus travelled through Germany in disguise to Poland, and concealed himself in the house of the French ambassador at Warsaw. As the day of election approached, the imperial, Russian, and Prussian ministers delivered in their several declarations, by way of protest against the contingent election of Stanislaus, as a person proscribed, disqualified, depending upon a foreign power, and connected with the Turks and other infidels. The Russian General Lasci entered Poland at the head of fifty thousand men: the diet of the election was opened with the usual ceremony on the twenty-fifth day of August. Prince Vicsnzowski, chief of the Saxon interest, retired to the other side of the Vistula with three thousand men, including some of the nobility who adhered to that party. Nevertheless, the primate proceeded to the election: Stanislaus was unanimously chosen king; and appeared in the electoral field, where he was received with loud acclamations. The opposite party soon increased to ten thousand men; protested against the election, and joined the Russian army, which advanced by speedy marches. King Stanislaus, finding himself unable to cope with such adversaries, retired with the primate and French ambassador to Dantzic, leaving the Palatine of Kiow at Warsaw. This general attacked the Saxon palace, which was surrendered upon terms: then the soldiers and inhabitants plundered the houses belonging to the grandees who had declared for Augustus, as well as the hotel of the Russian minister. In the mean time, the Poles, who had joined the Muscovites, finding it impracticable to pass the Vistula before the expiration of the time fixed for the session of the diet, erected a kelo at Cracow, where the Elector of Saxony was chosen, and proclaimed by the Bishop of Cracow, King of Poland, under the name of Augustus III., on the sixth day of October. They afterwards passed the river, and the Palatine of Kiow retiring towards Cracow, they took possession of Warsaw, where in their turn they plundered the palaces and houses belonging to the opposite party.

During these transactions, the French king concluded a treaty with Spain and Sardinia, by which those powers agreed to declare war against the emperor. Manifestos were published reciprocally by all the contracting powers. The Duke of Berwick passed the Rhine in October, and undertook the siege of fort Kehl, which in a few days was surrendered on capitulation; then he repassed the river and returned to Versailles. The King of Sardinia, having declared war against the emperor, joined a body of French forces commanded by Mareschal de Villars, and drove the imperialists out of the Milanese. His imperial majesty, dreading the effects of such a powerful confederacy against him, offered to compromise all differences with the crown of Spain, under the mediation of the King of Great Britain; and Mr. Keen, the British minister at Madrid, proposed an accommodation. Philip expressed his acknowledgments to the King of England, declaring, however, that the emperor's advances were too late; and that his own resolutions were already taken. Nevertheless, he sent orders to the Count de Montijo, his ambassador at London, to communicate to his Britannic majesty the motives which had induced him to take these resolutions. In the mean time he detached a powerful armament to Italy, where they invested the imperial fortress of Aula, the garrison of which was obliged to surrender themselves prisoners of war. The republic of Venice declared she would take no share in the disputes of Italy; the States-General signed a neutrality with the French king for the Austrian Netherlands, without consulting the emperor or the King of Great Britain; and the English councils seemed to be altogether pacific.

*The Kings of France, Spain, and Sardinia join against the emperor.*

In November the Prince of Orange arrived at Greenwich, in order to espouse the princess royal: but the marriage was postponed on account of his being taken ill; and he repaired to Bath, in Somersetshire, to drink the waters for the recovery of his strength.

*The Prince of Orange arrives in England.*

Henrietta, the young Duchess of Marlborough, dying about this time, the title devolved to her sister's son, the Earl of Sunderland. Lord King resigning his office of chancellor, it was conferred upon Mr. Talbot, solicitor-general, together with the title of baron; a promotion that reflected honour upon those by whom it was advised. He possessed the spirit of a Roman senator, the elegance of an Atticus, and the integrity of a Cato. At the meeting of the Parliament in January, the king told them, in his speech, that though he was no way engaged in the war which had begun to rage in Europe, except by the good offices he had employed among the contending powers, he could not sit regardless of the present events, or be unconcerned for the consequences of a war undertaken and supported by such a powerful alliance. He said, he had thought proper to take time to examine the facts alleged on both sides, and to wait the result of the councils of those powers that were more immediately interested in the consequences of the rupture. He declared he would concert with his allies, more particularly with the States-General of the United Provinces, such measures as should be thought most advisable for their common safety, and for restoring the peace of Europe. In the mean time, he expressed his hope that they would make such provision as should secure his kingdom, rights, and possessions from all dangers and insults, and maintain the respect due to the British nation. He said, that whatever part it might in the end be most reasonable for him to act, it would in all views be necessary, when all Europe was preparing for arms, to put his kingdoms in a posture of defence. The motion for an address of thanks produced, as usual, a debate in both Houses, which, it must be owned, appears to have proceeded from a spirit of cavilling, rather than from any reasonable cause of objection.

The House of Commons resolved to address his majesty for a copy of the treaty of Vienna. Sir John Rushout moved for another, desiring that the letters and instructions relating to the execution of the treaty of Seville should be submitted to the inspection of the Commons; but after a hard struggle, it was overruled. The next motion was made by Mr. Sandys, a gentleman who had for some time appeared strenuous in the opposition, and wrangled with great perseverance. He proposed that the House should examine the instructions which had been given to the British minister in Poland some years before the death of King Augustus, that they might be the better able to judge of the causes which produced this new rupture among the powers of Europe. The motion being opposed by all the court members, a contest ensued, in the course of which Mr. Pulteney compared the ministry to an empiric, and the constitution of England to his patient. This pretender in physic (said he), being consulted, tells the distempered person, there were but two or three ways of treating his disease: and he was afraid that none of them would succeed. A vomit might throw him into convulsions that would occasion immediate death; a purge might bring on a diarrhœa that would carry him off in a short time; and he had been already bled so much, and so often, that he could bear it no longer. The unfortunate patient, shocked at this declaration, replies, "Sir, you have always pretended to be a regular doctor, but now I find you are an arrant quack. I had an excellent constitution when I first fell into your hands, but you have quite destroyed it: and now I have no other chance for saving my life, but by calling for the help of some regular physician." In the debate, the members on both sides seemed to wander from the question, and indulged themselves with ludicrous personalities. Mr. H. Walpole took occasion to say, that the opposition treated the ministry as he himself was treated by some of his acquaintance with respect to his dress. "If I am in plain clothes (said he), then they call me a slovenly, dirty fellow; and if by chance I wear a laced suit, they cry, What, shall such an awkward fellow wear fine clothes?" He continued to sport in this kind of idle buffoonery. He compared the present administration to a ship at sea. As long as the wind was fair, and proper for carrying us to our destined port, the word was "Steady, steady!" but when the wind began to shift and change, the word was necessarily altered to "Thus, thus, and no nearer." The motion was overpowered by the majority; and this was the fate of several other proposals made by the members in the opposition. Sir John Barnard presented a petition from the druggists, and other dealers in tea, complaining of the insults and oppression to which they were subjected by the excise laws, and imploring relief. Sir John and Mr. Perry, another of the city members, explained the grievous hardships which those traders sustained, and moved that the petition might be referred to the consideration of the whole House.

They were opposed by Mr. Winnington, Sir W. Yonge, and other partisans of the ministry; and these skirmishes brought on a general engagement of the two parties, in which every weapon of satire, argument, reason, and truth, was wielded against that odious, arbitrary, and oppressive method of collecting the public revenue. Nevertheless the motion in favour of the sufferers was rejected.

When the Commons deliberated upon the supply, Mr. Andrews, deputy-paymaster of the army, moved for an addition of eighteen hundred men to the number of land-forces which had been continued since the preceding year. The members in the opposition disputed this small augmentation with too much heat and eagerness. It must be acknowledged, they were by this time irritated into such personal animosity against the minister, that they resolved to oppose all his measures, whether they might or might not be necessary for the safety and advantage of the kingdom. Nor indeed were they altogether blameable for acting on this maxim, if their sole aim was to remove from the confidence and councils of their sovereign a man whose conduct they thought prejudicial to the interests and liberties of their country. They could not, however, prevent the augmentation proposed; but they resolved, if they could not wholly stop the career of the ministry, to throw in such a number of rubs as should at least retard their progress. The Duke of Bolton and Lord Cobham had been deprived of the regiments they commanded, because they refused to concur in every project of the administration. It was in consequence of their dismission, that Lord Morpeth moved for a bill to prevent any commission-officer, not above the rank of a colonel, from being removed, unless by a court-martial, or by address of either House of Parliament. Such an attack on the prerogative might have succeeded in the latter part of the reign of the first Charles; but at this juncture could not fail to miscarry; yet it was sustained with great vigour and address. When the proposal was set aside by the majority, Mr. Sandys moved for an address to the king, desiring to know who advised his majesty to remove the Duke of Bolton and Lord Cobham from their respective regiments. He was seconded by Mr. Pulteney and Sir William Wyndham: but the ministry, foreseeing another tedious dispute, called for the question, and the motion was carried in the

*[margin: Debate about the removal of the Duke of Bolton and Lord Viscount Cobham from their respective regiments.]*

negative. The next source of contention was a bill for securing the freedom of Parliament, by limiting the number of officers in the House of Commons. It was read a first and second time; but, when a motion was made for its being committed, it met with a powerful opposition, and produced a warm debate that issued in a question, which, like the former, passed in the negative. A clergyman having insinuated in conversation that Sir William Milner, baronet, member for York, received a pension from the ministry, the House took cognizance of this report; the clergyman acknowledged at the bar that he might have dropped such a hint from hearsay. The accused member protested, upon his honour, that he never did, nor ever would, receive place, pension, gratuity, or reward from the court, either directly or indirectly, for voting in Parliament, or upon any other account whatever. The accusation was voted false and scandalous, and the accuser taken into custody; but in a few days he was discharged upon his humble petition, and his begging pardon of the member whom he had calumniated. The duty on salt was prolonged for eight years; and a bill passed against stock-jobbing.

But the subject which of all others employed the eloquence and abilities on both sides to the most vigorous exertion, was a motion made by Mr. Bromley, who proposed that a bill should be brought in for repealing the septennial act, and for the more frequent meeting and calling of Parliaments. The arguments for and against septennial Parliaments have already been stated. The ministry now insisted upon the increase of Papists and Jacobites, which rendered it dangerous to weaken the hands of the government: they challenged the opposition to produce one instance in which the least encroachment had been made on the liberties of the people since the septennial act took place; and they defied the most ingenious malice to prove that his present majesty had ever endeavoured to extend any branch of the prerogative beyond its legal bounds. Sir John Hinde Cotton affirmed, that in many parts of England the Papists had already begun to use all their influence in favour of those candidates who were recommended by the ministers as members in the ensuing Parliament. With respect to his majesty's conduct, he said he would not answer one word; but as to the grievances introduced since the law was enacted for septennial Parliaments, he thought himself more at liberty to declare his sentiments. He asserted, that the septennial law itself was an encroachment on the rights of the people; a law passed by a Parliament that made itself septennial. He observed, that the laws of treason with regard to trials were altered since that period: that in former times a man was tried by a jury of his neighbours, within the county where the crimes alleged against him were said to be committed; but by an act of a septennial Parliament he might be removed and tried in any place where the crown, or rather the ministry, could find a jury proper for their purpose; where the prisoner could not bring any witnesses in his justification, without an expense which, perhaps, his circumstances would not bear. He asked, if the riot act was not an encroachment on the rights of the people? An act by which a little dirty justice of the peace, the meanest and vilest tool a minister can use, who, perhaps, subsists by his being in the commission, and may be deprived of that subsistence at the pleasure of his patron, had it in his power to put twenty or thirty of the best subjects in England to immediate death, without any trial or form but that of reading a proclamation. "Was not the fatal South-Sea scheme (said he) established by the act of a septennial Parliament? And can any man ask, whether that law was attended with any inconvenience? To the glorious catalogue I might have added the late excise bill, if it had passed into a law; but, thank Heaven, the septennial Parliament was near expiring before that famous measure was introduced."

Conclusion of a remarkable speech by Sir W. Wyndham.

Sir William Wyndham concluded an excellent speech, that spoke him the unrivalled orator, the uncorrupted Briton, and the unshaken patriot, in words to this effect: "Let us suppose a man abandoned to all notions of virtue and honour, of no great family, and but a mean fortune, raised to be chief minister of state by the concurrence of many whimsical events; afraid, or unwilling, to trust any but creatures of his own making; lost to all sense of shame and reputation; ignorant of his country's true interest; pursuing no aim but that of aggrandizing himself and his favourites; in foreign affairs trusting none but those who, from the nature of their education, cannot possibly be qualified for the service of their country, or give weight and credit to their negotiations. Let us suppose the true interest of the nation, by such means, neglected or misunderstood, her honour tarnished, her importance lost, her trade insulted, her merchants plundered, and her sailors murdered; and all these circumstances overlooked, lest his administration should be endangered. Suppose him next possessed of immense wealth, the plunder of the nation, with a Parliament chiefly composed of members whose seats are purchased, and whose votes are bought at the expense of the public treasure. In such a Parliament, suppose all attempts made to inquire into his conduct, or to relieve the nation from the distress which has been entailed upon it by his administration. Suppose him screened by a corrupt majority of his creatures, whom he retains in daily pay, or engages in his particular interest by distributing among them those posts and places which ought never to be bestowed upon any but for the good of the public. Let him plume himself upon his scandalous victory, because he has obtained a Parliament like a packed jury, ready to acquit him at all adventures. Let us suppose him domineering with insolence over all the men of ancient families, over all the men of sense, figure, or fortune, in the nation; as he has no virtue of his own, ridiculing it in others, and endeavouring to destroy or corrupt it in all. With such a minister, and such a Parliament, let us suppose a case which I hope will never happen: a prince upon the throne, uninformed, ignorant, and unacquainted with the inclinations and true interest of his people, weak, capricious, transported with unbounded ambition, and possessed with insatiable avarice. I hope such a case will never occur; but as it possibly may, could any greater curse happen to a nation, than such a prince on the throne, advised, and solely advised, by such a minister, and that minister supported by such a Parliament? The nature of mankind cannot be altered by human laws; the existence of such a prince or such a minister we cannot prevent by act of Parliament; but the existence of such a Parliament I think we may prevent; as it is much more likely to exist, and may do more mischief, while the septennial law remains in force, than if it were repealed: therefore, I am heartily for its being repealed." Notwithstanding the most warm, the most nervous, the most pathetic remonstrances in favour of the motion, the question was put, and it was suppressed by mere dint of number.

The triumph of the ministry was still more complete in

the success of a message delivered from the crown in the latter end of the session, when a great many members of the other party had retired to their respective habitations in the country. Sir Robert Walpole delivered this commission to the House, importing that his majesty might be enabled to augment his forces, if occasion should require such an augmentation, between the dissolution of this Parliament and the election of another. Such an important point, that was said to strike at the foundation of our liberties, was not tamely yielded; but, on the contrary, contested with uncommon ardour. The motion for taking the message into consideration was carried in the affirmative; and an address presented to the king, signifying their compliance with his desire. In consequence of a subsequent message they prepared and passed a bill, enabling his majesty to settle an annuity of five thousand pounds for life on the princess royal, as a mark of his paternal favour and affection.

The opposition in the House of Peers kept pace with that in the House of Commons, and was supported with equal abilities, under the auspices of the Lords Bathurst and Carteret, the Earls of Chesterfield and Abingdon. The Duke of Marlborough made a motion for a bill to regulate the army, equivalent to that which had been rejected in the Lower House; and it met with the same fate after a warm dispute. Then Lord Carteret moved for an address to the king, that he would be graciously pleased to acquaint the House who advised his majesty to remove the Duke of Bolton and Lord Viscount Cobham from their respective regiments; and what crimes were laid to their charge. This proposal was likewise rejected, at the end of a debate in which the Duke of Argyle observed, that two lords had been removed, but only one soldier lost his commission. Such a great majority of the Scottish representatives had always voted for the ministry, since the accession of the late king, and so many of these enjoyed places and preferments in the gift of the crown, that several attempts were made by the lords in the opposition to prevent for the future the ministerial influence from extending itself to the elections of North Britain. Accordingly two motions for this purpose were made by the Earl of Marchmont and the Duke of

Bedford; and sustained by the Earls of Chesterfield, Winchelsea, and Stair, Lords Willoughby de Broke, Bathurst, and Carteret. They were opposed by the Dukes of Newcastle and Argyle, the Earl of Cholmondeley, Earl Paulet, Lord Hervey, now called up by writ to the House of Peers, and Lord Talbot. The question being put on both, they were of course defeated; and the Earl of Stair was deprived of his regiment of dragoons, after having performed the most signal services to the royal family, and exhausted his fortune in supporting the interest and dignity of the crown. Strenuous protests were entered against the decision of the majority concerning the king's message, demanding a power to augment his forces during the recess of Parliament; as also against a bill for enabling his majesty to apply the sum of one million two hundred thousand pounds out of the sinking-fund for the service of the current year. The business of the session being despatched, the king repaired to the House of Lords on the sixteenth day of April, and having passed all the bills that were ready for the royal assent, took leave of this Parliament, with the warmest acknowledgment of their zeal, duty, and affection. It was at first prorogued, then dissolved, and another convoked by the same proclamation. On the fourteenth day of March, the nuptials of the Prince of Orange and the princess royal were solemnized with great magnificence; and this match was attended with addresses of congratulation to his majesty from different parts of the kingdom.

The powers at war upon the continent acted with surprising vigour. The Russian and Saxon army invested the city of Dantzic, in hopes of securing the person of King Stanislaus. The town was strong, the garrison numerous, and, animated by the examples of the French and Poles, made a very obstinate defence. For some time they were supplied by sea with recruits, arms, and ammunition. On the eleventh day of May a reinforcement of fifteen hundred men was landed from two French ships of war and some transports under fort Wechselmunde, which was so much in want of provisions that they were not admitted; they therefore re-embarked, and sailed back to Copenhagen. But afterwards a larger number was landed in the same place, and attacked the Russian intrenchments, in order to force their way into the city. They were repulsed in this attempt, but retired in good order. At length

*Dantzic besieged by the Russians.*

the Russian fleet arrived, under the command of Admiral Gordon; and now the siege was carried on with great fury. Fort Wechselmunde was surrendered; the French troops capitulated, and were embarked in the Russian ships, to be conveyed to some port in the Baltic. Stanislaus escaped in the disguise of a peasant to Marienwarder in the Prussian territories. The city of Dantzic submitted to the dominion of Augustus III., King of Poland, and was obliged to defray the expense of the war to the Russian general, Count de Munich, who had assumed the command after the siege was begun. The Polish lords at Dantzic signed an act of submission to King Augustus, who, on the tenth day of July, arrived at the convent of Oliva. There a council was held in his presence. The recusant noblemen took the oath which he proposed. Then a general amnesty was proclaimed; and the king set out on his return to Dresden.

On the Rhine the French arms bore down all resistance. The Count de Belleisle besieged and took Traerbach. The Duke of Berwick, at the head of sixty thousand men, invested Philipsburgh, while Prince Eugene was obliged to remain on the defensive in the strong camp at Heilbron, waiting for the troops of the empire. On the twelfth day of June, the Duke of Berwick, in visiting the trenches, was killed by a cannon-ball, and the command devolved upon the Marquis d'Asfeldt, who carried on the operations of the siege with equal vigour and capacity. Prince Eugene, being joined by the different reinforcements he expected, marched towards the French lines; but found them so strong that he would not hazard an attack; and such precautions taken, that with all his military talents he could not relieve the besieged. At length General Watgenau, the governor, capitulated, after having made a noble defence, and obtained the most honourable conditions. Prince Eugene retired to Heidelberg; and the campaign ended about the beginning of October. The imperial arms were not more successful in Italy. The Infant Don Carlos had received so many invitations from the Neapolitan nobility, that he resolved to take possession of that kingdom. He began his march in February, at the head of the Spanish forces; published a manifesto, declaring he was sent by his father to relieve the kingdom of Naples from the oppression under which it groaned; and entered the capital amidst the acclamations of the people; while the Count de Visconti, the German viceroy, finding himself unable to cope with the invaders, thought proper to retire, after having thrown succours into Gaeta and Capua. When he arrived at Nocera, he began to assemble the militia, with intent to form a camp at Barletta. The Count de Montemar marched with a body of forces against this general, and obtained over him a complete victory at Bitonto in Apuglia, on the twenty-fifth of May, when the imperialists were entirely routed, and a great number of principal officers taken prisoners. Don Carlos being proclaimed, and acknowledged King of Naples, created the Count de Montemar Duke of Bitonto; reduced Gaeta, and all other parts of the kingdom which were garrisoned with imperial troops; and resolved to subdue the island of Sicily. About twenty thousand troops, being destined for this expedition, were landed in the road of Solanto in August, under the command of the new Duke of Bitonto, who, being favoured by the natives, proceeded in his conquests with great rapidity. The people acknowledged Don Carlos as their sovereign, and took arms in support of his government; so that the imperial troops were driven before them, and the Spaniards possessed the whole kingdom, except Messina, Syracuse, and Trepani, when the infant determined to visit the island in person.

While Don Carlos was thus employed in the conquest of Naples and Sicily, the imperialists were hard pressed Battle of in Lombardy by the united forces of France and Parma. Piedmont, commanded by the King of Sardinia and the old Mareschal Duke de Villars. In the month of January they undertook the siege of Tortona, which they reduced; while the troops of the emperor began to pour in great numbers into the Mantuan. In the beginning of May, Count Merci, who commanded them, passed the Po in the face of the allies, notwithstanding all the skill of Villars, obliged him to retreat from the banks of that river, and took the Castle of Colorno. The old French general, being taken ill, quitted the army, and retired to Turin, where in a little time he died; and the King of Sardinia retiring to the same place, the command of the allied forces devolved upon the Mareschal de Coigny. The confederates were posted at Sanguina, and the imperialists at Sorbola, when the Count de Merci made a motion to San Prospero, as if he intended either to attack the enemy, or take possession of Parma. The Mareschal de Coigny forthwith made a disposition for an engagement; and, on the twenty-ninth day of June, the imperial general, having passed the Parma, began the attack with great impetuosity. He charged in person at the head of his troops, and was killed soon after the battle began. Nevertheless, the Prince of Wirtemberg assuming the command, both armies fought with great obstinacy, from eleven in the forenoon till four in the afternoon, when the imperialists retired towards Monte Cirugalo, leaving five thousand men dead on the field of battle, and among these many officers of distinction. The loss of the allies was very considerable, and they reaped no solid fruits from their victory.

The imperial forces retreated to Reggio, and from thence moved to the plains of Carpi, on the right of the Secchia, where they received some reinforcements: then General Count Konigsegg, arriving in the camp, took upon himself the command of the army. His first step was to take post at Quingentolo, by which motion he secured Mirandola, that was threatened with a siege. On the fifteenth of February he forded the river Secchia, and surprised the quarters of Mareschal de Broglio, who escaped, in his shirt, with great difficulty. The French retired with such precipitation, that they left all their baggage behind, and above two thousand were taken prisoners. They posted themselves under Guastalla, where, on the nineteenth day of the month, they were vigorously attacked by the imperialists, and a general engagement ensued. Konigsegg made several desperate efforts to break the French cavalry, upon which, however, he could make no impression. The infantry on both sides fought with uncommon ardour for six hours, and the field was covered with carnage. At length the imperial general retreated to Lazara, after having lost above five thousand men, including the Prince of Wirtemberg, the Generals Valpareze and Colminero, with many other officers of distinction: nor was the damage sustained by the French greatly inferior to that of the Germans, who repassed the Po, and took post on the banks of the Oglio. The allies crossed the same river, and the Marquis de Mallebois was sent with a detachment to attack Mirandola; but the imperialists, marching to the relief of the place, compelled him to abandon the enterprise: then he rejoined his rmy, which retired under the walls of Cremona, to wait

*[sidenote: The imperialists are again worsted at Guastalla. An edict in France compelling the British subjects in that kingdom to enlist in the French army.]*

for succours from Don Carlos. So little respect did the French court pay to the British nation at this juncture, that in the month of November an edict was published at Paris, commanding all the British subjects in France, who were not actually in employment, from the age of eighteen to fifty, to quit the kingdom in fifteen days, or enlist in some of the Irish regiments, on pain of being treated as vagabonds, and sent to the galleys. This edict was executed with the utmost rigour. The prisons of Paris were crowded with the subjects of Great Britain, who were surprised and cut off from all communication with their friends, and must have perished by cold and hunger, had not they been relieved by the active charity of the Jansenists. The Earl of Waldegrave, who then resided at Paris as ambassador from the King of Great Britain, made such vigorous remonstrances to the French ministry upon this unheard-of outrage against a nation with which they had been so long in alliance, that they thought proper to set the prisoners at liberty, and publish another edict, by which the meaning of the former was explained away.

While these transactions occurred on the continent, the King of Great Britain augmented his land-forces; and warm contests were maintained through the whole united kingdom in electing representatives for the new Parliament. But in all these struggles the ministerial power predominated; and the new members appeared with the old complexion. The two Houses assembled on the fourteenth day of January, and Mr. Onslow was re-elected speaker. The leaders of both parties in all debates were the self-same persons who had conducted those of the former Parliament; and the same measures were pursued in the same manner. The king, in his speech at the opening of the session, gave them to understand, that he had concerted with the States-General of the united provinces such measures as were thought most advisable for their common safety, and for restoring the peace of Europe: that they had considered on one side the pressing applications made by the imperial court both in England and Holland for obtaining succours against the powers at war with the House of Austria; and, on the other side, the repeated professions made by the allies of their sincere disposition to put an end to the present troubles upon honourable and solid terms; that he and the States-General had concurred in a resolution to employ their joint and earnest instances to bring matters to a speedy and happy accommodation: that their good offices were at length accepted; and in a short time a plan would be offered to the consideration of all parties engaged in the war, as a basis for a general negotiation for peace. He told them he had used the power vested in him by the last Parliament with great moderation; and concluded a treaty with the crown of Denmark of great importance in the present conjuncture. He observed that whilst many of the principal powers of Europe were actually engaged in a war, Great Britain must be more or less affected with the consequences; and as the best concerted measures are liable to uncertainty, the nation ought to be prepared against all events. He therefore expressed his hope, that his good subjects would not repine at the necessary means of procuring the blessings of peace and universal tranquillity, or of putting him in a condition to act that part which it might be necessary and incumbent upon him to take. The address of thanks produced a dispute as usual, which ended with an acquiescence in the motion. The House, in a grand committee on the supply, resolved, that thirty thousand seamen should be employed for the service of the ensuing year; and that the land forces should be augmented to the number of twenty-five thousand seven hundred and forty-four effective men. But these resolutions were not taken without dispute and division. The minister's opponents not only reproduced all the reasons which had been formerly advanced against a standing army, but they opposed this augmentation with extraordinary ardour, as a huge stride towards the establishment of arbitrary power. They refuted those fears of external broils on which the ministry pretended to ground the necessity of such an augmentation; and they exposed the weak conduct of the administration, in having contributed to destroy the balance of power, by assisting Spain against the emperor in Italy, so as to aggrandize the house of Bourbon.

Sir William Wyndham moved, that the estimate of the navy for the ensuing year might be referred to a select committee. He expressed his surprise, that notwithstanding the vast sums which had been yearly raised, and the long continuance of the peace, the people had not been quite delivered of any one tax incurred in the preceding war. He said, he could not comprehend

*Debate on a subsidy to Denmark.*

how it was possible to find pretences for exposing the nation to such exorbitant charges; and he took notice of some unconscionable articles in the account of the navy debt that lay upon the table. He was seconded by Mr. Sandys, and supported by Sir Joseph Jekyll and Mr. Pulteney; but, after some debate, the motion was carried in the negative. When the new treaty with Denmark fell under consideration in a grand committee, Mr. H. Walpole moved, that the sum of fifty-six thousand two hundred and fifty pounds should be granted to his majesty as a subsidy to the Dane, pursuant to the said treaty, for the service of the ensuing year. The demand did not meet with immediate compliance. All the leaders in the opposition exclaimed against the subsidy as unnecessary and unreasonable. They observed, that as the English had no particular interest of their own for inducing them to engage in the present war, but only the danger to which the balance of power might be exposed by that event; and as all the powers of Europe were as much, if not more, interested than the English in the preservation of that balance, should it ever be really endangered, they would certainly engage in its defence without receiving any valuable consideration from Great Britain; but should the English be always the first to take the alarm upon any rupture, and offer bribes and pensions to all the princes in Europe, the whole charge of preserving that balance would fall upon Great Britain: every state would expect a gratification from her, for doing that which it would otherwise be obliged to do for its own preservation: even the Dutch might at last refuse to assist in trimming this balance, unless Britain should submit to make the grand pensionary of Holland a pensionary of England, and take a number of their forces into English pay. The debate having had its free course, the question was put, and the motion approved by the majority. The ministry allowed a bill to be brought in for limiting the number of officers in the House of Commons; but at the second reading it was rejected upon a division, after a learned debate, in which it appeared that the opposition had gained a valuable auxiliary in the person of Lord Polwarth, son to the Earl of Marchmont, a nobleman of elegant parts, keen penetration, and uncommon vivacity, who spoke with all the fluency and fervour of elocution.

The minority in the House of Lords were not less vigilant and resolute in detecting and opposing every measure which they thought would redound to the prejudice of their country. But the most remarkable object that employed their attention during this session was a very extraordinary petition, subscribed by the Dukes of Hamilton, Queensberry, and Montrose, the Earls of Dundonald, Marchmont, and Stair, representing that undue influence had been used for carrying on the election of the sixteen peers for Scotland. The Duke of Bedford, who delivered their petition to the House, proposed a day for taking it into consideration; and to this they agreed. It was afterwards moved, that the consideration of it should be adjourned to a short day, before which the petitioners should be ordered to declare whether they intended to controvert the last election of all the sixteen peers, or the election of any, and which of them. This affair was of such an unprecedented nature, that the House seemed to be divided in opinion about the manner in which they ought to proceed. The partisans of the ministry would have willingly stifled the inquiry in the beginning; but the petitioners were so strenuously supported in their claim to some notice, by the Earls of Chesterfield, Abingdon, and Strafford, the Lords Bathurst and Carteret, that they could not dismiss it at once with any regard to decorum. The order of the House, according to the motion explained above, being communicated by the lord chancellor to the petitioners, they waited on him with a declaration, importing that they did not intend to controvert the election or return of the sixteen peers for Scotland; but they thought it their duty to lay before their lordships the evidence of such facts and undue methods as appeared to them to be dangerous to the constitution; and might in future elections equally affect the right of the present sixteen peers, as that of the other peers of Scotland, if not prevented by a proper remedy. This declaration being repeated to the House, the Duke of Devonshire made a motion, that the petitioners might be ordered to lay before the House, in writing, instances of those undue methods and illegal practices upon which they intended to proceed, and the names of the persons they suspected to be guilty. He was warmly opposed by the country party; and a long debate ensued; after which the question was carried in favour of the motion, and the order signified to the petitioners. Next day their answer was read to the House to this effect: that as they had no intention to state themselves accusers, they could not take upon them to name particular persons who might have been concerned in those illegal practices; but who they were would undoubtedly appear to their lordships upon their taking the proper examinations; nevertheless, they did humbly acquaint their lordships, that the petition was laid before them upon information, that the list of the sixteen peers for Scotland had been framed, previous to the election, by persons in high trust under the crown: that this list was shown to peers, as a list approved by the crown; and was called the king's list, from which there was to be no variation, unless to make way for one or two particular peers, on condition they should conform to measures: that peers were solicited to vote for this list, without the liberty of making any alteration: that endeavours were used to engage peers to vote for this list by promise of pensions, and offices civil and military, to themselves and relations, as well as by offers of money: that sums were given for this purpose: that pensions, offices, and releases of debts owing to the crown, were actually granted to peers who concurred in voting for this list, and to their relations: that on the day of election a battalion of his majesty's troops were drawn up in the Abbey-court of Edinburgh, contrary to custom, and without any apparent cause but that of overawing the electors. This answer gave rise to another violent dispute; but the majority voted it unsatisfactory, and the petition was rejected, though the resolution was clogged with a vigorous protest.

Notwithstanding this discouragement, the Earl of Abingdon moved, that although the petition was dismissed, an inquiry might be set on foot touching an affair of such consequence to the liberties of the kingdom. The Earl of Ilay declaring his belief that no such illegal methods had been practised, the other produced a pamphlet, entitled "The Protests of a great Number of noble Lords, entered by them at the last Election of Peers for Scotland." Exceptions being taken to a pamphlet, as an object unworthy of their notice, Lord Bathurst exhibited an authentic copy of those protests, extracted from the journal of that election, signed by the two principal clerks, and witnessed by two gentlemen then attending in the lobby. These were accordingly read, and plainly demonstrated the truth of the allegations contained in the petition. Nothing could be more scandalous, arrogant,

*1735. Bill explaining an act of the Scottish Parliament touching wrongous imprisonment.*

and shamefully flagrant than the conduct and deportment of those who acted the part of understrappers to the ministry on this occasion. But all this demonstration, adorned and enforced by the charms and energy of eloquence, was like preaching in a desert. A motion was made for adjourning, and carried in the affirmative: a protest was entered, and the whole affair consigned to oblivion. Divers other motions were made successively by the lords in the opposition, and rejected by the invincible power of a majority. The uninterrupted success of the ministry did not, however, prevent them from renewing the struggle as often as an opportunity offered. They disputed the continuation of the salt-tax, and the bill for enabling the king to apply the sum of one million out of the sinking-fund for the service of the current year, though success did not attend their endeavours. They supported with all their might a bill sent up from the Commons, explaining and amending an act of the Scottish Parliament, for preventing wrongous imprisonment, and against undue delays in trials. This was all the natives of Scotland had in lieu of the habeas corpus act, though it did not screen them from oppression. Yet the Earl of Ilay undertook to prove they were on a footing with their neighbours of England in this respect; and the bill was thrown out on a division. The session was closed on the fifteenth of May, when the king, in his speech to both Houses, declared that the plan of pacification concerted between him and the States-General had not produced the desired effect. He thanked the Commons for the supplies they had granted with such cheerfulness and despatch. He signified his intention to visit his German dominions; and told them he should constitute the queen regent of the realm in his absence. Immediately after the prorogation his majesty embarked for Holland, in his way to Hanover.

By this time the good understanding between the courts of Madrid and Lisbon was destroyed by a remarkable incident. The Portuguese ambassador at Madrid having allowed his servants to rescue a criminal from the officers of justice, all the servants concerned in that rescue were dragged from his house to prison, by the Spanish king's order, with circumstances of rigour and disgrace. His Portuguese majesty, being informed of this outrage, ordered reprisals to be made upon the servants of the Spanish ambassador

*Misunderstanding between the courts of Spain and Portugal. Sir John Norris sails with a strong squadron to Lisbon.*

at Lisbon. The two ministers withdrew abruptly to their respective courts. The two monarchs expressed their mutual resentment. The King of Spain assembled a body of troops on the frontiers of Portugal; and his Portuguese majesty had recourse to the assistance of King George. Don Marcos Antonio d'Alzeveda was despatched to London with the character of envoy extraordinary; and succeeded in his commission according to his wish. In a little time after the king's departure from England, Sir John Norris sailed from Spithead, with a powerful squadron, in order to protect the Portuguese against the Spaniards; and on the ninth day of June arrived at Lisbon, where he was welcomed as a deliverer. Mr. Keene, the British envoy at the court of Spain, had communicated to his Catholic majesty the resolution of his master to send a powerful squadron to Lisbon, with orders to guard that coast from insults, and secure the Brazil fleet, in which the merchants of Great Britain were deeply interested. Don Joseph Patinho, minister of his Catholic majesty, delivered a memorial to Mr. Keene, representing that such an expedition would affect the commerce of Spain, by intimidating foreign merchants from embarking their merchandise in the flota. But in all probability, it prevented a rupture between the two crowns, and disposed the King of Spain to listen to terms of accommodation.

The powers in alliance against the house of Austria, having rejected the plan of pacification concerted by the King of Great Britain and the States-General, Mr. Walpole, ambassador at the Hague, presented a memorial to their high mightinesses, desiring they would, without loss of time, put themselves in a posture of defence by an augmentation of their forces at sea and land; that they might take such vigorous steps in concert with Great Britain, as the future conjuncture of affairs might require. But before they would subject themselves to such expense, they resolved to make further trial of their influence with the powers in alliance against the emperor; and conferences were renewed with the ministers of those allies. The affairs of Poland became more and more unfavourable to the interest of Stanislaus; for though a great number of the Polish nobility engaged in a confederacy to support his claim, and made repeated efforts in his behalf, the Palatine of Kiow submitted to Augustus; and even his brother the primate, after having sustained a long imprisonment and many extraordinary hardships, was obliged to acknowledge that prince his sovereign. In Italy the arms of the allies still continued to prosper. Don Carlos landed in Sicily, and reduced the whole island, almost without opposition; while the imperialists were forced to abandon all the territories they possessed in Italy, except the Mantuan. The emperor, being equally unable to cope with the French armies on the Rhine, implored succours of the czarina, who sent thirty thousand men to his assistance. This vigorous interposition, and the success of Augustus in Poland, disposed the court of Versailles to a pacification. A secret negotiation was begun between France and the house of Austria; and the preliminaries were signed without the concurrence or knowledge of Spain, Sardinia, and the maritime powers. In these articles it was stipulated, that France should restore all the conquests she had made in Germany: that the reversion of the dukedom of Tuscany should be vested in the Duke of Lorraine: that Lorraine should be allotted to King Stanislaus; and after his death be united to the crown of France: that the emperor should possess the Milanese, the Mantuan, and Parma: that the King of Sardinia should enjoy Vigevano and Novara: that Don Carlos should be acknowledged King of Naples and Sicily, and retain the island of Elba, with all the Spanish territories on the coast of Tuscany: and that France should guarantee the pragmatic sanction.

*Proceedings in Parliament.*
The King of Great Britain returned from Hanover to England in the month of November; and on the fifteenth day of January opened the session of Parliament. On this occasion he congratulated them on the near prospect of a general peace in Europe, in consequence of the preliminary articles in which the emperor and the King of France had agreed; and of which he had expressed his approbation, as they did not differ in any essential point from the plan of pacification which he and the States-General had offered to the belligerent powers. He told them that he had already ordered a considerable reduction to be made in his forces both by sea and land; but at the same time observed, it would be necessary to continue some extraordinary expense, until a more perfect reconciliation should be established among the several powers of Europe. An address of thanks was unanimously voted, presented, and graciously received. After the House had received several petitions from different counties and gentle-

men, complaining of undue influence in elections for members of Parliament, it proceeded to consider of the supply, and Sir Charles Wager moving that fifteen thousand seamen should be employed for the service of the ensuing year, the proposal was approved without opposition. But this was not the case with a motion made by Mr. Pulteney, "That the ordinary estimate of the navy should be referred to a select committee." The ministry discouraged all such prying measures: a debate was produced, the House divided, and the motion was rejected. Such was the fate of a motion for raising the supplies within the year, made by Mr. Sandys, and supported by Sir John Barnard, Mr. Willimot, and other patriots, who demonstrated, that this was a speedy and practicable expedient for discharging the national debt, lowering the interest of money, reducing the price of labour, and encouraging a spirit of commerce.

The bill for limiting the number of officers in the House of Commons was again revived. The king was empowered to borrow six hundred thousand pounds, chargeable on the sinking-fund, for the service of the ensuing year, though this power was not easily granted; and the House resolved to lay a duty of twenty shillings per gallon on all spirituous liquors, after it had appeared to the committee appointed for that purpose, that those spirits were pernicious to the health and morals of the people. To this resolution was added another, which amounted to a total prohibition, namely, that fifty pounds should be yearly paid to his majesty for a licence to be annually taken out by every person who should vend, barter, or utter any such spirituous liquors. Mr. Walter Plumer, in a well-concerted speech, moved for the repeal of some clauses in the test act: these he represented as a species of persecution, in which Protestant dissenters were confounded with the Roman Catholics and enemies to the establishment. He was sustained by Lord Polwarth and Mr. Heathcote; but Sir Robert Walpole was joined by Mr. Shippen against the motion as dangerous to the established church; and the question being put, it was carried in the negative. When Sir Joseph Jekyll presented to the House, according to order, a bill founded on the resolutions they had taken against spirituous liquors, Sir Robert Walpole acquainted them, by his majesty's command, that as the alterations proposed to be made by

*Bill for preventing the retail of spirituous liquors. Another for the relief of Quakers in the article of tithes.*

1736.

that bill in the duties charged upon all spirituous liquors might, in a great degree, affect some part of the civil-list revenues, his majesty, for the sake of remedying so great an evil as was intended by that bill to be prevented, did consent to accept any other revenue of equal value, to be settled and appropriated in lieu of his interest in the said duties. The bill was read a second time, and consigned to a committee of the whole House; but that for limiting the number of officers in the House of Commons was thrown out at the second reading. Petitions against the bill touching the retail of spirituous liquors were presented by the traders to the British sugar colonies, by the merchants of Bristol and Liverpool, representing the hardships to which they would be exposed by a law which amounted to a prohibition of rum and spirits distilled from molasses. In consequence of these remonstrances, a mitigating clause was inserted in favour of the composition known by the name of punch, and distillers were permitted to exercise any other employment. The sum of seventy thousand pounds was voted for making good the deficiencies that might happen in the civil-list by this bill, which at length passed through the House, though not without reiterated disputes and warm altercation. Violent opposition was likewise made to a bill for the relief of the people called Quakers, who offered a petition, representing, that though from motives of conscience they refused the payment of tithes, church-rates, oblations, and ecclesiastical dues, they were exposed to grievous sufferings by prosecution in the exchequer, ecclesiastical, and other courts, to the imprisonment of their persons, and the ruin of them and their families. A bill, being prepared for their relief, was read and printed: then petitions were preferred against it by the clergy of Middlesex, and of many other parts of the kingdom. Counsel was heard in behalf of these petitioners, and several alterations proposed in the bill, which, after long and repeated debates, surmounted all opposition, and was sent up to the Lords.

In the month of February the king had sent two members of the privy-council to the Prince of Wales, with a message, proposing a marriage between his royal highness and the Princess of Saxegotha. The proposal being agreeable to the prince, the marriage was celebrated on the twenty-seventh day of April. Upon this occasion Mr. Pulteney moved for an address of congratulation to his

*Mortmain act.*

majesty, and was supported by Mr. George Lyttelton and Mr. William Pitt, who seized this opportunity of pronouncing elegant panegyrics on the Prince of Wales and his amiable consort. These two young members soon distinguished themselves in the House by their eloquence and superior talents. The attention of the House was afterwards converted to a bill for the preventing of smuggling; and another for explaining the act for the more effectual preventing of bribery and corruption in the election of members to serve in Parliament. Both made their way through the Lower House, and were sent up to the Lords for their concurrence. The number of land-forces voted for the service of the current year was reduced to seventeen thousand seven hundred and four effective men. The supplies were raised by the malt-tax and land-tax at two shillings in the pound, additional duties on mum, cider, and perry, stamped vellum, parchment, and paper; and by an act empowering his majesty to borrow six hundred thousand pounds from the sinking-fund. In this session the Parliament repealed the old statutes of England and Scotland against conjuration, witchcraft, and dealing with evil spirits. The Commons likewise prepared a bill to restrain the disposition of lands in mortmain, whereby they became unalienable. Against this measure petitions were presented by the two universities, the colleges of Eton, Winchester, and Westminster, and divers hospitals that subsisted by charitable donations. In favour of the universities and colleges, a particular exempting clause was inserted. Several other amendments were made in the bill, which passed through both Houses, and obtained the royal assent. Among the acts passed in this session, was one for naturalizing her royal highness the Princess of Wales; and another for building a bridge across the Thames from New Palace-yard, in the city of Westminster, to the opposite shore in the county of Surrey. The points chiefly debated in the House of Lords were the address of thanks for his majesty's speech, the mortmain bill, the Quakers' bill, which was thrown out, and that for the prevention of smuggling, which did not pass without division and protest. On the twentieth day of May the king closed the session with a speech, in which he told both Houses, that a further convention, touching the execution of the preliminaries, had been made and communicated to him by the emperor and Most Christian king;

and that negotiations were carrying on by the several powers engaged in the late war, in order to settle a general pacification. He expressed great concern at seeing such seeds of dissatisfaction sown among his people: he protested it was his desire, and should be his care, to preserve the present constitution in church and state as by law established: he recommended harmony and mutual affection among all Protestants of the nation, as the great security of that happy establishment; and signified his intention to visit his German dominions. Accordingly the Parliament was no sooner prorogued than he set out for Hanover, after having appointed the queen regent in his absence.

Such a decree of licentiousness prevailed over the whole nation, that the kingdom was filled with tumult and riots, which might have been prevented by proper regulations of the civil government in the due execution of the laws. The most remarkable of these disturbances happened at Edinburgh, on the seventh day of September. John Porteous, who commanded the guard paid by that city, a man of brutal disposition and abandoned morals, had, at the execution of a smuggler, been provoked by some insults from the populace to order his men, without using the previous formalities of the law, to fire with shot among the crowd; by which precipitate order several innocent persons lost their lives. Porteous was tried for murder, convicted, and received sentence of death; but the queen, as guardian of the realm, thought proper to indulge him with a reprieve. The common people of Edinburgh resented this lenity shown to a criminal who was the object of their detestation. They remembered that pardons had been granted to divers military delinquents in that country, who had been condemned by legal trial. They seemed to think those were encouragements to oppression: they were fired by a national jealousy; they were stimulated by the relations and friends of those who had been murdered; and they resolved to wreak their vengeance on the author of that tragedy, by depriving him of life on the very day which the judges had fixed for his execution. Thus determined, they assembled in different bodies, about ten o'clock at night. They blocked up the gates of the city, to prevent the admission of the troops that were quartered in the suburbs. They surprised and disarmed the town guards; they broke open the prison doors; dragged Porteous from thence to the place of execution; and, leaving him hanging by the neck on a dyer's pole, quietly dispersed to their several habitations. This exploit was performed with such conduct and deliberation as seemed to be the result of a plan formed by some persons of consequence; it therefore became the object of a very severe inquiry.

During this summer a rupture happened between the Turks and the Russians, which last reduced the city of Asoph, on the Black Sea, and overran the greatest part of Crim Tartary. The czarina declared war against the Ottoman Porte, because the Tartars of the Crimea had made incursions upon her frontiers; and when she complained of these disorders to the vizir, she received no satisfaction; besides, a large body of Tartars had, by order of that minister, marched through the Russian provinces in despite of the empress, and committed terrible havoc in their route. The emperor was obliged to engage as a party in this war, by a treaty offensive and defensive, which he had many years before concluded with the czarina. Yet, before he declared himself, he joined the maritime powers in offering his mediation to the sultan, who was very well disposed to peace; but the czarina insisted upon her retaining Asoph, which her forces had reduced; and this preliminary article being rejected, as dishonourable to the Ottoman empire, the court of Vienna began to make preparations for war. By this time all the belligerent powers in Italy had agreed to the preliminaries of peace concluded between the emperor and France. The Duke of Lorraine had espoused the emperor's eldest daughter, the Archduchess Maria Theresa, and ceded Lorraine to France, even before he succeeded to Tuscany. Don Carlos was crowned King of Sicily; Stanislaus abdicated the crown of Poland; and Augustus was universally acknowledged sovereign of that kingdom. The preliminaries were approved and accepted by the diet of the empire: the King of Spain sent orders for his troops to evacuate Tuscany; and the provinces in Italy yielded to the house of Austria. Prince Eugene, who had managed the interests of the emperor on this occasion, did not live to see the happy fruits of this negotiation. He died at Vienna in April, at the age of seventy-three, leaving behind him the character of an invincible hero and consummate politician. He was not long survived by Count Staremberg, another imperial general, who ranked next to the prince in military reputation. About the same time Great Britain sustained a national loss in the death of Lord Chancellor Talbot, who, by his worth, probity, and acquired accomplishments, had dignified the great office to which he had been raised. He died universally lamented, in the month of February, at the age of fifty-two, and was succeeded on the bench by Lord Hardwicke.

<small>The session of Parliament opened by commission.</small> The king being indisposed, in consequence of having been fatigued by a very tempestuous passage from Holland, the Parliament was prorogued from the twenty-first day of January to the first of February, and then the session was opened by commission. The lord chancellor, as one of the peers authorized by this commission, made a speech in his majesty's name to both Houses. With respect to foreign affairs, he told them, that the respective acts of cession being exchanged, and orders given for the evacuation and possession of the several countries and places by the powers concerned, according to the allotment and disposition of the preliminary articles, the great work of re-establishing the general tranquillity was far advanced: that, however, common prudence called upon them to be very attentive to the final conclusion of the new settlement. He said, his majesty could not, without surprise and concern, observe the many contrivances and attempts carried on, in various shapes and in different parts of the nation, tumultuously to resist and obstruct the execution of the laws, and to violate the peace of the kingdom. He observed, that the consideration of the height to which these audacious practices might rise, if not timely suppressed, afforded a melancholy prospect, and required particular attention, lest they should affect private persons in the quiet enjoyment of their property, as well as the general peace and good order of the whole. After the Commons had agreed to an address, and heard counsel on some controverted elections, they proceeded to take the supply into consideration. They voted ten thousand men for the sea-service. They continued for the land-service the same number they had maintained in times of tranquillity, amounting to seventeen thousand seven hundred and four: but this measure was not adopted without opposition; the money was raised by the land and malt-taxes, reinforced with one million granted out of the sinking-fund.

The chief subject of contention that presented itself in the course of this session, was a motion which Mr. Pulteney made for an address to his majesty, that he would be pleased to settle one hundred thousand pounds a year upon the Prince of Wales. He represented that such provision was conformable to the practice of ancient time: that what he proposed had been enjoyed by his present majesty in the lifetime of his father; and that a settlement of this nature was reasonable and necessary to ascertain the independency of the apparent heir to the crown. The motion was vigorously opposed by Sir Robert Walpole, as an encroachment on the prerogative; as an officious intermeddling in the king's family affairs; and as an effort to set his majesty and the prince at variance. But a misunderstanding, it seems, had already happened in the royal family. The minister in the midst of his harangue told the House, by his majesty's command, that on the preceding day the king had sent a message to the prince by several noblemen of the first quality, importing that his majesty had given orders for settling a jointure upon the Princess of Wales, suitable to her high rank and dignity, which he would in a proper time lay before Parliament, in order to be rendered more certain and effectual: that although his royal highness had not thought fit, by any application to his majesty, to desire that his allowance of fifty thousand pounds might be rendered less precarious, the king, to prevent the bad consequences which he apprehended might follow from the undutiful measures which his majesty was informed the prince had been advised to pursue, would grant to his royal highness, for his majesty's life, the said fifty thousand pounds per annum, to be issued out of the civil-list revenues, over and above the prince's revenues arising from the duchy of Cornwall, which his majesty thought a very competent allowance, considering his own numerous issue, and the great expense which did and must necessarily attend an honourable provision for the whole royal family; that the prince, by a verbal answer, desired their lordships to lay him with all humility at his majesty's feet; to assure him that he did, and ever should, retain the utmost duty for his royal person: that he was very thankful for any instance of his majesty's goodness to him or to the princess, and particularly for his majesty's gracious intention of settling a jointure upon her royal highness; but that, as to the message, the affair was now out of his hands, and therefore he could give no answer to it: that his royal highness afterwards used many dutiful expressions towards his majesty, adding, " Indeed, my lords, it is in other hands, and I am sorry for it;" or words to that effect. Sir Robert Walpole then endeavoured to demonstrate, that the annual sum of fifty thousand pounds was as much as the king could afford to allow for the prince's maintenance; and he expatiated upon the bad consequences that might ensue, if the son should be rendered altogether independent of the father.

These suggestions did not pass unanswered. Sir Robert Walpole had asserted, that the Parliament had no right to interfere in the creation or maintenance of a Prince of Wales; and that in the case of Richard II., who, upon the death of his father, the Black Prince, was created Prince of Wales, in consequence of an address or petition from Parliament, that measure was in all probability directed by the king himself. In answer to this assertion it was observed, that probably the king would not have been so forward in creating his grandson Prince of Wales, if he had not been forced into this step by his Parliament; for Edward in his old age fell into a sort of love dotage, and gave himself entirely up to the management of his mistress, Alice Pierce, and his second son, the Duke of Lancaster; a circumstance that raised a most reasonable jealousy in the Black Prince, at that time on his death-bed, who could not but be anxious about the safety and right of his only son, whom he found he was soon to leave a child in the hands of a doting grandfather, and an ambitious, aspiring uncle. The supporters of the motion observed, that the allowance of fifty thousand pounds was not sufficient to defray the prince's yearly expense, without allotting one shilling for acts of charity and munificence; and that the several deductions for land-taxes and fees reduced it to forty-three thousand pounds. They affirmed that his whole income, including the revenues of the duchy of Cornwall, did not exceed fifty-two thousand pounds a year, though, by his majesty's own regulation, the expense of the prince's household amounted to sixty-three thousand. They proved, that the produce of the civil-list exceeded nine hundred thousand pounds, a sum above one hundred thousand pounds a year more than was enjoyed by

*Fierce debate on this subject.*

his late majesty; and that, in the first year of the late king, the whole expense of his household and civil government did not much exceed four hundred and fifty thousand pounds a year. They observed, that the Parliament added one hundred and forty thousand pounds annually for acts of charity and bounty, together with the article of secret service money; and allowed one hundred thousand pounds for the maintenance of the Prince of Wales: that the article of secret service money had prodigiously increased in the late reign: by an account which happened to be laid before the Parliament, it appeared that vast sums of money had been given for purposes which nobody understood, and to persons whom nobody knew. In the beginning of the following session several members proposed that this extraordinary account should be taken into consideration; but the inquiry was warded off by the other party, who declared that the Parliament could not examine any account which had been presented to a former session. The debate was fierce and long; and ended in a division, by which the motion was rejected. A motion of the same nature was made by Lord Carteret in the House of Peers, and gave rise to a very keen dispute, maintained by the same arguments, and issuing in the same termination.

The next remarkable contest was occasioned by a motion of Sir R. Walpole, who proposed that the sum of one million should be granted to his majesty, towards redeeming the like sum of the increased capital of the South-Sea Company, commonly called South-Sea annuities. Several members argued for the expediency of applying this sum to the payment of the debt due to the bank, as a part of that incumbrance was saddled with an interest of six per cent., whereas the interest paid for the other sums that constituted the public debt did not exceed four per cent. Many plausible arguments were offered on both sides of the question; and at length the motion was carried in the affirmative. The House having resolved itself into a committee to consider of the national debt, Sir John Barnard made a motion, for enabling his majesty to raise money either by the sale of annuities, or by borrowing at an interest not exceeding three per cent., to be applied towards redeeming the South-Sea annuities; and that such of the said annuitants as should be inclined to subscribe their respective annuities should be preferred to all others. He said, that even those public securities which bore an interest of three per cent. only were sold at a premium in Change-alley; he was therefore persuaded, that all those who were willing to give a premium for a three per cent. security would gladly lend their money to the government at the same interest, should books of subscription be opened for that purpose, with an assurance that no part of the principal should be paid off for fourteen years. He expatiated upon the national advantages that would accrue from a reduction of interest. From easy and obvious calculations he inferred, that in a very little time the interest upon all the South-Sea annuities would be reduced from four to three per cent. without any danger to public credit, or breach of public faith: that then the produce of the sinking-fund would amount to fourteen hundred thousand pounds per annum, to be applied only towards redeeming the capital of the several trading companies: he proved that this measure would bring every one of them so much within the power of Parliament, that they would be glad to accept of three per cent. interest on any reasonable terms; in which case the sinking-fund would rise to one million six hundred thousand pounds per annum. Then the Parliament might venture to annihilate one half of it by freeing the people from the taxes upon coals, candles, soap, leather, and such other impositions as lay heavy upon the poor labourers and manufacturers: the remaining part of the sinking-fund might be applied towards the discharge of those annuities and public debts which bore an interest of three per cent. only, and afterwards towards diminishing the capitals of the several trading companies, till the term of fourteen years should be expired; then the sinking-fund would again amount to above a million yearly, which would be sufficient for paying them off, and freeing the nation entirely from all its incumbrances. This salutary scheme was violently opposed by Alderman Heathcote, and other partisans of the ministry; yet all their objections were refuted; and, in order to defeat the project, they were obliged to have recourse to artifice. Mr. Winnington moved, that all the public creditors, as well as the South-Sea annuitants, should be comprehended. Sir John Barnard demonstrated, that it might be easy for the government to borrow money at three per cent. sufficient for paying off such of the proprietors of four-and-twenty millions as were not willing to accept of that interest, but it would be extremely difficult to borrow enough to satisfy the proprietors of four-and-forty millions, who might choose to have their principal rather than such an interest. Nevertheless, resolutions were founded on this and other alterations of the original scheme; and a bill was immediately prepared. It produced many other debates, and was at last postponed by dint of ministerial influence. The same venerable patriot, who projected this scheme, moved that as soon as the interest of all the national redeemable debt should be reduced to three per cent. the House would take off some of the heavy taxes which oppressed the poor and the manufacturers; but this motion was rejected by the majority.

The last disputes of this session were excited by a bill sent down from the Lords for punishing the magistrates and city of Edinburgh, on account of the murder of John Porteous. In the beginning of the session Lord Carteret recapitulated the several tumults and riots which had lately happened in different parts of the kingdom. He particularly insisted upon the atrocious murder of Captain Porteous, as a flagrant insult upon the government, and a violation of the public peace, so much the more dangerous, as it seemed to have been concerted and executed with deliberation and decency. He suspected that some citizens of Edinburgh had been concerned in the murder, not only from this circumstance, but likewise because, notwithstanding the reward of two hundred pounds, which had been offered by proclamation for the discovery of any person who acted in that tragedy, not one individual had as yet been detected. He seemed to think that the magistrates had encouraged the riot, and that the city had forfeited its charter; and he proposed a minute inquiry into the particulars of the affair. He was seconded by the Duke of Newcastle and the Earl of Ilay; though this last nobleman differed in opinion from him with respect to the charter of the city, which, he said could not be justly forfeited by the fault of the magistracy. The Lords resolved, that the magistrates and other persons from whom they might obtain the necessary information concerning this riot should be ordered to attend; and that an address should be presented to his majesty, desiring that the different accounts and papers relating to the murder of Captain Porteous might be sub-

*1737. Bill against the city of Edinburgh.*

mitted to the perusal of the House. These documents being accordingly examined, and all the witnesses arrived, including three Scottish judges, a debate arose about the manner in which these last should be interrogated, whether at the bar, at the table, or on the woolsacks. Some Scottish lords asserted that they had a right to be seated next to the judges of England; but after a long debate this claim was rejected, and the judges of Scotland appeared at the bar in their robes. A bill was brought in to disable Alexander Wilson, Esquire, lord provost of Edinburgh, from enjoying any office or place of magistracy in the city of Edinburgh, or elsewhere in Great Britain; for imprisoning the said Alexander Wilson; for abolishing the guard of that city; and for taking away the gates of the Nether-bow-port, so as to open a communication between the city and suburbs, in which the king's troops are quartered. The Duke of Argyle, in arguing against this bill, said he could not think of a proceeding more harsh or unprecedented than the present, as he believed there was no instance of the whole weight of parliamentary indignation, for such he called a proceeding by a bill *ex post facto*, falling upon any single person, far less upon any community, for crimes that were within the reach of the inferior courts of justice; for this reason he observed, that if the lord provost and citizens of Edinburgh should suffer in the terms of the present bill, they would suffer by a cruel, unjust, and fantastical proceeding; a proceeding of which the worst use might be made, if ever the nation should have the misfortune to fall under a partial, self-interested administration. He told them he sat in the Parliament of Scotland when that part of the treaty of union relating to the privileges of the royal burghs was settled on the same footing as religion; that is, they were made unalterable by any subsequent Parliament of Great Britain. Notwithstanding the eloquence and warmth of his remonstrance, the bill was sent down to the House of Commons, where it produced a violent contest. The Commons set on foot a severe scrutiny into the particular circumstances that preceded and attended the murder of Porteous: from the examination of the witnesses, it appeared that no freeman or citizen of Edinburgh was concerned in the riot, which was chiefly composed of country people, excited by the relations of some unhappy persons whom Porteous and his men had slain at the execution of the smuggler; and these were assisted by prentice-boys, and the lowest class of vagabonds that happened to be at Edinburgh: that the lord provost had taken all the precautions to prevent mischief that his reflection suggested; that he even exposed his person to the rage of the multitude, in his endeavour to disperse them; and that, if he had done amiss, he erred from want of judgment, rather than from want of inclination to protect the unhappy Porteous. It likewise appeared that Mr. Lindsay, member for the city of Edinburgh, had gone in person to General Moyle, commander of the forces in North Britain, informed him of the riot, implored his immediate assistance, and promised to conduct his troops into the city; and that his suit was rejected, because he could not produce a written order from the magistracy, which he neither could have obtained in such confusion, nor ventured to carry about his person through the midst of an enraged populace. The Scottish members exerted themselves with uncommon vivacity in defence of their capital. They were joined by Sir John Barnard, Lord Cornbury, Mr. Shippen, and Mr. Oglethorpe. Lord Polwarth declared, that if any gentleman would show where one argument in the charge against the lord provost and the city of Edinburgh had been proved, he would that instant give his vote for the commitment of the bill. He said, if gentlemen would lay their hands upon their hearts, and ask themselves whether they would have voted in this manner had the case of Edinburgh been that of the city of Bristol, York, or Norwich, he was persuaded they would have required that every tittle of the charge against them should have been fully and undeniably proved. Some amendments and mitigations being inserted in the bill, it passed the House, was sent back to the Lords, who agreed to the alterations, and then received the royal assent.

The next effort of the minister was obliquely levelled at the liberty of the press, which it was much for his interest to abridge. The errors of his conduct, the mystery of that corruption which he had so successfully reduced to a system, and all the blemishes of his administration, had been exposed and ridiculed, not only in political periodical writings produced by the most eminent hands, but likewise in a succession of theatrical pieces, which met with uncommon success among the people. He either wanted judgment to distinguish men of genius, or could find none that would engage in his service: he therefore employed a

*[margin: Playhouse bill.]*

set of wretched authors, void of understanding and ingenuity. They undertook the defence of his ministry, and answered the animadversions of his antagonists. The match was so extremely unequal, that, instead of justifying his conduct, they exposed it to additional ridicule and contempt, and he saw himself in danger of being despised by the whole nation. He resolved so seize the first opportunity to choke those canals through which the torrent of censure had flowed upon his character. The manager of a playhouse communicated to him a manuscript farce, entitled the Golden Rump, which was fraught with treason and abuse upon the government, and had been presented to the stage for exhibition. This performance was produced in the House of Commons. The minister descanted upon the insolence, the malice, the immorality, and the seditious calumny, which had been of late propagated in theatrical pieces. A bill was brought in to limit the number of playhouses; to subject all dramatic writers to the inspection of the lord chamberlain; and to compel them to take out a licence for every production before it could appear on the stage. Notwithstanding a vigorous opposition, this bill passed through both Houses with extraordinary despatch, and obtained the royal sanction. In this debate the Earl of Chesterfield distinguished himself by an excellent speech, that will ever endear his character to all the friends of genius and literature, to all those who are warmed with zeal for the liberties of their country. "Our stage (said he) ought certainly to be kept within due bounds; but, for this purpose, our laws as they stand at present are sufficient. If our stage-players at any time exceed those bounds, they ought to be prosecuted; they may be punished. We have precedents, we have examples of persons punished for things less criminal than some pieces which have been lately represented: a new law must, therefore, be unnecessary; and in the present case it cannot be unnecessary without being dangerous. Every unnecessary restraint is a fetter upon the legs, is a shackle upon the hands of liberty. One of the greatest blessings we enjoy, one of the greatest blessings a people can enjoy, is liberty. But every good in this life has its allay of evil. Licentiousness is the allay of liberty. It is an ebullition, an excrescence; it is a speck upon the eye of the political body, which I can never touch but with a gentle, with a trembling hand; lest I destroy the body, lest I injure the eye, upon which it is apt to appear. If the stage becomes at any time licentious, if a play appears to be a libel upon the government, or upon any particular man, the king's courts are open: the law is sufficient to punish the offender. If poets and players are to be restrained, let them be restrained as other subjects are, by the known laws of their country: if they offend, let them be tried as every Englishman ought to be, by God and their country. Do not let us subject them to the arbitrary will and pleasure of any one man. A power lodged in the hands of a single man to judge and determine without limitation, control, or appeal, is a sort of power unknown to our laws, inconsistent with our constitution. It is a higher, a more absolute power than we trust even to the king himself; and, therefore, I must think we ought not to vest any such power in his majesty's lord chamberlain." His arguments had no effect, though the House admired his elocution; and the playhouse bill passed into a law. On the twenty-first day of June the king made a short speech to both Houses, and the lord chancellor prorogued the Parliament.

## CHAPTER XVII.

THE RUSSIANS TAKE OCZAKOW. — DEATH OF GASTON DE MEDICIS, DUKE OF TUSCANY. — DEATH OF CAROLINE, QUEEN CONSORT OF ENGLAND. — DISPUTE IN PARLIAMENT ABOUT THE STANDING ARMY. — SPANISH DEPREDATIONS. — MOTIVES OF THE MINISTER FOR AVOIDING A WAR. — ADDRESS TO THE KING ON THE SUBJECT OF THE DEPREDATIONS. — BILL FOR SECURING THE TRADE OF HIS MAJESTY'S SUBJECTS IN AMERICA. — DEBATES IN THE HOUSE OF LORDS. — BIRTH OF PRINCE GEORGE. — ADMIRAL HADDOCK SAILS WITH A SQUADRON TO THE MEDITERRANEAN. — PROGRESS OF THE WAR AGAINST THE TURKS. — DISPUTES AND RUPTURE BETWEEN HANOVER AND DENMARK. — SIR ROBERT WALPOLE EXTOLS THE CONVENTION IN THE HOUSE OF COMMONS. — MOTION FOR AN ADDRESS, THAT THE REPRESENTATIONS, LETTERS, &C., RELATING TO THE SPANISH DEPREDATIONS SHOULD BE LAID BEFORE THE HOUSE. — PETITIONS AGAINST THE CONVENTION. — SUBSTANCE OF THAT AGREEMENT. — DEBATE IN THE HOUSE OF COMMONS ON THE CONVENTION. — SECESSION OF THE CHIEF MEMBERS IN THE OPPOSITION. — DEBATE IN THE HOUSE OF LORDS UPON AN ADDRESS TO HIS MAJESTY TOUCHING THE CONVENTION. — MESSAGE FROM THE THRONE TOUCHING A SUBSIDY TO DENMARK, AND A POWER TO AUGMENT THE FORCES OF THE KINGDOM. — PARLIAMENT PROROGUED. — THE KING OF SPAIN PUBLISHES A MANIFESTO. — THE EMPEROR AND CZARINA CONCLUDE A PEACE WITH THE TURKS. — PREPARATIONS FOR WAR IN ENGLAND. — APOLOGY IN THE HOUSE OF COMMONS FOR THE SECEDING MEMBERS. — PENSION-BILL REVIVED AND LOST. — PORTOBELLO TAKEN BY ADMIRAL VERNON. — HARD FROST. — MARRIAGE OF THE PRINCESS MARY TO THE PRINCE OF HESSE. — STRONG ARMAMENT SENT TO THE WEST INDIES. — DEATH OF THE EMPEROR AND CZARINA. — PROCEEDINGS IN PARLIAMENT. — SEAMEN'S BILL. — DISCONTENTS AGAINST THE MINISTRY. — MOTION FOR REMOVING SIR ROBERT WALPOLE FROM HIS MAJESTY'S COUNCILS AND PRESENCE FOR EVER. — DEBATE ON THE MUTINY BILL. — PROCEEDINGS IN THE HOUSE OF LORDS. — CLOSE OF THE LAST SESSION OF THIS PARLIAMENT.

A CONGRESS had been opened at Niemerow, in Poland, to compromise the differences between the czarina and the grand signor; but this proving ineffectual, the emperor declared war against the Turks, and demanded assistance from the diet of the empire. He concerted the operations of the campaign with the Empress of Muscovy. It was agreed that the imperialists, under Count Seckendorf, should attack Widin, in Servia, while the Russians, commanded by Count de Munich, should penetrate to the Ukraine, and besiege Oczakow, on the Boristhenes. They accordingly advanced against this place, which was garrisoned by twenty thousand men; and on the side of the Boristhenes defended by eighteen galleys. The Muscovites carried on their approaches with such impetuosity and perseverance, that the Turks were terrified at their valour, and in a few days capitulated. Among those who signalized themselves by uncommon marks of prowess in these attacks

*1737.*
*The Russians take Oczakow.*

was General Keith, now field-marshal in the Prussian service, who was dangerously wounded on this occasion. Meanwhile Count Seckendorf, finding it impossible to reduce Widin without a squadron of ships on the Danube, turned his arms against Nissa, which was surrendered to him on the eight-and-twentieth day of July; but this was the farthest verge of his good fortune. The Turks attacked the post which the imperialists occupied along the Danube. They took the fort of Padudil, burned the town of Ilas in Wallachia, and plundered the neighbouring villages. The Prince of Saxe-Hildburghausen, who had invested Bagnalack in Bosnia, was defeated, and obliged to repass the Saave. Count Seckendorf was recalled to Vienna; and the command of the army devolved upon Count Philippi. Count Kevenhuller was obliged to retreat from Servia; and Nissa was retaken by the Mussulmen. The conferences at Niemerow were broken off; and the Turkish plenipotentiaries returned to Constantinople.

The kingdom of Poland now enjoyed the most perfect repose under the dominion of Augustus. Ferdinand, the old Duke of Courland, dying without issue, the succession was disputed by the Teutonic order and the kingdom of Poland, while the states of Courland claimed a right of election, and sent deputies to Petersburg, imploring the protection of the czarina. A body of Russian troops immediately entered that country; and the states elected the Count de Biron, high chamberlain to the Empress of Muscovy. The Elector of Cologn, as grand master of the Teutonic order, protested against this election; but the King of Poland agreed to it, on certain conditions settled at Dantzic with the commissaries of the new duke and those of the czarina. In the month of July, John Gaston de Medicis, Great Duke of Tuscany, died at Florence; and the Prince de Craon took possession of his territories, in the name of the Duke of Lorraine, to whom the emperor had already granted the eventual investiture of that duchy. *Death of Gaston de Medicis, Duke of Tuscany.*

In England, the attention of the public was attracted by an open breach in the royal family. The Princess of Wales had advanced to the very last month of her pregnancy before the king and queen were informed of her being with child. She was twice conveyed from Hampton-court to the palace of St. James's, when her labour-pains were supposed to be approaching; *Death of Caroline, Queen Consort of England.*

and at length was delivered of a princess in about two hours after her arrival. The king, being apprised of this event, sent a message by the Earl of Essex to the prince, expressing his displeaure at the conduct of his royal highness, as an indignity offered to himself and the queen. The prince deprecated his majesty's anger in several submissive letters, and implored the queen's mediation. The princess joined her entreaties to those of his royal highness; but all their humility and supplication proved ineffectual. The king, in another message sent by the Duke of Grafton, observed, that the prince had removed the princess twice in the week immediately preceding the day of her delivery from the place of his majesty's residence, in expectation of her labour; and both times, on his return, industriously concealed from the knowledge of the king and queen every circumstance relating to this important affair: that at last, without giving any notice to their majesties, he had precipitately hurried the princess from Hampton-court, in a condition not to be named: that the whole tenor of his conduct, for a considerable time, had been so entirely void of all real duty to the king, that his majesty had reason to be highly offended with him. He gave him to understand, that until he should withdraw his regard and confidence from those by whose instigation and advice he was directed and encouraged in his unwarrantable behaviour to his majesty and the queen, and return to his duty, he should not reside in the palace: he therefore signified his pleasure that he should leave St. James's with all his family, when it could be done without prejudice or inconvenience to the princess. In obedience to this order the prince retired to Kew, and made other efforts to be re-admitted into his majesty's favour, which, however, he could not retrieve. Whatever might have been his design in concealing so long from the king and queen the pregnancy of the princess, and afterwards hurrying her from place to place in such a condition, to the manifest hazard of her life, his majesty had certainly cause to be offended at this part of his conduct; though the punishment seems to have been severe, if not rigorous; for he was not even admitted into the presence of the queen his mother, to express his duty to her, in her last moments, to implore her forgiveness, and receive her last blessing. She died of a mortification in her bowels, on the twentieth day of November, in the fifty-fifth year of her age, regretted as a princess of uncommon sagacity, and as a pattern of conjugal virtue.

The king opened the session of Parliament on the twenty-fourth day of January, with a short speech, recommending the despatch of the public business with prudence and unanimity. Each House presented a warm address of condolence on the queen's death, with which he seemed to be extremely affected. Though the House of Commons unanimously sympathized with the king in his affliction, the minister still met with contradiction in some of his favourite measures. One would imagine that all the arguments for and against a standing army in time of peace had been already exhausted; but, when it was moved that the same number of land-forces which they had voted in the preceding year should be continued in pay for the ensuing year, the dispute was renewed with surprising vivacity, and produced some reasons which had not been suggested before. The adherents of the minister fairly owned, that if the army should be disbanded, or even considerably reduced, they believed the tory interest would prevail; that the present number of forces was absolutely necessary to maintain the peace of the kingdom, which was filled with clamour and discontent, as well as to support the whig interest; and that they would vote for keeping up four times the number, should it be found expedient for that purpose. The members in the opposition replied, that this declaration was a severe satire on the ministry, whose conduct had given birth to such a spirit of discontent. They said it was in effect a tacit acknowledgment, that what they called the whig interest was no more than an inconsiderable party, which had engrossed the administration by indirect methods; which acted contrary to the sense of the nation; and depended for support upon a military power, by which the people in general were overawed, and consequently enslaved. They affirmed, that the discontent of which the ministry complained was in a great measure owing to that very standing army, which perpetuated their taxes, and hung over their heads as the instruments of arbitrary power and oppression. Lord Polwarth explained the nature of whig principles, and demonstrated that the party which distinguished itself by this appellation no longer retained the maxims by which the whigs were originally characterized. Sir John Hynde Cotton, who spoke with the courage and freedom of an old English baron, declared he never knew a member of that House, who acted on true whig principles, vote for a standing army in time of peace: "I have heard of whigs (said he) who opposed all unlimited votes of credit: I have heard of whigs who looked upon corruption as the greatest curse that could befall any nation: I have heard of whigs who esteemed the liberty of the press to be the most valuable privilege of a free people, and triennial Parliaments as the greatest bulwark of their liberties; and I have heard of a whig administration which has resented injuries done to the trade of the nation, and revenged insults offered to the British flag." The ministry triumphed as usual, and the same number of forces was continued.

Ever since the treaty of Seville, the Spaniards in America had almost incessantly insulted and distressed the commerce of Great Britain. They disputed the right of English traders to cut logwood in the bay of Campeachy, and gather salt on the island of Tortugas; though that right was acknowledged by implication in all the treaties which had been lately concluded between the two nations. The captains of their armed vessels, known by the name of guarda-costas, had made a practice of boarding and plundering British ships, on pretence of searching for contraband commodities, on which occasions they had behaved with the utmost insolence, cruelty, and rapine. Some of their ships of war had actually attacked a fleet of English merchant ships at the island of Tortugas, as if they had been at open enmity with England. They had seized and detained a great number of British vessels, imprisoned their crews, and confiscated their cargoes, in violation of treaties, in defiance of common justice and humanity. Repeated memorials were presented to the court of Spain by the British ambassador at Madrid. He was amused with evasive answers, vague promises of inquiry, and cedulas of instructions sent to the Spanish governors in America, to which they paid no sort of regard. Not but that the Spaniards had reason to complain, in their turn, of the illicit commerce which the English traders from Jamaica and other islands carried on with their subjects on the continent of South America; though this could not justify the depredations and cruelties which the commanders of the guarda-costas had committed, without provocation or pretence.

The merchants of England loudly complained of these

outrages; the nation was fired with resentment, and cried for vengeance; but the minister appeared cold, phlegmatic, and timorous. He knew that a war would involve him in such difficulties as must of necessity endanger his administration. The treasure which he now employed for domestic purposes must in that case be expended in military armaments: the wheels of that machine on which he had raised his influence would no longer move: the opposition would of consequence gain ground, and the imposition of fresh taxes, necessary for the maintenance of the war, would fill up the measure of popular resentment against his person and ministry. Moved by these considerations, he industriously endeavoured to avoid a rupture, and to obtain some sort of satisfaction by dint of memorials and negotiations, in which he betrayed his own fears to such a degree, as animated the Spaniards to persist in their depredations, and encouraged the court of Madrid to disregard the remonstrances of the British ambassador. But this apprehension of war did not proceed from Spain only: the two branches of the house of Bourbon were now united by politics as well as by consanguinity: and he did not doubt that, in case of a rupture with Spain, they would join their forces against Great Britain. Petitions were delivered to the House by merchants from different parts of the kingdom, explaining the repeated violences to which they had been exposed, and imploring relief of the Parliament. These were referred to a committee of the whole House; and an order was made to admit the petitioners, if they should think fit, to be heard by themselves or by counsel. Sir John Barnard moved for an address to the king, that all the memorials and papers relating to the Spanish depredations should be laid before the House; and this, with some alteration proposed by Sir Robert Walpole, was actually presented. In compliance with this request, an enormous multitude of letters and memorials was produced.

The House, in a grand committee, proceeded to hear counsel for the merchants, and examine evidence; by which it appeared that amazing acts of wanton cruelty and injustice had been perpetrated by Spaniards on the subjects of Great Britain. Mr. Pulteney expatiated upon these circumstances of barbarity. He demonstrated, from treaties, the right of the British traders to the logwood of Campeachy, and to the salt of

Tortugas: he exposed the pusillanimity of the minister, and the futility of his negotiations: he moved for such resolutions as would evince the resentment of an injured nation, and the vigour of a British Parliament. These were warmly combated by Sir Robert Walpole, who affirmed, they would cramp the ministers in their endeavours to compromise these differences: that they would frustrate their negotiations, intrench upon the king's prerogative, and precipitate the nation into an unnecessary and expensive war. Answers produced replies, and a general debate ensued. A resolution was reported; but the question, being put for re-committing it, was carried in the negative. The House, however, agreed to an address, beseeching his majesty to use his endeavours to obtain effectual relief for his injured subjects, to convince the court of Spain that his majesty could no longer suffer such constant and repeated insults and injuries to be carried on, to the dishonour of his crown, and to the ruin of his trading subjects; and assuring him, that in case his royal and friendly instances with the catholic king should miscarry, the House would effectually support his majesty in taking such measures as honour and justice should make it necessary for him to pursue. To this address the king made a favourable answer.

The next important subject on which both sides exercised their talents, was a bill prepared and brought in by Mr. Pulteney, for the more effectual securing the trade of his majesty's subjects in America. This was no other than the revival of part of two acts passed in the reign of Queen Anne, by which the property of all prizes taken from the enemy was vested in the captors; while the sovereign was empowered to grant commissions or charters to any persons or societies, for taking any ships, goods, harbours, lands, or fortifications of the nation's enemies in America, and for holding and enjoying the same as their own property and estate for ever. The ministry endeavoured to evade the discussion of this bill, by amusing the House with other business, until an end should be put to the session. A mean artifice was practised with this view; and some severe altercation passed between Sir Robert Walpole and Mr. Pulteney. At length the bill was read, and gave rise to a very long and warm contest, in which the greatest orators of both sides found opportunities to display their eloquence and satire. Mr.

Pulteney defended the bill with all the ardour of paternal affection; but, notwithstanding his warmest endeavours, it was rejected upon a division.

When the mutiny bill was sent up to the House of Lords, a long debate arose upon the number of troops voted for the ensuing year. Lord Carteret explained the situation of affairs in almost every nation of Europe with great conciseness and precision. He demonstrated the improbability of a rupture between Great Britain and any power against which a land army could be of any service. He examined the domestic circumstances of the nation; and proved, that whatever discontents there might be in the kingdom, there was little or no disaffection, and no seeming design to overturn or disturb the government. In answer to an argument, that such a number of regular forces was necessary for preventing or quelling tumults, and for enabling the civil magistrate to execute the laws of his country, he expressed his hope that he should never see the nation reduced to such unfortunate circumstances: he said, a law which the civil power was unable to execute, must either be in itself oppressive, or such a one as afforded a handle for oppression. In arguing for a reduction of the forces, he took notice of the great increase of the national expense. He observed, that before the Revolution, the people of England did not raise above two millions for the whole of the public charge; but now what was called the current expense, for which the Parliament annually provided, exceeded that sum; besides the civil-list, the interest due to the public creditors, and the sinking-fund, which, added together, composed a burden of six millions yearly. The Earl of Chesterfield, on the same subject, affirmed, that slavery and arbitrary power were the certain consequences of keeping up a standing army for any number of years. It is the machine by which the chains of slavery are riveted upon a free people. They may be secretly prepared by corruption; but, unless a standing army protected those that forged them, the people would break them asunder, and chop off the polluted hands by which they were prepared. By degrees a free people must be accustomed to be governed by an army; by degrees that army must be made strong enough to hold them in subjection. England had for many years been accustomed to a standing army, under pretence of its being necessary to assist the civil power; and by degrees the number and strength of it have been increasing. At the accession of the late king it did not exceed six thousand: it soon amounted to double that number, which has been since augmented under various pretences. He therefore concluded, that slavery, under the disguise of an army for protecting the liberties of the people, was creeping in upon them by degrees; if no reduction should be made, he declared he should expect in a few years to hear some minister, or favourite of a minister, terrifying the House with imaginary plots and invasions, and making the tour of Europe in search of possible dangers, to show the necessity of keeping up a mercenary standing army, three times as numerous as the present. In spite of these suggestions, the standing army maintained its ground. The same noblemen, assisted by Lord Bathurst, distinguished themselves in a debate upon the Spanish depredations, which comprehended the same arguments that were used in the House of Commons. They met with the same success in both. Resolutions equivalent to those of the Lower House were taken: an address was presented; and his majesty assured them he would repeat, in the most pressing manner, his instances at the court of Spain in order to obtain satisfaction and security for his subjects trading to America. This assurance was renewed in his speech at the close of the session, on the twentieth of May, when the Parliament was prorogued.

At this period the Princess of Wales was delivered of a son, who was baptized by the name of George, now King of Great Britain. His birth was celebrated with uncommon rejoicings: addresses of congratulation were presented to the king by the two universities, and by almost all the cities and communities of the kingdom. But the Prince of Wales still laboured under the displeasure of his majesty, who had ordered the lord chamberlain to signify in the gazette, that no person who visited the prince should be admitted to the court of St. James's. His royal highness was divested of all the external marks of royalty, and lived like a private gentleman, cultivating the virtues of a social life, and enjoying the best fruits of conjugal felicity. In the latter end of this month, Rear-Admiral Haddock set sail with a strong squadron for the Mediterranean, which it was hoped would give weight to the negotiation of the

*Birth of Prince George. Admiral Haddock sails with a squadron to the Mediterranean.*

British minister at the court of Madrid. The act to discourage the retail of spirituous liquors had incensed the populace to such a degree as occasioned numberless tumults in the cities of London and Westminster. They were so addicted to the use of that pernicious compound, known by the appellation of gin or geneva, that they ran all risks rather than forego it entirely; and so little regard was paid to the law by which it was prohibited, that in less than two years twelve thousand persons within the bills of mortality were convicted of having sold it illegally. Nearly one-half of that number were cast in the penalty of one hundred pounds; and three thousand persons paid ten pounds each, for an exemption from the disgrace of being committed to the house of correction.

The war maintained by the emperor and the czarina against the Ottoman Porte had not yet produced any decisive event. Count Seckendorf was disgraced and confined on account of his ill success in the last campaign. General Doxat was tried by a council of war at Belgrade, and condemned to death, for having surrendered to the enemy the town of Nissa, in which he commanded. The diet of the empire granted a subsidy of fifty Roman months to the emperor, who began to make vigorous preparations for the ensuing campaign; but, in the mean time, Ragotski, Vaivode of Transylvania, revolted against the house of Austria, and brought a considerable army into the field, under the protection of the grand signor. He was immediately proclaimed a rebel, and a price set upon his head by the court of Vienna. The Turks, taking the field early, reduced the fort of Usitz and Meadia, and undertook the siege of Orsova, which, however, they abandoned at the approach of the imperial army, commanded by the Grand Duke of Tuscany, assisted by Count Konigsegg. The Turks, being reinforced, marched back, and attacked the imperialists, by whom they were repulsed after an obstinate engagement. The Germans, notwithstanding this advantage, repassed the Danube; and then the infidels made themselves masters of Orsova, where they found a fine train of artillery, designed for the siege of Widin. By the conquest of this place the Turks laid the Danube open to their galleys and vessels: and the Germans retired under the cannon of Belgrade. In the Ukraine, the Russians under General Count Munich obtained the advantage over the Turks in two engagements; and General Lacy routed the Tartars of the Crimea; but they returned in greater numbers, and harassed the Muscovites in such a manner, by intercepting their provisions and destroying the country, that they were obliged to abandon the lines of Precops.

In the month of October, an affair of very small importance produced a rupture between the King of Denmark and the Elector of Hanover. A detachment of Hanoverians took by assault the castle of Steinhorst, belonging to the privy counsellor Wederkop, and defended by thirty Danish dragoons, who had received orders to repel force by force. Several men were killed on both sides before the Hanoverians could enter the place, when the garrison was disarmed and conducted to the frontiers. This petty dispute, about a small territory, which did not yield the value of one thousand pounds a year, had well nigh involved Hanover in a war, which, in all probability, Great Britain must have maintained; but this dispute was compromised by a convention between the Kings of England and Denmark.

*Dispute and rupture between Hanover and Denmark.*

The session of Parliament was opened on the first day of February, when the king in his speech to both Houses gave them to understand, that a convention was concluded and ratified between him and the King of Spain, who had obliged himself to make reparation to the British subjects for their losses, by certain stipulated payments: the plenipotentiaries were named and appointed for regulating, within a limited time, all those grievances and abuses which had hitherto interrupted the commerce of Great Britain in the American seas; and for settling all matters of dispute, in such a manner as might for the future prevent and remove all new causes and pretences of complaint. The motion for an address of approbation was disputed as usual. Though the convention was not yet laid before the House, the nature of it was well known to the leaders of the opposition. Sir William Wyndham observed, that if the ministry had made the resolutions taken by the Parliament in the last session the foundation of their demands; if they had discovered a resolution to break off all treating, rather than depart from the sense of Parliament; either a defensive treaty might have been obtained, or by this time the worst would have been known; but, by

*Sir Robert Walpole extols the convention in the House of Commons.*

what appeared from his majesty's speech, the convention was no other than a preliminary; and, in all probability, a very bad preliminary. He supposed the minister had ventured to clothe some of his creatures with full powers to give up the rights of the nation; for they might do it if they durst. Sir Robert Walpole, in answer to these suggestions, affirmed, that the ministry had on this occasion obtained more than ever on like occasions was known to be obtained: that they had reconciled the peace of their country with her true interest: that this peace was attended with all the advantages that the most successful arms could have procured: that future ages would consider this as the most glorious period of our history, and do justice to the counsels that produced the happy event, which every gentleman divested of passion and prejudice was ready to do: and which he believed the present age, when rightly informed, would not refuse. In a word, he extolled his own convention with the most extravagant encomiums.

The House resolved to address the king, that copies of all the memorials, representations, letters, and papers, presented to his majesty, or his secretary of state, relating to depredations, should be submitted to the perusal of the House; but some members in the opposition were not contented with this resolution. Then Mr. Sandys, who may be termed the "motion maker," moved for an address, desiring that the House might inspect all letters written, and instructions given, by the secretaries of state, or commissioners of the Admiralty, to any of the British governors in America, or any commander-in-chief, or captains of his majesty's ships of war, or his majesty's minister at the court of Spain, or any of his majesty's consuls in Europe, since the treaty of Seville, relating to the losses which the British subjects had sustained by means of depredations committed by the subjects of Spain in Europe and America. This was an unreasonable proposal, suggested by the spirit of animosity and faction. Mr. H. Walpole justly observed, that a compliance with such an address might lay open the most private transactions of the cabinet, and discover secrets that ought, for the good of the kingdom, to be concealed. It would discover to the court of Spain the *ultimatum* of the king's demands and concessions, and the nation would thereby be deprived of many advantages which it might

*Motion for an address, that the representations, letters, &c., relating to the Spanish depredations, should be laid before the House.*

reap, were no such discovery made. He said, that as soon as the differences betwixt the two courts should arrive at such a crisis, and not before, the consuls were instructed to give notice to the merchants, that they might retire in time with their effects; but should such instructions come to the knowledge of the Spaniards, it would be a kind of watchword to put them on their guard, and unavoidably occasion the ruin of many thousands of British subjects. Certain it is, no government could act either in external or domestic affairs with proper influence, dignity, and despatch, if every letter and instruction relating to an unfinished negotiation should be exposed to the view of such a numerous assembly, composed of individuals actuated by motives in themselves diametrically opposite. The motion being rejected by the majority, the same gentleman moved again for an address, that his majesty would give directions for laying before the House copies of such memorials or representations as had been made, either to the King of Spain or to his ministers, since the treaty of Seville, relating to the depredations committed in Europe or America. A debate ensued; and, upon a division, the question passed in the negative.

*Petitions against the convention.* The House, in a committee of supply, voted twelve thousand seamen for the service of the ensuing year, and the standing army was continued without reduction, though powerfully attacked by the whole strength of the opposition. The Commons likewise ordered an address to his majesty, for the copies of several memorials since the treaty of Seville, touching the rights of Great Britain, or any infraction of treaties which had not been laid before them. These were accordingly submitted to the inspection of the House. By this time the convention itself was not only presented to the Commons, but also published for the information of the people. Divers merchants, planters, and others trading to America, the cities of London and Bristol, the merchants of Liverpool, and owners of sundry ships which had been seized by the Spaniards, offered petitions against the convention, by which the subjects of Spain were so far from giving up their groundless and unjustifiable practice of visiting and searching British ships sailing to and from the British plantations, that they appeared to have claimed the power of doing it as a right; for they insisted that the differences which had arisen concerning it should be referred to plenipotentiaries, to be discussed by them without even agreeing to abstain from such visitation and search during the time that the discussion of this affair might last. They therefore prayed, that they might have an opportunity of being heard, and allowed to represent the great importance of the British trade to and from the plantations in America; the clear indisputable right which they had to enjoy it, without being stopped, visited, or searched by the Spaniards, on any pretence whatsoever; and the certain inevitable destruction of all the riches and strength derived to Great Britain from that trade, if a search of British ships sailing to and from their own plantations should be tolerated upon any pretext, or under any restrictions, or even if the freedom of this navigation should continue much longer in a state of uncertainty. These petitions were referred to the committee appointed to consider of the convention. Another remonstrance was likewise presented by the trustees for establishing the colony of Georgia, setting forth, that the King of Spain claimed that colony as part of his territories; and that by the convention, the regulation of the limits of Carolina and Florida was referred to the determination of plenipotentiaries; so that the colony of Georgia, which undoubtedly belonged to the crown of Great Britain, was left in dispute, while the settlers remained in the most precarious and dangerous situation. It was moved, that the merchants should be heard by their counsel; but the proposal was strenuously opposed by the ministry, and rejected upon a division.

This famous convention, concluded at the Pardo on the fourteenth day of January, imported, that within six weeks, to be reckoned from the day on which the ratifications were exchanged, two ministers plenipotentiaries should meet at Madrid, to confer, and finally regulate the respective pretensions of the two crowns, with relation to the trade and navigation in America and Europe, and to the limits of Florida and Carolina, as well as concerning other points which remained likewise to be adjusted, according to the former treaties subsisting between the two nations: that the plenipotentiaries should finish their conferences within the space of eight months: that in the mean time no progress should be made in the fortifications of Florida and Carolina: that his Catholic majesty should pay to the King of Great Britain the sum of ninety-five thousand pounds, for a balance due to the crown and subjects of Great

*Substance of that agreement.*

Britain, after deduction made of the demands of the crown and subjects of Spain: that this sum should be employed for the satisfaction, discharge, and payment of the demands of the British subjects upon the crown of Spain: that this reciprocal discharge, however, should not extend or relate to the accounts and differences which subsisted and were to be settled between the crown of Spain and the Assiento company, nor to any particular or private contracts that might subsist between either of the two crowns, or their ministers, with the subjects of the other; or between the subjects and subjects of each nation respectively: that his Catholic majesty should cause the sum of ninety-five thousand pounds to be paid at London within four months, to be reckoned from the day on which the ratifications were exchanged. Such was the substance of that convention, which alarmed and provoked the merchants and traders of Great Britain, excited the indignation of all those who retained any regard for the honour of their country, and raised a general cry against the minister who stood at the helm of administration.

The eyes of the whole kingdom were now turned upon the House of Commons. The two contending parties summoned their whole force for the approaching dispute: on the day appointed for considering the convention, four hundred members had taken their seats by eight in the morning. In a committee of the whole House, certain West India merchants and planters were heard against the convention; so that this and the following day were employed in reading papers and obtaining information. On the eighth day of March, Mr. H. Walpole, having launched out in the praise of that agreement, moved for an address of approbation to his majesty. He was seconded by Mr. Campbell, of Pembrokeshire; and the debate began with extraordinary ardour. He who first distinguished himself in the lists was Sir Thomas Sanderson, at that time treasurer to the Prince of Wales, afterwards Earl of Scarborough. All the officers and adherents of his royal highness had joined the opposition; and he himself on this occasion sat in the gallery, to hear the debate on such an important transaction. Sir Thomas Sanderson observed, that the Spaniards by the convention, instead of giving us reparation, had obliged us to give them a general release. They had not allowed the word satisfaction to be so much as once mentioned in the treaty. Even the Spanish pirate who had cut off the ear of

*Debate in the House of Commons on the convention.*

Captain Jenkins,[a] and used the most insulting expression towards the person of the king—an expression which no British subject could decently repeat—an expression which no man that had a regard for his sovereign could ever forgive—even this fellow lived to enjoy the fruits of his rapine, and remained a living testimony of the cowardly tameness and mean submission of Great Britain, of the triumphant haughtiness and stubborn pride of Spain. Lord Gage, one of the most keen, spirited, and sarcastic orators in the House, stated in this manner the account of the satisfaction obtained from the court of Spain by the convention: the losses sustained by the Spanish depredations amounted to three hundred and forty thousand pounds; the commissary, by a stroke of his pen, reduced this demand to two hundred thousand pounds; then forty-five thousand were struck off for prompt payment: he next allotted sixty thousand pounds as the remaining part of a debt pretended to be due to Spain, for the destruction of her fleet by Sir George Byng, though it appeared by the instructions on the table, that Spain had been already amply satisfied on that head: these deductions reduced the balance to ninety-five thousand pounds; but the King of Spain insisted upon the South-Sea Company's paying immediately the sum of sixty-eight thousand pounds, as a debt due to him on one head of accounts, though, in other articles, his Catholic majesty was indebted to the company a million over and above this demand: the remainder to be paid by Spain did not exceed seven-and-twenty thousand pounds, from which she insisted upon deducting whatever she might have already given in satisfaction for any of the British ships that had been taken; and on being allowed the value of the St. Theresa, a Spanish ship which had been seized in the port of Dublin. Mr. W. Pitt, with an energy

---

[a] Captain Jenkins was master of a Scottish merchant-ship. He was boarded by the captain of a Spanish guarda-costa, who treated him in the most barbarous manner. The Spaniards, after having rummaged his vessel for what they called contraband commodities, without finding any thing to justify their search, insulted Jenkins with the most opprobrious invectives. They tore off one of his ears, bidding him carry it to his king, and tell him they would serve him in the same manner should an opportunity offer: they tortured him with the most shocking cruelty, and threatened him with immediate death. This man was examined at the bar of the House of Commons, and being asked by a member what he thought when he found himself in the hands of such barbarians? "I recommended my soul to God," said he, "and my cause to my country." The behaviour of this brave seaman, the sight of his ear, which was produced, with his account of the indignities which had been offered to the nation and sovereign of Great Britain, filled the whole House with indignation. Jenkins was afterwards employed in the service of the East India Company: he approved himself worthy of his good fortune in a long engagement with the pirate Angria, during which he behaved with extraordinary courage and conduct, and saved his own ship, with three others that were under his convoy.

of argument and diction peculiar to himself, declaimed against the convention, as insecure, unsatisfactory, and dishonourable to Great Britain. He said the great national objection, the searching of British ships, was not admitted, indeed, in the preamble; but stood there as the reproach of the whole, as the strongest evidence of the fatal submission that followed: on the part of Spain, an usurpation, an inhuman tyranny claimed and exercised over the American seas; on the part of England, an undoubted right, by treaties, and from God and nature, declared and asserted in the resolutions of Parliament, were now referred to the discussion of plenipotentiaries, upon one and the same equal foot. This undoubted right was to be discussed and regulated; and if to regulate be to prescribe rules, as in all construction it is, that right was, by the express words of the convention, to be given up and sacrificed; for it must cease to be any thing from the moment it is submitted to limitation. Mr. Lyttelton, with equal force and fluency, answered the speech of Mr. H. Walpole. "After he had used many arguments to persuade us to peace (said he), to any peace, good or bad, by pointing out the dangers of a war, dangers I by no means allow to be such as he represents them, he crowned all those terrors with the name of the pretender. It would be the cause of the pretender. The pretender would come. Is the honourable gentleman sensible what this language imports? The people of England complain of the greatest wrongs and indignities: they complain of the interruption, the destruction, of their trade; they think the peace has left them in a worse condition than before; and, in answer to all these complaints, what are they told? Why, that their continuing to suffer all this, is the price they must pay to keep the king and his family on the throne of these realms. If this were true, it ought not to be owned; but it is far from truth; the very reverse is true. Nothing can weaken the family, nothing shake the establishment, but such measures as these, and such language as this." He affirmed, that if the ministers had proceeded conformably to the intentions of Parliament, they would either have acted with vigour, or have obtained a real security in an express acknowledgment of our right not to be searched as a preliminary, *sine qua non*, to our treating at all. Instead of this, they had referred it to plenipotentiaries. "Would you, sir, (said he,) submit to a reference, whether you may travel unmolested from your house in town to your house in the country? Your right is clear and undeniable, why would you have it discussed? but much less would you refer it, if two of your judges belonged to a gang which has often stopped and robbed you in your way thither before."—The ministers, in vindication of the convention, asserted, that the satisfaction granted by Spain was adequate to the injury received; that it was only the preliminary of a treaty which would remove all causes of complaint; that war was always expensive and detrimental to a trading nation, as well as uncertain in its events; that France and Spain would certainly join their forces in case of a rupture with Great Britain; that there was not one power in Europe upon which the English could depend for effectual assistance; and that war would favour the cause and designs of a popish pretender. The House, upon a division, agreed to the address; but when a motion was made for its being recommitted, the two parties renewed the engagement with redoubled eagerness and impetuosity. Sir William Wyndham and Mr. Pulteney poured all the thunder of their eloquence against the insolence of Spain and the concessions of the British ministry. Sir Robert Walpole exerted all his fortitude and dexterity in defence of himself and his measures, and the question being put, the resolutions for the address were carried by a small majority.

Then Sir William Wyndham, standing up, made a pathetic remonstrance upon this determination. "This address (said he) is intended to convince mankind, that the treaty under our consideration is a reasonable and an honourable treaty. But if a majority of twenty-eight in such a full house should fail of that success; if the people should not implicitly resign their reason to a vote of this House, what will be the consequence? Will not the Parliament lose its authority? Will it not be thought, that even in the Parliament we are governed by a faction? and what the consequence of this may be, I leave to those gentlemen to consider, who are now to give their vote for this address: for my own part I will trouble you no more, but with these my last words, I sincerely pray to Almighty God, who has so often wonderfully protected these kingdoms, that he will graciously continue his protection over them, by preserving us from that impending danger which threatens the nation from without, and like-

*Secession of the chief members in the opposition.*

wise from that impending danger which threatens our constitution from within." The minister was on this occasion deserted by his usual temper, and even provoked into personal abuse. He declared, that the gentleman who was now the mouth of his opponents, had been looked upon as the head of those traitors who twenty-five years before conspired the destruction of their country and of the royal family, in order to set a popish pretender upon the throne; that he was seized by the vigilance of the then government, and pardoned by its clemency; but all the use he had ungratefully made of that clemency, was to qualify himself according to law, that he and his party might some time or other have an opportunity to overthrow all law. He branded them all as traitors, and expressed his hope that their behaviour would unite all the true friends of the present happy establishment. To such a degree of mutual animosity were both sides inflamed, that the most eminent members in the minority actually retired from Parliament; and were by the nation in general revered as martyrs to the liberty of the people.

*Debate in the House of Lords upon an address to his majesty touching the convention.*

The dispute occasioned by the convention in the House of Lords was maintained with equal warmth, and perhaps with more abilities. After this famous treaty had been considered, Lord Carteret suggested, that possibly one of the contracting powers had presented a protest or declaration, importing that she acceded to such or such a measure, only upon condition that the terms of that protest or declaration should be made good. He said, that until his mind should be free from the most distant suspicion that such a paper might exist in the present case, he could not form a just opinion of the transaction himself, nor communicate to their lordships any light which might be necessary for that purpose. The adherents to the ministry endeavoured to evade his curiosity in this particular by general assertions; but he insisted on his suspicion with such perseverance, that at length the ministry produced the copy of a declaration made by the King of Spain before he ratified the convention, signifying that his Catholic majesty reserved to himself, in its full force, the right of being able to suspend the assiento of negroes, in case the company should not pay within a short time the sum of sixty-eight thousand pounds sterling, owing to Spain on the duty of negroes, or on the profit of the ship Caroline; that under the validity and force of this protest, the signing of the said convention might be proceeded on, and in no other manner. In the debate that ensued, Lord Carteret displayed a surprising extent of political knowledge, recommended by all the graces of elocution, chaste, pure, dignified, and delicate. Lord Bathust argued against the articles of convention with his usual spirit, integrity, and good sense, particularly animated by an honest indignation which the wrongs of his country had inspired. The Earl of Chesterfield attacked this inglorious measure with all the weight of argument, and all the poignancy of satire. The Duke of Argyle, no longer a partisan of the ministry, inveighed against it as infamous, treacherous, and destructive, with all the fire, impetuosity, and enthusiasm of declamation. It was defended with unequal arms by the Duke of Newcastle, the Earl of Cholmondeley, Lord Hervey, the lord chancellor, the Bishop of Salisbury, and in particular by the Earl of Ilay, a nobleman of extensive capacity and uncommon erudition; remarkable for his knowledge of the civil law, and seemingly formed by nature for a politician; cool, discerning, plausible, artful, and enterprising, staunch to the minister, and invariably true to his own interest. The dispute was learned, long, and obstinate; but ended as usual in the discomfiture of those who had stigmatized the treaty. The House agreed to an address, in which they thanked his majesty for his gracious condescension in laying before them the convention. They acknowledged his great prudence in bringing the demands of his subjects for their past losses, which had been so long depending, to a final adjustment; in procuring an express stipulation for a speedy payment; and in laying a foundation for accomplishing the great and desirable ends of obtaining future security, and preserving the peace between the two nations. They declared their confidence in his royal wisdom, that in the treaty to be concluded, in pursuance of the convention, proper provisions would be made for the redress of the grievances of which the nation had so justly complained: they assured his majesty, that in case his just expectations should not be answered, the House would heartily and zealously concur in all such measures as should be necessary to vindicate his majesty's honour, and to preserve to his subjects the full enjoyment of all those rights to which they were entitled by treaty and the law of nations. This was a hard-won victory. At the head of those who voted against the address we find the Prince of Wales. His example was followed by six dukes, two-and-twenty earls, four viscounts, eighteen barons, four bishops; and their party was reinforced by sixteen proxies. A spirited protest was entered, and subscribed by nine-and-thirty peers, comprehending all the noblemen of the kingdom who were most eminent for their talents, integrity, and virtue.

1739.

A message having been delivered to the House from his majesty, importing that he had settled nine-and-thirty thousand pounds per annum on the younger children of the royal family; and desiring their lordships would bring in a bill to enable his majesty to make that provision good out of the hereditary revenues of the crown; some lords in the opposition observed, that the next heir to the crown might look upon this settlement as a mortgage of his revenue, which a Parliament had no power to make: that formerly no daughter of the royal family was ever provided for by Parliament, except the eldest, and that never was by way of annuity, but an express provision of a determinate sum of money paid by way of dowry. These objections were overruled; and the House complied with his majesty's request. Then the Duke of Newcastle produced a subsidy-treaty, by which his majesty obliged himself to pay to the King of Denmark seventy thousand pounds per annum, on condition of the Dane's furnishing to his Britannic majesty a body of six thousand men when demanded. At the same time, his grace delivered a message from the king, desiring the House would enable him to fulfil this engagement; and also to raise what money and troops the exigency of affairs, during the approaching recess, might require. Another vehement dispute arose from this proposal. With respect to the treaty, Lord Carteret observed, that no use could be made of the Danish troops in any expedition undertaken against Spain, because it was stipulated in the treaty, that they should not be used either in Italy, or on board of the fleet, or be transported in whole or in part beyond sea, after they should have marched out of the territories of Denmark, except for the defence of the kingdoms of Great Britain and Ireland: nay, should France join against the English, the Danes could not act against

*Message from the throne touching a subsidy to Denmark, and a power to augment the forces of the kingdom.*

that power or Spain, except as part of an army formed in Germany or Flanders. This body of Danes may be said, therefore, to have been retained for the defence and protection of Hanover; or, if the interest of Britain was at all consulted in the treaty, it must have been in preventing the Danes from joining their fleets to those of France and Spain. Then he argued against the second part of the message with great vivacity. He said nothing could be more dangerous to the constitution than a general and unlimited vote of credit. Such a demand our ancestors would have heard with amazement, and rejected with scorn. He affirmed that the practice was but of modern date in England; that it was never heard of before the Revolution; and never became frequent until the nation was blessed with the present wise administration. He said, if ever a general vote of credit and confidence should become a customary compliment from the Parliament to the crown at the end of every session, or as often as the minister might think fit to desire it, Parliaments would grow despicable in the eyes of the people; then a proclamation might be easily substituted in its stead, and happy would it be for the nation if that should be sufficient; for when a Parliament ceases to be a check upon ministers, it becomes an useless and unnecessary burden on the people. The representatives must always be paid some way or other: if their wages are not paid openly and surely by their respective constituents, as they were formerly, a majority of them may in future times be always ready to accept of wages from the administration, and these must come out of the pockets of the people. The Duke of Argyle and the Earl of Chesterfield enlarged upon the same topics. Nevertheless, the House complied with the message; and presented an address, in which they not only approved of the treaty with Denmark, but likewise assured his majesty they would concur with his measures, and support him in fulfilling his engagements, as well as in making such further augmentation of his forces by sea and land, as he should think necessary for the honour, interest, and safety of these kingdoms.

The same message being communicated to the Commons, they voted seventy thousand five hundred and eighty-three pounds for the subsidy to Denmark, and five hundred thousand pounds for augmenting the forces on any emergency. As Great Britain stood engaged by the convention to pay to the crown of Spain the sum of sixty thousand pounds in consideration of the ships taken and destroyed by Sir George Byng, which sum was to be applied to the relief of the British merchants who had suffered by the Spanish depredations, the Commons inserted in a bill a clause providing for this sum to be paid by the Parliament. When the bill was read in the House of Lords, a motion was made by Lord Bathurst for an address, to know whether Spain had paid the money stipulated by the convention, as the time limited for the payment of it was now expired. The Duke of Newcastle, by his majesty's permission, acquainted the House that it was not paid, and that Spain had as yet given no reason for the non-payment. Then a day was appointed to consider the state of the nation, when Lord Carteret moved for a resolution, that the failure of Spain in this particular was a breach of the convention, a high indignity to his majesty, and an injustice to the nation; but, after a warm debate, this motion was overruled by the majority. The minister, in order to atone in some measure for the unpopular step he had taken in the convention, allowed a salutary law to pass for the encouragement of the woollen manufacture, and two bills in behalf of the sugar colonies: one permitting them for a limited time to export their produce directly to foreign parts, under proper restrictions; and the other making more effectual provisions for securing the duties laid upon the importation of foreign sugars, rum, and molasses, into Great Britain, and his majesty's plantations in America. The supplies being voted, the funds established, and the crown gratified in every particular, the king closed the session with a speech on the fourteenth day of June, when the chancellor in his majesty's name prorogued the Parliament.[b]

Letters of marque and reprisal were granted against the Spaniards; a promotion was made of general officers; the troops were augmented; a great fleet was assembled at Spit-

[b] Among the laws enacted in the course of this session was an act against gaming, which had become universal through all ranks of people, and likely to prove destructive of all morals, industry, and sentiment. Another bill passed, for granting a reward to Joanna Stevens, on her discovering, for the benefit of the public, a nostrum for the cure of persons afflicted with the stone; a medicine which has by no means answered the expectations of the legislature.

In the House of Lords, complaint was made by Lord Delawar of a satire, entitled Manners, written by Mr. Whitehead; in which some characters of distinction were severely lashed, in the true spirit of poetry. It was voted a libel: a motion was made to take the author into custody; but he having withdrawn himself, the resentment of the House fell upon R. Dodsley, the publisher of the work, who was committed to the usher of the black-rod, though Lord Carteret, the Earl of Abingdon, and Lord Talbot, spoke in his behalf.

head; a reinforcement sent out to Admiral Haddock; and an embargo laid on all merchant-ships outward bound. Notwithstanding these preparations of war, Mr. Keene, the British minister at Madrid, declared to the court of Spain that his master, although he had permitted his subjects to make reprisals, would not be understood to have broken the peace; and that this permission would be recalled as soon as his Catholic majesty should be disposed to make the satisfaction which had been so justly demanded. He was given to understand, that the King of Spain looked upon those reprisals as acts of hostility; and that he hoped, with the assistance of heaven and his allies, he should be able to support a good cause against his adversaries. He published a manifesto in justification of his own conduct, complaining that Admiral Haddock had received orders to cruize with his squadron between the capes St. Vincent and St. Mary, in order to surprise the assogue ships; that letters of reprisal had been published at London in an indecent style, and even carried into execution in different parts of the world. He excused his non-payment of the ninety-five thousand pounds stipulated in the convention, by affirming that the British court had first contravened the articles of that treaty, by the orders sent to Haddock; by continuing to fortify Georgia; by reinforcing the squadron at Jamaica; and by eluding the payment of the sixty-eight thousand pounds due to Spain from the South-Sea Company, on the assiento for negroes. The French ambassador at the Hague declared that the king his master was obliged by treaties to assist his Catholic majesty by sea and land, in case he should be attacked; he dissuaded the States-General from espousing the quarrel of Great Britain; and they assured him they would observe a strict neutrality, though they could not avoid furnishing his Britannic majesty with such succours as he could demand, by virtue of the treaties subsisting between the two powers. The people of England were inspired with uncommon alacrity at the near prospect of war, for which they had so long clamoured; and the ministry, seeing it unavoidable, began to be earnest and effectual in their preparations.

The events of war were still unfavourable to the emperor. He had bestowed the command of his army upon Veldt-Mareschal Count Wallis, who assembled his forces in the neighbourhood of Belgrade; and advanced towards Crotska, where he was attacked by the Turks with such impetuosity and perseverance, that he was obliged to give ground, after a long and obstinate engagement, in which he lost above six thousand men. The Earl of Crawford, who served as a volunteer in the imperial army, signalized his courage in an extraordinary manner on this occasion, and received a dangerous wound, of which he never perfectly recovered. The Turks were afterwards worsted at Jabouka; nevertheless, their grand army invested Belgrade on the side of Servia, and carried on the operations of the siege with extraordinary vigour. The emperor, dreading the loss of this place, seeing his finances exhausted, and his army considerably diminished, consented to a negotiation for peace, which was transacted under the mediation of the French ambassador at the Ottoman Porte. The Count de Neuperg, as imperial plenipotentiary, signed the preliminaries on the first day of September. They were ratified by the emperor, though he pretended to be dissatisfied with the articles; and declared that his minister had exceeded his powers. By this treaty the house of Austria ceded to the grand signor, Belgrade, Sabatz, Servia, Austrian Wallachia, the isle and fortress of Orsova, with the fort of St. Elizabeth; and the contracting powers agreed that the Danube and the Saave should serve as boundaries to the two empires. The emperor published a circular letter, addressed to his ministers at all the courts in Europe, blaming Count Wallis for the bad success of the last campaign, and disowning the negotiations of Count Neuperg; nay, these two officers were actually disgraced, and confined in different castles. This, however, was no other than a sacrifice to the resentment of the czarina, who loudly complained that the emperor had concluded a separate peace, contrary to his engagements with the Russian empire. Her general, Count Munich, had obtained a victory over the Turks at Choczim, in Moldavia, and made himself master of that place, in which he found two hundred pieces of artillery; but the country was so ruined by the incursions of the Tartars, that the Muscovites could not subsist in it during the winter. The czarina, finding herself abandoned by the emperor, and unable to cope with the whole power of the Ottoman empire, took the first opportunity of putting an end to the war upon honourable terms. After a short negotiation, the conferences ended in a treaty, by which she was left in possession of Asoph, on condition that its fortifications should be demolished; and the ancient limits were re-established between the two empires.

A rupture between Great Britain and Spain was now become inevitable. The English squadron in the Mediterranean had already made prize of two rich Caracca ships. The king had issued orders for augmenting his land-forces and raising a body of marines; and a great number of ships of war were put in commission. Admiral Vernon had been sent to the West Indies, to assume the command of the squadron in those seas, and to annoy the trade and settlements of the Spaniards. This gentleman had rendered himself considerable in the House of Commons, by loudly condemning all the measures of the ministry, and bluntly speaking his sentiments, whatever they were, without respect of persons, and sometimes without any regard to decorum. He was counted a good officer, and this boisterous manner seemed to enhance his character. As he had once commanded a squadron in Jamaica, he was perfectly well acquainted with those seas; and in a debate upon the Spanish depredations, he chanced to affirm, that Porto Bello, on the Spanish main, might be easily taken; nay, he even undertook to reduce it with six ships only. This offer was echoed from the mouths of all the members in the opposition. Vernon was extolled as another Drake or Raleigh: he became the idol of a party, and his praise resounded from all corners of the kingdom. The minister, in order to appease the clamours of the people on this subject, sent him as commander-in-chief to the West Indies. He was pleased with an opportunity to remove such a troublesome censor from the House of Commons; and, perhaps, he was not without hope, that Vernon would disgrace himself and his party, by failing in the exploit he had undertaken. His Catholic majesty having ordered all the British ships in his harbours to be seized and detained, the King of England would keep measures with him no longer, but denounced war against him on the twenty-third day of October. Many English merchants began to equip privateers, and arm their trading vessels, to protect their own commerce, as well as to distress that of the enemy. The session of Parliament was opened in November, when the king, in his speech to both Houses, declared that he had augmented his forces by sea and land, pursuant to the power vested in him by Parliament for the security of his dominions, the protection of trade, and the annoyance of the enemy; and he expressed his apprehension, that the heats and animosities which had been industriously fomented throughout the kingdom, encouraged Spain to act in such a manner as rendered it necessary for him to have recourse to arms. In answer to this speech, affectionate addresses were presented by both Houses, without any considerable opposition.

*Apology in the House of Commons for the seceding members.*

The seceding members had again resumed their seats in the House of Commons; and Mr. Pulteney thought proper to vindicate the extraordinary step which they had taken. He said, they thought that step was necessary, as affairs then stood, for clearing their characters to posterity from the imputation of sitting in an assembly, where a determined majority gave a sanction to measures evidently to the disgrace of his majesty and the nation. He observed, that their conduct was so fully justified by the declaration of war against Spain, that any further vindication would be superfluous; for every assertion contained in it had been almost in the same words insisted upon by those who opposed the convention: " Every sentence in it (added he) is an echo of what was said in our reasonings against that treaty: every positive truth which the declaration lays down was denied with the utmost confidence by those who spoke for the convention; and since that time there has not one event happened which was not then foreseen and foretold." He proposed, that in maintaining the war, the Spanish settlements in the West Indies should be attacked; and that the ministry should not have the power to give up the conquests that might be made. He said he heartily wished, for his majesty's honour and service, that no mention had been made of heats and animosities in the king's speech; and gave it as his opinion, that they should take no notice of that clause in their address. He was answered by Sir Robert Walpole, who took occasion to say, he was in no great concern lest the service of his majesty or the nation should suffer by the absence of those members who had quitted the House: he affirmed, the nation was generally sensible, that the many useful and popular acts which passed towards the end of the last session were greatly forwarded and facilitated by the secession of those gentlemen ; and, if they were returned only to oppose and perplex, he should not be at all sorry to see them secede again.

Mr. Pulteney revived the bill which he had formerly prepared for the encouragement of seamen. After a long dispute, and eager opposition by the ministry, it passed both Houses, and obtained the royal assent. Mr. Sandys, having observed that there could be no immediate use for a great number of forces in the kingdom, and explained how little service could be expected from raw and undisciplined men, proposed an address to the king, desiring that the body of marines should be composed of drafts from the old regiments; that as few officers should be appointed as the nature of the case would permit; and he expressed his hope that the House would recommend this method to his majesty, in tender compassion to his people, already burdened with many heavy and grievous taxes. This scheme was repugnant to the intention of the ministry, whose aim was to increase the number of their dependents, and extend their parliamentary interest, by granting a great number of commissions. The proposal was, therefore, after a long debate, rejected by the majority. Motions were made for an inquiry into the conduct of those who concluded the convention, but they were overruled. The pension bill was revived, and so powerfully supported by the eloquence of Sir William Wyndham, Mr. Pulteney, and Mr. Lyttelton, that it made its way through the Commons to the Upper House, where it was again lost, upon a division, after a very long debate. As the seamen of the kingdom expressed uncommon aversion to the service of the government, and the fleet could not be manned without great difficulty, the ministry prepared a bill, which was brought in by Sir Charles Wager, for registering all seamen, watermen, fishermen, and lightermen throughout his majesty's dominions. Had this bill passed into a law, a British sailor would have been reduced to the most abject degree of slavery : had he removed from a certain district allotted for the place of his residence, he would have been deemed a deserter, and punished accordingly ; he must have appeared, when summoned, at all hazards, whatever might have been the circumstances of his family, or the state of

*Pension-bill revived and lost.*

his private affairs: had he been encumbered with debt, he must either have incurred the penalties of this law, or lain at the mercy of his creditors: had he acquired by industry, or received by inheritance, an ample fortune, he would have been liable to be torn from his possessions, and subjected to hardships which no man would endure but from the sense of fear or indigence. The bill was so vigorously opposed by Sir John Barnard and others, as a flagrant encroachment on the liberties of the people, that the House rejected it on the second reading.

The king having by message communicated to the House *Porto Bello taken by Admiral Vernon.* his intention of disposing the Princess Mary in marriage to Prince Frederick of Hesse; and expressing his hope, that the Commons would enable him to give a suitable portion to his daughter, they unanimously resolved to grant forty thousand pounds for that purpose; and presented an address of thanks to his majesty, for having communicated to the House this intended marriage. On the thirteenth day of March a ship arrived from the West Indies, despatched by Admiral Vernon, with an account of his having taken Porto Bello, on the isthmus of Darien, with six ships only, and demolished all the fortifications of the place. The Spaniards acted with such pusillanimity on this occasion, that their forts were taken almost without bloodshed. The two Houses of Parliament joined in an address of congratulation upon the success of his majesty's arms; and the nation in general was wonderfully elated by an exploit which was magnified much above its merit. The Commons granted every thing the crown thought proper to demand. They provided for eight-and-twenty thousand land forces, besides six thousand marines. They enabled his majesty to equip a very powerful navy; they voted the subsidy to the King of Denmark; and they empowered their sovereign to defray certain extraordinary expenses not specified in the estimates. To answer these uncommon grants, they imposed a land-tax of four shillings in the pound; and enabled his majesty to deduct twelve hundred thousand pounds from the sinking fund; in a word, the expense of the war, during the course of the ensuing year, amounted to about four millions. The session was closed on the twenty-ninth day of April, when the king thanked the Commons for the supplies they had so liberally granted, and recommended union and moderation to both Houses.

During the greatest part of this winter, the poor had been grievously afflicted in consequence of a severe frost, which began at Christmas, and continued till the latter end of February. The river Thames was covered with such a crust of ice that a multitude of people dwelled upon it in tents, and a great number of booths were erected for the entertainment of the populace. The navigation was entirely stopped: the watermen and fishermen were disabled from earning a livelihood: the fruits of the earth were destroyed by the cold, which was so extreme that many persons were chilled to death; and this calamity was the more deeply felt, as the poor could not afford to supply themselves with coals and fuel, which were advanced in price, in proportion to the severity and continuance of the frost. The lower class of labourers, who worked in the open air, were now deprived of all means of subsistence: many kinds of manufacture were laid aside, because it was found impracticable to carry them on. The price of all sorts of provisions rose almost to a dearth; even water was sold in the streets of London. In this season of distress, many wretched families must have perished by cold and hunger, had not those of opulent fortunes been inspired with a remarkable spirit of compassion and humanity. Nothing can more redound to the honour of the English nation than did those instances of benevolence and well-conducted charity which were then exhibited. The liberal hand was not only opened to the professed beggar, and the poor that owned their distress; but uncommon pains were taken to find out and relieve those more unhappy objects, who, from motives of false pride or ingenuous shame, endeavoured to conceal their misery. These were assisted almost in their own despite. The solitary habitations of the widow, the fatherless, and the unfortunate, were visited by the beneficent, who felt for the woes of their fellow-creatures; and, to such as refused to receive a portion of the public charity, the necessaries of life were privately conveyed, in such a manner as could least shock the delicacy of their dispositions.

In the beginning of May the King of Great Britain set out for Hanover, after having appointed a regency, and concerted vigorous measures for distressing the enemy. In a few days after his departure, the espousals of the Princess Mary were celebrated by proxy, the Duke of Cumberland representing the Prince of Hesse; and in June the princess embarked for the continent. About the same time, a sloop arrived in England with despatches from Admiral Vernon, who, since his adventure at Porto Bello, had bombarded Carthagena, and taken the fort of San Lorenzo, on the river of Chagre, in the neighbourhood of his former conquest. This month was likewise marked by the death of his Prussian majesty, a prince by no means remarkable for great or amiable qualities. He was succeeded on the throne by Frederick his eldest son, the late king of that realm, who has so eminently distinguished himself as a warrior and legislator. In August, the King of Great Britain concluded a treaty with the Landgrave of Hesse, who engaged to furnish him with a body of six thousand men for four years, in consideration of an annual subsidy of two hundred and fifty thousand crowns.

Meanwhile, preparations of war were vigorously carried on by the ministry in England. They had wisely resolved to annoy the Spaniards in their American possessions. Three ships of war, cruising in the bay of Biscay, fell in with a large Spanish ship of the line strongly manned, and took her after a very obstinate engagement; but the assogue ships arrived, with the treasure, in Spain, notwithstanding the vigilance of the English commanders, who were stationed in a certain latitude to intercept that flota. One camp was formed on Hounslow-heath; and six thousand marines lately levied were encamped on the Isle of Wight, in order to be embarked for the West Indies. Intelligence being received, that a strong squadron of Spanish ships of war waited at Ferrol for orders to sail to their American settlements, Sir John Norris sailed with a powerful fleet from Spithead, to dispute their voyage; and the Duke of Cumberland served in person as a volunteer in this expedition; but after divers fruitless efforts, he was, by contrary winds, obliged to lie inactive for the greatest part of the summer in Torbay; and, upon advice that the French and Spanish squadrons had sailed to the West Indies in conjunction, the design against Ferrol was wholly laid aside. In September, a small squadron of ships, commanded by Commodore Anson, set sail for the South-Sea, in order to act against the enemy on the coast of Chili and Peru, and co-operate occasionally with Admiral Vernon across the isthmus of

*Strong armament sent to the West Indies.*

Darien. The scheme was well laid, but ruined by unnecessary delays and unforeseen accidents. But the hopes of the nation centred chiefly in a formidable armament designed for the northern coast of New Spain, and his Catholic majesty's other settlements on that side of the Atlantic. Commissions had been issued for raising a regiment of four battalions in the English colonies of North America, that they might be transported to Jamaica, and join the forces from England. These, consisting of the marines, and detachments from some old regiments, were embarked in October at the Isle of Wight, under the command of Lord Cathcart, a nobleman of approved honour, and great experience in the art of war; and they sailed under convoy of Sir Chaloner Ogle, with a fleet of seven-and-twenty ships of the line, besides frigates, fire-ships, bomb-ketches, and tenders. They were likewise furnished with hospital-ships, and store-ships, laden with provisions, ammunition, all sorts of warlike implements, and every kind of convenience. Never was an armament more completely equipped; and never had the nation more reason to hope for extraordinary success.

On the twentieth day of October, Charles VI. Emperor of Germany, the last prince of the house of Austria, died at Vienna, and was succeeded in his hereditary dominions by his eldest daughter, the Archduchess Maria Theresa, married to the Grand Duke of Tuscany. Though this princess succeeded as Queen of Hungary, by virtue of the pragmatic sanction guaranteed by all the powers in Europe, her succession produced such contests as kindled a cruel war in the empire. The young King of Prussia was no sooner informed of the emperor's death, than he entered Silesia at the head of twenty thousand men; seized certain fiefs to which his family laid claim; and published a manifesto, declaring that he had no intention to contravene the pragmatic sanction. The Elector of Bavaria refused to acknowledge the archduchess as Queen of Hungary and Bohemia; alleging, that he himself had pretensions to those countries, as the descendant of the Emperor Ferdinand I., who was head of the German branch of the house of Austria. Charles VI. was survived but a few days by his ally, the Czarina Anne Iwanowna, who died in the forty-fifth year of her age, after having bequeathed her crown to Iwan, or John, the infant son of her niece, the Princess Anne of Mecklenburgh, who had been married to Anthony Ulrick, Duke of Brunswick Lunenbourg-Bevern. She appointed the Duke of Courland regent of the empire, and even guardian of the young czar, though his own parents were alive; but this disposition was not long maintained.

*Proceedings in Parliament.* The King of Great Britain having returned to England from his German dominions, the session of Parliament was opened in November. His majesty assured them, on this occasion, that he was determined to prosecute the war vigorously, even though France should espouse the cause of Spain, as her late conduct seemed to favour this supposition. He took notice of the emperor's death, as an event which in all likelihood would open a new scene of affairs in Europe; he therefore recommended to their consideration the necessary supplies for putting the nation in such a posture, that it should have nothing to fear from any emergency. Finally, he desired them to consider of some proper regulations for preventing the exportation of corn, and for more effectual methods to man the fleet at this conjuncture. The Commons, after having voted an address of thanks, brought in a bill for prohibiting the exportation of corn and provisions, for a limited time, out of Great Britain, Ireland, and the American plantations. This was a measure calculated to distress the enemy, who were supposed to be in want of these necessaries. The French had contracted for a very large quantity of beef and pork in Ireland for the use of their own and the Spanish navy; and an embargo had been laid upon the ships of that kingdom. The bill met with a vigorous opposition; yet the House unanimously resolved, that his majesty should be addressed to lay an immediate embargo upon all ships laden with corn, grain, starch, rice, beef, pork, and other provisions to be exported to foreign parts. They likewise resolved that the thanks of the House should be given to Vice-Admiral Vernon, for the services he had done to his king and country in the West Indies. One William Cooley was examined at the bar of the House, and committed to prison, after having owned himself author of a paper, entitled " Considerations upon the Embargo on Provision of Victual." The performance contained many shrewd and severe animadversions upon the government, for having taken a step which, without answering the purpose of distressing the enemy, would prove a grievous discouragement to trade, and ruin all the graziers of Ireland. Notwithstanding the arguments used in this remonstrance, and several petitions that were presented against the corn-bill, it passed by mere dint of ministerial influence. The other party endeavoured, by various motions, to set on foot an inquiry into the orders, letters, and instructions, which had been sent to Admiral Vernon and Admiral Haddock; but all such investigations were carefully avoided.

A very hot contest arose from a bill which the ministry brought in under the specious title of "A bill for the encouragement and increase of seamen, and for the better and speedier manning his majesty's fleet." This was a revival of the oppressive scheme which had been rejected in the former session; a scheme by which the justices of the peace were empowered to issue warrants to constables and headboroughs, to search by day or night for such seafaring men as should conceal themselves within their respective jurisdictions. These searchers were vested with authority to force open doors in case of resistance; and encouraged to this violence by a reward for every seaman they should discover; while the unhappy wretches so discovered were dragged into the service, and their names entered in a register to be kept at the navy or the admiralty office. Such a plan of tyranny did not pass uncensured. Every exceptionable clause produced a warm debate, in which Sir John Barnard, Mr. Pulteney, Mr. Sandys, Lord Gage, Mr. Pitt, and Mr. Lyttelton, signalized themselves nobly in defending the liberties of their fellow-subjects. Mr. Pitt having expressed a laudable indignation at such a large stride towards despotic power, in justification of which nothing could be urged but the plea of necessity, Mr. H. Walpole thought proper to attack him with some personal sarcasms. He reflected upon his youth; and observed that the discovery of truth was very little promoted by pompous diction and theatrical emotion. These insinuations exposed him to a severe reply. Mr. Pitt, standing up again, said, "He would not undertake to determine whether youth could be justly imputed to any man as a reproach; but he affirmed, that the wretch, who, after having seen the consequences of repeated errors, continues still to blunder, and whose age has only added obstinacy to stupidity, is surely the object of either abhorrence or contempt, and deserves not that his gray head should secure him from insults; much more is he, to be abhorred, who, as he has advanced in age, has receded from virtue, and becomes more wicked with less temptation; who prostitutes himself for money which he cannot enjoy; and spends the remains of his life in the ruin of his country." Petitions were presented from the city of London, and county of Gloucester, against the bill, as detrimental to the trade and navigation of the kingdom, by discouraging rather than encouraging sailors, and destructive to the liberties of the subject; but they were both rejected as insults upon the House of Commons. After very long debates, maintained on both sides with extraordinary ardour and emotion, the severe clauses were dropped, and the bill passed with amendments.

But the most remarkable incident of this session was an open and personal attack upon the minister, who was become extremely unpopular all over the kingdom. The people were now more than ever sensible of the grievous taxes under which they groaned; and saw their burdens daily increasing. No effectual attempt had as yet been made to annoy the enemy. Expensive squadrons had been equipped, had made excursions, and returned without striking a blow. The Spanish fleet had sailed first from Cadiz, and then from Ferrol, without any interruption from Admiral Haddock, who commanded the British squadron in the Mediterranean, and who was supposed to be restricted by the instructions he had received from the ministry, though in fact his want of success was owing to accident. Admiral Vernon had written from the West Indies to his private friends, that he was neglected, and in danger of being sacrificed. Notwithstanding the numerous navy which the nation maintained, the Spanish privateers made prize of the British merchant-ships with impunity. In violation of treaties, and in contempt of that intimate connexion which had been so long cultivated between the French and English ministry, the King of France had ordered the harbour and fortifications of Dunkirk to be repaired; his fleet had sailed to the West Indies, in conjunction with that of Spain; and the merchants of England began to tremble for Jamaica: finally, commerce was in a manner suspended, by the practice of pressing sailors into the service, and by the embargo which had been laid upon ships, in all the ports of Great Britain and Ireland. These causes of popular discontent, added to other complaints which had been so long repeated against the minister, exaggerated and inculcated by his enemies with unwearied industry, at length rendered him so universally odious, that his name was seldom or never mentioned with decency, except by his own dependents.

The country party in Parliament seized this opportunity of vengeance. Mr. Sandys went up to Sir Robert Walpole in the House, and told him, that on Friday next he should bring a charge against him in public. The minister seemed to be surprised at this unexpected intimation; but, after a short pause, thanked him politely for this previous notice, and said he desired no favour, but fair play.* Mr. Sandys, at the time which he had appointed for this accusation, stood up, and in a studied speech entered into a long deduction of the minister's misconduct. He insisted upon the discontents of the nation, in consequence of the measures which had been for many years pursued at home and abroad. He professed his belief that there was not a gentleman in the House who did not know that one single person in the administration was the chief, if not the sole adviser and promoter of all those measures. "This (added he) is known without doors, as well as within; therefore, the discontents, the reproaches, and even the curses of the people, are all directed against that single person. They complain of present measures; they have suffered by past measures; they expect no redress; they expect no alteration or amendment, whilst he has a share in directing or advising our future administration. These, sir, are the sentiments of the people in regard to that minister: these sentiments we are in honour and duty bound to represent to his majesty; and the proper method for doing this, as established by our constitution, is to address his majesty to remove him from his councils." He then proceeded to explain the particulars of the minister's misconduct in the whole series of his negotiations abroad. He charged him with having endeavoured to support his own interest, and to erect a kind of despotic government, by the practice of corruption; with having betrayed the interest and honour of Great Britain in the late convention; with having neglected to prosecute the war against Spain; and he concluded with a motion for an address to the king, that

*Motion for removing Sir Robert Walpole from his majesty's councils and presence for ever.*

---

* Upon this occasion he misquoted Horace. "As I am not conscious of any crime (said he), I do not doubt of being able to make a proper defence." *Nil conscire sibi, nulli pallescere culpæ.* He was corrected by Mr. Pulteney; but insisted upon his being in the right, and actually laid a wager on the justness of his quotation.

he would be pleased to remove Sir Robert Walpole from his presence and councils for ever. He was answered by Mr. Pelham, who undertook to defend or excuse all the measures which the other had condemned; and acquitted himself as a warm friend and unshaken adherent. Against this champion Sir John Barnard entered the lists, and was sustained by Mr. Pulteney, who, with equal spirit and precision, pointed out and exposed all the material errors and mal-practices of the administration. Sir Robert Walpole spoke with great temper and deliberation in behalf of himself. With respect to the article of bribery and corruption, he said, if any one instance had been mentioned; if it had been shown that he ever offered a reward to any member of either House, or ever threatened to deprive any member of his office or employment, in order to influence his voting in Parliament, there might have been some ground for this charge; but when it was so generally laid, he did not know what he could say to it, unless to deny it as generally and as positively as it had been asserted.—Such a declaration as this, in the hearing of so many persons, who not only knew, but subsisted by his wages of corruption, was a strong proof of the minister's being dead to all sense of shame, and all regard to veracity. The debate was protracted by the court members till three o'clock in the morning, when, about sixty of the opposite party having retired, the motion was rejected by a considerable majority.

<small>Debate on the mutiny bill.</small> A bill was brought in for prohibiting the practice of insuring ships belonging to the enemies of the nation; but it was vigorously opposed by Sir John Barnard and Mr. Willimot, who demonstrated that this kind of traffic was advantageous to the kingdom; and the scheme was dropped. Another warm contest arose upon a clause of the mutiny bill, relating to the quartering of soldiers upon innkeepers and publicans, who complained of their being distressed in furnishing those guests with provisions and necessaries at the rates prescribed by law or custom. There were not wanting advocates to expatiate upon the nature of this grievance, which, however, was not redressed. A new trade was at this time opened with Persia, through the dominions of the czar, and vested with an exclusive privilege in the Russian company, by an act of Parliament. The Commons voted forty thousand seamen for the service of the ensuing year, and about thirty thou-

sand men for the establishment of land-forces. They provided for the subsidies granted to the King of Denmark and the Landgrave of Hesse-Cassel; and took every step which was suggested for the ease and the convenience of the government.

The parties in the House of Lords were influenced by the same motives which actuated the Commons. The Duke of Argyle, who had by this time resigned all his places, declared open war against the ministry. *Proceedings in the House of Lords.* In the beginning of the session, the king's speech was no sooner reported by the chancellor, than this nobleman stood up, and moved that a general address of thanks should be presented to his majesty, instead of a recapitulation of every paragraph of the king's speech re-echoed from the Parliament to the throne, with expressions of blind approbation, implying a general concurrence with all the measures of the minister. He spoke on this subject with an astonishing impetuosity of eloquence, that rolled like a river which had overflowed its banks and deluged the whole adjacent country. The motion was supported by Lord Bathurst, Lord Carteret, the Earl of Chesterfield, and Lord Gower, who, though they displayed all the talents of oratory, were outvoted by the opposite party, headed by the Duke of Newcastle, the Earl of Cholmondeley, Lord Hervey, and the Lord Chancellor. The motion was rejected, and the address composed in the usual strain. The same motions for an inquiry into orders and instructions, which had miscarried in the Lower House, were here repeated with the same bad success: in the debates which ensued, the young Earls of Halifax and Sandwich acquired a considerable share of reputation, for the strength of argument and elocution with which they contended against the adherents of the ministry. When the House took into consideration the state of the army, the Duke of Argyle, having harangued with equal skill and energy on military affairs, proposed that the forces should be augmented by adding new levies to the old companies, without increasing the number of officers; as such an augmentation served only to debase the dignity of the service, by raising the lowest of mankind to the rank of gentlemen; and to extend the influence of the minister, by multiplying his dependents. He therefore moved for a resolution, that the augmenting the army by raising regiments, as it is the most unnecessary and most expensive method of augmentation, was also the most dangerous to the liberties of the nation. This proposal was likewise overruled, after a short though warm contention. This was the fate of all the other motions made by the lords in the opposition, though the victory of the courtiers was always clogged with a nervous and spirited protest. Two days were expended in the debate produced by Lord Carteret's motion for an address, beseeching his majesty to remove Sir Robert Walpole from his presence and councils for ever. The speech that ushered in this memorable motion would not have disgraced a Cicero. It contained a retrospect of all the public measures which had been pursued since the Revolution. It explained the nature of every treaty, whether right or wrong, which had been concluded under the present administration. It described the political connexions subsisting between the different powers in Europe. It exposed the weakness, the misconduct, and the iniquity of the minister, both in his foreign and domestic transactions. It was embellished with all the ornaments of rhetoric, and warmed with a noble spirit of patriotic indignation. The Duke of Argyle, Lord Bathurst, and his other colleagues, seemed to be animated with uncommon fervour, and even inspired, by the subject. A man of imagination, in reading their speeches, will think himself transported into the Roman senate, before the ruin of that republic. Nevertheless, the minister still triumphed by dint of numbers; though his victory was dearly purchased. Thirty peers entered a vigorous protest; and Walpole's character sustained such a rude shock from this opposition, that his authority seemed to be drawing near a period. Immediately after this contest was decided, the Duke of Marlborough moved for a resolution, that any attempt to inflict any kind of punishment on any person, without allowing him an opportunity to make his defence, or without any proof of any crime or misdemeanour committed by him, is contrary to natural justice, the fundamental laws of the realm, and the ancient established usage of Parliament; and is a high infringement of the liberties of the subject. It was seconded by the Duke of Devonshire and Lord Lovel; and opposed by Lord Gower, as an intended censure on the proceedings of the day. This sentiment was so warmly espoused by Lord Talbot, who had distinguished himself in the former debate, that he seemed to be transported beyond the bounds of moderation. He was interrupted by the Earl of Cholmondeley, who charged him with having violated the order and decorum which ought to be preserved in such an assembly. His passion was inflamed by this rebuke; he declared himself an independent lord; a character which he would not forfeit for the smiles of a court, the profit of an employment, or the reward of a pension: he said, when he was engaged on the side of truth, he would trample on the insolence that should command him to suppress his sentiments.—On a division, however, the motion was carried.

In the beginning of April, the king, repairing to the House of Peers, passed some acts that were ready for the royal assent. Then, in his speech to both Houses, he gave them to understand, that the Queen of Hungary had made a requisition of the twelve thousand men stipulated by treaty; and that he had ordered the subsidy-troops of Denmark and Hesse-Cassel to be in readiness to march to her assistance. He observed, that in this complicated and uncertain state of affairs many incidents might arise, and render it necessary for him to incur extraordinary expenses for maintaining the pragmatic sanction, at a time when he could not possibly have recourse to the advice and assistance of his Parliament. He therefore demanded of the Commons such a supply as might be requisite for these ends; and promised to manage it with all possible frugality. The Lower House, in their address, approved of all his measures; declared they would effectually support him against all insults and attacks that might be made upon any of his territories, though not belonging to the crown of Great Britain; and that they would enable him to contribute, in the most effectual manner, to the support of the Queen of Hungary. Sir Robert Walpole moved, that an aid of two hundred thousand pounds should be granted to that princess. Mr. Shippen protested against any interposition in the affairs of Germany. He expressed his dislike of the promise which had been made to defend his majesty's foreign dominions; a promise, in his opinion, inconsistent with that important and inviolable law, the act of settlement; a promise which, could it have been foreknown, would perhaps have for ever precluded from the succession that illustrious family to which the nation owed such numberless blessings, such continued felicity. The motion however passed, though not without further opposi-

*Close of the last session of this Parliament.*

tion; and the House resolved that three hundred thousand pounds should be granted to his majesty, to enable him effectually to support the Queen of Hungary. Towards the expense of this year, a million was deducted from the sinking-fund; and the land-tax continued at four shillings in the pound. The preparations for this war had already cost five millions. The session was closed on the twenty-fifth day of April, when the king took his leave of this Parliament, with warm expressions of tenderness and satisfaction. Henry Bromley, Stephen Fox, and John Howe, three members of the Lower House, who had signalized themselves in defence of the minister, were now ennobled, and created Barons of Montfort, Ilchester, and Chedworth. A camp was formed near Colchester; and the king, having appointed a regency, set out in May for his German dominions.[d]

[d] Sir William Wyndham died in the preceding year, deeply regretted as an orator, a patriot, and a man, the constant asserter of British liberty, and one of the chief ornaments of the English nation. In the course of the same year, General Oglethorpe, governor of Georgia, had, with some succours obtained from the colony of Carolina, and a small squadron of the king's ships, made an attempt upon Fort Augustine, the capital of Spanish Florida; and actually reduced some small forts in the neighbourhood of the place; but the Carolinians withdrawing in disgust, dissensions prevailing among the sea-officers, the hurricane months approaching, and the enemy having received a supply and reinforcements, he abandoned the enterprise, and returned to Georgia.

## CHAPTER XVIII.

THE ARMY UNDER LORD CATHCART AND SIR CHALONER OGLE PROCEEDS TO THE WEST INDIES. — NATURE OF THE CLIMATE ON THE SPANISH MAIN. — ADMIRAL VERNON SAILS TO CARTHAGENA. — ATTACK OF FORT LAZAR. — EXPEDITION TO CUBA. — RUPTURE BETWEEN THE QUEEN OF HUNGARY AND THE KING OF PRUSSIA. — BATTLE OF MOLWITZ. — THE KING OF GREAT BRITAIN CONCLUDES A TREATY OF NEUTRALITY WITH FRANCE FOR THE ELECTORATE OF HANOVER. — A BODY OF FRENCH FORCES JOINS THE ELECTOR OF BAVARIA. — HE IS CROWNED KING OF BOHEMIA AT PRAGUE. — FIDELITY OF THE HUNGARIANS. — WAR BETWEEN RUSSIA AND SWEDEN. — REVOLUTION IN RUSSIA. — THE SPANISH AND FRENCH SQUADRONS PASS UNMOLESTED BY THE ENGLISH ADMIRAL IN THE MEDITERRANEAN. — INACTIVITY OF THE NAVAL POWER OF GREAT BRITAIN. — OBSTINATE STRUGGLE IN ELECTING MEMBERS IN THE NEW PARLIAMENT. — REMARKABLE MOTION IN THE HOUSE OF COMMONS BY LORD NOEL SOMERSET. — THE COUNTRY PARTY OBTAIN A MAJORITY IN THE HOUSE OF COMMONS. — SIR ROBERT WALPOLE CREATED EARL OF ORFORD. — CHANGE IN THE MINISTRY. — INQUIRY INTO THE ADMINISTRATION OF SIR ROBERT WALPOLE. — OBSTRUCTED BY THE NEW MINISTRY. — REPORTS OF THE SECRET COMMITTEE. — THE ELECTOR OF BAVARIA CHOSEN EMPEROR. — THE KING OF PRUSSIA GAINS THE BATTLE OF CZASLAU. — TREATY AT BRESLAU. — THE FRENCH TROOPS RETIRE UNDER THE CANNON OF PRAGUE. — A FRESH BODY SENT WITH THE MARESCHAL DE MAILLEBOIS TO BRING THEM OFF. — EXTRAORDINARY RETREAT OF M. DE BELLEISLE. — THE KING OF GREAT BRITAIN FORMS AN ARMY IN FLANDERS. — PROGRESS OF THE WAR BETWEEN RUSSIA AND SWEDEN. — THE KING OF SARDINIA DECLARES FOR THE HOUSE OF AUSTRIA. — MOTIONS OF THE SPANIARDS IN ITALY AND SAVOY. — CONDUCT OF ADMIRAL MATTHEWS IN THE MEDITERRANEAN. — OPERATIONS IN THE WEST INDIES. — THE ATTENTION OF THE MINISTRY TURNED CHIEFLY ON THE AFFAIRS OF THE CONTINENT. — EXTRAORDINARY MOTION IN THE HOUSE OF LORDS BY EARL STANHOPE. — WARM AND OBSTINATE DEBATE ON THE REPEAL OF THE GIN ACT. — BILL FOR QUIETING CORPORATIONS. — CONVENTION BETWEEN THE EMPEROR AND THE QUEEN OF HUNGARY. — DIFFERENCE BETWEEN THE KING OF PRUSSIA AND THE ELECTOR OF HANOVER. — THE KING OF GREAT BRITAIN OBTAINS A VICTORY OVER THE FRENCH AT DETTINGEN. — TREATY OF WORMS. — CONCLUSION OF THE CAMPAIGN. — AFFAIRS IN THE NORTH. — BATTLE OF CAMPO-SANTO. — TRANSACTIONS OF THE BRITISH FLEET IN THE MEDITERRANEAN. — UNSUCCESSFUL ATTEMPTS UPON THE SPANISH SETTLEMENTS IN THE WEST INDIES.

THE British armament had by this time proceeded to action in the West Indies. Sir Chaloner Ogle, who sailed from Spithead, had been overtaken by a tempest in the bay of Biscay, by which the fleet, consisting of about one hundred and seventy sail, were scattered and dispersed. Nevertheless, he prosecuted his voyage, and anchored with a view to provide wood and water in the neutral island of Dominica, where the intended expedition sustained a terrible shock in the death of the gallant Lord Cathcart, who was carried off by a dysentery. The loss of this nobleman was the more severely felt, as the command of the land-forces devolved upon

1741. The army under Lord Cathcart and Sir Chaloner Ogle proceeds to the West Indies.

General Wentworth, an officer without experience, authority, or resolution. As the fleet sailed along the island of Hispaniola, in its way to Jamaica, four large ships of war were discovered; and Sir Chaloner detached an equal number of his squadron to give them chase, while he himself proceeded on his voyage. As those strange ships refused to bring to, Lord Augustus Fitzroy, the commodore of the four British ships, saluted one of them with a broadside, and a smart engagement ensued. After they had fought during the best part of the night, the enemy hoisted their colours in the morning, and appeared to be part of the French squadron, which had sailed from Europe, under the command of the Marquis d'Antin, with orders to assist the Spanish Admiral de Torres, in attacking and distressing the English ships and colonies. War was not yet declared between France and England; therefore hostilities ceased: the English and French commanders complimented each other; excused themselves mutually for the mistake which had happened; and parted as friends, with a considerable loss of men on both sides.

In the mean time Sir Chaloner Ogle arrived at Jamaica, where he joined Vice-Admiral Vernon, who now found himself at the head of the most formidable fleet and army that ever visited those seas, with full power to act at discretion. The conjoined squadrons consisted of nine-and-twenty ships of the line, with almost an equal number of frigates, fire-ships, and bomb-ketches, well manned and plentifully supplied with all kinds of provisions, stores, and necessaries. The number of seamen amounted to fifteen thousand; that of the land-forces, including the American regiment of four battalions, and a body of negroes enlisted at Jamaica, did not fall short of twelve thousand. Had this armament been ready to act in the proper season of the year, under the conduct of wise, experienced officers, united in councils, and steadily attached to the interest and honour of their country, the Havannah and the whole island of Cuba might have been easily reduced; the whole treasure of the Spanish West Indies would have been intercepted; and Spain must have been humbled into the most abject submission. But several unfavourable circumstances concurred to frustrate the hopes of the public. The ministry had detained Sir Chaloner Ogle at Spithead without any visible cause, until the season for action was almost exhausted; for, on the continent of New Spain, the periodical rains begin about the end of April; and this change in the atmosphere is always attended with epidemical distempers, which render the climate extremely unhealthy; besides, the rain is so excessive, that for the space of two months no army can keep the field.

Sir Chaloner Ogle arrived at Jamaica on the ninth day of January; and Admiral Vernon did not sail on his intended expedition till towards the end of the month. Instead of directing his course to the Havannah, which lay to leeward, and might have been reached in less than three days, he resolved to beat up against the wind to Hispaniola, in order to observe the motions of the French squadron commanded by the Marquis d'Antin. The fifteenth day of February had elapsed before he received certain information that the French admiral had sailed for Europe, in great distress, for want of men and provisions, which he could not procure in the West Indies. Admiral Vernon, thus disappointed, called a council of war, in which it was determined to proceed for Carthagena. The fleet, being supplied with wood and water at Hispaniola, set sail for the continent of New Spain, and on the fourth of March anchored in Playa Grande, to the windward of Carthagena. Admiral de Torres had already sailed to the Havannah; but Carthagena was strongly fortified, and the garrison reinforced by the crews of a small squadron of large ships commanded by Don Blas de Leso, an officer of experience and reputation. Here the English admiral lay inactive till the ninth, when the troops were landed on the island of Tierra Bomba, near the mouth of the harbour, known by the name of Bocachica, or Little-mouth, which was surprisingly fortified with castles, batteries, booms, chains, cables, and ships of war. The British forces erected a battery on shore, with which they made a breach in the principal fort, while the admiral sent in a number of ships to divide the fire of the enemy, and co-operate with the endeavours of the army. Lord Aubrey Beauclerc, a gallant officer, who commanded one of these ships, was slain on this occasion. The breach being deemed practicable, the forces advanced to the attack; but the forts and batteries were abandoned; the Spanish ships that lay athwart the harbour's mouth were destroyed or taken; the passage was opened, and the fleet entered without further opposition. Then the forces were re-embarked with the artillery, and landed within a mile of Carthagena, where they were opposed by about seven hundred Spaniards, whom they obliged to retire. The admiral and general had contracted a hearty contempt for each other, and took all opportunities of expressing their mutual dislike: far from acting vigorously in concert, for the advantage of the community, they maintained a mutual reserve, and separate cabals; and each proved more eager for the disgrace of his rival, than zealous for the honour of the nation.

The general complained that the fleet lay idle while his troops were harassed and diminished by hard duty and distemper. The admiral affirmed, that his ships could not lie near enough to batter the town of Carthagena: he upbraided the general with inactivity and want of resolution to attack the fort of St. Lazar, which commanded the town, and might be taken by scalade. Wentworth, stimulated by these reproaches, resolved to try the experiment. His forces marched up to the attack; but the guides being slain, they mistook their route, and advanced to the strongest part of the fortification, where they were moreover exposed to the fire of the town. Colonel Grant, who commanded the grenadiers, was mortally wounded: the scaling ladders were found too short: the officers were perplexed for want of orders and directions: yet the soldiers sustained a severe fire for several hours with surprising intrepidity, and at length retreated, leaving about six hundred killed or wounded on the spot. Their number was now so much reduced, that they could no longer maintain their footing on shore; besides, the rainy season had begun with such violence, as rendered it impossible for them to live in camp: they were, therefore, re-embarked; and all hope of further success immediately vanished. The admiral, however, in order to demonstrate the impracticability of taking the place by sea, sent in the Gallicia, one of the Spanish ships which had been taken at Boca-chica, to cannonade the town, with sixteen guns mounted on one side, like a floating battery. This vessel, manned by detachments of volunteers from different ships, and commanded by Captain Hoare, was warped into the inner harbour, and moored before day, at a considerable distance from the walls, in very shallow water. In this position she stood the fire of several batteries for some

*Attack of Fort Lazar.*

hours, without doing or sustaining much damage: then the admiral ordered the men to be brought off in boats, and the cables to be cut; so that she drove with the sea-breeze upon a shoal, where she was soon filled with water. This exploit was absurd, and the inference which the admiral drew from it altogether fallacious: he said it plainly proved that there was not depth of water in the inner harbour sufficient to admit large ships near enough to batter the town with any prospect of success. This, indeed, was the case in that part of the harbour to which the Gallicia was conducted; but a little farther to the left, he might have stationed four or five of his largest ships abreast, within pistol-shot of the walls; and if this step had been taken, when the land-forces marched to the attack of St. Lazar, in all probability the town would have been surrendered.

After the re-embarkation of the troops, the distempers peculiar to the climate and season began to rage *Expedition to Cuba.* with redoubled fury; and great numbers of those who escaped the vengeance of the enemy perished by a more painful and inglorious fate. Nothing was heard but complaints and execrations; the groans of the dying, and the service for the dead: nothing was seen but objects of woe, and images of dejection. The conductors of this unfortunate expedition agreed in nothing but the expediency of a speedy retreat from this scene of misery and disgrace. The fortifications of the harbour were demolished, and the fleet returned to Jamaica.—The miscarriage of this expedition, which had cost the nation an immense sum of money, was no sooner known in England, than the kingdom was filled with murmurs and discontent, and the people were depressed in proportion to that sanguine hope by which they had been elevated. Admiral Vernon, instead of undertaking any enterprise which might have retrieved the honour of the British arms, set sail from Jamaica with the forces in July, and anchored at the south-east part of Cuba, in a bay on which he bestowed the appellation of Cumberland Harbour. The troops were landed, and encamped at the distance of twenty miles further up the river, where they remained totally inactive, and subsisted chiefly on salt and damaged provisions, till the month of November, when, being considerably diminished by sickness, they were put on board again, and reconveyed to Jamaica.

He was afterwards reinforced from England by four ships of war, and about three thousand soldiers; but he performed nothing worthy of the reputation he had acquired; and the people began to perceive that they had mistaken his character.

The affairs on the continent of Europe were now more than ever embroiled. The King of Prussia had demanded of the court of Vienna part of Silesia, by virtue of old treaties of co-fraternity, which were either obsolete or annulled; and promised to assist the queen with all his forces, in case she should comply with his demand; but this being rejected with disdain, he entered Silesia at the head of an army, and prosecuted his conquests with great rapidity. In the mean time the Queen of Hungary was crowned at Presburgh, after having signed a capitulation, by which the liberties of that kingdom were confirmed; and the grand duke, her consort, was, at her request, associated with her for ten years in the government. At the same time the states of Hungary refused to receive a memorial from the Elector of Bavaria. During these transactions, his Prussian majesty made his public entrance into Breslau, and confirmed all the privileges of the inhabitants. One of his generals surprised the town and fortress of Jablunka, on the confines of Hungary: Prince Leopold of Anhalt-Dessau, who commanded another army, which formed the blockade of Great Glogau, on the Oder, took the place by scalade, made the Generals Wallis and Reyski prisoners, with a thousand men that were in garrison: here, likewise, the victor found the military chest, fifty pieces of brass cannon, and a great quantity of ammunition.

*Rupture between the Queen of Hungary and the King of Prussia.*

The Queen of Hungary had solicited the maritime powers for assistance, but found them fearful and backward. Being obliged, therefore, to exert herself with the more vigour, she ordered Count Neuperg to assemble a body of forces, and endeavour to stop the progress of the Prussians in Silesia. The two armies encountered each other in the neighbourhood of Neiss, at a village called Molwitz; and, after an obstinate dispute, the Austrians were obliged to retire, with the loss of four thousand men, killed, wounded, or taken. The advantage was dearly purchased by the King of Prussia. His kinsman, Frederick, Margrave of Brandenburgh, and Lieutenant-General

*Battle of Molwitz.*

Schuylemberg, were killed in the engagement, together with a great number of general officers, and about two thousand soldiers. After this action, Brieg was surrendered to the Prussian, and he forced the important pass of Fryewalde, which was defended by four thousand Austrian hussars. The English and Dutch ministers, who accompanied him in his progress, spared no pains to effect an accommodation; but the two sovereigns were too much irritated against each other to acquiesce in any terms that could be proposed. The Queen of Hungary was incensed to find herself attacked, in the day of her distress, by a prince to whom she had given no sort of provocation; and his Prussian majesty charged the court of Vienna with a design either to assassinate, or carry him off by treachery; a design which was disowned with expressions of indignation and disdain. Count Neuperg being obliged to abandon Silesia, in order to oppose the Bavarian arms in Bohemia, the King of Prussia sent thither a detachment to join the elector, under the command of Count Deslau, who, in his route, reduced Glatz and Neiss, almost without opposition; then his master received the homage of the Silesian states at Breslau, and returned to Berlin. In December the Prussian army was distributed in winter-quarters in Moravia, after having taken Olmutz, the capital of that province; and in March his Prussian majesty formed a camp of observation in the neighbourhood of Magdeburgh.

The Elector of Hanover was alarmed at the success of the King of Prussia, in apprehension that he would become too formidable a neighbour. A scheme was said to have been proposed to the court of Vienna for attacking that prince's electoral dominions, and dividing the conquest; but it never was put in execution. Nevertheless, the troops of Hanover were augmented: the auxiliary Danes and Hessians in the pay of Great Britain were ordered to be in readiness to march; and a good number of British forces encamped and prepared for embarkation. The subsidy of three hundred thousand pounds granted by Parliament, was remitted to the Queen of Hungary; and every thing seemed to presage the vigorous interposition of his Britannic majesty. But in a little time after his arrival at Hanover, that spirit of action seemed to flag, even while her Hungarian majesty tottered on the verge of ruin. *The King of Great Britain concludes a treaty of neutrality with France for the electorate of Hanover.*

France resolved to seize this opportunity of crushing the house of Austria. In order to intimidate the Elector of Hanover, Mareschal Maillebois was sent with a numerous army into Westphalia; and this expedient proved effectual. A treaty of neutrality was concluded; and the King of Great Britain engaged to vote for the Elector of Bavaria at the ensuing election of an emperor. The design of the French court was to raise this prince to the imperial dignity, and furnish him with such succours as should enable him to deprive the Queen of Hungary of her hereditary dominions.

While the French minister at Vienna endeavoured to amuse the queen with the strongest assurances of his master's friendship, a body of five-and-thirty thousand men began their march for Germany, in order to join the Elector of Bavaria: another French army was assembled upon the Rhine; and the Count de Belleisle, being provided with large sums of money, was sent to negotiate with different electors. Having thus secured a majority of voices, he proceeded to Munich, where he presented the Elector of Bavaria with a commission, appointing him generalissimo of the French troops marching to his assistance; and now the treaty of Nymphenburgh was concluded. The French king engaged to assist the elector with his whole power, towards raising him to the imperial throne: the elector promised, that after his elevation he would never attempt to recover any of the towns or provinces of the empire which France had conquered: that he would in his imperial capacity renounce the barrier-treaty; and agree that France should irrevocably retain whatever places she should subdue in the Austrian Netherlands. The next step of Belleisle was to negotiate another treaty between France and Prussia, importing, that the Elector of Bavaria should possess Bohemia, Upper Austria, and the Tyrolese; that the King of Poland should be gratified with Moravia and Upper Silesia; and that his Prussian majesty should retain Lower Silesia, with the town of Neiss and the county of Glatz. These precautions being taken, the Count de Belleisle repaired to Frankfort in quality of ambassador and plenipotentiary from France, at the imperial diet of election. It was in this city that the French king published a declaration, signifying that as the King of Great Britain had assembled an army to influence the approaching election of an emperor, his most Christian majesty, as guarantee of the treaty of Westphalia, had ordered some troops to advance towards the Rhine, with a view to maintain the tranquillity of the Germanic body, and secure the freedom of the imperial election.

In July, the Elector of Bavaria, being joined by the French forces under Mareschal Broglio, surprised the imperial city of Passau, upon the Danube; and entering Upper Austria, at the head of seventy thousand men, took possession of Lintz, where he received the homage of the states of that country. *He is crowned King of Bohemia at Prague.* Understanding that the garrison of Vienna was very numerous, and that Count Palfi had assembled thirty thousand Hungarians in the neighbourhood of this capital, he made no further progress in Austria, but marched into Bohemia, where he was reinforced by a considerable body of Saxons, under the command of Count Rutowski, natural son to the late King of Poland. By this time his Polish majesty had acceded to the treaty of Nymphenburgh, and declared war against the Queen of Hungary, on the most frivolous pretences. The Elector of Bavaria advanced to Prague, which was taken in the night by scalade; an achievement in which Maurice Count of Saxe, another natural son of the King of Poland, distinguished himself at the head of the French forces. In December the Elector of Bavaria made his public entry into his capital, where he was proclaimed King of Bohemia, and inaugurated with the usual solemnities; then he set out for Frankfort, to be present at the diet of election.

At this period the Queen of Hungary saw herself abandoned by all her allies, and seemingly devoted to destruction. She was not, however, forsaken by her courage; nor destitute of good officers and an able ministry. *Fidelity of the Hungarians.* She retired to Presburgh, and, in a pathetic Latin speech to the states, expressed her confidence in the loyalty and valour of her Hungarian subjects. The nobility of that kingdom, touched with her presence and distress, assured her, unanimously, that they would sacrifice their lives and fortunes in her defence. The ban being raised, that brave people crowded to her standard; and the diet expressed their resentment against her enemy by a public edict, excluding for ever the electoral house of Bavaria from the succession to the crown of Hungary: yet, without the subsidy she received from Great Britain, their courage and attachment would have proved ineffectual. By this supply she was enabled to pay her army, erect magazines, complete her warlike preparations, and put her strong places in a posture of defence. In December, her generals, Berenclau and Mentzel, defeated Count Thoring, who commanded eight thousand men, at the pass of Scardingen, and opening their way into Bavaria, laid the whole country under contribution: while Count Khevenhuller retook the city of Lintz, and drove the French troops out of Austria. The grand signor assured the Queen of Hungary, that, far from taking advantage of her troubles, he should seize all opportunities to convince her of his friendship: the pope permitted her to levy a tenth on the revenues of the clergy within her dominions, and even to use all the church-plate for the support of the war.

As the czarina expressed an inclination to assist this unfortunate princess, the French court resolved to find her employment in another quarter. They had already gained over to their interest Count Gyllenburgh, prime minister and president of the chancery in Sweden. A dispute happening between him and Mr. Burnaby, the British resident at Stockholm, some warm altercation passed: Mr. Burnaby was forbid the court, and published a memorial in his own vindication; on the other hand, the King of Sweden justified his conduct in a rescript sent to all the foreign ministers. The King of Great Britain had proposed a subsidy-treaty to Sweden, which, from the influence of French counsels, was rejected. The Swedes, having assembled a numerous army in Finland, and equipped a large squadron of ships, declared war against Russia upon the most trifling pretences; and the fleet, putting to sea, commenced hostilities by blocking up the Russian ports in Livonia. A body of eleven thousand Swedes, commanded by General Wrangle, having advanced to Willmenstrand, were in August attacked and defeated by General Lasci, at the head of thirty thousand Russians. Count Lewenhaupt, who commanded the main army of the Swedes, resolved to take vengeance for this disgrace, after the Russian troops had retired into winter-quarters. In December he marched towards Wybourg; but receiving letters from the Prince of Hesse-Hombourg and the Marquis de la Chetardie, the French ambassador at Petersburgh, informing him of the surprising revolution which had just happened in Russia, and proposing a suspension of hostilities, he retreated with his army in order to wait for further instructions; and the two courts agreed to a cessation of arms for three months.

The Russians had been for some time discontented with their government. The late czarina was influenced chiefly by German counsels, and employed a great number of foreigners in her service. These causes of discontent produced factions and conspiracies; and when they were discovered, the empress treated the authors of them with such severity as increased the general disaffection. Besides, they were displeased at the manner in which she had settled the succession. The Prince of Brunswick-Lunenburgh Bevern, father to the young czar, was not at all agreeable to the Russian nobility; and his consort, the Princess Anne of Mecklenburgh, having assumed the reins of government during her son's minority, seemed to follow the maxims of her aunt, the late czarina. The Russian grandees and generals, therefore, turned their eyes upon the Princess Elizabeth, who was daughter of Peter the Great, and the darling of the empire. The French ambassador gladly concurred in a project for deposing a princess who was well affected to the house of Austria. General Lasci approved of the design, which was chiefly conducted by the Prince of Hesse-Hombourg, who, in the reigns of the Empress Catherine and Peter II., had been generalissimo of the Russian army. The good-will and concurrence of the troops being secured, two regiments of guards took possession of all the avenues of the imperial palace at Petersburgh. The Princess Elizabeth, putting herself at the head of one thousand men, on the fifth day of December entered the winter-palace, where the Princess of Mecklenburgh and the infant czar resided. She advanced into the chamber where the princess and her consort lay, and desired them to rise and quit the palace, adding that their persons were safe, and that they could not justly blame her for asserting her right. At the same time the Counts Osterman, Golofkin, Mingden, and Munich, were arrested; their papers and effects were seized, and their persons conveyed to Schlisselbourg, a fortress on the Neva. Early in the morning the senate assembling, declared all that had passed since the reign of Peter II. to be usurpation; and that the imperial dignity belonged of right to the Princess Elizabeth: she was immediately proclaimed Empress of all the Russias, and recognized by the army in Finland. She forthwith published a general act of indemnity: she created the Prince of Hesse-Hombourg generalissimo of her armies: she restored the Dolgorucky family to their honours and estates: she recalled and rewarded all those who had been banished for favouring her pretensions: she mitigated the exile of the Duke of Courland, by indulging him with a maintenance more suitable to his rank: she released General Wrangle, Count Wasaburgh, and the other Swedish officers, who had been taken at the battle of Willmenstrand; and the Princess Anne of Mecklenburgh, with her consort and children, were sent under a strong guard to Riga, the capital of Livonia.

*The Spanish and French squadrons pass unmolested by the English admiral in the Mediterranean.*

Amidst these tempests of war and revolution, the States General wisely determined to preserve their own tranquillity. It was doubtless their interest to avoid the dangers and expense of a war, and to profit by that stagnation of commerce which would necessarily happen among their neighbours that were at open enmity with each other; besides, they were overawed by the declarations of the French monarch on one side; by the power, activity, and pretensions of his Prussian majesty on the other; and they dreaded the prospect of a stadtholder at the head of their army. These at least were the sentiments of many Dutch patriots, reinforced by others that acted under French influence. But the Prince of Orange numbered among his partisans and adherents many persons of dignity and credit in the commonwealth: he was adored by the populace, who loudly exclaimed against their governors, and clamoured for a war, without ceasing. This national spirit, joined to the remonstrances and requisitions made by the courts of Vienna and London, obliged the states to issue orders for an augmentation of their forces: but these were executed so slowly, that neither France nor Prussia had much cause to take umbrage at their preparations. In Italy, the King of Sardinia declared for the house of Austria: the republic of Genoa was deeply engaged in the French interest: the pope, the Venetians, and the dukedom of Tuscany were neutral: the King of Naples resolved to support the claim of his family to the Austrian dominions in Italy, and began to make preparations accordingly. His mother, the Queen of Spain, had formed a plan for erecting these dominions into a monarchy for her second son Don Philip; and a body of fifteen thousand men, being embarked at Barcelona, were transported to Orbitello, under the convoy of the united squadrons of France and Spain. While Admiral Haddock, with twelve ships of the line, lay at anchor in the bay of Gibraltar, the Spanish fleet passed the straits in the night, and was joined by the French squadron from Toulon. The British admiral, sailing from Gibraltar, fell in with them in a few days, and found both squadrons drawn up in line of battle. As he bore down upon the Spanish fleet, the French admiral sent a flag of truce, to inform him that, as the French and Spaniards were engaged in a joint expedition, he should be obliged to act in concert with his master's allies. This interposition prevented an engagement. The combined fleet amounting to double the number of the English squadron, Admiral Haddock was obliged to desist, and proceeded to Port Mahon, leaving the enemy to prosecute their voyage without molestation. The people of England were incensed at this transaction, and did not scruple to affirm, that the hands of the British admiral were tied up by the neutrality of Hanover.[a]

The court of Madrid seemed to have shaken off that indolence and phlegm which had formerly disgraced the councils of Spain. They no sooner learned the destination of Commodore Anson, who had sailed from Spithead in the course of the preceding year, than they sent Don Pizarro, with a more powerful squadron, upon the same voyage, to defeat his design. He accordingly steered the same course, and actually fell in with one or two ships of the British armament, near the straits of Magellan; but he could not weather a long and furious tempest through which Mr. Anson proceeded into the South-Sea. One of the Spanish ships perished at sea: another was wrecked on the coast of Brazil: and Pizarro bore away for the Rio de la Plata, where he arrived with the three remaining ships in a shattered

*Inactivity of the naval power of Great Britain.*

---

[a] In the month of July two ships of Haddock's squadron falling in with three French ships of war, Captain Barnet, the English commodore, supposing them to be Spanish register ships, fired a shot in order to bring them to; and they refusing to comply with this signal, a sharp engagement ensued: after they had fought several hours, the French commander ceased firing, and thought proper to come to an explanation, when he and Barnet parted with mutual apologies.

In the course of this year a dangerous conspiracy was discovered at New York, in North America. One Hewson, a low publican, had engaged several negroes in a design to destroy the town, and massacre the people. Fire was set to several parts of the city; nine or ten negroes were apprehended, convicted, and burned alive. Hewson, with his wife, and a servant maid privy to the plot, were found guilty and hanged, though they died protesting their innocence.

condition, after having lost twelve hundred men by sickness and famine. The Spaniards exerted the same vigilance and activity in Europe. Their privateers were so industrious and successful, that in the beginning of this year they had taken, since the commencement of the war, four hundred and seven ships belonging to the subjects of Great Britain, valued at near four millions of piastres. The traders had, therefore, too much cause to complain, considering the formidable fleets which were maintained for the protection of commerce. In the course of the summer, Sir John Norris had twice sailed towards the coast of Spain, at the head of a powerful squadron, without taking any effectual step for annoying the enemy, as if the sole intention of the ministry had been to expose the nation to the ridicule and contempt of its enemies. The inactivity of the British arms appears the more inexcusable, when we consider the great armaments which had been prepared. The land-forces of Great Britain, exclusive of the Danish and Hessian auxiliaries, amounted to sixty thousand men; and the fleet consisted of above one hundred ships of war, manned by fifty-four thousand sailors.

*Obstinate struggle in electing members in the new Parliament.*

The general discontent of the people had a manifest influence upon the election of members for the new Parliament, which produced one of the most violent contests between the two parties which had happened since the Revolution. All the adherents of the Prince of Wales concurred with the country party, in opposition to the ministry; and the Duke of Argyle exerted himself so successfully among the shires and boroughs of Scotland, that the partisans of the ministry could not secure six members out of the whole number returned from North Britain. They were, however, much more fortunate in the election of the sixteen peers, who were chosen literally according to the list transmitted from court. Instructions were delivered by the constituents to a great number of members returned for cities and counties, exhorting and requiring them to oppose a standing army in time of peace; to vote for the mitigation of excise laws, for the repeal of septennial Parliaments, and for the limitation of placemen in the House of Commons. They likewise insisted upon their examining into the particulars of the public expense, and endeavouring to redress the grievances of the nation. Obstinate struggles were maintained in all parts of the united kingdom with uncommon ardour and perseverance: and such a national spirit of opposition prevailed, that, notwithstanding the whole weight of ministerial influence, the country interest seemed to preponderate in the new Parliament.

The king returned to England in the month of October; and on the first day of December the session was opened. Mr. Onslow being rechosen speaker was approved of by his majesty, who spoke in the usual style to both Houses. He observed, that the former Parliament had formed the strongest resolutions in favour of the Queen of Hungary, for the maintenance of the pragmatic sanction; for the preservation of the balance of power, and the peace and liberties of Europe; and that if the other powers which were under the like engagements with him had answered the just expectations so solemnly given, the support of the common cause would have been attended with less difficulty. He said he had endeavoured, by the most proper and early applications, to induce other powers that were united with him by the ties of common interest, to concert such measures as so important and critical a conjuncture required: that where an accommodation seemed necessary, he had laboured to reconcile princes whose union would have been the most effectual means to prevent the mischiefs which had happened, and the best security for the interest and safety of the whole. He owned his endeavours had not hitherto produced the desired effect; though he was not without hope, that a just sense of approaching danger would give a more favourable turn to the counsels of other nations. He represented the necessity of putting the kingdom in such a posture of defence as would enable him to improve all opportunities of maintaining the liberties of Europe, and defeat any attempts that should be made against him and his dominions; and he recommended unanimity, vigour, and despatch. The House of Commons having appointed their several committees, the speaker reported the king's speech; and Mr. Herbert moved for an address of thanks, including an approbation of the means by which the war had been prosecuted. The motion being seconded by Mr. Trevor, Lord Noel Somerset stood up and moved, that the House would in their address desire his majesty not to engage these kingdoms in a war for the preservation of his foreign

*Remarkable motion in the House of Commons by Lord Noel Somerset.*

dominions. He was supported by that incorruptible patriot, Mr. Shippen, who declared he was neither ashamed nor afraid to affirm, that thirty years had made no change in any of his political opinions. He said he was grown old in the House of Commons; that time had verified the predictions he had formerly uttered; and that he had seen his conjectures ripened into knowledge. "If my country (added he) has been so unfortunate as once more to commit her interest to men who propose to themselves no advantage from their trust but that of selling it, I may, perhaps, fall once more under censure for declaring my opinion, and be once more treated as a criminal, for asserting what they who punish me cannot deny; for maintaining that Hanoverian maxims are inconsistent with the happiness of this nation; and for preserving the caution so strongly inculcated by those patriots who framed the act of settlement, and conferred upon the present royal family their title to the throne." He particularized the instances in which the ministry had acted in diametrical opposition to that necessary constitution; and he insisted on the necessity of taking some step to remove the apprehensions of the people, who began to think themselves in danger of being sacrificed to the security of foreign dominions. Mr. Gibbon, who spoke on the same side of the question, expatiated upon the absurdity of returning thanks for the prosecution of a war which had been egregiously mismanaged. "What! (said he) are our thanks to be solemnly returned for defeats, disgrace, and losses, the ruin of our merchants, the imprisonment of our sailors, idle shows of armaments, and useless expenses?" Sir Robert Walpole, having made a short speech in defence of the first motion for an address, was answered by Mr. Pulteney, who seemed to be animated with a double proportion of patriot indignation. He asserted, that from a review of that minister's conduct since the beginning of the dispute with Spain, it would appear that he had been guilty not only of single errors, but of deliberate treachery: that he had always co-operated with the enemies of his country, and sacrificed to his private interest the happiness and honour of the British nation. He then entered into a detail of that conduct against which he had so often declaimed; and being transported by an overheated imagination, accused him of personal attachment and affection to the enemies of the kingdom. A charge that was doubtless the result of exaggerated animosity, and served only to invalidate the other articles of imputation that were much better founded. His objections were overruled; and the address, as at first proposed, was presented to his majesty.

This small advantage, however, the minister did not consider as a proof of his having ascertained an undoubted majority in the House of Commons. There was a great number of disputed elections; and the discussion of these was the point on which the people had turned their eyes, as the criterion of the minister's power and credit. *The country party obtain a majority in the House of Commons.* In the first, which was heard at the bar of the House, he carried his point by a majority of six only; and this he looked upon as a defeat rather than a victory. His enemies exulted in their strength, as they knew they should be joined, in matters of importance, by several members who voted against them on this occasion. The inconsiderable majority that appeared on the side of the administration plainly proved that the influence of the minister was greatly diminished, and seemed to prognosticate his further decline. This consideration induced some individuals to declare against him as a setting sun, from whose beams they could expect no further warmth. His adherents began to tremble; and he himself had occasion for all his art and equanimity. The court interest was not sufficient to support the election of their own members for Westminster. The high-bailiff had been guilty of some illegal practices at the poll; and three justices of the peace had, on pretence of preventing riots, sent for a military force to overawe the election. A petition presented by the electors of Westminster was taken into consideration by the House; and the election was declared void by a majority of four voices. The high-bailiff was taken into custody: the officer who ordered the soldiers to march, and the three justices who signed the letter, in consequence of which he acted, were reprimanded on their knees at the bar of the House.

The country party maintained the advantage they had gained in deciding upon several other controverted elections; and Sir Robert Walpole tottered on the brink of ruin. *Sir Robert Walpole created Earl of Orford.* He knew that the majority of a single vote would at any time commit him prisoner to the Tower, should ever the motion be made: and he saw that his safety could be effected by no other expedient but that of dividing the opposition. Towards the accomplishment of this purpose he employed all his credit and dexterity. His emissaries did not fail to tamper with those members of the opposite party who were the most likely to be converted by their arguments. A message was sent by the Bishop of Oxford to the Prince of Wales, importing, that if his royal highness would write a letter of condescension to the king, he and all his counsellors should be taken into favour; that fifty thousand pounds should be added to his revenue; four times that sum be disbursed immediately for the payment of his debts; and suitable provision be made in due time for all his followers. The prince declined this proposal. He declared that he would accept no such conditions while Sir Robert Walpole continued to direct the public affairs: that he looked upon him as a bar between his majesty and the affections of his people; as the author of the national grievances both at home and abroad; and as the sole cause of that contempt which Great Britain had incurred in all the courts of Europe. His royal highness was now chief of this formidable party, revered by the whole nation—a party which had gained the ascendency in the House of Commons; which professed to act upon the principles of public virtue; which demanded the fall of an odious minister, as a sacrifice due to an injured people; and declared that no temptation could shake their virtue; that no art could dissolve the cement by which they were united. Sir Robert Walpole, though repulsed in his attempt upon the Prince of Wales, was more successful in his other endeavours. He resolved to try his strength once more in the House of Commons, in another disputed election; and had the mortification to see the majority augmented to sixteen voices. He declared he would never more sit in that House; and next day, which was the third of February, the king adjourned both Houses of Parliament to the eighteenth day of the same month. In this interim, Sir Robert Walpole was created Earl of Orford, and resigned all his employments.

*Change in the ministry.* At no time of his life did he acquit himself with such prudential policy as he now displayed. He found means to separate the parts that composed the opposition, and to transfer the popular odium from himself to those who had professed themselves his keenest adversaries. The country party consisted of the tories, reinforced by discontented whigs, who had either been disappointed in their own ambitious views, or felt for the distresses of their country, occasioned by a weak and worthless administration. The old patriots, and the whigs whom they had joined, acted upon very different, and, indeed, upon opposite principles of government: and therefore they were united only by the ties of convenience. A coalition was projected between the discontented whigs, and those of the same denomination who acted in the ministry. Some were gratified with titles and offices; and all were assured that in the management of affairs a new system would be adopted, according to the plan they themselves should propose. The court required nothing of them, but that the Earl of Orford should escape with impunity. His place of chancellor of the exchequer was bestowed upon Mr. Sandys, who was likewise appointed a lord of the treasury; and the Earl of Wilmington succeeded him as first commissioner of that board. Lord Harrington, being dignified with the title of Earl, was declared president of the council; and in his room Lord Carteret became secretary of state. The Duke of Argyle was made master-general of the ordnance, colonel of his majesty's royal regiment of horseguards, field-marshal and commander-in-chief of all the forces in South Britain; but, finding himself disappointed in his expectations of the coalition, he in less than a month renounced all these employments. The Marquis of Tweeddale was appointed secretary of state for Scotland, a post which had been long suppressed; Mr. Pulteney was sworn of the privy-council, and afterwards created Earl of Bath. The Earl of Winchelsea and Nottingham was preferred to the head of the Admiralty, in the room of Sir Charles Wager; and after the resignation of the Duke of Argyle, the Earl of Stair was appointed field-marshal of all his majesty's forces, as well as ambassador extraordinay to the States-General. On the seventeenth day of February the Prince of Wales, attended by a numerous retinue of his adherents, waited on his majesty, who received him graciously, and ordered his guards to be restored. Lord Carteret and Mr. Sandys were the first who embraced the offers of the court, without the consent or privity of any other leaders in the opposition, except that of Mr. Pulteney;

but they declared to their friends, they would still proceed upon patriot principles; that they would concur in promoting an inquiry into past measures; and in enacting necessary laws to secure the constitution from the practices of corruption. These professions were believed, not only by their old coadjutors in the House of Commons, but also by the nation in general. The reconciliation between the king and the Prince of Wales, together with the change in the ministry, were celebrated with public rejoicings all over the kingdom; and immediately after the adjournment nothing but concord appeared in the House of Commons.

But this harmony was of short duration. It soon appeared that those who had declaimed the loudest for the liberties of their country had been actuated solely by the most sordid, and even the most ridiculous, motives of self-interest. Jealousy and mutual distrust ensued between them and their former confederates.

*Inquiry into the administration of Sir Robert Walpole.*

The nation complained that, instead of a total change of men and measures, they saw the old ministry strengthened by this coalition; and the same interest in Parliament predominating with redoubled influence. They branded the new converts as apostates and betrayers of their country; and in the transport of their indignation, they entirely overlooked the old object of their resentment. That a nobleman of pliant principles, narrow fortune, and unbounded ambition, should forsake his party for the blandishments of affluence, power, and authority, will not appear strange to any person acquainted with the human heart; but the sensible part of mankind will always reflect with amazement upon the conduct of a man who, seeing himself idolized by his fellow-citizens as the first and firmest patriot in the kingdom, as one of the most shining ornaments of his country, could give up all his popularity, and incur the contempt or detestation of mankind, for the wretched consideration of an empty title, without office, influence, or the least substantial appendage. One cannot, without an emotion of grief, contemplate such an instance of infatuation; one cannot but lament that such glory should have been so weakly forfeited; that such talents should been lost to the cause of liberty and virtue. Doubtless he flattered himself with the hope of one day directing the councils of his sovereign; but this was never accomplished, and he remained a solitary monument of blasted ambition. Before the change in the ministry, Mr. Pulteney moved that the several papers relating to the conduct of the war, which had been laid before the House, should be referred to a select committee, who should examine strictly into the particulars, and make a report to the House of their remarks and objections. The motion introduced a debate; but, upon a division, was rejected by a majority of three voices. Petitions having been presented by the merchants of London, Bristol, Liverpool, Glasgow, and almost all the trading towns in the kingdom, complaining of the losses they had sustained by the bad conduct of the war, the House resolved itself into a committee, to deliberate on these remonstrances. The articles of the London petition were explained by Mr. Glover, an eminent merchant of that city. Six days were spent in perusing papers and examining witnesses: then the same gentleman summed up the evidence, and in a pathetic speech endeavoured to demonstrate that the commerce of Great Britain had been exposed to the insults and rapine of the Spaniards, not by inattention or accident, but by one uniform and continued design. This inquiry being resumed after the adjournment, copies of instructions to admirals and captains of cruising ships were laid before the House: the Commons passed several resolutions, upon which a bill was prepared for the better protecting and securing the trade and navigation of the kingdom. It made its way through the Lower House, but was thrown out by the Lords. The pension-bill was revived, and sent up to the Peers, where it was again rejected; Lord Carteret voting against that very measure which he had so lately endeavoured to promote. On the ninth day of March, Lord Limerick made a motion for appointing a committee to inquire into the conduct of affairs for the last twenty years; he was seconded by Sir John St. Aubyn, and supported by Mr. Velters Cornwall, Mr. Phillips, Mr. W. Pitt, and Lord Percival, the new member for Westminster, who had already signalized himself by his eloquence and capacity. The motion was opposed by Sir Charles Wager, Mr. Pelham, and Mr. Henry Fox, surveyor-general to his majesty's works, and brother to Lord Ilchester. Though the opposition was faint and frivolous, the proposal was rejected by a majority of two voices. Lord Limerick, not yet discouraged, made a motion, on the twenty-third day of March, for an inquiry into the conduct of Robert Earl of Orford for the last ten years of his administration; and after a sharp debate, it was carried in the affirmative. The House resolved to choose a secret committee by ballot; and in the mean time presented an address to the king, assuring him of their fidelity, zeal, and affection.

Sir Robert Godschall having moved for leave to bring in a bill to repeal the act for septennial Parliaments, he was seconded by Sir John Barnard; but warmly opposed by Mr. Pulteney and Mr. Sandys; and the question passed in the negative. The committee of secrecy, being chosen, began to examine evidence, and Mr. Paxton, solicitor to the treasury, refusing to answer such questions as were put to him, Lord Limerick, chairman of the committee, complained to the House of his obstinacy. He was first taken into custody; and still persisting in his refusal, committed to Newgate. Then his lordship moved, that leave should be given to bring in a bill for indemnifying evidence against the Earl of Orford; and it was actually prepared by a decision of the majority. In the House of Lords it was vigorously opposed by Lord Carteret, and as strenuously supported by the Duke of Argyle; but fell upon a division, by the weight of superior numbers. Those members in the House of Commons who heartily wished that the inquiry might be prosecuted, were extremely incensed at the fate of this bill. A committee was appointed to search the journals of the Lords for precedents: their report being read, Lord Strange, son of the Earl of Derby, moved for a resolution, "that the Lords refusing to concur with the Commons of Great Britain, in an indemnification necessary to the effectual carrying on the inquiry now depending in Parliament, is an obstruction to justice, and may prove fatal to the liberties of this nation." This motion, which was seconded by Lord Quarendon, son of the Earl of Lichfield, gave rise to a warm debate; and Mr. Sandys declaimed against it, as a step that would bring on an immediate dissolution of the present form of government. It is really amazing to see with what effrontery some men can shift their maxims, and openly contradict the whole tenor of their former conduct. Mr. Sandys did not pass uncensured: he sustained some severe sarcasms on his apostasy from Sir John Hynde Cotton, who refuted all his objections; nevertheless, the motion passed in the negative. Notwithstanding this great obstruction, purposely thrown in the way of the

*Obstructed by the new ministry.*

inquiry, the secret committee discovered many flagrant instances of fraud and corruption in which the Earl of Orford had been concerned. It appeared that he had granted fraudulent contracts for paying the troops in the West Indies: that he had employed iniquitous arts to influence elections: that for secret service, during the last ten years, he had touched one million four hundred fifty-three thousand four hundred pounds of the public money: that above fifty thousand pounds of this sum had been paid to authors and printers of newspapers and political tracts written in defence of the ministry; that on the very day which preceded his resignation, he had signed orders on the civil-list revenues for above thirty thousand pounds; but as the cash remaining in the exchequer did not much exceed fourteen thousand pounds, he had raised the remaining part of the thirty thousand by pawning the orders to a banker. The committee proceeded to make further progress in their scrutiny, and had almost prepared a third report, when they were interrupted by the prorogation of Parliament.

The ministry, finding it was necessary to take some step for conciliating the affection of the people, gave way to a bill for excluding certain officers from seats in the House of Commons. They passed another for encouraging the linen manufacture; a third for regulating the trade of the plantations; and a fourth to prevent the marriage of lunatics. They voted forty thousand seamen and sixty-two thousand five hundred landmen for the service of the current year. They provided for the subsidies to Denmark and Hesse-Cassel, and voted five hundred thousand pounds to the Queen of Hungary. The expense of the year amounted to near six millions, raised by the land-tax at four shillings in the pound, by the malt-tax, by one million from the sinking fund, by annuities granted upon it for eight hundred thousand pounds, and a loan of one million six hundred thousand pounds from the bank. In the month of July, John Lord Gower was appointed keeper of his majesty's privy-seal; Allen Lord Bathurst was made captain of the band of pensioners; and on the fifteenth day of the month, Mr. Pulteney took his seat in the House of Peers as Earl of Bath. The king closed the session in the usual way, after having given them to understand that a treaty of peace was concluded between the Queen of Hungary and the King of Prussia, under his mediation; and that the late successes of the Austrian arms were in a great measure owing to the generous assistance afforded by the British nation.

By this time great changes had happened in the affairs of the continent. The Elector of Bavaria was chosen emperor of Germany at Frankfort on the Maine, and crowned by the name of Charles VII. on the twelfth day of February. Thither the imperial diet was removed from Ratisbon: they confirmed his election, and indulged him with a subsidy of fifty Roman months, amounting to about two hundred thousand pounds sterling. In the mean time, the Austrian General Khevenhuller ravaged his electorate, and made himself master of Munich, the capital of Bavaria; he likewise laid part of the Palatinate under contribution, in resentment for that elector's having sent a body of his troops to reinforce the imperial army. In March, Count Saxe, with a detachment of French and Bavarians, reduced Egra; and the Austrians were obliged to evacuate Bavaria, though they afterwards returned. Khevenhuller took post in the neighbourhood of Passau, and detached General Bernclau to Dinglesing on the Iser, to observe the motions of the enemy, who were now become extremely formidable. In May, a detachment of French and Bavarians advanced to the castle of Hilkersbergh on the Danube, with a view to take possession of a bridge over the river: the Austrian garrison immediately marched out to give them battle, and a severe action ensued, in which the imperialists were defeated.

*The Elector of Bavaria chosen emperor.*

In the beginning of the year the Queen of Hungary had assembled two considerable armies in Moravia and Bohemia. Prince Charles of Lorraine, at the head of fifty thousand men, advanced against the Saxons and Prussians, who thought proper to retire with precipitation from Moravia, which they had invaded. Then the Prince took the road to Bohemia; and Mareschal Broglio, who commanded the French forces in that country, must have fallen a sacrifice, had not the King of Prussia received a strong reinforcement, and entered that kingdom before his allies could be attacked. The two armies advanced towards each other; and on the seventeenth of May joined battle at Czaslau, where the Austrians at first gained a manifest advantage, and penetrated as far as the Prussian baggage: then the irregulars began to plunder so eagerly, that

*The King of Prussia gains the battle of Czaslau. Treaty at Breslau.*

they neglected every other consideration. The Prussian infantry took this opportunity to rally: the battle was renewed, and, after a very obstinate contest, the victory was snatched out of the hands of the Austrians, who were obliged to retire, with the loss of five thousand men killed, and twelve hundred taken by the enemy. The Prussians paid dear for the honour of remaining on the field of battle; and from the circumstances of this action the king is said to have conceived a disgust to the war. When the Austrians made such progress in the beginning of the engagement, he rode off with great expedition, until he was recalled by a message from his general, the Count de Schwerin, assuring his majesty that there was no danger of a defeat. Immediately after this battle, he discovered an inclination to accommodate all differences with the Queen of Hungary. The Earl of Hyndford, ambassador from the court of Great Britain, who accompanied him in this campaign, and was vested with full powers by her Hungarian majesty, did not fail to cultivate this favourable disposition; and on the first day of June, a treaty of peace between the two powers was concluded at Breslau. The queen ceded to his Prussian majesty the Upper and Lower Silesia, with the county of Glatz in Bohemia; and he charged himself with the payment of the sum lent by the merchants of London to the late emperor, on the Silesian revenues. He likewise engaged to observe a strict neutrality during the war, and to withdraw his forces from Bohemia in fifteen days after the ratification of the treaty, in which were comprehended the King of Great Britain, Elector of Hanover, the Czarina, the King of Denmark, the States-General, the house of Wolfenbuttel, and the King of Poland, Elector of Saxony, on certain conditions, which were accepted.

The King of Prussia recalled his troops; while Mareschal Broglio, who commanded the French auxiliaries in that kingdom, and the Count de Belleisle, abandoned their magazines and baggage, and retired with precipitation under the cannon of Prague. There they intrenched themselves in an advantageous situation; and Prince Charles, being joined by the other body of Austrians, under Prince Lobkowitz, encamped in sight of them, on the hills of Girinsnitz. The Grand Duke of Tuscany arrived in the Austrian army, of which he took the command; and the French generals offered to surrender Prague, Egra, and all

*The French troops retire under the cannon of Prague.*

the other places they possessed in Bohemia, provided they might be allowed to march off with their arms, artillery, and baggage. The proposal was rejected, and Prague invested on all sides about the end of July. Though the operations of the siege were carried on in an awkward and slovenly manner, the place was so effectually blocked up, that famine must have compelled the French to surrender at discretion had not very extraordinary efforts been made for their relief. The emperor had made advances to the Queen of Hungary. He promised that the French forces should quit Bohemia, and evacuate the empire; and he offered to renounce all pretensions to the kingdom of Bohemia, on condition that the Austrians would restore Bavaria; but these conditions were declined by the court of Vienna. The King of France was no sooner apprised of the condition to which the Generals Broglio and Belleisle were reduced, than he sent orders to Mareschal Maillebois, who commanded his army on the Rhine, to march to their relief. His troops were immediately put in motion; and when they reached Amberg in the Upper Palatinate, were joined by the French and imperialists from Bavaria. Prince Charles of Lorraine, having received intelligence of their junction and design, left eighteen thousand men to maintain the blockade of Prague, under the command of General Festititz, while he himself, with the rest of his army, advanced to Haydon on the frontiers of Bohemia. There he was joined by Count Khevenhuller, who from Bavaria had followed the enemy, now commanded by Count Seckendorff, and the Count de Saxe. Seckendorff, however, was sent back to Bavaria, while Mareschal Maillebois entered Bohemia on the twenty-fifth day of September: but he marched with such precaution that Prince Charles could not bring him to an engagement. Meanwhile, Festititz, for want of sufficient force, was obliged to abandon the blockade of Prague; and the French generals, being now at liberty, took post at Leutmaritz. Maillebois advanced as far as Kadan; but seeing the Austrians possessed of all the passes of the mountains, he marched back to the Palatinate, and was miserably harassed in his retreat by Prince Charles, who had left a strong body with Prince Lobkowitz, to watch the motions of Belleisle and Broglio.

These generals, seeing themselves surrounded on all hands,

returned to Prague, from whence Broglio made his escape in the habit of a courier, and was sent to command the army of Maillebois, who was by this time disgraced. Prince Lobkowitz, who now directed the blockade of Prague, had so effectually cut off all communication between that place and the adjacent country, that in a little time the French troops were reduced to great extremity, both from the severity of the season and the want of provision. They were already reduced to the necessity of eating horse-flesh and unclean animals; and they had no other prospect but that of perishing by famine or war, when their commander formed the scheme of a retreat, which was actually put in execution. Having taken some artful precautions to deceive the enemy, he, in the middle of December, departed from Prague at midnight, with about fourteen thousand men, thirty pieces of artillery, and some of the principal citizens as hostages for the safety of nine hundred soldiers whom he had left in garrison. Notwithstanding the difficulties he must have encountered at that season of the year, in a broken and unfrequented road, which he purposely chose, he marched with such expedition, that he had gained the passes of the mountains before he was overtaken by the horse and hussars of Prince Lobkowitz. The fatigue and hardships which the miserable soldiers underwent are inexpressible. A great number perished in the snow, and many hundreds, fainting with weariness, cold, and hunger, were left to the mercy of the Austrian irregulars, consisting of the most barbarous people on the face of the earth. The Count de Belleisle, though tortured with the hip-gout, behaved with surprising resolution and activity. He caused himself to be carried in a litter to every place where he thought his presence was necessary, and made such dispositions, that the pursuers never could make an impression upon the body of his troops; but all his artillery, baggage, and even his own equipage, fell into the hands of the enemy. On the twenty-ninth day of December he arrived at Egra, from whence he proceeded to Alsace without further molestation: but, when he returned to Versailles, he met with a very cold reception, notwithstanding the gallant exploit which he had performed. After his escape, Prince Lobkowitz returned to Prague, and the small garrison which Belleisle had left in that place surrendered upon honourable terms; so that this capital reverted to the house of Austria.

*Extraordinary retreat of M. de Belleisle.*

*The King of Great Britain forms an army in Flanders.*

The King of Great Britain, resolving to make a powerful diversion in the Netherlands, had in the month of April ordered sixteen thousand effective men to be embarked for that country; but, as this step was taken without any previous concert with the States-General, the Earl of Stair, destined to the command of the forces in Flanders, was in the mean time appointed ambassador extraordinary and plenipotentiary to their high mightiness, in order to persuade them to co-operate vigorously in the plan which his Britannic majesty had formed; a plan by which Great Britain was engaged as a principal in a foreign dispute, and entailed upon herself the whole burden of an expensive war, big with ruin and disgrace. England, from being the umpire, was now become a party in all continental quarrels; and instead of trimming the balance of Europe, lavished away her blood and treasure in supporting the interest and allies of a puny electorate in the north of Germany. The King of Prussia had been at variance with the Elector of Hanover. The duchy of Mecklenburgh was the avowed subject of dispute; but his Prussian majesty is said to have had other more provoking causes of complaint, which, however, he did not think proper to divulge. The King of Great Britain found it convenient to accommodate these differences. In the course of this summer, the two powers concluded a convention; in consequence of which the troops of Hanover evacuated Mecklenburgh, and three regiments of Brandenburgh took possession of those bailiwicks that were mortgaged to the King of Prussia. The Elector of Hanover being now secured from danger, sixteen thousand troops of that country, together with the six thousand auxiliary Hessians, began their march for the Netherlands; and about the middle of October arrived in the neighbourhood of Brussels, where they encamped. The Earl of Stair repaired to Ghent, where the British forces were quartered: a body of Austrians was assembled; and though the season was far advanced, he seemed determined upon some expedition: but all of a sudden the troops were sent into winter-quarters. The Austrians retired to Luxembourg; the English and Hessians remained in Flanders; and the Hanoverians marched into the county of Liege, without paying any regard to the bishop's protestation.

The States-General had made a considerable augmentation of their forces by sea and land; but, notwithstanding the repeated instances of the Earl of Stair, they resolved to adhere to their neutrality: they dreaded the neighbourhood of the French; and they were far from being pleased to see the English get footing in the Netherlands. *Progress of the war between Russia and Sweden.* The friends of the house of Orange began to exert themselves: the states of Groningen and West Friesland protested, in favour of the prince, against the promotion of foreign generals which had lately been made; but his interest was powerfully opposed by the provinces of Zealand and Holland, which had the greatest weight in the republic. The revolution in Russia did not put an end to the war with Sweden. These two powers had agreed to an armistice of three months, during which the czarina augmented her forces in Finland. She likewise ordered the Counts Osterman and Munich, with their adherents, to be tried: they were condemned to death, but pardoned on the scaffold, and sent in exile to Siberia. The Swedes, still encouraged by the intrigues of France, refused to listen to any terms of accommodation, unless Carelia, and the other conquests of the Czar Peter, should be restored. The French court had expected to bring over the new empress to their measures; but they found her as well disposed as her predecessor to assist the house of Austria. She remitted a considerable sum of money to the Queen of Hungary; and at that same time congratulated the Elector of Bavaria on his elevation to the imperial throne. The ceremony of her coronation was performed in May, with great solemnity, at Moscow; and in November she declared her nephew, the Duke of Holstein-Gottorp, her successor, by the title of Grand Prince of all the Russias. The cessation of arms being expired, General Lasci reduced Fredericksheim, and obliged the Swedish army, commanded by Count Lewenhaupt, to retire before him, from one place to another, until at length they were quite surrounded near Helsingfors. In this emergency, the Swedish general submitted to a capitulation, by which his infantry were transported by sea to Sweden; his cavalry marched by land to Abo; and his artillery and magazines remained in the hands of the Russians. The King of Sweden being of an advanced age, the diet assembled in order to settle the succession; and the Duke of Holstein-Gottorp, as grandson to the eldest sister to Charles XII., was declared next heir to the crown,

A courier was immediately despatched to Moscow, to notify to the duke this determination of the diet; and this message was followed by a deputation; but when they understood that he had embraced the religion of the Greek church, and been acknowledged successor to the throne of Russia, they annulled his election for Sweden, and resolved that the succession should not be re-established, until a peace should be concluded with the czarina. Conferences were opened at Abo for this purpose. In the mean time, the events of the war had been so long unfortunate for Sweden, that it was absolutely necessary to appease the indignation of the people with some sacrifice. The Generals Lewenhaupt and Bodenbrock were tried by a court-martial for misconduct: being found guilty, and condemned to death, they applied to the diet, by which the sentence was confirmed. The term of the subsidy-treaty between Great Britain and Denmark expiring, his Danish majesty refused to renew it; nor would he accede to the peace of Breslau. On the other hand, he became subsidiary to France, with which also he concluded a new treaty of commerce.

*The King of Sardinia declares for the house of Austria.*

The court of Versailles were now heartily tired of maintaining the war in Germany, and had actually made equitable proposals of peace to the Queen of Hungary, by whom they were rejected. Thus repulsed, they redoubled their preparations; and endeavoured, by advantageous offers, to detach the King of Sardinia from the interest of the house of Austria. This prince had espoused a sister to the grand duke, who pressed him to declare for her brother, and the Queen of Hungary promised to gratify him with some territories in the Milanese: besides, he thought the Spaniards had already gained too much ground in Italy; but, at the same time, he was afraid of being crushed between France and Spain, before he could be properly supported. He therefore temporized, and protracted the negotiation, until he was alarmed at the progress of the Spanish arms in Italy, and fixed in his determination by the subsidies of Great Britain. The Spanish army assembled at Rimini, under the Duke de Montemar; and being joined by the Neapolitan forces, amounted to sixty thousand men, furnished with a large train of artillery. About the beginning of May they entered the Bolognese: then the King of Sardinia, declaring against them, joined the Austrian army commanded by

Count Traun; marched into the duchy of Parma; and understanding that the Duke of Modena had engaged in a treaty with the Spaniards, dispossessed that prince of his dominions. The Duke de Montemar, seeing his army diminished by sickness and desertion, retreated to the kingdom of Naples, and was followed by the King of Sardinia as far as Rimini.

Here he received intelligence that Don Philip, third son of his Catholic majesty, had made an irruption into Savoy with another army of Spaniards, and already taken possession of Chamberri, the capital. He forthwith began his march for Piedmont. Don Philip abandoned Savoy at his approach, and retreating into Dauphiné, took post under the cannon of Fort Barreaux. The king pursued him thither, and both armies remained in sight of each other till the month of December, when the Marquis de Minas, an active and enterprising general, arrived from Madrid, and took upon him the command of the forces under Don Philip. This general's first exploit was against the castle of Aspremont, in the neighbourhood of the Sardinian camp. He attacked it so vigorously, that the garrison was obliged to capitulate in four-and-forty hours. The loss of this important post compelled the king to retire into Piedmont, and the Spaniards marched back into Savoy, where they established their winter-quarters. In the mean time, the Duke de Montemar, who directed the other Spanish army, though the Duke of Modena was nominal generalissimo, resigned his command to Count Gages, who attempted to penetrate into Tuscany; but was prevented by the vigilance of Count Traun, the Austrian general. In December he quartered his troops in the Bolognese and Romagna; while the Austrians and Piedmontese were distributed in the Modenese and Parmesan. The pope was passive during the whole campaign: the Venetians maintained their neutrality, and the King of the two Sicilies was overawed by the British fleet in the Mediterranean.

*Motions of the Spaniards in Italy and Savoy.*

The new ministry in England had sent out Admiral Matthews to assume the command of this squadron, which had been for some time conducted by Lestock, an inferior officer, as Haddock had been obliged to resign his commission on account of his ill state of health. Matthews was likewise invested with the

*Conduct of Admiral Matthews in the Mediterranean.*

character of minister-plenipotentiary to the King of Sardinia and the states of Italy. Immediately after he had taken possession of his command, he ordered Captain Norris to destroy five Spanish galleys which had put into the bay of St. Tropez; and this service was effectually performed. In May he detached Commodore Rowley, with eight sail, to cruise off the harbour of Toulon; and a great number of merchant-ships belonging to the enemy fell into his hands. In August he sent Commodore Martin with another squadron into the bay of Naples to bombard that city, unless his Sicilian majesty would immediately recall his troops which had joined the Spanish army, and promise to remain neuter during the continuance of the war. Naples was immediately filled with consternation; the king subscribed to these conditions; and the English squadron rejoined the admiral in the road of Hieres, which he had chosen for his winter station. Before this period he had landed some men at St. Remo in the territories of Genoa, and destroyed the magazines that were erected for the use of the Spanish army. He had likewise ordered two of his cruisers to attack a Spanish ship of the line, which lay at anchor in the port of Ajaccio, in the island of Corsica: but the Spanish captain set his men on shore, and blew up his ship, rather than she should fall into the hands of the English.

In the course of this year Admiral Vernon and General Wentworth made another effort in the West Indies. They had in January received a reinforcement from England, and planned a new expedition, in concert with the governor of Jamaica, who accompanied them in their voyage. Their design was to disembark the troops at Porto Bello, and march across the isthmus of Darien, to attack the rich town of Panama. They sailed from Jamaica on the ninth day of March, and on the twenty-eighth arrived at Porto Bello. There they held a council of war, in which it was resolved that, as the troops were sickly, the rainy season begun, and several transports not yet arrived, the intended expedition was become impracticable. In pursuance of this determination the armament immediately returned to Jamaica, exhibiting a ridiculous spectacle of folly and irresolution.[b] In August,

*Operations in the West Indies.*

---

[b] In May, two English frigates, commanded by Captain Smith and Captain Stuart, fell in with three Spanish ships of war, near the island of St. Christopher's. They forthwith

a ship of war was sent from thence, with about three hundred soldiers, to the small island of Rattan, in the bay of Honduras, of which they took possession. In September, Vernon and Wentworth received orders to return to England with such troops as remained alive: these did not amount to a tenth part of the number which had been sent abroad in that inglorious service. The inferior officers fell ignobly by sickness and despair, without an opportunity of signalizing their courage, and the commanders lived to feel the scorn and reproach of their country. In the month of June the new colony of Georgia was invaded by an armament from St. Augustine, commanded by Don Marinel de Monteano, governor of that fortress. It consisted of six-and-thirty ships, from which four thousand men were landed at St. Simon's; and began their march for Frederica. General Oglethorpe, with a handful of men, took such wise precautions for opposing their progress, and harassed them in their march with such activity and resolution, that, after two of their detachments had been defeated, they retired to their ships, and totally abandoned the enterprise.

In England the merchants still complained that their commerce was not properly protected, and the people clamoured against the conduct of the war. They said their burdens were increased to maintain quarrels with which they had no concern; to defray the enormous expense of inactive fleets and pacific armies. Lord C. had by this time insinuated himself into the confidence of his sovereign, and engrossed the whole direction of public affairs. The war with Spain was now become a secondary consideration, and neglected accordingly; while the chief attention of the new minister was turned upon the affairs of the continent. The dispute with Spain concerned Britain only. The interests of Hanover were connected with the troubles of the empire. By pursuing this object he soothed the wishes of his master, and opened a more ample field for his own ambition. He had studied the policy of the continent with peculiar eager-

*The attention of the ministry turned chiefly on the affairs of the continent.*

---

engaged, and the action continued till night, by the favour of which the enemy retired to Porto Rico, in a shattered condition.

In the month of September the Tilbury ship of war, of sixty guns, was accidentally set on fire, and destroyed, off the island of Hispaniola, on which occasion one hundred and twenty-seven men perished; the rest were saved by Captain Hoare, of the Defiance, who happened to be on the same cruise.

ness. This was the favourite subject of his reflection, upon which he thought and spoke with a degree of enthusiasm. The intolerable taxes, the poverty, the ruined commerce of his country, the iniquity of standing armies, votes of credit, and foreign connexions, upon which he had so often expatiated, were now forgotten, or overlooked. He saw nothing but glory, conquest, and acquired dominion. He set the power of France at defiance; and, as if Great Britain had felt no distress, but teemed with treasure which she could not otherwise employ, he poured forth her millions with a rash and desperate hand, in purchasing beggarly allies, and maintaining mercenary armies. The Earl of Stair had arrived in England towards the end of August, and conferred with his majesty. A privy-council was summoned; and in a few days that nobleman returned to Holland. Lord Carteret was sent with a commission to the Hague in September; and when he returned, the baggage of the king and the Duke of Cumberland, which had been shipped for Flanders, was ordered to be brought on shore. The Parliament met on the sixteenth day of November, when his majesty told them, that he had augmented the British forces in the Low Countries with sixteen thousand Hanoverians and the Hessian auxiliaries, in order to form such a force, in conjunction with the Austrian troops, as might be of service to the common cause at all events. He extolled the magnanimity and fortitude of the Queen of Hungary, as well as the resolute conduct of the King of Sardinia, and that prince's strict adherence to his engagements, though attacked in his own dominions. He mentioned the requisition made by Sweden, of his good offices for procuring a peace between that nation and Russia, the defensive alliances which he had concluded with the czarina, and with the King of Prussia, as events which could not have been expected, if Great Britain had not manifested a seasonable spirit and vigour, in defence and assistance of her ancient allies, and in maintaining the liberties of Europe. He said the honour and interest of his crown and kingdoms, the success of the war with Spain, the re-establishment of the balance and tranquillity of Europe, would greatly depend on the prudence and vigour of their resolutions. The Marquis of Tweeddale moved for an address of thanks, which was opposed by the Earl of Chesterfield, for the reasons so often urged on the same occasion; but supported by Lord C. on his new adopted maxims, with those specious arguments which he could at all times produce, delivered with amazing serenity and assurance. The motion was agreed to, and the address presented to his majesty. About this period a treaty of mutual defence and guarantee between his majesty and the King of Prussia was signed at Westminster. In the House of Commons Mr. Lyttelton made a motion for reviving the place-bill; but it was opposed by a great number of members who had formerly been strenuous advocates for this measure, and rejected upon a division. This was also the fate of a motion made to renew the inquiry into the conduct of Robert Earl of Orford. As many strong presumptions of guilt had appeared against him in the reports of the secret committee, the nation had reason to expect that this proposal would have been embraced by a great majority; but several members, who in the preceding session had been loud in their demands of justice, now shamefully contributed their talents and interest in stifling the inquiry.

When the House of Lords took into consideration the several estimates of the expense occasioned by the forces in the pay of Great Britain, Earl Stanhope, at the close of an elegant speech, moved for an address, to beseech and advise his majesty, that, in compassion to his people, loaded already with such numerous and heavy taxes, such large and growing debts, and greater annual expenses than the nation at any time before had ever sustained, he would exonerate his subjects of the charge and burden of those mercenaries who were taken into the service last year, without the advice or consent of Parliament. The motion was supported by the Earl of Sandwich, who took occasion to speak with great contempt of Hanover, and, in mentioning the royal family, seemed to forget that decorum which the subject required. He had, indeed, reason to talk with asperity on the contract by which the Hanoverians had been taken into the pay of Great Britain. Levy-money was charged to the account, though they were engaged for one year only, and though not a single regiment had been raised on this occasion: they had been levied for the security of the electorate; and would have been maintained if England had never engaged in the affairs of the continent. The Duke of Bedford enlarged upon the same subject. He said it had been suspected, nor was the suspicion without foundation, that the measures

*Extraordinary motion in the House of Lords by Earl Stanhope.*

of the English ministry had long been regulated by the interest of his majesty's electoral territories: that these had been long considered as a gulf into which the treasures of Great Britain had been thrown: that the state of Hanover had been changed, without any visible cause, since the accession of its princes to the throne of England: affluence had begun to wanton in their towns, and gold to glitter in their cottages, without the discovery of mines, or the increase of their commerce; and new dominions had been purchased, of which the value was never paid from the revenues of Hanover. The motion was hunted down by the new minister, the patriot Lord Bathurst, and the Earl of Bath, which last nobleman declared, that he considered it as an act of cowardice and meanness to fall passively down the stream of popularity, to suffer his reason and integrity to be overborne by the noise of vulgar clamours, which had been raised against the measures of government by the low arts of exaggeration, fallacious reasonings, and partial representations. This is the very language which Sir Robert Walpole had often used against Mr. Pulteney and his confederates in the House of Commons. The associates of the new secretary pleaded the cause of Hanover, and insisted upon the necessity of a land-war against France, with all the vehemence of declamation. Their suggestions were answered; their conduct was severely stigmatized by the Earl of Chesterfield, who observed, that the assembling an army in Flanders, without the concurrence of the States-General, or any other power engaged by treaty, or bound by interest, to support the Queen of Hungary, was a rash and ridiculous measure: the taking sixteen thousand Hanoverians into British pay, without consulting the Parliament, seemed highly derogatory to the rights and dignity of the great council of the nation, and a very dangerous precedent to future times: that these troops could not be employed against the emperor, whom they had already recognized: that the arms and wealth of Britain alone were altogether insufficient to raise the house of Austria to its former strength, dominion, and influence: that the assembling an army in Flanders would engage the nation as principals in an expensive and ruinous war, with a power which it ought not to provoke, and could not pretend to withstand in that manner: that while Great Britain exhausted herself almost to ruin, in pursuance of schemes founded on engagements to the Queen of Hungary, the electorate of Hanover, though under the same engagements, and governed by the same prince, did not appear to contribute any thing as an ally to her assistance, but was paid by Great Britain for all the forces it had sent into the field, at a very exorbitant price: that nothing could be more absurd and iniquitous than to hire these mercenaries, while a numerous army lay inactive at home, and the nation groaned under such intolerable burdens. "It may be proper (added he) to repeat what may be forgotten in the multitude of other objects, that this nation, after having exalted the Elector of Hanover from a state of obscurity to the crown, is condemned to hire the troops of that electorate to fight their own cause; to hire them at a rate which was never demanded before; and to pay levy-money for them, though it is known to all Europe that they were not raised for this occasion." All the partisans of the old ministry joined in the opposition to Earl Stanhope's motion, which was rejected by the majority. Then the Earl of Scarborough moved for an address, to approve of the measures which had been taken on the continent; and this was likewise carried by dint of numbers. It was not however a very eligible victory: what they gained in Parliament they lost with the people. The new ministers became more odious than their predecessors; and the people began to think public virtue was an empty name.

But the most severe opposition they underwent was in their endeavours to support a bill which they had concerted, and which had passed through the House of Commons with great precipitation: it repealed certain duties on spirituous liquors, and licences for retailing these liquors; and imposed others at an easier rate. *Warm and obstinate debate on the repeal of the gin-act.* When those severe duties, amounting almost to a prohibition, were imposed, the populace of London were sunk into the most brutal degeneracy, by drinking to excess the pernicious spirit called gin, which was sold so cheap that the lowest class of the people could afford to indulge themselves in one continued state of intoxication, to the destruction of all morals, industry, and order. Such a shameful degree of profligacy prevailed, that the retailers of this poisonous compound set up painted boards in public, inviting people to be drunk for the small expense of one penny; assuring them they might be dead drunk for two-pence, and have straw for nothing. They accordingly provided cellars and places strewed with straw, to which they conveyed those wretches who were overwhelmed with intoxication. In these dismal caverns they lay until they had recovered some use of their faculties, and then they had recourse to the same mischievous potion; thus consuming their health and ruining their families, in hideous receptacles of the most filthy vice, resounding with riot, execration, and blasphemy. Such beastly practices too plainly denoted a total want of all police and civil regulations, and would have reflected disgrace upon the most barbarous community. In order to restrain this evil, which was become intolerable, the legislature enacted that law which we have already mentioned. But the populace soon broke through all restraint. Though no licence was obtained, and no duty paid, the liquor continued to be sold in all corners of the streets; informers were intimidated by the threats of the people; and the justices of the peace, either from indolence or corruption, neglected to put the law in execution. The new ministers foresaw that a great revenue would accrue to the crown from a repeal of this act; and this measure they thought they might the more decently take, as the law had proved ineffectual; for it appeared that the consumption of gin had considerably increased every year since those heavy duties were imposed. They therefore pretended that, should the price of the liquor be moderately raised, and licences granted at twenty shillings each to the retailers, the lowest class of people would be debarred the use of it to excess; their morals would of consequence be mended; and a considerable sum of money might be raised for the support of the war, by mortgaging the revenue arising from the duty and the licences. Upon these maxims the new bill was founded, and passed through the Lower House without opposition; but among the Peers it produced the most obstinate dispute which had happened since the beginning of this Parliament. The first assault it sustained was from Lord Hervey, who had been divested of his post of privy-seal, which was bestowed on Lord Gower; and these two noblemen exchanged principles from that instant. The first was hardened into a sturdy patriot; the other suppled into an obsequious courtier. Lord Hervey on this occasion made a florid harangue upon the pernicious effects of that destructive spirit they were about to let loose upon their fellow-creatures. Several prelates expatiated on the same topics; but the Earl of

Chesterfield attacked the bill with the united powers of reason, wit, and ridicule. Lord Carteret, Lord Bathurst, and the Earl of Bath, were numbered among its advocates; and shrewd arguments were advanced on both sides of the question. After very long, warm, and repeated debates, the bill passed without amendments, though the whole bench of bishops voted against it; and we cannot help owning that it has not been attended with those dismal consequences which the lords in the opposition foretold. When the question was put for committing this bill, and the Earl of Chesterfield saw the bishops join in his division, "I am in doubt (said he) whether I have not got on the other side of the question; for I have not had the honour to divide with so many lawn sleeves for several years."

By the report of the secret committee it appeared that the then minister had commenced prosecutions against the mayors of boroughs who opposed his influence in the elections of members of Parliament. These prosecutions were founded on ambiguities in charters, or trivial informalities in the choice of magistrates. An appeal on such a process was brought into the House of Lords; and this evil falling under consideration, a bill was prepared for securing the independency of corporations; but as it tended to diminish the influence of the ministry, they argued against it with their usual eagerness and success; and it was rejected on a division. The mutiny bill and several others passed through both Houses. The Commons granted supplies to the amount of six millions, raised by the land-tax, the malt-tax, duties on spirituous liquors and licences, and a loan from the sinking-fund. In two years the national debt had suffered an increase of two millions four hundred thousand pounds. On the twenty-first day of April the session was closed in the usual manner. The king, in his speech to both Houses, told them that, at the requisition of the Queen of Hungary, he had ordered his army, in conjunction with the Austrians, to pass the Rhine for her support and assistance; that he continued one squadron of ships in the Mediterranean, and another in the West Indies. He thanked the Commons for the ample supplies they had granted; and declared it was the fixed purpose of his heart to promote the true interest and happiness of his kingdoms. Immediately after the prorogation of Parliament he embarked for Germany, accompanied by the

Duke of Cumberland, Lord Carteret, and other persons of distinction.

At this period the Queen of Hungary seemed to triumph over all her enemies. The French were driven out of Bohemia and part of the Upper Palatinate; and their forces under Mareschal Broglio were posted on the Danube. Prince Charles of Lorraine, at the head of the Austrian army, entered Bavaria; and in April obtained a victory over a body of Bavarians at Braunau: at the same time, three bodies of Croatians penetrating through the passes of the Tyrolese, ravaged the whole country to the very gates of Munich. The emperor pressed the French general to hazard a battle; but he refused to run the risk, though he had received a strong reinforcement from France. His imperial majesty, thinking himself unsafe in Munich, retired to Augsburgh: Mareschal Seckendorf retreated with the Bavarian troops to Ingoldstadt, where he was afterwards joined by Mareschal Broglio, whose troops had in this retreat been pursued and terribly harassed by the Austrian cavalry and hussars. Prince Charles had opened a free communication with Munich, which now for the third time fell into the hands of the Queen of Hungary. Her arms likewise reduced Friedberg and Landsperg, while Prince Charles continued to pursue the French to Donawert, where they were joined by twelve thousand men from the Rhine. Broglio still avoided an engagement, and retreated before the enemy to Hailbron. The emperor, being thus abandoned by his allies, and stripped of all his dominions, repaired to Frankfort, where he lived in indigence and obscurity. He now made advances towards an accommodation with the Queen of Hungary. His general, Seckendorf, had an interview with Count Khevenhuller at the convent of Lowersconfield, where a convention was signed. This treaty imported, that the emperor should remain neuter during the continuance of the present war; and that his troops should be quartered in Franconia: that the Queen of Hungary should keep possession of Bavaria till the peace: that Braunau and Scarding should be delivered up to the Austrians: that the French garrison of Ingoldstadt should be permitted to withdraw, and be replaced by Bavarians; but that the Austrian general should be put in possession of all the artillery, magazines, and warlike stores belonging to the French, which should be found in the place. The governors of Egra and Ingoldstadt refusing to acquiesce in the capitulation, the Austrians had recourse to the operations of war; and both places were reduced. In Ingoldstadt they found all the emperor's domestic treasure, jewels, plate, pictures, cabinets, and curiosities, with the archives of the house of Bavaria, the most valuable effects belonging to the nobility of that electorate, a prodigious train of artillery, and a vast quantity of provisions, arms, and ammunition.

The French king, baffled in all the efforts he had hitherto made for the support of the emperor, ordered his minister at Frankfort to deliver a declaration to the diet, professing himself extremely well pleased to hear they intended to interpose their mediation for terminating the war. He said, he was no less satisfied with the treaty of neutrality which the emperor had concluded with the Queen of Hungary; an event of which he was no sooner informed, than he had ordered his troops to return to the frontiers of his dominions, that the Germanic body might be convinced of his equity and moderation. To this declaration the Queen of Hungary answered in a rescript, that the design of France was to embarrass her affairs, and deprive her of the assistance of her allies: that the Elector of Bavaria could not be considered as a neutral party in his own cause: that the mediation of the empire could only produce a peace either with or without the concurrence of France: that in the former case no solid peace could be expected; in the latter, it was easy to foresee that France would pay no regard to a peace in which she should have no concern. She affirmed, that the aim of the French king was solely to gain time to repair his losses, that he might afterwards revive the troubles of the empire. The Elector of Mentz, who had favoured the emperor, was now dead, and his successor inclined to the Austrian interest. He allowed this rescript to be entered in the journal of the diet, together with the protests which had been made when the vote of Bohemia was suppressed in the late election. The emperor complained in a circular letter of this transaction, as a stroke levelled at his imperial dignity; and it gave rise to a warm dispute among the members of the Germanic body. Several princes resented the haughty conduct, and began to be alarmed at the success, of the house of Austria; while others pitied the deplorable situation of the emperor.

*Difference between the King of Prussia and the Elector of Hanover.*

The Kings of Great Britain and Prussia, as Electors of Hanover and Brandenburgh, espoused opposite sides in this contest. His Prussian majesty protested against the investiture of the duchy of Saxe Lawenburgh, claimed by the King of Great Britain: he had an interview with General Seckendorf at Anspach; and was said to have privately visited the emperor at Frankfort.

*The King of Great Britain obtains a victory over the French at Dettingen.* The troops which the King of Great Britain had assembled in the Netherlands, began their march for the Rhine in the latter end of February; and in May they encamped near Hoech on the river Mayne, under the command of the Earl of Stair. This nobleman sent Major-General Bland to Frankfort, with a compliment to the emperor, assuring him, in the name of his Britannic majesty, that the respect owing to his dignity should not be violated, nor the place of his residence disturbed. Notwithstanding this assurance, the emperor retired to Munich, though he was afterwards compelled to return, by the success of the Austrians in Bavaria. The French king, in order to prevent the junction of the British forces with Prince Charles of Lorraine, ordered the Mareschal de Noailles to assemble sixty thousand men upon the Mayne; while Coigny was sent into Alsace with a numerous army, to defend that province, and oppose Prince Charles, should he attempt to pass the Rhine. The Mareschal de Noailles, having secured the towns of Spire, Worms, and Oppenheim, passed the Rhine in the beginning of June, and posted himself on the east side of that river, above Frankfort. The Earl of Stair advanced towards him, and encamped at Killenbach, between the river Mayne and the forest of D'Armstadt; from this situation he made a motion to Aschaffenburgh, with a view to secure the navigation of the Upper Mayne; but he was anticipated by the enemy, who lay on the other side of the river, and had taken possession of the posts above, so as to intercept all supplies. They were posted on the other side of the river, opposite to the allies, whose camp they overlooked; and they found means, by their parties and other precautions, to cut off the communication by water between Frankfort and the confederates. The Duke of Cumberland had already come to make his first campaign, and his majesty arrived in the camp on the ninth day of June. He found his army, amounting to about forty thousand men, in danger of starving: he received intelligence that a reinforcement of twelve thousand Hanoverians and Hessians had reached Hanau; and he resolved to march thither, both with a view to effect a junction, and to procure provision for his forces. With this view he decamped on the twenty-sixth day of June. He had no sooner quitted Aschaffenburgh than it was seized by the French general: he had not marched above three leagues, when he perceived the enemy, to the number of thirty thousand, had passed the river farther down, at Selingenstadt, and were drawn up in order of battle at the village of Dettingen, to dispute his passage. Thus he found himself cooped up in a very dangerous situation. The enemy had possessed themselves of Aschaffenburgh behind, so as to prevent his retreat: his troops were confined in a narrow plain, bounded by hills and woods on the right, flanked on the left by the river Mayne, on the opposite side of which the French had erected batteries that annoyed the allies on their march; in the front a considerable part of the French army was drawn up, with a narrow pass before them, the village of Dettingen on their right, a wood on their left, and a morass in the centre. Thus environed, the confederates must either have fought at a very great disadvantage, or surrendered themselves prisoners of war, had not the Duke de Gramont, who commanded the enemy, been instigated by the spirit of madness to forego these advantages. He passed the defile, and advancing towards the allies, a battle ensued. The French horse charged with great impetuosity, and some regiments of British cavalry were put in disorder; but the infantry of the allies behaved with such intrepidity and deliberation, under the eye of their sovereign, as soon determined the fate of the day: the French were obliged to give way, and repass the Mayne with great precipitation, having lost about five thousand men killed, wounded, or taken. Had they been properly pursued before they recollected themselves from their first confusion, in all probability they would have sustained a total overthrow. The Earl of Stair proposed that a body of cavalry should be detached on this service; but his advice was overruled. The loss of the allies in this action amounted to two thousand men. The Generals Clayton and Monroy were killed: the Duke of Cumberland, who exhibited uncommon proofs of courage, was shot through the calf of the leg: the Earl of Albemarle, General Huske, and several other officers of distinction, were wounded. The king exposed his person to a severe fire of cannon as well as musketry: he rode between the first and second lines with his sword drawn, and encouraged the troops to fight for the honour of England. Immediately after the action he continued his march to Hanau, where he was joined by the reinforcement. The Earl of Stair sent a trumpeter to Mareschal de Noailles, recommending to his protection the sick and wounded that were left on the field of battle; and these the French general treated with great care and tenderness. Such generosity softens the rigours of war, and does honour to humanity.

<small>Treaty of Worms.</small> The two armies continued on different sides of the river till the twelfth day of July, when the French general receiving intelligence that Prince Charles of Lorraine had approached the Neckar, he suddenly retired and repassed the Rhine between Worms and Oppenheim. The King of Great Britain was visited by Prince Charles and Count Khevenhuller at Hanau, where the future operations of the campaign were regulated. On the twenty-seventh day of August, the allied army passed the Rhine at Mentz, and the king fixed his head-quarters in the episcopal palace at Worms. Here the forces lay encamped till the latter end of September, when they advanced to Spire, where they were joined by twenty thousand Dutch auxiliaries from the Netherlands. Mareschal Noailles having retreated into Upper Alsace, the allies took possession of Germersheim, and demolished the intrenchments which the enemy had raised on the Queich; then they returned to Mentz, and in October were distributed into winter-quarters, after an inactive campaign that redounded very little to the honour of those by whom the motions of the army were conducted. In September a treaty had been concluded at Worms between his Britannic majesty, the King of Sardinia, and the Queen of Hungary. She engaged to maintain thirty thousand men in Italy: the King of Sardinia obliged himself to employ forty thousand infantry and five thousand horse, in consideration of his commanding the combined army, and receiving an annual subsidy of two hundred thousand pounds from Great Britain. As a further gratification, the queen yielded to him the city of Placentia, with several districts in the duchy of Pavia, and in the Novarese; and all her right and pretensions to Final, at present possessed

by the republic at Genoa, which they hoped would give it up on being repaid the purchase-money, amounting to three hundred thousand pounds. This sum the King of England promised to disburse; and moreover to maintain a strong squadron in the Mediterranean, the commander of which should act in concert with his Sardinian majesty. Finally, the contracting powers agreed that Final should be constituted a free port, like that of Leghorn. Nothing could be more unjust than this treaty, by which the Genoese were negotiated out of their property. They had purchased the marquisate of Final of the late emperor for a valuable consideration, and the purchase had been guaranteed by Great Britain. It could not, therefore, be expected that they would part with this acquisition to a prince whose power they thought already too formidable; especially, on condition of its being made a free port, to the prejudice of their own commerce. They presented remonstrances against this article by their ministers at the courts of London, Vienna, and Turin; and, as very little regard was paid to their representations, they threw themselves into the arms of France and Spain for protection.

After the battle of Dettingen, Colonel Mentzel, at the head of a large body of irregulars belonging to the Queen of Hungary, made an irruption into Lorraine, part of which they ravaged without mercy. *Conclusion of the campaign.*
In September, Prince Charles, with the Austrian army, entered the Brisgaw, and attempted to pass the Rhine; but Mareschal Coigny had taken such precautions for guarding it on the other side, that he was obliged to abandon his design, and, marching back into the Upper Palatinate, quartered his troops in that country, and in Bavaria. By this time the Earl of Stair had solicited and obtained leave to resign his command. He had for some time thought himself neglected; and was unwilling that his reputation should suffer on account of measures in which he had no concern. In October the King of Great Britain returned to Hanover, and the army separated. The troops in British pay marched back to the Netherlands, and the rest took the route to their respective countries. The States-General still wavered between their own immediate interest and their desire to support the house of Austria. At length, however, they supplied her with a subsidy, and ordered twenty thousand men to march to her assistance, notwithstanding the intrigues

of the Marquis de Fenelon, the French ambassador at the Hague, and the declaration of the King of Prussia, who disapproved of this measure, and refused them a passage through his territories to the Rhine.

Affairs in the north.
Sweden was filled with discontents, and divided into factions. The Generals Bodenbrock and Lewenhaupt were beheaded, having been sacrificed as scapegoats for the ministry. Some unsuccessful efforts by sea and land were made against the Russians. At last the peace of Abo was concluded; and the Duke of Holstein-Utin, uncle to the successor of the Russian throne, was chosen as next heir to the crown of Sweden. A party had been formed in favour of the Prince of Denmark; and the order of the peasants actually elected him as successor. The debates in the college of nobles rose to a very dangerous degree of animosity, and were appeased by an harangue in Swedish verse, which one of the senators pronounced. The peasants yielded the point, and the succession was settled on the Duke of Holstein. Denmark, instigated by French counsels, began to make preparations for war against Sweden; but a body of Russian auxiliaries arriving in that kingdom, under the command of General Keith, and the czarina declaring she would assist the Swedes with her whole force, the King of Denmark thought proper to disarm. It had been an old maxim of French policy to embroil the courts of the north, that they might be too much employed at home to intermeddle in the affairs of Germany, while France was at war with the house of Austria. The good understanding between the czarina and the Queen of Hungary was at this period destroyed, in consequence of a conspiracy which had been formed by some persons of distinction at the court of Petersburgh, for removing the Empress Elizabeth, and recalling the Princess Anne to the administration. This design being discovered, the principal conspirators were corporally punished, and sent in exile to Siberia. The Marquis de Botta, the Austrian minister, who had resided at the court of the czarina, was suspected of having been concerned in the plot; though the grounds of this suspicion did not appear till after he was recalled, and sent as ambassador to the court of Berlin. The empress demanded satisfaction of the Queen of Hungary, who appointed commissioners to inquire into his conduct, and he was acquitted; but the czarina was not at all

satisfied of his innocence. In February a defensive treaty of alliance was concluded between this princess and the King of Great Britain.

By this time France was deprived of her ablest minister, in the death of the Cardinal de Fleury, who had for many years managed the affairs of that kingdom. He is said to have possessed a lively genius, and an insinuating address; to have been regular in his deportment, and moderate in his disposition; but at the same time he has been branded as deceitful, dissembling, and vindictive. His scheme of politics was altogether pacific: he endeavoured to accomplish his purposes by raising and fomenting intrigues at foreign courts: he did not seem to pay much regard to the military glory of France; and he too much neglected the naval power of that kingdom. Since Broglio was driven out of Germany, the French court affected uncommon moderation. They pretended that their troops had only acted as auxiliaries while they remained in the empire: being, however, apprehensive of an irruption into their own dominions, they declared, that those troops were no longer to be considered in that light, but as subjects acting in the service of France. The campaign in Italy proved unfavourable to the Spaniards. In the beginning of February, Count Gages, who commanded the Spanish army in the Bolognese, amounting to four-and-twenty thousand men, passed the Penaro, and advanced to Campo-Santo, where he encountered the imperial and Piedmontese forces, commanded by the Counts Traun and Aspremont. The strength of the two armies was nearly equal. The action was obstinate and bloody, though indecisive. The Spaniards lost about four thousand men killed, wounded, or taken. The damage sustained by the confederates was not quite so great. Some cannon and colours were taken on both sides; and each claimed the victory. Count Gages repassed the Penaro, retreated suddenly from Bologna, and marched to Rimini in the ecclesiastical state, where he fortified his camp in an advantageous situation, after having suffered severely by desertion. Count Traun remained inactive in the Modenese till September, when he resigned his command to Prince Lobkowitz. This general entered the Bolognese in October, and then advanced towards Count Gages, who, with his forces, now reduced to seven thousand, retreated to Fano; but afterwards took possession of Pesaro, and fortified

*Battle of Campo-Santo.*

all the passes of the river Foglia. The season was far advanced before the Spanish troops, commanded by Don Philip, in Savoy, entered upon action. In all probability, the courts of Versailles and Madrid carried on some private negotiation with the King of Sardinia. This expedient failing, Don Philip decamped from Chamberri in the latter end of August, and, defiling through Dauphiné towards Briançon, was joined by the Prince of Conti, at the head of twenty thousand French auxiliaries. Thus reinforced, he attacked the Piedmontese lines at Chateau-Dauphiné; but was repulsed in several attempts, and obliged to retreat with considerable loss. The French established their winter-quarters in Dauphiné and Provence; and the Spaniards maintained their footing in Savoy.

The British fleet, commanded by Admiral Matthews, overawed all the states that bordered on the Mediterranean. This officer, about the end of June, understanding that fourteen xebecks, laden with artillery and ammunition for the Spanish army, had arrived at Genoa, sailed thither from the road of Hieres, and demanded of the republic that they would either oblige these vessels with the stores to quit their harbour, or sequester their lading until a general peace should be established. After some dispute, it was agreed that the cannon and stores should be deposited in the castle of Bonifacio, situated on a rock at the south end of Corsica; and that the xebecks should have leave to retire without molestation. The Corsicans had some years before revolted, and shaken off the dominion of the Genoese, under which their island had remained for many centuries. They found themselves oppressed, and resolved to assert their freedom. They conferred the sovereign authority on a German adventurer, who was solemnly proclaimed by the name of King Theodore. He had supplied them with some arms and ammunition, which he had brought from Tunis; and amused them with promises of being assisted by foreign powers in retrieving their independency; but as these promises were not performed, they treated him so roughly, that he had thought proper to quit the island, and they submitted again to their old masters. The troubles of Corsica were now revived. Theodore revisited his kingdom, and was recognized by the principal chiefs of the island. He published a manifesto; he granted a general pardon to all his subjects who should

*Transactions of the British fleet in the Mediterranean.*

return to their obedience: he pretended to be countenanced and supported by the King of Great Britain and the Queen of Hungary. He was certainly thought a proper instrument to perplex and harass the Genoese, and was supplied at this juncture with a sum of money to purchase arms for the Corsicans; but a change soon happened in the British ministry, and then he was suffered to relapse into his original obscurity. Admiral Matthews, though he did not undertake any expedition of importance against the maritime towns of Spain, continued to assert the British empire at sea through the whole extent of the Mediterranean. The Spanish army under Don Philip was no sooner in motion, than the English admiral ordered some troops and cannon to be disembarked for the security of Villa-Franca. Some stores having been landed at Civita Vecchia, for the use of the Spanish forces under Count Gages, Matthews interpreted this transaction into a violation of the neutrality which the pope had professed; and sent thither a squadron to bombard the place. The city of Rome was filled with consternation; and the pope had recourse to the good offices of his Sardinian majesty, in consequence of which the English squadron was ordered to withdraw. The captains of single cruising ships, by their activity and vigilance, wholly interrupted the commerce of Spain; cannonaded and burned some towns on the sea-side; and kept the whole coast in continual alarm.[e]

In the West Indies some unsuccessful efforts were made by an English squadron, commanded by Commodore Knowles. He attacked La Gueira on the coast of Caraccas, in the month of February; but met with such a warm reception, that he was obliged to desist, and make the best of his way for the Dutch island Curaçoa, where he repaired the damage he had sustained. His ships being refitted, he made another attempt upon

*Unsuccessful attempts upon the Spanish settlements in the West Indies.*

[e] In May a dreadful plague broke out at Messina in Sicily. It was imported in cotton and other commodities brought from the Morea; and swept off such a multitude of people, that the city was almost depopulated: all the galley slaves, who were employed in burying the dead, perished by the contagion; and this was the fate of many priests and monks who administered to those who were infected. The dead bodies lay in heaps in the streets, corrupting the air, and adding fresh fuel to the rage of the pestilence. Numbers died miserably, for want of proper attendance and necessaries; and all was horror and desolation. At the beginning of winter it ceased, after having destroyed near fifty thousand inhabitants of Messina, and of the garrisons in the citadel and castle. It was prevented from spreading in Sicily by a strong barricado drawn from Melazzo to Tuormina; but it was conveyed to Reggio in Calabria, by the avarice of a broker of that place, who bought some goods at Messina. The King of Naples immediately ordered lines to be formed, together with a chain of troops, which cut off all communication between that place and the rest of the continent.

Porto Cavallo in April, which like the former miscarried. Twelve hundred marines, being landed in the neighbourhood of that place, were seized with such a panic that it was found necessary to re-embark them without delay. Then the commodore abandoned the enterprise, and sailed back to his station at the Leeward Islands, without having added much to his reputation, either as to conduct or resolution. On the continent of America the operations of the war were very inconsiderable. General Oglethorpe, having received intelligence that the Spaniards prepared for another invasion from St. Augustine, assembled a body of Indians, as a reinforcement to part of his own regiment, with the highlanders and rangers, and in the spring began his march, in order to anticipate the enemy. He encamped for some time in the neighbourhood of St. Augustine, by way of defiance; but they did not think proper to hazard an engagement; and as he was in no condition to undertake a siege, he returned to Georgia. In October the Princess Louisa, youngest daughter of his Britannic majesty, was married by proxy, at Hanover, to the Prince Royal of Denmark, who met her at Altona, and conducted her to Copenhagen.

## CHAPTER XIX.

DEBATE IN PARLIAMENT AGAINST THE HANOVERIAN TROOPS. — SUPPLIES GRANTED. — PROJECTED INVASION OF GREAT BRITAIN. — A FRENCH SQUADRON SAILS UP THE ENGLISH CHANNEL. — THE KINGDOM IS PUT IN A POSTURE OF DEFENCE. — THE DESIGN OF THE FRENCH DEFEATED. — WAR BETWEEN FRANCE AND ENGLAND. — BILL AGAINST THOSE WHO SHOULD CORRESPOND WITH THE SONS OF THE PRETENDER. — NAVAL ENGAGEMENT OFF TOULON. — ADVANCES TOWARDS PEACE MADE BY THE EMPEROR. — TREATY OF FRANKFORT. — PROGRESS OF THE FRENCH KING IN THE NETHERLANDS. — PRINCE CHARLES OF LORRAINE PASSES THE RHINE. — THE KING OF PRUSSIA MAKES AN IRRUPTION INTO BOHEMIA. — CAMPAIGN IN BAVARIA AND FLANDERS. — THE KING OF NAPLES JOINS COUNT GAGES IN ITALY. — BATTLE OF COMI. — RETURN OF COMMODORE ANSON. — SIR JOHN BALCHEN PERISHES AT SEA. — REVOLUTION IN THE BRITISH MINISTRY. — SESSION OF PARLIAMENT. — DEATH OF THE EMPEROR CHARLES VII. — ACCOMMODATION BETWEEN THE QUEEN OF HUNGARY AND THE YOUNG ELECTOR OF BAVARIA. — THE KING OF PRUSSIA GAINS TWO SUCCESSIVE BATTLES AT FRIEDBERG AND SOHR, OVER THE AUSTRIAN AND SAXON FORCES. — TREATY OF DRESDEN. — THE GRAND DUKE OF TUSCANY ELECTED EMPEROR OF GERMANY. — THE ALLIES ARE DEFEATED AT FONTENOY. — THE KING OF SARDINIA IS ALMOST STRIPPED OF HIS DOMINIONS. — THE ENGLISH FORCES TAKE CAPE BRETON. — THE IMPORTANCE OF THIS CONQUEST. — PROJECT OF AN INSURRECTION IN GREAT BRITAIN. — THE ELDEST SON OF THE CHEVALIER DE ST. GEORGE LANDS IN SCOTLAND. — TAKES POSSESSION OF EDINBURGH. — DEFEATS SIR JOHN COPE AT PRESTON PANS. — EFFORTS OF THE FRIENDS OF GOVERNMENT IN SCOTLAND. — PRECAUTIONS TAKEN IN ENGLAND. — THE PRINCE PRETENDER REDUCES CARLISLE, AND PENETRATES AS FAR AS DERBY. — CONSTERNATION OF THE LONDONERS. — THE REBELS RETREAT INTO SCOTLAND. — THEY INVEST THE CASTLE OF STIRLING. — THE KING'S TROOPS UNDER HAWLEY ARE WORSTED AT FALKIRK. — THE DUKE OF CUMBERLAND ASSUMES THE COMMAND OF THE FORCES IN SCOTLAND. — THE REBELS UNDERTAKE THE SIEGE OF FORT WILLIAM.

THE discontents of England were artfully inflamed by antiministerial writers, who not only exaggerated the burdens of the people, and drew frightful pictures of the distress and misery which, they said, impended over the nation, but also employed the arts of calumny and misrepresentation, to excite a jealousy and national quarrel between the English and Hanoverians. They affirmed that in the last campaign the British general had been neglected and despised; while the counsels of foreign officers, greatly inferior to him in capacity, quality, and reputation, had been followed, to the prejudice of the common cause: that the British troops sustained daily insults from their own mercenaries, who were indulged with particular marks of royal favour: that the sovereign himself appeared at Dettingen in a Hanoverian scarf; and that his electoral troops were of very

*1743. Debate in Parliament against the Hanoverian troops.*

little service in that engagement. Though the most material of these assertions were certainly false, they made a strong impression on the minds of the people, already irritated by the enormous expense of a continental war maintained for the interest of Germany. When the Parliament met in the beginning of December, a motion was made in the House of Peers, by the Earl of Sandwich, for an address, beseeching his majesty to discontinue the Hanoverian troops in British pay, in order to remove the popular discontent, and stop the murmurs of the English troops abroad. He was supported by the Duke of Bedford, the Earl of Chesterfield, and all the leaders in the opposition, who did not fail to enumerate and insist upon all the circumstances we have mentioned. They moreover observed, that better troops might be hired at a smaller expense: that it would be a vain and endless task to exhaust the national treasure, in enriching a hungry and barren electorate: that the popular dissatisfaction against these mercenaries was so general, and raised to such violence, as nothing but their dismission could appease: that if such hirelings should be thus continued from year to year, they might at last become a burden entailed upon the nation, and be made subservient, under some ambitious prince, to purposes destructive of British liberty. These were the suggestions of spleen and animosity; for, granting the necessity of a land war, the Hanoverians were the most natural allies and auxiliaries which Great Britain could engage and employ. How insolent soever some few individual generals of that electorate might have been in their private deportment, certain it is, their troops behaved with great sobriety, discipline, and decorum; and in the day of battle did their duty with as much courage and alacrity as any body of men ever displayed on the like occasion. The motion was rejected by the majority; but, when the term for keeping them in the British pay was nearly expired, and the estimates for their being continued the ensuing year were laid before the House, the Earl of Sandwich renewed his motion. The lord chancellor, as speaker of the House, interposing, declared, that by their rules a question once rejected could not be revived during the same session. A debate ensued, and the second motion was overruled. The Hanoverian troops were voted in the House of Commons: nevertheless, the same nobleman moved in the Upper House, that the continuing sixteen thousand Hanoverians in British pay was prejudicial to his majesty's true interest, useless to the common cause, and dangerous to the welfare and tranquillity of the nation. He was seconded by the Duke of Marlborough, who had resigned his commission in disgust; and the proposal gave birth to another warm dispute; but victory declared, as usual, for the ministry.

In the House of Commons they sustained divers attacks. A motion was made for laying a duty of eight shillings in the pound on all places and pensions. *Supplies granted.* Mr. Grenville moved for an address, to beseech his majesty, that he would not engage the British nation any further in the war on the continent, without the concurrence of the States-General on certain stipulated proportions of force and expense, as in the late war. These proposals begat vigorous debates, in which the country party were always foiled by dint of superior numbers. Such was the credit and influence of the ministry in Parliament, that, although the national debt was increased by above six millions since the commencement of the war, the Commons indulged them with an enormous sum for the expense of the ensuing year. The grants specified in the votes amounted to six millions and a half: to this sum were added three millions and a half paid to the sinking-fund in perpetual taxes; so that this year's expense rose to ten millions. The funds established for the annual charge were the land and malt taxes; one million paid by the East India Company for the renewal of their charter, twelve hundred thousand pounds by annuities, one million from the sinking-fund, six-and-thirty thousand pounds from the coinage, and six hundred thousand pounds by a lottery; an expedient which for some time had been annually repeated, and which, in a great measure, contributed to debauch the morals of the public, by introducing a spirit of gaming, destructive of all industry and virtue.

The dissensions of the British Parliament were suddenly suspended by an event that seemed to unite both parties in the prosecution of the same measures. *Projected invasion of Great Britain.* This was the intelligence of an intended invasion. By the parliamentary disputes, the loud clamours, and the general dissatisfaction of the people in Great Britain, the French ministry were persuaded that the nation was ripe for a revolt. This belief was corroborated by the assertions of their emissaries in different parts of Great Britain and Ireland. These were Papists and Jacobites of strong prejudices and warm imaginations, who saw things through the medium of passion and party, and spoke rather from extravagant zeal than from sober conviction. They gave the court of Versailles to understand, that if the Chevalier de St. George, or his eldest son, Charles Edward, should appear at the head of a French army in Great Britain, a revolution would instantly follow in his favour. This intimation was agreeable to Cardinal de Tencin, who, since the death of Fleury, had borne a share in the administration of France. He was of a violent enterprising temper. He had been recommended to the purple by the Chevalier de St. George, and was seemingly attached to the Stuart family. His ambition was flattered with the prospect of giving a king to Great Britain; of performing such eminent service to his benefactor; and of restoring to the throne of their ancestors a family connected by the ties of blood with all the greatest princes of Europe. The ministry of France foresaw, that even if this aim should miscarry, a descent upon Great Britain would make a considerable diversion from the continent in favour of France, and embroil and embarrass his Britannic majesty, who was the chief support of the house of Austria and all its allies. Actuated by these motives, he concerted measures with the Chevalier de St. George at Rome, who, being too much advanced in years to engage personally in such an expedition, agreed to delegate his pretensions and authority to his son Charles, a youth of promising talents, sage, secret, brave, and enterprising, amiable in his person, grave, and even reserved in his deportment. He approved himself in the sequel composed and moderate in success, wonderfully firm in adversity; and though tenderly nursed in all the delights of an effeminate country and gentle climate, patient, almost beyond belief, of cold, hunger, and fatigue. Such was the adventurer now destined to fill the hope which the French ministry had conceived, from the projected invasion of Great Britain.

Count Saxe was appointed by the French king commander of the troops designed for this expedition, which amounted to fifteen thousand men. They began their march to Picardy, and a great number of vessels was assembled for their embarkation at Dunkirk, Calais, and Boulogne. It was determined that they should be landed in Kent, under convoy of a strong squadron equipped at Brest, and commanded by Monsieur de Roquefeuille, an officer of experience and capacity. The Chevalier de St. George is said to have required the personal service of the Duke of Ormond, who excused himself on account of his advanced age: be that as it will, Prince Charles departed from Rome about the end of December, in the disguise of a Spanish courier, attended by one servant only, and furnished with passports by Cardinal Aquaviva. He travelled through Tuscany to Genoa, from whence he proceeded to Savona, where he embarked for Antibes, and, prosecuting his journey to Paris, was indulged with a private audience of the French king; then he set out incognito for the coast of Picardy. The British ministry, being apprized of his arrival in France, at once comprehended the destination of the armaments prepared at Brest and Boulogne. Mr. Thomson, the English resident at Paris, received orders to make a remonstrance to the French ministry, on the violation of those treaties by which the pretender to the crown of Great Britain was excluded from the territories of France. But he was given to understand, that his Most Christian Majesty would not explain himself on that subject, until the King of England should have given satisfaction on the repeated complaints which had been made to him, touching the infractions of those very treaties which had been so often violated by his orders. In the month of January, M. de Roquefeuille sailed from Brest, directing his course up the English channel with twenty ships of war. They were immediately discovered by an English cruiser, which ran into Plymouth; and the intelligence was conveyed by land to the board of Admiralty. Sir John Norris was forthwith ordered to take the command of the squadron at Spithead, with which he sailed round to the Downs, where he was joined by some ships of the line from Chatham, and then he found himself at the head of a squadron considerably stronger than that of the enemy.

Several regiments marched to the southern coast of England: all governors and commanders were ordered to repair immediately to their respective posts: the forts at the mouths of the Thames and Medway were put in a posture of defence; and directions were issued to assemble the Kentish militia, to defend the coast in case of an invasion. On the fifteenth day of February the king sent a message to both Houses of Parliament, intimating the arrival of the pretender's son in France, the preparations at Dunkirk, and the appearance of a French fleet in the English channel. They joined in an address, declaring their indignation and abhorrence of the design formed in favour of a popish pretender; and assuring his majesty, that they would, with the warmest zeal and unanimity, take such measures as would enable him to frustrate and defeat so desperate and insolent an attempt. Addresses of the same kind were presented by the city of London, both universities, the principal towns of Great Britain, the clergy, the dissenting ministers, the quakers, and almost all the corporations and communities of the kingdom. A requisition was made of the six thousand auxiliaries which the States-General were by treaty obliged to furnish on such occasions; and these were granted with great alacrity and expedition. The Earl of Stair, forgetting his wrongs, took this opportunity of offering his services to government, and was invested with the chief command of the forces in Great Britain. His example was followed by several noblemen of the first rank. The Duke of Montague was permitted to raise a regiment of horse; and orders were sent to bring over six thousand of the British troops from Flanders, in case the invasion should actually take place. His majesty was, in another address from Parliament, exhorted to augment his forces by sea and land: the habeas corpus act was suspended for six months, and several persons of distinction were apprehended on suspicion of treasonable practices: a proclamation was issued for putting the laws in execution against papists and nonjurors, who were commanded to retire ten miles from London; and every precaution was taken which seemed necessary for the preservation of the public tranquillity.

Meanwhile the French court proceeded with their preparations at Boulogne and Dunkirk, under the eye of the young pretender; and seven thousand men were actually embarked. M. de Roquefeuille sailed up the channel as far as Dungeness, a promontory on the coast of Kent, after having detached M. de Barreil, with five ships, to hasten the embarkation

*The design of the French War between France and England defeated.*

at Dunkirk. While the French admiral anchored off Dungeness, he perceived, on the twenty-fourth day of February, the British fleet under Sir John Norris, doubling the South Foreland from the Downs; and though the wind was against him, taking the opportunity of the tide to come up and engage the French squadron. Roquefeuille, who little expected such a visit, could not be altogether composed, considering the great superiority of his enemies; but the tide failing, the English admiral was obliged to anchor two leagues short of the enemy. In this interval, M. de Roquefeuille called a council of war, in which it was determined to avoid an engagement, weigh anchor at sunset, and make the best of their way to the place from whence they had set sail. This resolution was favoured by a very hard gale of wind, which began to blow from the north-east, and carried them down the channel with incredible expedition. But the same storm which, in all probability, saved their fleet from destruction, utterly disconcerted the design of invading England. A great number of their transports were driven ashore and destroyed, and the rest were so damaged that they could not be speedily repaired. The English were now masters at sea, and their coast was so well guarded that the enterprise could not be prosecuted with any probability of success. The French generals nominated to serve in this expedition returned to Paris, and the young pretender resolved to wait a more favourable opportunity. In the mean time he remained in Paris, or that neighbourhood, incognito, and almost totally neglected by the court of France. Finding himself in this disagreeable situation, and being visited by John Murray of Broughton, who magnified the power of his friends in Great Britain, he resolved to make some bold effort even without the assistance of Louis, in whose sincerity he had no faith, and forthwith took proper measures to obtain exact information touching the number, inclinations, and influence of his father's adherents in England and Scotland. The French king no longer preserved any measures with the court of London: the British resident at Paris was given to understand, that a declaration of war must ensue; and this was actually published on the twentieth day of March. The King of Great Britain was taxed with having dissuaded the court of Vienna from entertaining any thoughts of an accommodation; with having infringed the convention of Hanover; with having exercised piracy upon the subjects of France; and with having blocked up the harbour of Toulon. On the thirty-first day of March, a like denunciation of war against France was published at London, amidst the acclamations of the people.

<small>1744.
Bill against those who should correspond with the sons of the pretender.</small>

The Commons of England, in order to evince their loyalty, brought in a bill, denouncing the penalties of high treason against those who should maintain correspondence with the sons of the pretender. In the Upper House, Lord Hardwicke, the chancellor, moved, that a clause should be inserted, extending the crime of treason to the posterity of the offenders, during the lives of the pretender's sons. The motion, which was supported by the whole strength of the ministry, produced a warm debate, in which the Duke of Bedford, the Earl of Chesterfield, the Lords Talbot and Hervey, argued against it in the most pathetic manner, as an illiberal expedient, contrary to the dictates of humanity, the law of nature, the rules of common justice, and the precepts of religion; an expedient that would involve the innocent with the guilty, and tend to the augmentation of ministerial power, for which purpose it was undoubtedly calculated. Notwithstanding these suggestions, the clause was carried in the affirmative, and the bill sent back to the Commons, where the amendment was vigorously opposed by Lord Strange, Lord Guernsey, Mr. W. Pitt, and other members, by whom the original bill had been countenanced;* the majority, however, declared for the amendment, and the bill obtained the royal assent. The session of Parliament was closed in May, when the king told them, that the French had made vast preparations on the side of the Netherlands; and that the States-General had agreed to furnish the succours stipulated by treaties.

<small>Naval engagement of Toulon.</small>

By this time an action had happened in the Mediterranean, between the British fleet commanded by Admiral Matthews, and the combined squadrons of France and Spain, which had been for some time blocked up in the harbour of Toulon. On the ninth day of February they were perceived standing out of the road, to

---

* The opposition had sustained a heavy blow in the death of the Duke of Argyle, a nobleman of shining qualifications for the senate and the field, whose character would have been still more illustrious, had not some parts of his conduct subjected him to the suspicion of selfishness and inconstancy. He was succeeded in that title by his brother, Archibald, Earl of Ilay.

the number of four-and-thirty sail: the English admiral immediately weighed from Hieres bay; and on the eleventh, part of the fleets engaged. Matthews attacked the Spanish admiral, Don Navarro, whose ship, the Real, was a first-rate, mounted with above a hundred guns. Rear-Admiral Rowley singled out M. de Court, who commanded the French squadron; and a very few captains followed the example of their commanders: but Vice-Admiral Lestock, with his whole division, remained at a great distance astern: and several captains who were immediately under the eye of Matthews, behaved in such a manner as reflected disgrace upon their country. The whole transaction was conducted without order or deliberation. The French and Spaniards would have willingly avoided an engagement, as the British squadron was superior to them in strength and number. M. de Court, therefore, made the best of his way towards the Straits' mouth, probably with intention to join the Brest quadron; but he had orders to protect the Spanish fleet; and as they sailed heavily, he was obliged to wait for them at the hazard of maintaining a battle with the English. Thus circumstanced, he made sail and lay-to by turns; so that the British admiral could not engage them in proper order; and as they outsailed his ships, he began to fear they would escape him altogether, should he wait for Vice-Admiral Lestock, who was so far astern. Under this apprehension he made the signal for engaging, while that for the line of battle was still displayed; and this inconsistency naturally introduced confusion. The fight was maintained with great vivacity by the few who engaged. The Real being quite disabled, and lying like a wreck upon the water, Mr. Matthews sent a fire-ship to destroy her; but the expedient did not take effect. The ship ordered to cover this machine did not obey the signal; so that the captain of the fire-ship was exposed to the whole fire of the enemy. Nevertheless, he continued to advance until he found the vessel sinking; and being within a few yards of the Real, he set fire to the fusees. The ship was immediately in flames, in the midst of which he and his lieutenant, with twelve men, perished. This was likewise the fate of a Spanish launch, which had been manned with fifty sailors, to prevent the fire-ship from running on board the Real. One ship of the line belonging to the Spanish squadron struck to Captain Hawke, who sent a lieutenant to take possession of her: she was afterwards retaken by the French squadron; but was found so disabled that they left her deserted, and she was next day burned by order of Admiral Matthews. At night the action ceased; and the admiral found his own ship so much damaged that he moved his flag into another. Captain Cornwall fell in the engagement, after having exhibited a remarkable proof of courage and intrepidity; but the loss of men was very inconsiderable. Next day the enemy appeared to leeward, and the admiral gave chase till night, when he brought to, that he might be joined by the ships astern. They were perceived again on the thirteenth at a considerable distance, and pursued till the evening. In the morning of the fourteenth, twenty sail of them were seen distinctly, and Lestock with his division had gained ground of them considerably by noon; but Admiral Matthews displayed the signal for leaving off chase, and bore away for Port Mahon, to repair the damage he had sustained. Meanwhile the combined squadrons continued their course towards the coast of Spain. M. de Court, with his division, anchored in the road of Alicant; and Don Navarro sailed into the harbour of Carthagena. Admiral Matthews, on his arrival at Minorca, accused Lestock of having misbehaved on the day of action; suspended him from his office, and sent him prisoner to England, where, in his turn, he accused his accuser. Long before the engagement, these two officers had expressed the most virulent resentment against each other. Matthews was brave, open, and undisguised; but proud, imperious, and precipitate. Lestock had signalized his courage on many occasions, and perfectly understood the whole discipline of the navy; but he was cool, cunning, and vindictive. He had been treated superciliously by Matthews, and, in revenge, took advantage of his errors and precipitation. To gratify this passion he betrayed the interest and glory of his country; for it is not to be doubted but that he might have come up in time to engage; and in that case, the fleets of France and Spain would in all likelihood have been destroyed: but he intrenched himself within the punctilios of discipline, and saw with pleasure his antagonist expose himself to the hazard of death, ruin, and disgrace. Matthews himself, in the sequel, sacrificed his duty to his resentment, in restraining Lestock from pursuing and attacking the combined squadrons on the third day after the engagement, when they appeared disabled, and in manifest disorder, and would have fallen an easy prey, had they been vigorously attacked. One can hardly, without indignation, reflect upon these instances, in which a community has so severely suffered from the personal animosity of individuals. The miscarriage of Toulon became the subject of a parliamentary inquiry in England. The Commons, in an address to the throne, desired that a court-martial might be appointed to try the delinquents. By this time Lestock had accused Matthews, and all the captains of his division who misbehaved on the day of battle. The court-martial was constituted, and proceeded to trial. Several commanders of ships were cashiered: Vice-Admiral Lestock was honourably acquitted; and Admiral Matthews rendered incapable of serving for the future in his majesty's navy. All the world knew that Lestock kept aloof, and that Matthews rushed into the hottest part of the engagement. Yet the former triumphed on his trial, and the latter narrowly escaped the sentence of death for cowardice and misconduct. Such decisions are not to be accounted for, except from prejudice and faction.

The war in Germany, which had been almost extinguished in the last campaign, began to revive, and raged with redoubled violence. The emperor had solicited the mediation of his Britannic majesty for compromising the differences between him and the court of Vienna. *Advances towards peace made by the emperor.* Prince William of Hesse-Cassel had conferred with the King of England on this subject; and a negotiation was begun at Hanau. The emperor offered to dismiss the French auxiliaries, provided the Austrians would evacuate his hereditary dominions. Nay, Prince William and Lord Carteret, as plenipotentiaries, actually agreed to preliminaries, by which his imperial majesty engaged to renounce the alliance of France, and throw himself into the arms of the maritime powers; to resign all pretensions to the succession of the house of Austria; and to revive the vote of Bohemia in the electoral college; on condition of his being re-established in the possession of his dominions, recognized as emperor by the Queen of Hungary, and accommodated with a monthly subsidy for his maintenance, as his own territories were exhausted and impoverished by the war. By a separate article, the King of Great Britain promised to furnish him with three hundred thousand crowns, and to interpose his good offices with the Queen of Hungary, that his electoral dominions should be favourably treated. These preliminaries, though settled, were not signed. The court of Vienna was unwilling to part with their conquests in Bavaria and the Upper Palatinate. The queen trusted too much to the valour of her troops, and the wealth of her allies, to listen to such terms of accommodation; and whatever arguments were used by the King of Great Britain, certain it is the negotiation was dropped, on pretence that the articles were disapproved by the ministry of England. The emperor, environed with distress, renewed his application to the King of Great Britain; and even declared that he would refer his cause to the determination of the maritime powers; but all his advances were discountenanced; and the treaty of Worms dispelled all hope of accommodation. In this manner did the British ministry reject the fairest opportunity that could possibly occur of terminating the war in Germany with honour and advantage, and of freeing their country from that insufferable burden of expense under which she groaned.

The inflexibility of the house of Austria and its chief ally proved serviceable to the emperor. The forlorn situation of this unfortunate prince excited the compassion of divers princes: they resented the insolence with which the head of the empire had been treated by the court of Vienna; and they were alarmed at the increasing power of a family noted for pride, tyranny, and ambition. These considerations gave rise to the treaty of Frankfort, concluded in May between the emperor, the King of Prussia, the King of Sweden as Landgrave of Hesse-Cassel, and the Elector Palatine. They engaged to preserve the constitution of the empire, according to the treaty of Westphalia, and to support the emperor in his rank and dignity. They agreed to employ their good offices with the Queen of Hungary, that she might be induced to acknowledge the emperor, to restore his hereditary dòminions, and give up the archives of the empire that were in her possession. They guaranteed to each other their respective territories; the disputes about the succession of the late emperor they referred to the decision of the states of the empire: they promised to assist one another in case of being attacked; and they invited the King of Poland, the Elector of Cologn, and the Bishop of Liege, to accede to this treaty. Such was the confederacy that broke all the measures which had been concerted between the King of Great Britain and her Hungarian majesty, for the operations of the campaign. In the mean time, the French king declared war against this princess, on pretence that she was obstinately deaf to all terms of accommodation, and determined to carry the war into the territories of France. In her counter-declaration she taxed Louis with having infringed the most solemn engagement with respect to the pragmatic sanction; with having spirited up different pretenders, to lay claim to the succession of the late emperor; with having endeavoured to instigate the common enemy of Christendom against her; and with having acted the incendiary in the north of Europe, that the czarina might be prevented from assisting the house of Austria, while his numerous armies overspread the empire, and desolated her hereditary countries. These recriminations were literally true. The houses of Bourbon and Austria have, for many centuries, been the common disturbers and plagues of Europe.

The King of France, though in himself pacific and unenterprising, was stimulated by his ministry to taste the glory of conquest in the Netherlands, where he had assembled an army of one hundred and twenty thousand men, provided with a very formidable train of artillery. *Progress of the French king in the Netherlands.* The chief command was vested in the Mareschal Count de Saxe, who possessed great military talents, and proved to be one of the most fortunate generals of the age in which he lived. The allied forces, consisting of English, Hanoverians, Dutch, and Austrians, to the number of seventy thousand effective men, were in the month of May assembled in the neighbourhood of Brussels, from whence they marched towards Oudenarde, and posted themselves behind the Schelde, being unable to retard the progress of the enemy. The French monarch, attended by his favourite ladies, with all the pomp of eastern luxury, arrived at Lisle on the twelfth day of the same month; and in the adjacent plain reviewed his army. The States-General, alarmed at his preparations, had, in a conference with his ambassador at the Hague, expressed their apprehensions, and entreated his most Christian majesty would desist from his design of attacking their barrier. Their remonstrances having proved ineffectual, they now sent a minister to wait upon that monarch, to enforce their former representations, and repeat their entreaties; but no regard was paid to his request. The French king told him, he was determined to prosecute the war with vigour, as his moderation hitherto had served to no other purpose but that of rendering his enemies more intractable. Accordingly, his troops invested Menin, which was in seven days surrendered upon capitulation. Ypres, Fort Knock, and Furnes, underwent the same fate; and on the twenty-ninth day of June the King of France entered Dunkirk in triumph.

He had taken such precautions for the defence of Alsace, which was guarded by considerable armies under the command of Coigny and Seckendorf, that he thought he had nothing to fear from the Austrians in that quarter: besides, he had received secret assurances that the King of Prussia would declare for the emperor; so that he resolved to pursue his conquests in the Netherlands. But all his measures were defeated by the activity of Prince Charles of Lorraine, and his officers, who found means to pass the Rhine, and oblige the French and Bavarian generals to retire to Lampertheim, that they might cover Strasburgh. The Austrians made themselves masters of Haguenau and Saverne; they secured the passes of Lorraine; and laid all the country of Lower Alsace under contribution. The King of France was no sooner apprised of the prince's having passed the Rhine, and penetrated into this province, than he sent off a detachment of thirty thousand men from his army in Flanders to reinforce that under the Mareschal de Coigny; and he himself began his journey from the Rhine, that he might in person check the progress of the enemy; but this design was anticipated by a severe distemper that overtook him at Mentz in Lorraine. The physicians despaired of his life. The queen, with her children, and all the princes of the blood, hastened from Versailles to pay their last duties to their dying sovereign, who, as a true penitent, dismissed his concubines, and began to prepare himself for death: yet the strength of his constitution triumphed over the fever, and his recovery was celebrated all over his dominions with uncommon marks of joy and affection.

*Prince Charles of Lorraine passes the Rhine.*

In the mean time the schemes of the Austrian general were frustrated by the King of Prussia, who, in the month of August, entered the electorate of Saxony, at the head of a numerous army. There he declared, in a public manifesto, that his aims were only to re-establish the peace of the empire, and to support the dignity of its head. He assured the inhabitants that they might depend upon his protection, in case they should remain quiet; but threatened them with fire and sword should they presume to oppose his arms. In a rescript, addressed to his ministers at foreign courts, he accused the Queen of Hungary of obstinacy, in refusing to acknowledge the emperor, and restore his hereditary dominions: he said he had engaged in the league of Frankfort, to hinder the head of the empire from being oppressed: that he had no intention to violate the peace of Breslau, or enter as a principal into this war: he affirmed that his design was to act as auxiliary to the emperor, and establish the quiet of Germany. He penetrated into Bohemia, and undertook the siege of Prague, the governor of which surrendered himself and his garrison prisoners of war on the sixteenth day of September. He afterwards reduced Tabor, Bodweis, and Teyn, and, in a word, subdued the greatest part of the kingdom; the Austrian forces in that country being in no condition to stop his progress. Nevertheless, he was soon obliged to relinquish his conquests. Prince Charles of Lorraine was recalled from Alsace, and repassed the Rhine in the face of the French army, commanded by the Mareschals de Coigny, Noailles, and Belleisle. Then he marched to the Danube, laid the Upper Palatinate under contribution, and entering Bohemia, joined the troops under Bathiani at Merotitz. The King of Poland, Elector of Saxony, at this juncture, declared in favour of her Hungarian majesty. A convention for the mutual guarantee of their dominions had been signed between those two powers in December; and now Prince Charles of Lorraine was reinforced by twenty thousand Saxon troops, under the conduct of the Duke of Saxe-Wessenfels. The combined army was superior to that of his Prussian majesty, whom they resolved to engage. But he retired before them, and having evacuated all the places he had garrisoned in Bohemia, retreated with precipitation into Silesia. There his troops were put into winter-quarters; and he himself returned to Berlin, extremely mortified at the issue of the campaign.

During these transactions, Count Seckendorff marched

into Bavaria at the head of a strong army, drove the Austrians out of the electorate, and the emperor regained possession of Munich, his capital, on the twenty-second day of October. In August, the French army passed the Rhine at Fort Louis, and invested the strong and important city of Fribourg, defended by General Demnitz, at the head of nine thousand veterans. The King of France arrived in the camp on the eleventh day of October, and the siege was carried on with uncommon vigour. The Austrian governor made incredible efforts in the defence of the place, which he maintained until it was reduced to a heap of ruins, and one half of the garrison destroyed. At length, however, they were obliged to surrender themselves prisoners of war, after the trenches had been open five-and-forty days, during which they had killed above fifteen thousand of the besiegers. With this conquest the French king closed the campaign, and his army was cantoned along the Rhine, under the inspection of the Count de Maillebois. By the detachments drawn from the French army in Flanders, Count Saxe had found himself considerably weaker than the confederates: he threw up strong intrenchments behind the Lys, where he remained on the defensive, until he was reinforced by the Count de Clermont, who commanded a separate body on the side of Newport. The allies, to the number of seventy thousand, passed the Schelde, and advanced towards Helchin; but the enemy being so advantageously posted that they could not attack him with any prospect of advantage, they filed on in sight of Tournay; and on the eighth day of August encamped in the plains of Lisle, in hope of drawing Count Saxe from the situation in which he was so strongly fortified. Here they foraged for several days, and laid the open country under contribution: however, they made no attempt on the place itself, which in all probability would have fallen into their hands, had they invested it at their first approach, for then there was no other garrison but two or three battalions of militia: but Count Saxe soon threw in a considerable reinforcement. The allies were unprovided with a train of battering cannon; and their commanders would not deviate from the usual form of war. Besides, they were divided in their opinions, and despised one another. General Wade, who commanded the English and Hanoverians, was a vain, weak man, without confidence, weight, or authority; and the Austrian general, the Duke d'Aremberg, was a proud rapacious glutton, devoid of talents and sentiment. After having remained for some time in sight of Lisle, and made a general forage without molestation, they retired to their former camp on the Schelde, from whence they soon marched into winter quarters. Count Saxe at length quitted his lines; and by way of retaliation sent out detachments to ravage the Low Countries to the very gates of Ghent and Bruges. The conduct of the allied generals was severely censured in England, and ridiculed in France, not only in private conversation, but also on their public theatres, where it became the subject of farces and pantomimes.

The campaign in Italy produced divers vicissitudes of fortune. The King of Naples, having assembled an army, joined Count Gages, and published a manifesto in vindication of his conduct, which was a direct violation of the neutrality he had promised to observe. *The King of Naples joins Count Gages in Italy.* He maintained that his moderation had been undervalued by the courts of London and Vienna; that his frontiers were threatened with the calamities of war; and that the Queen of Hungary made no secret of her intention to invade his dominions. This charge was not without foundation. The emissaries of the house of Austria endeavoured to excite a rebellion in Naples, which Prince Lobkowitz had orders to favour by an invasion. This general was encamped at Monte Rotundo, in the neighbourhood of Rome, when, in the month of June, the confederates advanced to Velletri. While the two armies remained in sight of each other, Prince Lobkowitz detached a strong body of forces, under Count Soro and General Gorani, who made an irruption into the province of Abruzzo, and took the city of Aquilla, where they distributed a manifesto, in which the Queen of Hungary exhorted the Neapolitans to shake off the Spanish yoke, and submit again to the house of Austria. This step, however, produced little or no effect, and the Austrian detachment retired at the approach of the Duke of Vieuville, with a superior number of forces. In August, Count Brown, at the head of an Austrian detachment, surprised Velletri in the night; and the King of the Two Sicilies, with the Duke of Modena, were in the utmost danger of being taken. They escaped by a postern with great difficulty, and repaired to the quarters of Count Gages, who performed the part of a great general on this occasion. He rallied the fugitives, dispelled the panic and confusion which had begun to prevail in his camp, and made a disposition for cutting off the retreat of the Austrians. Count Brown, finding himself in danger of being surrounded, thought proper to secure his retreat, which he effected with great art and gallantry, carrying off a prodigious booty. Three thousand Spaniards are said to have fallen in this action; and eight hundred men were taken, with some standards and colours. Count Mariani, a Neapolitan general, was among the prisoners. The Austrians lost about six hundred men; and General Novati fell into the hands of the enemy; but the exploit produced no consequence of importance. The heats of autumn proved so fatal to the Austrians, who were not accustomed to the climate, that Prince Lobkowitz saw his army mouldering away, without any possibility of its being recruited: besides, the country was so drained that he could no longer procure subsistence. Impelled by these considerations, he meditated a retreat. On the eleventh day of November he decamped from Faiola, marched under the walls of Rome, passed the Tiber at Ponte Molle, formerly known by the name of Pons Milvius, which he had just time to break down behind him when the vanguard of the Spaniards and Neapolitans appeared. Part of his rearguard, however, was taken, with Count Soro who commanded it, at Nocera; and his army suffered greatly by desertion. Nevertheless, he continued his retreat with equal skill and expedition, passed the mountains of Gubio, and by the way of Viterbo reached the Bolognese. The pope was altogether passive. In the beginning of the campaign he had caressed Lobkowitz; and now he received the King of the Two Sicilies with marks of the warmest affection. That prince, having visited the chief curiosities of Rome, returned to Naples, leaving part of his troops under the command of Count Gages.

Fortune likewise favoured his brother Don Philip, in Savoy and Piedmont. He was, early in the season, joined at Antibes by the French army, under the conduct of the Prince of Conti. In the latter end of March the combined forces passed the Var, reduced the castle of Aspremont, and entered the city of Nice, without opposition. In April, they attacked the King of Sardinia, who, with twenty thousand men, was strongly intrenched among the

*Battle of Coni.*

mountains of Villa Franca. The action was obstinate and bloody; but their numbers and perseverance prevailed. He was obliged to abandon his posts, and embark on board of the British squadron, which transported him and his troops to Vado. The intention of Don Philip was to penetrate through the territories of Genoa into the Milanese; but Admiral Matthews, who hovered with a strong squadron on that coast, sent a message to the republic, declaring that, should the combined army be suffered to pass through her dominions, the King of Great Britain would consider such a step as a breach of their neutrality. The senate, intimidated by this intimation, entreated the princes to desist from their design, and they resolved to choose another route. They defiled towards Piedmont, and assaulted the strong post of Chateau Dauphiné, defended by the King of Sardinia in person. After a desperate attack, in which they lost four thousand men, the place was taken: the garrison of Demont surrendered at discretion, and the whole country of Piedmont was laid under contribution. His Sardinian majesty was not in a condition to hazard a battle; and therefore posted himself at Saluzzes, in order to cover his capital. The combined army advanced to the strong and important town of Coni, which was invested in the beginning of September. Baron Leutrum the governor made an obstinate defence, and the situation of the place was such as rendered the siege difficult, tedious, and bloody. The King of Sardinia, being reinforced by ten thousand Austrians, under General Pallavicini, advanced to its relief, and a battle ensued. The action was maintained with great vigour on both sides, till night, when his majesty, finding it impracticable to force the enemy's intrenchments, retired in good order to his camp at Murasso. He afterwards found means to throw a reinforcement and supply of provisions into Coni; and the heavy rains that fell at this period not only retarded, but even dispirited the besiegers. Nevertheless, the princes persisted in their design, notwithstanding a dearth of provisions, and the approach of winter, till the latter end of November, when the Chevalier de Soto entered the place with six hundred fresh men. This incident was no sooner known than the princes abandoned their enterprise; and, leaving their sick and wounded to the mercy of the Piedmontese, marched back to Demont. Having dismantled the fortifications of this place, they retreated with great precipitation to Dauphiné, and were dreadfully harassed by the Vaudois and light troops in the service of his Sardinian majesty, who now again saw himself in possession of Piedmont. The French troops were quartered in Dauphiné; but Don Philip still maintained his footing in Savoy, the inhabitants of which he fleeced without mercy.

<small>Return of Commodore Anson. Sir John Balchen perishes at sea.</small> After the action at Toulon, nothing of consequence was achieved by the British squadron in the Mediterranean; and indeed the naval power of Great Britain was, during the summer, quite inactive. In the month of June, Commodore Anson returned from his voyage of three years and nine months, in which he had surrounded the terraqueous globe. We have formerly observed that he sailed with a small squadron to the South-Sea, in order to annoy the Spanish settlements of Chili and Peru. Two of his large ships, having been separated from him in a storm before he weathered Cape Horn, had put in at Rio de Janeiro, on the coast of Brazil, from whence they returned to Europe. A frigate, commanded by Captain Cheap, was shipwrecked on a desolate island in the South-Sea. Mr. Anson, having undergone a dreadful tempest which dispersed his fleet, arrived at the island of Juan Fernandez, where he was joined by the Gloucester, a ship of the line, a sloop, and a pink loaded with provisions. These were the remains of his squadron. He made prize of several vessels; took and burned the little town of Payta; set sail from the coast of Mexico, for the Philippine Isles: and in this passage the Gloucester was abandoned and sunk: the other vessels had been destroyed for want of men to navigate them, so that nothing now remained but the commodore's own ship, the Centurion, and that but very indifferently manned; for the crews had been horribly thinned by sickness. Incredible were the hardships and misery they sustained from the shattered condition of the ships and the scorbutic disorder, when they reached the plentiful island of Tinian, where they were supplied with the necessary refreshments. Thence they prosecuted their voyage to the river of Canton in China, where the commodore ordered the ship to be sheathed, and found means to procure a reinforcement of sailors. The chief object of his attention was the rich annual ship that sails between Acapulco in Mexico, and Manilla, one of the Philippine Islands. In hopes of intercepting her, he set sail from Canton, and steered his course back to the

straits of Manilla, where she actually fell into his hands, after a short but vigorous engagement. The prize was called Nuestra Signora de Cabodonga, mounted with forty guns, manned with six hundred sailors, and loaded with treasure and effects to the value of three hundred and thirteen thousand pounds sterling: with this windfall he returned to Canton, from whence he proceeded to the Cape of Good Hope, and prosecuted his voyage to England, where he arrived in safety. Though this fortunate commander enriched himself by an occurrence that may be termed almost accidental, the British nation was not indemnified for the expense of the expedition; and the original design was entirely defeated. Had the Manilla ship escaped the vigilance of the English commodore, he might have been, at his return to England, laid aside as a superannuated captain, and died in obscurity; but his great wealth invested him with considerable influence, and added lustre to his talents. He soon became the oracle which was consulted in all naval deliberations; and the king raised him to the dignity of a peerage. In July, Sir John Balchen, an admiral of approved valour and great experience, sailed from Spithead with a strong squadron, in quest of an opportunity to attack the French fleet at Brest, under the command of M. de Rochambault. In the bay of Biscay he was overtaken by a violent storm that dispersed the ships, and drove them up the English channel. Admiral Stewart, with the greater part of them, arrived at Plymouth; but Sir John Balchen's own ship, the Victory, which was counted the most beautiful first-rate in the world, foundered at sea; and this brave commander perished, with all his officers, volunteers, and crew, amounting to eleven hundred choice seamen. On the fourth day of October, after the siege of Fribourg, the Marshal Duke de Belleisle, and his brother, happened, in their way to Berlin, to halt at a village in the forest of Hartz, dependent on the Electorate of Hanover. There they were apprehended by the bailiff of the place, and conducted as prisoners to Osterode; from whence they were removed to Stade on the Elbe, where they embarked for England. They resided at Windsor till the following year, when they were allowed the benefit of the cartel which had been established between Great Britain and France at Frankfort, and released accordingly, after they had been treated by the British nobility with that respect and hospitality which was due to their rank and merit.[b]

*Revolution in the British ministry. Session of Parliament.*

The dissensions in the British cabinet were now ripened into another revolution in the ministry. Lord Carteret, who was by this time Earl Granville, in consequence of his mother's death, had engrossed the royal favour so much, that the Duke of N—— and his brother are said to have taken umbrage at his influence and greatness. He had incurred the resentment of those who were distinguished by the appellation of patriots, and entirely forfeited his popularity. The two brothers were very powerful by their parliamentary interest; they knew their own strength, and engaged in a political alliance with the leading men in the opposition, against the prime minister and his measures. This coalition was dignified with the epithet of "The Broad Bottom," as if it had been established on a true constitutional foundation, comprehending individuals of every class, without distinction of party. The appellation, however, which they assumed was afterwards converted into a term of derision. The Earl of Granville, perceiving the gathering storm, and foreseeing the impossibility of withstanding such an opposition in Parliament, wisely avoided the impending danger and disgrace, by a voluntary resignation of his employments. The Earl of Harrington succeeded him as secretary of state. The Duke of Bedford was appointed first lord of the admiralty, and the Earl of Chesterfield declared lord lieutenant of Ireland. The Lords Gower and Cobham were re-established in the offices they had resigned: Mr. Lyttelton was admitted as a commissioner of the treasury: even Sir John Hynde Cotton accepted of a place at court; and Sir John Philips sat at the board of trade and plantations, though he soon renounced this employment. This was rather a change of men than of measures, and turned out to the ease and advantage of the sovereign; for his views were no longer thwarted by an obstinate opposition in Parliament. The session was opened on the twenty-eighth day of November, in the usual manner. The Commons unanimously granted about six millions and a half for the service of the ensuing year, to be raised by the land, the malt, and the salt taxes,

[b] Mr. Pope, the celebrated poet, died in the month of June. In October, the old Duchess of Marlborough resigned her breath, in the eighty-fifth year of her age, immensely rich, and very little regretted, either by her own family, or the world in general.

the sinking fund, and an additional duty on wines. In January, the Earl of Chesterfield set out for the Hague, with the character of ambassador extraordinary, to persuade, if possible, the States-General to engage heartily in the war. About the same time, a treaty of quadruple alliance was signed at Warsaw, by the Queen of Hungary, the King of Poland, and the maritime powers. This was a mutual guarantee of the dominions belonging to the contracting parties: but his Polish majesty was paid for his concurrence with an annual subsidy of one hundred and fifty thousand pounds, two-thirds of which were defrayed by England, and the remainder was disbursed by the United Provinces.*

The business of the British Parliament being discussed, the session was closed in the beginning of May, and, immediately after the prorogation, the king set out for Hanover. The death of the Emperor Charles VII., which happened in the month of January, had entirely changed the face of affairs in the empire, and all the princes of Germany were in commotion. The Grand Duke of Tuscany, consort to her Hungarian majesty, was immediately declared a candidate for the imperial crown; while his pretensions were warmly opposed by the French king and his allies. The court of Vienna, taking advantage of the late emperor's death, sent an army to invade Bavaria in the month of March, under the conduct of General Bathiani, who routed the French and Palatine troops at Psiffenhoven; took possession of Rain; surrounded and disarmed six thousand Hessians in the neighbourhood of Ingoldstadt; and drove the Bavarian forces out of the electorate. The young elector was obliged to abandon his capital, and retire to Augsburgh, where he found himself in danger of losing all his dominions. In this emergency he yielded to the earnest solicitations of the empress his mother, enforced by the advice of his uncle, the Elector of Cologn, and of his general, Count Seckendorf, who exhorted him to be reconciled to the court of Vienna. A negotiation was immediately begun at Fuessen, where, in April, the treaty was concluded.

1745. Death of the Emperor Charles VII. Accommodation between the Queen of Hungary and the young Elector of Bavaria.

* Robert, Earl of Orford, late prime minister, died in March, after having for a very short time enjoyed a pension of four thousand pounds granted by the crown, in consideration of his past services. Though he had for such a length of time directed the application of the public treasure, his circumstances were not affluent; he was liberal in his disposition, and had such a number of rapacious dependants to gratify, that little was left for his own private occasions.

The queen consented to recognize the imperial dignity, as having been vested in the person of his father; to acknowledge his mother as empress dowager; to restore his dominions, with all the fortresses, artillery, stores, and ammunition which she had taken; on the other hand, he renounced all claim to the succession of her father, and became guarantee of the pragmatic sanction: he acknowledged the validity of the electoral vote of Bohemia in the person of the queen; and engaged to give his voice for the grand duke, at the ensuing election of the King of the Romans. Until that should be determined, both parties agreed that Ingoldstadt should be garrisoned by neutral troops; and that Braunau and Schardingen, with all the country lying between the Inn and the Saltza, should remain in the queen's possession, though without prejudice to the civil government, or the elector's revenue. In the mean time he dismissed the auxiliaries that were in his pay, and they were permitted to retire without molestation.

The court of Vienna had now secured the votes of all the electors, except those of Brandenburgh and the Palatinate. Nevertheless, France assembled a powerful army in the neighbourhood of Frankfort, in order to influence the election. But the Austrian army, commanded by the grand duke in person, marched thither from the Danube; and the Prince of Conti was obliged to repass the Rhine at Nordlingen. Then the grand duke repaired to Frankfort, where, on the second day of September, he was by a majority of voices declared King of the Romans and Emperor of Germany. Meanwhile the King of Prussia had made great progress in the conquest of Silesia. The campaign began in January, when the Hungarian insurgents were obliged to retire into Moravia. In the following month the Prussian General Lehwald defeated a body of twelve thousand Austrians, commanded by General Helsrich; the town of Ratibor was taken by assault; and the king entered Silesia, in May, at the head of seventy thousand men. Prince Charles of Lorraine, being joined by the Duke of Saxe-Wessenfels and twenty thousand Saxons, penetrated into Silesia by the defiles of Landshut, and were attacked by his Prussian majesty in the plains of Striegau, near Friedberg. The battle was maintained from morning till noon, when the Saxons giving way, Prince Charles was

*[sidenote: The king of Prussia gains two successive battles at Frielberg and Sohr, over the Austrian and Saxon forces.]*

obliged to retire with the loss of twelve thousand men, and a great number of colours, standards, and artillery. This victory, obtained on the fourth day of June, complete as it was, did not prove decisive; for, though the victor transferred the seat of the war into Bohemia, and maintained his army by raising contributions in that country, the Austrians resolved to hazard another engagement. Their aim was to surprise him in his camp at Sohr, which they attacked on the thirtieth of September, at daybreak, but they met with such a warm reception, that, notwithstanding their repeated efforts during the space of four hours, they were repulsed with considerable damage, and retreated to Jaromire, leaving five thousand killed upon the spot, besides two thousand that were taken, with many standards, and twenty pieces of cannon. The loss of this battle was in a great measure owing to the avarice of the irregulars, who, having penetrated into the Prussian camp, began to pillage with great eagerness, giving the king an opportunity to rally his disordered troops, and restore the battle: nevertheless, they retired with the plunder of his baggage, including his military chest, the officers of his chancery, his own secretary, and all the papers of his cabinet.

After this action, his Prussian majesty returned to Berlin, and breathed nothing but peace and moderation. In August he had signed a convention with the King of Great Britain, who became guarantee of his possessions in Silesia, as yielded by the treaty of Breslau; and he promised to vote for the Grand Duke of Tuscany at the election of an emperor. This *Treaty of Dresden. The Grand Duke of Tuscany elected Emperor of Germany.* was intended as the basis of a more general accommodation. But he now pretended to have received undoubted intelligence that the King of Poland and the Queen of Hungary had agreed to invade Brandenburgh with three different armies; and that, for this purpose, his Polish majesty had demanded of the czarina the succours stipulated by treaty between the two crowns. Alarmed, or seemingly alarmed, at this information, he solicited the maritime powers to fulfil their engagements, and interpose their good offices with the court of Petersburgh. Yet, far from waiting for the result of these remonstrances, he made a sudden irruption into Lusatia, took possession of Gorlitz, and obliged Prince Charles of Lorraine to retire before him into Bohemia. Then he entered Leipsic, and laid Saxony under contribution. The King of Poland, unable to resist the torrent, quitted his capital, and took refuge in Prague. His troops, reinforced by a body of Austrians, were defeated at Pirna on the fifteenth day of December; and his Prussian majesty became master of Dresden without further opposition. The King of Poland, thus deprived of his hereditary dominions, was fain to acquiesce in such terms as the conqueror thought proper to impose; and the treaty of Dresden was concluded under the mediation of his Britannic majesty. By this convention the King of Prussia retained all the contributions he had levied in Saxony; and was entitled to a million of German crowns, to be paid by his Polish majesty at the next fair of Leipsic. He and the Elector Palatine consented to acknowledge the grand duke as Emperor of Germany; and this last confirmed to his Prussian majesty certain privileges *de non evocando*, which had been granted by the late emperor, with regard to some territories possessed by the King of Prussia, though not belonging to the electorate of Brandenburgh. Immediately after the ratification of this treaty, the Prussian troops evacuated Saxony; and the peace of Germany was restored.

Though the French King could not prevent the elevation of the grand duke to the imperial throne, he resolved to humble the house of Austria by making a conquest of the Netherlands. A prodigious army was there assembled, under the auspices of Mareschal Count de Saxe; and his most Christian majesty, with the dauphin, arriving in the camp, they invested the strong town of Tournay on the thirtieth day of April. The Dutch garrison consisted of eight thousand men, commanded by the old Baron Dorth, who made a vigorous defence. The Duke of Cumberland assumed the chief command of the allied army assembled at Soignies: he was assisted with the advice of the Count Konigseg, an Austrian general, and the Prince of Waldeck, commander of the Dutch forces. Their army was greatly inferior in number to that of the enemy; nevertheless, they resolved to march to the relief of Tournay. They accordingly advanced to Leuse; and on the twenty-eighth day of April took post at Maulbre, in sight of the French army, which was encamped on an eminence, from the village of Antoine to a large wood beyond Vezon, having Fontenoy in their front. Next day was employed by the allies in driving the enemy from some outposts, and clearing

*The allies are defeated at Fontenoy.*

the defiles through which they were obliged to advance to
the attack; while the French completed their batteries, and
made the most formidable preparations for their reception.
On the thirtieth day of April, the Duke of Cumberland,
having made the proper dispositions, began his march to
the enemy at two o'clock in the morning: a brisk cannonade ensued; and about nine both armies were engaged.
The British infantry drove the French beyond their lines;
but the left wing failing in the attack on the village of
Fontenoy, and the cavalry forbearing to advance on the
flanks, they measured back their ground with some disorder,
from the prodigious fire of the French batteries. They
rallied, however, and returning to the charge with redoubled ardour, repulsed the enemy to their camp with
great slaughter, but, being wholly unsupported by the other
wing, and exposed both in front and flank to a dreadful fire,
which did great execution, the duke was obliged to make
the necessary dispositions for a retreat about three o'clock
in the afternoon; and this was effected in tolerable order.
The battle was fought with great obstinacy, and the carnage on both sides was very considerable. The allies lost
about twelve thousand men, including a good number of
officers; among these were Lieutenant-General Campbell,
and Major-General Ponsonby. The victory cost the French
almost an equal number of lives; and no honour was lost
by the vanquished. Had the allies given battle on the preceding day, before the enemy had taken their measures and
received all their reinforcements, they might have succeeded
in their endeavours to relieve Tournay. Although the attack was generally judged rash and precipitate, the British
and Hanoverian troops fought with such intrepidity and perseverance, that if they had been properly sustained by the
Dutch forces, and their flanks covered by the cavalry, the
French, in all likelihood, would have been obliged to abandon
their enterprise. The Duke of Cumberland left his sick and
wounded to the humanity of the victors; and retiring to
Aeth, encamped in an advantageous situation at Lessines.
The garrison of Tournay, though now deprived of all hope
of succour, maintained the place to the twenty-first day of
June, when the governor obtained an honourable capitulation. After the conquest of this frontier, which was dismantled, the Duke of Cumberland, apprehending the enemy
had a design upon Ghent, sent a detachment of four thou-

sand men to reinforce the garrison of that city; but they fell into an ambuscade at Pas-du-mêle, and were killed or taken, except a few dragoons that escaped to Ostend: on that very night, which was the twelfth of June, Ghent was surprised by a detachment of the French army. Then they invested Ostend, which, though defended by an English garrison, and open to the sea, was, after a short siege, surrendered by capitulation on the fourteenth day of August. Dendermonde, Oudenarde, Newport, and Aeth underwent the same fate; while the allied army lay intrenched beyond the canal of Antwerp. The French king, having subdued the greatest part of the Austrian Netherlands, returned to Paris, which he entered in triumph.

<small>The King of Sardinia is almost stripped of his dominions.</small> The campaign in Italy was unpropitious to the Queen of Hungary and the King of Sardinia. Count Gages passed the Apennines, and entered the state of Lucca; from thence he proceeded by the eastern coast of Genoa to Lestride-Levante. The junction of the two armies was thus accomplished, and reinforced with ten thousand Genoese: meanwhile Prince Lobkowitz decamped from Modena and took post at Parma; but he was soon succeeded by Count Schuylemberg, and sent to command the Austrians in Bohemia. The Spaniards entered the Milanese without further opposition. Count Gages, with thirty thousand men, took possession of Serravalle; and advancing towards Placentia, obliged the Austrians to retire under the cannon of Tortona; but when Don Philip, at the head of forty thousand troops, made himself master of Acqui, the King of Sardinia and the Austrian general, unable to stem the torrent, retreated behind the Tanaro. The strong citadel of Tortona was taken by the Spaniards, who likewise reduced Parma and Placentia; and forcing the passage of the Tanaro, compelled his Sardinian majesty to take shelter on the other side of the Po. Then Pavia was won by scalade; and the city of Milan submitted to the infant, though the Austrian garrison still maintained the citadel; all Piedmont, on both sides of the Po, as far as Turin, was reduced, and even that capital threatened with a siege; so that by the month of October the territories belonging to the house of Austria, in Italy, were wholly subdued, and the King of Sardinia stripped of all his dominions; yet he continued firm and true to his engagements, and deaf to all proposals of a separate accommodation.

The naval transactions of Great Britain were in the course of this year remarkably spirited. In the Mediterranean, Admiral Rowley had succeeded Matthews in the command; Savona, Genoa, Final, St. Remo, with Bastia, the capital of Corsica, were bombarded; several Spanish ships were taken; but he could not prevent the safe arrival of their rich Havannah squadron at Corunna. Commodore Barnet, in the East Indies, made prize of several French ships richly laden; and Commodore Townshend, in the latitude of Martinico, took about thirty merchantships belonging to the enemy, under convoy of four ships of war, two of which were destroyed. The English privateers likewise met with uncommon success. But the most important achievement was the conquest of Louisbourg on the isle of Cape Breton, in North America; a place of great consequence, which the French had fortified at a prodigious expense. The scheme of reducing this fortress was planned in Boston, recommended by their general assembly, and approved by his majesty, who sent instructions to Commodore Warren, stationed off the Leeward Islands, to sail for the northern parts of America, and to co-operate with the forces of New England in this expedition. A body of six thousand men was formed under the conduct of Mr. Pepperel, a trader of Piscataquay, whose influence was extensive in that country, though he was a man of little or no education, and utterly unacquainted with military operations. In April Mr. Warren arrived at Canso with ten ships of war; and the troops of New England, being embarked in transports, sailed immediately for the isle of Cape Breton, where they landed without opposition. The enemy abandoned their grand battery, which was detached from the town; and the immediate seizure of it contributed in a good measure to the success of the enterprise. While the American troops, reinforced by eight hundred marines, carried on their approaches by land, the squadron blocked up the place by sea in such a manner that no succours could be introduced. A French ship of the line, with some smaller vessels destined for the relief of the garrison, were intercepted and taken by the British cruisers; and, indeed, the reduction of Louisbourg was chiefly owing to the vigilance and activity of Mr. Warren, one of the bravest and best officers in the service of England. The operations of the siege were wholly conducted by the engineers and officers who commanded the British marines; and the Americans, being ignorant of war, were contented to act under their directions. The town being considerably damaged by the bombs and bullets of the besiegers, and the garrison despairing of relief, the governor capitulated on the seventeenth day of June, when the city of Louisbourg and the isle of Cape Breton were surrendered to his Britannic majesty. The garrison and inhabitants engaged that they would not bear arms for twelve months against Great Britain or her allies; and being embarked in fourteen cartel ships, were transported to Rochefort. In a few days after the surrender of Louisbourg, two French East India ships, and another from Peru, laden with treasure, sailed into the harbour, on the supposition that it still belonged to France, and were taken by the English squadron.

The news of this conquest being transmitted to England, Mr. Pepperel was preferred to the dignity of a baronet of Great Britain, and congratulatory addresses were presented to the king on the success of his majesty's arms. The possession of Cape Breton was doubtless a valuable acquisition to Great Britain. It not only distressed the French in their fishery and navigation, but removed all fears of encroachment and rivalship from the English fishers on the banks of Newfoundland. It freed New England from the terrors of a dangerous neighbour, overawed the Indians of that country, and secured the possession of Acadia to the crown of Great Britain. The plan of this conquest was originally laid by Mr. Auchmuty, judge-advocate of the court of Admiralty in New England. He demonstrated that the reduction of Cape Breton would put the English in sole possession of the fishery of North America, which would annually return to Great Britain two millions sterling for the manufactures yearly shipped to the plantations; employ many thousand families that were otherwise unserviceable to the public; increase the shipping and mariners; extend navigation; cut off all communication between France and Canada by the river St. Laurence; so that Quebec would fall of course into the hands of the English, who might expel the French entirely from America, open a correspondence with the remote Indians, and render themselves masters of the profitable fur trade, which was now engrossed by the enemy. The natives of New England acquired great glory from the success of this enterprise. Britain, which had in some instances behaved like a stepmother to her own colonies, was now convinced of their importance, and treated those as brethren whom she had too long considered as aliens and rivals. Circumstanced as the nation is, the legislature cannot too tenderly cherish the interests of the British plantations in America. They are inhabited by a brave, hardy, industrious people, animated with an active spirit of commerce, inspired with a noble zeal for liberty and independence. The trade of Great Britain, clogged with heavy taxes and impositions, has for some time languished in many valuable branches. The French have undersold our cloths, and spoiled our markets in the Levant. Spain is no longer supplied as usual with the commodities of England: the exports to Germany must be considerably diminished by the misunderstanding between Great Britain and the house of Austria; consequently, her greatest resource must be in her communication with her own colonies, which consume her manufactures, and make immense returns in sugar, rum, tobacco, fish, timber, naval stores, iron, furs, drugs, rice, and indigo. The southern plantations likewise produce silk; and, with due encouragement, might furnish every thing that could be expected from the most fertile soil and the happiest climate. The continent of North America, if properly cultivated, will prove an inexhaustible fund of wealth and strength to Great Britain; and perhaps it may become the last asylum of British liberty. When the nation is enslaved by domestic despotism or foreign dominion; when her substance is wasted, her spirit broken, and the laws and constitution of England are no more; then those colonies, sent off by our fathers, may receive and entertain their sons as hapless exiles and ruined refugees.

While the continent of Europe and the isles of America were thus exposed to the ravages of war, and subjected to such vicissitudes of fortune, Great Britain underwent a dangerous convulsion in her own bowels. The son of the Chevalier de St. George, fired with ambition, and animated with the hope of ascending the throne of his ancestors, resolved to make an effort for that purpose, which, though it might not be crowned with success, should at least astonish all Christendom. The Jacobites in England and Scotland had promised, that if

*Project of an insurrection in Great Britain.*

he would land in Britain at the head of a regular army, they would supply him with provisions, carriages, and horses, and a great number of them declared they would take up arms and join his standard; but they disapproved of his coming over without forces, as a dangerous enterprise, that would in all probability end in the ruin of himself and all his adherents. This advice, including an exact detail of his father's interest, with the dispositions of his particular friends in every town and county, was transmitted to London in January, in order to be forwarded to Prince Charles; but the person with whom it was entrusted could find no safe method of conveyance; so that he sent it back to Scotland, from whence it was despatched to France; but before it reached Paris, Charles had left that kingdom. Had the paper come to his hands in due time, perhaps he would not have embarked in the undertaking, though he was stimulated to the attempt by many concurring motives. Certain it is, he was cajoled by the sanguine misrepresentations of a few adventurers, who hoped to profit by the expedition. They assured him that the whole nation was disaffected to the reigning family; that the people could no longer bear the immense load of taxes, which was daily increasing; and that the most considerable persons of the kingdom would gladly seize the first opportunity of crowding to his standard. On the other hand, he knew the British government had taken some effectual steps to alienate the friends of his house from the principles they had hitherto professed. Some of them had accepted posts and pensions; others were preferred in the army; and the Parliament were so attached to the reigning family, that he had nothing to hope from their deliberations. He expected no material succour from the court of France: he foresaw that delay would diminish the number of his adherents in Great Britain; and therefore resolved to seize the present occasion, which in many respects was propitious to his design. Without doubt, had he been properly supported, he could not have found a more favourable opportunity of exciting an intestine commotion in Great Britain; for Scotland was quite unfurnished with troops; King George was in Germany; the Duke of Cumberland, at the head of the British army, was employed in Flanders; and a great part of the Highlanders were keen for insurrection. Their natural principles were on this occasion stimulated by the suggestions of revenge. At the beginning of the war a regiment of those people had been formed, and transported with the rest of the British troops to Flanders. Before they were embarked a number of them deserted with their arms, on pretence that they had been decoyed into the service by promises and assurances that they should never be sent abroad: and this was really the case. They were overtaken by a body of horse, persuaded to submit, brought back to London pinioned like malefactors, and tried for desertion. Three were shot to death *in terrorem;* and the rest were sent in exile to the plantations. Those who suffered were persons of some consequence in their own country; and their fate was deeply resented by the clans to which they belonged. It was considered as a national outrage; and the Highlanders, who are naturally vindictive, waited impatiently for an opportunity of vengeance.

The young pretender, being furnished with a sum of money, and a supply of arms, on his private credit, without the knowledge of the French court, wrote letters to his friends in Scotland, explaining his design and situation, intimating the place where he intended to land, communicating a private signal, and assuring them he should be with them by the middle of June. *The eldest son of the Chevalier de St. George lands in Scotland.* These precautions being taken, he embarked on board of a small frigate at Port St. Nazaire, accompanied by the Marquis of Tullibardine, Sir Thomas Sheridan, Sir John Macdonald, with a few other Irish and Scottish adventurers; and setting sail on the fourteenth of July, was joined off Belleisle by the Elizabeth, a French ship of war, mounted with sixty-six guns, as his convoy.[d] Their design was to sail round Ireland, and land in the western part of Scotland; but falling in with the Lion, an English ship of the line, a very obstinate and bloody action ensued. The Elizabeth was so disabled that she could not prosecute the voyage, and with difficulty reached the harbour of Brest; but the Lion was shattered to such a degree, that she floated like a wreck upon the water. The disaster of the Elizabeth was a great misfortune to the adventurer, as by her being disabled he lost a great quantity of arms, and about one hundred able officers, who were embarked on board of her for the benefit of his

---

[d] The Elizabeth, a king's ship, was procured as a convoy by the interest of Mr. Walsh, an Irish merchant at Nantes; and on board of her fifty French young gentlemen embarked as volunteers.

expedition. Had this ship arrived in Scotland, she could easily have reduced Fort William, situate in the midst of the clans attached to the Stuart family. Such a conquest, by giving lustre to the prince's arms, would have allured many to his standard, who were indifferent in point of principle, and encouraged a great number of Highlanders to join him who were restricted by the apprehension, that their wives and families would be subject to insults from the English garrison of this fortress. Prince Charles, in the frigate, continued his course to the western isles of Scotland. After a voyage of eighteen days, he landed on a little island between Barra and South Inst, two of the Hebrides; then he re-embarked, and in a few days arrived at Borodale in Arnsacy, on the confines of Lochnannach, where he was in a little time joined by a considerable number of hardy mountaineers, under their respective chiefs or leaders. On the nineteenth day of August, the Marquis of Tullibardine erected the pretender's standard at Glensinnan. Some of those, however, on whom Charles principally depended now stood aloof, either fluctuating in their principles, astonished at the boldness of the undertaking, or startled at the remonstrances of their friends, who did not fail to represent, in aggravated colours, all the dangers of embarking in such a desperate enterprise. Had the government acted with proper vigour when they received intelligence of his arrival, the adventurer must have been crushed in embryo before any considerable number of his adherents could have been brought together; but the lords of the regency seemed to slight the information, and even to suspect the integrity of those by whom it was conveyed. They were soon convinced of their mistake. Prince Charles, having assembled about twelve hundred men, encamped in the neighbourhood of Fort William; and immediately hostilities were commenced. A handful of Keppoch's clan, commanded by Major Donald Mac Donald, even before they joined the pretender, attacked two companies of new raised soldiers, who, with their officer, were disarmed after an obstinate dispute: another captain of the king's forces, falling into their hands, was courteously dismissed with one of the pretender's manifestoes, and a passport for his personal safety. The administration was now effectually alarmed. The lords of the regency issued a proclamation, offering a reward of thirty thousand pounds to any person who should apprehend the prince adventurer.

The same price was set upon the head of the Elector of Hanover, in a proclamation published by the pretender. A courier was despatched to Holland to hasten the return of his majesty, who arrived in England about the latter end of August. A requisition was made of the six thousand Dutch auxiliaries; and several British regiments were recalled from the Netherlands. A loyal address was presented to the king by the city of London; and the merchants of this metropolis resolved to raise two regiments at their own expense. Orders were issued to keep the trained bands in readiness; to array the militia of Westminster; and instructions to the same effect were sent to all the lords-lieutenants of the counties throughout the kingdom. The principal noblemen of the nation made a tender of their services to their sovereign; and some of them received commissions to levy regiments towards the suppression of the rebellion. Bodies of volunteers were incorporated in London, and many other places; associations were formed, large contributions raised in different towns, counties, and communities; and a great number of eminent merchants in London agreed to support the public credit, by receiving, as usual, bank-notes in payment for the purposes of traffic. The Protestant clergy of all denominations exerted themselves with extraordinary ardour in preaching against the religion of Rome and the pretender; and the friends of the government were encouraged, animated, and confirmed in their principles, by several spiritual productions published for the occasion.

In a word, the bulk of the nation seemed unanimously bent upon opposing the enterprise of the pretender, who, nevertheless, had already made surprising progress. His arrival in Scotland was no sooner confirmed, than Sir John Cope, who commanded the troops in that kingdom, assembled what force he could bring together, and advanced against the rebels. Understanding, however, that they had taken possession of a strong pass, he changed his route, and proceeded northward as far as Inverness, leaving the capital and southern parts of North Britain wholly exposed to the incursions of the enemy. The Highlanders forthwith marched to Perth, where the Chevalier de St. George was proclaimed King of Great Britain, and the public money seized for his use: the same steps were taken at Dundee and other places. Prince Charles was joined by the nobleman who assumed the title of Duke of Perth, the Viscount

*Takes possession of Edinburgh.*

Strathallan, Lord Nairn, Lord George Murray, and many persons of distinction, with their followers. The Marquis of Tullibardine, who had accompanied him from France, took possession of Athol, as heir of blood to the titles and estates which his younger brother enjoyed in consequence of his attainder; and met with some success in arming the tenants for the support of that cause which he avowed. The rebel army, being considerably augmented, though very ill provided with arms, crossed the Forth in the neighbourhood of Stirling, and advanced towards Edinburgh, where they were joined by Lord Elcho, son of the Earl of Wemyss, and other persons of some distinction. On the sixteenth day of September Charles summoned the town to surrender. The inhabitants were divided by faction and distracted by fear: the place was not in a posture for defence, and the magistrates would not expose the people to the uncertain issue of an assault. Several deputations were sent from the town to the pretender, in order to negotiate terms of capitulation. In the mean time, one of the gates being opened for the admission of a coach, Cameron of Lochiel, one of the most powerful of the highland chiefs, rushed into the place with a party of his men, and secured it without opposition. Next morning the whole rebel army entered, and their prince took possession of the royal palace of Holyrood-house in the suburbs. Then he caused his father to be proclaimed at the market-cross: there also the manifesto was read, in which the Chevalier de St. George declared his son Charles regent of his dominions, promised to dissolve the union, and redress the grievances of Scotland. His being in possession of the capital encouraged his followers, and added reputation to his arms: but the treasure belonging to the two banks of that kingdom had been previously conveyed into the castle, a strong fortress, with a good garrison, under the command of General Guest, an old officer of experience and capacity.

During these transactions, Sir John Cope marched back from Inverness to Aberdeen, where he embarked with his troops, and on the seventeenth day of September landed at Dunbar, about twenty miles to the eastward of Edinburgh. Here he was joined by two regiments of dragoons, which had retired with precipitation from the capital at the approach of the Highland army. With this reinforcement his troops amounted to near three thousand men; and he began his march to Edinburgh in order

*Defeats Sir John Cope at Preston Pans.*

to give battle to the enemy. On the twentieth day of the month he encamped in the neighbourhood of Preston Pans, having the village of Tranent in his front, and the sea in his rear. Early next morning he was attacked by the young pretender, at the head of about two thousand four hundred Highlanders half armed, who charged them sword in hand with such impetuosity, that in less than ten minutes after the battle began, the king's troops were broken and totally routed. The dragoons fled in the utmost confusion at the first onset; the general officers, having made some unsuccessful efforts to rally them, thought proper to consult their own safety by an expeditious retreat towards Coldstream on the Tweed. All the infantry were either killed or taken; and the colours, artillery, tents, baggage, and military chests, fell into the hands of the victor, who returned in triumph to Edinburgh. Never was victory more complete, or obtained at a smaller expense; for not above fifty of the rebels lost their lives in the engagement. Five hundred of the king's troops were killed on the field of battle, and among these Colonel Gardiner, a gallant officer, who disdained to save his life at the expense of his honour. When abandoned by his own regiment of dragoons, he alighted from his horse, joined the infantry, and fought on foot, until he fell covered with wounds in sight of his own threshold. Prince Charles bore his good fortune with moderation. He prohibited all rejoicings for the victory he had obtained: the wounded soldiers were treated with humanity; and the officers were sent into Fife and Angus, where they were left at liberty on their parole, which the greater part of them shamefully broke in the sequel. From this victory the pretender reaped manifold and important advantages. His followers were armed, his party encouraged, and his enemies intimidated. He was supplied with a train of field-artillery, and a considerable sum of money, and saw himself possessed of all Scotland, except the fortresses, the reduction of which he could not pretend to undertake without proper implements and engineers. After the battle he was joined by a small detachment from the Highlands; and some chiefs, who had hitherto been on the reserve, began to exert their influence in his favour. But he was not yet in a condition to take advantage of that consternation which his late success had diffused through the kingdom of England.

Charles continued to reside in the palace of Holyrood-house,* and took measures for cutting off the communication between the castle and the city. General Guest declared that he would demolish the city, unless the blockade should be raised, so as that provision might be carried into the castle. After having waited the return of an express which he had found means to despatch to court, he began to put his threats into execution by firing upon the town. Some houses were beaten down, and several persons killed even at the market-cross. The citizens, alarmed at this disaster, sent a deputation to the prince, entreating him to raise the blockade; and he complied with their request. He levied a regiment in Edinburgh and the neighbourhood. He imposed taxes; seized the merchandise that was deposited in the king's warehouses at Leith, and other places; and compelled the city of Glasgow to accommodate him with a large sum, to be repaid when the peace of the kingdom should be re-established. The number of his followers daily increased; and he received considerable supplies of money, artillery, and ammunition, by single ships that arrived from France, where his interest seemed to rise in proportion to the success of his arms. The greater and richer part of Scotland was averse to his family and pretensions; but the people were unarmed and undisciplined, consequently passive under his dominion. By this time, however, the prince-pretender was joined by the Earl of Kilmarnock, the Lords Elcho, Balmerino, Ogilvie, Pitsligo; and the eldest son of Lord Lovat had begun to assemble his father's clan, in order to reinforce the victor, whose army lay encamped at Duddingston, in the neighbourhood of Edinburgh. Kilmarnock and Balmerino were men of broken and desperate fortune: Elcho and Ogilvie were sons to the Earls of Wemyss and Airly; so that their influence was far from being extensive. Pitsligo was a nobleman of very amiable character, as well as of great personal interest; and great dependence was placed upon the power and attachment of Lord Lovat, who had entered into private engagements with the Chevalier de St. George, though he still wore the mask of loyalty to the government, and disavowed the conduct of his son when he

*Efforts of the friends of government in Scotland.*

---

* While he resided at Edinburgh, some of the presbyterian clergy continued to preach in the churches of that city, and publicly prayed for King George, without suffering the least punishment or molestation. One minister in particular, of the name of Mac Vicar, being solicited by some Highlanders to pray for their prince, promised to comply with their request, and performed his promise in words to this effect: "And as for the young prince, who is come hither in quest of an earthly crown, grant, O Lord, that he may speedily receive a crown of glory."

declared for the pretender. This old nobleman is the same Simon Fraser whom we have had occasion to mention as a partisan and emissary of the court of St. Germain's, in the year one thousand seven hundred and three. He had renounced his connexions with that family, and in the rebellion immediately after the accession of King George I. approved himself a warm friend to the Protestant succession. Since that period he had been induced, by disgust and ambition, to change his principles again, and was in secret an enthusiast in Jacobitism. He had greatly augmented his estate, and obtained a considerable interest in the Highlands, where, however, he was rather dreaded than beloved. He was bold, enterprising, vain, arbitrary, rapacious, cruel, and deceitful; but his character was chiefly marked by a species of low cunning and dissimulation, which, however, overshot his purpose, and contributed to his own ruin. While Charles resided at Edinburgh, the Marquis de Guilles arrived at Montrose, as envoy from the French king, with several officers, some cannon, and a considerable quantity of small arms for the use of that adventurer.'

While the young pretender endeavoured to improve the advantages he had gained, the ministry of Great Britain took every possible measure to retard his progress. Several powerful chiefs in the Highlands were attached to the government, and exerted themselves in its defence. The Duke of Argyle began to arm his vassals; but not before he had obtained the sanction of the legislature. Twelve hundred men were raised by the Earl of Sutherland: the Lord Rae brought a considerable number to the field: the Grants and Monroes appeared under their respective leaders for the service of his majesty: Sir Alexander Macdonald declared for King George, and the Laird of Macleod sent two thousand hardy islanders from Skie to strengthen the same interest. These gentlemen, though supposed to be otherwise affected, were governed and directed by the advice of Duncan Forbes, president of the college of justice at Edinburgh, a man of extensive knowledge, agreeable manners, and unblemished integrity. He procured commissions for raising twenty independent companies, and some of these he bestowed upon individuals who were either attached by principle, or engaged by promise, to the pre-

*Precautions taken in England.*

---

' He solicited, and is said to have obtained of the Chevalier de St. George, the patent of a duke, and a commission for being lord lieutenant of all the Highlands.

tender. He acted with indefatigable zeal for the interest of the reigning family; and greatly injured an opulent fortune in their service. He confirmed several chiefs who began to waver in their principles: some he actually converted by the energy of his arguments, and brought over to the assistance of the government which they had determined to oppose: others he persuaded to remain quiet, without taking any share in the present troubles. Certain it is, this gentleman, by his industry and address, prevented the insurrection of ten thousand Highlanders, who would otherwise have joined the pretender; and, therefore, he may be said to have been one great cause of that adventurer's miscarriage. The Earl of Loudon repaired to Inverness, where he completed his regiment of Highlanders; directed the conduct of the clans who had taken arms in behalf of his majesty; and, by his vigilance, overawed the disaffected chieftains of that country, who had not yet openly engaged in the rebellion. Immediately after the defeat of Cope, six thousand Dutch troops* arrived in England, and three battalions of guards, with seven regiments of infantry, were recalled from Flanders, for the defence of the kingdom. They forthwith began their march to the north, under the command of General Wade, who received orders to assemble an army, which proceeded to Newcastle. The Parliament meeting on the sixteenth day of October, his majesty gave them to understand that an unnatural rebellion had broken out in Scotland, towards the suppression of which he craved their advice and assistance. He found both Houses cordial in their addresses, and zealous in their attachment to his person and government. The Commons forthwith suspended the habeas corpus act; and several persons were apprehended on suspicion of treasonable practices. Immediately after the session was opened, the Duke of Cumberland arrived from the Netherlands, and was followed by another detachment of dragoons and infantry. The train-bands of London were reviewed by his majesty; the county regiments were completed; the volunteers in different parts of the kingdom employed themselves industriously in the exercise of arms; and the whole English nation seemed to rise up as one man against this formidable invader. The government, being

* They were composed of the forces who had been in garrison at Tournay and Dendermonde when those places were taken, and engaged by capitulation that they should not perform any military function before the first day of January in the year 1747: so they could not have acted in England without the infringement of a solemn treaty.

apprehensive of a descent from France, appointed Admiral Vernon to command a squadron in the Downs, to observe the motions of the enemy by sea, especially in the harbours of Dunkirk and Boulogne; and his cruisers took several ships laden with soldiers, officers, and ammunition, destined for the service of the pretender in Scotland.

This enterprising youth, having collected about five thousand men, resolved to make an irruption into England, which he accordingly entered by the west border on the sixth day of November. Carlisle was invested, and in less than three days surrendered: the keys were delivered to him at Brampton, by the mayor and aldermen on their knees. Here he found a considerable quantity of arms: his father was proclaimed King of Great Britain, and himself regent, by the magistrates in their formalities. General Wade, being apprised of his progress, decamped from Newcastle, and advanced across the country as far as Hexham, though the fields were covered with snow, and the roads almost impassable. There he received intelligence that Carlisle was reduced, and forthwith returned to his former station. In the mean time orders were issued for assembling another army in Staffordshire, under the command of Sir John Ligonier. Prince Charles, notwithstanding this formidable opposition, determined to proceed. He had received assurances from France, that a considerable body of troops would be landed on the southern coast of Britain, to make a diversion in his favour; and he never doubted but that he should be joined by all the English malecontents, as soon as he could penetrate into the heart of the kingdom. Leaving a small garrison in the castle of Carlisle, he advanced to Penrith, marching on foot in the Highland garb, at the head of his forces; and continued his route through Lancaster and Preston to Manchester, where, on the twenty-ninth day of the month, he established his head-quarters. There he was joined by about two hundred Englishmen, who were formed into a regiment, under the command of Colonel Townley. The inhabitants seemed to receive him with marks of affection; and his arrival was celebrated by illuminations, and other public rejoicings. His supposed intention was to prosecute his march by the way of Chester into Wales, where he hoped to find a great number of adherents; but all the bridges over the river Mersey being broken down, he chose

the route to Stockport, and forded the river at the head of
his division, though the water rose to his middle. He passed
through Macclesfield and Congleton; and on the fourth day
of December entered the town of Derby, in which his army
was quartered, and his father proclaimed with great formality. He had now advanced within one hundred miles of
the capital, which was filled with terror and confusion. Wade
lingered in Yorkshire; the Duke of Cumberland had assumed the command of the other army assembled in the
neighbourhood of Lichfield. He had marched from Stafford
to Stone; so that the rebels, in turning off from Ashbourne to
Derby, had gained a march between him and London. Had
Charles proceeded in his career with that expedition which
he had hitherto used, he might have made himself master of
the metropolis, where he would have been certainly joined
by a considerable number of his well-wishers, who waited
impatiently for his approach: yet this exploit could not have
been achieved without hazarding an engagement, and running the risk of being enclosed within three armies, each
greatly superior to his own in number and artillery. Orders
were given for forming a camp on Finchley-common, where
the king resolved to take the field in person, accompanied by
the Earl of Stair, field-mareschal, and commander-in-chief
of the forces in South Britain. Some Romish priests were
apprehended: the militia of London and Middlesex were kept
in readiness to march: double watches were posted at the
city gates, and signals of alarm appointed. The volunteers
of the city were incorporated into a regiment: the practi-
tioners of the law, headed by the judges, the weavers of
Spitalfields, and other communities, engaged in association;
and even the managers of the theatres offered to raise a body
of their dependents for the service of the government.
Notwithstanding these precautions and appearances of unanimity, the trading part of the city, and those concerned in
the money corporations, were overwhelmed with fear and
dejection. They reposed very little confidence in the courage or discipline of their militia and volunteers: they had
received intelligence that the French were employed in
making preparations at Dunkirk and Calais for a descent
upon England: they dreaded an insurrection of the Roman
Catholics, and other friends of the house of Stuart; and they
reflected that the Highlanders, of whom by this time they
had conceived a most terrible idea, were within four days'

march of the capital. Alarmed by these considerations, they prognosticated their own ruin in the approaching revolution; and their countenances exhibited the plainest marks of horror and despair. On the other hand, the Jacobites were elevated to an insolence of hope, which they were at no pains to conceal; while many people, who had no private property to lose, and thought no change would be for the worse, waited the issue of this crisis with the most calm indifference.

This state of suspense was of short duration. The young pretender found himself miserably disappointed in his expectations. He had now advanced into the middle of the kingdom, and, except a few that joined him at Manchester, not a soul appeared in his behalf; one would have imagined that all the Jacobites of England had been annihilated. The Welsh took no step to excite an insurrection in his favour: the French made no attempt towards an invasion: his court was divided into factions: the highland chiefs began to murmur, and their clans to be unruly: he saw himself with a handful of men, hemmed in between two considerable armies, in the middle of winter, and in a country disaffected to his cause. He knew he could not proceed to the metropolis without hazarding a battle, and that a defeat would be attended with the inevitable destruction of himself and all his adherents; and he had received information that his friends and officers had assembled a body of forces in the north, superior in number to those by whom he was attended. He called a council at Derby, and proposed to advance towards London: the proposal was supported by Lord Nairn with great vehemence; but, after violent disputes, the majority determined that they should retreat to Scotland with all possible expedition. Accordingly, they abandoned Derby on the sixth day of December, early in the morning, and measured back the route by which they had advanced. On the ninth their vanguard arrived at Manchester: on the twelfth they entered Preston, and continued their march northwards. The Duke of Cumberland, who was encamped at Meriden, when first apprised of their retreat, detached the horse and dragoons in pursuit of them; while General Wade began his march from Ferrybridge into Lancashire, with a view of intercepting them in their route: but at Wakefield he understood that they had already reached Wigan; he, therefore, repaired to his old

*The rebels retreat into Scotland.*

post at Newcastle, after having detached General Oglethorpe, with his horse and dragoons, to join those who had been sent off from the duke's army. They pursued with such alacrity, that they overtook the rear of the rebels, with which they skirmished, in Lancashire. The militia of Cumberland and Westmoreland were raised and armed by the duke's order to harass them in their march. The bridges were broken down, the roads damaged, and the beacons lighted to alarm the country. Nevertheless, they retreated regularly with their small train of artillery. They were overtaken at the village of Clifton, in the neighbourhood of Penrith, by two regiments of dragoons. These alighted, and lined the hedges, in order to harass part of the enemy's rear-guard, commanded by Lord John Murray, who at the head of the Macphersons, attacked the dragoons sword in hand, and repulsed them with some loss. On the nineteenth day of the month, the Highland army reached Carlisle, where the majority of the English in the service of the pretender were left, at their own desire. Charles, having reinforced the garrison of the place, crossed the rivers Eden and Solway into Scotland, having thus accomplished one of the most surprising retreats that ever was performed. But the most remarkable circumstance of this expedition was the moderation and regularity with which those ferocious people conducted themselves in a country abounding with plunder. No violence was offered; no outrage committed; and they were effectually restrained from the exercise of rapine. Notwithstanding the excessive cold, the hunger and fatigue to which they must have been exposed, they left behind no sick, and lost a very few stragglers; but retired with deliberation, and carried off their cannon in the face of their enemy. The Duke of Cumberland invested Carlisle with his whole army on the twenty-first day of December, and on the thirtieth the garrison surrendered on a sort of capitulation made with the Duke of Richmond. The prisoners, amounting to about four hundred, were imprisoned in different gaols in England, and the duke returned to London.

The pretender proceeded by the way of Dumfries to Glasgow, from which last city he exacted severe contributions, on account of its attachment to the government, for whose service it had raised a regiment of nine hundred men under the command of the Earl of Home. Having continued several days at Glasgow, he advanced to-

*They invest the castle of Stirling.*

wards Stirling, and was joined by some forces which had been assembled in his absence by Lords Lewis Gordon and John Drummond, brothers to the Dukes of Gordon and Perth. This last nobleman had arrived from France in November, with a small reinforcement of French and Irish, and a commission as general of these auxiliaries. He fixed his head-quarters at Perth, where he was reinforced by the Earl of Cromartie, and other clans, to the number of two thousand, and he was accommodated with a small train of artillery. They had found means to surprise a sloop of war at Montrose, with the guns of which they fortified that harbour. They had received a considerable sum of money from Spain. They took possession of Dundee, Dumblaine, Downcastle, and laid Fife under contribution. The Earl of Loudon remained at Inverness, with about two thousand Highlanders in the service of his majesty. He convoyed provisions to Fort Augustus and Fort William; he secured the person of Lord Lovat, who still temporized, and at length this cunning veteran accomplished his escape. The Laird of Macleod, and Mr. Munro of Culcairn, being detached from Inverness towards Aberdeenshire, were surprised and routed by Lord Lewis Gordon at Inverary; and that interest seemed to preponderate in the north of Scotland. Prince Charles, being joined by Lord John Drummond, invested the castle of Stirling, in which General Blakeney commanded; but his people were so little used to enterprises of this kind that they made very little progress in their operations.

By this time a considerable body of forces were assembled at Edinburgh, under the conduct of General Hawley, who determined to relieve Stirling castle, and advanced to Linlithgow on the thirteenth day of January: next day his whole army rendezvoused at Falkirk, while the rebels were cantoned about Bannockburn. On the seventeenth day of the month, they began their march in two columns to attack the king's forces, and had forded the water of Carron, within three miles of Hawley's camp, before he discovered their intention. Such was his obstinacy, self-conceit, or contempt of the enemy, that he slighted the repeated intelligence he had received of their motions and design, firmly believing they durst not hazard an engagement. At length, perceiving they had occupied the rising ground to the southward of Falkirk, he ordered his cavalry to advance, and drive them from the eminence; *The king's troops under Hawley are worsted at Falkirk.*

while his infantry formed, and were drawn up in order of battle. The Highlanders kept up their fire, and took aim so well, that the assailants were broken by the first volley: they retreated with precipitation, and fell in amongst the infantry, which were likewise discomposed by the wind and rain beating with great violence in their faces, wetting their powder, and disturbing their eyesight. Some of the dragoons rallied, and advanced again to the charge, with part of the infantry which had not been engaged; then the pretender marched up at the head of his corps de reserve, consisting of the regiment of Lord John Drummond, and the Irish piquets. These reinforcing the Camerons and the Stuarts in the front line, immediately obliged the dragoons to give way a second time; and they again disordered the foot in their retreat. They set fire to their camp, and abandoned Falkirk with their baggage and train, which last had never reached the field of battle. The rebels followed their first blow, and great part of the royal army, after one irregular discharge, turned their backs, and fled in the utmost consternation. In all probability few or none of them would have escaped, had not General Huske and Brigadier Cholmondeley rallied part of some regiments, and made a gallant stand, which favoured the retreat of the rest to Falkirk, from whence they retired in confusion to Edinburgh, leaving the field of battle, with part of their tents and artillery, to the rebels: but their loss of men did not exceed three hundred, including Sir Robert Monro, Colonel Whitney, and some other officers of distinction. It was at this period that the officers who had been taken at the battle of Preston Pans, and conveyed to Angus and Fife, finding themselves unguarded, broke their parole, and returned to Edinburgh, on pretence of their having been forcibly released by the inhabitants of those parts.[b]

*The Duke of Cumberland assumes the command of the forces in Scotland.* General Hawley, who had boasted that, with two regiments of dragoons, he would drive the rebel army from one end of the kingdom to the other, incurred abundance of censure for the disposition he made, as well as for his conduct before and after the action; but he found means to vindicate himself to the satisfaction of his sovereign. Nevertheless,

---

[b] Sir Peter Halket, Captain Lucy Scot, Lieutenants Farquharson and Cumming, with a few other gentlemen, adhered punctually to their parole, and their conduct was approved by his majesty.

it was judged necessary that the army in Scotland should be commanded by a general in whom the soldiers might have some confidence; and the Duke of Cumberland was chosen for this purpose. Over and above his being beloved by the army, it was suggested that the appearance of a prince of the blood in Scotland might have a favourable effect upon the minds of people in that kingdom; he, therefore, began to prepare for his northern expedition. Meanwhile the French minister at the Hague having represented to the States-General that the auxiliaries which they had sent into Great Britain were part of the garrisons of Tournay and Dendermonde, and restricted by the capitulation from bearing arms against France for a certain term, the states thought proper to recall them, rather than come to an open rupture with his most Christian majesty. In the room of those troops, six thousand Hessians were transported from Flanders to Leith, where they arrived in the beginning of February, under the command of their prince, Frederick of Hesse, son-in-law to his Britannic majesty. By this time the Duke of Cumberland had put himself at the head of the troops in Edinburgh, consisting of fourteen battalions of infantry, two regiments of dragoons, and twelve hundred Highlanders from Argyleshire, under the command of Colonel Campbell. On the last day of January his royal highness began his march to Linlithgow; and the enemy, who had renewed the siege of Stirling castle, not only abandoned that enterprise, but crossed the river Forth with precipitation. Their prince found great difficulty in maintaining his forces, that part of the country being quite exhausted. He hoped to be reinforced in the Highlands, and to receive supplies of all kinds from France and Spain; he, therefore, retired by Badenoch towards Inverness, which the Earl of Loudon abandoned at his approach. The fort was surrendered to him almost without opposition, and here he fixed his head-quarters. His next exploit was the siege of Fort Augustus, which he in a little time reduced. The Duke of Cumberland, having secured the important posts of Stirling and Perth, with the Hessian battalions, advanced with the army to Aberdeen, where he was joined by the Duke of Gordon, the Earls of Aberdeen and Findlater, the Laird of Grant, and other persons of distinction.

While he remained in this place, refreshing his troops and

preparing magazines, a party of the rebels surprised a detachment of Kingston's horse, and about seventy Argyleshire Highlanders, at Keith, who were either killed or taken. Several advanced parties of that militia met with the same fate in different places. Lord George Murray invested the castle of Blair, which was defended by Sir Andrew Agnew, until a body of Hessians marched to its relief, and obliged the rebels to retire. The prince pretender ordered all his forces to assemble, in order to begin their march for Aberdeen, to attack the Duke of Cumberland; but, in consequence of a remonstrance from the clans, who declined leaving their families at the mercy of the king's garrison in Fort William, he resolved previously to reduce that fortress, the siege of which was undertaken by Brigadier Stapleton, an engineer in the French service; but the place was so vigorously maintained by Captain Scot, that in the beginning of April they thought proper to relinquish the enterprise. The Earl of Loudon had retired into Sutherland, and taken post at Dornoch, where his quarters were beaten up by a strong detachment of the rebels, commanded by the Duke of Perth: a major and sixty men were taken prisoners; and the earl was obliged to take shelter in the isle of Skye. These little checks were counterbalanced by some advantages which his majesty's arms obtained. The sloop of war which the rebels had surprised at Montrose was retaken in Sutherland, with a considerable sum of money and a great quantity of arms on board, which she had brought from France for the use of the pretender. In the same county the Earl of Cromartie fell into an ambuscade, and was taken by the militia of Sutherland, who likewise defeated a body of the rebels at Goldspie. This action happened on the very day which has been rendered famous by the victory obtained at Culloden.

## CHAPTER XX.

THE REBELS ARE TOTALLY DEFEATED AT CULLODEN. — THE DUKE OF CUMBERLAND TAKES POSSESSION OF INVERNESS, AND AFTERWARDS ENCAMPS AT FORT AUGUSTUS. — THE PRINCE PRETENDER ESCAPES TO FRANCE. — CONVULSION IN THE MINISTRY. — LIBERALITY OF THE COMMONS. — TRIAL OF THE REBELS. — KILMARNOCK, BALMERINO, LOVAT, AND MR. RATCLIFFE, ARE BEHEADED ON TOWER-HILL. — THE STATES-GENERAL ALARMED AT THE PROGRESS OF THE FRENCH IN THE NETHERLANDS. — COUNT SAXE SUBDUES ALL FLANDERS, BRABANT, AND HAINAULT. — REDUCES THE STRONG FORTRESS OF NAMUR, AND DEFEATS THE ALLIED ARMY AT ROCOUX. — THE FRENCH AND SPANIARDS ARE COMPELLED TO ABANDON PIEDMONT AND THE MILANESE. — DON PHILIP IS WORSTED AT CADOGNO, AND AFTERWARDS AT PORTO FREDDO. — THE AUSTRIANS TAKE POSSESSION OF GENOA. — COUNT BROWN PENETRATES INTO PROVENCE. — THE GENOESE EXPEL THE AUSTRIANS FROM THEIR CITY. — MADRAS IN THE EAST INDIES TAKEN BY THE FRENCH. — EXPEDITION TO THE COAST OF BRETAGNE, AND ATTEMPT UPON PORT L'ORIENT. — NAVAL TRANSACTIONS IN THE WEST INDIES. — CONFERENCES AT BREDA. — VAST SUPPLIES GRANTED BY THE COMMONS OF ENGLAND. — PARLIAMENT DISSOLVED. — THE FRENCH AND ALLIES TAKE THE FIELD IN FLANDERS. — THE PRINCE OF ORANGE ELECTED STADTHOLDER, CAPTAIN-GENERAL, AND ADMIRAL OF THE UNITED PROVINCES. — THE CONFEDERATES DEFEATED AT LAFFELDT. — SIEGE OF BERGEN-OP-ZOOM. — THE AUSTRIANS UNDERTAKE THE SIEGE OF GENOA, WHICH, HOWEVER, THEY ABANDON. — THE CHEVALIER DE BELLEISLE SLAIN IN THE ATTACK OF EXILES. — A FRENCH SQUADRON DEFEATED AND TAKEN BY THE ADMIRALS ANSON AND WARREN. — ADMIRAL HAWKE OBTAINS ANOTHER VICTORY OVER THE FRENCH AT SEA. — OTHER NAVAL TRANSACTIONS. — CONGRESS AT AIX-LA-CHAPELLE. — COMPLIANT TEMPER OF THE NEW PARLIAMENT. — PRELIMINARIES SIGNED. — PREPARATIONS FOR THE CAMPAIGN IN THE NETHERLANDS. — SIEGE OF MAESTRICHT. — CESSATION OF ARMS. — TRANSACTIONS IN THE EAST AND WEST INDIES. — CONCLUSION OF THE DEFINITIVE TREATY AT AIX-LA-CHAPELLE.

IN the beginning of April the Duke of Cumberland began his march from Aberdeen, and on the twelfth passed the deep and rapid river Spey, without opposition from the rebels, though a detachment of them appeared on the opposite side. Why they did not dispute the passage is not easy to be conceived; but, indeed, from this instance of neglect, and their subsequent conduct, we may conclude they were under a total infatuation. His royal highness proceeded to Nairn, where he received intelligence that the enemy had advanced from Inverness to Culloden, about the distance of nine miles from the royal army, with intention to give him battle. The design of Charles was to march in the night from Culloden, and surprise the duke's army at daybreak: for this purpose the English camp had been reconnoitred; and on the night of the fifteenth the Highland army began to march in two columns.

*1746.*
*The rebels are totally defeated at Culloden.*

Their design was to surround the enemy, and attack them at once on all quarters; but the length of the columns embarrassed the march, so that the army was obliged to make many halts: the men had been under arms during the whole preceding night, were faint with hunger and fatigue, and many of them overpowered with sleep. Some were unable to proceed; others dropped off unperceived in the dark; and the march was retarded in such a manner that it would have been impossible to reach the duke's camp before sunrise. The design being thus frustrated, the prince pretender was with great reluctance prevailed upon by his general officers to measure back his way to Culloden: at which place he had no sooner arrived, than great numbers of his followers dispersed in quest of provision; and many, overcome with weariness and sleep, threw themselves down on the heath, and along the park walls. Their repose, however, was soon interrupted in a very disagreeable manner. Their prince, receiving intelligence that his enemies were in full march to attack him, resolved to hazard an engagement, and ordered his troops to be formed for that purpose. On the sixteenth day of April the Duke of Cumberland, having made the proper dispositions, decamped from Nairn early in the morning, and after a march of nine miles perceived the Highlanders drawn up in order of battle, to the number of four thousand men, in thirteen divisions, supplied with some pieces of artillery. The royal army, which was much more numerous, the duke immediately formed into three lines, disposed in excellent order; and about one o'clock in the afternoon the cannonading began. The artillery of the rebels was ill served, and did very little execution; but that of the king's troops made dreadful havoc among the enemy. Impatient of this fire, their front line advanced to the attack, and about five hundred of the clans charged the duke's left wing with their usual impetuosity. One regiment was disordered by the weight of this column; but two battalions, advancing from the second line, sustained the first, and soon put a stop to their career, by a severe fire that killed a great number. At the same time, the dragoons under Hawley, and the Argyleshire militia, pulled down a park wall that covered their right flank, and the cavalry falling in among the rebels sword in hand completed their confusion. The French piquets on their left covered the retreat of the Highlanders by a close and regular fire;

and then retired to Inverness, where they surrendered themselves prisoners of war. An entire body of the rebels marched off the field in order, with their pipes playing, and the pretender's standard displayed; the rest were routed with great slaughter; and their prince was with reluctance prevailed upon to retire. In less than thirty minutes they were totally defeated, and the field covered with the slain. The road, as far as Inverness, was strewed with dead bodies; and a great number of people, who from motives of curiosity had come to see the battle, were sacrificed to the undistinguishing vengeance of the victors. Twelve hundred rebels were slain or wounded on the field, and in the pursuit. The Earl of Kilmarnock was taken; and in a few days Lord Balmerino surrendered to a country gentleman, at whose house he presented himself for this purpose. The glory of the victory was sullied by the barbarity of the soldiers. They had been provoked by their former disgraces to the most savage thirst of revenge. Not contented with the blood which was so profusely shed in the heat of action, they traversed the field after the battle, and massacred those miserable wretches who lay maimed and expiring: nay, some officers acted a part in this cruel scene of assassination, the triumph of low illiberal minds, uninspired by sentiment, untinctured by humanity. The vanquished adventurer rode off the field, accompanied by the Duke of Perth, Lord Elcho, and a few horsemen: he crossed the water of Nairn, and retired to the house of a gentleman in Stratharick, where he conferred with old Lord Lovat; then he dismissed his followers, and wandered about, a wretched and solitary fugitive, among the isles and mountains, for the space of five months, during which he underwent such a series of dangers, hardships, and misery, as no other person ever outlived. Thus, in one short hour all his hope vanished, and the rebellion was entirely extinguished. One would almost imagine the conductors of this desperate enterprise had conspired their own destruction, as they certainly neglected every step that might have contributed to their safety or success. They might have opposed the Duke of Cumberland at the passage of the Spey; they might by proper conduct have afterwards attacked his camp in the night, with a good prospect of success. As they were greatly inferior to him in number, and weakened with hunger and fatigue, they might have retired to the hills and fastnesses, where they would have found plenty of live cattle for provision, recruited their regiments, and been joined by a strong reinforcement, which was actually in full march to their assistance. But they were distracted by dissensions and jealousies: they obeyed the dictates of despair, and wilfully devoted themselves to ruin and death. When the news of the battle arrived in England, the nation was transported with joy, and extolled the Duke of Cumberland as a hero and deliverer. Both Houses of Parliament congratulated his majesty on the auspicious event. They decreed, in the most solemn manner, their public thanks to his royal highness, which were transmitted to him by the speakers; and the Commons, by bill, added five-and-twenty thousand pounds per annum to his former revenue.

Immediately after the decisive action at Culloden, the duke took possession of Inverness, where six-and-thirty deserters, convicted by a court-martial, were ordered to be executed; then he detached several parties to ravage the country. One of these apprehended the Lady Mackintosh, who was sent prisoner to Inverness. They did not plunder her house, but drove away her cattle, though her husband was actually in the service of government. The castle of Lord Lovat was destroyed. The French prisoners were sent to Carlisle and Penrith: Kilmarnock, Balmerino, Cromartie, and his son the Lord Macleod, were conveyed by sea to London; and those of an inferior rank were confined in different prisons. The Marquis of Tullibardine, together with a brother of the Earl of Dunmore, were seized and transported to the Tower of London, to which the Earl of Traquaire had been committed on suspicion: in a few months after the battle of Culloden, Murray, the pretender's secretary, was apprehended; and the eldest son of Lord Lovat, having surrendered himself, was imprisoned in the castle of Edinburgh. In a word, all the gaols of Great Britain, from the capital northwards, were filled with those unfortunate captives; and great numbers of them were crowded together in the holds of ships, where they perished in the most deplorable manner, for want of necessaries, air, and exercise. Some rebel chiefs escaped in two French frigates, which had arrived on the coast of Lochaber about the end of April, and engaged three vessels belonging to his Britannic majesty, which they obliged to retire. Others embarked on board of a

*The Duke of Cumberland takes possession of Inverness, and afterwards encamps at Fort Augustus.*

ship on the coast of Buchan, and were conveyed to Norway; from whence they travelled to Sweden. In the month of May, the Duke of Cumberland advanced with the army into the Highlands, as far as Fort Augustus, where he encamped; and sent off detachments on all hands, to hunt down the fugitives, and lay waste the country with fire and sword. The castles of Glengary and Lochiel were plundered and burned; every house, hut, or habitation, met with the same fate, without distinction: all the cattle and provision were carried off: the men were either shot upon the mountains, like wild beasts, or put to death in cold blood, without form of trial: the women, after having seen their husbands and fathers murdered, were subjected to brutal violation, and then turned out naked, with their children, to starve on the barren heaths. One whole family was enclosed in a barn, and consumed to ashes. Those ministers of vengeance were so alert in the execution of their office, that in a few days there was neither house, cottage, man, nor beast, to be seen in the compass of fifty miles: all was ruin, silence, and desolation.

The humane reader cannot reflect upon such a scene without grief and horror; what then must have been the sensation of the fugitive prince, when he beheld these spectacles of woe, the dismal fruit of his ambition? He was now surrounded by armed troops, that chased him from hill to dale, from rock to cavern, and from shore to shore. Sometimes he lurked in caves and cottages, without attendants, or any other support but that which the poorest peasant could supply. Sometimes he was rowed in fisher-boats from isle to isle, among the Hebrides, and often in sight of his pursuers. For some days he appeared in woman's attire, and even passed through the midst of his enemies unknown. But, understanding his disguise was discovered, he assumed the habit of a travelling mountaineer, and wandered about among the woods and heaths, with a matted beard and squalid looks, exposed to hunger, thirst, and weariness, and in continual danger of being apprehended. He was obliged to trust his life to the fidelity of above fifty individuals, and many of these were in the lowest paths of fortune. They knew that a price of thirty thousand pounds was set upon his head; and that, by betraying him, they should enjoy wealth and affluence: but they detested the thought of obtaining riches on such infamous terms, and ministered to his necessities, with the utmost zeal and fidelity, even at the hazard of their own destruction. In the course of these peregrinations, he was more than once hemmed in by his pursuers, in such a manner as seemed to preclude all possibility of escaping; yet he was never abandoned by his hope and recollection: he still found some expedient that saved him from captivity and death; and through the whole course of his distresses maintained the most amazing equanimity and good humour. At length a privateer of St. Malo, hired by the young Sheridan and some other Irish adherents, arrived in Lochnannach; and on the twentieth day of September this unfortunate prince embarked in the habit which he wore for disguise. His eye was hollow, his visage wan, and his constitution greatly impaired by famine and fatigue. He was accompanied by Cameron of Lochiel and his brother, with a few other exiles. They set sail for France, and after having passed unseen, by means of a thick fog, through a British squadron, commanded by Admiral Lestock, and been chased by two English ships of war, arrived in safety at Roscau, near Morlaix, in Bretagne. Perhaps he would have found it still more difficult to escape, had not the vigilance and eagerness of the government been relaxed, in consequence of a report that he had already fallen among some persons that were slain by a volley from one of the duke's detachments.

Having thus explained the rise, progress, and extinction of the rebellion, it will be necessary to take a retrospective view of the proceedings in Parliament.

*Convulsion in the ministry.*

The necessary steps being taken for quieting the intestine commotions of the kingdom, the two Houses began to convert their attention to the affairs of the continent. On the fourteenth day of January the king repaired to the House of Peers, and, in a speech from the throne, gave his Parliament to understand, that the States-General had made pressing instances for his assistance in the present conjuncture, when they were in such danger of being oppressed by the power of France in the Netherlands; that he had promised to co-operate with them towards opposing the further progress of their enemies; and even concerted measures for that purpose. He declared it was with regret that he asked any further aids of his people: he exhorted them to watch over the public credit; and expressed his entire dependence on their zeal and unanimity. He was favoured with loyal addresses, couched in the warmest terms of duty and affection: but the supplies were retarded by new convulsions in the ministry. The Earl of Granville had made an effort to retrieve his influence in the cabinet, and his sovereign favoured his pretensions. The two brothers, who knew his aspiring genius, and dreaded his superior talents, refused to admit such a colleague into the administration; they even resolved to strengthen their party, by introducing fresh auxiliaries into the offices of state. Some of these were personally disagreeable to his majesty, who accordingly rejected the suit by which they were recommended. The Duke of Newcastle and his brother, with all their adherents, immediately resigned their employments. The Earl of Granville was appointed secretary of state, and resumed the reins of administration; but finding himself unequal to the accumulated opposition that preponderated against him; foreseeing that he should not be able to secure the supplies in Parliament; and dreading the consequences of that confusion which his restoration had already produced, he, in three days, voluntarily quitted the helm; and his majesty acquiesced in the measures proposed by the opposite party. The seals were re-delivered to the Duke of Newcastle and the Earl of Harrington: Mr. Pelham, and all the rest who had resigned, were reinstated in their respective employments; and offices were conferred on several individuals who had never before been in the service of the government. William Pitt, Esq., was appointed vice-treasurer of Ireland, and soon promoted to the place of paymaster-general of the forces; at the same time the king declared him a privy-counsellor. This gentleman had been originally designed for the army, in which he actually bore a commission; but fate reserved him for a more important station. In point of fortune he was barely qualified to be elected member of Parliament, when he obtained a seat in the House of Commons, where he soon outshone all his compatriots. He displayed a surprising extent and precision of political knowledge, an irresistible energy of argument, and such power of elocution as struck his hearers with astonishment and admiration. It flashed like the lightning of heaven against the ministers and sons of corruption, blasting where it smote, and withering the nerves of opposition: but his more substantial praise was founded upon his disinterested integrity, his incorruptible heart, his unconquerable spirit of independence, and his invariable attachment to the interest and liberty of his country.

*Liberality of the Commons.* The quiet of the ministry being re-established, the House of Commons provided for forty thousand seamen, nearly the same number of land forces, besides fifteen regiments raised by the nobility, on account of the rebellion, and about twelve thousand marines. They settled funds for the maintenance of the Dutch and Hessian troops that were in England, as well as for the subsidy to the landgrave. They granted three hundred thousand pounds to the King of Sardinia; four hundred thousand pounds to the Queen of Hungary; three hundred and ten thousand pounds to defray the expense of eighteen thousand Hanoverians; about three-and-thirty thousand pounds in subsidies to the Electors of Mentz and Cologn; and five hundred thousand pounds in a vote of credit and confidence to his majesty. The whole charge of the current year amounted to seven millions two hundred and fifty thousand pounds, which was raised by the land and malt-taxes, annuities on the additional duties imposed on glass and spirituous liquors, a lottery, a deduction from the sinking fund, and exchequer bills, chargeable on the first aids that should be granted in the next session of Parliament.

*Trial of the rebels. Kilmarnock, Balmerino, Lovat, and Mr. Radcliffe are beheaded on Tower-hill.* The rebellion being quelled, the legislature resolved to make examples of those who had been concerned in disturbing the peace of their country. In June, an act of attainder was passed against the principal persons who had embarked in that desperate undertaking; and courts were opened in different parts of England for the trial of the prisoners. Seventeen persons who had borne arms in the rebel army were executed at Kennington-common, in the neighbourhood of London, and suffered with great constancy under the dreadful tortures which their sentence prescribed: nine were put to death, in the same manner, at Carlisle; six at Brompton, seven at Penrith, and eleven at York: of these a considerable number were gentlemen, and had acted as officers; about fifty had been executed as deserters in different parts of Scotland; eighty-one suffered the pains of the law as traitors. A few obtained pardons, and a considerable number were transported to the plantations. Bills of indictment for high treason were found by the county of Surrey against the Earls of Kilmarnock and Cromartie, and Lord Balmerino. These noblemen were tried by their Peers in Westminster-hall, the lord chancellor presiding as lord high steward for the occasion. The two earls confessed their crimes, and in pathetic speeches recommended themselves to his majesty's mercy. Lord Balmerino pleaded not guilty: he denied his having been at Carlisle at the time specified in the indictment, but this exception was overruled: then he moved a point of law in arrest of judgment, and was allowed to be heard by his counsel. They might have expatiated on the hardship of being tried by an *ex post facto* law, and claimed the privilege of trial in the county where the act of treason was said to have been committed. The same hardship was imposed upon all the imprisoned rebels: they were dragged in captivity to a strange country, far from their friends and connexions, destitute of means to produce evidence in their favour, even if they had been innocent of the charge. Balmerino waived this plea, and submitted to the court, which pronounced sentence of death upon him and his two associates. Cromartie's life was spared; but the other two were beheaded, in the month of August, on Tower-hill. Kilmarnock was a nobleman of fine personal accomplishments; he had been educated in revolution principles, and engaged in the rebellion, partly from the desperate situation of his fortune, and partly from resentment to the government, on his being deprived of a pension which he had for some time enjoyed. He was convinced of his having acted criminally, and died with marks of penitence and contrition. Balmerino had been bred to arms, and acted upon principle: he was gallant, brave, rough, and resolute; he eyed the implements of death with the most careless familiarity, and seemed to triumph in his sufferings. In November, Mr. Radcliffe, the titular Earl of Derwentwater, who had been taken in a ship bound to Scotland, was arraigned on a former sentence, passed against him in the year one thousand seven hundred and sixteen: he refused to acknowledge the authority of the court, and pleaded that he was a subject of France, honoured with a commission in the service of his most Christian majesty. The identity of his person being proved, a rule was made for his execution; and on the eighth day of December he suffered decapitation, with the most perfect composure and serenity. Lord Lovat, now turned of fourscore, was impeached by the Commons, and tried in Westminster-hall before the lord high steward. John Murray, secretary to the prince pretender, and some of his own domestics, appearing against him, he was convicted of high treason, and condemned. Notwithstanding his age, infirmities, and the recollection of his conscience, which was supposed to be not altogether void of offence, he died like an old Roman, exclaiming, "*Dulce et decorum est pro patria mori.*" He surveyed the crowd with attention, examined the axe, jested with the executioner, and laid his head upon the block with the utmost indifference. From this last scene of his life, one would have concluded that he had approved himself a patriot from his youth, and never deviated from the paths of virtue.

The flame of war on the continent did not expire at the election of an emperor, and the re-establishment of peace among the princes of the empire. On the contrary, it raged with double violence in consequence of these events: for the force that was before divided, being now united in one body, exerted itself with great vigour and rapidity. The States-General were overwhelmed with consternation. Notwithstanding the pains they had taken to avoid a war, and the condescension with which they had soothed and supplicated the French monarch in repeated embassies and memorials, they saw themselves stripped of their barrier, and once more in danger of being overwhelmed by that ambitious nation. The city of Brussels had been reduced during the winter; so that the enemy were in possession of all the Austrian Netherlands, except a few fortresses. Great part of the forces belonging to the republic were restricted from action by capitulations, to which they had subscribed. The States were divided in their councils between the two factions which had long subsisted. They trembled at the prospect of seeing Zealand invaded in the spring. The Orange party loudly called for an augmentation of their forces by sea and land, that they might prosecute the war with vigour. The common people, fond of novelty, dazzled by the splendour of greatness, and fully persuaded that nothing but a chief was wanting to their security, demanded the Prince of Orange as their stadtholder; and even mingled menaces with their demands. The opposite faction dreaded alike the

*The States-General alarmed at the progress of the French in the Netherlands.*

power of a stadtholder, the neighbourhood of a French army, and a seditious disposition of the populace. An ambassador was sent to London with representations of the imminent dangers which threatened the republic, and he was ordered to solicit in the most pressing terms the assistance of his Britannic majesty, that the allies might have a superiority in the Netherlands by the beginning of the campaign. The king was very well disposed to comply with their request; but the rebellion in his kingdom, and the dissensions in his cabinet, had retarded the supplies, and embarrassed him so much, that he found it impossible to make those early preparations that were necessary to check the career of the enemy.

The King of France, with his general the Count de Saxe, took the field in the latter end of April, at the head of one hundred and twenty thousand men, and advanced towards the allies, who, to the number of four-and-forty thousand, were intrenched behind the Demer, under the conduct of the Austrian General Bathiani, who retired before them, and took post in the neighbourhood of Breda, the capital of Dutch Brabant. Mareschal Saxe immediately invested Antwerp, which in a few days was surrendered. Then he appeared before the strong town of Mons in Hainault, with an irresistible train of artillery, an immense quantity of bombs and warlike implements. He carried on his approaches with such unabating impetuosity, that, notwithstanding a very vigorous defence, the garrison was obliged to capitulate on the twenty-seventh day of June, in about eight-and-twenty days after the place had been invested. Sieges were not now carried on by the tedious method of sapping. The French king found it much more expeditious and effectual to bring into the field a prodigious train of battering cannon and enormous mortars, that kept up such a fire as no garrison could sustain, and discharged such an incessant hail of bombs and bullets, as in a very little time reduced to ruins the place, with all its fortifications. St. Guisland and Charleroy met with the fate of Mons and Antwerp; so that by the middle of July the French king was absolute master of Flanders, Brabant, and Hainault.

Prince Charles of Lorraine had by this time assumed the command of the confederate army at Terheyde, which, being reinforced by the Hessian troops from Scotland, and a fresh body of Austrians under Count Palfi, amounted to eighty-seven thousand men, including the Dutch forces commanded by the Prince of Waldeck. The generals, supposing the next storm would fall upon Namur, marched towards that place, and took post in an advantageous situation on the eighteenth day of July, in sight of the French army, which was encamped at Gemblours. Here they remained till the eighth day of August, when a detachment of the enemy, commanded by Count Lowendahl, took possession of Huy, where he found a large magazine belonging to the confederates; and their communication with Maestricht was cut off. Mareschal Saxe, on the other side, took his measures so well that they were utterly deprived of all subsistence. Then Prince Charles, retiring across the Maese, abandoned Namur to the efforts of the enemy, by whom it was immediately invested. The trenches were opened on the second day of September; and the garrison, consisting of seven thousand Austrians, defended themselves with equal skill and resolution: but the cannonading and bombardment were so terrible, that in a few days the place was converted into a heap of rubbish; and on the twenty-third day of the month the French monarch took possession of this strong fortress, which had formerly sustained such dreadful attacks. Meanwhile the allied army encamped at Maestricht were joined by Sir John Ligonier, with some British and Bavarian battalions; and Prince Charles resolved to give the enemy battle. With this view he passed the Maese on the thirteenth day of September, and advanced towards Mareschal Saxe, whom he found so advantageously posted at Tongres, that he thought proper to march back to Maestricht. On the twenty-sixth day of September he crossed the Jaar in his retreat; and his rear was attacked by the enemy, who were repulsed. But Count Saxe, being reinforced by a body of troops, under the Count de Clermont, determined to bring the confederates to an engagement. On the thirteenth day of the month he passed the Jaar: while he took possession of the villages of Liers, Warem, and Roucoux, they drew up their forces in order of battle, and made preparations for giving him a warm reception. On the first day of October the enemy advanced in three columns; and a terrible cannonading began about noon. At two o'clock Prince Waldeck on the left was charged with great fury; and after an obstinate defence

*Reduces the strong fortress of Namur, and defeats the allied army at Roucoux.*

overpowered by numbers. The villages were attacked in columns, and as one brigade was repulsed, another succeeded; so that the allies were obliged to abandon these posts, and retreat towards Maestricht, with the loss of five thousand men, and thirty pieces of artillery. The victory, however, cost the French general a much greater number of lives; and was attended with no solid advantage. Sir John Ligonier, the Earls of Crawford* and Rothes, Brigadier Douglas, and other officers of the British troops, distinguished themselves by their gallantry and conduct on this occasion. This action terminated the campaign. The allies, passing the Maese, took up their winter quarters in the duchies of Limburgh and Luxemburgh; while the French cantoned their troops in the places which they had newly conquered.

The campaign in Italy was altogether unfavourable to the French and Spaniards. The house of Austria, being no longer pressed on the side of Germany, was enabled to make the stronger efforts in this country; and the British subsidy encouraged the King of Sardinia to act with redoubled vivacity. Mareschal Maillebois occupied the greater part of Piedmont with about thirty thousand men. Don Philip and the Count de Gages were at the head of a greater number in the neighbourhood of Milan; and the Duke of Modena, with eight thousand, secured his own dominions. The King of Sardinia augmented his forces to six-and-thirty thousand; and the Austrian army, under the Prince of Lichtenstein, amounted to a much greater number; so that the enemy were reduced to the necessity of acting on the defensive, and retired

*The French and Spaniards are compelled to abandon Piedmont and the Milanese.*

---

* This nobleman, so remarkable for his courage and thirst of glory, exhibited a very extraordinary instance of presence of mind on the morning that preceded this battle. He and some volunteers, accompanied by his aide-du-camp, and attended by two orderly dragoons, had rode out before day to reconnoitre the situation of the enemy; and fell in upon one of their advanced guards. The sergeant who commanded it immediately turned out his men, and their pieces were presented when the earl first perceived them. Without betraying the least mark of disorder, he rode up to the sergeant, and, assuming the character of a French general, told him in that language that there was no occasion for such ceremony. Then he asked if they had perceived any of the enemy's parties? and being answered in the negative, "Very well, (said he,) be upon your guard; and if you should be attacked, I will take care that you shall be sustained." So saying, he and his company retired before the sergeant could recover himself from the surprise occasioned by this unexpected address. In all probability he was soon sensible of his mistake; for the incident was that very day publicly mentioned in the French army. The Prince of Tingray, an officer in the Austrian service, having been taken prisoner in the battle that ensued, dined with Mareschal Count Saxe, who dismissed him on his parole, and desired he would charge himself with a facetious compliment to his old friend the Earl of Crawford. He wished his lordship joy of being a French general, and said he could not help being displeased with the sergeant, as he had not procured him the honour of his lordship's company at dinner.

VOL. II.—S. Y

towards the Mantuan. In February, Baron Leutrum, the Piedmontese general, invested and took the strong fortress of Aste. He afterwards relieved the citadel of Alexandria, which the Spaniards had blocked up in the winter, reduced Casal, recovered Valencia, and obliged Maillebois to retire to the neighbourhood of Genoa. On the other side, Don Philip and Count Gages abandoned Milan, Pavia, and Parma, retreating before the Austrians with the utmost precipitation to Placentia, where they were joined on the third of June by the French forces under Maillebois.

Before this junction was effected, the Spanish general Pignatelli had passed the river Po in the night with a strong detachment, and beaten up the quarters of seven thousand Austrians posted at Codogno. Don Philip, finding himself at the head of two-and-fifty thousand men by his junction with the French general, resolved to attack the Austrians in their camp at San Lazaro, before they should be reinforced by his Sardinian majesty. Accordingly, on the fourth day of June, in the evening, he marched with equal silence and expedition, and entered the Austrian trenches about eleven, when a desperate battle ensued. The Austrians were prepared for the attack, which they sustained with great vigour till morning. Then they quitted their intrenchments, and charged the enemy in their turn with such fury, that after an obstinate resistance the combined army was broken, and retired with precipitation to Placentia, leaving on the field fifteen thousand men killed, wounded, and taken, together with sixty colours, and ten pieces of artillery. In a few weeks the Austrians were joined by the Piedmontese: the King of Sardinia assumed the chief command; and Prince Lichtenstein being indisposed, his place was supplied by the Marquis de Botta. Don Philip retired to the other side of the Po, and extended his conquests in the open country of the Milanese. The King of Sardinia called a council of war, in which it was determined that he should pass the river with a strong body of troops, in order to straiten the enemy on one side; while the Marquis de Botta should march up the Tydone, to cut off their communication with Placentia. They forthwith quitted all the posts they had occupied between the Lambro and Adda, resolving to repass the Po, and retreat to Tortona. With this view they threw bridges of boats over that river, and began to pass on the ninth day of August, in the evening.

*Don Philip is worsted at Codogno, and afterwards at Porto Freddo.*

They were attacked at Rotto Freddo by a detachment of Austrians, under General Serbelloni, who maintained the engagement till ten in the morning, when Botta arrived: the battle was renewed with redoubled rage, and lasted till four in the afternoon, when the enemy retired in great disorder to Tortona, with the loss of eight thousand men, a good number of colours and standards, and eighteen pieces of cannon. This victory cost the Austrians four thousand men killed upon the spot, including the gallant General Bernclau. The victors immediately summoned Placentia to surrender; and the garrison, consisting of nine thousand men, were made prisoners of war: Don Philip continued his retreat, and of all his forces brought six-and-twenty thousand only into the territories of Genoa.

The Piedmontese and Austrians, rejoining in the neighbourhood of Pavia, advanced to Tortona, of which they took possession without resistance, while the enemy sheltered themselves under the cannon of Genoa. They did not long continue in this situation; for on the twenty-second day of August they were again in motion, and retired into Provence. The court of Madrid, imputing the bad success of this campaign to the misconduct of Count Gages, recalled that general, and sent the Marquis de las Minas to resume the command of the forces. In the mean time, the victorious confederates appeared before Genoa on the fourth day of December; and the senate of that city, thinking it incapable of defence, submitted to a very mortifying capitulation, by which the gates were delivered up to the Austrians, together with all their arms, artillery, and ammunition; and the city was subjected to the most cruel contributions. The Marquis de Botta being left at Genoa with sixteen thousand men, the King of Sardinia resolved to pass the Var, and pursue the French and Spaniards into Provence; but, that monarch being seized with the small-pox, the conduct of this expedition was intrusted to Count Brown, an Austrian general of Irish extract, who had given repeated proofs of uncommon valour and capacity. He was on this occasion assisted by Vice-Admiral Medley, who commanded the British squadron in the Mediterranean. The French forces had fortified the passes of the Var, under the conduct of the Mareschal de Belleisle, who thought proper to abandon his posts at the approach of Count Brown; and this general, at the head of fifty thousand men, passed the river, without opposition, on the ninth day of November. While he advanced as far as Draguignan, laying the open country under contribution, Baron Roth, with four-and-twenty battalions, invested Antibes, which was at the same time bombarded on the side of the sea by the British squadron. The trenches were opened on the twentieth day of September; but Belleisle having assembled a numerous army, superior to that of the confederates, and the Genoese having expelled their Austrian guests, Count Brown abandoned the enterprise, and repassed the Var, not without some damage from the enemy.

The court of Vienna, which has always patronised oppression, exacted such heavy contributions from the Genoese, and its exactions were so rigorously put into execution, that the people were reduced to despair; and resolved to make a last effort for the recovery of their liberty and independence. Accordingly, they took arms in secret, seized several important posts of the city; surprised some battalions of the Austrians; surrounded others, and cut them in pieces; and, in a word, drove them out with great slaughter. The Marquis de Botta acted with caution and spirit; but being overpowered by numbers, and apprehensive of the peasants in the country, who were in arms, he retreated to the pass of the Brochetta on the side of Lombardy, where he secured himself in an advantageous situation, until he could receive reinforcements. The loss he had sustained at Genoa did not hinder him from reducing Savona, a sea-port town belonging to that republic; and he afterwards made himself master of Gavi. The Genoese, on the contrary, exerted themselves with wonderful industry in fortifying their city, raising troops, and in taking other measures for a vigorous defence, in case they should again be insulted.

*The Genoese expel the Austrians from their city.*

The naval transactions of this year reflected very little honour on the British nation. Commodore Peyton, who commanded six ships of war in the East Indies, shamefully declined a decisive engagement with a French squadron of inferior force; and abandoned the important settlement of Madras, on the coast of Coromandel, which was taken without opposition in the month of September by the French commodore, De la Bourdonnais. Fort St. David, and the other British factories in India, would probably have shared the same fate, had not the

*Madras in the East Indies taken by the French.*

enemy's naval force in that country been shattered and partly destroyed by a terrible tempest. No event of consequence happened in America, though it was a scene that seemed to promise the greatest success to the arms of England. The reduction of Cape Breton had encouraged the ministry to project the conquest of Quebec, the capital of Canada, situated upon the river St. Laurence. Commissions were sent to the governors of the British colonies in North America, empowering them to raise companies to join the armament from England; and eight thousand troops were actually raised in consequence of these directions; while a powerful squadron and transports, having six regiments on board, were prepared at Portsmouth for this expedition. But their departure was postponed by unaccountable delays, until the season was judged too far advanced to risk the great ships on the boisterous coast of North America. That the armament, however, might not be wholly useless to the nation, it was employed in making a descent upon the coast of Bretagne, on the supposition that Port L'Orient, the repository of all the stores and ships belonging to the French East India Company, might be surprised; or, that this invasion would alarm the enemy, and, by making a diversion, facilitate the operations of the Austrian general in Provence.

The naval force intended for this service consisted of sixteen great ships, and eight frigates, besides bomb-ketches and store-ships, commanded by Richard Lestock, appointed admiral of the blue division. Six battalions of land troops, with a detachment of matrosses and bombardiers, were embarked in thirty transports under the conduct of Lieutenant-General Sinclair; and the whole fleet set sail from Plymouth on the fourteenth day of September. On the twentieth the troops were landed in Quimperlay bay, at the distance of ten miles from Port L'Orient. The militia, reinforced by some detachments from different regiments, were assembled to the number of two thousand, and seemed resolved to oppose the disembarkation; but, seeing the British troops determined to land at all events, they thought proper to retire. Next day General Sinclair advanced into the country, skirmishing with the enemy in his route; and arriving at the village of Plemure, within half a league from Port L'Orient, summoned that place to surrender.

*Expedition to the coast of Bretagne, and attempt upon Port L'Orient.*

He was visited by a deputation from the town, which offered to admit the British forces, on condition that they should be restrained from pillaging the inhabitants, and touching the magazines; and that they should pay a just price for their provisions. These terms being rejected, the inhabitants prepared for a vigorous defence; and the English general resolved to besiege the place in form, though he had neither time, artillery, nor forces sufficient for such an enterprise. This strange resolution was owing to the declaration of the engineers, who promised to lay the place in ashes in the space of four-and-twenty hours. All his cannon amounted to no more than a few field-pieces; and he was obliged to wait for two iron guns, which the sailors dragged up from the shipping. Had he given the assault on the first night after his arrival, when the town was filled with terror and confusion, and destitute of regular troops, in all probability it would have been easily taken by scalade; but the reduction of it was rendered impracticable by his delay. The ramparts were mounted with cannon from the ships in the harbour; new works were raised with great industry; the garrison was reinforced by several bodies of regular troops; and great numbers were assembling from all parts: so that the British forces were in danger of being surrounded in an enemy's country. Notwithstanding these discouragements, they opened a small battery against the town, which was set on fire in several places by their bombs and red-hot bullets: they likewise repulsed part of the garrison which had made a sally to destroy their works: but their cannon producing no effect upon the fortifications, the fire from the town daily increasing, the engineers owning they could not perform their promise, and Admiral Lestock declaring in repeated messages, that he could no longer expose the ships on an open coast at such a season of the year, General Sinclair abandoned the siege. Having caused the two iron pieces of cannon and the mortars to be spiked, he retreated in good order to the sea-side, where his troops were re-embarked, having sustained very inconsiderable damage since their first landing. He expected reinforcements from England, and was resolved to wait a little longer for their arrival, in hopes of being able to annoy the enemy more effectually. In the beginning of October the fleet sailed to Quiberon bay, where they destroyed the Ardent, a French ship of war of sixty-four guns; and a detachment of the forces, being landed, took possession of a fort on the peninsula; while the little islands of Houat and Heydic were reduced by the sailors. In this situation the admiral and general continued till the seventeenth day of the month, when the forts being dismantled, and the troops re-embarked, the fleets sailed from the French coast: the admiral returned to England, and the transports with the soldiers proceeded to Ireland, where they arrived in safety.

This expedition, weak and frivolous as it may seem, was resented by the French nation as one of the greatest insults they had ever sustained; and demonstrated the possibility of hurting France in her tenderest parts, by means of an armament of this nature, well timed, and vigorously conducted. Indeed, nothing could be more absurd or precipitate than an attempt to distress the enemy by landing a handful of troops, without draught-horses, tents, or artillery, from a fleet of ships lying on an open beach, exposed to the uncertainty of weather in the most tempestuous season of the year, so as to render the retreat and re-embarkation altogether precarious. The British squadrons in the West Indies performed no exploit of consequence in the course of this year. The commerce was but indifferently protected. Commodore Lee, stationed off Martinico, allowed a French fleet of merchant ships and their convoy to pass by his squadron unmolested; and Commodore Mitchel behaved scandalously in a rencounter with the French squadron, under the conduct of Monsieur de Conflans, who in his return to Europe took the Severn, an English ship of fifty guns. The cruisers on all sides, English, French, and Spaniards, were extremely alert; and though the English lost the greater number of ships, this difference was more than overbalanced by the superior value of the prizes taken from the enemy. In the course of this year two-and-twenty Spanish privateers, and sixty-six merchant vessels, including ten register ships, fell into the hands of the British cruisers: from the French they took seven ships of war, ninety privateers, and about three hundred ships of commerce. The new King of Spain[b] being sup-

*Naval transactions in the West Indies. Conferences at Breda.*

---

[b] In the month of July, Philip King of Spain dying, in the sixty-third year of his age, was succeeded by his eldest son Ferdinand, born of Maria-Louisa Gabriela, sister to the late King of Sardinia. He espoused Donna Maria Magdalena, Infanta of Portugal, but had no issue. Philip was but two days survived by his daughter, the Dauphiness of France. The same month was remarkable for the death of Christiern VI. King of Denmark

posed well affected to the British nation, an effort was made to detach him from the interest of France, by means of the Marquis de Tabernega, who had formerly been his favourite, and resided many years as a refugee in England. This nobleman proceeded to Lisbon, where a negotiation was set on foot with the court of Madrid. But his efforts miscarried: and the influence of the queen-mother continued to predominate in the Spanish councils. The States-General had for some years endeavoured to promote a pacification by remonstrances, and even entreaties, at the court of Versailles: the French king at length discovered an inclination to peace, and in September a congress was opened at Breda, the capital of Dutch Brabant, where the plenipotentiaries of the emperor, Great Britain, France, and Holland, were assembled; but the French were so insolent in their demands that the conferences were soon interrupted.

The Parliament of Great Britain meeting in November, the king exhorted them to concert with all possible expedition the proper measures for pursuing the war with vigour, that the confederate army in the Netherlands might be seasonably augmented; he likewise gave them to understand that the funds appropriated for the support of his civil government had for some years past fallen short of the revenue intended and granted by Parliament; and said he relied on their known affection to find out some method to make good this deficiency. As all those who had conducted the opposition were now concerned in the administration, little or no objection was made to any demand or proposal of the government and its ministers. The Commons, having considered the estimates, voted forty thousand seamen for the service of the ensuing year, and about sixty thousand land forces, including eleven thousand five hundred marines. They granted four hundred and thirty-three thousand pounds to the Empress Queen of Hungary; three hundred thousand pounds to the King of Sardinia; four hundred and ten thousand pounds for the maintenance of eighteen thousand Hanoverian auxiliaries; one hundred and sixty-one thousand six hundred and seven pounds for six thousand Hessians; subsidies to the Electors of Cologn, Mentz, and Bavaria; and the sum of five hundred thousand pounds to enable his majesty to prosecute the war

mark, succeeded by his son Frederick V., who had married the Princess Louisa, youngest daughter to the King of Great Britain.

with advantage. In a word, the supplies amounted to nine millions four hundred twenty-five thousand two hundred and fifty-four pounds; a sum almost incredible, if we consider how the kingdom had been already drained of its treasure. It was raised by the usual taxes, reinforced with new impositions on windows, carriages, and spirituous liquors, a lottery, and a loan from the sinking fund. The new taxes were mortgaged for four millions by transferable annuities, at an interest of four, and a premium of ten per centum. By reflecting on these enormous grants, one would imagine the ministry had been determined to impoverish the nation; but, from the eagerness and expedition with which the people subscribed for the money, one would conclude that the riches of the kingdom were inexhaustible. It may not be amiss to observe, that the supplies of this year exceeded, by two millions and a half, the greatest annual sum that was raised during the reign of Queen Anne, though she maintained as great a number of troops as was now in the pay of Great Britain, and her armies and fleets acquired every year fresh harvests of glory and advantage; whereas this war had proved an almost uninterrupted series of events big with disaster and dishonour. During the last two years, the naval expense of England had exceeded that of France above five millions sterling; though her fleets had not obtained one single advantage over the enemy at sea, nor been able to protect her commerce from their depredations. She was at once a prey to her declared adversaries and professed friends. Before the end of summer, she numbered among her mercenaries two empresses, five German princes, and a powerful monarch, whom she hired to assist her in trimming the balance of Europe, in which they themselves were immediately interested, and she had no more than a secondary concern. Had these fruitless subsidies been saved; had the national revenue been applied with economy to national purposes; had it been employed in liquidating gradually the public incumbrances; in augmenting the navy, improving manufactures, encouraging and securing the colonies, and extending trade and navigation; corruption would have become altogether unnecessary, and disaffection would have vanished; the people would have been eased of their burdens, and ceased to complain: commerce would have flourished, and produced such affluence as must have raised Great Britain to the highest pinnacle of maritime power,

above all rivalship or competition. She would have been
dreaded by her enemies; revered by her neighbours; oppressed nations would have crept under her wings for protection; contending potentates would have appealed to her
decision; and she would have shone the universal arbitress
of Europe. How different is her present situation! her
debts are enormous, her taxes intolerable, her people discontented, and the sinews of her government relaxed. Without
conduct, confidence, or concert, she engages in blundering
negotiations; she involves herself rashly in foreign quarrels,
and lavishes her substance with the most dangerous precipitation; she is even deserted by her wonted vigour, steadiness, and intrepidity; she grows vain, fantastical, and pusil-
lanimous; her arms are despised by her enemies; and her
counsels ridiculed through all Christendom.

The king, in order to exhibit a specimen of his desire to
diminish the public expense, ordered the third and
fourth troops of his life guards to be disbanded, and
reduced three regiments of horse to the quality of dragoons.
The House of Commons presented an address of thanks for
this instance of economy, by which the annual sum of seventy
thousand pounds was saved to the nation. Notwithstanding
this seeming harmony between the king and the great council
of the nation, his majesty resolved, with the advice of his
council, to dissolve the present Parliament, though the term
of seven years was not yet expired since its first meeting.
The ministry affected to insinuate, that the States-General
were unwilling to concur with his majesty in vigorous measures against France, during the existence of a Parliament
which had undergone such a vicissitude of complexion. The
allies of Great Britain, far from being suspicious of this
assembly, which had supplied them so liberally, saw with
concern that, according to law, it would soon be dismissed;
and they doubted whether another could be procured equally
agreeable to their purposes. In order to remove this doubt,
the ministry resolved to surprise the kingdom with a new
election, before the malecontents should be prepared to oppose the friends of the government. Accordingly, when the
business of the session was despatched, the king, having
given the royal assent to the several acts they had prepared,
dismissed them in the month of June with an affectionate
speech, that breathed nothing but tenderness and gratitude.
The Parliament was immediately dissolved by proclamation,

and new writs were issued for convoking another. Among the laws passed in this session, was an act abolishing the heritable jurisdictions, and taking away the tenure of wardholdings in Scotland, which were reckoned among the principal sources of those rebellions that had been excited since the Revolution. In the Highlands, they certainly kept the common people in subjection to their chiefs, whom they implicitly followed and obeyed in all their undertakings. By this act these mountaineers were legally emancipated from slavery; but as the tenants enjoyed no leases, and were at all times liable to be ejected from their farms, they still depended on the pleasure of their lords, notwithstanding this interposition of the legislature, which granted a valuable consideration in money to every nobleman and petty baron who was thus deprived of one part of his inheritance. The forfeited estates, indeed, were divided into small farms, and let by the government on leases at an under value; so that those who had the good fortune to obtain such leases tasted the sweets of independence: but the Highlanders in general were left, in their original indigence and incapacity, at the mercy of their superiors. Had manufactures and fisheries been established in different parts of their country, they would have seen and felt the happy consequences of industry, and in a little time been effectually detached from all their slavish connexions.

The operations of the campaign had been concerted in the winter at the Hague, between the Duke of Cumberland and the States-General of the United Provinces, who were by this time generally convinced of France's design to encroach upon their territories. They therefore determined to take effectual measures against that restless and ambitious neighbour. The allied powers agreed to assemble a vast army in the Netherlands; and it was resolved that the Austrians and Piedmontese should once more penetrate into Provence. The Dutch patriots, however, were not roused into this exertion until all their remonstrances had failed at the court of Versailles; until they had been urged by repeated memorials of the English ambassador, and stimulated by the immediate danger to which their country was exposed: for France was by this time possessed of all the Austrian Netherlands, and seemed bent upon penetrating into the territories of the United Provinces. In February, the Duke of Cumberland began to assemble the allied forces; and in the latter end of March they took the field in three separate bodies. His royal highness, with the English, Hanoverians, and Hessians, fixed his head-quarters at the village of Tilberg: the Prince of Waldeck was posted with the Dutch troops at Breda; and Mareschal Bathiani collected the Austrians and Bavarians in the neighbourhood of Venlo. The whole army amounted to one hundred and twenty thousand men, who lay inactive six weeks, exposed to the inclemency of the weather, and almost destitute of forage and provision. Count Saxe, by this time created Mareschal-General of France, continued his troops within their cantonments at Bruges, Antwerp, and Brussels, declaring, that when the allied army should be weakened by sickness and mortality, he would convince the Duke of Cumberland, that the first duty of a general is to provide for the health and preservation of his troops. In April this fortunate commander took the field, at the head of one hundred and forty thousand men; and the Count de Clermont commanded a separate body of nineteen battalions and thirty squadrons. Count Lowendahl was detached on the sixteenth day of the month, with seven-and-twenty thousand men, to invade Dutch Flanders: at the same time, the French minister at the Hague presented a memorial to the states, intimating that his master was obliged to take this step by the necessity of war; but that his troops should observe the strictest discipline, without interfering with the religion, government, or commerce of the republic: he likewise declared, that the countries and places of which he might be obliged to take possession should be detained no otherwise than as a pledge, to be restored as soon as the United Provinces should give convincing proofs that they would no longer furnish the enemies of France with succours.

While the states deliberated upon this declaration, Count Lowendahl entered Dutch Brabant, and invested the town and fortress of Sluys, the garrison of which surrendered themselves prisoners of war on the nineteenth day of April. This was likewise the fate of Sasvan-Ghent; while the Marquis de Contades, with another detachment, reduced the forts Perle and Leifkensboek, with the town of Philippine, even within hearing of the confederate army. The fort of Sanberg was vigorously defended by two English battalions; but they were overpowered, and obliged to retire to Welsthoorden; and Count Lowendahl undertook the siege of Hulst, which was shamefully surrendered by La Roque, the Dutch governor, though he knew that a reinforcement of nine battalions was on the march to his relief. Then the French general took possession of Axel and Terneuse, and began to prepare flat-bottomed boats for a descent on the island of Zealand. The Dutch people were now struck with consternation. They saw the enemy at their doors, and owed their immediate preservation to the British squadron stationed at the Swin, under the command of Commodore Mitchel,\* who, by means of his sloops, tenders, and small craft, took such measures as defeated the intention of Lowendahl. The common people in Zealand, being reduced to despair, began to clamour loudly against their governors, as if they had not taken the proper measures for their security. The friends of the Prince of Orange did not neglect this opportunity of promoting his interest. They encouraged their discontent, and exaggerated the danger: they reminded them of the year one thousand six hundred and seventy-two, when the French king was at the gates of Amsterdam, and the republic was saved by the choice of a stadtholder: they exhorted them to turn their eyes on the descendant of those heroes who had established the liberty and independence of the United Provinces; they extolled his virtue and ability, his generosity, his justice, his unshaken love to his country. The people in several towns, inflamed by such representations to tumult and sedition, compelled their magistrates to declare the Prince of Orange stadtholder. He himself, in a letter to the states of Zealand, offered his services for the defence of the province. On the twenty-eighth day of April he was nominated Captain-General and Admiral of Zealand. Their example was followed by Rotterdam and the whole province of Holland; and on the second day of May, the Prince of Orange was, in the assembly of the States-General, invested with the power and dignity of Stadtholder, Captain-General, and Admiral of the United Provinces. The vigorous consequences of this resolution immediately appeared. All commerce and contracts with the French were prohibited: the peasants were armed and exercised: a resolution passed for making a considerable augmentation of the army: a council of war was established

\* Not the person who commanded in the West Indies.

for inquiring into the conduct of the governors who had given up the frontier places: and orders were issued to commence hostilities against the French both by sea and land.

Meanwhile, the Duke of Cumberland took post with his whole army between the two Nethes, to cover Bergen-op-Zoom and Maestricht; and Mareschal Saxe called in his detachments, with a view to hazard a general engagement. In the latter end of May, the French king arrived at Brussels; and his general resolved to undertake the siege of Maestricht. For this purpose he advanced towards Louvain; and the confederates, perceiving his drift, began their march to take post between the town and the enemy. On the twentieth day of June, they took possession of their ground, and were drawn up in order of battle, with their right at Bilsen, and their left extending to Wirle, within a mile of Maestricht, having in the front of their left wing the village of Laffeldt, in which they posted several battalions of British infantry. The French had taken possession of the heights of Herdceren, immediately above the allies; and both armies cannonaded each other till the evening. In the morning, the enemy's infantry marched down the hill, in a prodigious column, and attacked the village of Laffeldt, which was well fortified, and defended with amazing obstinacy. The assailants suffered terribly in their approach from the cannon of the confederates, which was served with surprising dexterity and success; and they met with such a warm reception from the British musketry as they could not withstand; but when they were broken and dispersed, fresh brigades succeeded with astonishing perseverance. The confederates were driven out of the village; yet, being sustained by three regiments, they measured back their ground, and repulsed the enemy with great slaughter. Nevertheless, Count Saxe continued pouring in other battalions, and the French regained and maintained their footing in the village after it had been three times lost and carried. The action was chiefly confined to this post, where the field exhibited a horrible scene of carnage. At noon the Duke of Cumberland ordered the whole left wing to advance against the enemy, whose infantry gave way: Prince Waldeck led up the centre: Mareschal Bathiani made a motion with the right wing towards Herdceren, and victory seemed ready to declare for the confederates, when the fortune of the day took a sudden turn to their prejudice. Several squadrons of Dutch horse, posted in the centre, gave way, and flying at full gallop, overthrew five battalions of infantry that were advancing from the body of reserve. The French cavalry charged them with great impetuosity, increasing the confusion that was already produced, and penetrating through the lines of the allied army, which was thus divided about the centre. The Duke of Cumberland, who exerted himself with equal courage and activity in attempting to remedy this disorder, was in danger of being taken; and the defeat would in all probability have been total, had not Sir John Ligonier taken the resolution of sacrificing himself and a part of the troops to the safety of the army. At the head of three British regiments of dragoons, and some squadrons of imperial horse, he charged the whole line of the French cavalry with such intrepidity and success that he overthrew all that opposed him, and made such a diversion as enabled the Duke of Cumberland to effect an orderly retreat to Maestricht. He himself was taken by a French carabineer, after his horse had been killed; but the regiments he commanded retired with deliberation. The confederates retreated to Maestricht, without having sustained much damage from the pursuit, and even brought off all their artillery, except sixteen pieces of cannon. Their loss did not exceed six thousand men killed and taken; whereas the French general purchased the victory at a much greater expense. The common cause of the confederate powers is said to have suffered from the pride and ignorance of their generals. On the eve of the battle, when the detachment of the Count de Clermont appeared on the hill of Herdeeren, Mareschal Bathiani asked permission of the commander-in-chief to attack them before they should be reinforced, declaring he would answer for the success of the enterprise. No regard was paid to this proposal; but the superior asked in his turn, where the mareschal would be in case he should be wanted? He replied, "I shall always be found at the head of my troops," and retired in disgust. The subsequent disposition has likewise been blamed, inasmuch as not above one half of the army could act, while the enemy exerted their whole force.

The confederates passed the Maese, and encamped in the duchy of Limburgh, so as to cover Maestricht; while the

French king remained with his army in the neighbourhood of Tongres. Mareschal Saxe, having amused the allies with marches and counter-marches, at length detached Count Lowendahl with six-and-thirty thousand men to besiege Bergen-op-Zoom, the strongest fortification of Dutch Brabant, the favourite work of the famous engineer Coehorn, never conquered, and generally esteemed invincible. It was secured with a garrison of three thousand men, and well provided with artillery, ammunition, and magazines. The enemy appeared before it on the twelfth day of July, and summoned the governor to surrender. The Prince of Saxe-Hilburghausen was sent to its relief, with twenty battalions and fourteen squadrons of the troops that could be most conveniently assembled: he entered the lines of Bergen-op-Zoom, where he remained in expectation of a strong reinforcement from the confederate army; and the old Baron Cronstrom, whom the stadtholder had appointed Governor of Brabant, assumed the command of the garrison. The besiegers carried on their operations with great vivacity; and the troops in the town defended it with equal vigour. The eyes of all Europe were turned upon this important siege: Count Lowendahl received divers reinforcements; and a considerable body of troops was detached from the allied army, under the command of Baron Schwartzemberg, to co-operate with the Prince of Saxe-Hildburghausen. The French general lost a great number of men by the close and continual fire of the besieged; while he, in his turn, opened such a number of batteries, and plied them so warmly, that the defences began to give way. From the sixteenth day of July to the fifteenth of September, the siege produced an unintermitting scene of horror and destruction; desperate sallies were made, and mines sprung with the most dreadful effects: the works began to be shattered; the town was laid in ashes; the trenches were filled with carnage: nothing was seen but fire and smoke; nothing heard but one continued roar of bombs and cannon. But still the damage fell chiefly on the besiegers, who were slain in heaps; while the garrison suffered very little, and could be occasionally relieved or reinforced from the lines. In a word, it was generally believed that Count Lowendahl would be baffled in his endeavours; and by this belief the governor of Bergen-op-Zoom seems to have been lulled into a blind security. At length, some inconsiderable breaches were made in one ravelin and two bastions, and these the French general resolved to storm, though Cronstrom believed they were impracticable; and on that supposition presumed that the enemy would not attempt an assault. For this very reason Count Lowendahl resolved to hazard the attack before the preparations should be made for his reception. He accordingly regulated his dispositions, and at four o'clock in the morning, on the sixteenth day of September, the signal was made for the assault. A prodigious quantity of bombs being thrown into the ravelin, his troops threw themselves into the fossé, mounted the breaches, forced open a sallyport, and entered the place almost without resistance. In a word, they had time to extend themselves along the curtains, and form in order of battle, before the garrison could be assembled. Cronstrom was asleep, and the soldiers upon duty had been surprised by the suddenness and impetuosity of the attack. Though the French had taken possession of the ramparts, they did not gain the town without opposition. Two battalions of the Scottish troops, in the pay of the States-General, were assembled in the market-place, and attacked them with such fury, that they were driven from street to street, until fresh reinforcements arriving, compelled the Scots to retreat in their turn; yet they disputed every inch of ground, and fought until two thirds of them were killed on the spot. Then they brought off the old governor, abandoning the town to the enemy: the troops that were encamped in the lines retreating with great precipitation, all the forts in the neighbourhood immediately surrendered to the victors, who now became masters of the whole navigation of the Schelde. The French king was no sooner informed of Lowendahl's success, than he promoted him to the rank of Mareschal of France, appointed Count Saxe governor of the conquered Netherlands, and returned in triumph to Versailles. In a little time after this transaction, both armies were distributed into winter quarters, and the Duke of Cumberland embarked for England.

In Italy, the French arms did not triumph with equal success, though the Mareschal de Belleisle saw himself at the head of a powerful army in Provence. In April he passed the Var without opposition, and took possession of Nice. He met with little or no resistance in reducing Montalban, Villafranca, and Ventimiglia; while General Brown, with eight-and-twenty thousand Austrians, retired towards *The Austrians undertake the siege of Genoa, which, however, they abandon.*

Final and Savona. In the mean time another large body, under Count Schuylemberg, who had succeeded the Marquis de Botta, co-operated with fifteen thousand Piedmontese in an attempt to recover the city of Genoa. The French king had sent them supplies, succours, and engineers, with the Duke de Boufflers, as ambassador to the republic, who likewise acted as commander in chief of the forces employed for its defence. The Austrian general assembled his troops in the Milanese: having forced the passage of the Bochetta on the thirteenth of January, he advanced into the territories of Genoa, and the Riviera was ravaged without mercy. On the last day of March he appeared before the city, at the head of forty thousand men, and summoned the revolters to lay down their arms. The answer he received was, that the republic had fifty-four thousand men in arms, two hundred and sixty cannon, thirty-four mortars, with abundance of ammunition and provision; that they would defend their liberty with their last blood, and be buried in the ruins of their capital, rather than submit to the clemency of the court of Vienna, except by an honourable capitulation guaranteed by the Kings of Great Britain and Sardinia, the republic of Venice, and the United Provinces. In the beginning of May, Genoa was invested on all sides; a furious sally was made by the Duke de Boufflers, who drove the besiegers from their posts; but the Austrians rallying, he was repulsed in his turn with the loss of seven hundred men. General Schuylemberg carried on his operations with such skill, vigour, and intrepidity, that he made himself master of the suburbs of Bisagno; and in all probability would have reduced the city, had he not been obliged to desist, in consequence of the repeated remonstrances made by the King of Sardinia and Count Brown, who represented the necessity of his abandoning his enterprise, and drawing off his army, to cover Piedmont and Lombardy from the efforts of Mareschal de Belleisle. Accordingly, he raised the siege on the tenth day of June, and returned into the Milanese, in order to join his Sardinian majesty; while the Genoese made an irruption into the Parmesan and Placentin, where they committed terrible outrages, in revenge for the mischiefs they had undergone.

While the Mareschal de Belleisle remained at Ventimiglia, his brother, at the head of four-and-thirty thousand French and Spaniards, attempted to penetrate into Piedmont: on the sixth day of July he arrived at the pass of Exiles, a strong fortress on the frontiers of Dauphiné, situated on the north side of the river Doria. The defence of this important post the King of Sardinia had committed to the care of the Count de Brigueras, who formed an encampment behind the lines, with fourteen battalions of Piedmontese and Austrians, while divers detachments were posted along the passes of the Alps. On the eighth day of the month the Piedmontese intrenchments were attacked by the Chevalier de Belleisle with incredible intrepidity; but the columns were repulsed with great loss in three successive attacks. Impatient of this obstinate opposition, and determined not to survive a miscarriage, this impetuous general seized a pair of colours, and advancing at the head of his troops, through a prodigious fire, pitched them with his own hand on the enemy's intrenchments. At that instant he fell dead, having received two musket-balls and the thrust of a bayonet in his body. The assailants were so much dispirited by the death of their commander, that they forthwith gave way, and retreated with precipitation towards Sestrieres, having lost near five thousand men in the attack. The mareschal was no sooner informed of his brother's misfortune, than he retreated towards the Var to join the troops from Exiles, while the King of Sardinia, having assembled an army of seventy thousand men, threatened Dauphiné with an invasion; but the excessive rains prevented the execution of his design. General Leutrum was detached with twenty battalions, to drive the French from Ventimiglia; but Belleisle marching back, that scheme was likewise frustrated; and thus ended the campaign.

*The Chevalier de Belleisle slain in the attack of Exiles.*

In this manner was the French king baffled in his projects upon Italy; nor was he more fortunate in his naval operations. He had, in the preceding year, equipped an expensive armament, under the command of the Duke d'Anville, for the recovery of Cape Breton; but it was rendered ineffectual by storms, distempers, and the death of the commander. Not yet discouraged by these disasters, he resolved to renew his efforts against the British colonies in North America, and their settlements in the East Indies. For these purposes, two squadrons were prepared at Brest, one to be

*A French squadron defeated and taken by the Admirals Anson and Warren.*

commanded by the Commodore de la Jonquiere; and the
other, destined for India, by Monsieur de St. George. The
ministry of Great Britain, being apprised of these measures,
resolved to intercept both squadrons, which were to set
sail together. For this purpose Vice-Admiral Anson and
Rear-Admiral Warren took their departure from Plymouth
with a formidable fleet, and steered their course to Cape
Finisterre on the coast of Gallicia. On the third day of
May they fell in with the French squadrons, commanded
by La Jonquiere and St. George, consisting of six large
ships of war, as many frigates, and four armed vessels
equipped by their East India company, having under their
convoy about thirty ships laden with merchandize. Those
prepared for war immediately shortened sail, and formed a
line of battle; while the rest, under the protection of the
six frigates, proceeded on their voyage with all the sail
they could carry. The British squadron was likewise drawn
up in line of battle; but Mr. Warren, perceiving that the
enemy began to sheer off, now their convoy was at a considerable distance, advised Admiral Anson to haul in the
signal for the line, and hoist another for giving chase and
engaging, otherwise the French would, in all probability,
escape by favour of the night. The proposal was embraced;
and in a little time the engagement began with great fury
about four o'clock in the afternoon. The enemy sustained
the battle with equal conduct and valour, until they were
overpowered by numbers, and then they struck their colours.
The admiral detached three ships in pursuit of the convoy,
nine sail of which were taken; but the rest were saved
by the intervening darkness. About seven hundred of
the French were killed and wounded in this action. The
English lost about five hundred; and amongst these Captain Granville, commander of the ship Defiance. He was
nephew to the Lord Viscount Cobham, a youth of the most
amiable character and promising genius, animated with
the noblest sentiments of honour and patriotism. Eager
in the pursuit of glory, he rushed into the midst of the
battle, where both his legs were cut off by a cannon ball.
He submitted to his fate with the most heroic resignation,
and died universally lamented and beloved. The success
of the British arms in this engagement was chiefly owing
to the conduct, activity, and courage of the rear-admiral.
A considerable quantity of bullion was found in the prizes,

which was brought to Spithead in triumph; and the treasure, being landed, was conveyed in twenty waggons to the bank of London. Admiral Anson was ennobled, and Mr. Warren honoured with the Order of the Bath.

About the middle of June, Commodore Fox, with six ships of war, cruising in the latitude of Cape Ortegal in Gallicia, took above forty French ships, richly laden from St. Domingo, after they had been abandoned by their convoy. But the French king sustained another more important loss at sea in the month of October. Rear-Admiral Hawke sailed from Plymouth in the beginning of August, with fourteen ships of the line, to intercept a fleet of French merchant-ships bound for the West Indies. He cruised for some time on the coast of Bretagne; and at length the French fleet sailed from the isle of Aix, under convoy of nine ships of the line, besides frigates, commanded by Monsieur de Letendeur. On the fourteenth day of October the two squadrons were in sight of each other, in the latitude of Belleisle. The French commodore immediately ordered one of his great ships, and the frigates, to proceed with the trading ships, while he formed the line of battle, and waited the attack. At eleven in the forenoon Admiral Hawke displayed the signal to chase, and in half an hour both fleets were engaged. The battle lasted till night, when all the French squadron, except the Intrepide and Tonant, had struck to the English flag. These two capital ships escaped in the dark, and returned to Brest in a shattered condition. The French captains sustained the unequal fight with uncommon bravery and resolution; and did not yield until their ships were disabled. Their loss in men amounted to eight hundred; the number of English killed in this engagement did not exceed two hundred, including Captain Saumarez, a gallant officer, who had served under Lord Anson in his expedition to the Pacific Ocean. Indeed it must be owned, for the honour of that nobleman, that all the officers formed under his example, and raised by his influence, approved themselves in all respects worthy of the commands to which they were preferred. Immediately after the action, Admiral Hawke despatched a sloop to Commodore Legge, whose squadron was stationed at the Leeward Islands, with intelligence of the French fleet of merchant-ships, outward-bound, that he might take

*Admiral Hawke obtains another victory over the French at sea.*

the proper measures for intercepting them in their passage to Martinique, and the other French islands. In consequence of this advice, he redoubled his vigilance, and a good number of them fell into his hands. Admiral Hawke conducted his prizes to Spithead; and in his letter to the board of Admiralty declared, that all his captains behaved like men of honour during the engagement, except Mr. Fox, whose conduct he desired might be subjected to an inquiry. That gentleman was accordingly tried by a court-martial, and suspended from his command, for having followed the advice of his officers, contrary to his own better judgment; but he was soon restored, and afterwards promoted to the rank of admiral; while Mr. Matthews, whose courage never incurred suspicion, still laboured under a suspension for that which had been successfully practised in both these late actions, namely, engaging the enemy without any regard to the line of battle.

In the Mediterranean, Vice-Admiral Medley blocked up the Spanish squadron in Carthagena; assisted the Austrian general on the coast of Villafranca; and intercepted some of the succours sent from France to the assistance of the Genoese. At his death, which happened in the beginning of August, the command of that squadron devolved upon Rear-Admiral Byng, who proceeded on the same plan of operation. In the summer, two British ships of war, having under their convoy a fleet of merchant-ships bound to North America, fell in with the Glorioso, a Spanish ship of eighty guns, in the latitude of the Western Isles. She had sailed from the Havannah, with an immense treasure on board, and must have fallen a prize to the English ships, had each captain done his duty. Captain Erskine, in the Warwick of sixty guns, attacked her with great intrepidity, and fought until his ship was entirely disabled; but being unsustained by his consort, he was obliged to haul off, and the Glorioso arrived in safety at Ferrol: there the silver was landed, and she proceeded on her voyage to Cadiz, which, however, she did not reach. She was encountered by the Dartmouth, a British frigate of forty guns, commanded by Captain Hamilton, a gallant youth, who, notwithstanding the inequality of force, engaged her without hesitation: but in the heat of the action, his ship, being set on fire by accident, was blown up, and he perished with all his crew, except a midshipman, and ten or eleven sailors, who were taken up alive by a privateer that happened to be in sight. Favourable as this accident may seem to the Glorioso, she did not escape. An English ship of eighty guns, under the command of Captain Buckle, came up, and obliged the Spaniards to surrender, after a short but vigorous engagement. Commodore Griffin had been sent, with a reinforcement of ships, to assume the command of the squadron in the East Indies; and although his arrival secured Fort St. David's, and the other British settlements in that country, from the insults of Monsieur de la Bourdonnais, his strength was not sufficient to enable him to undertake any enterprise of importance against the enemy: the ministry of England, therefore, resolved to equip a fresh armament, that, when joined by the ships in India, should be in a condition to besiege Pondicherry, the principal settlement belonging to the French on the coast of Coromandel. For this service a good number of independent companies was raised, and set sail, in the sequel, with a strong squadron under the conduct of Rear-Admiral Boscawen, an officer of unquestioned valour and capacity. In the course of this year the British cruisers were so alert and successful, that they took six hundred and forty-four prizes from the French and Spaniards; whereas the loss of Great Britain in the same time did not exceed five hundred and fifty.

All the belligerent powers were by this time heartily tired of a war which had consumed an immensity of treasure, had been productive of so much mischief, and in the events of which all, in their turns, had found themselves disappointed. *Congress of Aix-la-Chapelle.* Immediately after the battle of Laffeldt, the King of France had, in a personal conversation with Sir John Ligonier, expressed his desire of a pacification; and afterwards his minister at the Hague presented a declaration on the same subject to the deputies of the States-General. The signal success of the British arms at sea confirmed him in these sentiments, which were likewise reinforced by a variety of other considerations. His finances were almost exhausted, and his supplies from the Spanish West Indies rendered so precarious by the vigilance of the British cruisers, that he could no longer depend upon their arrival. The trading part of his subjects had sustained such losses, that his kingdom was filled with bankruptcies: and the best part of his navy now contributed to strengthen the fleets of his enemies. The election of a stadtholder had united the whole power of the States-General against him, in taking the most resolute measures for their own safety: his views in Germany were entirely frustrated by the elevation of the grand duke to the imperial throne, and the re-establishment of peace between the houses of Austria and Brandenburgh: the success of his arms in Italy had not at all answered his expectation; and Genoa was become an expensive ally. He had the mortification to see the commerce of Britain flourish in the midst of war, while his own people were utterly impoverished. The Parliament of England granted, and the nation paid, such incredible sums as enabled their sovereign not only to maintain invincible navies and formidable armies, but likewise to give subsidies to all the powers of Europe. He knew that a treaty of this kind was actually upon the anvil between his Britannic majesty and the czarina, and he began to be apprehensive of seeing an army of Russians in the Netherlands. His fears from this quarter were not without foundation. In the month of November, the Earl of Hyndford, ambassador from the King of Great Britain at the court of Russia, concluded a treaty of subsidy, by which the czarina engaged to hold in readiness thirty thousand men, and forty galleys, to be employed in the service of the confederates, on the first requisition. The States-General acceded to this agreement, and even consented to pay one-fourth of the subsidy. His most Christian Majesty, moved by these considerations, made further advances towards an accommodation, both at the Hague and in London; and the contending powers agreed to another congress, which was actually opened in March at Aix-la-Chapelle, where the Earl of Sandwich and Sir Thomas Robinson assisted as plenipotentiaries from the King of Great Britain.

The elections for the new Parliament in England had been conducted so as fully to answer the purposes of the Duke of Newcastle, and his brother Mr. Pelham, who had for some time wholly engrossed the administration. Both Houses were assembled on the tenth day of November, when Mr. Onslow was unanimously re-elected Speaker of the Commons. The session was opened, as usual, by a speech from the throne, congratulating them on the signal successes of the British navy, and the happy alteration in the government of the

*Compliant temper of the new Parliament. Preliminaries signed.*

United Provinces. His majesty gave them to understand that a congress would be speedily opened at Aix-la-Chapelle, to concert the means for effecting a general pacification; and reminded them that nothing would more conduce to the success of this negotiation than the vigour and unanimity of their proceedings. He received such addresses as the ministers were pleased to dictate. Opposition now languished at their feet. The Duke of Bedford was become a courtier, and in a little time appointed secretary of state, in the room of the Earl of Chesterfield, who had lately executed that office, which he now resigned; and the Earl of Sandwich no longer harangued against the administration. This new House of Commons, in imitation of the liberality of their predecessors, readily gratified all the requests of the government. They voted forty thousand seamen, forty-nine thousand land-forces, besides eleven thousand five hundred marines; the subsidies for the Queen of Hungary, the czarina, the King of Sardinia, the Electors of Mentz and Bavaria, the Hessians, and the Duke of Wolfenbuttel: the sum of two hundred thirty-five thousand seven hundred and forty-nine pounds was granted to the provinces of New England, to re-imburse them for the expense of reducing Cape Breton: five hundred thousand pounds were given to his majesty for the vigorous prosecution of the war; and about one hundred and fifty-two thousand pounds to the Scottish claimants in lieu of their jurisdiction. The supplies for the ensuing year fell very little short of nine millions, of which the greater part was raised on a loan by subscription, chargeable on a new subsidy of poundage exacted from all merchandise imported into Great Britain. Immediately after the rebellion was suppressed, the legislature had established some regulations in Scotland, which were thought necessary to prevent such commotions for the future. The Highlanders were disarmed, and an act passed for abolishing their peculiarity of garb, which was supposed to keep up party distinctions, to encourage their martial disposition, and to preserve the memory of the exploits achieved by their ancestors. In this session a bill was brought in to enforce the execution of that law, and passed with another act for the more effectual punishment of high-treason in the Highlands of Scotland. The practice of insuring French and Spanish ships at London being deemed the sole circumstance that prevented a total stagnation of commerce in those countries, it was prohibited by law under severe penalties; and this step of the British Parliament accelerated the conclusion of the treaty. Several other prudent measures were taken in the course of this session for the benefit of the public; and among these we may reckon an act for encouraging the manufacture of indigo in the British plantations of North America; an article for which Great Britain used to pay two hundred thousand pounds yearly to the subjects of France. The session was closed on the thirteenth day of May, when the king declared to both Houses, that the preliminaries of a general peace were actually signed at Aix-la-Chapelle by the ministers of Great Britain, France, and the United Provinces; and that the basis of this accommodation was a general restitution of the conquests which had been made during the war. Immediately after the prorogation of Parliament, his majesty set out for his German dominions, after having appointed a regency to rule the realm in his absence.

1748.

The articles might have been made much less unfavourable to Great Britain and her allies, had the ministry made a proper use of the treaty with the czarina; and if the confederates had acted with more vigour and expedition in the beginning of the campaign. The Russian auxiliaries might have been transported by sea to Lubeck, before the end of the preceding summer, in their own galleys, which had been lying ready for use since the month of July. Had this expedient been used, the Russian troops would have joined the confederate army before the conclusion of the last campaign. But this easy and expeditious method of conveyance was rejected for a march by land, of incredible length and difficulty, which could not be begun before the month of January, nor accomplished till midsummer. The operations of the campaign had been concerted at the Hague, in January, by the respective ministers of the allies, who resolved to bring an army of one hundred and ninety thousand men into the Netherlands, in order to compel the French to abandon the barrier which they had conquered. The towns of Holland became the scenes of tumult and insurrection. The populace plundered the farmers of the revenue, abolished the taxes, and insulted the magistrates; so that the States-General, seeing their country on the brink of anarchy and confusion, authorized

*Preparations for the campaign in the Netherlands.*

the Prince of Orange to make such alterations as he should see convenient. They presented him with a diploma, by which he was constituted hereditary stadtholder and captain-general of Dutch Brabant, Flanders, and the upper quarter of Guelderland; and the East India company appointed him director and governor-general of their commerce and settlements in the Indies. Thus invested with authority unknown to his ancestors, he exerted himself with equal industry and discretion in new modelling, augmenting, and assembling the troops of the republic. The confederates knew that the Count de Saxe had a design upon Maestricht: the Austrian general Bathiani made repeated remonstrances to the British ministry, entreating them to take speedy measures for the preservation of that fortress. He in the month of January proposed that the Duke of Cumberland should cross the sea, and confer with the Prince of Orange on this subject: he undertook, at the peril of his head, to cover Maestricht with seventy thousand men, from all attacks of the enemy; but his representations seemed to have made very little impression on those to whom they were addressed. The Duke of Cumberland did not depart from England till towards the latter end of February; part of March was elapsed before the transports sailed from the Nore with the additional troops and artillery; and the last draughts from the foot-guards were not embarked till the middle of August.

The different bodies of the confederate forces joined each other, and encamped in the neighbourhood of Ruremond, to the number of one hundred and ten thousand men; and the French army invested Maestricht without opposition, on the third day of April. The garrison consisted of imperial and Dutch troops, under the conduct of the governor, Baron d'Aylva, who defended the place with extraordinary skill and resolution. He annoyed the besiegers in repeated sallies; but they were determined to surmount all opposition, and prosecuted their approaches with incredible ardour. They assaulted the covered way, and there effected a lodgment, after an obstinate dispute, in which they lost two thousand of their best troops; but next day they were entirely dislodged by the gallantry of the garrison. These hostilities were suddenly suspended, in consequence of the preliminaries signed at Aix-la-Chapelle. The plenipotentiaries agreed, that, for the glory of his

*Siege of Maestricht. Cessation of arms.*

Christian Majesty's arms, the town of Maestricht should be surrendered to his general, on condition that it should be restored with all the magazines and artillery. He accordingly took possession of it on the third day of May, when the garrison marched out with all the honours of war; and a cessation of arms immediately ensued. By this time the Russian auxiliaries to the number of thirty-seven thousand, commanded by Prince Repnin, had arrived in Moravia, where they were reviewed by their imperial majesties; then they proceeded to the confines of Franconia, where they were ordered to halt, after they had marched seven hundred miles since the beginning of the year. The French king declared, that, should they advance farther, he would demolish the fortifications of Maestricht and Bergen-op-Zoom. This dispute was referred to the plenipotentiaries, who, in the beginning of August, concluded a convention, importing, that the Russian troops should return to their own country; and that the French king should disband an equal number of his forces. The season being far advanced, the Russians were provided with winter quarters in Bohemia and Moravia, where they continued till the spring, when they marched back to Livonia. In the mean time seven-and-thirty thousand French troops were withdrawn from Flanders into Picardy, and the two armies remained quiet till the conclusion of the definitive treaty. The suspension of arms was proclaimed at London, and in all the capitals of the contracting powers: orders were sent to the respective admirals in different parts of the world to refrain from hostilities; and a communication of trade and intelligence was again opened between the nations which had been at variance. No material transaction distinguished the campaign in Italy. The French and Spanish troops who had joined the Genoese in the territories of the republic amounted to thirty thousand men, under the direction of the Duke de Richelieu, who was sent from France to assume that command on the death of the Duke de Boufflers; while Mareschal de Belleisle, at the head of fifty thousand men, covered the western Riviera, which was threatened with an invasion by forty thousand Austrians and Piedmontese, under General Leutrum. At the same time General Brown, with a more numerous army, prepared to re-enter the eastern Riviera, and recommence the siege of Genoa. But these intended operations were prevented by an armistice, which took place as soon as the belligerent powers had acceded to the preliminaries.

In the East Indies, Rear-Admiral Boscawen undertook the siege of Pondicherry, which, in the month of August, he blocked up by sea with his squadron, and invested by land with a small army of four thousand Europeans, and about two thousand natives of that country. He prosecuted the enterprise with great spirit, and took the fort of Area Coupan, at the distance of three miles from the town: then he made his approaches to the place, against which he opened batteries, while it was bombarded and cannonaded by the shipping. But the fortifications were so strong, the garrison so numerous, and the engineers of the enemy so expert in their profession, that he made very little progress, and sustained considerable damage. At length, his army being diminished by sickness, and the rainy season approaching, he ordered the artillery and stores to be reembarked; and raising the siege on the sixth day of October, returned to Fort St. David, after having lost about a thousand men in this expedition. In the sequel, several ships of his squadron, and above twelve hundred sailors, perished in a hurricane. The naval force of Great Britain was more successful in the West Indies. Rear-Admiral Knowles, with a squadron of eight ships, attacked Fort Louis on the south side of Hispaniola, which, after a warm action of three hours, was surrendered on capitulation, and dismantled. Then he made an abortive attempt upon St. Jago de Cuba, and returned to Jamaica, extremely chagrined at his disappointment, which he imputed to the misconduct of Captain Dent, who was tried in England by a court-martial and honourably acquitted. On the first day of October, the same admiral, cruising in the neighbourhood of the Havannah, with eight ships of the line, encountered a Spanish squadron of nearly the same strength, under the command of the Admirals Reggio and Spinola. The engagement began between two and three o'clock in the afternoon, and continued with intervals till eight in the evening, when the enemy retired to the Havannah, with the loss of two ships; one of which struck to the British admiral, and the other was, two days after, set on fire by her own commander, that she might not fall into the hands of the English. Mr. Knowles taxed some of his captains with misbehaviour, and they recriminated on his conduct. On their return to England, a court-martial was the consequence of their mutual accusations. Those who adhered to the commander, and the others whom he impeached, were inflamed against each other with the most rancorous resentment. The admiral himself did not escape uncensured: two of his captains were reprimanded; but Captain Holmes, who had displayed uncommon courage, was honourably acquitted. Their animosities did not end with a court-martial. A bloodless encounter happened between the admiral and Captain Powlett: but Captain Innes and Captain Clarke meeting by appointment in Hyde-Park with pistols, the former was mortally wounded, and died next morning; the latter was tried, and condemned for murder, but indulged with his majesty's pardon. No naval transaction of any consequence happened in the European seas during the course of this summer. In January, indeed, the Magnanime, a French ship of the line, was taken in the channel by two English cruisers, after an obstinate engagement; and the privateers took a considerable number of merchant-ships from the enemy.

The plenipotentiaries still continued at Aix-la-Chapelle, discussing all the articles of the definitive treaty, which was at length concluded and signed on the seventh day of October. It was founded on former treaties, which were now expressly confirmed, from that of Westphalia to the last concluded at London and Vienna. The contracting parties agreed, that the prisoners on each side should be mutually released without ransom, and all conquests restored: that the duchies of Parma, Placentia, and Guastalla, should be ceded as a settlement to the Infant Don Philip, and the heirs male of his body; but in case of his ascending the throne of Spain, or of the Two Sicilies, or his dying without male issue, that they should revert to the house of Austria: that the King of Great Britain should, immediately after the ratification of this treaty, send two persons of rank and distinction to reside in France, as hostages, until restitution should be made of Cape Breton, and all the other conquests which his Britannic majesty should have achieved in the East or West Indies, before or after the preliminaries were signed: that the assiento contract, with the article of the annual ship, should be confirmed for four years, during which the enjoyment of that privilege was suspended since the commencement of the present war: that Dunkirk should remain fortified on the land side, and towards the sea continue on the footing of former treaties. All the contracting powers became guarantees to the King of Prussia for the duchy of Silesia and the county of Glatz, as he at present possessed them; and they likewise engaged to secure the Empress Queen of Hungary and Bohemia in possession of her hereditary dominions, according to the pragmatic sanction. The other articles regulated the forms and times fixed for the mutual restitution, as well as for the termination of hostilities in different parts of the world. But the right of English subjects to navigate in the American seas, without being subject to search, was not once mentioned, though this claim was the original source of the differences between Great Britain and Spain: nor were the limits of Acadia ascertained. This and all other disputes were left to the discussion of commissaries. We have already observed, that, after the troubles of the empire began, the war was no longer maintained on British principles. It became a continental contest, and was prosecuted on the side of the allies without conduct, spirit, or unanimity. In the Netherlands they were outnumbered and outwitted by the enemy. They never hazarded a battle without sustaining a defeat. Their vast armies, paid by Great Britain, lay inactive, and beheld one fortress reduced after another, until the whole country was subdued; and as their generals fought, their plenipotentiaries negotiated. At a time when their affairs began to wear the most promising aspect, when the arrival of the Russian auxiliaries would have secured an undoubted superiority in the field, when the British fleets had trampled on the naval power of France and Spain, intercepted the supplies of treasure, and cut off all their resources of commerce, the British ministers seemed to treat without the least regard to the honour and advantage of their country. They left her most valuable and necessary rights of trade unowned and undecided; they subscribed to the insolent demand of sending the nobles of the realm to grace the court and adorn the triumphs of her enemy; and they tamely gave up her conquests in North America, of more consequence to her traffic than all the other dominions for which the powers at war contended: they gave up the important isle of Cape Breton, in exchange for a petty factory in the East Indies, belonging to a private company, whose existence had been deemed prejudicial to the commonwealth. What then were the fruits which Britain reaped from this long and desperate war? A dreadful expense of blood and treasure,[d] disgrace upon disgrace, an additional load of grievous impositions, and the national debt accumulated to the enormous sum of eighty millions sterling.

[d] Such an expensive war could not be maintained without a very extraordinary exertion of a commerical spirit: accordingly we find that Great Britain, since the death of King William, has risen under her pressures with increased vigour and perseverance. Whether it be owing to the natural progression of trade extending itself from its origin to its acme, or *ne plus ultra*, or to the encouragement given by the administration to monied men of all denominations; or to necessity, impelling those who can no longer live on small incomes to risk their capitals in traffic, that they may have a chance for bettering their fortunes; or, lastly, to a concurrence of all these causes; certain it is, the national exports and imports have been sensibly increasing for those forty years: the yearly medium of woollen exports, from the year 1738 to 1743 inclusive, amounted to about three millions and a half, which was a yearly increase on the medium, of five hundred thousand pounds above the medium from 1718 to 1724. From this article, the reader will conceive the prodigious extent and importance of the British commerce.

## CHAPTER XXI.

REFLECTIONS ON THE PEACE. — THE PRINCE OF WALES'S ADHERENTS JOIN THE OPPOSITION. — CHARACTER OF THE MINISTRY. — SESSION OPENED. — DEBATE ON THE ADDRESS. — SUPPLIES GRANTED. — EXORBITANT DEMAND OF THE EMPRESS QUEEN OPPOSED. — VIOLENT CONTEST CONCERNING THE SEAMEN'S BILL. — OBJECTIONS TO THE MUTINY BILL. — BILL FOR LIMITING THE TERM OF A SOLDIER'S SERVICE. — MEASURES TAKEN WITH RESPECT TO THE AFRICAN TRADE. — SCHEME FOR IMPROVING THE BRITISH FISHERY. — ATTEMPT TO OPEN THE COMMERCE TO HUDSON'S BAY. — PLAN FOR MANNING THE NAVY. — FRUITLESS MOTIONS MADE BY THE OPPOSITION. — SEVERITIES EXERCISED UPON SOME STUDENTS AT OXFORD. — DUKE OF NEWCASTLE CHOSEN CHANCELLOR OF THE UNIVERSITY OF CAMBRIDGE. — TUMULTS IN DIFFERENT PARTS OF THE KINGDOM. — SCHEME FOR A SETTLEMENT IN NOVA SCOTIA. — TOWN OF HALIFAX FOUNDED. — FRENCH ATTEMPT TO SETTLE THE ISLAND OF TOBAGO. — REJOICINGS FOR THE PEACE OF AIX-LA-CHAPELLE. — PRETENDER'S ELDEST SON ARRESTED AT PARIS. — APPEARANCE OF A RUPTURE BETWEEN RUSSIA AND SWEDEN. — INTERPOSITION OF THE KING OF PRUSSIA. — MEASURES TAKEN BY THE FRENCH MINISTRY. — CONDUCT OF THE DIFFERENT EUROPEAN POWERS. — INSOLENCE OF THE BARBARY CORSAIRS. — DISTURBANCES IN ENGLAND. — SESSION OPENED. — SUBJECTS OF DEBATE. — SCHEME FOR REDUCING THE INTEREST OF THE NATIONAL DEBT. — ACT PASSED FOR THAT PURPOSE. — NEW MUTINY BILL. — BILL FOR ENCOURAGING THE IMPORTATION OF IRON FROM AMERICA. — ERECTION OF THE BRITISH HERRING FISHERY. — NEW AFRICAN COMPANY. — WESTMINSTER ELECTION. — EARTHQUAKES IN LONDON. — PESTILENTIAL FEVER AT THE SESSION IN THE OLD BAILEY. — DISPUTES BETWEEN RUSSIA AND SWEDEN. — PLAN FOR ELECTING THE ARCHDUKE JOSEPH KING OF THE ROMANS. — OPPOSITION OF THE KING OF PRUSSIA. — DISPUTES WITH THE FRENCH ABOUT THE LIMITS OF NOVA SCOTIA. — TREATY WITH SPAIN. — SESSION OPENED. — DEBATE ON THE ADDRESS. — SUPPLIES GRANTED. — DEATH AND CHARACTER OF THE PRINCE OF WALES. — SETTLEMENT OF A REGENCY, IN CASE OF A MINOR SOVEREIGN. — GENERAL NATURALIZATION BILL. — CENSURE PASSED UPON A PAPER ENTITLED CONSTITUTIONAL QUERIES. — PROCEEDINGS OF THE COMMONS ON THE WESTMINSTER ELECTION. — MR. MURRAY SENT PRISONER TO NEWGATE. — SESSION CLOSED. — STYLE ALTERED.

THE peace of Aix-la-Chapelle, however unstable or inglorious it might appear to those few who understood the interests, and felt for the honour of their country, was nevertheless not unwelcome to the nation in general. The British ministry will always find it more difficult to satisfy the people at the end of a successful campaign, than at the conclusion of an unfortunate war. The English are impatient of miscarriage and disappointment, and too apt to be intoxicated with victory. At this period they were tired of the burdens, and sick of the disgraces, to which they had been exposed in the course of seven tedious campaigns. They had suffered considerable losses and interruptions in the article of commerce, which was the source of their national opulence and power; they knew it would necessarily be clogged with additional duties for the maintenance of a continental war, and the support of foreign subsidiaries; and they drew very faint presages of future success either from the conduct of their allies, or the capacity of their commanders. To a people influenced by these considerations, the restoration of a free trade, the respite from that anxiety and suspense which the prosecution of a war never fails to engender, and the prospect of a speedy deliverance from discouraging restraints and oppressive impositions, were advantages that sweetened the bitter draught of a dishonourable treaty, and induced the majority of the nation to acquiesce in the peace, not barely without murmuring, but even with some degree of satisfaction and applause.

*The Prince of Wales's adherents join the opposition.* Immediately after the exchange of ratifications at Aix-la-Chapelle the armies were broken up; the allies in the Netherlands withdrew their several proportions of troops; the French began to evacuate Flanders; and the English forces were re-embarked for their own country. His Britannic majesty returned from his German dominions in November, having landed near Margate, in Kent, after a dangerous passage; and on the twenty-ninth of the same month he opened the session of Parliament. By this time the misunderstanding between the first two personages of the royal family had been increased by a fresh accession of matter. The Prince of Wales had held a court of Stannary, in quality of Duke of Cornwall; and revived some claims attached to that dignity, which, had they been admitted, would have greatly augmented his influence among the Cornish boroughs. These efforts roused the jealousy of the administration, which had always considered them as an interest wholly dependent on the crown; and, therefore, the pretensions of his royal highness were opposed by the whole weight of the ministry. His adherents, resenting these hostilities as an injury to their royal master, immediately joined the remnant of the former opposition in Parliament, and resolved to counteract all the ministerial measures that should fall under their cognizance; at least they determined to seize every opportunity of thwarting the servants of the crown, in every scheme or proposal that had not an evident tendency to the advantage of the nation. This band of auxiliaries was headed by the Earl of E—t, Dr. Lee, and Mr. N—t. The first possessed a species of eloquence rather plausible than powerful: he spoke with fluency and fire; his spirit was bold and enterprising, his apprehension quick, and his repartee severe. Dr. Lee was a man of extensive erudition, and irreproachable morals, particularly versed in the civil law, which he professed, and perfectly well acquainted with the constitution of his country. Mr. N—t was an orator of middling abilities, who harangued upon all subjects indiscriminately, and supplied with confidence what he wanted in capacity: he had been at some pains to study the business of the House, as well as to understand the machine of government; and was tolerably well heard, as he generally spoke with an appearance of good humour, and hazarded every whimsical idea as it arose in his imagination. But Lord Bolingbroke is said to have been the chief spring, which, in secret, actuated the deliberations of the prince's court. That nobleman, seemingly sequestered from the tumults of a public life, resided at Battersea, where he was visited like a sainted shrine by all the distinguished votaries of wit, eloquence, and political ambition. There he was cultivated and admired for the elegance of his manners, and the charms of his conversation. The prince's curiosity was first captivated by his character, and his esteem was afterwards secured by the irresistible address of that extraordinary personage, who continued in a regular progression to insinuate himself still further and further into the good graces of his royal patron. How far the conduct of his royal highness was influenced by the private advice of this nobleman we shall not pretend to determine; but, certain it is, the friends of the ministry propagated a report, that he was the dictator of those measures which the prince adopted; and that, under the specious pretext of attachment to the heir apparent of the crown, he concealed his real aim, which was to perpetuate the breach in the royal family. Whatever his sentiments and motives might have been, this was no other than a revival of the old ministerial clamour, that a man cannot be well affected to the king, if he pretends to censure any measure of the administration.

The weight which the opposition derived from these new confederates in the House of Commons was still greatly overbalanced by the power, influence, and ability that sustained every ministerial project. *Character of the ministry.*

Mr. Pelham, who chiefly managed the helm of affairs, was generally esteemed as a man of honesty and candour, actuated by a sincere love for his country, though he had been educated in erroneous principles of government, and in some measure obliged to prosecute a fatal system, which descended to him by inheritance. At this time he numbered Mr. Pitt among his fellow-ministers, and was moreover supported by many other individuals of distinguished abilities: among whom the first place in point of genius was due to Mr. M., who executed the office of solicitor-general. This gentleman, the son of a noble family in North Britain, had raised himself to great eminence at the bar, by a most keen intuitive spirit of apprehension, that seemed to seize every object at first glance; an innate sagacity, that saved the trouble of intense application; and an irresistible stream of eloquence, that flowed pure and classical, strong and copious, reflecting, in the most conspicuous point of view, the subjects over which it rolled, and sweeping before it all the slime of formal hesitation, and all the entangling weeds of chicanery. Yet the servants of the crown were not so implicitly attached to the first minister as to acquiesce in all his plans, and dedicate their time and talents to the support of every court measure indiscriminately. This was one material point in which Mr. Pelham deviated from the maxims of his predecessor, who admitted of no contradiction from any of his adherents or fellow-servants, but insisted on sacrificing their whole perception and faculties to his conduct and disposal. That sordid deference to a minister no longer characterised the subordinate instruments of the administration. It was not unusual to see the great officers of the government divided in a parliamentary debate, and to hear the secretary at war opposing with great vehemence a clause suggested by the chancellor of the exchequer. After all, if we coolly consider those arguments which have been bandied about, and retorted with such eagerness and acrimony in the House of Commons, and divest them of those passionate tropes and declamatory metaphors which the spirit of opposition alone had produced, we shall find very little left for the subject of dispute, and sometimes be puzzled to discover any material source of disagreement.

In the month of November his majesty opened the session of Parliament with a speech, acquainting them, That the definitive treaty of peace was at length signed by all the parties concerned: that he had made the most effectual provision for securing the rights and interests of his own subjects; and procured for his allies the best

*Session opened.*

conditions which, in the present situation of affairs, could be obtained. He said he had found a general good disposition in all parties to bring the negotiation to a happy conclusion; and observed, that we might promise ourselves a long enjoyment of the blessings of peace. Finally, after having remarked that times of tranquillity were the proper seasons for lessening the national debt, and strengthening the kingdom against future events, he recommended to the Commons the improvement of the public revenue, the maintenance of a considerable naval force, the advancement of commerce, and the cultivation of the arts of peace. This speech, as usual, was echoed back by an address to the throne from both Houses, containing general expressions of the warmest loyalty and gratitude to his majesty, and implying the most perfect satisfaction and acquiescence in the articles of the treaty of Aix-la-Chapelle.

The members in the opposition, according to custom, cavilled at the nature of this address. They observed, that the late pacification was the worst and most inglorious of all the bad treaties to which the English nation had ever subscribed: that it was equally disgraceful, indefinite, and absurd: they said, the British navy had gained such an ascendancy over the French at sea, that the sources of their wealth were already choked up; that the siege of Maestricht would have employed their arms in the Low Countries till the arrival of the Russians; and that the accession of these auxiliaries would have thrown the superiority into the scale of the allies. They did not fail to take notice, that the most important and original object of the war was left wholly undecided; and demonstrated the absurdity of their promising, in the address, to make good such engagements as his majesty had entered into with his allies, before they knew what those engagements were. In answer to these objections, the ministers replied, That the peace was in itself rather better than could be expected; and that the smallest delay might have proved fatal to the liberties of Europe. They affirmed, that the Dutch were upon the point of concluding a neutrality, in consequence of which their troops would have been withdrawn from the allied army; and in that case, even the addition of the Russian auxiliaries would not have rendered it a match for the enemy. They asserted, that if the war had been prolonged another year, the national credit of

Great Britain must have been entirely ruined, many of the public funds having sunk below par in the preceding season, so that the ministry had begun to despair of seeing the money paid in on the new subscription. With respect to the restoration of Cape Breton, the limits of Nova Scotia, and the right of navigating without search in the American seas, which right had been left unestablished in the treaty, they declared that the first was an unnecessary expense, of no consequence to Great Britain; and that the other two were points in dispute, to be amicably settled in private conferences by commissaries duly authorized; but by no means articles to be established by a general treaty.

*Supplies granted.* What the opposition wanted in strength, it endeavoured to make up with spirit and perseverance. Every ministerial motion and measure was canvassed, sifted, and decried with uncommon art and vivacity: but all this little availed against the single article of superior numbers; and accordingly, this was the source of certain triumph in all debates in which the servants of the crown were united. The nation had reason to expect an immediate mitigation in the article of annual expense, considering the number of troops and ships of war which had been reduced at the ratification of the treaty; but they were disagreeably undeceived in finding themselves again loaded with very extraordinary impositions, for the payment of a vast debt which government had contracted in the course of the war, notwithstanding the incredible aids granted by Parliament. The committee of supply established four points of consideration, in their deliberations concerning the sums necessary to be raised; namely, for fulfilling the engagements which the Parliament had entered into with his majesty, and the services undertaken for the success of the war; for discharging debts contracted by government for making good deficiencies; and for defraying the current expense of the year. It appeared, that the nation owed four-and-forty thousand pounds to the Elector of Bavaria; above thirty thousand to the Duke of Brunswick; the like sum to the Landgrave of Hesse-Cassel; and near nine thousand pounds to the Elector of Mentz. The Queen of Hungary claimed an arrear of one hundred thousand pounds. The city of Glasgow, in North Britain, presented a petition praying to be reimbursed the sum of ten thousand pounds, extorted from that corporation by the son of the pretender, during the rebellion. One hundred and twelve thousand pounds were owing to the forces in North America and the East Indies; besides near half a million due on extraordinary expenses incurred by the land forces in America, Flanders, and North Britain, by the office of ordnance, and other services of the last year, to which the parliamentary provision did not extend. The remaining debt of the ordnance amounted to above two hundred and thirty thousand pounds: but the navy bills could not be discharged for less than four millions. An addition of two millions three hundred and seventy-four thousand three hundred thirty-three pounds fifteen shillings and two pence was also required for the current service of the year. In a word, the whole annual supply exceeded eight millions sterling—a sum at which the whole nation expressed equal astonishment and disgust. It was charged upon the duties on malt, mum, cider, and perry, the land-tax at four shillings in the pound, annuities on the sinking-fund, an application of one million from that deposit, and a loan of the like sum to be charged on the first aids of next session. The number of seamen was reduced to seventeen thousand, and that of the land forces to eighteen thousand eight hundred and fifty-seven, including guards and garrisons.

Every article of expense, however, was warmly disputed by the anti-courtiers; especially the demand of the Queen of Hungary, which was deemed unreasonably exorbitant and rapacious, considering the seas of blood which we had shed, and the immensity of treasure we had exhausted for her benefit; and surely the subjects of this nation had some reason to complain of an indulgence of this nature, granted to a power which they had literally snatched from the brink of ruin—a power whose quarrel they had espoused with a degree of enthusiasm that did much more honour to their gallantry than to their discretion—a power that kept aloof, with a stateliness of pride peculiar to herself and family; and beheld her British auxiliaries fighting her battles at their own expense; while she squandered away, in the idle pageantry of barbarous magnificence, those ample subsidies which they advanced in order to maintain her armies, and furnish out her proportion of the war. The leaders of the opposition neglected no opportunity of embittering the triumphs of their adversaries; they inveighed against the extravagance

*Exorbitant demand of the empress queen opposed.*

of granting sixteen thousand pounds for the pay of general and staff officers, during a peace that required no such establishment, especially at a juncture when the national incumbrances rendered it absolutely necessary to practise every expedient of economy. They even combated the request of the city of Glasgow, to be indemnified for the extraordinary exaction it underwent from the rebels, though it appeared from unquestionable evidence, that this extraordinary contribution was exacted on account of that city's peculiar attachment to the reigning family; that it had always invariably adhered to revolution principles; and, with an unequalled spirit of loyalty and zeal for the Protestant succession, distinguished itself both in the last and preceding rebellion.

But the most violent contest arose on certain regulations which the ministry wanted to establish in two bills, relating to the sea and land service. The first, under the title of a bill for amending, explaining, and reducing into one act of Parliament the laws relating to the navy, was calculated solely with a view of subjecting half-pay officers to martial law—a design which not only furnished the opposition with a plausible handle for accusing the ministers, as intending to encroach upon the constitution, in order to extend the influence of the crown; but also alarmed the sea-officers to such a degree, that they assembled to a considerable number, with a view to deliberate upon the proper means of defending their privileges and liberties from invasion. The result of their consultations was a petition to the House of Commons, subscribed by three admirals and forty-seven captains, not members of Parliament, representing, that the bill in agitation contained several clauses, tending to the injury and dishonour of all naval officers, as well as to the detriment of his majesty's service; and that the laws already in force had been always found effectual for securing the service of officers on half-pay upon the most pressing occasions: they, therefore, hoped that they should not be subjected to new hardships and discouragements; and begged to be heard by their counsel, before the committee of the whole House, touching such parts of the bill as they apprehended would be injurious to themselves and the other officers of his majesty's navy. This petition was presented to the House by Sir John Norris, and the motion for its being read was seconded by Sir Peter

*Violent contest concerning the seamen's bill.*

Warren, whose character was universally esteemed and beloved in the nation. This measure had like to have produced very serious consequences. Many commanders and subalterns had repaired to the Admiralty, and threatened, in plain terms, to throw up their commissions in case the bill should pass into a law; and a general ferment was begun among all the subordinate members of the navy. A motion was made, That the petitioners, according to their request, should be heard by their counsel; and this proposal was strongly urged by the first orators of the anti-ministerial association; but the minister, confiding in his own strength, reinforced by the abilities of Mr. Pitt, Mr. Lyttelton, and Mr. Fox, the secretary at war, strenuously opposed the motion, which, upon a division, was thrown out by a great majority. The several articles of the bill were afterwards separately debated with great warmth; and though Mr. Pelham had, with the most disinterested air of candour, repeatedly declared that he required no support even from his own adherents, but that which might arise from reason unrestrained, and full conviction, he on this occasion reaped all the fruit from their zeal and attachment which could be expected from the most implicit complaisance. Some plausible amendments of the most exceptionable clauses were offered, particularly of that which imposed an oath upon the members of every court-martial, that they should not, on any account, disclose the opinions or transactions of any such tribunal. This was considered as a sanction, under which any court-martial might commit the most flagrant acts of injustice and oppression, which even Parliament itself could not redress, because it would be impossible to ascertain the truth, eternally sealed up by this absurd obligation. The amendment proposed was, that the members of a court-martial might reveal the transactions and opinions of it in all cases wherein the courts of justice, as the law now stands, have a right to interfere, if required thereto by either House of Parliament: a very reasonable mitigation, which, however, was rejected by the majority. Nevertheless, the suspicion of an intended encroachment had raised such a clamour without doors, and diffused the odium of this measure so generally, that the minister thought proper to drop the projected article of war, subjecting the reformed officers of the navy to the jurisdiction of courts-martial; and the bill being also softened in other particulars, during its passage through the Upper House, at length received the royal assent.

<small>Objections to the mutiny bill.</small> The flame which this act had kindled was rather increased than abated on the appearance of a new mutiny-bill replete with divers innovations, tending to augment the influence of the crown, as well as the authority and power of a military jurisdiction. All the articles of war established since the reign of Charles the Second were submitted to the inspection of the Commons; and in these appeared a gradual spirit of encroachment, almost imperceptibly deviating from the civil institutes of the English constitution, towards the establishment of a military dominion. By this new bill a power was vested in any commander-in-chief to revise and correct any legal sentence of a court-martial, by which the members of such a court, corresponding with the nature of a civil jury, were rendered absolutely useless, and the commander in a great measure absolute; for he had not only the power of summoning such officers as he might choose to sit on any trial, a prerogative unknown to any civil court of judicature; but he was also at liberty to review and alter the sentence; so that a man was subject to two trials for the same offence, and the commander-in-chief was judge both of the guilt and the punishment. By the final clause of this bill, martial law was extended to all officers on half-pay; and the same arguments which had been urged against this article in the navy bill, were now repeated and reinforced with redoubled fervour. Many reasons were offered to prove that the half-pay was allotted as a recompense for past services; and the opponents of the bill affirmed, that such an article, by augmenting the dependents of the crown, might be very dangerous to the constitution. On the other hand, the partisans of the ministry asserted, that the half-pay was granted as a retaining fee, and that originally all those who enjoyed this indulgence were deemed to be in actual service, consequently subject to martial law. Mr. Pitt, who at this time exercised the office of paymaster-general with a rigour of integrity unknown to the most disinterested of all his predecessors in that department, espoused the clause in dispute, as a necessary extension of military discipline, which could never be attended with any bad consequence to the liberty of the nation. The remarks which he made on this occasion implied an opinion that our liberties wholly existed in depen-

dence upon the discretion of the sovereign, and the virtue of the army. "To that virtue (said he) we trust even at this hour, small as our army is—to that virtue we must have trusted, had this bill been modelled as its warmest opposers could have wished; and without this virtue, should the Lords, the Commons, and the people of England, entrench themselves behind parchment up to the teeth, the sword will find a passage to the vitals of the constitution." All the disputed articles of the bill being sustained on the shoulders of a great majority, it was conveyed to the Upper House, where it excited another violent contest. Upon the question whether officers on half-pay had not been subject to martial law, the judges were consulted, and divided in their sentiments. The Earl of Bath declared his opinion, that martial law did not extend to reformed officers; and opened all the sluices of his ancient eloquence. He admitted a case which was urged, of seven officers on half-pay, who, being taken in actual rebellion at Preston, in the year 1745, had been executed on the spot by martial law, in consequence of the king's express order. He candidly owned, that he himself was secretary at war at that period; that he had approved of this order, and even transmitted it to General Carpenter, who commanded at Preston; but now his opinion was entirely changed. He observed, that when the forementioned rebellion first broke out, the House presented an address to the king, desiring his majesty would be pleased to employ all half-pay officers, and gratify them with whole pay; and, indeed, all such officers were voted on whole pay by the House of Commons. They were afterwards apprized of this vote by an advertisement in the gazette, and ordered to hold themselves in readiness to repair to such places as should be appointed; and finally commanded to repair by such a day to those places, on pain of being struck off the half-pay list. These precautions would have been unnecessary, had they been deemed subject to martial law; and the penalty for non-obedience would not have been merely a privation of their pensions, but they would have fallen under the punishment of death, as deserters from the service. His lordship distinguished, with great propriety and precision, between a step which had been precipitately taken in a violent crisis, when the public was heated with apprehension and resentment, and a solemn law concerted at leisure, during the most profound tranquillity. Notwithstanding the spirited opposition of this nobleman, and some attempts to insert additional clauses, the bill, having undergone a few inconsiderable amendments, passed by a very considerable majority.

Immediately after the mutiny-bill had passed the Lower House, another fruitless effort was made by the opposition. The danger of a standing army, on whose virtue the constitution of Great Britain seemed to depend, did not fail to alarm the minds of many who were zealously attached to the liberties of their country, and gave birth to a scheme, which, if executed, would have enabled the legislature to establish a militia that must have answered many national purposes, and acted as a constitutional bulwark against the excesses and ambition of a military standing force, under the immediate influence of government. The scheme which patriotism conceived was, in all probability, adopted by party. A bill was brought in, limiting the time beyond which no soldier, or non-commissioned officer, should be compelled to continue in the service. Had this limitation taken place, such a rotation of soldiers would have ensued among the common people, that in a few years every peasant, labourer, and inferior tradesman in the kingdom would have understood the exercise of arms; and perhaps the people in general would have concluded that a standing army was altogether unnecessary. A project of this nature could not, for obvious reasons, be agreeable to the administration, and therefore the bill was rendered abortive; for, after having been twice read, it was postponed from time to time, till the Parliament was prorogued, and never appeared in the sequel. Such were the chief subjects of debate between the ministry and the opposition, composed, as we have already observed, of the prince's servants and the remains of the country party, this last being headed by Lord Strange, son of the Earl of Derby, and Sir Francis Dashwood: the former, a nobleman of distinguished abilities, keen, penetrating, eloquent, and sagacious; the other frank, spirited, and sensible.

*Bill for limiting the term of a soldier's service.*

It must be owned, however, for the honour of the ministry, that if they carried a few unpopular measures with a high hand, they seemed earnestly desirous of making amends to the nation, by promoting divers regulations for the benefit and improvement of commerce, which actually took place in the ensuing session of

*Measures taken with respect to the African trade.*

Parliament. One of the principal objects of this nature which fell under their cognizance was the trade to the coast of Guinea; a very important branch of traffic, whether considered as a market for British manufactures, or as the source that supplied the English plantations with negroes. This was originally monopolized by a joint-stock company, which had from time to time derived considerable sums from the legislature, for enabling them the better to support certain forts or castles on the coast of Africa, to facilitate the commerce and protect the merchants. In the sequel, however, the exclusive privilege having been judged prejudicial to the national trade, the coast was laid open to all British subjects indiscriminately, on condition of their paying a certain duty towards defraying the expense of the forts and factories. This expedient did not answer the purposes for which it had been contrived. The separate traders, instead of receiving any benefit from the protection of the company, industriously avoided their castles, as the receptacles of tyranny and oppression. The company, whether from the misconduct or knavery of their directors, contracted such a load of debts as their stock was unable to discharge. They seemed to neglect the traffic, and allowed their castles to decay. In a word, their credit being exhausted, and their creditors growing clamorous, they presented a petition to the House of Commons, disclosing their distresses, and imploring such assistance as should enable them not only to pay their debts, but also to maintain the forts in a defensible condition. This petition, recommended to the House in a message from his majesty, was corroborated by another in behalf of the company's creditors. Divers merchants of London, interested in the trade of Africa and the British plantations in America, petitioned the House, that, as the African trade was of the utmost importance to the nation, and could not be supported without forts and settlements, some effectual means should be speedily taken for protecting and extending this valuable branch of commerce. A fourth was offered by the merchants of Liverpool, representing that the security and the protection of the trade of Africa must always principally depend upon his majesty's ships of war being properly stationed on that coast, and seasonably relieved: and that such forts and settlements as might be judged necessary, for marks of sovereignty and possession, would prove a nuisance and a burden to the trade, should they remain in the hands of any joint-stock company, whose private interest always had been, and ever would be, found incompatible with the interest of the separate and open trader. They therefore prayed, that the said forts might either be taken into his majesty's immediate possession, and supported by the public, or committed to the merchants trading on that coast, in such a manner as the House should judge expedient, without vesting in them any other advantage, or right to the commerce, but what should be common to all his majesty's subjects. This remonstrance was succeeded by another to the same effect, from the master, wardens, assistants, and commonalty of the society of merchant adventurers within the city of Bristol. All these petitions were referred to a committee appointed to deliberate on this subject; who agreed to certain resolutions, implying, That the trade to Africa should be free and open; that the British forts and settlements on that coast ought to be maintained, and put under proper direction; and that, in order to carry on the African trade in the most beneficial manner to these kingdoms, all the British subjects trading to Africa should be united in one open company, without any joint-stock, or power to trade as a corporation. A bill was immediately founded on these resolutions, which alarmed the company to such a degree, that they had recourse to another petition, demonstrating their right to the coast of Africa, and expressing their reliance on the justice of the House, that they should not be deprived of their property without an adequate consideration. In a few days a second address was offered by their creditors, complaining of the company's mismanagement, promising to surrender their right, as the wisdom of Parliament should prescribe; praying that their debts might be inquired into; and that the equivalent to be granted for the company's possessions might be secured and applied, in the first place, for their benefit. The Commons, in consequence of this petition, ordered the company to produce a list of their debts, together with a copy of their charter, and two remonstrances, which their creditors had presented to them before this application to Parliament. A committee of the whole House, having deliberated on these papers and petitions, and heard the company by their counsel, resolved to give them a reasonable compensation for their charter, lands, forts, settlements, slaves, and effects, to be, in the first place, applied towards the payment of their creditors. A bill, being formed accordingly, passed the Commons, and was conveyed to the Upper House, where a great many objections were started; and for the present it was dropped, until a more unexceptionable plan should be concerted. In the mean time, their lordships addressed his majesty, That the lords commissioners for trade and plantations might be directed to prepare a scheme on this subject, to be laid before both Houses of Parliament at the beginning of the next session: that instant orders should be given for the preserving and securing the forts and settlements on the coast of Guinea belonging to Great Britain: and, that proper persons should be appointed to examine into the condition of those forts, as well as of the military stores, slaves, and vessels belonging to the African company, so as to make a faithful report of these particulars, with all possible expedition.

The ministry having professed an inclination, and indeed shown a disposition, to promote and extend the commerce of the kingdom, the Commons resolved to take some steps for encouraging the white fishery along the northern coast of the island, which is an inexhaustible source of wealth to our industrious neighbours the Dutch, who employ annually a great number of hands and vessels in this branch of commerce. The sensible part of the British people, reflecting on this subject, plainly foresaw that a fishery under due regulations, undertaken with the protection and encouragement of the legislature, would not only prove a fund of national riches, and a nursery of seamen; but likewise, in a great measure, prevent any future insurrections in the highlands of Scotland, by diffusing a spirit of industry among the natives of that country, who, finding it in their power to become independent on the fruits of their own labour, would soon enfranchise themselves from that slavish attachment, by which they had been so long connected with their landlords the chieftains. Accordingly, a committee was appointed to deliberate on the state of the British fishery; and upon their report a bill was founded for encouraging the whale fishery on the coast of Spitzbergen, by a bounty of forty shillings per ton for every ship equipped for that undertaking. The bill having made its way through both Houses, and obtained the royal assent, the merchants in different parts of the kingdom, particularly in North Britain, began to build and fit out ships of great burden, and peculiar

*Scheme for improving the British fishery.*

structure, for the purposes of that fishery, which ever since hath been carried on with equal vigour and success. Divers merchants and traders of London having presented to the House of Commons a petition, representing the benefits that would accrue to the community from a herring and cod fishery, established on proper principles, and carried on with skill and integrity, this remonstrance was referred to a committee, upon whose resolutions a bill was formed; but, before this could be discussed in the House, the Parliament was prorogued, and of consequence this measure proved abortive.

The next regulation proposed in favour of trade was that of laying open the commerce of Hudson's Bay, in the most northern parts of America, where a small monopoly maintained a few forts and settlements, and prosecuted a very advantageous fur-trade with the Indians of that continent. It was suggested, that the company had long ago enriched themselves by their exclusive privilege; that they employed no more than four annual ships; that, contrary to an express injunction in their charter, they discouraged all attempts to discover a north-west passage to the East Indies; that they dealt cruelly and perfidiously with the poor Indians, who never traded with them, except when compelled by necessity, so that the best part of the fur-trade had devolved to the enemies of Great Britain; and that their exclusive patent restricted to very narrow limits a branch of commerce, which might be cultivated to a prodigious extent, as well as to the infinite advantage of Great Britain. Petitions, that the trade of Hudson's Bay might be laid open, were presented to the House by the merchants of London, Great Yarmouth, and Wolverhampton; and a committee was appointed to deliberate upon this subject. On the other hand, the company exerted themselves in petitions and private applications for their own preservation. The committee examined many papers and records; and the report was taken into consideration by the whole House. Many evidences were interrogated, and elaborate speeches made, on both sides of the question. At length a majority seemed satisfied that the traffic on the coast of Hudson's Bay could not be preserved without forts and settlements, which must be maintained either by an exclusive company, or at the public expense; and as this was not judged a proper juncture to encumber the nation with any

*Attempt to open the commerce to Hudson's Bay.*

charge of that kind, the design of dissolving the company was laid aside till a more favourable opportunity.

The government had, during the war, found great difficulty in pressing men for the service of the navy— a practice, which, however sanctioned by necessity, is nevertheless a flagrant encroachment on the liberty of the subject, and a violent outrage against the constitution of Great Britain. The ministry, therefore, had employed some of their agents to form a scheme for retaining in time of peace, by means of a certain allowance, a number of seamen who should be registered for the purpose, and be ready to man a squadron upon any emergency. Such a plan, properly regulated, would have been a great advantage to commerce, which is always distressed by the practice of pressing seamen; and at the same time, a great security to the kingdom in dangerous conjunctures, when it may be necessary to equip an armament at a minute's warning. The House of Commons being moved upon this subject, agreed to divers resolutions, as a foundation for the bill; but the members in the opposition affecting to represent this measure in an odious light, as an imitation of the French method of registering seamen without their own consent, Mr. Pelham dropped it, as an unpopular project. *Plan for manning the navy.*

Information having been received that the French intended to settle the neutral islands of St. Lucia, Dominica, St. Vincent, and Tobago, in the West Indies, the nation had taken the alarm in the beginning of the year; and a motion was made in the House of Commons to address his majesty, that he would be graciously pleased to give directions for laying before the House copies of the instructions given to the governors of Barbadoes for ten years last past, so far as they related to these neutral islands; but whether the minister was conscious of a neglect in this particular, or thought such inquiries trenched upon the prerogative, he opposed the motion with all his might; and after some debate, the previous question passed in the negative. This was also the fate of another motion made by the Earl of E—t for an address, entreating his majesty would submit to the inspection of the House all the proposals of peace that had been made by the French king since the year which preceded the last rebellion, to that in which the definitive treaty was concluded at Aix-la-Chapelle. This they proposed as a previous step to the Parliament's forming any *Fruitless motions made by the opposition.*

VOL. II.—S. 2 B

opinion concerning the utility or necessity of the peace which had been established. Violent debates ensued, in which the opposition was as much excelled in oratory as out-numbered in votes. Such were the material transactions of this session, which in the month of June was closed as usual with a speech from the throne; in which his majesty signified his hope, that the Parliament, at their next meeting, would be able to perfect what they had now begun for advancing the trade and navigation of the kingdom. He likewise expressed his satisfaction at seeing public credit flourish at the end of an expensive war; and recommended unanimity as the surest bulwark of national security.

While the ministry, on some occasions, exhibited all the external signs of moderation and good-humour, they on others manifested a spirit of jealousy and resentment, which seems to have been childish and illiberal. Two or three young riotous students at Oxford, trained up in prejudice, and heated with intemperance, uttered some expressions over their cups, implying their attachment to the family of the pretender. The report of this indiscretion was industriously circulated by certain worthless individuals, who, having no reliance on their own intrinsic merit, hoped to distinguish themselves as the tools of party, and to obtain favour with the ministry by acting as volunteers in the infamous practice of information. Though neither the rank, age, nor connexions of the delinquents were such as ought to have attracted the notice of the public, the vice-chancellor, heads of houses, and proctors of the university, knowing the invidious scrutiny to which their conduct was subjected, thought proper to publish a declaration, signifying their abhorrence of all seditious practices, their determined resolution to punish all offenders to the utmost severity and rigour of the statutes; and containing peremptory orders for the regulation of the university. Notwithstanding these wise and salutary precautions, the three boys, who, in the heat of their intoxication, had drunk the pretender's health, were taken into custody by a messenger of state; and two of them being tried in the court of King's Bench, and found guilty, were sentenced to walk through the courts of Westminster with a specification of their crime fixed to their foreheads; to pay a fine of five nobles each; to be imprisoned for two years, and find security for their good behaviour for the term of seven years after their enlargement. Many people thought they saw the proceedings of the Star-Chamber revived in the severity of this punishment. The administration, not yet satisfied with the vengeance which had been taken on these three striplings, seemed determined to stigmatize the university to which they belonged. The cry of Jacobitism was loudly trumpeted against the whole community. The address of the university congratulating his majesty on the establishment of the peace was rejected with disdain, and an attempt was made to subject their statutes to the inspection of the king's council; but this rule, being argued in the court of King's Bench, was dismissed, in consequence of the opinions given by the judges. Finally, the same tribunal granted an information against Dr. Purnel, the vice-chancellor, for his behaviour in the case of the rioters above-mentioned; but this was countermanded in the sequel, his conduct appearing unexceptionable upon a more cool and impartial inquiry.

In proportion as Oxford declined, her sister university rose in the favour of the administration, which she at this period cultivated by an extraordinary mark of compliance and attachment. The dignity of chancellor of the university being vacated by the death of the Duke of Somerset, the nation in general seemed to think it would naturally devolve upon the Prince of Wales, as a compliment at all times due to that rank; but more especially to the then heir apparent, who had eminently distinguished himself by the virtues of a patriot and a prince. He had even pleased himself with the hope of receiving this mark of attachment from a seminary for which he entertained a particular regard. But the ruling members, seeing no immediate prospect of advantage in glorifying even a prince who was at variance with the ministry, wisely turned their eyes upon the illustrious character of the Duke of Newcastle, whom they elected without opposition, and installed with great magnificence; learning, poetry, and eloquence, joining their efforts in celebrating the shining virtues and extraordinary talents of their new patron. *Duke of Newcastle chosen chancellor of the university of Cambridge.*

Although opposition lay gasping at the feet of power in the House of Commons, the people of England did not yet implicitly approve all the measures of the administration; and the dregs of faction, still agitated by an internal ferment, threw up some ineffectual *Tumults in different parts of the kingdom.*

bubbles in different parts of the kingdom. Some of those who made no secret of their disaffection to the reigning family, determined to manifest their resentment and contempt of certain noblemen and others, who were said to have abandoned their ancient principles, and to have sacrificed their consciences to their interest. Many individuals, animated by the fumes of inebriation, now loudly extolled that cause which they durst not avow when it required their open approbation and assistance; and though they industriously avoided exposing their lives and fortunes to the chance of war in promoting their favourite interest when there was a possibility of success, they betrayed no apprehension in celebrating the memory of its last effort, amidst the tumult of a riot, and the clamours of intemperance. In the neighbourhood of Lichfield the sportsmen of the party appeared in the highland taste of variegated drapery; and their zeal descending to a very extraordinary exhibition of practical ridicule, they hunted with hounds clothed in plaid, a fox dressed in a red uniform. Even the females at their assembly, and the gentlemen at the races, affected to wear the chequered stuff by which the prince-pretender and his followers had been distinguished. Divers noblemen on the course were insulted as apostates; and one personage, of high rank, is said to have undergone a very disagreeable flagellation.

*Scheme for a settlement in Nova Scotia.* As the public generally suffers at the end of a war by the sudden dismission of a great number of soldiers and seamen, who, having contracted a habit of idleness, and finding themselves without employment and the means of subsistence, engage in desperate courses, and prey upon the community, it was judged expedient to provide an opening, through which these unquiet spirits might exhale without damage to the commonwealth. The most natural was that of encouraging them to become members of a new colony in North America, which, by being properly regulated, supported, and improved, might be the source of great advantages to its mother country. Many disputes had arisen between the subjects of England and France, concerning the limits of Nova Scotia, which no treaty had as yet properly ascertained. A fort had been raised, and a small garrison maintained, by the King of Great Britain, at a part of this very country, called Annapolis Royal, to overawe the French neutrals settled in the neighbourhood : but this did not answer the purpose for which it was intended. Upon every rupture or dispute between the two crowns, these planters, forgetting their neutrality, intrigued with the Indians, communicated intelligence to their own countrymen, settled at St. John's and Cape Breton, and did all the ill offices their hatred could suggest against the colonies and subjects of Great Britain. A scheme was now formed for making a new establishment on the same peninsula, which should further confirm and extend the property and dominion of the crown of Great Britain in that large tract of country, clear the uncultivated grounds, constitute communities, diffuse the benefits of population and agriculture, and improve the fishery of that coast, which might be rendered a new source of wealth and commerce to Old England. The particulars of the plan being duly considered, it was laid before his majesty, who approved of the design, and referred the execution of it to the board of trade and plantations, over which the Earl of Halifax presided. This nobleman, endued by nature with an excellent capacity, which had been diligently and judiciously cultivated, animated with liberal sentiments, and fired with an eager spirit of patriotism, adopted the plan with the most generous ardour, and cherished the infant colony with paternal affection. The commissioners for trade and plantations immediately advertised, under the sanction of his majesty's authority, that proper encouragement would be given to such of the officers and private men, lately dismissed from the land and sea service, as were willing to settle with or without families, in the province of Nova Scotia; that the fee-simple, or perpetual property, of fifty acres of land should be granted to every private soldier or seaman, free from the payment of any quit-rents or taxes, for the term of ten years ; at the expiration of which no person should pay more than one shilling per annum for every fifty acres so granted: that, over and above these fifty, each person should receive a grant of ten acres for every individual, including women and children, of which his family should consist: that further grants should be made to them as the number should increase, and in proportion as they should manifest their abilities in agriculture; that every officer under the rank of ensign in the land-service, or lieutenant in the navy, should be gratified with fourscore acres on the same conditions: that two hundred acres should be bestowed upon ensigns, three hundred upon lieutenants, four hundred upon captains, and six hundred on every officer above that degree, with proportionable considerations for the number and increase of every family: that the lands should be parcelled out as soon as possible after the arrival of the colonists, and a civil government established; by virtue of which they should enjoy all the liberties and privileges of British subjects, with proper security and protection: that the settlers, with their families, should be conveyed to Nova Scotia, and maintained for twelve months after their arrival at the expense of the government; which should also supply them with arms and ammunition, as far as should be judged necessary for their defence, with proper materials and utensils for clearing and cultivating their land, erecting habitations, exercising the fishery, and such other purposes as should be judged necessary for their support.

Town of Halifax founded. The scheme was so feasible, and the encouragement so inviting, that in a little time about four thousand adventurers, with their families, were entered, according to the directions of the board of trade, who in the beginning of May set sail from England, under the command of Colonel Cornwallis, whom the king had appointed their governor, and towards the latter end of June arrived at the place of their destination, which was the harbour of Chebuctou, on the sea-coast of the peninsula, about midway between Cape Canceau and Cape Sable. It is one of the most secure and commodious havens in the whole world, and well situated for the fishery; yet the climate is cold, the soil barren, and the whole country covered with woods of birch, fir, pine, and some oak, unfit for the purposes of timber; but at the same time extremely difficult to remove and extirpate. Governor Cornwallis no sooner arrived in this harbour than he was joined by two regiments of infantry from Cape Breton, and a company of rangers from Annapolis. Then he pitched upon a spot for the settlement, and employed his people in clearing the ground for laying the foundation of a town; but some inconveniences being discovered in this situation, he chose another to the northward, hard by the harbour, on an easy ascent, commanding a prospect of the whole peninsula, and well supplied with rivulets of fresh and wholesome water. Here he began to build a town on a regular plan, to which he gave the name of Halifax, in honour of the nobleman who had the greatest share in founding the colony; and before the approach of winter above three hundred comfortable wooden houses were built, the whole surrounded by a strong palisade. This colony, however, has by no means answered the sanguine expectations of the projectors; for notwithstanding the ardour with which the interests of it were promoted by its noble patron, and the repeated indulgence it has reaped from the bounty of the legislature, the inhabitants have made little or no progress in agriculture: the fishery is altogether neglected, and the settlement entirely subsists on the sums expended by the individuals of the army and navy, whose duty obliges them to reside in this part of North America.

The establishment of such a powerful colony in Nova Scotia could not fail giving umbrage to the French in that neighbourhood, who, though they did not think proper to promulgate their jealousy and disgust, nevertheless employed their emissaries clandestinely in stimulating and exciting the Indians to harass the colonists with hostilities, in such a manner as should effectually hinder them from extending their plantations, and perhaps induce them to abandon the settlement. Nor was this the only part of America in which the French court countenanced such perfidious practices. More than ever convinced of the importance of a considerable navy, and an extensive plantation trade, they not only exerted uncommon industry in re-establishing their marine, which had suffered so severely during the war; but they resolved, if possible, to extend their plantations in the West Indies, by settling the neutral islands, which we have already mentioned. In the beginning of the year the governor of Barbadoes, having received intelligence that the French had begun to settle the island of Tobago, sent Captain Tyrrel thither in a frigate, to learn the particulars. That officer found above three hundred men already landed, secured by two batteries and two ships of war, and in daily expectation of a further reinforcement from the Marquis de Caylus, governor of Martinique; who had published an ordonnance, authorizing the subjects of the French king to settle the island of Tobago, and promising to defend them from the attempts of all their enemies. This assurance was in answer to a proclamation issued by Mr. Grenville, governor of Barbadoes, and stuck up in different parts of the island, commanding all the inhabitants to remove, in thirty days, on pain of undergoing military execution. Captain Tyrrel, with a spirit that became a commander in the British navy, gave the French officers to understand, that his most Christian majesty had no right to settle the island, which was declared neutral by treaties; and that if they would not desist, he should be obliged to employ force in driving them from their new settlement. Night coming on, and Mr. Tyrrel's ship falling to leeward, the French captain seized that opportunity of sailing to Martinique; and next day the English commander returned to Barbadoes, having no power to commit hostilities. These tidings, with a copy of the French governor's ordonnance, were no sooner transmitted to the ministry, than they despatched a courier to the English envoy at Paris, with directions to make representations to the court of Versailles on this subject. The ministry of France, knowing they were in no condition to support the consequences of an immediate rupture, and understanding how much the merchants and people of Great Britain were alarmed and incensed at their attempts to possess these islands, thought proper to disown the proceedings of the Marquis de Caylus, and to grant the satisfaction that was demanded, by sending him orders to discontinue the settlement, and evacuate the island of Tobago. At the same time, however, that the court of Versailles made this sacrifice for the satisfaction of England, the Marquis de Puysieux, the French minister, observed to the English resident, that France was undoubtedly in possession of that island towards the middle of the last century. He ought in candour to have added, that although Louis XIV. made a conquest of this island from the Hollanders, during his war with that republic, it was restored to them by the treaty of Nimeguen, and since that time France could not have the least shadow of a claim to number it among her settlements. It was before this answer could be obtained from the court of Versailles, that the motion, of which we have already taken notice, was made in the House of Commons, relating to the subject of the neutral islands; a motion discouraged by the court, and defeated by the majority.

The peace of Aix-la-Chapelle was celebrated by fireworks,

illuminations, and rejoicings, in which the English, French, and Dutch, seemed to display a spirit of emulation in point of taste and magnificence; and, in all probability, these three powers were sincerely pleased at the cessation of the war. England enjoyed a respite from intolerable supplies, exorbitant insurance, and interrupted commerce; Holland was delivered from the brink of a French invasion; and France had obtained a breathing time for re-establishing her naval power, for exerting that spirit of intrigue, by dint of which she had often embroiled her neighbours, and for executing plans of insensible encroachment, which might prove more advantageous than the progress of open hostilities. In the affair of Tobago the French king had manifested his inclination to avoid immediate disputes with England; and had exhibited another proof of the same disposition in his behaviour to the prince-pretender, who had excited such a dangerous rebellion in the island of Great Britain.

*Rejoicings for the peace of Aix-la-Chapelle.*

Among those princes and powers who excepted against different articles of the treaty of Aix-la-Chapelle, the Chevalier de St. George, foreseeing that none of the plenipotentiaries would receive his protest, employed his agents to fix it up in the public places of Aix-la-Chapelle; a precaution of very little service to his cause, which all the states of Christendom seemed now to have abandoned. So little was the interest of his family considered in this negotiation, that the contracting powers agreed, without reserve, to a literal insertion of the fifth article of the quadruple alliance; by which it was stipulated, that neither the pretender nor any of his descendants should be allowed to reside within the territories belonging to any of the subscribing parties. At the same time the plenipotentiaries of France promised to those of Great Britain, that Prince Charles-Edward should be immediately obliged to quit the dominions of his most Christian majesty. Notice of this agreement was accordingly given by the court of Versailles to the young adventurer; and as he had declared he would never return to Italy, Mons. de Courteille, the French envoy to the Cantons of Switzerland, was directed by his sovereign to demand an asylum for Prince Edward in the city of Fribourg. The regency having complied in this particular with the earnest request of his most Christian majesty, Mr. Burnaby, the British minister to the Helvetic body, took the alarm, and presented the magis-

*Pretender's eldest son arrested at Paris.*

tracy of Fribourg with a remonstrance, couched in such terms as gave offence to that regency, and drew upon him a severe answer. In vain had the French king exerted his influence in procuring this retreat for the young pretender, who, being pressed with repeated messages to withdraw, persisted in refusing to quit the place, to which he had been so cordially invited by his cousin the King of France, and where he said that monarch had solemnly promised, on the word of a king, that he would never forsake him in his distress, nor abandon the interests of his family. Louis was not a little perplexed at this obstinacy of Prince Edward, which was the more vexatious, as that youth appeared to be the darling of the Parisians; who not only admired him for his own accomplishments, and pitied him for his sufferings, but also revered him, as a young hero lineally descended from their renowned Henry the Fourth. At length, the two English noblemen arriving at Paris, as hostages for the performance of the treaty, and seeing him appear at all public places of diversion, complained of this circumstance, as an insult to their sovereign, and an infringement of the treaty so lately concluded. The French king, after some hesitation between punctilio and convenience, resolved to employ violence upon the person of this troublesome stranger, since milder remonstrances had not been able to influence his conduct; but this resolution was not taken till the return of a courier whom he despatched to the Chevalier de St. George; who, being thus informed of his son's deportment, wrote a letter to him, laying strong injunctions upon him to yield to the necessity of the times, and acquiesce with a good grace in the stipulations which his cousin of France had found it necessary to subscribe for the interest of his realm. Edward, far from complying with this advice and injunction, signified his resolution to remain in Paris; and even declared, that he would pistol any man who should presume to lay violent hands on his person. In consequence of this bold declaration, an extraordinary council was held at Versailles, when it was determined to arrest him without further delay, and the whole plan of this enterprise was finally adjusted. That same evening, the prince entering the narrow lane that leads to the opera, the barrier was immediately shut, and the serjeant of the guard called "To arms;" on which Monsieur de Vaudreuil, exempt of the French guards, advancing to Edward, "Prince, (said he,) I arrest you in the king's name, by virtue of this order." At that instant the youth was surrounded by four grenadiers, in order to prevent any mischief he might have done with a case of pocket-pistols which he always carried about him; and a guard was placed at all the avenues and doors of the opera-house, lest any tumult should have ensued among the populace. These precautions being taken, Vaudreuil, with an escort, conducted the prisoner through the garden of the Palais Royal to a house where the Duke de Biron waited with a coach and six to convey him to the castle of Vincennes, whither he was immediately accompanied by a detachment from the regiment of French guards, under the command of that nobleman. He had not remained above three days in his confinement when he gave the French ministry to understand, that he would conform himself to the king's intentions; and was immediately enlarged upon giving his word and honour that he would, without delay, retire from the dominions of France. Accordingly, he set out in four days from Fontainebleau, attended by three officers, who conducted him as far as Pont-Beauvoisin on the frontiers, where they took their leave of him, and returned to Versailles. He proceeded for some time in the road to Chamberri; but soon returned into the French dominions, and passing through Dauphiné, repaired to Avignon, where he was received with extraordinary honours by the pope's legate. In the mean time, his arrest excited great murmurings at Paris; the inhabitants blaming, without scruple, their king's conduct in this instance, as a scandalous breach of hospitality, as well as a mean proof of condescension to the King of England; and many severe pasquinades relating to this transaction were fixed up in the most public places of that metropolis.

Although peace was now re-established among the principal powers of the continent, yet another storm seemed ready to burst upon the northern parts of Europe, in a fresh rupture between Russia and Sweden. Whether the czarina had actually obtained information that the French faction meditated some revolution of government at Stockholm, or she wanted a pretence for annexing Finland to her empire; certain it is, she affected to apprehend that the prince-successor of Sweden waited only for the decease of the reigning king, who was very old and infirm, to change the form of government, and resume that absolute authority which some of the monarchs, his predecessors, had enjoyed. She seemed to think that a prince thus vested with arbitrary power, and guided by the counsels of France and Prussia, with which Sweden had lately engaged in close alliance, might become a very troublesome and dangerous neighbour to her in the Baltic; she, therefore, recruited her armies, repaired her fortifications, filled her magazines, ordered a strong body of troops to advance towards the frontiers of Finland, and declared in plain terms to the court of Stockholm, that if any step should be taken to alter the government, which she had bound herself by treaty to maintain, her troops should enter the territory of Sweden, and she would act up to the spirit of her engagements. The Swedish ministry, alarmed at these peremptory proceedings, had recourse to their allies; and, in the mean time, made repeated declarations to the court of Petersburgh, that there was no design to make the least innovation in the nature of their established government: but little or no regard being paid to these representations, they began to put the kingdom in a posture of defence; and the old king gave the czarina to understand that if, notwithstanding the satisfaction he had offered, her forces should pass the frontiers of Finland, he would consider their march as an hostile invasion, and employ the means which God had put in his power for the defence of his dominions.

*Interposition of the King of Prussia.* This declaration in all probability did not produce such effect as the interposition of his Prussian majesty, the most enterprising prince of his time, at the head of one hundred and forty thousand of the best troops that Germany ever trained. Perhaps he was not sorry that the empress of Muscovy furnished him with a plausible pretence for maintaining such a formidable army, after the peace of Europe had been ascertained by a formal treaty, and all the surrounding states had diminished the number of their forces. He now wrote a letter to his uncle the King of Great Britain, complaining of the insults and menaces which had been offered by the czarina to Sweden; declaring, that he was bound by a defensive alliance, to which France had acceded, to defend the government at present established in Sweden; and that he would not sit still, and tamely see that kingdom attacked by any power whatsoever without acting up to his engagements; he therefore entreated his Britannic majesty to interpose his good offices, in conjunction with France and him, to compromise the disputes which threatened to embroil the northern parts of Europe. By this time the Russian army had approached the frontiers of Finland; the Swedes had assembled their troops, replenished their magazines, and repaired their marine; and the King of Denmark, jealous of the czarina's designs with regard to the duchy of Sleswick, which was contested with him by the prince-successor of Russia, kept his army and navy on the most respectable footing. At this critical juncture, the courts of London, Versailles, and Berlin co-operated so effectually by remonstrances and declarations at Petersburgh and Stockholm, that the Empress of Russia thought proper to own herself satisfied, and all those clouds of trouble were immediately dispersed. Yet, in all probability, her real aim was disappointed; and, however she might dissemble her sentiments, she never heartily forgave the King of Prussia for the share he had in this transaction. That monarch, without relaxing in his attention to the support of a very formidable military power, exerted very extraordinary endeavours in cultivating the civil interests of his country. He reformed the laws of Brandenburgh, and rescued the administration of justice from the frauds of chicanery. He encouraged the arts of agriculture and manufacture; and even laid the foundation of naval commerce, by establishing an East India company in the port of Embden.

Nor did the French ministry neglect any measure that might contribute to repair the damage which the kingdom had sustained in the course of the war. One half of the army was disbanded; the severe imposition of the tenth penny was suspended by the king's edict; a scheme of economy was proposed with respect to the finances; and the utmost diligence used in procuring materials, as well as workmen, for ship-building, that the navy of France might speedily retrieve its former importance. In the midst of these truly patriotic schemes, the court of Versailles betrayed a littleness of genius, and a spirit of tyranny, joined to fanaticism, in quarrelling with their Parliament about superstitious forms of religion. The sacraments had been denied to a certain person on his deathbed, because he refused to subscribe to the bull Unigenitus. The nephew of the defunct preferred a complaint to the Parliament, whose province it was to take cognizance of the affair: a deputation of that body attended the king with the report of the resolutions; and his majesty commanded them to

*Measures taken by the French ministry.*

suspend all proceedings relating to a matter of such consequence, concerning which he would take an opportunity of signifying his royal pleasure. This interposition was the source of disputes between the crown and Parliament, which had like to have filled the whole kingdom with intestine troubles.

<small>Conduct of the different European powers.</small> At Vienna the empress-queen was not more solicitous in promoting the trade and internal manufactures of her dominions, by sumptuary regulations, necessary restrictions on foreign superfluities, by opening her ports in the Adriatic, and giving proper encouragement to commerce, than she was careful and and provident in reforming the economy of her finances, maintaining a respectable body of forces, and guarding, by defensive alliances, against the enterprises of his Prussian majesty, on whose military power she looked with jealousy and distrust. In Holland, all the authority and influence of the stadtholder were scarcely sufficient to allay the ferments excited among the people, by the provisional taxation which had succeeded the abolition of the pachters, and was indeed very grievous to the subject. As this was no more than a temporary expedient, the Prince of Orange proposed a more equitable plan, which was approved by the States, and established with great difficulty. In Italy the system of politics seemed to change its complexion. The King of Sardinia effected a match between one of the Infantas of Spain and the Prince of Piedmont; and whether irritated by the conduct of the Austrians in the last war, or apprehensive of such a powerful neighbour in the Milanese, he engaged with the Kings of France and Spain in a defensive alliance, comprehending the King of the Two Sicilies, the Republic of Genoa, and the Dukes of Modena and Parma. His most Catholic majesty, sincerely disposed to cultivate the arts of peace, and encourage every measure that could contribute to the advantage of his country, was no sooner released from the embarrassments of war, than he began to execute plans of internal economy; to reduce unnecessary pensions, discharge the debts contracted in the war, replenish his arsenals, augment his navy, promote manufactures, and encourage an active commerce by sea, the benefits of which the kingdom of Spain had not known since the first discovery and conquest of the West Indies.

The preparations for refitting and increasing the navy

of Spain were carried on with such extraordinary vigour, that other nations believed an expedition was intended against the corsairs of Algiers, who had for some time grievously infested the trade and coasts of the Mediterranean. *Insolence of the Barbary corsairs.* The existence of this and other predatory republics, which entirely subsist upon piracy and rapine, petty states of barbarous ruffians, maintained as it were in the midst of powerful nations, which they insult with impunity, and of which they even exact an annual contribution, is a flagrant reproach upon Christendom; a reproach the greater, as it is founded upon a low, selfish, illiberal maxim of policy. All the powers that border on the Mediterranean, except France and Tuscany, are at perpetual war with the Moors of Barbary, and for that reason obliged to employ foreign ships for the transportation of their merchandise. This employment naturally devolves to those nations whose vessels are in no danger from the depredations of the barbarians; namely, the subjects of the maritime powers, who, for this puny advantage, not only tolerate the piratical states of Barbary, but even supply them with arms and ammunition, solicit their passes, and purchase their forbearance with annual presents, which are, in effect, equivalent to a tribute : whereas, by one vigorous exertion of their power, they might destroy all their ships, lay their towns in ashes, and totally extirpate those pernicious broods of desperate banditti. Even all the condescension of those who disgrace themselves with the title of allies to these miscreants is not always sufficient to restrain them from acts of cruelty and rapine. At this very period four cruisers from Algiers made a capture of an English packet-boat, in her voyage from Lisbon, and conveyed her to their city, where she was plundered of money and effects to the amount of one hundred thousand pounds, and afterwards dismissed. In consequence of this outrage, Commodore Keppel was sent with seven ships of war to demand satisfaction, as well as to compromise certain differences which had arisen on account of arrears claimed of the English by the Dey of Algiers. The Mussulman frankly owned that the money having been divided among the captors could not possibly be refunded. The commodore returned to Gibraltar ; and in the sequel, an Algerine ambassador arrived in London with some presents of wild beasts for his Britannic majesty. This transaction was succeeded by another injurious affront offered by the governor or alcayde of Tetuan to Mr. Latton, an English ambassador, sent thither to redeem the British subjects, who had been many years enslaved in the dominions of the King of Morocco. A revolution having lately happened in this empire, Muley Abdallah, the reigning ruffian, insisted upon the ambassador's paying a pretended balance for the ransom of the captives, as well as depositing a considerable sum, which had already been paid to a deceased bashaw; alleging, that as he (the emperor) received no part of it, the payment was illegal. Mr. Latton refusing to comply with this arbitrary demand, his house was surrounded by a detachment of soldiers, who violently dragged his secretary from his presence, and threw him into a dismal subterranean dungeon, where he continued twenty days. The English slaves, to the number of twenty-seven, were condemned to the same fate; the ambassador himself was degraded from his character, deprived of his allowance, and sequestered from all communication. All the letters directed to him were intercepted, and interpreted to the alcayde: two negro porters were entrusted with the keys of all his apartments, and a couple of soldiers posted at his chamber-door; nay, this Moorish governor threatened to load him with irons, and violently seized part of the presents designed by his Britannic majesty for the emperor. At length, finding that neither Mr. Latton nor the Governor of Gibraltar, to whom he had written, would deposit the money, without fresh instructions from the court of London, the barbarian thought proper to relax in his severity: the prisoners were enlarged, the restrictions removed from the person of the ambassador, and after all these indignities offered to the honour of the British nation, the balance was paid, and the affair quietly adjusted.

Britain, in the meanwhile, was altogether barren of events which might deserve a place in a general history. Commerce and manufacture flourished again to such a degree of increase as had never been known in the island; but this advantage was attended with an irresistible tide of luxury and excess, which flowed through all degrees of the people, breaking down all the mounds of civil policy, and opening a way for licence and immorality. The highways were infested with rapine and assassination; the cities teemed with the brutal votaries of lewdness, intem-

*Disturbances in England.*

perance, and profligacy. The whole land was overspread with a succession of tumult, riot, and insurrection, excited in different parts of the kingdom by the erection of new turnpikes, which the legislature judged necessary for the convenience of inland carriage. In order to quell these disturbances, recourse was had to the military power; several individuals were slain, and some were executed as examples.

In the month of November the session of Parliament was opened with a speech from the throne, in which his majesty expressed a particular pleasure in meeting them at a time when the perfect re-establishment of a general peace had restored to his people the blessings of quiet and tranquillity. He said, the good effects of these already appeared in the flourishing condition of national commerce, and in the rise of public credit, which were the foundations of strength and prosperity to these kingdoms. He declared that, during the summer, he had used every opportunity of cementing and securing the peace; that it was his firm resolution to do every thing in his power for the preservation of it, and religiously adhere to the engagements into which he had entered. Finally, he took notice of the good disposition he had found in the other contracting parties to the treaty of Aix-la-Chapelle to cherish the public tranquillity of Europe; and he earnestly recommended to the two Houses the maintenance of a strong naval power, as the bulwark of national security. *Session opened.*

When the motion was made for an address of thanks in the House of Commons, the first paragraph of his majesty's speech furnished the opposition with a handle to declaim against the late treaty. Sir John Hynde Cotton observed, that the peace could not be properly styled complete, as nothing had been stipulated with respect to the article of "no search;" alluding to the interruption our commerce had sustained from the Spaniards in the West Indies; a stipulation, without which both Houses of Parliament had formerly voted that there should be no peace with that kingdom. In the present conjuncture of affairs such an objection savoured rather of party than of patriotism; and indeed Sir John declared, that the remarks he made upon the occasion were rather in discharge of the duty he owed to his country, than in hope of seeing his sentiments espoused by the majority. Some sharp altercation was used in the debate which arose *Subjects of debate.*

on this subject; and many severe invectives were levelled at those who negotiated, as well as at those who approved and confirmed the treaty. But Mr. Pelham, who sustained the whole weight of the debate on the side of administration, answered every objection with equal candour and ability; and if he failed in proving that the terms of peace were as favourable as could be expected, considering the unfortunate events of the war, and the situation of the contending powers; he at least demonstrated, that it would be the interest of the kingdom to acquiesce for the present in the treaty which had been concluded, and endeavoured to remedy its imperfections by subsequent conventions, amicably opened among those powers between whom any cause of dispute remained. With respect to the vote of both Houses, mentioned by Sir John Hynde Cotton, he declared that he had never approved of that step when it was first taken; or, if he had, times and circumstances, which could not be foreseen, would have justified his deviating from it in the re-establishment of peace. He reminded them, that a Parliament of Great Britain had once voted "no peace while any part of the West Indies should remain in possession of the Spanish king;" yet a train of incidents, which they could not possibly foresee, afterwards rendered it expedient to adopt a peace, without insisting upon the accomplishment of that condition. In a word, we must own, that in the majority of debates excited in the course of this session, the ministry derived their triumphs from the force of reason, as well as from the weight of influence. We shall always, however, except the efforts that were made for reducing the number of land-forces to fifteen thousand, and maintaining a greater number of seamen than the ministry proposed. On these constitutional points the Earl of Egmont, and the other chiefs of the opposition, expatiated with all the energy of eloquence, which, however, was frustrated by the power of superior numbers. Ten thousand seamen were voted for the service of the ensuing year, notwithstanding his majesty's injunction to maintain a considerable navy; and the number of land-forces was continued at eighteen thousand eight hundred and fifty-seven. The sums granted for making good his majesty's engagements with the Electors of Bavaria and Mentz, and the Duke of Brunswick Wolfenbuttle, amounted to fifty-three thousand two hundred and twenty-five pounds sterling. The services done by the colonies in North America, during the war, were gratified with the sum of one hundred twenty-two thousand two hundred forty-six pounds. The expense incurred by the new colony of Nova Scotia exceeded seventy-six thousand pounds. A small sum was voted for the improvement of Georgia; and ten thousand pounds were granted towards the support of the British forts and settlements on the coast of Africa. The sum total granted in this session arose to four millions one hundred forty-one thousand six hundred sixty-one pounds nine shillings and eleven pence halfpenny, to be raised by the land-tax, at three shillings in the pound; the malt, and other duties, the surplus of divers impositions remaining in the bank and exchequer; one million by annuities, at three per cent. charged on the sinking fund, until redeemed by Parliament; and nine hundred thousand pounds out of the excess or overplus of moneys denominated the sinking-fund.

But the capital measure which distinguished this session of Parliament was the reduction of the interest on the public funds; a scheme which was planned and executed by the minister, without any national disturbance or disquiet, to the astonishment of all Europe; the different nations of which could not comprehend how it would be possible for the government, at the close of a long and expensive war, which had so considerably drained the country, and augmented the enormous burden of national debt, to find money for paying off such of the public creditors as might choose to receive their principal, rather than submit to a reduction of the interest. It was not very much for the honour of the opposition, that some of its leading members endeavoured to impede this great machine of civil economy, by taking opportunities of affirming in Parliament, in opposition to his majesty's speech, that the nation, far from being in a flourishing condition, was almost entirely exhausted: that commerce drooped and declined; that public credit stood tottering on the brink of ruin; and that all the treaties lately concluded among the different powers of Europe were, in effect, disadvantageous and prejudicial to the interests of Great Britain. In answer to these assertions, Mr. Pelham undertook to prove, from the register of exports and imports, that the commerce of the kingdom was more extensive at this than at any former period; and that the public credit was strong enough to admit of an experiment, which he would not presume to hazard, except upon a moral certainty of its being firmly rooted, beyond the power of accident and faction to shake or overturn. He declared, that his design of reducing the interest upon the funds was the result of the love he bore his country, and an opinion that it was the duty of the servants of the crown to ease the burdens of the people. He said he had conferred on this subject with persons of the most approved knowledge and undoubted experience; and chose to promulgate the method proposed for alleviating the load of the national debt, that the public, in knowing the particulars of the scheme, might have time to consider them at leisure, and start such objections as should occur to their reflection, before it might be too late to adopt amendments. He observed, that nothing could more clearly demonstrate the vigour of public credit, and the augmentation of national commerce, than the price of stock, which had within three years risen to a very considerable increase; and the duties on imports, which in nine months had added one million to the sinking-fund, notwithstanding a very extraordinary sum which had been paid as bounties for exported corn. He expressed great tenderness and regard for the interests of those who had advanced their money for the service of the government; declaring that his aim was to contrive a fair, honest, and equitable method for lessening the national incumbrances, by lowering the interest, conformable to parliamentary faith, and agreeable to the rules of eternal justice. His plan was accordingly communicated, canvassed, and approved in the House of Commons, and an act passed for reducing the interest of the funds which constitute the national debt.* In pursuance of this act, for the reduc-

* The resolutions of the Commons on this head were printed by authority in the London Gazette, signifying, That those who were, or should be, proprietors of any part of the public debt, redeemable by law, incurred before Michaelmas, in the year one thousand seven hundred and forty-nine, carrying an interest of four per centum per annum, who should, on or before the twenty-eighth day of February in that year, subscribe their names, signifying their consent to accept of an interest of three pounds per centum, to commence from the twenty-fifth day of December, in the year one thousand seven hundred and fifty-seven, subject to the same provisions, notices, and clauses of redemption, to which their respective sums at four per centum were then liable, should, in lieu of their present interest, be entitled to four per centum till the twenty-fifth day of December, in the year one thousand seven hundred and fifty; and after that day to three pounds ten shillings per centum per annum, till the twenty-fifth day of December one thousand seven hundred and fifty-seven: and no part of that debt, except what was due to the East India Company, should be redeemable to this period: That if any part of the national debt, incurred before last Michaelmas, redeemable by law, and carrying an interest of four per centum, should remain unsubscribed on or before the thirtieth day of May, the government should pay off the principal. For this purpose his majesty was enabled to borrow of any person or persons, bodies politic or corporate, any sum or sums of money not exceeding that part

tion of the interest, the greater part of the creditors complied with the terms proposed, and subscribed their respective annuities before the end of February; but the three great companies at first kept aloof, and refused to subscribe any part of their capital.

About the middle of March the Commons ordered the proper officers to lay before them an account of the sums which had been subscribed, and these were taken into consideration by a committee of the whole House. It was then that Mr. Pelham, as chancellor of the exchequer, observed, that besides the debts due to the three great companies in their corporate capacity, all the rest, carrying four per centum interest, had been subscribed, except about eight or nine millions, the proprietors of which had forfeited the favour designed them by Parliament; but as many of these had been misled by evil counsellors, who perhaps were more intent on distressing the government, than solicitous to serve their friends; and as many were foreigners, residing beyond sea, who had not time to take proper advice, and give the necessary instructions; and as these could not possibly be distinguished from such as refuse to subscribe from mere obstinacy or disaffection, it might be thought cruel to take the most rigorous advantage of the forfeiture they had incurred. With respect to the proprietors of the stock or capital belonging to the three great companies, he asserted, that many of them would willingly have subscribed their properties within the time limited, but were necessarily excluded by the majority on the ballot; and as it was equally impossible to know those who were against the question on the ballot, he thought that some tenderness was due even to the proprietors of those three companies: his opinion, therefore, was, that they, and the uncomplying annuitants, should be indulged with further time to complete their subscriptions; but in order to preserve the authority of Parliament, and the respect due to that august assembly, they ought not to be gratified with such advantageous terms as were allowed to the annuitants who at first cheerfully complied with the

1750.

*Act passed for that purpose.*

---

of the national debt which might remain unsubscribed, to be charged on the sinking-fund, upon any terms not exceeding the rate of interest in the foregoing proposal.

All the duties appropriated to the payment of the interest were still continued, and the surplus of those incorporated with the sinking fund for the discharge of the principal. Books were opened for the subscription at the Exchequer, the Bank of England, and the South-Sea House; and copies of those resolutions transmitted to the directors of all the monied corporations.

proposals offered by the legislature. For these reasons he proposed, that although the term of subscribing should be protracted till the thirtieth day of May, the encouragement of three pounds ten shillings per centum per annum should not be continued to the second subscribers longer than till the fifth day of December, in the year one thousand seven hundred and fifty-five. The proposal being approved, a bill was framed for this purpose, as well as for redeeming such annuities as should not be subscribed, which passed through both Houses, and was enacted into a law, after having received an additional clause, empowering the East India Company, in case they should subscribe all their stock bearing an interest of four per centum, to borrow, with the consent of the treasury, any sums not exceeding four millions two hundred thousand pounds, after the several rates of interest before proposed to be paid by the public, and one million more at three per centum per annum. They were also vested with a power to raise money by bonds as formerly; yet so as the whole, including the annuities, should not exceed what they were by former acts empowered to borrow. The objections to the execution of this project, which by many were deemed insurmountable, entirely vanished before the fortitude, perseverance, and caution of the minister; who had secured, among the monied men of the nation, the promise of such sums as would have been sufficient to pay off the capital belonging to those creditors who might refuse to accept the interest thus reduced. The second subscription had the desired effect. The three great companies acquiesced, and their example was followed by the other scrupulous annuitants; the national burden was comfortably lightened, and the sinking-fund considerably increased, without producing the least perplexity or disturbance in the commonwealth; a circumstance that could not fail to excite the admiration and envy of all Christendom.

The mutiny-bill for the ensuing year was mitigated with an essential alteration, relating to the oath of secrecy imposed upon the members of every court-martial, who were now released from this reserve, if required to give evidence, by due course of law, in any court of judicature; and whereas, by the former mutiny-bill, a general was empowered to order the revisal of any sentence by court-martial as often as he pleased, and, on that pretence, to keep in

*New Mutiny-bill.*

confinement a man who had been acquitted upon a fair trial, it was now enacted, that no sentence pronounced by any court-martial, and signed by the president, should be more than once liable to revisal. Colonel George Townshend, son of Lord Viscount Townshend, who had equally distinguished himself by his civil and military accomplishments, proposed another clause, for preventing any non-commissioned officer being broke or reduced into the ranks, or any soldier being punished, but by the sentence of a court-martial. He gave the House to understand, that certain persons attended at the door, who from the station of non-commissiond officers had been broke, and reduced into the ranks, without trial, or any cause assigned; and he expatiated not only upon the iniquity of such proceedings, but also upon the danger of leaving such arbitrary power in the hands of an individual officer. A warm debate was the consequence of this motion, which, however, was overruled by the majority.

Among other regulations made in the course of this session for the encouragement of the British manufactures, a large duty was laid upon Irish sail-cloth, which, being sold at an under price, was found to interfere with the same species of commodity fabricated in the island of Great Britain; and, for the further benefit of this last, the bounty upon the exportation of it, which had been deducted from a defective fund, was now made payable out of the customs. This measure, however, was not of such importance to the nation, as the act which they passed for encouraging the importation of pig and bar-iron from the British colonies in North America. Every well-wisher to his country reflected with concern on the nature of the British trade with Sweden, from which kingdom the subjects of his Britannic majesty imported more iron and steel than all the other countries in Europe. For this article they paid a very great balance in ready money, which the Swedes again expended in purchasing from the French, and other mercantile powers, those necessaries and superfluities with which they might have been as cheaply furnished by Great Britain. In the mean time the English colonies in America were restricted by severe duties from making advantage of their own produce, in exchanging their iron for such commodities as they were under the necessity of procuring from their mother-country. Such restriction was not only a cruel grievance upon our own settlements, but also attended with

*Bill for encouraging the importation of iron from America.*

manifest prejudice to the interest of Great Britain, annually drained of great sums in favour of an ungrateful nation, from which no part of them returned; whereas the iron imported from America must of necessity come in exchange for our own manufactures. The Commons, having appointed a day for taking this affair into consideration, carefully examined into the state of the British commerce carried on with Sweden, as well as into the accounts of iron imported from the plantations in America; and a committee of the whole House having resolved, that the duties on American pig and bar-iron should be removed, a bill [b] was brought in for that purpose, containing a clause, however, to prevent his majesty's subjects from making steel, and establishing mills for slitting and rolling iron, within the British colonies of America; this precaution being taken, that the colonists

[b] The most remarkable circumstance attending the progress of this bill, which made its way through both Houses, and obtained the royal assent, was the number of contradictory petitions in favour and in prejudice of it, while it remained under consideration. The tanners of leather in and about the town of Sheffield, in Yorkshire, represented, that if the bill should pass, the English iron would be undersold; consequently a great number of furnaces and forges would be discontinued; in that case the woods used for fuel would stand uncut, and the tanners be deprived of oak bark sufficient for the continuance and support of their occupation. They nevertheless owned, that should the duty be removed from pig-iron only, no such consequences could be apprehended; because, should the number of furnaces be lessened, that of forges would be increased. This was likewise the plea urged in divers remonstrances by masters of iron-works, gentlemen, and freeholders, who had tracts of wood-land in their possession. The owners, proprietors, and farmers of furnaces and iron forges, belonging to Sheffield and its neighbourhood, enlarged upon the great expense they had incurred in erecting and supporting iron-works, by means of which great numbers of his majesty's subjects were comfortably supported. They expressed their apprehension, that should the bill pass into a law, it could not in any degree lessen the consumption of Swedish iron, which was used for purposes which neither the American nor British iron would answer; but that the proposed encouragement, considering the plenty and cheapness of wood in America, would enable the colonies to undersell the British iron, a branch of traffic which would be totally destroyed, to the ruin of many thousand labourers, who would be compelled to seek their livelihood in foreign countries. They likewise suggested, that if all the iron manufacturers of Great Britain should be obliged to depend upon a supply of iron from the plantations, which must ever be rendered precarious by the hazard of the seas and the enemy, the manufacture would probably decay for want of materials, and many thousand families be reduced to want and misery. On the other hand, the ironmongers and smiths belonging to the flourishing town of Birmingham, in Warwickshire, presented a petition, declaring, that the bill would be of great benefit to the trade of the nation, as it would enable the colonists to make larger returns of their own produce, and encourage them to take a greater quantity of the British manufactures. They affirmed, that all the iron-works in the island of Great Britain did not supply half the quantity of that metal sufficient to carry on the manufacture; that if this deficiency could be supplied from the colonies in America, the importation would cease, and considerable sums of money be saved to the nation. They observed, that the importation of iron from America could no more affect the iron-works and freeholders of the kingdom than the like quantity imported from any other country; but they prayed that the people of America might be restrained from erecting slitting or rolling mills, or forges for plating iron, as they would interfere with the manufactures of Great Britain.

Many remonstrances to the same effect were presented from different parts of the kingdom; and it appeared, upon the most exact inquiry, that the encouragement of American iron would prove extremely beneficial to the kingdom, as it had been found, upon trial, applicable to all the uses of Swedish iron, and as good in every respect as the produce of that country.

might not interfere with the manufactures of their mother-country.

The next commercial improvement, of which we shall take notice, was the bill for the encouragement of the British white herring and cod fisheries. This was likewise the result of mature deliberation, importing, that a bounty of thirty shillings per ton should be granted, and paid out of the customs to all new vessels from twenty to four-score tons burden, which should be built for that purpose, and actually employed in the fishery: that a society should be incorporated, under the name of the Free British Fishery, by a charter, not exclusive, with power to raise a capital not exceeding five hundred thousand pounds; and that three pounds ten shillings per centum per annum should be granted and paid out of the customs to the proprietors for fourteen years, for so much of the capital as should be actually employed in the said fisheries. Corresponding chambers were proposed to be erected in remote parts of North Britain, for taking in subscriptions, and prosecuting the trade, under the directions of the company at London; and the nation in general seemed eager to dispute this branch of commerce with the subjects of Holland, whom they considered as ungrateful interlopers. In the House of Peers, however, the bill met with a formidable opposition from the Earl of Winchelsea and Lord Sandys, who justly observed, that it was a crude, indigested scheme, which, in the execution, would never answer the expectations of the people: that in contending with the Dutch, who are the patterns of unwearied industry, and the most rigid economy, nothing could be more absurd than a joint-stock company, which is always clogged with extraordinary expense; or than the resolution of fitting out vessels at the port of London, where all sorts of materials, labour, and seamen are so much dearer than in any other part of the united kingdom, exclusive of the great distance and dangerous voyage between the metropolis and the Sound of Brassa in Shetland, the rendezvous at which all the herring-busses were to assemble in the beginning of the fishing season. They likewise took notice of the heavy duty on salt, used in curing the fish for sale, and the beef for provision to the mariners; a circumstance of itself sufficient to discourage adventurers from embarking in a commerce which, at best, yields but very slender profits to the trade in particular, how important soever it might prove to the community in general. These objections were answered by the Duke of Argyle and the Earl of Granville, who seemed to think that this branch of trade could not be fairly set on foot without such a considerable sum of money as no single individual would care to advance; that a joint-stock company would be able to prosecute the fishery at a smaller expense than that which particular traders must necessarily incur; that the present spirit of the nation, which was eagerly bent upon trying the experiment, ought not to be balked by delay, lest it should evaporate; and, that though the plan was not unexceptionable, the defects of it might in the sequel be remedied by the legislature. In a word, the bill was adopted by the majority, with a small amendment in the title, which produced some disquiets in the Lower House; but this dispute was compromised, and it was enacted into a law towards the close of the session. Nothing could be more agreeable to the public than the sanction of the legislature to this favourite plan, which was ardently promoted and patronized by men of the greatest eminence for wealth and popularity. The company chose for their governor the Prince of Wales, who received this proof of their attachment and respect with particular marks of satisfaction: the president and vice-president were both aldermen of London; and the council was composed of thirty gentlemen, the majority of whom were members of Parliament. Great pains were taken, and some artifice was used, to learn the Dutch method of curing the fish. People crowded with their subscriptions; a number of hands were employed in building and equipping the busses or vessels used in the fishery; and the most favourable consequences were expected from the general vigour and alacrity which animated these preparations.* But the success did not gratify the sanguine hopes of the projectors and adventurers. The objections made in the House of Lords soon appeared to have been well founded: these co-operating with mismanagement in the directors, the spirit of the company began to flag, the natural consequences of commercial disappointment, and now the British fishery seems to languish under the neglect of the legislature.

Touching the trade to the coast of Africa, petitions were

*New African Company.* renewed by the company and its creditors, the merchants of Bristol, Liverpool, and Lancaster; and a remonstrance was presented by the planters and merchants interested in the British sugar settlements in America: but the Commons adhered to their former resolutions of laying open the trade, maintaining the forts at the public expense, and regulating the commerce by a committee of merchants, representing the chief trading towns in the kingdom, to be superintended by the board of trade and plantations. The bill was accordingly framed and presented, and having proceeded through both Houses without opposition, obtained the royal assent. Over and above these wise, salutary, and patriotic measures for the improvement of commerce, they encouraged the importation of raw silk by an act, reducing the duties formerly payable on that which was the growth of China to the same that is raised on the raw silk from Italy, and allowing the same drawback upon the exportation of the one which had been usually granted on the other. A second bill was brought in for the encouragement of the growth and culture of silk in Carolina and Georgia, where it had been lately produced with extraordinary success, by freeing from all duties that which should be imported from his majesty's dominions in America; and a third was framed, permitting raw silk of the growth or produce of Persia, purchased in Russia, to be imported into Great Britain, from any port or place belonging to the empire of Russia. Divers efforts were made, by different members in the opposition, to rectify certain abuses in the army and administration: some bills were brought in, and several petitions were left on the table; but all of them proved abortive, from the power and influence of the minister, who seemed resolved that no benefit should flow upon the nation through any channel but his own. Nevertheless it must be acknowledged, for the honour of his memory, that there is no session on record so productive as this was of measures advantageous to the community.

The people, however, were not entirely satisfied with the conduct of the administration, if we may judge from the ferment and commotions raised during the progress of an election for a citizen to represent the city of Westminster in Parliament. The seat which had been filled by Lord Trentham, eldest son of Earl Gower, having become vacant, in consequence of that nobleman's accepting a place at the board of admiralty, he again declared himself a candidate, and met with a violent opposition. Those who styled themselves the independent electors of Westminster, being now incensed to an uncommon degree of turbulence by the interposition of ministerial influence, determined to use their utmost endeavours to baffle the designs of the court, and at the same time take vengeance on the family of Earl Gower, who had entirely abandoned the opposition, of which he was formerly one of the most respected leaders. With this view they held consultations, agreed to resolutions, and set up a private gentleman, named Sir George Vandeput, as the competitor of Lord Trentham, declaring that they would support his pretensions at their own expense, being the more encouraged to this enterprise by the countenance and assistance of the Prince of Wales and his adherents. They accordingly opened houses of entertainment for their partisans, solicited votes, circulated remonstrances, and propagated abuse: in a word, they canvassed, with surprising spirit and perseverance, against the whole interest of St. James's. Mobs were hired, and processions made, on both sides, and the city of Westminster was filled with tumult and uproar. The mutual animosity of the parties seemed every day to increase during the election, and a great number of unqualified votes were presented on both sides; all the powers of insinuation, obloquy, and ridicule, were employed to vilify and depreciate both candidates. At length, the poll being closed, a majority of votes appeared in behalf of Lord Trentham; but a scrutiny being demanded by the other side, the returning officer complied with their request. The speaker of the Lower House had issued his warrant for a new writ of election about the middle of November; and towards the end of February Mr. Fox, secretary at war, standing up, and observing that no return had yet been made, thought proper to move, that the clerk of the crown, the messenger extraordinary attending the great seal, the under-sheriff of Middlesex, and the high-bailiff of Westminster, should attend next morning, and give an account of their issuing, delivering, and executing the writ of election. These being examined, and the high-bailiff declaring that he would proceed with all possible despatch in the scrutiny, which had been demanded and was begun, Mr. Speaker explained to him some particulars of his duty; in the discharge of which, he was given to understand he might depend upon the protection of the House, should he meet with any obstruction which he could not otherwise surmount. By the violence and caprice with which a great number of votes were contested on both sides, the scrutiny was protracted a long time, and the return attended with some extraordinary consequences, which shall be particularized among the transactions of the next year. In the mean time, the present session of Parliament was closed on the twelfth day of April, with a speech from the throne, commending the Commons for having seized the very first opportunity of reducing the interest of the national debt, without the least infringement upon the faith of Parliament; and congratulating them on the flourishing state of the public credit, which could not fail to add strength and reputation to the government, both at home and abroad. Immediately after the rising of the Parliament, his majesty appointed a regency to govern the kingdom in his absence, and embarked for the continent, in order to visit his German dominions.

The month of January and the beginning of February were distinguished, the first day, by a very remarkable aurora borealis, appearing at night to the north-east, of a deep and dusky red colour, like the reflection of some great fire, for which it was by many people mistaken; and the coruscations, unlike those that are generally observed, did not meet in the zenith, but in a point some degrees to the southward. February was ushered in by terrible peals of thunder, flashes of lightning, and such a tempest of wind, hail, and rain, as overwhelmed with fear and consternation the inhabitants of Bristol, where it chiefly raged. On the eighth day of the same month, between twelve and one in the afternoon, the people of London were still more dreadfully alarmed by the shock of an earthquake, which shook all the houses with such violence, that the furniture rocked on the floors, the pewter and porcelain rattled on the shelves, the chamber-bells rang, and the whole of this commotion was attended with a clap or noise resembling that produced by the fall of some heavy piece of furniture. The shock extended through the cities of London and Westminster, and was felt on both sides the river Thames, from Greenwich to the westward of London; but not perceptible at any considerable distance. On the very same day of the next month, between five and six o'clock in the morning, the inhabitants of the metropolis were again affrighted by a second shock, more violent than the first, and abundantly more alarming, as it waked the greater part of the people from their repose. It was pre-

*Earthquakes in London.*

ceded by a succession of thick low flashes of lightning, and a rumbling noise, like that of a heavy carriage rolling over a hollow pavement. The shock itself consisted of repeated vibrations, which lasted some seconds, and violently shook every house from top to bottom. Again the chairs rocked, the shelves clattered, the small bells rang, and in some places public clocks were heard to strike. Many persons, roused by this terrible visitation, started naked from their beds, and ran to their doors and windows in distraction: yet no life was lost, and no house overthrown by this concussion, though it was so dreadful as to threaten an immediate dissolution of the globe. The circumstance, however, did not fail to make a deep impression upon ignorant, weak, and superstitious minds, which were the more affected by the consideration that the two shocks were periodical; that the second, which happened exactly one month after the first, had been the more violent; and that the next, increasing in proportion, might be attended with the most dismal consequences. This general notion was confirmed, and indeed propagated, among all ranks of people, by the admonitions of a fanatic soldier, who publicly preached up repentance, and boldly prophesied that the next shock would happen on the same day in April, and totally destroy the cities of London and Westminster. Considering the infectious nature of fear and superstition, and the emphatic manner in which the imagination had been prepared and prepossessed, it was no wonder that the prediction of this illiterate enthusiast should have contributed, in a great measure, to augment the general terror. The churches were crowded with penitent sinners: the sons of riot and profligacy were overawed into sobriety and decorum. The streets no longer resounded with execrations, or the noise of brutal licentiousness; and the hand of charity was liberally opened. Those whom fortune had enabled to retire from the devoted city, fled to the country with hurry and precipitation, insomuch that the highways were encumbered with horses and carriages. Many who had, in the beginning, combated these groundless fears with the weapons of reason and ridicule, began insensibly to imbibe the contagion, and felt their hearts fail in proportion as the hour of probation approached: even science and philosophy were not proof against the unaccountable effects of this communication. In after-ages it will hardly be believed that, on the evening of the eighth, day of April, the open fields that skirted the metropolis were filled with an incredible number of people assembled in chairs, in chaises, and coaches, as well as on foot, who waited in the most fearful suspense until morning, and the return of day, disproved the truth of the dreaded prophecy. Then their fears vanished : they returned to their respective habitations in a transport of joy ; and were soon reconciled to their abandoned vices, which they seemed to resume with redoubled affection, and once more bade defiance to the vengeance of Heaven.

By this time all the gaols in England were filled with the refuse of the army and navy, which, having been dismissed at the peace, and either averse to labour, or excluded from employment, had naturally preyed upon the commonwealth. Great numbers of those wretches who, by proper regulations, might have been rendered serviceable to the community, were executed as examples ; and the rest perished miserably, amidst the stench and horrors of noisome dungeons. Even the prison of Newgate was rendered so infectious by the uncommon crowds of confined felons, stowed together in close apartments, that the very air they breathed acquired a pestilential degree of putrefaction. It was this putrified air which, adhering to the clothes of the malefactors brought to trial at the bar of the Old Bailey in May, produced among the audience a pestilential fever, which infected and proved fatal to the lord mayor of London, to one alderman, two of the judges, divers lawyers who attended the session, the greatest part of the jury, and a considerable number of the spectators. In order to prevent such disasters for the future, the gaols were cleansed, and accommodated with ventilators, which exhaust the foul and supply a circulation of fresh air; and other humane precautions were taken for the benefit of the prisoners.

*Pestilential fever at the session in the Old Bailey.*

The affairs of the continent underwent no remarkable alteration. An ambassador extraordinary being sent to Petersburgh from the court of London, declared to the czarina's minister, that in case of a rupture between Russia and Sweden, occasioned by the hostilities committed by the former power, his Britannic majesty would consider Russia as the aggressor, and the czarina could not expect that he would supply her with the succours which he was engaged by treaty to furnish for her

*Disputes between Russia and Sweden.*

defence, in case she should be attacked. A declaration of the same nature was made by the ambassador of her imperial majesty the Queen of Hungary, while the ministers of France and Prussia, who were in strict alliance with Sweden, gave her to understand, that they would punctually fulfil their engagements with the court of Stockholm, should she actually invade the Swedish territories of Finland. The spirit with which the King of Prussia exerted himself on this occasion gave infinite umbrage to the czarina, who, indeed, expressed her resentment, by treating the minister of Brandenburgh with contemptuous neglect, and even refused to favour him with an audience, till he should be vested with the character of ambassador. Thus were sown the seeds of misunderstanding between those two powers, which, in the sequel, grew up to the most bitter animosity, and served to inflame those dissensions which have desolated the fairest provinces of Germany. The remonstrance of his Prussian majesty with respect to the troubles of the north was couched in such terms as gave dissatisfaction to the court of Petersburgh. The Russian minister retired from Berlin without the ceremony of taking leave, and the Prussian ambassador Warendorf was recalled from the court of the czarina.

The attention of his Britannic majesty was not wholly engrossed by the disputes between Russia and Sweden. He had another object in view, which more nearly concerned the interest of his German dominions; and had set on foot two negotiations of the utmost importance to the commerce and advantage of Great Britain. His first and principal aim was, in conjunction with the court of Vienna, to take such measures as would secure the succession of the imperial dignity to the Archduke Joseph, eldest son and heir to the reigning emperor. As the previous step to that elevation, it was proposed to elect this young prince King of the Romans; and for this purpose it was necessary to procure a majority not only of the electors, but also in the diet of the empire, through which the proposal must have passed. No stone was left unturned to reconcile this expedient to the German princes. Subsidies were offered by the maritime powers of England, and the States-General, to the Electors of Mentz and Cologn; and a treaty of the same nature was concluded with the Elector of Bavaria, who, in consideration of an

*Plan for electing the Archduke Joseph King of the Romans.*

annual subsidy, amounting to forty thousand pounds sterling, two-thirds to be paid by Great Britain, and the rest by the States-General, engaged to keep in readiness a body of six thousand infantry, as auxiliaries to the maritime powers, though not to act against the emperor or empire; and to join the interest of his Britannic majesty in the diet, as well as in the electoral college. In order to render the King of Poland, Elector of Saxony, propitious to this design, he was accommodated with the loan of a very considerable sum upon the mortgage of certain bailiwicks and lordships belonging to the Saxon dominions. Thus a majority of the electors was secured, and such foundations were laid for the success of this project, that it was generally believed it would be accomplished in his Britannic majesty's next visit to his German dominions. Hopes, it was said, were given to the King of Sweden, that his concurrence would be gratified by erecting the House of Hesse-Cassel, of which he was head, into a tenth electorate. Arguments of an interesting nature were used by the King of Prussia and the Elector Palatine, that, if possible, the diet might unanimously approve of this measure, so necessary for establishing the peace of the empire, and preventing such troubles as arose from a disputed succession at the death of Charles the Sixth. These endeavours, however, did not succeed in their full extent.

The King of Prussia, as Elector of Brandenburgh, opposed the election as unnecessary and improper, on account of the health and vigour of the reigning emperor, and the tender years of the archduke. This monarch had set himself up as a balance to the power of the house of Austria, which had long aspired to absolute dominion over its co-estates, and endeavoured to establish an hereditary right of succession to the empire; he, therefore, employed all his influence to frustrate the measure proposed, either actuated by a spirit of pure patriotism, or inspired with designs which he had not yet thought proper to declare. The opposition was joined by the Elector Palatine, and countenanced by the French king, who protested that, for the sake of peace, he would not oppose this election, though contrary to the Golden Bull, provided it should be confirmed by the unanimous consent of the electoral college; but should any one member signify his dissent, and he or any state of the empire claim the protection and assistance of his most Christian majesty, he could not dispense with

*Opposition of the King of Prussia.*

granting both, in consequence of his being guarantee of the treaty of Westphalia; an engagement by which he was obliged to succour those princes and states of the empire who might have recourse to him, in case of any grievance they suffered contrary to what was stipulated in that constitution. This declaration co-operating with the known character of his Prussian majesty, whose great army overawed Hanover and Bohemia, in all probability damped that vigour with which the courts of Vienna and Herenhausen had hitherto prosecuted this important negotiation.

Disputes with the French about the limits of Nova Scotia. The second object that employed the attention of the British ministry was the establishment of the precise limits of Acadia or Nova Scotia, where the new colony had suffered great mischief and interruption from the incursions of the Indians, excited to these outrages by the subjects and emissaries of France. Commissaries had been appointed by both crowns to meet at Paris, and compromise these disputes; but the conferences were rendered abortive by every art of cavilling, chicanery, and procrastination, which the French commissioners opposed to the justice and perspicuity of the English claims. They not only misinterpreted treaties, though expressed with the utmost precision, and perplexed the conferences with difficulties and matter foreign to the subject, but they carried the finesse of perfidy so far as to produce false charts and maps of the country, in which the rivers and boundaries were misplaced and misrepresented. At this time also the insincerity of the French court appeared in affected delays and artful objections, with respect to the evacuation of the neutral islands in the West Indies; and the governors of the British plantations, in different parts of North America, transmitted intelligence, that the French had begun to make encroachments on the back of the English colonies.

Treaty with Spain. Perhaps the precarious footing on which the peace stood between Great Britain and France at this juncture, and the critical situation of affairs in Germany, determined the ministry of England to compromise all differences with Spain, upon such terms as at any other time they would hardly have embraced. In order to discuss those points between the two nations, which had not been settled by the treaty of Aix-la-Chapelle, conferences were also begun at Madrid, and carried on by Mr. Keene, plenipotentiary of his Britannic majesty, and Don Joseph de Carvajal and Lancastro, the Spanish king's minister. At length a treaty was concluded on these conditions: the King of Spain engaged to pay in three months, to the South Sea Company of England, one hundred thousand pounds sterling, as an indemnification for all claims upon his crown by virtue of the assiento. In other respects, the trade and navigation of the English to the ports of Spain were regulated by former treaties. It was stipulated, that they should pay no other duties than those that were exacted of them in the reign of Charles II. of Spain: that they should be treated on the footing of the most favoured nations; and continue to enjoy the privilege of taking salt at the island of Tortuga. But there was no article restricting the Spanish guarda-costas from searching the British vessels on the high seas: although, as we have already observed, this insolent prerogative, assumed without right, and exercised without humanity, was, in effect, the original and sole cause of the late rupture, which had been attended with such enormous expense to the nation. It must be owned, however, that his Catholic majesty was at this period extremely well disposed to live upon good terms with Great Britain. He was resolved to indulge his people with the blessings of peace, to propagate a spirit of industry throughout his dominions, and, in particular, to encourage commerce, which he foresaw would prove a much more certain and inexhaustible source of wealth, power, and influence, than all the treasures he could drain from the mines of Mexico and Peru. His resolutions on this interesting subject were chiefly directed by Don Ricardo Wall, who now acted as his minister at London; a gentleman of Irish extract, who had distinguished himself in the field as well as in the cabinet, and possessed the joint qualifications of a general and a statesman. He had, by virtue of a passport, come over privately to England before the peace, in order to pave the way for the treaty, by a secret negotiation with the English ministers; but immediately after the peace was proclaimed, he appeared in the character of ambassador. He was possessed of the most insinuating address, shrewd, penetrating, and inquisitive. While he resided in London, he spared no pains in learning the nature of those manufactures, and that commerce, by which Great Britain had been so remarkably aggrandized: and on his return to Spain, where in a little time he was placed at the helm of affairs, he turned the knowledge he had thus acquired to the advantage of his country. He not only promoted the useful arts within the kingdom of Spain, but demonstrated the infinite advantage that would accrue from an active trade, which the Spaniards had for many years neglected; and in a few years their ships were seen to swarm in all the commercial ports of Europe. Of other foreign events which distinguished this summer, the most remarkable was the death of John, King of Portugal, who perfectly understood, and steadily pursued, the true interest of his country, and in whom many princely qualities were debased by a cruel spirit of bigotry and superstition. He was succeeded by his eldest son, Joseph, who, if he has fallen short of his father in some respects, cannot be justly charged with having inherited this paternal weakness.

The King of Great Britain, having returned to England, opened the session of Parliament in January with a speech, importing, that he had concluded a treaty with the King of Spain, and amicably adjusted such differences as could not be so properly compromised in a general treaty: that the commerce of this nation with that country was re-established upon the most advantageous and sure foundations; and that there was the greatest reason to hope the ancient friendship between Great Britain and Spain would, from mutual inclination as well as interest, be now effectually restored. He told them that, in conjunction with the empress-queen and the States-General, he had concluded a treaty with the Elector of Bavaria; and was employed in taking such further measures as might best tend to strengthen and secure the tranquillity of the empire, support its system, and timely anticipate such events as had been found by experience to endanger the common cause, involve Europe in the calamities of war, and occasion the loss of much blood and treasure to these kingdoms. He promised, that both these treaties should be subjected to their perusal; he gave them to understand, that he had received from all the other contracting powers in the definitive treaty of Aix-la-Chapelle the most full and clear declarations of their resolution to preserve the general peace; and that he had taken care to consolidate the ties of union and friendship between him and his allies, the better to secure their mutual interests, maintain the peace already subsisting, and prevent the occasion of any future rupture. Finally, he recommended unanimity, the improvement of commerce, and the effectual suppression of such outrages and violences as are inconsistent with good order and government, and endanger the lives and properties of the subject, whose happiness and flourishing condition he had at heart.

When the motion was made for an address of thanks, couched in terms that savoured of the most implicit complaisance, approbation, and acquiescence in the measures which the crown had taken, the Earl of Eg—t, and some other anti-courtiers, affirmed, that such an address would be equally servile and absurd. They observed, that nothing could be more preposterous than a blind approbation of measures which they did not know: that nothing could be more ridiculous than their congratulations on the present happy tranquillity, when almost every day's newspapers informed them of some British ships being seized by the Spaniards, or some new attack made by the French on our infant colony in Nova Scotia. With respect to the continent of Europe, they affirmed, that the tranquillity of Germany would have been upon a much more solid foundation, had England never interposed in the affairs of the empire; in that case the princes would of themselves have supported the constitution of their own country: that the election of an infant for the King of the Romans was much more likely to disturb than establish the tranquillity of Europe; because it would help to overturn the constitution of the empire, by rendering the imperial dignity hereditary in one house, instead of being the result of a free election. They took notice, that the constitution had provided vicars to govern the empire during the vacancy of the imperial throne; but had made no provision of regents, protectors, or guardians for a minor emperor, because it was never supposed that a minor would be chosen. They inveighed against the late treaty with Spain; in which, they said, the ministry, for the paltry sum of one hundred thousand pounds, had given up the claims of the South Sea Company, and other British merchants, who had suffered from depredations to the amount of one million three hundred thousand pounds; and bartered away the freedom of our trade and navigation, by leaving untouched that prerogative which the Spaniards have assumed of searching the British ships in the open seas, and confiscating them should they find on board the least particle of what they called contraband merchandise. They produced an instance of an English ship, lately driven by stress of weather into one of the ports of the Spanish West Indies, where she was searched, seized, and condemned, under this pretence. They recapitulated the conduct of the French, who, in the midst of their declarations of peace and moderation, were still employed in fortifying their settlements on the neutral islands, as well as in harassing and encroaching upon our plantations in North America. They exclaimed against the treaty of subsidy with the Elector of Bavaria, or any other prince in time of peace; observing, that for some years the nation had paid such pensions to the Danes and the Hessians; but, in the course of the late war, the former abandoned our interests, and the latter actually took arms against Great Britain. They affirmed, that the subsidy was greater than the nation could spare; for, unless the land-tax should be continued at four shillings in the pound, they could not afford a shilling to any prince in Germany, without encroaching upon the sinking-fund. "At such a juncture (said a certain member) will any gentleman presume to propose the continuation of such an imposition on the landholder, for the sake of bribing the princes of Germany to do what?—to preserve the freedom and independency of their native country. I say, princes of Germany, because this subsidy to Bavaria would signify nothing unless we take half a score more of them into our pay: and when we have thus indulged them for seven years of peace, they may give us the slip, as others have done, whenever another war should be declared." Against these objections the motion was supported by William Pitt, at this time an advocate for the ministry. He observed that the address was no more than the usual compliment to the throne, which did not imply an obligation on the Parliament to approve of measures which they might find cause to censure upon further inquiry. He said, the trivial disputes still subsisting between this nation and the Spaniards, or France, would soon be terminated amicably, and could never affect the general tranquillity of Europe, which was to be established upon a firm alliance between his majesty and such a confederacy upon the continent as would be an overmatch for the house of Bourbon. He expatiated upon his majesty's wisdom in taking off from the French interest such a powerful prince as the Elector of Bavaria, and concerting other salutary measures for preserving the balance of power on the continent. He defended the articles of the late treaty with Spain; observing, that what remained of the assiento contract was a matter of very little consequence to the South Sea Company; that the demands of this company and other British merchants were all cancelled by the rupture with Spain, and more than recompensed to the nation by a great balance of captures during the war, as well as by the great traffic carried on with the Spanish settlements in the West Indies, after it had been laid open by the demolition of their fortresses. He asserted, that by this treaty the court of Spain had made many important concessions: they had condescended to pay a great sum to the South Sea Company; they had consented to the re-establishment of the British trade in Spain, upon a very advantageous and solid footing, by agreeing that the subjects of Great Britain should pay no other duties on merchandise than those exacted of his Catholic majesty's own subjects, and to abolish all innovations that had been introduced into the commerce. He affirmed that the article of No Search was a stipulation which it would have been ridiculous to insist upon; and thought proper to obviate a reproach which he foresaw the opposition would throw upon him, from the circumstance of his having, upon a former occasion, heartily concurred in a motion for an address, that no treaty of peace with Spain should be admitted, unless such a stipulation should be first obtained as a preliminary. He owned he had strenuously contended for such a motion, because at that time, being very young and sanguine, he thought it right and reasonable; but he was now ten years older, had considered matters more coolly, and was convinced that the privilege of No Search, with respect to British vessels sailing near the American shore, would never be obtained, unless Spain should be brought so low as to acquiesce in any terms we, as victors, might propose. He likewise signified his conviction, that all addresses from the House of Commons, during the course of a war, for prescribing terms of peace, were in themselves ridiculous; and that every such address was an encroachment on the king's prerogative, which had always been attended with unlucky consequences. How far these arguments are satisfactory, conclusive, and consistent, we shall leave to the reader's determination. Certain it is, they were adopted by the majority, and the address was presented without further opposition.

*Supplies granted.* The two grand committees appointed to discuss the supplies for the ensuing year, and the funds upon which they were to be raised, proceeded, as usual, under the direction of the ministry; yet not without some vehement opposition, in which certain servants of the crown expressed the most hearty concurrence. When a motion was made for reducing the number of seamen to eight thousand, Mr. W. Pitt, Mr. Lyttelton, and Mr. G. Grenville, opposed it with all their might of argument and elocution; but they were overruled. Annual debates were also revived, with the same success, upon the number of troops constituting the standing army; but the other resolutions of the grand committees met with little or no opposition. The number of seamen for the ensuing year was limited to eight thousand; and that of the standing forces continued at eighteen thousand eight hundred and fifty-seven effective men, including one thousand eight hundred and fifteen invalids. The Commons granted a considerable sum of money for paying off the principal of such redeemable stocks as had not been subscribed, in pursuance of two acts passed in the last session for reducing the interest of annuities. Thirty thousand pounds were given for fulfilling the king's engagement with the Elector of Bavaria: large grants were made for supplying deficiencies, and replacing sums borrowed from the sinking-fund. The expense incurred by the new colony in Nova Scotia, not provided for by Parliament, exceeded fifty-seven thousand pounds; and the maintenance of it for the ensuing year was fixed at fifty-three thousand nine hundred and twenty-seven pounds, fourteen shillings, and four pence. An enormous charge! if we consider to how little purpose all this bounty was bestowed. A fund was established under the sanction of Parliament for the relief and maintenance of the widows of sea-officers, by allowing, upon the books of every ship of war in sea-pay, the wages and victuals of one man for every hundred of which the complement shall consist, for such time only as the number of men employed in the service of the royal navy shall not exceed twenty thousand. This was an additional indulgence, over and above the allowance of one man granted by a former act of Parliament. On the whole, the provisions of this year amounted to five millions one hundred twenty-five thousand twenty-three pounds, eleven shillings, and seven pence, to be raised by the usual duties: the sum of one million twenty-six thousand four hundred seventy-six pounds, four shillings, and six pence, advanced by the bank of England, to pay off their own unsubscribed annuities, for which they accepted exchequer-bills at three per cent. interest; by the land-tax at three shillings in the pound; a lottery and annuities, at the rate of three per cent. per ann. to be charged on the sinking-fund, redeemable by Parliament. The annual measure called the mutiny-bill was not passed without dispute and altercation: some alterations were proposed, but not adopted; and the sentences of court-martials still subjected to one revision.

In the midst of these deliberations the kingdom was alarmed with an event which overwhelmed the people with grief and consternation. His royal highness the Prince of Wales, in consequence of a cold caught in his garden at Kew, was seized with a pleuritic disorder; and, after a short illness, expired on the twentieth day of March, to the unspeakable affliction of his royal consort, and the unfeigned sorrow of all who wished well to their country. This excellent prince, who now died in the forty-fifth year of his age, was possessed of every amiable quality which could engage the affection of the people, a tender and obliging husband, a fond parent, a kind master, liberal, generous, candid, and humane; a munificent patron of the arts, an unwearied friend to merit; well disposed to assert the rights of mankind in general, and warmly attached to the interest of Great Britain. The nation could not but be afflicted at seeing a prince of such expectations ravished from their hopes; and their grief was the better founded, as the king had already attained to an advanced age, and the heir-apparent, George, now Prince of Wales, was a minor. *Death and character of the Prince of Wales.*

His majesty, foreseeing all the inconveniences which might arise from a minority, deliberated with his council on this subject, and resolved to obtain a parliamentary sanction for the measures judged necessary to secure the succession. With this view he sent a *1751. Settlement of a regency, in case of a minor sovereign.*

message to both Houses on the twenty-sixth day of April, importing, that nothing could conduce so much to the preservation of the Protestant succession in his royal family as proper provisions for the tuition of the person of his successor, and for the regular administration of the government, in case the successor should be of tender years: his majesty, therefore, earnestly recommended this weighty affair to the deliberation of Parliament; and proposed, that when the imperial crown of these realms should descend to any of the late prince's sons, being under the age of eighteen years, his mother, the Princess Dowager of Wales, should be guardian of his person, and regent of these kingdoms, until he should attain the age of majority, with such powers and limitations as should appear necessary and expedient for these purposes. This message produced a very affectionate address, promising to take the affair into their serious consideration; and in the beginning of May the Duke of Newcastle presented to the House of Peers a bill to provide for the administration of government, in case the crown should descend to a minor. The bill was read a second time, and committed, when a second message arrived from his majesty, recommending to their consideration the settlement of such a council of regency as the bill proposed, consisting of his royal highness the Duke of Cumberland, who at that time commanded the army, the Archbishop of Canterbury, the Lord Chancellor, the Lord High Treasurer, or first Lord Commissioner of the Treasury, the President of the Council, the Lord Privy-Seal, the Lord High Admiral of Great Britain, or first Commissioner of the Admiralty, the two principal Secretaries of State, and the Lord Chief Justice of the King's Bench; all these great officers, except his royal highness the duke, for the time being. This bill did not pass through the Lower House without violent debate and bitter sarcasms. The council of regency, though espoused by all the ministry, including the paymaster-general, met with fierce opposition, as an unnecessary and fatal restriction, that would impede the machine of government, and, as the council was constituted, might be productive of the most pernicious consequence. Some of the members ventured even to insinuate the danger of leaving at the head of a large standing army a prince of the blood vested with a share of the regency, possessed of great personal influence, the darling of the soldiery, brave, popular, and enterprising; supposed not wholly devoid of ambition, and not at all remarkable for any symptoms of extraordinary affection towards the person of the heir-apparent. The history of England was ransacked for invidious instances of royal uncles and regents, who had injured the sovereigns, and distressed the government, by their pride, cruelty, and ambition. The characters of John Lackland, and John of Gaunt, Humphrey and Richard Dukes of Gloucester, were called in review, canvassed, compared, and quoted, with some odious applications; but the majority, being convinced of the loyalty, virtue, integrity, and great abilities of his royal highness, to whom the nation owed obligations of the most important nature, passed the bill with a few amendments, in which the Lords acquiesced; and in a little time it received the royal sanction.

The death of the Prince of Wales was fatal to a bill which had been brought into the House of Commons, for naturalizing all foreign Protestants who should settle within the dominions of Great Britain. Political arithmeticians have generally taken it for granted, that to every commercial nation an increase of people is an increase of opulence; and this maxim is certainly true, on the supposition that every individual is industrious, and that there is a sufficient field for employment; but all these general maxims ought to be received under certain qualifications. When all branches of manufacture are overstocked, an addition of workmen will doubtless be an additional incumbrance on the community. In the debates which this bill produced, the members of the ministry were divided among themselves. The measure was enforced by the chancellor of the exchequer, Mr. W. Pitt, and Mr. Lyttelton; and in opposing it the Earl of Egmont was joined by Mr. Fox, secretary at war. Petitions and counter-petitions were presented by the merchants of London, Bristol, and other trading towns of the kingdom. All merchants and traders of foreign extraction exerted themselves vigorously in its behalf, and it was without doubt countenanced by the administration; but the project was odious to the people in general. The lord-mayor, aldermen, and commons of London, in common council assembled, composed a remonstrance to the Lower House, setting forth the danger and inutility of a general naturalization of foreign Protestants. A petition of the merchants and principal inhabitants of Bristol represented

*General naturalization-bill.*

that such a law would be prejudicial to the trade and commerce of this kingdom, by preventing many industrious artificers from procuring a sufficient support for themselves and their families, and of consequence increasing the rates of the poor: that the introduction of such a number of foreigners, instead of being a support to the present happy establishment, might endanger the very basis of our constitution: that it would greatly tend to the diminution of our manufactures, as many strangers would doubtless come and reside in England for a time, in order to learn the methods and management of our manufacturers and artificers; and, after having obtained this instruction, return to their native countries, where they would establish and carry on works of the same nature. The twentieth day of March being appointed for the third reading of the bill, it was postponed, in consequence of the unfortunate death of the Prince of Wales; and other petitions from different cities of the kingdom being mustered against it in the sequel, the ministry did not think proper to persist in any unpopular measure at such a delicate conjuncture; so the bill was no more brought upon the carpet. Divers other regulations, relating to civil policy as well as to the commerce of Great Britain, were propounded in the House of Commons; but these proposals proved abortive, either because they appeared crude and indigested in themselves, or the House could not obtain proper information touching the allegations they contained.

There were no other transactions in this session, except the concurrence of both Houses in stigmatizing a printed paper, entitled "Constitutional Queries, earnestly recommended to the serious Consideration of every true Briton;" and the steps taken by the Commons, in consequence of the commotions occasioned by the Westminster election. The above-mentioned paper, which had been conveyed by letter to the majority of both Houses, was communicated to the Lords in the month of January by the Duke of Marlborough, who moved for resolutions against it as a seditious libel, and that the concurrence of the Commons might be desired. A conference accordingly ensued, and both Houses concurred in voting the paper a false, malicious, scandalous, infamous, and seditious libel, containing the most false, audacious, and abominable calumnies and indignities upon his majesty, and the most

*[marginal note: Censure passed upon a paper entitled Constitutional Queries.]*

presumptuous and wicked insinuations that our laws, liberties, and properties, and the excellent constitution of this kingdom, were in danger under his majesty's legal, mild, and gracious government, with intent to instil groundless suspicions and jealousies into the minds of his majesty's good subjects, and to alienate their affections from his majesty and the royal family. It was therefore resolved by the Lords spiritual and temporal and Commons in Parliament assembled, that in abhorrence and detestation of such abominable and seditious practices, the paper should be burnt by the hands of the common hangman in the new Palace-yard of Westminster; and this sentence was executed accordingly. Then they presented an address to his majesty, desiring that the most effectual means might be taken for discovering the author, printer, or publisher, that he or they might be brought to condign punishment. Directions were given for this purpose; but without effect. Those concerned in writing, printing, and circulating the paper had acted with such caution that not one of them was ever discovered.

The proceedings of the Commons with respect to the election of a burgess for Westminster were attended with some extraordinary circumstances, which we shall now record for the edification of those who pique themselves on the privileges of a British subject. We have already observed that a majority appearing on the poll for Lord Trentham, the adherents of the other candidate, Sir George Vandeput, demanded a scrutiny, which was granted by the high-bailiff of Westminster, the returning officer. During this tedious investigation, which turned chiefly on the qualifications of voters, he acted with such address and seeming candour as gave entire satisfaction to both parties, till at length he determined in favour of Lord Trentham, whom he returned as duly elected. Those who styled themselves the independent electors did not acquiesce in this determination without clamour, reproach, menaces, and riot. They taxed Mr. Leigh, the high-bailiff, with partiality and injustice: they loudly affirmed, that ministerial influence had been used in the most scandalous manner; and, finally, joined Sir George Vandeput in a petition to the Lower House, complaining of an undue election and return of a member for the city of Westminster. The Commons, instead of inquiring into the merits of these petitions, ordered them to lie upon the table; and without any complaint from any person whatever, a motion was made that Leigh, the high-bailiff, should attend the House immediately, in order to make them acquainted with what he had done in pursuance of the directions he had formerly received from that House, touching the execution of the writ for electing a new member to represent the city of Westminster. As this motion had been preconcerted, Leigh was attending in the lobby, and immediately called into the House to be examined on this subject. Having, in the course of his examination, alleged that the election had been protracted by affected delays, he was asked by whom, and by what means; but before he could answer, the Earl of Egmont, interposing, objected to the question as improper, and moved for the order of the day. A debate immediately ensued, in which the impropriety of the question was demonstrated by Mr. Henley, afterwards lord-keeper, Dr. Lee, and some others, the most sensible and moderate members of the House; but they were opposed with great violence by Lord Viscount Corke, Henry Fox, Esq., Sir William Yonge, Colonel Lyttelton, and the weight of the ministry; so that the motion for the order of the day was carried in the negative, and the high-bailiff required to answer the question. Thus interrogated, he declared that he had been impeded in the scrutiny, and maltreated, by Mr. Crowle, who had acted as counsel for Sir George Vandeput, by the Honourable Alexander Murray, brother to Lord Elibank, and one Gibson, an upholsterer, who had been very active, zealous, and turbulent in his endeavours to promote the interest of Sir George Vandeput, or rather to thwart the pretensions of the other candidate, who was supposed to be countenanced by the ministry. These three persons, thus accused, were brought to the bar of the House, notwithstanding the strenuous remonstrances of several members, who opposed this method of proceeding as a species of oppression equally arbitrary and absurd. They observed, that, as no complaint had been preferred, they had no right to take cognizance of the affair: that if any undue influence had been used, it would naturally appear when the merits of the election should fall under their inquiry: that a complaint having been lodged already against the returning officer, it was their duty to investigate his conduct and punish him, if he should be found delinquent; but that nothing could be more flagrantly unjust, and apparently partial, than their neglecting the petitions of the other candidate and electors, and encouraging the high-bailiff, who stood charged with iniquity, to recriminate upon his accusers, that they might be disabled from giving evidence on the inquiry into the merits of the election. What difference is it to the subject, whether he is oppressed by an arbitrary prince, or by the despotic insolence of a ministerial majority? Mr. Crowle alleged, in his own vindication, that he had been employed as counsel by the electors of Westminster, and attended the scrutiny in that character; that after the high-bailiff had, in the course of the last session, received the order of the House to expedite the election, he hurried on the scrutiny with such precipitation as, he apprehended, was unjust, and prejudicial to his clients; that, in this apprehension, he (Mr. Crowle) insisted upon the high-bailiff's proceeding with more deliberation, and in so doing he thought he did his duty to his employers. Some evidence, being examined against him, declared he had not only protracted the scrutiny, but also spoken disrespectful words of the House of Commons: he was, therefore, reprimanded on his knees by the speaker, and discharged.

Mr. Murray being charged with having uttered some threatening and affronting expressions, the House adjourned the consideration of this affair for some days, at the expiration of which Mr. Murray was to be heard by his counsel; but, in the mean time, they ordered him to be taken into custody by the serjeant at arms attending the House. This step, however, was not taken without a warm opposition by some of the most sedate and intelligent members of the House, who considered it as a cruel act of oppression. They observed, that in cases of breach of privilege, no person complained of was ever taken into custody until after he had been fully heard in his defence; that this was literally prejudging the cause before it had been examined; and the oppression was the greater, as the alleged offence consisted entirely of words, of which no complaint or information had been made for above eight months after the supposed offence had been committed; and, even then, not till an accusation had been lodged against the informant, upon the trial of which accusation the persons informed against might very probably be the most material witnesses. They observed, that in one of the highest offences which can be committed by words, namely, that of denying the king's

*Mr. Murray sent prisoner to Newgate.*

right to the crown, or renouncing the Trinity, the information must be brought in three or four days after the words are spoken; the words must be proved to have been spoken maliciously, directly, and advisedly, and the prosecution must commence in three months after the information. These suggestions made no more impression than if they had been uttered in a desert. Those who were secure in their number asserted, that the House of Commons was not restricted by the forms of proceedings at common law; and that it was necessary to vindicate their own honour and dignity, by making examples of those who seemed to hold them in contempt. Mr. Murray was committed to the custody of the serjeant at arms, and found bail; and Gibson was sent prisoner to Newgate, from whence he was in a few days released, upon presenting a humble petition, professing his sorrow for having incurred the displeasure of the House, to the bar of which he was brought, and received a reprimand on his knees from the speaker. In the mean time divers witnesses, being examined before the House, declared, that Mr. Murray had been seen, about the time of the return of a member for Westminster, heading and exciting a tumult to acts of violence against the high-bailiff. The majority, therefore, after a long and warm debate, agreed, that for his dangerous and seditious practices, in violation and contempt of the privileges of the House, and of the freedom of elections, he should be committed close prisoner to Newgate. Then, in the close of another violent debate, they resolved, that he should be brought to the bar of the House, to receive that sentence on his knees. He accordingly appeared, and being directed by the speaker to kneel, refused to comply. He knew that he could not be discharged from Newgate during the session, without petitioning, acknowledging his offence, and making such concessions as he thought would imply a consciousness of guilt: he considered this whole transaction as an oppressive exertion of arbitrary power, and, being apprised of the extent of their authority, determined to bear the brunt of their indignation, rather than make submissions which he deemed beneath the dignity of his character. When he refused to humble himself, the whole House was in commotion; he was no sooner removed from the bar than they resolved, that his having in a most insolent and audacious manner refused to be on his knees at the bar of that House, in consequence of their former resolution, was a high and most dangerous contempt of the authority and privilege of the Commons: it was therefore ordered, that he should be committed close prisoner to Newgate, debarred the use of pen, ink, and paper; and that no person should have access to him without the leave of the House. Finally, a committee was appointed to consider what methods might be proper to be taken by them, in relation to this instance of contempt. Meanwhile the petitioners against the return made by the high-bailiff, perceiving the temper of the House, and the complexion of the majority, withdrew their petition; and the order which had passed for hearing the merits of the election was discharged. Mr. Murray being taken dangerously ill in Newgate, application was made to the Commons by some of his relations, that he might be removed to a more convenient situation; and his physician, being examined, gave it as his opinion that he was infected with the gaol distemper. Upon this representation the House agreed that the speaker should issue a warrant for removing him from Newgate to the custody of the serjeant at arms, but this favour he refused to accept, and expressed the warmest resentment against those relations who had applied to the Commons in his behalf. Thus he remained sequestered even from his own brother and sister, under the displeasure of the Commons of England, who condescended so far as to make resolutions touching the physician, apothecary, and nurse who attended this prisoner. But the prorogation of Parliament having put an end to their authority for that session, Mr. Murray was discharged of course, and conducted by the sheriffs from Newgate to his own house, in procession, with flags and streamers exhibiting the emblems of liberty.

In the month of June the session was closed with a speech from the throne, in which his majesty thanked both Houses for the zeal and affection they had manifested towards him and his government; and congratulated the Commons in particular, upon their firmness and prudence in reducing the interest of the national debt, a measure as agreeable to him as essential to the strength and welfare of the kingdom.°—The interior economy of Great

*Session closed. Style altered.*

° One of the most remarkable acts which passed in the course of this session was that for regulating the commencement of the year, and correcting the calendar, according to the Gregorian computation, which had been adopted by all other nations in Europe. By this new law it was decreed that the new year should begin on the first day of January, and that eleven intermediate nominal days, between the second and fourteenth days of September, 1752, should for that time be omitted, so that the day succeeding the second should be denominated the fourteenth of that month. By this establishment of the new

Britain produced within the circle of this year nothing else worthy of historical regard, except a series of enormous crimes, arising from the profligacy of individuals, which reflected disgrace upon the morals and polity of the nation. Rapine and robbery had domineered without intermission ever since the return of peace, which was attended with a reduction of the army and navy; but now crimes of a deeper dye seemed to lift up their heads in contempt of law and humanity.[d] Every day almost produced fresh instances of perjury, forgery, fraud, and circumvention; and the kingdom exhibited a most amazing jumble of virtue and vice, honour and infamy, compassion and obduracy, sentiment and brutality.

style, the equinoxes and solstice will happen nearly on the same nominal days on which they fell in the year 325, at the council of Nice; and the correspondence between the English merchants and those of foreign countries will be greatly facilitated with respect to the dates of letters and accounts.

[d] An indulgent parent was poisoned by his only daughter, on whom, besides other marks of tenderness and paternal affection, he had bestowed a liberal education, which greatly aggravated her guilt and ingratitude. Another young woman was concerned in the assassination of her own uncle, who had been her constant benefactor and sole guardian. A poor old woman, having, from the ignorance and superstition of her neighbours, incurred the suspicion of sorcery and witchcraft, was murdered in Hertfordshire by the populace, with all the wantonness of barbarity. Rape and murder were perpetrated upon an unfortunate woman in the neighbourhood of London, and an innocent man suffered death for this complicated outrage, while the real criminals assisted at his execution, heard him appeal to heaven for his innocence, and in the character of friends embraced him, while he stood on the brink of eternity.

# CHAPTER XXII.

DEATH OF THE QUEEN OF DENMARK AND PRINCE OF ORANGE.—MISUNDERSTANDING BETWEEN THE CZARINA AND KING OF PRUSSIA.—MEASURES FOR ELECTING A KING OF THE ROMANS.—DEATH OF THE KING OF SWEDEN.—SESSION OPENED.—ANIMOSITY OF THE COMMONS TOWARDS MR. MURRAY.—PROCEEDINGS UPON A PAMPHLET, ENTITLED THE CASE OF MR. MURRAY.—SUPPLIES GRANTED.—CIVIL REGULATIONS.—LAW RELATING TO THE FORFEITED ESTATES IN SCOTLAND.—NEW CONSOLIDATIONS OF FUNDS.—TWO PORTS OPENED FOR THE IMPORTATION OF IRISH WOOL.—THE KING SETS OUT FOR HANOVER.—AFFAIRS OF THE CONTINENT.—DISPUTE BETWEEN HANOVER AND PRUSSIA, CONCERNING EAST FRIEZELAND.—MISUNDERSTANDING BETWEEN THE COURTS OF LONDON AND BERLIN.—IMPROVEMENT OF POMERANIA.—TREATY WITH THE ELECTOR PALATINE.—SESSION OPENED.—SUPPLIES GRANTED.—GAME ACT.—ACT FOR PERFORMING QUARANTINE—AND FOR PREVENTING THE PLUNDERING OF SHIPWRECKED VESSELS.—BILL RELATING TO THE BOUNTY ON CORN EXPORTED.—TURKEY TRADE LAID OPEN.—NATURALIZATION OF THE JEWS.—MARRIAGE ACT.—DELIBERATIONS CONCERNING THE SUGAR COLONIES.—FATE OF THE REGISTER BILL.—SIR HANS SLOANE'S MUSEUM PURCHASED BY PARLIAMENT.—STORY OF ELIZABETH CANNING.—EXECUTION OF DR. CAMERON.—TUMULTS IN DIFFERENT PARTS OF THE KINGDOM.—DISTURBANCES IN FRANCE.—PROCEEDINGS OF THE DIET RELATIVE TO EAST FRIEZELAND.—TREATY BETWEEN THE COURT OF VIENNA AND THE DUKE OF MODENA.—CONFERENCES WITH RESPECT TO NOVA SCOTIA BROKEN UP.—DESCRIPTION OF NOVA SCOTIA.—DISPUTES CONCERNING ITS LIMITS.

THE royal family of England had sustained three severe shocks in the compass of a few months. Besides the loss of the Prince of Wales, which the nation lamented as irreparable, his majesty was deeply afflicted by the untimely death of his youngest daughter, the Queen of Denmark, who died at Copenhagen, on the nineteenth day of December, in the prime of youth. She was one of the most amiable princesses of the age in which she lived, whether we consider the virtues of her heart, or the accomplishments of her person; generous, mild, and tender-hearted; beloved even almost to adoration by her royal consort, to whom she had borne a prince and two princesses; and universally admired and revered by the subjects of his Danish majesty. Her death had been preceded about two months by that of her brother-in-law, the Prince of Orange, no less regretted by the natives of the United Provinces, for his candour, integrity, and hereditary love to his country. Though he had not distinguished himself by the lustre of a superior genius, he had been at great pains to cultivate his understanding, and study the true interest of that community, of which he was a member.

*1751. Death of the Queen of Denmark and Prince of Orange.*

He had always approved himself a good and zealous citizen, and, since his elevation to the stadtholdership, taken many salutary steps for the advantage of his country. Among other excellent schemes which he suggested, he left a noble plan with the States-General for restoring their commerce to its former lustre, and lived long enough to receive their warmest acknowledgments for this last proof of his prudence and patriotism. His son and daughter being both infants, the administration of the government devolved upon the princess, as governante during her son's minority; and as such she succeeded to all the power which her husband had enjoyed.

With respect to the affairs of the continent, the peace of the North seemed still as precarious as ever; for though the difference between Russia and Sweden had been compromised, the mutual disgust between the czarina and the King of Prussia had gained such accession from reciprocal insults, ill offices, and inflammatory declarations, that these two powers seemed to be on the eve of a rupture, and each was employed in making extraordinary preparations for war. The courts of Vienna and Great Britain, foreseeing that such a rupture would embroil the empire, and raise insurmountable obstructions to their favourite scheme of electing the Archduke Joseph King of the Romans, resolved to employ all their influence, in order to effect a reconciliation between the courts of Petersburgh and Berlin. His Prussian majesty had signified to the King of Great Britain, and the States-General, the situation in which he stood with the czarina, and solicited their interposition, that the difference might be amicably accommodated. At the same time he sent an envoy extraordinary to Versailles, to negotiate with the French king for a very considerable body of auxiliaries, in case he should be attacked. These circumstances induced the maritime powers, and the court of Vienna, to use their utmost endeavours for the prevention of a rupture; and accordingly they made remonstrances on this subject by their ministers at Petersburgh, proposing that the quarrel should be terminated without bloodshed, and all causes of animosity be buried in oblivion.

*Misunderstanding between the czarina and King of Prussia.*

*Measures for electing a king of the Romans.*

In the mean time, they eagerly prosecuted the design of the election; and the imperial minister at Berlin not only communicated to his Prussian majesty the sentiments of the King of England on this expedient, but even solicited his vote for the Archduke Joseph, when the election of a King of the Romans should be proposed in the electoral college. To this proposal he replied, that he was extremely well disposed to manifest his regard for their imperial majesties, and to give the most genuine proofs of it, even in the proposed election of a King of the Romans, considering the great merit of the present candidate, the Archduke Joseph: but he left it to the consideration of their imperial majesties, whether the election would not be a little premature, if transacted at a time when his imperial majesty was in the flower of his age; enjoying perfect health: and when all Europe, particularly the empire, was hushed in the bosom of tranquillity, so that no circumstance seemed to prognosticate the necessity of such an election; or of putting in execution the motives mentioned in the capitulation of the reigning emperor's election; especially as the examination of these motives belonged to the whole empire, and ought to precede the election by virtue of the eighth article of the treaty of Westphalia. He observed, that, in case of the emperor's death, Germany would find herself in a very disagreeable situation, under the government of a minor. For these reasons, he said, he could not help advising their imperial majesties to wait until the archduke should be of age, when his election might be carried on more conformably to the laws and constitutions of the empire, and more suitably to the majesty of the whole Germanic body. This reply he circulated among the electors, and in particular transmitted it to the King of Great Britain, desiring they would deliberate maturely on this subject, and confer together in a body, as well as in private, that they might proceed according to the ancient custom of the electoral college, and take such measures as should be judged expedient for the honour and advantage of the community. This circular letter was answered both by the King of England and the Elector of Bavaria, who demonstrated, that it was the privilege of the electoral college only, without any participation of the other princes of the empire, to elect a King of the Romans during the life of the emperor, in order to maintain the peace and preserve the liberties of Germany; and that the neglect of this wise precaution had produced bloody wars, and many fatal consequences to the empire. They observed, that nothing could more contribute to the establishment of the public tranquillity than this measure, so ardently desired by the majority of the German princes; and that, although the Archduke Joseph wanted a few years of being of age, and it might possibly happen that the reigning emperor should die during that prince's minority, yet it would be much less prejudicial to the empire to have a minor chief, than to see the succession altogether unsettled. His Prussian majesty received a declaration to the same purpose from the Elector of Mentz; and understanding that this prince, as archchancellor of the empire, intended to convoke an electoral diet, in order to propose the election of a King of the Romans, he wrote an elaborate letter to his electoral highness, explaining at more length his reasons for postponing the election. He quoted that sentence of the treaty of Westphalia which expressly declares, that the election of a King of the Romans shall be discussed and ordained by the common consent of the states of the empire; and, therefore, he could not conceive what right the electoral college had to arrogate this privilege to themselves, excluding the other states of the empire. He observed, that the imperial capitulations, which were the only laws of the empire that treated of this subject, mentioned only three cases in which it was lawful to proceed to such an election; namely, the emperor's leaving, and long absence from, Germany; his advanced age, or an indisposition, rendering him incapable of managing the reins of government; and any case of emergency in which the preservation of the empire's prosperity is interested. He affirmed, that none of these motives at present existed: that, in case the imperial crown should devolve to a minor, many mischiefs and disorders must ensue, as the constitutions of the empire have established no regulations nor regency in that event: that an election of this nature, carried on under the power, influence, and authority of the head of the empire, would strike at the fundamental privileges of the princes and states; consequently, in time overturn the constitution of the empire, which, from being an elective dignity, conferred by the free and independent suffrages of the electoral college and states of Germany, under certain capitulations, obliging the prince thus chosen to govern according to law, would become an hereditary succession, perpetuated in one family, which, of course, must be aggrandized to the prejudice of its co-estates and the ruin of the Germanic liberties. In a word, all Germany in general, and Ratisbon in particular, was filled with writings published on both sides: by the emperor and his adherents, to demonstrate that the election of a King of the Romans, during the life of the emperor, had often happened, and at this present time was necessary, and would be advantageous to the empire: while the King of Prussia and his friends laboured to prove that such an election, at the present juncture, would be ill-timed, irregular, and of dangerous consequence. Perhaps, if the truth was known, this enterprising prince had projected some great scheme, with the execution of which this proposed establishment would have interfered. Certain it is, he exerted himself with that spirit and perseverance which were peculiar to his character, to frustrate the intention of the courts of Vienna and London in this particular, and was assisted with all the intrigue of the French ministry. Their joint endeavours were so effectual, that the Elector of Cologn renounced his subsidiary treaty with the maritime powers, and once more threw himself into the arms of France. The Elector Palatine, being solicited by the empress-queen and his Britannic majesty to co-operate with their views, insisted, as a preliminary article, upon being indemnified by the court of Vienna for the ravages committed in his territories by the Austrian troops, during the course of the last war: the King of Poland, Elector of Saxony, made the same demand of the like indemnification, which was granted by the mediation of King George; and then he subscribed to a subsidy-treaty, obliging himself to furnish a body of six thousand auxiliaries, in case they should be required by the maritime powers; and to act as elector, in concert with the house of Austria, in every thing relating to the welfare of his country that should square with the fundamental laws of the empire. The courts of London and Vienna had this election so much at heart, that they sounded almost all the powers of Europe, to know how they stood affected towards the measure proposed. The King of Spain declined intermeddling in a domestic affair of the empire. The French king returned an ambiguous answer; from whence it was concluded, that nothing but opposition could be expected from that quarter. The Swedish monarch was rendered propitious to the project, by assurances that the house of Hesse-Cassel, of which he was the head, should be elevated into an electorate. They even endeavoured to soften his Prussian majesty, by consenting, at last, that the treaty of Dresden, confirming to him the possession of Silesia, should be guaranteed by the diet of the empire; a sanction which he now actually obtained, together with the ratification of his imperial majesty. Notwithstanding this indulgence, he still persisted in raising fresh objections to the favourite project, on pretence of concerting measures for preventing the inconveniences that might result from a minority; for regulating the capitulations to be agreed on with the King of the Romans, securing the freedom of future elections, and preserving the prerogatives and privileges of the Germanic body in all its members. In consequence of these obstacles, joined to the apostasy of the Elector of Cologn, the obstinacy of the Elector Palatine, and the approaching diet of Hungary, at which their imperial majesties were obliged personally to preside, the measures for the election were suspended till next summer, when his Britannic majesty was expected at Hanover, to put the finishing stroke to this great event in favour of the house of Austria.

Another disappointment, with respect to this election, the promoters of it sustained in the death of his Swedish majesty, who expired in a good old age, and was succeeded by Adolphus Frederick, Duke of Holstein Eutin, Bishop of Lubeck, upon whom the succession had been settled for some years, by the unanimous concurrence of the states of the kingdom. This prince ascended the throne of Sweden without the least disturbance; and, of his own accord, took an oath in full senate, that he would never attempt to introduce a despotic authority; but maintain their liberties with his blood, and govern his subjects in all respects according to the laws, and the form of government established in Sweden. This public act, which was communicated to all the foreign ministers, and particularly to the envoy from Petersburgh, met with such a favourable reception from the czarina, that she expressed her satisfaction in a public declaration; and the good understanding between the two courts was perfectly restored.

*Death of the King of Sweden.*

When the Parliament of England was opened, in the month of November, the king, in his speech from the throne, gave them to understand, that for the same purposes which suggested the treaty with the Elector of Bavaria, he had now, in conjunction with the States-General, concluded another with the King of Poland, Elector of Saxony. He told them, that the unfortunate death of the Prince of Orange had made no alteration in the state of affairs in Holland; and that he had received the strongest assurances from the states of their firm resolution to maintain the intimate union and friendship happily subsisting between his majesty and those ancient and natural allies of his crown. He exhorted both Houses to consider seriously of some effectual provisions, to suppress those audacious crimes of robbery and violence, grown so frequent about the capital, proceeding in a great measure from that profligate spirit of irreligion, idleness, gaming, and extravagance, which had of late extended itself in an uncommon degree, to the dishonour of the nation, and the great offence and prejudice of the sober and industrious part of the people. The paragraphs of this speech were, as usual, echoed back to the throne in addresses replete with expressions of loyalty, affection, and approbation. Opposition was by this time almost extinguished; and the proceedings of both Houses took place with such unanimity as was hardly ever known before this period in a British Parliament. The Commons, however, seem to have assembled with such sentiments as did no great honour to their temper and magnanimity. In a few days after the session opened, Lord Viscount C——e, a young nobleman, whose character entitled him to very little regard or influence among men of sense and probity, made a motion, that Mr. Murray, who had been so severely persecuted in the last session for refusing to humble himself on his knees before them, should be again committed close prisoner to Newgate for the same offence. This proposal, which supposed a power that the Commons had never before exercised, was sharply disputed by the Earl of Egmont, and others, who had not resigned all sense of moderation; but the majority adopted the measure with great eagerness, and the speaker was ordered to issue his warrant accordingly. Then the House resolved, that the said Alexander Murray should receive the sentence, for his now being committed close prisoner to his majesty's gaol of Newgate, at the bar of the House, upon his knees; and the serjeant at arms was commanded to take him into custody for this purpose. Their indignation, however, was eluded by the caution of the delinquent, who, having foreseen the effects of their resentment, had prudently retired to another country. They determined, nevertheless, to proceed against him as a person of some consequence in the commonwealth; for, being informed of his retreat, they condescended so far as to present an address to his majesty, desiring that his royal proclamation might be issued for apprehending the said Mr. Murray, promising a reward to him who should have the good fortune to apprehend this fugitive—a request with which his majesty most graciously complied.

Nor was this the only address presented to the king upon such an important subject. A pamphlet, entitled "The Case of the Hon. Alexander Murray, Esquire, in an Appeal to the People of Great Britain," was first stigmatized in a complaint to the House, and was afterwards produced, and read at the table. The piece was written with great acrimony, and abounded with severe animadversions, not only upon the conduct of the returning officer, but also on the proceedings of the Commons. The violent members immediately took fire, and the flame extended itself to the majority. Nay, the House unanimously resolved, that the pamphlet was an impudent, malicious, scandalous, and seditious libel, falsely and most injuriously reflecting upon and aspersing the proceedings of the House, tending to create misapprehensions in the minds of the people, to the great dishonour of the said House, and in violation of the privileges thereof. They furthermore presented an address to the king, desiring his majesty would be graciously pleased to give directions to his attorney-general to prosecute the authors or author, the printers or printer, and the publishers or publisher of the said scandalous libel, that they might be brought to condign punishment. Directions were accordingly given for this purpose, and a prosecution commenced against the publisher, who had some reason to be dismayed, considering the great weight of influence he was doomed to encounter—influence arising from a prosecution of the crown, instituted at the request, and founded on a vote, of the House of Commons. Nevertheless, when the cause was heard before the lord chief justice of England, a jury of free-born Englishmen, citizens of London, asserted their privilege of judging the law as well as the fact, and acquitted the defendant with a truly admirable spirit of independency. They considered the pamphlet as an appeal against oppression; and, convinced that the contents were true, they could not in conscience adjudge it a false libel, even though it had been so declared by one of the branches of the legislature.

The Commons, in regulating the supplies of the ensuing year, voted the continuation of eighteen thousand eight hundred and fifty-seven men for the land service, though not without some opposition from certain patriots, who, rather from a sense of duty than from any hope of influencing the majority, affirmed that sixteen thousand men in time of peace would answer all the ends proposed by a standing army. The number of seamen was fixed at ten thousand: large sums were granted to make up deficiencies, and fulfil the engagements of the crown with the Electors of Bavaria and Saxony, as well as for the maintenance of Nova Scotia and Georgia, and the castles on the coast of Guinea; and one hundred and twelve thousand one hundred and fifty-two pounds, three shillings, and three pence were voted, as a full compensation to the old royal African company for their exclusive charter and property, to be applied for the relief of their creditors.\* *Supplies granted.*

The laws enacted for the encouragement of traffic, and the regulation of civil polity, consisted in an act for licensing pawnbrokers, and for the more effectual preventing the receiving of stolen goods: another for preventing thefts and robberies, by which places of entertainment, dancing, and music in London, Westminster, and within twenty miles of the capital, were suppressed and prohibited, unless the proprietors of them could obtain licences from the justices of the peace, empowered for that purpose: a third for annexing the forfeited estates in Scotland unalienably in the crown, after having made satisfaction to the lawful creditors; establishing a method of leasing these estates, and applying the rents and profits of them for the better civilizing and improving the Highlands, and preventing future disorders in that part of the united kingdom. Nothing could be more salutary than the purposes of these *1752. Civil regulations.*

---

\* These expenses were defrayed by a continuation of the duties on malt, &c.; a land-tax at three shillings in the pound; a duty on licences, to be yearly paid by pawnbrokers and dealers in second-hand goods, within the bills of mortality; the sum of one million four hundred thousand pounds advanced by the Bank, according to a proposal made for that purpose; five hundred thousand pounds to be issued from the sinking-fund; a duty laid on gum senega; and the continuation of divers other occasional impositions. The grants for the year amounted to something less than four millions, and the provisions made for this expense exceeded it in the sum of two hundred seventy-one thousand twenty-four pounds, ten shillings, and sixpence halfpenny.

regulations. The suburbs of the metropolis abounded with an incredible number of public-houses, which continually resounded with the noise of riot and intemperance; they were the haunts of idleness, fraud, and rapine, and the seminaries of drunkenness, debauchery, extravagance, and every vice incident to human nature; yet the suppression of these receptables of infamy was attended with an inconvenience, which, in some cases, arose even to a degree of oppression. The justices, being vested by the legislature with the power of granting or refusing licences, were constituted, in effect, the arbiters on whose decision the fortunes and livelihood of many individuals absolutely depended. Many of those who exercised this species of magistracy within the bills of mortality were, to the reproach of government, men of profligate lives, needy, mean, ignorant, and rapacious, and often acted from the most scandalous principles of selfish avarice.

*Law relating to the forfeited estates in Scotland.* The law relating to the Highlands of Scotland was well calculated for promoting, among the inhabitants of that country, such a spirit of industry as might detach them from their dangerous connexions, and gradually supersede that military genius which had been so productive of danger and alarm to the southern parts of Great Britain. The king, by this act, was empowered to appoint commissioners for managing the forfeited estates; who were enabled to grant leases of small farms, not above twenty pounds a-year, to individuals, who should take an oath to government to reside upon and cultivate the lands thus let. It was also provided, that no lease should be granted for a longer term than twenty-one years; and that the lessees should not pay above three-fourths of the annual value. Although these forfeited estates were generally encumbered with claims beyond their real value, and the act directed that they should be disposed of by public sale; yet, as they lay in the most disaffected parts of the Highlands, it was thought necessary that they should remain in the possession of the crown, because, in case of their being publicly sold, they might be purchased in trust for the families of the persons by whom they were forfeited, and thus the spirit of disaffection would still survive. A valuation, therefore, was made by the court of session in Scotland, at the joint suit of the crown and the creditors; and the value being ascertained, the just claimants were paid out of the next aids granted by parliament. The bill met with considerable opposition in the House of Peers from the Duke of Bedford and the Earl of Bath, who probably foresaw that the good effects of this scheme, so laudable in itself, would be frustrated in the execution; and that the act, instead of answering the purposes for which it was intended, would serve only as a job to gratify the rapacious retainers to the government, and their emissaries, in that country. After a warm debate, however, it was adopted by a great majority, and obtained the royal assent.

A third law related to certain articles of the national debt, which was now converted into several joint stocks of annuities, transferable at the bank of England, to be charged on the sinking-fund. A great number of different funds for annuities, established at different times, and by different acts, subsisted at this period, so that it was necessary to keep many different accounts, which could not be regulated without considerable trouble and expense, for the removal of which the bill was calculated. *New consolidations of funds.*

In consequence of petitions from the woollen manufacturers of Westmoreland and Yorkshire, two bills were brought in, and passed through both Houses, by which the ports of Lancaster and Great Yarmouth were opened for the importation of wool and woollen yarn from Ireland; but why this privilege was not extended to all the frequented ports of the kingdom it is not easy to conceive, without supposing a little national jealousy on one hand, and a great deal of grievous restraint on the other. *Two ports opened for the importation of Irish wool.* Over and above these new laws, some unsuccessful endeavours were used in behalf of commerce and police. A bill was offered for laying further restrictions on pawnbrokers and brokers, that they might no longer suck the blood of the poor, and act as the accessaries of theft and robbery, which was canvassed, debated, and made its way through the Lower House; but the Lords rejected it as a crude scheme, which they could not amend, because it was a money bill, not cognizable by their House, without engaging in a dispute with the Commons. Another bill was prepared, for giving power to change the punishment of felony, in certain cases, to confinement and hard labour in dock-yards or garrisons. It was the opinion of many who wished well to their country, and were properly qualified to prosecute such inquiries, that the practice of consigning such a number of wretches to the hands of the executioner, served only, by its frequency, to defeat the purpose of the law, in robbing death of all its terror, and the public of many subjects, who might, notwithstanding their delinquency, be in some measure rendered useful to society. Such was the motive that influenced the promoters of this bill; by which it was proposed, in imitation of that economy practised in other countries, to confine felons convicted under certain circumstances to hard labour upon the public works of the kingdom. The scheme was adopted by the Lower House, but rejected by the Lords, who seemed apprehensive of its bringing such discredit upon his majesty's dock-yards, as would discourage persons who valued their reputation from engaging in such employment. Of still greater importance to the nation was the next measure proposed, in a bill for making the militia of England more useful, presented by Mr. Thornton, a gentleman of Yorkshire, who had distinguished himself by his loyalty and patriotism. It was canvassed in a committee of the whole House, and underwent divers amendments; but miscarried, through the aversion of the ministry to any project tending to remove or lessen the necessity of maintaining a standing army. A considerable number of petitions for different regulations, in respect to commerce and convenience of traffic, were presented, considered, and left upon the table. A remonstrance from the prisoners confined in the gaol of the King's Bench, complaining of their miserable situation, arising from want of room and other conveniences, being taken into consideration by a committee, among other evidences, they examined that remarkable personage who had signalized himself in different parts of Christendom, under the name of Theodore, King of Corsica. Though formerly countenanced and even treated as a sovereign prince by the British ministry, he was now reduced to the forlorn condition of a confined debtor; and, to the reproach of this kingdom, died in prison, surrounded with all the misery of indigence, and overwhelmed with the infirmities of old age. But the most remarkable circumstance of the parliamentary transactions that distinguished this session was a motion made in both Houses for an address to the King, beseeching his majesty, that in time of public tranquillity he would be graciously pleased to avoid entering into subsidiary treaties with foreign princes, which are so burdensome to this nation. This extraordinary

proposal was made and strenuously urged by the Duke of
B—, and a vehement debate ensued, in which the Earls
of G—, S—, and H—, opposed it with an exertion of
superior abilities, and the question, being put, was carried
in the negative without a division. The same fate attended
it in the House of Commons, where it was introduced by
Lord H—y, and supported by some distinguished orators.
The session ended in the latter end of March, when his
majesty, having given his assent to ninety-five public and
private bills, harangued both Houses, and prorogued the
Parliament.[b]

Immediately after the prorogation the king appointed a
regency, and set out for Hanover, in order to com-  *The king*
plete the great scheme he had projected for electing  *sets out for*
a King of the Romans. Great Britain, in the mean  *Hanover.*
time, produced no event of importance, nor any transaction
that deserves historical mention, except the ratification of
two treaties of peace and commerce with the states of Tripoli
and Tunis on the coast of Barbary, concluded by the British
consuls in those cities, under the influence and auspices of an
English squadron, commanded by Commodore Keppel, son to
the Earl of Albemarle. The tide of luxury still flowed with
an impetuous current, bearing down all the mounds of temperance and decorum; while fraud and profligacy struck out
new channels, through which they eluded the restrictions of
the law, and all the vigilance of civil policy. New arts of
deception were invented, in order to ensnare and ruin the
unwary; and some infamous practices in the way of commerce were countenanced by persons of rank and importance
in the commonwealth. A certain member of Parliament
was obliged to withdraw himself from his country, in consequence of a discovery, by which it appeared that he had
contrived and executed schemes for destroying his own ships
at sea, with a view to defraud the insurers.

In the course of this year the affairs of the continent did
not undergo any material alteration. In France,  *Affairs of*
the religious dispute concerning the doctrine of  *the conti-*
Jansenius still subsisted between the clergy and the  *nent.*
Parliament; and seemed to acquire additional fury from the

---

[b] Among the proceedings of this session, it may not be improper to mention a new act
for the prevention of murders, which had been shockingly frequent of late, importing,
that every criminal convicted of this horrid crime should be executed in one day after his
sentence, and his body delivered to the surgeons for dissection—an expedient which had
been found productive of very salutary consequences.

violence of the Archbishop of Paris, a haughty, turbulent prelate, whose pride and bigotry were sufficient to embroil one half of Christendom. The northern powers enjoyed a perfect tranquillity: the States-General of the United Provinces were engrossed by plans of national economy. Spain was intent upon extending her commerce, bringing her manufactures to perfection, and repressing the insolence of the Barbary corsairs. His Portuguese majesty endeavoured, by certain peremptory precautions, to check the exportation of gold coin from his dominions; and insisted upon inspecting the books of the British merchants settled at Lisbon; but they refused to comply with this demand, which was contrary to a treaty subsisting between the two crowns; and he thought proper to acquiesce in their refusal. He was much better employed, in obtaining from the pope an abolition of the annual procession called the *Auto da fe*, one of the most horrid triumphs of spiritual tyranny. The peace of Italy was secured by an offensive treaty concluded at Madrid between the emperor, his Catholic majesty, the King of the Two Sicilies, and the Duke of Parma; to which treaty the King of Sardinia afterwards acceded.

With respect to the great scheme of electing the Archduke Joseph King of the Romans, fresh objections seemed to rise from different quarters. The good understanding between the courts of Berlin and Hanover received an additional shock, from a dispute concerning the property of East Friezeland, which his Prussian majesty had secured as heir to the last possessor. His Britannic majesty, as Elector of Hanover, having pretensions to the same inheritance, his minister delivered a memorial to the diet of the empire, assembled at Ratisbon, demanding that the King of Prussia, as Elector of Brandenburgh, should be referred to the decision of the Aulic council, in regard to his claim to the estates of East Friezeland; but the king, being already in possession, refused to submit his right to the determination of that or any other tribunal; and when the diet presumed to deliberate on this affair, his envoy entered a strong protest against their proceedings. At the same time he presented the other ministers with a memorial, tending to refute the Elector of Hanover's pretensions to the principality in question.

*Dispute between Hanover and Prussia, concerning East Friezeland.*

At this juncture his Prussian majesty made no scruple of expressing his resentment against the court of London, which he seemed to consider as an officious cabal, that had no right to intermeddle in the affairs of Germany. His resident at London complained to the British ministry, that divers ships, sailing under the Prussian flag, had been stopped at sea, and even seized, by English cruisers; and that his subjects had been ill treated and oppressed: he therefore demanded reparation in a peremptory tone; and in the mean time discontinued the payment of the Silesian loan, which he had charged himself with by an article in the treaty of Breslau. This was a sum of money amounting to two hundred and fifty thousand pounds, which the Emperor Charles VI., father of the reigning empress, had borrowed of the subjects of Great Britain, on condition of paying an interest of six per cent. and mortgaging the silver-mines of Silesia for the repayment of the principal. These devolved to the King of Prussia with this incumbrance, and he continued to pay the interest punctually till this juncture, when the payment was stopped; and he published a paper, entitled "An Exposition of the Motives which influenced his Conduct on this Occasion." In his memorial to the ministry of Great Britain he alleged, that eighteen Prussian ships, and thirty-three neutral vessels, in which the subjects of Prussia were concerned, had been unjustly seized by English privateers: his account of damages amounted to a very considerable sum; and he demanded, in the most dogmatic terms, that the affair should be finally discussed in the term of three months from the date of his remonstrance. The exposition and memorial were subjected to the examination of the ablest civilians in England, who refuted every article of the charge with equal precision and perspicuity. They proved, that captures by sea fell properly under the cognizance of those powers under whose jurisdiction the seizures were made; and, therefore, his Prussian majesty could not, consistent with the laws of nations, determine these disputes in his own tribunals. They demonstrated, by undoubted evidence, the falsity of many facts alleged in the memorial, as well as the fairness of the proceedings by which some few of the Prussian vessels had been condemned; and made it appear, that no insult or injury had been offered to the subjects of Prussia. Finally, they observed, that the Silesian loan was a private transaction of such a nature, that, even if a war had happened between the Emperor Charles VI. and his Britannic majesty, this must have been held

*Misunderstanding between the courts of London and Berlin.*

sacred and inviolable: that when the empress-queen ceded Silesia to the King of Prussia, this monarch charged himself with the repayment of the loan, which, being a private debt and transferable, was now diffused into different countries, and become the property of many others besides the subjects of Great Britain. They wound up their chain of reasoning by observing, that, according to agreement with the emperor, the whole of this loan should have been repaid in the year one thousand seven hundred and forty-five; whereas the complaints specified in the Prussian memorial were founded on facts posterior to that period. Whether his Prussian majesty was convinced by these reasons, and desisted from principle, or thought proper to give up his claim upon other political considerations; certain it is, he no longer insisted upon satisfaction, but ordered the payments of the Silesian loan to be continued without further interruption: a report, indeed, was circulated, that advantage had been taken of the demur by a certain prince, who employed his agents to buy up great part of the loan at a considerable discount.

How much soever the King of Prussia may be the subject of censure on this occasion, it must be allowed that, with regard to his own subjects, he acted as a wise legislator, and the father of his country. He peopled the deserts of Pomerania, by encouraging with royal bounties a great number of industrious emigrants to settle in that province; the face of which, in a very few years, underwent the most agreeable alterations. Above sixty new villages arose amidst a barren waste, and every part of the country exhibited marks of successful cultivation. Those solitary and desolate plains, where no human footsteps had for many ages been seen, were now converted into fields of corn. The farms were regularly parcelled out; the houses multiplied, and teemed with population: the happy peasants, sheltered in a peculiar manner under their king's protection, sowed their grounds in peace, and reaped their harvests in security. The same care and indulgence were extended to the unpeopled parts of other provinces within the Prussian dominions; and extraordinary encouragement was granted to all French Protestants who should come and settle under the government of this political sage.

*Improvement of Pomerania.*

The courts of Vienna and Hanover still employed their chief attention upon the scheme of electing a King of the Romans; and the Elector of Mentz, influenced by the majority of the college, had convoked an electoral diet for that purpose; but strong protests against this convocation were entered by the Electors of Cologn and Palatine, insomuch that it was thought expedient to conciliate this last, by taking some steps in his favour, with respect to the satisfaction he demanded from the empress-queen and his Britannic majesty. His claim upon the court of Vienna amounted to three millions of florins, by way of indemnification for the losses he had sustained during the war. He demanded of the King of England twenty thousand pounds sterling, for provision and forage furnished to the British troops while they acted on the Maine; and the like sum for the like purposes from the States-General of the United Provinces. The empress-queen could not help remonstrating against this demand as exorbitant in itself, and the more unreasonable, as the Elector Palatine, at the death of her father, had openly declared against the Pragmatic Sanction, which he had guaranteed in the most solemn manner: she, therefore, observed, that the damage he had sustained, in consequence of that declaration, ought to be considered as the common fate of war. These reasons, though conclusive and irrefragable in the usual way of arguing, made no impression upon the Palatine, who perfectly well understood his own importance, and was determined to seize this opportunity of turning it to the best advantage. The court of Vienna, and the maritime powers, finding him thus obstinately attached to his own interest, resolved to bring him over to their views at any rate, and commenced a negotiation with him, which produced a formal treaty. By this convention his demands in money were fixed at twelve hundred thousand Dutch florins, to be paid at three instalments, five hundred thousand by the empress-queen, and the remaining seven hundred thousand by the King of Great Britain and the States-General, according to the proportion established in former treaties. The privilege of *Non appellendo* for the duchy of Deuxponts was confirmed to his electoral highness, together with some other rights and pretensions, in consideration of his concurring with the other electors in the choice of a King of the Romans, to be elected according to the customs prescribed by the laws and constitutions of the empire. He likewise engaged to join them in settling the articles of the capitulation with the King of the Romans, emperor *in futuro*. Yet, even after the concurrence of this prince was secured, the purposed election proved abortive, from the strong objections that were started, and the strenuous opposition which was made by his Prussian majesty, who perhaps aspired in secret at the imperial dignity, which the empress-queen took all this pains to perpetuate in her own family.

<small>1753. Session opened.</small> The King of Great Britain, returning from the continent, opened the session of Parliament on the eleventh day of January with a speech, implying, that all his views and negotiations had been calculated and directed to preserve and secure the duration of the general peace, so agreeable and necessary to the welfare of all Europe: that he had the satisfaction to be assured of a good disposition in all the powers that were his allies, to adhere to the same salutary object. He exhorted them to continue their attention to the reduction of the national debt, the augmentation of the sinking-fund, and the improvement of the public revenue. He recommended to their serious consideration what further laws and regulations might be necessary for suppressing those crimes and disorders, of which the public had so justly complained; and concluded with an assurance, that his hearty concurrence and endeavours should never be wanting in any measure that might promote their welfare and prosperity. The addresses in answer to this speech were couched in the usual form of implicit approbation; but that of the Commons did not pass without question. The Earl of E—— took exceptions to one paragraph, in which they acknowledged his majesty's wisdom, as well as goodness, in pursuing such measures as must contribute to maintain and render permanent the general tranquillity of Europe; and declared their satisfaction at the assurances his majesty had received from his allies, that they were all attached to the same salutary object. His lordship expatiated on the absurdity of these compliments at such a juncture, when the peace of Europe was so precarious, and the English nation had so much cause of complaint and dissatisfaction. He was seconded by some other individuals, who declaimed with great vivacity against continental connexions; and endeavoured to expose the weakness and folly of the whole system of foreign measures which our ministry had lately pursued. It must be owned, indeed, that they might have chosen a better opportunity to compliment their sovereign on the permanency of the peace than at this juncture, when they must have seen themselves on the very

brink of a new rupture with the most formidable power in Europe. But the truth is, these addresses to the throne had been long considered as compliments of course, implying no more than a respectful attachment to their sovereign; accordingly, both Houses agreed to their respective addresses without division. The two grand committees of supply and of ways and means being established, the business of the House was transacted without much altercation; and the people had great reason to be satisfied with their moderate proceedings. Ten thousand seamen, and the usual number of land forces, were retained for the service of the ensuing year. They provided for the maintenance of the new colony in Nova Scotia, the civil establishment of Georgia, the support of the castles on the coast of Guinea, and the erection of a new fort at Anamaboa, where the French had attempted to make a settlement; and they enabled his majesty to fulfil his engagements with the King of Poland and the Elector of Bavaria.

The supplies, including grants for formerd eficiencies and services, for which no provision had been made in the course of the last year, did not exceed two millions one hundred thirty-two thousand seven hundred and seven pounds, seventeen shillings, and two-pence halfpenny: in order to defray which expense they assigned the duty on malt, &c., the land-tax at two shillings in the pound, the surplus of certain funds in the exchequer, and the sum of four hundred and twenty thousand pounds out of the sinking-fund; so that the exceedings amounted to near three hundred thousand pounds.* As for the national debt, it now stood at the enormous sum of seventy-four millions three hundred sixty-eight thousand four hundred and fifty-one pounds, fifteen shillings, and one penny; and the sinking-fund produced one million seven hundred thirty-five thousand five hundred and twenty-nine pounds, six shillings, and ten-pence farthing. *Supplies granted.*

One of the first measures brought upon the carpet, in the course of this session, was an act containing regulations for the better preservation of the game, of which so great havoc had been made by poachers, and other *Game act.*

---

* Several duties on salt, as well as on red and white herrings delivered out for home consumption, were rendered perpetual, though subject to be redeemed by Parliament; and it was provided, that the debt contracted upon these duties being discharged, all the after produce of them should become part of the sinking-fund.

persons unqualified to enjoy that diversion, that the total extirpation of it was apprehended.

The next step taken by the Commons was an affair of much greater consequence to the community, being a bill for obliging ships the more effectually to perform quarantine, in order to prevent the plague from being imported from foreign countries into Great Britain. For this purpose it was ordained, that if this dreadful visitation should appear in any ship to the northward of Cape Finisterre, the master or commander should immediately proceed to the harbour of New Grimsby, in one of the islands of Scilly, and there communicate the discovery to some officer of the customs, who should, with the first opportunity, transmit this intelligence to another custom-house officer in the nearest port of England, to be by him forwarded to one of his majesty's principal secretaries of state. In the mean time the ship should remain at the said island, and not an individual presume to go ashore until his majesty's pleasure should be known. It was also provided, that in case the master of a ship thus infected should not be able to make the islands of Scilly, or be forced up either channel by violent winds, he should not enter any frequented harbour; but remain in some open road, until he could receive orders from his majesty, or the privy council: that during this interval, he should avoid all intercourse with the shore, or any person or vessel whatsoever, on pain of being deemed guilty of felony, and suffering death without benefit of clergy.

*Act for performing quarantine.*

In order the more effectually to repress the barbarous practice of plundering ships which have the misfortune to suffer shipwreck—a practice which prevailed upon many different parts of the British coast, to the disgrace of the nation, and the scandal of human nature—a bill was prepared, containing clauses to enforce the laws against such savage delinquents, who prowl along the shore, like hungry wolves, in hope of preying upon their fellow-creatures; and certain provisions for the relief of the unhappy sufferers.[d] When the mutiny-

*Act for preventing the plundering of shipwrecked vessels.*

---

[d] By the new law, the clerk of the peace in the county where the crime shall be committed is obliged, upon receiving proper information, to prosecute the offenders at the expense of the county. It was likewise proposed, that in case no prosecution of this nature should be commenced within a certain limited time after the information should have been legally given, in that case the county might be sued by the person who had sustained the damage, and obliged to indemnify him for his loss; but this clause was

bill fell under deliberation, the Earl of Egmont proposed a new clause for empowering and requiring regimental courts-martial to examine witnesses upon oath in all their trials. The proposal occasioned a debate, in which the ministry were pretty equally divided; but the clause was disapproved by the majority, and this annual bill was enacted into a law without any alteration.

The next bill was framed in consequence of divers petitions presented by the exporters of corn, who complained that the bounties were not paid, and prayed that the House would make proper provision for that purpose. A bill was accordingly brought in, importing, that interest after the rate of three per cent. should be allowed upon every debenture for the bounty on the exportation of corn, payable by the receiver-general or cashier of the customs, until the principal could be discharged out of such customs or duties as are appropriated for the payment of this bounty. This premium on the exportation of corn ought not to be granted, except when the lowness of the market price in Great Britain proves that there is a superabundance in the kingdom; otherwise the exporter will find his account in depriving our own labourers of their bread, in order to supply our rivals at an easier rate: for example, suppose wheat in England should sell at twenty shillings a quarter, the merchant might export it to France, and afford it to the people of that kingdom for eighteen shillings, because the bounty on exportation would, even at that rate, afford him a considerable advantage.

*Bill relating to the bounty on corn exported.*

A great number of merchants having presented petitions from different parts of the kingdom, representing that the trade of Turkey was greatly decreased, ascribing this diminution to the exclusive charter enjoyed by a monopoly, and praying that the trade might be laid open to all his majesty's subjects, one of the members for Liverpool moved for leave to bring in a bill for this purpose. Such a measure had been twice before proposed without success; but now it was adopted without opposition. A bill was immediately introduced; and, notwithstanding all the interest and efforts of the Turkey company, who petitioned the House against it, and were heard by their counsel, it passed through both Houses, and received the

*Turkey trade laid open.*

rejected by the majority; and the bill, having made its way through both Houses, received the royal assent.

royal sanction. By this regulation any British subject may obtain the freedom of the Turkey company, by paying or rendering a fine of twenty pounds; and all the members are secured from the tyranny of oppressive by-laws, contrived by any monopolizing cabal.*

But this session was chiefly distinguished by an act for naturalizing Jews, and a bill for the better preventing clandestine marriages. The first of these, which passed without much opposition in the House of Lords, from which it descended to the Commons, was entitled "An Act to permit Persons professing the Jewish Religion to be naturalized by Parliament, and for other Purposes therein mentioned." It was supported by some petitions of merchants and manufacturers, who, upon examination, appeared to be Jews, or their dependents; and countenanced by the ministry, who thought they foresaw, in the consequences of such naturalization, a great accession to the monied interest, and a considerable increase of their own influence among the individuals of that community. They boldly affirmed, that such a law would greatly conduce to the advantage of the nation; that it would encourage persons of wealth to remove with their effects from foreign parts into Great Britain, increase the commerce and the credit of the kingdom, and set a laudable example of industry, temperance, and frugality. Such, however, were not the sentiments of the lord mayor, aldermen, and commons of the city of London in common council assembled, who, in a petition to Parliament, expressed their apprehension that the bill, if passed into a law, would tend greatly to the dishonour of the Christian religion, endanger the excellent constitution, and be highly prejudicial to the interest and trade of the kingdom in general, and of the city of London in particular. Another petition to the same purpose was next day presented to the House, subscribed by merchants and traders of the city of London; who, among other allegations, observed, that the consequences of such a naturalization would greatly affect their trade

---

* Several other bills were passed—one for regulating the number of public-houses, and the more easy conviction of persons selling ale and strong liquors without a licence; an act which empowered the justices of peace to tyrannize over their fellow-subjects—a second, enabling the magistrates of Edinburgh to improve, enlarge, and adorn the avenues and streets of that city, according to a concerted plan, to be executed by voluntary subscription—a third, allowing the exportation of wool and woollen yarn from Ireland into any port of Great Britain—and a fourth, prescribing the breadth of the wheels belonging to heavy carriages, that the high roads of the kingdom might be the better preserved.

and commerce with foreign nations, particularly with Spain and Portugal. Counsel was heard, evidence examined, and the bill produced violent debates, in which there seemed to be more passion than patriotism, more declamation than argument. The adversaries of the bill affirmed, that such a naturalization would deluge the kingdom with brokers, usurers, and beggars; that the rich Jews, under the shadow of this indulgence, would purchase lands, and even advowsons; so as not only to acquire an interest in the legislature, but also to influence the constitution of the church of Christ, to which they were the inveterate and professed enemies: that the lower class of that nation, when thus admitted to the right of denizens, would interfere with the industrious natives who earn their livelihood by their labour; and by dint of the most parsimonious frugality, to which the English are strangers, work at an under price; so as not only to share, but even in a manner to exclude them from all employment: that such an adoption of vagrant Jews into the community, from all parts of the world, would rob the real subjects of their birthright, disgrace the character of the nation, expose themselves to the most dishonourable participation and intrusion, endanger the constitution both in church and state, and be an indelible reproach upon the established religion of the country. Some of these orators seemed transported even to a degree of enthusiasm. They prognosticated that the Jews would multiply so much in number, engross such wealth, and acquire so great power and influence in Great Britain, that their persons would be revered, their customs imitated, and Judaism become the fashionable religion of the English. Finally, they affirmed that such an act was directly flying in the face of the prophecy, which declares, that the Jews shall be a scattered people, without country or fixed habitation, until they shall be converted from their infidelity, and gathered together in the land of their forefathers. These arguments and apprehensions, which were in reality frivolous and chimerical, being industriously circulated among the vulgar, naturally prejudiced against the Jewish people, excited such a ferment throughout the nation, as ought to have deterred the ministry from the prosecution of such an unpopular measure; which, however, they had courage enough to maintain against all opposition. The bill passed the ordeal of both Houses, and his majesty vouchsafed the royal sanction to this law in favour of the Hebrew nation. The truth is, it might have increased the wealth, and extended the commerce, of Great Britain, had it been agreeable to the people; and as the naturalized Jews would still have been excluded from all civil and military offices, as well as from other privileges enjoyed by their Christian brethren, in all probability they would have gradually forsaken their own unprofitable and obstinate infidelity, opened their eyes to the shining truths of the gospel, and joined their fellow-subjects in embracing the doctrines of Christianity. But no ministry ought to risk an experiment, how plausible soever it might be, if they find it, as this was, an object of the people's unconquerable aversion. What rendered this unpopular measure the more impolitic, was the unseasonable juncture at which it was carried into execution, that is, at the eve of a general election for a new Parliament, when a minister ought carefully to avoid every step which may give umbrage to the body of the people. The Earl of Eg——t, who argued against the bill with equal power and vivacity, in describing the effect it might have upon that occasion, "I am amazed (said he) that this consideration makes no impression. When that day, which is not far off, shall arrive, I shall not fear to set my foot upon any ground of election in the kingdom, in opposition to any one man among you, or any new Christian, who has voted or appeared in favour of this naturalization."

Another bill, transmitted from the Upper House, met with a reception equally unfavourable among the Commons, though it was sustained on the shoulders of the majority, and thus forced its way to the throne, where it obtained the royal approbation. The practice of solemnizing clandestine marriages, so prejudicial to the peace of families, and so often productive of misery to the parties themselves thus united, was an evil that prevailed to such a degree as claimed the attention of the legislature. The sons and daughters of great and opulent families, before they had acquired knowledge and experience, or attained to the years of discretion, were every day seduced in their affections, and inveigled into matches big with infamy and ruin; and these were greatly facilitated by the opportunities that occurred of being united instantaneously by the ceremony of marriage, in the first transport of passion, before the destined victim had time to cool or deliberate on the subject. For this pernicious purpose, there was a band of profligate miscreants, the refuse of the clergy, dead to every sentiment of virtue, abandoned to all sense of decency and decorum, for the most part prisoners for debt or delinquency, and indeed the very outcasts of human society, who hovered about the verge of the Fleet-prison to intercept customers, plying like porters for employment, and performed the ceremony of marriage without licence or question, in cellars, garrets, or alehouses, to the scandal of religion, and the disgrace of that order which they professed. The ease with which this ecclesiastical sanction was obtained, and the vicious disposition of those wretches, open to the practices of fraud and corruption, were productive of polygamy, indigence, conjugal infidelity, prostitution, and every curse that could embitter the married state. A remarkable case of this nature having fallen under the cognizance of the Peers, in an appeal from an inferior tribunal, that House ordered the judges to prepare a new bill for preventing such abuses; and one was accordingly framed, under the auspices of Lord Hardwicke, at that time Lord High Chancellor of England. In order to anticipate the bad effects of clandestine marriages, this new statute enacted, that the banns should be regularly published, three successive Sundays, in the church of the parish where the parties dwell: that no licence should be granted to marry in any place where one of the parties has not dwelt at least a month, except a special licence by the archbishop: that if any marriage should be solemnized in any other place than a church or a chapel, without a special licence; or in a public chapel, without having published the banns, or obtained a licence of some person properly qualified, the marriage should be void, and the person who solemnized it transported for seven years: that marriages, by licence, of parties under age, without consent of parent or guardian should be null and void, unless the party under age be a widow, and the parent refusing consent a widow married again: that when the consent of a mother or guardian is refused from caprice, or such parent or guardian be *non compos mentis*, or beyond sea, the minor should have recourse for relief to the Court of Chancery: that no suit should be commenced to compel a celebration of marriage, upon pretence of any contract: that all marriages should be solemnized before two witnesses, and an entry be made in a book kept for that purpose, whether it was by banns or licence, whether either of the parties was under age, or the marriage celebrated with the consent of parent or guardian; and this entry to be signed by the minister, the parties, and the witnesses: that a false licence or certificate, or destroying register books, should be deemed felony, either in principal or accessary, and punished with death. The bill, when first considered in the Lower House, gave rise to a variety of debates; in which the members appeared to be divided rather according to their real sentiments, than by the rules of any political distinction; for some principal servants of the government freely differed in opinion from the minister, who countenanced the bill; while, on the other hand, he was, on this occasion, supported by certain chiefs of the opposition, and the disputes were maintained with extraordinary eagerness and warmth. The principal objections imported, that such restrictions on marriage would damp the spirit of love and propagation; promote mercenary matches, to the ruin of domestic happiness, as well as to the prejudice of posterity and population; impede the circulation of property, by preserving the wealth of the kingdom among a kind of aristocracy of opulent families, who would always intermarry within their own pale; subject the poor to many inconveniences and extraordinary expense, from the nature of the forms to be observed; and throw an additional power into the hands of the chancellor. They affirmed, that no human power had a right to dissolve a vow solemnly made in the sight of heaven; and that, in proportion as the bill prevented clandestine marriages, it would encourage fornication and debauchery, insomuch as the parties restrained from indulging their mutual passions in an honourable manner, would be tempted to gratify them by stealth, at the hazard of their reputation. In a word, they foresaw a great number of evils in the train of this bill, which have not yet been realized. On the other side, its advocates endeavoured to refute these arguments, and some of them spoke with great strength and precision. The bill underwent a great number of alterations and amendments; which were not effected without violent contest and altercation. At length, however, it was floated through both Houses on the tide of a great majority, and steered into the safe harbour of royal approbation. Certain it is, the abuse of clandestine marriage might have been removed upon much easier terms than those imposed upon the subject by this bill, which, after all, hath been found ineffectual, as it may be easily eluded by a short voyage to the continent, or a moderate journey to North Britain, where the indissoluble knot may be tied without scruple or interruption.

Over and above these new statutes, there were some other subjects which occasionally employed the attention of the Commons; such as the state of the British sugar-colonies, which was considered, in consequence of petitions presented by the sugar-refiners and grocers of London, Westminster, and Bristol, complaining of the exorbitant price demanded and given for sugars imported from Jamaica, desiring that the proprietors of land in Jamaica might be obliged to cultivate greater quantities of ground for raising sugar-canes, or that they (the petitioners) might have leave to import muscovado sugars from other countries, when the price of those imported from Jamaica should exceed a certain rate. This remonstrance was taken into consideration by a committee of the whole House; and a great number of evidences and papers being examined, they resolved, that the peopling of Jamaica with white inhabitants, and cultivating the lands thereof, would be the most proper measure for securing that island, and increasing the trade and navigation between it and Great Britain, and other parts of his majesty's dominions: that the endeavours hitherto used by the legislature of Jamaica to increase the number of white inhabitants, and enforce the cultivation of lands, in the manner that might best conduce to the security and defence of that island, had not been effectual for these purposes. The House ordered a bill to be founded on these resolutions; but this was postponed, until the ministry should receive more full information touching the true state of that island. The planters of Jamaica laboured under many grievances and hardships, from divers heavy impositions and restrictions; and a detail of these was transmitted in a representation to his majesty, which was referred to the consideration of the commissioners of trade and plantations. The cause of the planters was defended vigorously, and managed in the House of Commons by Alderman Beckford, a gentleman of vast possessions in the island of Jamaica, who perfectly well understood, and strenuously supported, the interest of that his native country.

*Deliberations concerning the sugar colonies.*

Abortive also proved the attempt to establish a law for keeping an annual register of marriages, births, deaths, the individuals who received alms, and the

*Fate of the register-bill.*

total number of people in Great Britain. A bill for this purpose was presented by Mr. Potter, a gentleman of pregnant parts and spirited elocution; who, enumerating the advantages of such a law, observed, that it would ascertain the number of the people, and the collective strength of the nation; consequently, point out those places where there is a defect or excess of population, and certainly determine whether a general naturalization would be advantageous or prejudicial to the community; that it would decide what number of men might, on any sudden emergency, be levied for the defence of the kingdom; and whether the nation is gainer or loser by sending its natives to settle, and our troops to defend, distant colonies; that it would be the means of establishing a local administration of civil government, or a police upon certain fixed principles, the want of which hath been long a reproach to the nation, a security to vice, and an encouragement to idleness; that in many cases where all other evidence is wanting, it would enable suitors to recover their rights in courts of justice, facilitate an equal and equitable assessment in raising the present taxes, and laying future impositions; specify the lineal descents, relations, and alliances of families; lighten the intolerable burdens incurred by the public, from innumerable and absurd regulations relating to the poor; provide for them by a more equal exertion of humanity, and effectually screen them from all risk of perishing by hunger, cold, cruelty, and oppression. Whether such a law would have answered the sanguine expectations of its patron, we shall not pretend to determine; though, in our opinion, it must have been attended with very salutary consequences, particularly in restraining the hand of robbery and violence, in detecting fraud, bridling the ferocity of a licentious people, and establishing a happy system of order and subordination. At first the bill met with little opposition, except from Mr. Thornton, member for the city of York, who inveighed against it with great fervour, as a measure that savoured of French policy, to which the English nation ever had the utmost aversion. He affirmed, that the method in which it was proposed this register should be kept would furnish the enemies of Great Britain with continual opportunities of knowing the strength or weakness of the nation; that it would empower an ill-designing minister to execute any scheme subversive of public liberty, invest parish and petty officers of the peace with exorbitant powers, and cost the nation above fifty thousand pounds a year to carry the scheme into execution. These arguments, which we apprehend are extremely frivolous and inconclusive, had great weight with a considerable number, who joined in the opposition, while the ministry stood neutral. Nevertheless, after having undergone some amendments, it was conveyed to the Lords, by whom it was, at the second reading, thrown out, as a scheme of very dangerous tendency. The legislature of Great Britain have, on some occasions, been more startled at the distant shadow of a bare possibility, than at the real approach of the most dangerous innovation.

From the usual deliberations on civil and commercial concerns, the attention of the Parliament, which had seldom or never turned upon literary avocations, was called off by an extraordinary subject of this nature. Sir Hans Sloane, the celebrated physician and naturalist, well known through all the civilized countries of Europe for his ample collection of rarities, culled from the animal, vegetable, and mineral kingdoms, as well as of antiquities and curiosities of art, had directed, in his last will, that his valuable museum, together with his numerous library, should be offered to the Parliament, for the use of the public, in consideration of their paying a certain sum, in compensation to his heirs. His terms were embraced by the Commons, who agreed to pay twenty thousand pounds for the whole, supposed to be worth four times that sum; and a bill was prepared for purchasing this museum, together with the Harleian collection of manuscripts, so denominated from its founder, Robert Harley, Earl of Oxford, Lord High Treasurer of England, and now offered to the public by his daughter, the Duchess of Portland. It was proposed that these purchases should be joined to the famous Cottonian library, and a suitable repository provided for them and the king's library, which had long lain neglected and exposed to the injuries of the weather in the old dormitory at Westminster. Accordingly, trustees and governors, consisting of the most eminent persons of the kingdom, were appointed, and regulations established for the management of this noble museum, which was deposited in Montagu-house, one of the most magnificent edifices in England, where it is subjected, without reserve, to the view of the public, under certain necessary restrictions, and ex-

*Sir Hans Sloane's Museum purchased by Parliament.*

hibits a glorious monument of national taste and liberality.¹ In the beginning of June the session of Parliament was closed by his majesty, who mentioned nothing particular in his speech, but that the state of foreign affairs had suffered no alteration since their meeting.

Story of Elizabeth Canning.
The genius of the English people is perhaps incompatible with a state of perfect tranquillity; if it is not ruffled by foreign provocations, or agitated by unpopular measures of domestic administration, it will undergo temporary fermentations from the turbulent ingredients inherent in its own constitution. Tumults are excited, and factions kindled into rage and inveteracy, by incidents of the most frivolous nature. At this juncture the metropolis of England was divided and discomposed in a surprising manner, by a dispute in itself of so little consequence to the community, that it would not deserve a place in a general history, if it did not serve to convey a characteristic idea of the English nation. In the beginning of the year an obscure damsel, of low degree, whose name was Elizabeth Canning, promulgated a report, which in a little time attracted the attention of the public. She affirmed that on the first day of the new year, at night, she was seized under Bedlam-wall by two ruffians, who having stripped her of her upper apparel, secured her mouth with a gag, and threatened to murder her should she make the least noise; that they conveyed her on foot about ten miles, to a place called Enfield-wash, and brought her to the house of one Mrs. Wells, where she was pillaged of her stays; and, because she refused to turn prostitute, confined in a cold, damp, separate, and unfurnished apartment; where she remained a whole month, without any other sustenance than a few stale crusts of bread, and about a gallon of water; till at length she forced her way through a window, and ran home to her mother's house, almost naked, in the night of the twenty-ninth of January. This story, improbable and unsupported, operated so strongly on the passions of the

---

¹ The library of Sir Hans Sloane consisted of above fifty thousand volumes, including about three hundred and fifty books of drawings, and three thousand five hundred and sixteen manuscripts, besides a multitude of prints. The museum comprehended an infinite number of medals, coins, urns, utensils, seals, cameos, intaglios, precious stones, vessels of agate and jasper, crystals, spars, fossils, metals, minerals, ores, earths, sands, salts, bitumens, sulphurs, amber, ambergrise, talcs, micæ, testacea, corals, sponges, echini, echonites, asteriæ, trochi, crustacea, stellæ marinæ, fishes, birds, eggs, and nests, vipers, serpents, quadrupeds, insects, human calculi, anatomical preparations, seeds, gums, roots, dried plants, pictures, drawings, and mathematical instruments. All these articles, with a short account of each, are specified in thirty-eight volumes in folio, and eight in quarto.

people in the neighbourhood of Aldermanbury, where Canning's mother lived, and particularly among fanatics of all denominations, that they raised voluntary contributions, with surprising eagerness, in order to bring the supposed delinquents to justice. Warrants were granted for apprehending Wells, who kept the house at Enfield-wash, and her accomplices, the servant-maid, whose name was Virtue Hall, and one Squires, an old gipsy-woman, which last was charged by Canning of having robbed her of her stays. Wells, though acquitted of the felony, was punished as a bawd. Hall turned evidence for Canning, but afterwards recanted. Squires, the gipsy, was convicted of the robbery, though she produced undoubted evidence to prove that she was at Abbotsbury in Dorsetshire that very night in which the felony was said to be committed, and Canning and her friends fell into divers contradictions during the course of the trial. By this time the prepossession of the common people in her favour had risen to such a pitch of enthusiasm, that the most palpable truths which appeared on the other side had no other effect than that of exasperating them to the most dangerous degree of rage and revenge. Some of the witnesses for Squires, though persons of unblemished character, were so intimidated, that they durst not enter the court; and those who had resolution enough to give evidence in her behalf, ran the risk of assassination from the vulgar that surrounded the place. On this occasion, Sir Crisp Gascoyne, Lord Mayor of London, behaved with that laudable courage and humanity which ought ever to distinguish the chief magistrate of such a metropolis. Considering the improbability of the charge, the heat, partiality, and blind enthusiasm with which it was prosecuted, and being convinced of the old woman's innocence by a great number of affidavits, voluntarily sent up from the country by persons of unquestionable credit, he, in conjunction with some other worthy citizens, resolved to oppose the torrent of vulgar prejudice. Application was made to the throne for mercy: the case was referred to the attorney and solicitor-general, who, having examined the evidences on both sides, made their report in favour of Squires to the king and council; and this poor old creature was indulged with his majesty's pardon. This affair was now swelled up into such a faction as divided the greater part of the kingdom, including the rich as well as the poor, the high as well as the humble. Pamphlets and pasquinades were published on both sides of the dispute, which became the general topic of conversation in all assemblies, and people of all ranks espoused one or other party with as much warmth and animosity as had ever inflamed the whigs and tories, even at the most rancorous period of their opposition. Subscriptions were opened, and large sums levied, on one side, to prosecute for perjury the persons on whose evidence the pardon had been granted. On the other hand, those who had interested themselves for the gipsy resolved to support her witnesses, and, if possible, detect the imposture of Canning. Bills of perjury were preferred on both sides. The evidences for Squires were tried and acquitted: at first Canning absconded; but afterwards surrendered to take her trial, and being, after a long hearing, found guilty, was transported to the British colonies. The zeal of her friends, however, seemed to be inflamed by her conviction; and those who carried on the prosecution against her were insulted, even to the danger of their lives. They supplied her with necessaries of all sorts, paid for her transportation in a private ship, where she enjoyed all the comforts and conveniences that could be afforded in that situation, and furnished her with such recommendations as secured to her a very agreeable reception in New England.

Next to this very remarkable transaction, the incident that principally distinguished this year in England was the execution of Dr. Archibald Cameron, a native of North Britain, and brother to Cameron of Lochiel, chief of that numerous and warlike tribe, who had taken the field with the prince-pretender. After the battle of Culloden, where he was dangerously wounded, he found means to escape to the continent. His brother, the doctor, had accompanied him in all his expeditions, though not in a military capacity, and was included with him in the act of attainder passed against those who had been concerned in the rebellion. Notwithstanding the imminent danger attending such an attempt, the doctor returned privately to Scotland, in order (as it was reported) to recover a sum of money belonging to the pretender, which had been embezzled by his adherents in that country. Whatever may have been his inducement to revisit his native country under such a predicament, certain it is, he was discovered, apprehended, conducted to London, confined in the Tower, examined by the privy-council, and produced in the court of King's Bench,

*Execution of Dr. Cameron.*

where his identity being proved by several witnesses, he received sentence of death, and was executed at Tyburn. The terror and resentment of the people, occasioned by the rebellion, having by this time subsided, their humane passions did not fail to operate in favour of this unfortunate gentleman: their pity was mingled with esteem, arising from his personal character, which was altogether unblemished, and his deportment on this occasion, which they could not help admiring, as the standard of manly fortitude and decorum. The populace, though not very subject to tender emotions, were moved to compassion, and even to tears, by his behaviour at the place of execution; and many sincere well-wishers to the present establishment thought that the sacrifice of this victim, at such a juncture, could not redound either to its honour or security.

The turbulent spirit, which is never totally extinguished in this island, manifested itself in sundry tumults that broke out in different parts of South Britain. The price of provisions, and bread in particular, being raised to an exorbitant rate, in consequence of an absurd exportation of corn, for the sake of the bounty, a formidable body of colliers, and other labouring people, raised an insurrection at Bristol, began to plunder the corn-vessels in the harbour, and commit such outrages in the city, that the magistrates were obliged to have recourse to the military power. A troop of dragoons were sent to their assistance, and the insurgents were quelled, though not without some bloodshed. Commotions of the same kind were excited in Yorkshire, Manchester, and several other places in the northern counties. At Leeds, a detachment of the king's troops were obliged in their own defence to fire upon the rioters, eight or nine of whom were killed on the spot; and, indeed, so little care had been taken to restrain the licentious insolence of the vulgar by proper laws and regulations, duly executed under the eye of civil magistracy, that a military power was found absolutely necessary to maintain the peace of the kingdom.

*Tumults in different parts of the kingdom.*

The tranquillity of the continent was not endangered by any new contest or disturbance; yet the breach between the clergy and the Parliament of Paris was every day more and more widened, and the people were pretty equally divided between superstition and a regard for civil liberty. The Parliament having

*Disturbances in France.*

caused divers ecclesiastics to be apprehended, for having refused to administer the sacraments to persons in extremity, who refused to subscribe to the bull Unigenitus, all of them declared they acted according to the direction of the Archbishop of Paris. Application being made to this haughty prelate, he treated the deputies of the Parliament with the most supercilious contempt, and even seemed to brave the power and authority of that body. They, on the other hand, proceeded to take cognizance of the recusant clergy, until their sovereign ordered them to desist. Then they presented remonstrances to his majesty, reminding him of their privileges, and the duty of their station, which obliged them to do justice on all delinquents. In the mean time, they continued to perform their functions, and even commenced a prosecution against the Bishop of Orleans, whom they summoned to attend their tribunal. Next day they received from Versailles a *lettre de cachet*, accompanied by letters patent, commanding them to suspend all prosecutions relating to the refusal of the sacraments; and ordered the letters patent to be registered. Instead of obeying these commands, they presented new remonstrances, for answers to which they were referred to the king's former declarations. In consequence of this intimation, they had spirit enough to resolve, "that whereas certain evil-minded persons had prevented truth from reaching the throne, the chambers remained assembled, and all other business should be suspended." The affair was now become very serious. His majesty, by fresh letters patent, renewed his orders, and commanded them to proceed with their ordinary business, on pain of incurring his displeasure. They forthwith came to another resolution, importing, that they could not obey this injunction without a breach of their duty and their oath. Next day *lettres de cachet* were issued, banishing to different parts of the kingdom all the members, except those of the great chamber, which the court did not find more tractable than their brethren. They forthwith resolved to abide by the two resolutions mentioned above; and, as an instance of their unshaken fortitude, ordered an ecclesiastic to be taken into custody for refusing the sacraments. This spirited measure involved them in the fate of the rest; for they were also exiled from Paris, the citizens of which did not fail to extol their conduct with the loudest encomiums, and at the same time to express their resentment against the clergy, who could not stir abroad without being exposed to violence or insult. The example of the Parliament of Paris was followed by that of Rouen, which had courage enough to issue orders for apprehending the Bishop of Évreux, because he had refused to appear when summoned to their tribunal. Their decrees on this occasion being annulled by the king's council of state, they presented a bold remonstrance, which, however, had no other effect than that of exasperating the ministry, A grand deputation being ordered to attend the king, they were commanded to desist from intermeddling in disputes relating to the refusal of the sacraments, and to register this injunction. At their return they had recourse to a new remonstrance; and one of their principal counsellors, who had spoken freely in the debates on this subject, was arrested by a party of dragoons, who carried him prisoner to the castle of Dourlens. In a word, the body of the people declared for the Parliament, in opposition to ecclesiastical tyranny; and, had they not been overawed by a formidable standing army, would certainly have taken up arms in defence of their liberties; while the monarch weakly suffered himself to be governed by priestly delusions; and, secure in his military appointment, seemed to set the rest of his subjects at defiance. Apprehensive, however, that these disputes would put an entire stop to the administration of justice, he, by letters patent, established a royal chamber for the prosecution of suits civil and criminal, which was opened with a solemn mass performed in the queen's chapel at the Louvre, where all the members assisted. On this occasion another difficulty occurred. The letters patent, constituting this new court, ought to have been registered by the Parliament, which was now no more. To remedy this defect, application was made to the inferior court of the Chatelet; which refusing to register them, one of its members was committed to the Bastile, and another absconded. Intimidated by this exertion of despotic power, they allowed the king's officers to enter the letters in their registers; but afterwards adopted more vigorous resolutions. The lieutenant-civil appearing in their court, all the counsellors rose up and retired, leaving him alone, and on the table an arrêt, importing, that whereas the confinement of one of their members, the prosecution of another who durst not appear, and the present calamities of the nation, gave them just apprehension for their own persons, they had, after mature deliberation, thought proper to retire. Thus a dangerous ferment was excited by the king's espousing the cause of spiritual insolence and oppression against the general voice of his people, and the plainest dictates of reason and common sense.

*Proceedings of the diet relative to East Friezeland.* The property of East Friezeland continued still to be the source of contention between the Electors of Brandenburgh and Hanover. The interests of his Britannic majesty being powerfully supported by the House of Austria, the minister of that power at the diet proposed that the affair should be taken into immediate consideration. He was seconded by the minister of Brunswick; but the envoy from Brandenburgh, having protested in form against this procedure, withdrew from the assembly, and the Brunswick minister made a counter protestation, after which he also retired. Then a motion being made, that this dispute should be referred to the decision of the Aulic council at Vienna, it was carried in the affirmative by a majority of fourteen voices. His Prussian majesty's final declaration with regard to this affair was afterwards presented to the diet, and answered in the sequel by a memorial from his Britannic majesty as Elector of Hanover. Some other petty disputes likewise happened between the regency of Hanover and the city of Munster; and the former, claiming some bailiwicks in the territories of Bremen, sequestered certain revenues belonging to this city, in Stade and Ferden, till these claims should be satisfied.

*Treaty between the court of Vienna and the Duke of Modena.* The court of Vienna having dropped for the present the scheme for electing a King of the Romans, concluded a very extraordinary treaty with the Duke of Modena, stipulating, that his serene highness should be appointed perpetual governor of the duchy of Milan, with a salary of ninety thousand florins, on condition that he should maintain a body of four thousand men, to be at the disposal of the empress-queen; that her imperial majesty should have a right to place garrisons in the citadels of Mirandola and Reggio, as well as in the castle of Massa Carrara; that the Archduke Peter Leopold, third son of their imperial majesties, should espouse the daughter of the hereditary Prince of Modena, by the heiress of Massa Carrara; and in case of her dying without heirs male, the estates of that house and the duchy of Mirandola should devolve to the archduke; but in case of her having male issue, that she should enjoy the principality of Fermia, and other possessions in Hungary, claimed by the Duke of Modena, for her fortune; finally, that on the extinction of the male branch of the house of Este, all the dominions of the Duke of Modena should devolve to the House of Austria.

While the powers on the continent of Europe were thus employed in strengthening their respective interests, and concerting measures for preventing any interruption of the general tranquillity, matters were fast ripening to a fresh rupture between the subjects of Great Britain and France, in different parts of North America. We have already observed that commissaries had been appointed, and conferences opened at Paris, to determine the disputes between the two crowns, relating to the boundaries of Nova Scotia; and we took notice in general of the little arts of evasion practised by the French commissaries, to darken and perplex the dispute, and elude the pretensions of his Britannic majesty. They persisted in employing these arts of chicanery and cavil with such perseverance, that the negotiation proved abortive, the conferences broke up, and every thing seemed to portend approaching hostilities. But, before we proceed to a detail of the incidents which were the immediate forerunners of the war, we will endeavour to convey a just idea of the dispute concerning Nova Scotia; which, we apprehend, is but imperfectly understood, though of the utmost importance to the interest of Great Britain.

*Conferences with respect to Nova Scotia broke up.*

Nova Scotia, called by the French Acadia, lies between the forty-fourth and fiftieth degrees of north latitude, having New England and the Atlantic Ocean to the south and south-west, and the river and gulf of St. Lawrence to the north and north-east. The winter, which continues near seven months in this country, is intensely cold; and, without the intervention of any thing that can be called spring, it is immediately succeeded by a summer, the heat of which is almost insupportable, but of no long continuance. The soil in general is thin and barren, though some parts of it are said to be equal to the best land in England. The whole country is covered with

*Description of Nova Scotia.*

a perpetual fog, even after the summer has commenced. It was first possessed by the French, before they made any establishment in Canada; who, by dint of industry and indefatigable perseverance, in struggling with many difficulties they necessarily laboured under in the infancy of this settlement, subsisted tolerably well, and increased considerably, with very little assistance from Europe; whilst we, even now, should lose the immense expense we have already been at to settle a colony there, and should see all our endeavours to that end defeated, if the support of the royal hand was withdrawn but for a moment. This country, by the possession of which an enemy would be enabled greatly to annoy all our other colonies, and if in the hands of the French, would be of singular service both to their fishery and their sugar-islands, has frequently changed hands from the French to the English, and from the English back again to the French, till our right to it was finally settled by the twelfth article of the treaty of Utrecht, by which all the country included within the ancient limits of what was called Nova Scotia or Acadia was ceded to the English. This article was confirmed by the treaty of Aix-la-Chapelle; but, for want of ascertaining distinctly what were the bounds intended to be fixed by the two nations with respect to this province, disputes arose, and commissaries, as we have observed, were appointed by both sides, to adjust the litigation.

The commissaries of the King of Great Britain conformed themselves to the rule laid down by the treaty itself, and assigned those as the ancient limits of this country which had always passed as such, from the very earliest time of any certainty, down to the conclusion of the treaty; which the two crowns had frequently declared to be such, and which the French had often admitted and allowed. These limits are, the southern bank of the river St. Lawrence to the north, and Pentagoet to the west: the country situated between these boundaries is that which the French received by the treaty of St. Germain's, in the year one thousand six hundred and thirty-two, under the general name of Acadia. Of this country, thus limited, they continued in possession from that period to the year one thousand six hundred and fifty-four, when a descent was made upon it, under the command of Colonel Sedgwick. That these were then the undisputed limits of

*Disputes concerning its limits.*

Acadia, his Britannic majesty's commissaries plainly proved, by a letter of Louis XIII. to the Sieurs Charnisay and La Tour, regulating their jurisdictions in Acadia; by the subsequent commissions of the French king to the same persons, as governors of Acadia, in the sequel; and by that which was afterwards granted to the Sieur Denys, in the year one thousand six hundred and fifty-four; all of which extend the bounds of this country from the river St. Lawrence to Pentagoet and New England. That these were the notions of the French with respect to the ancient limits of this province was further confirmed by the demand made by the ambassador, in the course of that same year, for the restitution of the forts Pentagoet, St. John's, and Port Royal, as forts situated in Acadia. In the year one thousand six hundred and sixty-two, upon the revival of the claim of France to the country of Acadia, which had been left undecided by the treaty of Westminster, the French ambassador, then at the court of London, assigned Pentagoet as the western, and the river St. Lawrence as the northern boundary of that country; and alleged the restitution of Acadia in the year one thousand six hundred and thirty-two, and the possession taken by France in consequence thereof, as well as the continuation of that possession, with the same limits, to the year one thousand six hundred and fifty-four, as proofs of the equity and validity of the claim he then made; in which claim, and in the manner of supporting it, he was particularly approved of by the court of France. The same court afterwards thought it so clear, upon former determinations, and her own former possessions, that the true ancient boundaries of Acadia were Pentagoet to the west, and the river St. Lawrence to the north, that she desired no specification of limits in the treaty of Breda, but was contented with the restitution of Acadia, generally named; and, upon a dispute which arose in the execution of this treaty, France re-asserted, and Great Britain, after some discussion, agreed to the above-mentioned limits of Acadia; and France obtained possession of that country, so bounded, under the treaty of Breda. The sense of France upon this subject, in the years one thousand six hundred and eighty-five, and one thousand six hundred and eighty-seven, was also clearly manifested, in the memorials delivered at that time, by the French ambassador at the court of London, complaining of some

encroachments made by the English upon the coast of
Acadia: he described the country as extending from isle
Percée, which lies at the entrance of the river St. Lawrence,
to St. George's island; and again, in a subsequent complaint, made by Mons. Barillon and Mons. de Bonrepaus to
the court of Great Britain, against the judge of Pema-
quid, for having seized the effects of a French merchant
at Pentagoet, which, said they, was situated in Acadia, as
restored to France by the treaty of Breda. To explain
the sense of France, touching the bounds of Acadia in the
year one thousand seven hundred, the British commissaries
produced a proposal of the French ambassador, then residing in Great Britain, to restrain the limits of that country
to the river St. George. They also instanced the surrender
of Port Royal in the year one thousand seven hundred
and ten, in which Acadia is described with the same limits
with which France had received it in the years one thousand
six hundred and thirty-two, and one thousand six hundred
and sixty-seven. And further to ascertain the sense of
both crowns, even at the treaty of Utrecht itself, they produced the Queen of Great Britain's instructions to her
ambassadors in the year one thousand seven hundred and
eleven, in which they were directed to insist, "That his
most Christian majesty should quit all claim or title, by
virtue of any former treaty, or otherwise, to the country
called Nova Scotia, and expressly to Port Royal, otherwise Annapolis Royal." To these they added a manifest
demonstration, founded on indisputable facts, proving that
the recital of the several sorts of right which France had
ever pretended to this country, and the specification of both
terms, Acadia or Nova Scotia, were intended by Great
Britain to obviate all doubts which had ever been made
concerning the limits of Acadia, and to comprehend with
more certainty all that country which France had ever
received as such: finally, to specify what France considered
as Acadia. During the treaty, they referred to the offers
of that crown in the year one thousand seven hundred and
twelve, in which she proposed to restrain the boundary of
Acadia to the river St. George, as a departure from its real
boundary, in case Great Britain would restore to her the
possession of that country. From all these facts it plainly
appears that Great Britain demanded nothing but what
the fair construction of the words of the treaty of Utrecht

necessarily implies; and that it is impossible for any thing to have more evident marks of candour and fairness in it, than the demand of the English on this occasion. From the variety of evidence brought in support of this claim, it evidently results, that the English commissaries assigned no limits as the ancient limits of Acadia, but those which France herself determined to be such, in the year one thousand six hundred and thirty-two; and which she possessed, in consequence of that determination, till the year one thousand six hundred and fifty-four: that in one thousand six hundred and sixty-two France claimed, and received in one thousand six hundred and sixty-nine, the country which Great Britain now claims as Acadia, restored to France by the treaty of Breda under that general denomination; that France never considered Acadia as having any other limits than those which were assigned to it from the year one thousand six hundred and thirty-two, to the year one thousand seven hundred and ten; and that, by the treaty of Utrecht, she engaged to transfer that very same country as Acadia, which France has always asserted and possessed, and Great Britain now claims as such. Should the crown of France, therefore, be ever willing to decide what are the ancient limits of Acadia, by her own declarations so frequently made in like discussions upon the same point, by her possessions of this country for almost a century, and by her description of Acadia, during the negotiation of that very treaty upon which this doubt is raised, she cannot but admit the claim of Great Britain to be conformable to the treaty of Utrecht, and to the description of the country transferred to Great Britain by the twelfth article of that treaty. There is a consistency in the claim of the English, and a completeness in the evidence brought in support of it, which is seldom seen in discussions of this sort; for it rarely happens in disputes of such a nature between two crowns, that either of them can safely offer to have its pretensions decided by the known and repeated declarations, or the possessions of the other. To answer the force of this detail of conclusive historical facts, and to give a new turn to the real question in dispute, the French commissaries, in their memorial, laid it down as a distinction made by the treaty of Utrecht, that the ancient limits of Acadia, referred to by that treaty, are different from any with which that country may have passed under the treaties of

St. Germain's and Breda; and then endeavoured to show, upon the testimonies of maps and historians, that Acadia and its limits were anciently confined to the south-eastern part of the peninsula. In support of this system, the French commissaries had recourse to ancient maps, and historians, who, as they asserted, had ever confined Acadia to the limits they assigned. They alleged, that those commissions of the French government over Acadia, which the English cited as evidence of the limits they claimed, were given as commissions over Acadia and the country around it, and not over Acadia only: that the whole of the country claimed by the English as Acadia could not possibly be supposed ever to be considered as such, because many parts of that territory always did, and still do, preserve particular and distinct names. They affirmed New France to be a province in itself; and argued that many parts of what we claim as Acadia can never have been in Acadia, because historians and the French commissions of government expressly place them in New France. They asserted that no evidence can be drawn of the opinion of any crown, with respect to the limits of any country, from its declaration during the negotiation of a treaty; and in the end, relying upon maps and historians for the ancient limits of Acadia, they pretended that the express restitution of St. Germain's and the possession taken by France in consequence of the treaty of Breda, after a long discussion of the limits and the declaration of France during the negotiation of the treaty of Utrecht, were foreign to the point in question. In refutation of these maxims, the English commissaries proved, from an examination of the maps and historians cited by the French in support of their system, that if this question was to be decided upon the authorities which they themselves allowed to belong, and to be applicable to this discussion, the limits which they assigned were utterly inconsistent with the best maps of all countries, which are authorities in point for almost every part of the claim of Great Britain. They showed that the French historians, Champlain and Denys, and particularly this last, with his commission in the year one thousand six hundred and fifty-five, assigned the same northern and western limits to Acadia which they did; and that Escarbot, another of their historians, as far as any evidence can be drawn from his writings, agrees entirely with the former two. They observed, that all these evidences fall in with and confirm the better authorities of treaties, and the several transactions between the two crowns for near a century past; and that the French commissaries, by deviating from treaties, and the late proceedings of the two crowns, to ancient historians and maps, only made a transition from an authentic to an insufficient sort of evidence, and led the English commissaries into an inquiry, which proved that both the proper and the improper, the regular and the foreign, evidence upon which this matter had been rested, equally confuted the limits alleged by the French commissaries as the ancient limits of Acadia.

# CHAPTER XXIII.

AMBITIOUS SCHEMES OF THE FRENCH IN NORTH AMERICA. — RISE AND CONDUCT OF THE OHIO COMPANY. — LETTER FROM THE GOVERNOR OF VIRGINIA TO THE FRENCH COMMANDER AT RIVIÈRE-AU-BŒUF. — PERFIDIOUS PRACTICES OF THE FRENCH IN NOVA SCOTIA. — MAJOR LAURENCE DEFEATS THE FRENCH NEUTRALS. — BRITISH AMBASSADOR AT PARIS AMUSED WITH GENERAL PROMISES. — SESSION OPENED. — SUPPLIES GRANTED. — REPEAL OF THE ACT FOR NATURALIZING JEWS. — MOTION FOR REPEALING A FORMER ACT FAVOURABLE TO THE JEWS. — EAST INDIA MUTINY-BILL. — CASE OF LE ———. — SESSION CLOSED. — DEATH OF MR. PELHAM. — CHANGE IN THE MINISTRY. — NEW PARLIAMENT ASSEMBLED AND PROROGUED. — DISPUTES IN THE IRISH PARLIAMENT. — TRANSACTIONS IN THE EAST INDIES. — ACCOUNT OF THE ENGLISH SETTLEMENTS ON THE MALABAR AND COROMANDEL COASTS. — DISPUTE ABOUT THE GOVERNMENT OF ARCOT. — MAHOMMED ALI KHAN SUPPORTED BY THE ENGLISH. — MR. CLIVE TAKES ARCOT — AND DEFEATS THE ENEMY IN THE PLAINS OF ARANI, AND AT KOVERIPACK. — HE REDUCES THREE FORTS, AND TAKES M. D'AUTEUIL. — CHUNDA SAIB TAKEN AND PUT TO DEATH, AND HIS ARMY ROUTED. — CONVENTION BETWEEN THE EAST INDIA COMPANIES OF ENGLAND AND FRANCE. — GENERAL VIEW OF THE BRITISH COLONIES IN NORTH AMERICA. — NEW ENGLAND AND NEW YORK. — NEW JERSEY. — PENNSYLVANIA. — MARYLAND. — VIRGINIA. — THE TWO CAROLINAS. — GEORGIA. — THE FRENCH SURPRISE LOGS TOWN, ON THE OHIO. — CONFERENCE WITH THE INDIANS AT ALBANY. — COLONEL WASHINGTON DEFEATED AND TAKEN BY THE FRENCH ON THE OHIO. — DIVISIONS AMONG THE BRITISH COLONIES. — THE HEREDITARY PRINCE OF HESSE-CASSEL PROFESSES THE ROMAN CATHOLIC RELIGION. — PARLIAMENT OF PARIS RECALLED FROM EXILE. — AFFAIRS OF SPAIN AND PORTUGAL. — SESSION OPENED. — SUPPLIES GRANTED. — BILL IN BEHALF OF CHELSEA PENSIONERS. — OXFORDSHIRE ELECTION. — MESSAGE FROM THE KING TO THE HOUSE OF COMMONS. — COURT OF VERSAILLES AMUSES THE ENGLISH MINISTRY. — SESSION CLOSED.

WHILE the British ministry depended upon the success of the conferences between the commissaries of the two crowns at Paris, the French were actually employed in executing their plans of encroachment upon the British colonies in North America. Their scheme was to engross the whole fur-trade of that continent; and they had already made great progress in extending a chain of forts connecting their settlements on the river Mississippi with their possessions in Canada, along the great lakes of Erie and Ontario, which last issues into the river St. Lawrence. By these means they hoped to exclude the English from all communication and traffic with the Indian nations, even those that lay contiguous to the British settlements, and confine them within a line of their drawing, beyond which they should neither extend their trade nor plantations. Their commercial spirit did not keep pace with the gigantic strides of their ambition: they could not supply

1753.
Ambitious schemes of the French in North America.

all those Indians with the necessaries they wanted, so that many of the natives had recourse to the English settlements; and this commerce produced a connexion, in consequence of which the British adventurers ventured to travel with merchandise as far as the banks of the river Ohio, that runs into the Mississippi, a great way on the other side of the Apalachian mountains, beyond which none of our colonists had ever attempted to penetrate. The tract of country lying along the Ohio is so fertile, pleasant, and inviting, and the Indians, called Twightees, who inhabit those delightful plains, were so well disposed towards a close alliance with the English, that, as far back as the year one thousand seven hundred and sixteen, Mr. Spotswood, governor of Virginia, proposed a plan for erecting a company to settle such lands upon this river as should be ceded to them by treaty with the natives; but the design was at that time frustrated, partly by the indolence and timidity of the British ministry, who were afraid of giving umbrage to the French, and partly by the jealousies and divisions subsisting between the different colonies of Great Britain. The very same circumstances encouraged the French to proceed in their project of invasion. At length they penetrated from the banks of the river St. Lawrence across lake Champlain, and upon the territory of New York built with impunity, and, indeed, without opposition, the fort of Crown Point, the most insolent and dangerous encroachment that they had hitherto carried into execution.

Governor Spotswood's scheme for an Ohio company was revived immediately after the peace of Aix-la-Chapelle, when certain merchants of London, who traded to Maryland and Virginia, petitioned the government on this subject, and were indulged not only with a grant of a great tract of ground to the southward of Pennsylvania, which they promised to settle, but also with an exclusive privilege of trading with the Indians on the banks of the river Ohio. This design no sooner transpired than the French governor of Canada took the alarm, and wrote letters to the governors of New York and Pennsylvania, giving them to understand that, as the English inland traders had encroached on the French territories and privileges, by trading with the Indians under the protection of his sovereign, he would seize them wherever they could be found, if they did not immediately desist from that illicit practice. No regard being paid

*Rise and conduct of the Ohio company.*

to this intimation, he next year caused three British traders to be arrested. Their effects were confiscated, and they themselves conveyed to Quebec, from whence they were sent prisoners to Rochelle in France, and there detained in confinement. In this situation they presented a remonstrance to the Earl of Albemarle, at that time English ambassador at Paris, and he claiming them as British subjects, they were set at liberty. Although, in answer to his lordship's memorial, the court of Versailles promised to transmit orders to the French governors in America to use all their endeavours for preventing any disputes that might have a tendency to alter the good correspondence established between the two nations: in all probability the directions given were seemingly the very reverse of these professions, for the French commanders, partisans, and agents in America, took every step their busy genius could suggest to strengthen their own power, and weaken the influence of the English, by embroiling them with the Indian nations. This task they found the more easy, as the natives had taken offence against the English, when they understood that their lands were given away without their knowledge, and that there was a design to build forts in their country, without their consent and concurrence. Indeed the person whom the new company employed to survey the banks of the Ohio concealed his design so carefully, and behaved in other respects in such a dark mysterious manner, as could not fail to rouse the jealousy of a people naturally inquisitive, and very much addicted to suspicion. How the company proposed to settle this acquisition in despite of the native possessors it is not easy to conceive, and it is still more unaccountable that they should have neglected the natives, whose consent and assistance they might have procured at a very small expense. Instead of acting such a fair, open, and honourable part, they sent a Mr. Gist to make a clandestine survey of the country, as far as the falls of the river Ohio; and, as we have observed above, his conduct alarmed both the French and Indians. The erection of this company was equally disagreeable to the separate traders of Virginia and Pennsylvania, who saw themselves on the eve of being deprived of a valuable branch of traffic, by the exclusive charter of a monopoly; and therefore they employed their emissaries to foment the jealousy of the Indians.

The French having in a manner commenced hostilities against the English, and actually built forts on the territories of the British allies at Niagara, and on the lake Erie, Mr. Hamilton, governor of Pennsylvania, communicated this intelligence to the Assembly of the province, and represented the necessity of erecting truck-houses, or places of strength and security, on the river Ohio, to which the traders might retire in case of insult or molestation. The proposal was approved, and money granted for the purpose; but the Assembly could not agree about the manner in which they should be erected; and in the mean time the French fortified themselves at leisure, and continued to harass the traders belonging to the British settlements. Repeated complaints of these encroachments and depredations being represented to Mr. Dinwiddie, governor of Virginia, he, towards the latter end of this very year, sent Major Washington with a letter to the commanding officer of a fort which the French had built on the Rivière-au-Bœuf, which falls into the Ohio, not far from the lake Erie. In this letter Mr. Dinwiddie expressed his surprise that the French should build forts and make settlements on the river Ohio, in the western part of the colony of Virginia, belonging to the crown of Great Britain. He complained of these encroachments, as well as of the injuries done to the subjects of Great Britain, in open violation of the law of nations, and of the treaties actually subsisting between the two crowns. He desired to know by whose authority and instructions his Britannic majesty's territories had been invaded; and required him to depart in peace, without further prosecuting a plan which must interrupt the harmony and good understanding which his majesty was desirous to continue and cultivate with the most Christian king. To this spirited intimation the officer replied, that it was not his province to specify the evidence, and demonstrate the right of the king his master to the lands situated on the river Ohio; but he would transmit the letter to the Marquis du Quesne, and act according to the answer he should receive from that nobleman. In the mean time, he said he did not think himself obliged to obey the summons of an English governor; that he commanded the fort by virtue of an order from his general, to which he was determined to conform with all the precision and resolution of a good officer. Mr. Dinwiddie expected no other reply, and therefore had projected a fort to be erected near the forks of the river. The province undertook to defray the expense, and the stores for that purpose were already provided; but, by some fatal oversight, the concurrence of the Indians was neither obtained nor solicited, and therefore they looked upon this measure with an evil eye, as a manifest invasion of their property.

While the French thus industriously extended their encroachments to the southward, they were not idle in the gulf of St. Lawrence, but seized every opportunity of distressing the English settlement of Nova Scotia. We have already observed, that the town of Halifax was no sooner built, than they spirited up the Indians of that neighbourhood to commit hostilities against the inhabitants, some of whom they murdered, and others they carried prisoners to Louisbourg, where they sold them for arms and ammunition, the French pretending that they maintained this traffic from motives of pure compassion, in order to prevent the massacre of the English captives, whom, however, they did not set at liberty without exacting an exorbitant ransom. As these skulking parties of Indians were generally directed and headed by French commanders, repeated complaints were made to the governor of Louisbourg, who still answered, that his jurisdiction did not extend over the Indians, and that their French conductors were chosen from the inhabitants of Annapolis, who thought proper to remain in that country after it was ceded to the English, and were, in fact, the subjects of Great Britain. Even while the conferences were carried on for ascertaining the limits of Nova Scotia, the governor of Canada detached M. la Corne, with some regular troops, and a body of militia, to fortify a post on the bay of Chignecto, on pretence that this and a great part of the peninsula belonged to his government. The possession of this post not only secured to the Indians of the continent a free entrance into the peninsula, and a safe retreat in case of pursuit; but also encouraged the French inhabitants of Annapolis to rise in open rebellion against the English government.

*Perfidious practices of the French in Nova Scotia.*

In the spring of the year one thousand seven hundred and fifty, General Cornwallis, governor of Halifax, detached Major Laurence with a few men to reduce them to obedience. At his approach they burned their towns to ashes, forsook their possessions, and threw themselves under the protection of M. la Corne, who, thus reinforced, found himself at the head of fifteen hundred

*Major Laurence defeats the French neutrals.*

men, well provided with arms and ammunition. Major Laurence, being unable to cope with him in the field, demanded an interview, at which he desired to know for what cause the French inhabitants of Nova Scotia had shaken off their allegiance to the crown of Great Britain, and violated the neutrality which they had hitherto affected to profess. The French officer, without pretending to account for their behaviour, gave him to understand, in general terms, that he had orders to defend his post, and these orders he was determined to obey. The English major, finding himself too weak to attack their united force, and having no orders to commit hostilities against any but the Indians and their open abettors, returned to Halifax, without having been able to fulfil the purpose of his expedition. Immediately after his retreat, the French neutrals (so they were called) returned to the habitations which they had abandoned; and, in conjunction with the Indians, renewed their depredations upon the inhabitants of Halifax, and its dependent settlements. The English governor, justly incensed at these outrages, and seeing they would neither submit to the English government themselves, nor allow others to enjoy it with tranquillity, resolved to expel them effectually from the country they so ill deserved to possess. Major Laurence was again detached with a thousand men, transported by sea to Chignecto, where he found the French and Indians entrenched, in order to dispute his landing. Notwithstanding this opposition, he made a descent with a few companies, received and returned a smart fire, and rushing into their entrenchments, obliged them to fly with the utmost precipitation, leaving a considerable number killed and wounded on the spot. The fugitives saved themselves by crossing a river, on the farther bank of which La Corne stood at the head of his troops, drawn up in order to receive them as friends and dependents. He had by this time erected a fort, which he denominated Beau Sejour; and now the English built another on the opposite side of the river, which was called after its founder St. Laurence. This being provided with a good garrison, served as a check upon the French, and in some measure restrained the incursions of their barbarians. Not that it effectually answered this purpose; for the Indians and neutrals still seized every opportunity of attacking the English in the interior parts of the peninsula. In the course of the succeeding year they surprised the little town of Dartmouth, on the other side of Halifax-bay, where they killed and scalped a great number of people, and carried off some prisoners. For these expeditions the French always supplied them with boats, canoes, arms, and ammunition; and indeed they were conducted with such care and secrecy, that it was almost impossible to prevent their success. One sure remedy against the sudden and stolen incursions of those savages might have been found in the use of stanch hounds, which would have run upon the foot, detected the skulking parties of the Indians, and frustrated all their ambuscades: but this expedient, so easy and practicable, was never tried, though frequently recommended in public to the attention of the government, and the consideration of the colonists. The Indians continued to plunder and massacre the British subjects with impunity, and were countenanced by the French government in that country, who now strengthened their lodgment on the neck of the peninsula with an additional fort, distinguished by the name of Baye-verte; and built a third at the mouth of St. John's river, on the north side of the bay of Fundy.

All these previous steps to a rupture with England were taken with great deliberation, while the commissaries of both nations were disputing about the limits of the very country which they thus arrogantly usurped; and they proceeded to perfect their chain of forts to the southward, without paying the least regard to the expostulations of the English governors, or to a memorial presented at Versailles by the Earl of Albemarle, the British minister. He demanded that express orders should be sent to M. de la Jonquiere, the commander for the French in America, to desist from violence against the British subjects in that country; that the fort of Niagara should be immediately razed; that the subjects of Great Britain, who had been made prisoners, should be set at liberty, and indemnified for the losses they had sustained; and that the persons who had committed these excesses should be punished in an exemplary manner. True it is, six Englishmen, whom they had unjustly taken, were immediately dismissed; and the ambassador amused with general promises of sending such instructions to the French governor in America, as should anticipate any cause of complaint for the future; but, far from having any intention to perform these promises, the court of Versailles, without all doubt, exhorted La Jonquiere to proceed in bringing its ambitious schemes to perfection.

Every incident in America seemed to prognosticate war when the session of Parliament was opened on the fifteenth day of November; yet his majesty, on this occasion, told them, that the events of the year had not made it necessary for him to offer any thing in particular to their consideration relating to foreign affairs. He even declared, that the continuance of the public tranquillity, and the general state of Europe, remained upon the same footing as when they last parted; and assured them of his steadiness in pursuing the most effectual measures to preserve to his people the blessings of peace. He expressed uncommon concern, that the horrid crimes of robbery and of murder were of late rather increased than diminished, and earnestly recommended this important object to their serious attention. Affectionate addresses were presented by both Houses in answer to this harangue; and, what was very remarkable, they were proposed and passed without question or debate. *Session opened.*

The Commons continued the same number of seamen and land-forces for the ensuing year, which had been granted in the last session, and made suitable provision for all the exigencies of the state. The whole supply amounted to two millions seven hundred and ninety-seven thousand nine hundred and sixteen pounds, ten shillings, and two pence, to be raised by a land-tax of two shillings in the pound, a malt-tax, a continuation of certain duties on wine, vinegar, cider, and beer imported, a sum taken from the sinking-fund, and the overplus of certain grants, funds, and duties. The provisions made considerably exceeded the grants: but this excess was chargeable with the interest of what should be borrowed upon the credit of the land or malt-tax, there being a clause of credit in both, as also with the deficiency (if any should happen) in the sums they were computed to produce. The House agreed to all these resolutions almost unanimously; indeed, no opposition was made to any of them, but that for continuing the same number of land-forces, which was carried by a great majority. *Supplies granted.*

The act permitting Jews to be naturalized, which had, during the last session, triumphed over such an obstinate opposition, was by this time become the subject of national horror and execration. Every *Repeal of the act for naturalizing Jews.*

part of the kingdom resounded with the reproach of the ministry who had enforced such an odious measure; and the two brothers, who engrossed the greater part of the administration, trembled at the prospect of what this clamour might produce at the general election, this being the last session of the present Parliament. So eager were the ministers to annul this unpopular measure, that, immediately after the peers had agreed to the nature and form of an address to his majesty, the Duke of Newcastle, with that precipitation so peculiar to his character, poured forth an abrupt harangue in that House, importing, that the disaffected had made a handle of the act passed last session in favour of the Jews, to raise discontents among many of his majesty's good subjects; and as the act was in itself of little importance, he was of opinion it ought to be repealed; for this purpose he presented a bill ready framed, which was read and committed, though not without some debate. The naturalization bill, now devoted as a sacrifice to the resentment of the people, contained a clause disabling all naturalized Jews from purchasing, inheriting, or receiving any advowson or presentation, or right to any ecclesiastical benefice or promotion, school, hospital, or donative, ; and by the first draft of the bill, which his grace now presented, it was intended that this clause should not be repealed. It was the opinion, however, of the majority, that such a clause standing unrepealed might imply that the Jews, by being thus expressly excluded from the possession of any ecclesiastical right of presentation, would be considered as having the power and privilege of purchasing and inheriting any lay property in the kingdom. On this consideration an amendment was made in the bill, the clause in question was left out, and the whole act of naturalization repealed without exception.\* Though the Lords in general concurred in the expediency of the repeal, it was opposed by some few, as too great a sacrifice to the idle and unfounded clamours of the multitude; and upon this side of the debate a great power of elocution was displayed by Earl Temple, (who had lately succeeded to this title on the death of his mother,) a nobleman of distinguished abilities, and the most amiable disposition, frank,

\* The reverend bench of bishops had, with a laudable spirit of Christian meekness and philanthropy, generally approved of the indulgence granted to their Hebrew brethren; and now they acquiesced in the proposed repeal with the same passive discretion, though one of the number contended for the saving clause which the Duke of N——had recommended.

liberal, humane, and zealously attached to the interest and honour of his country. In the Lower House, the members of both parties seemed to vie with each other in demonstrations of aversion to this unpopular act. On the very first day of the session, immediately after the motion for an address to his majesty, Sir James Dashwood, an eminent leader in the opposition, gave the Commons to understand, that he had a motion of very great importance to make, which would require the attention of every member, as soon as the motion for the address should be discussed; he therefore desired they would not quit the House, until he should have an opportunity to explain his proposal. Accordingly, they had no sooner agreed to the motion for an address of thanks to his majesty, than he stood up again; and having expatiated upon the just and general indignation which the act of the preceding session, in favour of the Jews, had raised among the people, he moved to order that the House should be called over on Tuesday the fourth day of December, for taking that act into consideration; but being given to understand, that it was not usual to appoint a call of the House for any particular purpose, he agreed that the motion should be general. It was seconded by Lord Parker, his opposite in political interests; the House agreed to it without opposition, and the call was ordered accordingly. They were anticipated, however, by the Lords, who framed and transmitted to them a bill on the same subject, to the purport of which the Commons made no objection; for every member, having the fear of the general election before his eyes, carefully avoided every expression which could give umbrage to his constituents; but violent opposition was made to the preamble, which ran in the following strain: " Whereas an act of Parliament was made and passed in the twenty-fifth year of his majesty's reign, entitled 'An Act to permit Persons professing the Jewish Religion to be naturalized by Parliament, and for other Purposes therein mentioned;' and whereas occasion has been taken, from the said act, to raise discontents and disquiets in the minds of his majesty's subjects, be it enacted," &c. This introduction was considered as an unjust reflection upon the body of the people in general, and in particular upon those who had opposed the bill in the course of the preceding session. Sir Roger Newdigate therefore moved, that the expression should be varied to this effect: " Whereas great discontents and disquietudes had from the said act arisen." The consequence of this motion was an obstinate debate, in which it was supported by the Earl of Egmont, and divers other able orators; but Mr. Pelham and Mr. Pitt were numbered among its opponents. The question being put for the proposed alteration, it was of course carried in the negative; the bill, after the third reading, passed *nemine contradicente*, and in due time obtained the royal assent.

<small>Motion for repealing a former act favourable to the Jews.</small> Even this concession of the ministry did not allay the resentment of the people, and their apprehensions of encroachment from the Jews. Another act still subsisted, by virtue of which any person professing the Jewish religion might become a free denizen of Great Britain, after having resided seven years in any of his majesty's colonies in America; and this was now considered as a law, having the same dangerous tendency, of which the other was now in a fair way of being convicted. It was moved, therefore, in the Lower House, that part of this former act might be read: then the same member made a motion for an address to his majesty, desiring that the House might have the perusal of the lists transmitted from the American colonies to the commissioners for trade and plantations, containing the names of all such persons professing the Jewish religion as had entitled themselves to the benefit of the said act, since the year one thousand seven hundred and forty. These lists were accordingly presented, and left upon the table for the perusal of the members; but as this act contained no limitation of time within which the benefit of it should be claimed, and as this claim was attended with a good deal of trouble and some expense, very few persons had availed themselves of it in that period. Nevertheless, as a great number of Jews were already entitled to claim this indulgence, and as it remained an open channel through which Great Britain might be deluged with those people, all of whom the law would hold as natural-born subjects, and their progeny as freed from all the restrictions contained in the act with respect to naturalized foreigners, Lord Harley moved for leave to bring in a bill to repeal so much of the said act as related to persons professing the Jewish religion, who should come to settle in any British colony after a certain time. The motion was seconded by Sir James Dashwood, and supported by the Earl of Egmont; but being found unequal to the interest

and elocution of Mr. Pelham and Mr. Pitt, was rejected by the majority.

The next object that claimed the attention of the Commons was a bill for improving the regulations already made to prevent the spreading of a contagious distemper, which raged among the horned cattle in different parts of the kingdom. The last bill of this session that had the good fortune to succeed was brought in for punishing mutiny and desertion of officers and soldiers in the service of the East India Company, and for the punishment of offences committed in the East Indies and the island of St. Helena. This being a measure of a very extraordinary nature, all the members were ordered to attend the House on the day fixed for the second reading; at the same time all charters, commissions, and authorities, by which any powers relative to a military jurisdiction, or the exercise of martial law, had been granted or derived from the crown to the said company, were submitted to the perusal of the members. The bill was by many considered as a dangerous extension of military power, to the prejudice of the civil rights enjoyed by British subjects, and as such violently contested by the Earl of Egmont, Lord Strange, and Mr. Alderman Beckford. Their objections were answered by the solicitor-general and Mr. Yorke. The bill, after some warm debates, being espoused by the ministry, was enacted into a law, and despatched to the East Indies by the first opportunity.

*1754. East India mutiny bill.*

Some other motions were made, and petitions presented, on different subjects, which, as they miscarried, it will be unnecessary to particularize. It may not be amiss, however, to record an exemplary act of justice done by the Commons on a person belonging to a public office, whom they detected in the practice of fraud and imposition. Notwithstanding the particular care taken in the last session to prevent the monopolizing of tickets in the state lottery, all those precautions had been eluded in a scandalous manner by certain individuals intrusted with the charge of delivering the tickets to the contributors, according to the intent of the act, which expressly declared that not more than twenty should be sold to any one person. Instead of conforming to these directions of the legislature, they and their friends engrossed great numbers, sheltering themselves under a false list of feigned names for the purpose; by which means

*Case of Le ——.*

they not only defeated the equitable intention of the Commons, but in some measure injured the public credit; inasmuch as their avarice had prompted them to subscribe for a greater number than they had cash to purchase, so that there was a deficiency in the first payment, which might have had a bad effect on the public affairs. These practices were so flagrant and notorious as to attract the notice of the Lower House, where an inquiry was begun, and prosecuted with a spirit of real patriotism, in opposition to a scandalous cabal, who endeavoured with equal eagerness and perseverance to screen the delinquents. All their efforts, however, proved abortive; and a committee, appointed to examine particulars, agreed to several severe resolutions against one Le ——, who had amassed a large fortune by this and other kinds of peculation. They voted him guilty of a breach of trust, and a direct violation of the lottery act; and an address was presented to his majesty, desiring he might be prosecuted by the attorney-general for these offences. He was accordingly sued in the court of King's Bench, and paid a fine of one thousand pounds, for having committed frauds by which he had gained forty times that sum; but he was treated with such gentleness as remarkably denoted the clemency of that tribunal.

The session ended in the beginning of April, when the king gave the Parliament to understand that he should say nothing at present on foreign affairs; but assured them of his fixed resolution to exert his whole power in maintaining the general tranquillity, and adhering to such measures for that purpose as he had hitherto pursued in conjunction with his allies. He in very affectionate terms thanked both Houses for the repeated proofs they had given of their zealous attachment and loyalty to his person and government. He enumerated the salutary measures they had taken for lessening the national debt, and augmenting the public credit, extending navigation and commerce, reforming the morals of the people, and improving the regulations of civil economy. He concluded with declaring, that he securely relied upon the loyalty and good affection of his people, and had no other aim than their permanent happiness. In a little time after the close of this session they were dissolved by proclamation, and new writs issued by the lord chancellor for convoking a new Parliament. The same ceremonies were practised with respect to the convo-

*Session closed.*

cations of Canterbury and York; though they no longer retained their former importance; nor, indeed, were they suffered to sit and deliberate upon the subjects which formerly fell under their cognizance and discussion.

In the beginning of March, the ministry of Great Britain had been left without a head by the death of Mr. Pelham, which was not only sincerely lamented by his sovereign, but also regretted by the nation in general, to whose affection he had powerfully recommended himself by the candour and humanity of his conduct and character, even while he pursued measures which they did not entirely approve. The loss of such a minister was the more deeply felt by the government at this juncture, being the eve of a general election for a new Parliament, when every administration is supposed to exert itself with redoubled vigilance and circumspection. He had already concerted the measures for securing a majority, and his plan was faithfully executed by his friends and adherents, who still engrossed the administration. His brother, the Duke of Newcastle, was appointed first lord commissioner of the treasury, and succeeded as secretary of state by Sir Thomas Robinson, who had long resided as ambassador at the court of Vienna. The other department of this office was still retained by the Earl of Holdernesse: and the function of chancellor of the exchequer was performed as usual by the lord chief justice of the King's Bench, until a proper person could be found to fill that important office; but in the course of the summer it was bestowed upon Mr. Legge, who acquitted himself with equal honour and capacity. Divers other alterations were made, of less importance to the public; Sir George Lyttelton was appointed cofferer, and the Earl of Hillsborough comptroller of the household. Mr. George Grenville, brother to Earl Temple, became treasurer of the navy; and Mr. Charles Townshend, of whom we shall have occasion to speak in the sequel, took place as a commissioner at the board of Admiralty, in the room of Lord Barrington, made master of the wardrobe. Lord Hardwicke, the chancellor, was promoted to the dignity of an earl. The place of lord chief justice of the King's Bench, becoming vacant by the death of Sir William Lee, was filled with Sir Dudley Rider, and he was succeeded by Mr. Murray in the office of attorney-general.

The elections for the new Parliament generally succeeded

according to the wish of the ministry; for opposition was now dwindled down to the lowest state of imbecility. It had received a mortal wound by the death of the late Prince of Wales, whose adherents were too wise to pursue an *ignis fatuus*, without any prospect of success or advantage. Some of them had prudently sung their palinodia to the ministry, and been gratified with profitable employments; while others, setting too great a price upon their own importance, kept aloof till the market was over, and were left to pine in secret over their disappointed ambition. The maxims of toryism had been relinquished by many, as the barren principles of a losing game; the body of the people were conciliated to the established government: and the harmony that now, for the first time, subsisted among all the branches of the royal family, had a wonderful effect in acquiring a degree of popularity which they had never before enjoyed. The writs being returned, the new Parliament was opened on the last day of May, by the Duke of Cumberland, and some other peers, who acted by virtue of a commission from his majesty. The Commons having chosen for their speaker the Right Hon. Arthur Onslow, who had honourably filled that high office in four preceding Parliaments, he was presented and approved by the commissioners. Then the lord high chancellor harangued both Houses, giving them to understand, that his majesty had indulged them with this early opportunity of coming together, in order to complete without loss of time certain parliamentary proceedings, which he judged would be for the satisfaction of his good subjects; but he did not think proper to lay before them any points of general business, reserving every thing of that nature to the usual time of their assembling in the winter. On the fifth day of June this short session was closed, and the Parliament prorogued by the lords commissioners.

In the beginning of this year violent disputes arose between the government and the House of Commons in Ireland, on the almost forgotten subjects of privilege and prerogative. The Commons conceived they had an undoubted right to apply the surplus of their revenue towards national purposes, without the consent of their sovereign; and, accordingly, in the year one thousand seven hundred and forty-nine, prepared a bill with this preamble: " Whereas on the twenty-fifth day of March last a considerable balance remained in the hands of the vice-treasurers or receivers-general of the kingdom, or their deputy or deputies, unapplied: and it will be for your majesty's service, and for the ease of your faithful subjects in this kingdom, that so much thereof as can be conveniently spared should be paid, agreeably to your majesty's most gracious intentions, in discharge of part of the national debt." This appropriation gave great offence to the advocates for prerogative in England, who affirmed that the Commons had no right to apply any part of the unappropriated revenue, or even to take any such affair into consideration, without the previous consent of the crown, expressed in the most explicit terms. It was in consequence of this doctrine that the Duke of Dorset, lord lieutenant of Ireland, told them in the next session of Parliament, held in the year one thousand seven hundred and fifty-one, he was commanded by the king to acquaint them, that his majesty, ever attentive to the ease and happiness of his subjects, would graciously consent and recommend it to them, that such a part of the money then remaining in his treasury, as should be thought consistent with the public service, be applied towards the further reduction of the national debt. This declaration alarmed the Commons, zealous as they were for the preservation of their privileges; and in their address of thanks, which, like that of the Parliament of Great Britain, used always to echo back the words of the speech, they made no mention of his majesty's consent; but only acknowledged his gracious attention to their ease and happiness, in recommending to them the application of the surplus. They accordingly resolved to apply one hundred and twenty thousand pounds of that overplus towards the discharge of the national debt; and, in the preamble of the bill framed for this purpose, made no mention of his majesty's consent, though before they had acknowledged his goodness in recommending this application. The ministry in England were highly offended at this purposed omission, which they construed into a wilful encroachment on the prerogative; and the bill was sent back with an alteration in the preamble, signifying his majesty's consent as well as recommendation. The Irish House of Commons, being at that time deeply engaged in a minute inquiry into the conduct of a gentleman, a servant of the crown, and a member of their own House, accused of having misapplied a large sum of money, with which he had been intrusted for rebuilding or repairing the barracks, were now unwilling to embroil themselves farther with the government, until this affair should be discussed. They, therefore, passed the bill with the alteration, and proceeded with their inquiry. The person was convicted of having misapplied the public money, and ordered to make the barracks fit for the reception and accommodation of the troops at his own expense. They did not, however, neglect to assert what they thought their rights and privileges, when the next opportunity occurred. The Duke of Dorset, when he opened the session of this year, repeated the expression of his majesty's gracious consent, in mentioning the surplus of the public money. They again omitted that word in their address; and resolved, in their bill of application, not only to sink this odious term, but likewise to abate in their complaisance to the crown, by leaving out that expression of grateful acknowledgment, which had met with such a cold reception above. By this time the contest had kindled up two violent factions, and diffused a general spirit of resentment through the whole Irish nation. The committee who prepared the bill, instead of inserting the usual compliments in the preamble, mentioned nothing but a recital of facts, and sent it over in a very plain dress, quite destitute of all embroidery. The ministry, intent upon vindicating the prerogative from such an unmannerly attack, filled up the omissions of the committee, and sent it back with this alteration: "And your majesty, ever attentive to the ease and happiness of your faithful subjects, has been graciously pleased to signify that you would consent, and to recommend it to us, that so much of the money remaining in your majesty's treasury as should be necessary to be applied to the discharge of the national debt, or such part thereof as should be thought expedient by Parliament." This then being the crisis which was to determine a constitutional point of such importance, namely, whether the people in Parliament assembled have a right to deliberate upon and vote the application of any part of the unappropriated revenue, without the previous consent of the crown; those who were the most zealously attached to the liberties of their country resolved to exert themselves in opposing what they conceived to be a violation of those liberties; and the bill, with its alterations, was rejected by a majority of five voices. The success of their endeavours was celebrated with the most extravagant rejoicings, as a triumph of patriotism over the arts of ministerial corruption; and, on the other hand, all the servants of the crown, who had joined the popular cry on this occasion, were in a little time dismissed from their employments. The rejection of the bill was a great disappointment to the creditors of the public, and the circulation of cash was almost stagnated. These calamities were imputed to arbitrary designs in the government; and the people began to be inflamed with an enthusiastic spirit of independency, which might have produced mischievous effects, had not artful steps been taken to bring over the demagogues, and thus divert the stream of popular clamour from the ministry to those very individuals who had been the idols of popular veneration. The speaker of the House of Commons was promoted to the dignity of an earl; and some other patriots were gratified with lucrative employments. His majesty's letter arrived for paying off seventy-five thousand five hundred pounds of the national debt. The circulation was thus animated, and the resentment of the populace subsiding, the kingdom retrieved its former tranquillity.

The ambition and intrigues of the French court, by which the British interest was invaded and disturbed on the continent of America, had also extended itself to the East Indies, where they endeavoured to embroil the English company with divers nabobs, or princes, who governed different parts of the peninsula intrà Gangem. That the reader may have a clear and distinct idea of these transactions, we shall exhibit a short sketch of the English forts and settlements in that remote country. The first of these we shall mention is Surat,[b] in the province so called, situated between the twenty-first and twenty-second degrees of north latitude; from hence the peninsula stretches into the Indian ocean as far as the latitude of eight north, ending in a point at Cape Comorin, which is the southern extremity. To the northward this peninsula joins to Indostan, and at its

*Transactions in the East Indies.*

---

[b] Several European nations had settlements at Surat, which was one of the most frequented cities of the East, from the great concourse of Mahometan pilgrims, who make it their road from India, in their visits to the tomb of their prophet at Mecca. In order to keep the seas clear of pirates between Surat and the gulf of Arabia and Persia, the mogul had been at the annual expense of a large ship fitted out on purpose to carry the pilgrims to Jadda, which is within a small distance of Mecca. For the security of this ship, as well as to protect the trade of Surat, he granted to his admiral, the *siddee* chief of a colony of caffrees, or blacks, a revenue called the tanka, to the value of three lacks of rupees, amounting to above thirty-seven thousand pounds, arising partly from the adjacent lands, and partly from the revenues of Surat, which were paid him yearly by the governor of the castle, who is appointed by the mogul to keep the city under proper subjection, without, however, interfering with the government of it.

greatest breadth extends seven hundred miles. Upon the west, east, and south, it is washed by the sea. It comprehends the kingdoms of Malabar, Decan, Golconda, and Bisnagar, with the principalities of Gingi, Tanjour, and Madura. The western side is distinguished by the name of the Malabar coast; the eastern takes the denomination of Coromandel; and, in different parts of this long sweep, from Surat round Cape Comorin to the bottom of the bay of Bengal, the English and other European powers have, with the consent of the mogul, established forts and trading settlements. All these kingdoms, properly speaking, belong to the mogul; but his power was so weakened by the last invasion of Kouli Khan, that he has not been able to assert his empire over this remote country; the tributary princes of which, and even the nabobs, who were originally governors appointed under their authority, have rendered themselves independent, and exert an absolute dominion over their respective territories, without acknowledging his superiority either by tribute or homage. These princes, when they quarrel among themselves, naturally have recourse to the assistance of such European powers as are settled in or near their dominions; and in the same manner the East Indian companies of the European powers, which happen to be at war with each other, never fail to interest the nabobs in the dispute.

Account of the English settlements on the Malabar and Coromandel coasts. The next English settlement to Surat, on the coast of the peninsula, is Bombay, in the kingdom of Decan, a small island, with a very convenient harbour, about five-and-forty leagues to the south of Surat. The town is very populous; but the soil is barren, and the climate unhealthy; and the commerce was rendered very precarious by the neighbourhood of the famous corsair Angria, until his fort of Geriah was taken, and his fortifications demolished. The English company likewise carry on some traffic at Dabul, about forty leagues farther to the south, in the province of Cuncan. In the same southerly progression, towards the point of the peninsula, we arrive at Carwar, in the latitude of fifteen degrees, where there is a small fort and factory belonging to the company, standing on the south side of a bay, with a river capable of receiving ships of pretty large burden. The climate here is remarkably salubrious: the country abounds with provisions of all sorts, and the best pepper of India grows in this neighbourhood. The next English settlement we find at Tillicherry, where the company has erected a fort, to defend their commerce of pepper and cardamoms from the insults of the rajah, who governs this part of Malabar. Hither the English trade was removed from Calicut, a large town that stands fifteen leagues to the southward of Tillicherry, and was as well frequented as any port on the coast of the Indian peninsula. The most southerly settlement which the English possess on the Malabar coast is that of Angengo, between the eighth and ninth degrees of latitude. It is defended by a regular fort, situated on a broad river, which falls into the sea, and would be very commodious for trade, were not the water on the bar too shallow to admit ships of considerable burden. Then turning the Cape, and passing through the strait of Chilao, formed by the island of Ceylon, we arrive on the coast of Coromandel, which forms the eastern side of the isthmus. Prosecuting our course in a northern direction, the first English factory we reach is that of Fort St. David's, formerly called Tegapatan, situated in the latitude of eleven degrees forty minutes north, within the kingdom of Gingi. It was, about six-and-twenty years ago, sold by a Mahratta prince to the East India Company, and, next to Bombay, is the most considerable settlement we have yet mentioned. Its territory extends about eight miles along the coast, and half that space up the country, which is delightfully watered by a variety of rivers: the soil is fertile, and the climate healthy. The fort is regular, well provided with cannon, ammunition, and a numerous garrison, which is the more necessary, on account of the neighbourhood of the French settlement of Pondicherry.\* But the chief settlement belonging to the company on this coast is that of Madras, or Fort St. George, standing farther to the northward, between the thirteenth and fourteenth degrees of latitude, and not a great way from the diamond mines of Golconda. It is seated on a flat, barren, scorching sand, so near the sea, that in bad weather the walls are endangered by the mighty surges rolled in from the ocean. As the soil is barren, the climate is so intensely hot that it would be altogether uninhabitable, were not the heat mitigated by the sea-breezes. On the land side it is defended by a salt-water river, which, while it contributes to the security of the place,

---

\* The trade consists of long cloths of different colours, sallampores, morees, dimities, ginghams, and succatoons.

robs the inhabitants of one great comfort, by obstructing the springs of fresh water. The fort is a regular square, the town surrounded with walls well mounted with artillery, and the place, including the Black Town, is very populous. Madras, with several villages in the neighbourhood, was purchased of the King of Golconda, before the mogul became sovereign of this country. The governor of this place is not only president of Fort St. George, but also of all the other settlements on the coasts of Malabar and Coromandel, as far as the island of Sumatra. He lives in great pomp, having inferior judges, who pass sentence of death occasionally on malefactors of any nation, except the subjects of Great Britain. All the company's affairs are directed by him and his council, who are invested with the power of inflicting corporal punishment, short of life and member, upon such Europeans as are in the service, and dispose of all places of trust and profit. By virtue of an act passed in the course of this very session, the military officers belonging to the company were permitted to hold courts-martial, and punish their soldiers according to the degree of their delinquency. In a word, Madras is of the utmost importance to the company for its strength, wealth, and the great returns it makes in calicoes and muslins. Towards the latter end of the last century the English company had a flourishing factory at Masulipatam, standing on the north side of the river Nagundi, which separates the provinces of Golconda and Bisnagar, in the latitude of sixteen degrees and thirty minutes; but now there is no European settlement here, except a Dutch factory, maintained for carrying on the chintz commerce. At Visagapatam, situated still farther to the northward, the English possess a factory, regularly fortified, on the side of a river, which, however, a dangerous bar has rendered unfit for navigation. The adjacent country affords cotton cloths, and the best striped muslins of India. It is chiefly for the use of this settlement that the company maintains a factory at Ganjam, the most eastern town in the province or kingdom of Golconda, situated in a country abounding with rice and sugar-canes. Still farther to the north coast, in the latitude of twenty-two degrees, the company maintains a factory at Balasore, which was formerly very considerable; but hath been of very little consequence since the navigation of the river Huguely was improved. At this place every European ship bound for Bengal and the

Ganges takes in a pilot. The climate is not counted very salubrious; but the adjacent country is fruitful to admiration, and here are considerable manufactures of cotton and silk. Without skilful pilots, the English would find it very difficult to navigate the different channels through which the river Ganges discharges itself into the sea at the bottom of the bay of Bengal. On the southern branch is a town called Pipely, where there was formerly an English factory; but this was removed to Huguely, one hundred and sixty miles farther up the river; a place which, together with the company's settlement at Calcutta, were the emporiums of their commerce for the whole kingdom of Bengal. Indeed Huguely is now abandoned by the English, and their whole trade centres at Calcutta or Fort William, which is a regular fortification, containing lodgings for the factors and writers, store-houses for the company's merchandise, and magazines for their ammunition. As for the governor's house, which likewise stands within the fort, it is one of the most regular structures in all India. Besides these settlements along the sea-coast of the peninsula, and on the banks of the Ganges, the English East India Company possess certain inland factories and posts for the convenience and defence of their commerce, either purchased of the nabobs and rajahs, or conquered in the course of the war. As the operations we propose to record were confined to the coasts of Malabar and Coromandel, or the interior countries which form the peninsula intrà Gangem, it will be unnecessary to describe the factory at Bencoolen, on the island of Sumatra, or any settlement which the English possess in other parts of the East Indies.

In order to understand the military transactions of the English company in India, the reader will take notice, that immediately after the peace of Aix-la-Chapelle, Monsieur Dupleix, who commanded for the French in that country, began by his intrigues to sow the seeds of dissension among the nabobs, that he might be the better able to fish in troubled waters. Nizam Almuluck, the mogul's viceroy of Decan, having the right of nominating a governor of the Carnatic, now more generally known by the name of the Nabob of Arcot, appointed Anaverdy Khan to that office in the year one thousand seven hundred and forty-five. The viceroy dying was succeeded in his viceroyalty, or subaship, by his second son Nazirzing, whom the mogul confirmed. He was op-

*Dispute about the government of Arcot.*

posed in his pretensions by his own cousin Muzapherzing, who had recourse to the assistance of M. Dupleix, and obtained from him a reinforcement of Europeans and artillery, in consideration of many presents and promises which he fulfilled in the sequel. Thus reinforced and joined by one Chunda Saib, an active Indian chief, he took the field against his kinsman Nazirzing, who was supported by a body of English troops under Colonel Laurence. The French, dreading an engagement, retired in the night; and Muzapherzing, seeing himself abandoned by all his own troops, appealed to the clemency of his cousin, who spared his life, but detained him as a state prisoner. In this situation he formed a conspiracy against his kinsman's life with Nazirzing's prime minister, and the Nabobs of Cadupab and Condancor, then in his camp: and the conspirators were encouraged in their scheme by Dupleix and Chunda Saib, who had retired to Pondicherry. Thus stimulated, they murdered Nazirzing in his camp, and proclaimed Muzapherzing Viceroy of Decan. In the tents of the murdered viceroy they found an immense treasure, of which a great share fell to M. Dupleix, whom Muzapherzing the usurper at this time associated in the government. By virtue of this association the Frenchman assumed the state and formalities of an eastern prince: and he and his colleague Muzapherzing appointed Chunda Saib Nabob of Arcot; Anaverdy Khan, the late nabob, had been, in the year one thousand seven hundred and forty-nine, defeated and slain by Muzapherzing and Chunda Saib, with the assistance of their French auxiliaries; and his son Mahommed Ali Khan had put himself under the protection of the English at Madras, and was confirmed by Nazirzing, as his father's successor in the nabobship, or government of Arcot. This government, therefore, was disputed between Mahommed Ali Khan, appointed by the legal Viceroy Nazirzing, supported by the English company, and Chunda Saib, nominated by the usurper Muzapherzing, and protected by Dupleix, who commanded at Pondicherry. Muzapherzing did not long survive his usurpation. In the year one thousand seven hundred and fifty-one, the same nabobs who had promoted him to his kinsman's place, thinking themselves ill rewarded for their services, fell upon him suddenly, routed his troops, and put him to death; and next day the chiefs of the army proclaimed Sallabatzing, brother to

Nazirzing, Viceroy of Decan: on the other hand, the mogul appointed Gauzedy Khan, who was the elder brother of Sallabatzing; and this prince confirmed Mahommed Ali Khan in the government of Arcot: but the affairs of the mogul's court were then in such confusion, that he could not spare an army to support the nomination he had made. Chunda Saib, Nabob of Arcot, having been deposed by the great mogul, who placed Anaverdy Khan in his room, he resolved to recover his government by force, and had recourse to the French general at Pondicherry, who reinforced him with two thousand sepoys, or soldiers of the country, sixty caffrees, and four hundred and twenty French troops, on condition that, if he proved successful in his enterprise, he should cede to the French the town of Velur, in the neighbourhood of Pondicherry, with its dependencies, consisting of forty-five villages. Thus reinforced, he defeated his rival Anaverdy Khan, who lost his life in the engagement, reassumed the government of Arcot, and punctually performed the conditions which had been stipulated by his French allies.

Mahommed Ali Khan, at the death of his father, had fled to Tiruchirapalli,[4] and solicited the assistance of the English, who favoured him with a reinforcement of money, men, and ammunition, under the conduct of Major Laurence, a brave and experienced officer. By dint of this supply he gained some advantages over the enemy, who were obliged to retreat; but no decisive blow was given. Mahommed afterwards repaired in person to Fort St. David's to demand more powerful succours, alleging that his fate was connected with the interest of the English company, which in time would be obliged to abandon the whole coast, should they allow the enemy to proceed in their conquests. In consequence of these representations, he received another strong reinforcement under the command of Captain Cope; but nothing of importance was attempted, and the English auxiliaries retired. Then Mahommed was attacked by the enemy, who obtained a complete victory over him. Finding it impossible to maintain his footing by his own strength, he entered into a close alliance with the English, and ceded

*Mahommed Ali Khan supported by the English.*

---

[4] Tiruchirapalli, commonly called Trichinopoly, situated near the river Cauveri, above two hundred miles to the southward of Madras, is the capital of a small kingdom belonging to the government of Arcot, and bounded on the east by the kingdom of Tanjore.

to them some commercial points which had been long in dispute. Then they detached Captain Cope to put Tiruchirapalli in a posture of defence; while Captain de Gingins, a Swiss officer, marched at the head of four hundred Europeans to the nabob's assistance. The two armies, being pretty equal in strength, lay encamped in sight of each other a whole month; during which nothing happened but a few skirmishes, which generally terminated to the advantage of the English auxiliaries. In order to make a diversion, and divide the French forces, the company resolved to send a detachment into the province of Arcot; and this was one of the first occasions upon which the extraordinary talents of Mr. Clive were displayed. He had entered into the service of the East India Company as a writer, and was considered as a person very indifferently qualified for succeeding in any civil station of life. He now offered his service in a military capacity, and actually began his march to Arcot, at the head of two hundred and ten Europeans, with five hundred sepoys.*

Mr. Clive takes Arcot. Such was the resolution, secrecy, and despatch with which he conducted this enterprise, that the enemy knew nothing of his motions until he was in possession of the capital, which he took without opposition. The inhabitants, expecting to be plundered, offered him a large sum to spare their city; but they derived their security from the generosity and discretion of the conqueror. He refused the proffered ransom, and issued a proclamation, intimating, that those who were willing to remain in their houses should be protected from insult and injury, and the rest have leave to retire with all their effects except provisions, for which he promised to pay the full value. By this sage conduct he conciliated the affections of the people so entirely, that even those who quitted the place supplied him with exact intelligence of the enemy's designs, when he was besieged in the sequel. The town was in a little time invested by Rajah Saib, son of Chunda Saib, at the head of a numerous army, and the operations of the siege were conducted by European engineers. Though their approaches were retarded by the repeated and resolute sallies of Mr. Clive, they at length effected two breaches supposed to be practicable; and on the fourteenth day of October, in the year one thousand seven

* The sepoys are the mercenaries of the country, who are hired as soldiers occasionally by all parties.

hundred and fifty-one, gave a general assault. Mr. Clive, having received intimation of their design, had made such preparations for their reception, that they were repulsed in every quarter with great loss, and obliged to raise the siege with the utmost precipitation.

This gallant Englishman, not contented with the reputation he had acquired from his noble defence, was no sooner reinforced by a detachment under Captain Kirkpatrick, from Trichinopoly, than he marched in pursuit of the enemy, whom he overtook in the plains of Arani. There, on the third day of December, he attacked them with irresistible impetuosity; and after an obstinate dispute, obtained a complete victory at a very small expense. The forts of Timery, Caujeveram, and Aranie, surrendered to the terror of his name, rather than to the force of his arms; and he returned to Fort St. David's in triumph. He had enjoyed a very few weeks of repose, when he was summoned to the field by fresh incursions of the enemy. In the beginning of the year one thousand seven hundred and fifty-two, he marched with a small detachment to Madras, where he was joined by a reinforcement from Bengal, the whole number not exceeding three hundred Europeans, and assembled a body of the natives, that he might have at least the appearance of an army. With these he proceeded to Koveripauk, about fifteen miles from Arcot, where he found the French and Indians, consisting of fifteen hundred sepoys, seventeen hundred horse, a body of natives, and one hundred and fifty Europeans, with eight pieces of cannon. Though they were advantageously posted and intrenched, and the day was already far advanced, Mr. Clive advanced against them with his usual intrepidity; but the victory remained for some time in suspense. It was now dark, and the battle doubtful, when Mr. Clive sent round a detachment to fall in the rear of the French battery. This attack was executed with great resolution, while the English in front entered the intrenchments with their bayonets fixed; and though very little tinctured with discipline, displayed the spirit and activity of hardy veterans. This double attack disconcerted the enemy in such a manner, that they soon desisted from all opposition. A considerable carnage ensued; yet the greater part of the enemy, both horse and foot, saved themselves by flight, under cover of the darkness. The French, to a man, threw down their arms, and surrendered themselves prisoners of war; and all the cannon and baggage fell into the hands of the victor.

The province of Arcot being thus cleared of the enemy, Mr. Clive with his forces returned to Fort St. David's, where he found Major Laurence just arrived from England,[f] to take upon him the command of the troops in the company's service. On the eighteenth day of March this officer, accompanied by Mr. Clive, took the field, and was joined by Captain de Gingins at Tiruchirapalli. From hence he detached Mr. Clive with four hundred European soldiers, a few Mahratta horse, and a body of sepoys, to cut off the enemy's retreat to Pondicherry. In the course of this expedition he dislodged a strong body of the foe posted at Samiaveram, and obliged Chunda Saib to throw a body of troops into a strong fortified temple, or pagoda, upon the river Koleroon, which was immediately invested. The commanding officer, in attempting to escape, was slain with some others, and the rest surrendered at discretion. They were still in possession of another fortified temple, which he also besieged in form, and reduced by capitulation. Having subdued these forts, he marched directly to Volconda, whither he understood the French commander D'Anteuil had retired. He found that officer intrenched in a village, from whence he drove him with precipitation, and made himself master of the French cannon. The enemy attempted to save themselves in the neighbouring fort; but the gates being shut against them by the governor, who was apprehensive that they would be followed pell-mell by the English, Mr. Clive attacked them with great fury, and made a considerable slaughter; but his humanity being shocked at this carnage, he sent a flag of truce to the vanquished, with terms of capitulation, which they readily embraced. These articles imported, that D'Anteuil, and three other officers, should remain prisoners on parole for one year, that the garrison should be exchanged, and the money and stores be delivered to the nabob whom the English supported.

During these transactions Chunda Saib lay encamped with an army of thirty thousand men at Syrinham, an island in the neighbourhood of Tiruchirapalli, which he longed eagerly to possess. Hither Major Laurence marched with his Indian allies,[g] and took his measures so well, that the enemy's

---
[f] Major Laurence had sailed for England in the year 1750.
[g] His army consisted of twelve hundred Europeans and Topasses in battalions, two

provisions were entirely intercepted. Chunda Saib, in attempting to fly, was taken prisoner by the Nabob of Tanjore, an ally of the English company, who ordered his head to be struck off, in order to prevent the disputes which otherwise would have arisen among the captors.[b] The main body of the army being attacked by Major Laurence, and totally defeated, the island of Syrinham was surrendered, and about a thousand European French soldiers, under the command of Mr. Law, nephew to the famous Law, who schemed the Mississippi company, fell into the hands of the conquerors, including thirty officers, with forty pieces of cannon, and ten mortars. M. Dupleix, though exceedingly mortified by this disaster, resolved to maintain the cause which he had espoused. He proclaimed Rajah Saib, the son of Chunda Saib, nabob of Arcot; and afterwards pretended that he himself had received from the mogul sanids or commissions appointing him governor of all the Carnatic, from the river Kristnah to the sea; but these sanids appeared in the sequel to be forged. In order to complete the comedy, a supposed messenger from Delhi was received at Pondicherry as ambassador from the mogul. Dupleix, mounted on an elephant, preceded by music and dancing women, in the oriental manner, received in public his commission from the hands of the pretended ambassador. He affected the eastern state, kept his darbar or court, where he appeared sitting cross-legged on a sofa, and received presents as prince of the country from his own council, as well as from the natives. In the mean time, hostilities continued between the forces of the two companies, as auxiliaries to the contending nabobs. The English, under Major Kinnier, made an unsuccessful attempt upon Ginge, a strong town situated to the west of Pondicherry. Major Laurence defeated a strong body of French and natives, commanded by Dupleix's nephew, M. de Kerjean, in the neighbourhood of Pondicherry, and took him prisoner, together with fifteen officers: after this success, Mr. Clive reduced the

---

thousand sepoys, with the forces of the nabob, the Kings of Tanjore, Muissack, and the Mahrattas, amounting to fifteen hundred horse and ten thousand infantry. Topasses are descendants from the Portuguese. The Mahrattas are native Indians of a very numerous and powerful nation, which hath more than once given law to the mogul.

[b] Chunda Saib demanded leave of the Tanjore general to pass through his camp to Tanjore, and this request was granted; but instead of being allowed to pass, he was detained prisoner, and as the allies could not agree about the manner in which he should be disposed of, some of the Tanjore officers, of their own accord, ended the dispute by cutting off his head.

forts of Covelong and Chengalput, the last very strong, situated about forty miles to the southward of Madras. On the other hand, M. Dupleix intercepted at sea Captain Schaub, with his whole Swiss company, whom he detained prisoners at Pondicherry, although the two nations were not at war with each other. During these transactions Sallabatzing, with a body of French under M. de Bussy, advanced towards Aurengabad, which was the seat of government; but he was opposed by a chief of the Mahrattas, at the head of a numerous army. In the mean time Gauzedy Khan, the elder brother of Sallabatzing, whom the mogul had appointed Viceroy of Decan, took possession of his government at Aurengabad, where, in fourteen days after his arrival, he was poisoned by his own sister. The mogul immediately appointed his son Schah Abadin Khan to succeed his father; and this prince actually raised an army to come and take possession; but the mogul's affairs requiring his presence at Delhi, he was obliged to postpone his design, so that Sallabatzing was left without a competitor, and made a present to the French of all the English settlements to the northward. Thus concluded the year one thousand seven hundred and fifty-two. Next campaign was chiefly confined to the neighbourhood of Trichinopoly, where Major Laurence made several vigorous attacks upon the enemy's army, and obtained many advantages, which, however, did not prove decisive, because he was so much outnumbered that he could never follow his blow.

In the course of this year the mogul was deposed by his general, Schah Abadin Khan, the Viceroy of Decan, who raised to the throne Allum Geer, another prince of the blood. In the succeeding year, a negotiation was set on foot by Mr. Saunders, Governor of Madras, and M. Dupleix; and conferences were opened at Sadrass, a Dutch settlement between Pondicherry and Fort St. George; but this proved abortive; and many other gallant efforts were made by Major Laurence in the territory of Trichinopoly, which still continued to be the scene of action. In the course of this year Admiral Watson arrived on the coast of Coromandel with a squadron of ships of war, having on board a regiment commanded by Colonel Aldercroon: at the same time the ships from France brought over to Pondicherry the Sieur Godeheu, commissary-general and governor-general of all their settlements, at whose arrival Dupleix departed for Europe. The new governor immediately wrote a letter to Mr. Saunders, professing the most pacific inclinations, and proposing a suspension of arms between the two companies until their disputes could be amicably adjusted. This proposal was very agreeable to the governor and council at Madras, and a cessation of arms actually took place in the month of October, in the year one thousand seven hundred and fifty-four. Deputies being sent to Pondicherry, a provisional treaty and truce were concluded, on condition that neither of the two companies should for the future interfere in any difference that might arise between the princes of the country. The other articles related to the places and settlements that should be retained or possessed by the respective companies, until fresh orders relating to this agreement should arrive from the courts of London and Versailles, transmitted by the two East India companies of France and England. Until such orders should arrive, it was stipulated that neither nation should be allowed to procure any new grant or cession, or to build forts for the defence of new establishments: and that they should not proceed to any cession, retrocession, or evacuation of what they then possessed; but every thing should remain on the footing of *uti possidetis*. How pacific soever the sentiments of the French subjects might have been at this period in the East Indies, certain it is, the designs of the French governors in America were altogether hostile, and their conduct hastening towards a rupture, which kindled up a bloody war in every division of the globe.

As this war may be termed a native of America, and the principal scenes of it were acted on that continent, we shall, for the information of the reader, sketch out the situation of the then British colonies as they bordered on each other, and extended along the sea-coast, from the gulf of St. Lawrence as far south as the country of Florida. We shall enumerate the Indian nations that lie scattered about their confines, and delineate the manner in which the French hemmed them in by a surprising line of fortifications. Should we comprehend Hudson's Bay, with the adjacent countries, and the banks of Newfoundland, in this geographical detail, we might affirm that Great Britain at that time possessed a territory along the sea-coast, extending seventeen hundred miles in a direct line, from the sixtieth to the thirty-first degree of northern latitude; but as these two countries were not concerned in this dispute, we shall advance from the northward to the southern side of the gulf of St. Lawrence; and, beginning with Acadia or Nova Scotia, describe our settlements as they lie in a southerly direction, as far as the gulf of Florida. This great tract of country, stretching fifteen degrees of latitude, is washed on the east by the Atlantic Ocean: the southern boundary is Spanish Florida; but to the westward the limits are uncertain, some affirming that the jurisdiction of the colonies penetrates through the whole continent, as far as the South Sea; while others, with more moderation, think they are naturally bounded by the river Illinois that runs into the Mississippi, and in a manner connects that river with the chain of lakes known by the names of Michigan, Huron, Erie, and Ontario, the three first communicating with each other, and the last discharging itself into the river St. Lawrence, which, running by Montreal and Quebec, issues into the bay of the same denomination, forming the northern boundary of Nova Scotia. The French, who had no legal claim to any lands on the south side of this river, nevertheless, with an insolence of ambition peculiar to themselves, not only extended their forts from the source of the St. Lawrence, through an immense tract of that country, as far as the Mississippi, which disembogues itself into the gulf of Florida; but also by a series of unparalleled encroachments, endeavoured to contract the English colonies within such narrow limits as would have cut off almost one-half of their possessions. As we have already given a geographical description of Nova Scotia, and mentioned the particulars of the new settlement of Halifax, we shall now only observe, that it is surrounded on three sides by the sea, the gulf, and river St. Lawrence; that its original boundary to the west was the river Pentagoet; but it is now contracted within the river St. Croix, because the crown of Great Britain did, in the year one thousand six hundred and sixty-three, grant to the Duke of York the territory of Sagadahack, stretching from St. Croix to the river of this name; which was in the sequel, by an express charter from the crown, annexed to the province of Massachusett's-bay, one of the four governments of New England. This country, situated next to Nova Scotia, lies between the forty-first and forty-fifth degrees of north latitude, extending near three hundred miles in length, and above two hundred in breadth, if we bound it by those tracts which the French possessed; no part of the settlements of this country, however, stretches above sixty miles from the sea. The summer is here intensely hot, and the winter proportionably severe; nevertheless the climate is healthy, and the sky generally serene. The soil is not favourable to any of the European kinds of grain, but produces great plenty of maize, which the people bake into bread, and brew into beer, though their favourite drink is made of molasses hopped, and impregnated with the tops of the spruce-fir, which is a native of this country. The ground raises good flax and tolerable hemp. Here are great herds of black cattle, some of them very large in size, a vast number of excellent hogs, a breed of small horses, graceful, swift, and hardy, and large flocks of sheep, whose wool, though not so fine as that of England, is manufactured with great success.

New England is composed of the four provinces known by the names of New Hampshire, Massachusett's-bay, Rhode-Island, and Connecticut. It is bounded on the south by New York, extending northerly on both sides of the river Hudson, about two hundred miles into the country possessed by the Indians of the Five Nations, whom the French distinguish by the name of the Irroquois; but in breadth this province does not exceed fifty miles, though it comprehends Long-island, lying to the southward of Connecticut. The capital, which derives from the province the name of New York, is situated on an excellent harbour in the island of Manahatton, extending fourteen miles in length, and five in breadth, at the mouth of the noble river Hudson, which is navigable for above two hundred miles. At the distance of one hundred and fifty miles from New York stands the town of Albany, upon the same river. In this place all the treaties and other transactions were negotiated between the English and the Irroquois, a confederacy of five Indian nations, who, by their union, courage, and military skill, had reduced a great number of other Indian tribes, and subdued a territory more extensive than the whole kingdom of France. They were about fourscore years ago able to bring ten thousand warriors into the field; but now their number is so greatly diminished by wars, epidemical diseases, and the use of spirituous liquors, that they cannot raise above fifteen hundred men, even

*New England and New York.*

though they have admitted into their confederacy the nation of the Tuscaroras, whom the English drove from the confines of Carolina. The Mohock Indians inhabit the country advanced from Albany. The northern extremities of New Hampshire and New York are divided by the lakes Champlain and Sacrament, between which the French had raised the fort of Crown Point.

<small>New Jersey.</small> Contiguous to New York, and lying along the coast, in a southerly direction, is the small province of New Jersey, bounded on the west by the river Delaware, which divides it from Pennsylvania, extending about one hundred and fifty miles in length, but in breadth not more than one-third of that extent. The climate, soil, and produce of these two provinces, as well as of Pennsylvania, are similar. They yield great quantities of grain, sheep, horses, hogs, and horned cattle; all kinds of poultry and game in great abundance; vegetables of every sort in perfection; and excellent fruit, particularly peaches and melons. Their vast forests abound with oak, ash, beech, chesnut, cedar, walnut-tree, cypress, hickery, sassafras, and pine; but the timber is not counted so fit for shipping as that of New England and Nova Scotia. These provinces produce great quantities of flax and hemp. New York affords mines of iron, and very rich copper ore is found in New Jersey.

<small>Pennsylvania.</small> Pennsylvania, lying to the southward of New York and New Jersey, is bounded on the other side by Maryland, stretching two hundred and fifty miles in length, two hundred in breadth, and having no communication with the sea, except by the mouth of the river Delaware. This province was originally settled by Quakers, under the auspices of the celebrated William Penn, whose descendants are still proprietaries of the country. Philadelphia, the capital, stands on a tongue of land, at the confluence of the two navigable rivers, the Delaware and the Schulkel, disposed in the form of a regular oblong, and designed by the original plan to extend from the one to the other. The streets, which are broad, spacious, and uniform, cross each other at right angles, leaving proper spaces for churches, markets, and other public edifices. The houses are neatly built of brick, the quays spacious and magnificent, the warehouses large and numerous, and the docks commodious and well contrived for ship-building. Pennsylvania is understood to extend as far northerly as the banks of

the lake Erie, where the French erected a fort. They also raised another at some distance to the southward of the Rivière-au-Bœuf, and made other encroachments on this colony.

Adjoining to part of Pennsylvania, on the sea-coast, lies the province of Maryland, a tract of land situated along the bay of Chesapeak, in length about one hundred and forty miles, and nearly of the same breadth, bounded on the north by Pennsylvania, on the east by the Atlantic Ocean, and by the river Potowmack on the south. This country was first planted with Roman Catholics, by Lord Baltimore, to whom Charles II. granted it by patent. In the sequel, however, people of all religions were admitted into this settlement, and indulged with liberty of conscience, and at present the reigning religion is that of the English church. The climate is very sultry in summer, and not very salubrious. The soil is fruitful, and produces a great quantity of tobacco, which the people cultivate as their staple commodity. The seat of government is established at Annapolis, a small town beautifully situated on the river Patuxent. *Maryland.*

Tracing the sea-coast still southerly, the next settlement is Virginia, watered on the north by the river Potowmack, which is the boundary between this and the colony last described, having the bay of Chesapeak to the east, bounded on the south by Carolina, and extending westward without any prescribed limits, though the plantations have reached no farther than the great Allegany mountains; so that the province, as now possessed, stretches in length about two hundred and forty miles, and in breadth not above two hundred, lying between the fifty-fifth and fortieth degrees of latitude. In sailing to Virginia, navigators steer through a strait formed by two points, called the Capes, into the bay of Chesapeak, a large inlet that runs three hundred miles into the country from south to north, covered from the Atlantic Ocean by the eastern side of Maryland, and a small portion of Virginia on the same peninsula. This noble bay is about eighteen miles broad for a considerable space, and seven at its narrowest part, yielding generally nine fathoms depth of water: on both sides it receives many navigable rivers, those on the Virginia side being known by the names of James-river, York-river, the Rappahannock, and Potowmack. This country, especially *Virginia.*

towards the sea, lies very low and swampy, and the soil is extremely fertile. The air and weather are variable, the heats of summer excessive, the frosts of winter sudden and intensely cold: so that, upon the whole, the climate is neither very agreeable nor healthy, the people being particularly subject to agues and pleuritic disorders. The province abounds with vast forests of timber; the plains are covered with a surprising luxuriancy of vegetables, flowers, and flowering shrubs, diffusing the most delicious fragrance. The ground yields plenty of corn, and every sort of fruit in great abundance and perfection. Horned cattle and hogs have here multiplied to admiration since they were first imported from Europe. The animals, natives of this and the neighbouring countries, are deer, panthers or tigers, bears, wolves, foxes, squirrels, racoons, and creatures called opossums, with an infinite variety of beautiful birds, and a diversity of serpents, among which the rattle-snake is the most remarkable.

Virginia is bounded to the south by the two Carolinas, situated between the forty-sixth and thirty-first degrees of latitude; the length amounting to upwards of four hundred miles, and the breadth extending near three hundred, as far as the Indian nations called the Catawbas, the Creeks, and the Cherokees. The country of Carolina is divided into two governments, of which the most northern is the most inconsiderable. The climate in both is the same, as well as the soil; the first is warm, though not unhealthy; the last extremely fertile, yielding every thing in plenty which is produced in Virginia, besides abundance of excellent oranges, and some commodities which are not found to the northward. North Carolina, though not so opulent, is more populous than the southern part. The colonists of North Carolina carry on a considerable traffic in tar, pitch, turpentine, staves, shingles, lumber, corn, peas, pork and beef, tobacco, deer-skins, indigo, wheat, rice, bees-wax, tallow, bacon, and hog's lard, cotton, and squared timber, live cattle, with the skins of beaver, racoon, fox, minx, wild cat, and otter. South Carolina is much better cultivated; the people are more civilized, and the commerce more important. The capital of this province, called Charlestown, is finely situated at the confluence of two navigable rivers, having the advantage of a commodious harbour. Their trade, exclusive of the articles we have already mentioned as common to this government and that of North Carolina, consists of two chief staple commodities, rice and indigo, which they cultivate with great success; and they have likewise made some progress in the culture of silk.

The most southern of all our settlements on this coast is Georgia, extending about sixty miles from north to south, along the sea-shore; but widening in the inland parts to above one hundred and fifty, and stretching almost three hundred from the sea to the Apalachian mountains. This country differs very little from that of South Carolina, with which it borders; yet the summer is here more hot, and the soil not so fertile. Savannah, the capital, stands commodiously for trade, about ten miles from the sea, on a river of the same name, navigable with large boats two hundred miles farther up to the second town called Augusta, a place that flourishes by the Indian trade of skins, which the inhabitants carry on with their neighbours the Creeks, the Chickesaws, and the Cherokees, who are the most numerous and powerful tribes in America. Georgia is bounded on the south by the river Attamaha, at no great distance from the Spanish fort of St. Augustin.

*Georgia.*

Having thus exhibited a succinct view of the British colonies in North America, for the information of the reader, we shall now resume the thread of our history, and particularize the transactions by which the present year was distinguished on this extensive continent. The government of England, having received nothing but evasive answers from the court of France, touching the complaints that were made of the encroachments in America, despatched orders to all the governors of that country to repel force by force, and drive the French from their settlements on the river Ohio. Accordingly, the provinces of Virginia and Pennsylvania took this important affair into their consideration: but, while they deliberated, the French vigorously prosecuted their designs on the other side of the mountains; they surprised Log's-town, which the Virginians had built upon the Ohio; made themselves masters of the Block-house and Truck-house, where they found skins and other commodities to the amount of twenty thousand pounds, and destroyed all the British traders, except two who found means to escape. At the same time, M. de Contrecœur, with a thousand men, and eighteen pieces of cannon, arrived in three hundred canoes from Venango, a fort they had raised

*The French surprise Log's-town on the Ohio.*

on the banks of the Ohio, and reduced by surprise a British fort which the Virginians had built on the forks of the Monangahela, that runs into the same river.

These hostilities were followed by divers skirmishes between the people of the two nations, which were fought with various success. At length the governors of the English settlements received orders from England to form a political confederacy for their mutual defence; and the governor of New York was directed to confer with the chiefs of the six nations, with a view to detach them from the French interest by dint of promises and presents of value, sent over for that purpose. A congress was accordingly appointed at Albany, to which place the Governor of New York repaired, accompanied by commissioners from all the other British settlements; but a very small number of Indians arrived, and even these seemed to be indifferent to the advances and exhortations that were made by the English orator. The truth is, the French had artfully weaned them from their attachment to the subjects of Great Britain. Nevertheless, they accepted the presents, renewed their treaties with the King of England, and even demanded his assistance in driving the French from the posts and possessions they had usurped within the Indian territories. It was in consequence of the measures here taken, that Colonel Washington was detached from Virginia with four hundred men, and occupied a post on the banks of the river Ohio, where he threw up some works, and erected a kind of occasional fort, in hopes of being able to defend himself in that situation, until he should be joined by a reinforcement from New York, which, however, did not arrive.

*Conference with the Indians at Albany.*

While he remained in this situation, De Viller, a French commander, at the head of nine hundred men, being on his march to dislodge Washington, detached one Jamonville, an inferior officer, with a small party, and a formal summons to colonel Washington, requiring him to quit the fort, which he pretended was built on ground belonging to the French, or their allies. So little regard was paid to this intimation, that the English fell upon this party, and, as the French affirm, without the least provocation, either slew or took the whole detachment. De Viller, incensed at these unprovoked hostilities, marched up to the attack, which Washington for some time sustained

*Colonel Washington defeated and taken by the French on the Ohio.*

under manifold disadvantages. At length, however, he surrendered the fort upon capitulation, for the performance of which he left two officers as hostages in the hands of the French; and in his retreat was terribly harassed by the Indians, who plundered his baggage, and massacred his people. This event was no sooner known in England, than the British ambassador at Paris received directions to complain of it to the French ministry, as an open violation of the peace; but this representation had no effect.

Both nations by this time foresaw that a rupture would be inevitable, and each resolved to make suitable preparations. France continued to send reinforcements of men, and supplies of ammunition, to Quebec, for the prosecution of her ambitious projects; and the ministry of Great Britain transmitted salutary cautions to the governors of the provinces of North America, exhorting them to join their endeavours for repelling the incursions of the enemy. Such an union as seemed necessary for their common preservation was not easily effected. The different colonies were divided by different views and interests, both religious and political: besides, every settlement was distracted into factions, formed by the governor and the demagogues of the assembly; in other words, an opposition like that in Parliament, and a continual struggle between the liberties of the people and the prerogative of the proprietor, whether sovereign or subject. Mr. Dinwiddie, Governor of Virginia, having demanded a certain perquisite or fee for every patent he should pass for land, the assembly voted his demand illegal, arbitrary, and oppressive. They declared that every man who paid it should be deemed an enemy to his country; and sent over an agent to London, to solicit the suppression of this imposition. The representatives of the people in Pennsylvania wasted the time in vain deliberations and violent disputes with their proprietors, while the enemy infested their frontiers. The colony of New York was filled with discontent and animosity. Sir Danvers Osborne, who had been appointed governor of this province, died immediately after his arrival at New York, and the instructions he had received were exposed to public censure. The preamble inveighed severely against the want of duty, allegiance, loyalty, and unanimity, which had lately appeared so notorious in the assembly of that province, who had violated the royal commission and instructions, by assuming to themselves the power to dispose of public money in the laws which they had occasionally passed. This gentleman was therefore directed to insist upon the reformation of all those public abuses, and upon the establishment of a certain supply for the service of the government, as well as upon the settlement of a salary for himself. Moreover, his majesty, in these instructions, signified his will and pleasure, that all money raised for the supply and support of government, or upon any emergency for immediate service, should be disposed and applied properly to the use for which it might be granted, by warrant from the governor, by and with the advice and consent of the council of the province, and no otherwise: that, nevertheless, the assembly should be permitted, from time to time, to view and examine the accounts of money disposed of, by virtue of laws which they had enacted: that if any member of the council, or officer holding place of trust or profit within the government, should, in any manner whatever, give his assent to, or in anywise advise or concur with the assembly in passing any act or vote, whereby the royal prerogative might be lessened or impaired, or any money be raised or disposed of for the public service, contrary to, or inconsistent with, the method prescribed by these instructions, the governor should forthwith remove or suspend such councillor or officer so offending, and give an immediate account of his proceedings to the commissioners of trade and plantations. These were peremptory injunctions, which plainly proved that the ministry was determined to support the prerogative with a high hand; but it must be owned, at the same time, that abundance of provocation had been given by the insolent opposition of some turbulent individuals, who had exerted all their influence in disturbing and distressing the views and designs of the government. While the British colonies in America were, by these divisions, in a great measure disabled from making vigorous efforts against the common enemy, the administration at home began to exert itself for their defence. Officers were appointed for two regiments, consisting of two battalions each, to be raised in America, and commanded by Sir William Pepperel and Governor Shirley, who had enjoyed the same command in the last war, and a body of troops was destined for the same service.

The most remarkable incident that marked this year, on

the continent of Europe, was the conversion of the hereditary Prince of Hesse-Cassel, who had espoused the Princess Mary of England. He now declared himself a Roman Catholic, and was supposed to have been cajoled to this profession by the promises of certain powers, who flattered his ambition, in order to weaken the Protestant interest in Germany. His father, though deeply affected by his son's apostasy, did not fail to take immediate measures for preventing the evil consequences which might otherwise have flowed from his defection. He forthwith assembled the states of the Landgraviate, in order to take such measures as might appear necessary to maintain the religion, laws, and constitution of the country; and the prince was laid under certain restrictions, which he did not find it an easy task to set aside. It was enacted, that when the regency should devolve to him by succession, he should not have it in his power to alter the established laws, or grant any church to persons of the Roman communion, for the public exercise of their religion; and that he should be excluded from all share in the education of his sons, the eldest of whom should be put in possession of the country of Hanau upon his father's accession to the regency of the Landgraviate. These resolutions were guaranteed by the Kings of Prussia and Denmark, by the maritime powers, and the evangelic body of the empire.

<small>The hereditary Prince of Hesse-Cassel professes the Roman Catholic religion.</small>

The exile of the Parliament of Paris, far from having intimidated the other tribunals from performing what they apprehended to be their duty, served only to inflame the discontents of the people, and to animate all the courts of justice to a full exertion of their authority. The Chatelet continued to prosecute those priests who refused the sacrament to persons whose consciences would not allow them to subscribe to the bull Unigenitus, even after three of their members were sent to the Bastile. The same prosecutions were carried on, and bold remonstrances published, by the Parliaments of Aix and Rouen. In a word, the whole kingdom was filled with such confusion as threatened a total suppression of justice, in a general spirit of disaffection, and universal anarchy. The prelates, meanwhile, seemed to triumph in the combustion they had raised. They entered into associations to support each other: they intrigued at court, and harassed the king with insolent declarations, till he grew tried of their proceedings, and opened

<small>Parliament of Paris recalled from exile.</small>

his eyes to the fatal consequences of their pride and obstinacy. He even took an opportunity of exhorting the Archbishop of Paris to act more suitably to the character of a clergyman. He recalled the Parliament from exile, and they returned in triumph, amidst the acclamations of the people, who celebrated their arrival at Paris with the most extravagant demonstrations of joy; and the archbishop, notwithstanding the king's express declaration to the contrary, still persisting in countenancing the recusant priests, was banished to Conflans-sous-Charenton.

In Spain, the interest of Great Britain was so warmly espoused, and so powerfully supported by Mr. Wall, who had been resident in England, that the French party, though countenanced by the queen-mother, and sustained with all the influence of the Marquis de la Ensenada, the prime minister, was totally defeated. The king, being convinced that it would be for the interest of his subjects to live on good terms with England, and well apprised of Ensenada's intrigues, ordered that minister to be arrested and confined, and bestowed upon Mr. Wall the best part of his employments. Nevertheless, the Spaniards in the West Indies continued to oppress the subjects of Great Britain, employed in cutting log-wood in the bay of Honduras; and representations on this head being made to the court of Madrid, the dispute was amicably adjusted between Mr. Wall and Sir Benjamin Keene, the British ambassador. While the interest of Britain thus triumphed in Spain, it seemed to lose ground at the court of Lisbon. His Portuguese majesty had formed vast projects of an active commerce, and even established an East India company: in the mean time he could not help manifesting his chagrin at the great quantities of gold which were yearly exported from his dominions, as the balance due from his subjects on English commodities. In his endeavours to check this traffic, which he deemed so detrimental to his subjects, he inflicted hardships on the British merchants settled at Lisbon: some were imprisoned on frivolous pretences; others deprived of their property, and obliged to quit the kingdom. He insisted upon laying an imposition of two per cent. on all the Portuguese gold that should be exported; but the profits of the trade would not bear such an exaction. Meanwhile, there being a scarcity of corn in Portugal, the kingdom was supplied from England; and the people having nothing but gold to purchase this

*Affairs of Spain and Portugal.*

necessary supply, the king saw the necessity of conniving at the exportation of his coin, and the trade reverted into its former channel.

On the fourteenth day of November, the King of Great Britain opened the session of Parliament with an harangue, which intimated nothing of an approach- *Session opened.* ing rupture. He said that the general state of affairs in Europe had undergone very little alteration since their last meeting; that he had lately received the strongest assurances from his good brother the King of Spain of friendship and confidence, which he would cultivate with harmony and good faith. He declared his principal view should be to strengthen the foundation, and secure the duration, of a general peace; to improve the present advantages of it for promoting the trade of his good subjects, and protecting those possessions which constituted one great source of their wealth and commerce. Finally, he exhorted them to complete their plan for appropriating the forfeited estates in the Highlands to the service of the public. He probably avoided mentioning the encroachments of France, that he might supply no handle for debates on the address, which was carried in both Houses almost without opposition. The government seemed determined to humble the insolence of the French councils; and this disposition was so agreeable to the people in general, that they grudged no expense, and heartily concurred with the demands of the ministry.

The Commons granted for the service of the ensuing year four millions seventy-three thousand seven hundred *Supplies* and twenty-nine pounds; one million of that sum *granted.* expressly given for enabling his majesty to augment his forces by land and sea. Thirty-two thousand pounds were allotted as a subsidy to the King of Poland, and twenty thousand to the Elector of Bavaria. These gratifications met with little or no opposition in the committee of supply; because it was taken for granted, that, in case of a rupture, France would endeavour to avail herself of her superiority by land, by invading his Britannic majesty's German dominions; and, therefore, it might be necessary to secure the assistance of such allies on the continent. That they prognosticated aright, with respect to the designs of that ambitious power, will soon appear in the course of this history; which will also demonstrate how little dependence is to be placed upon the professed attachment of subsidiary princes.

The supplies were raised by the standing branches of the revenue, the land-tax and malt-tax, and a lottery for one million; one hundred thousand pounds of it to be deducted for the service of the public, and the remaining nine hundred thousand to be charged on the produce of the sinking-fund, at the rate of three per cent. per annum, to commence from the fifth day of January, in the year one thousand seven hundred and fifty-six. The civil transactions of this session were confined to a few objects. Divers new regulations were made for encouraging and improving the whale and white herring fishery, as well as for finishing and putting in a proper state of defence a new fort, lately built at Anamaboe on the coast of Africa.

Mr. Pitt, the paymaster-general of the forces, brought in a bill, which will ever remain a standing monument of his humanity. The poor disabled veterans who enjoyed the pension of Chelsea hospital were so iniquitously oppressed by a set of miscreants, who supplied them with money per advance, at the most exorbitant rates of usury, that many of them, with their families, were in danger of starving; and the intention of government in granting such a comfortable subsistence was, in a great measure, defeated. Mr. Pitt, perceiving that this evil originally flowed from the delay of the first payment, which the pensioner could not touch till the expiration of a whole year after he had been put upon the list, removed this necessity of borrowing, by providing in the bill, that half a year's pension should be advanced half a year before it is due; and the practice of usury was effectually prevented by a clause, enacting that all contracts should be void by which any pension might be mortgaged. This humane regulation was unanimously approved, and having passed through both Houses with uncommon expedition, received the royal assent.

*Bill in behalf of Chelsea pensioners.*

Notwithstanding the unanimity manifested by the Commons, in every thing relating to the measures for acting vigorously against the common enemy of the nation, they were remarkably disturbed and divided by a contested election of members for Oxfordshire. In the course of this dispute, the strength and influence of what they called the old and new interest, or, to speak more intelligibly, of the tories and whigs in that county, were fully displayed. The candidates sustained on the shoulders of

*Oxfordshire election.*

the old interest were Lord Viscount Wenman and Sir James Dashwood; their competitors, whom the new interest supported, and of consequence the ministry countenanced, were Lord Parker and Sir Edward Turner. Never was any contention of this kind maintained with more spirit and animosity, or carried on at a greater expense. One would have imagined that each side considered it as a dispute which must have determined, whether the nation should enjoy its ancient liberty, or tamely submit to the fetters of corruption. Noblemen and gentlemen, clergymen and ladies, employed all their talents and industry in canvassing for either side, throughout every township and village in the county. Scandal emptied her whole quiver of insinuation, calumny, and lampoon: corruption was not remiss in promises and presents: houses of entertainment were opened: and nothing was for some time to be seen but scenes of tumult, riot, and intoxication. The revenue of many an independent prince on the continent would not have been sufficient to afford such sums of money as were expended in the course of this dispute. At length they proceeded to election, and the sheriff made a double return of all the four candidates, so that not one of them could sit, and the county remained without a representative until this ambiguous affair could be decided in the House of Commons. About the middle of November, petitions being presented by the four candidates, as well as by the gentlemen, clergy, and other freeholders of the county, complaining of an undue election, and double return, the matter of these petitions was heard at the bar of the House on the third day of December. The counsel for Lord Wenman and Sir James Dashwood alleged, that they had the majority of votes upon the poll, and this circumstance was admitted by the counsel on the other side; then they proceeded to prove by evidence, that, after closing the poll, the sheriff declared the majority of votes to be in favour of these two candidates, and adjourned the court from the twenty-third day of April to the eighth of May; so that the scrutiny demanded, and granted, on the behalf of Lord Parker and Sir Edward Turner, could not be discussed before the last day of the month, when the writ was returnable; that the scrutiny did not begin till the ninth day of May, when the time was protracted by disputes about the manner in which it should be carried on; that Lord Parker and Sir Edward Turner were allowed to object through the whole poll to the votes on the other side, on pretence that their competitors should be permitted to answer these objections, and, in their turn, object through the whole poll to the votes for Lord Parker and Sir Edward Turner, who should, in the last place, have leave to answer; that Lord Wenman and Sir James Dashwood had disapproved of this method, because they apprehended it might induce their competitors to make such a number of frivolous objections, that they should not have time to answer one half of them, much less to make objections of their own, before the writ should be returned; that, as they foresaw, such a number of frivolous objections were made, as engrossed the attention of the court till the twenty-seventh day of May, so that they could not begin to answer any of these objections till the twenty-eighth; and on the thirtieth the sheriff, having closed the scrutiny, made the double return. The proof being exhibited, the counsel insisted, that as they had established a majority on the poll, and demonstrated that this majority neither was nor could be overthrown by such an unfinished scrutiny, it was incumbent on the other side to proceed upon the merits of the election, by endeavouring to overthrow that majority of which their clients were in possession. A question in the House being carried to the same purpose, Lord Wenman and Sir James Dashwood objected to five hundred and thirty voters on the other side, whom they proposed to disqualify. Their counsel examined several witnesses, to prove the partiality of the sheriff in favour of Lord Parker and Sir Edward Turner, and to detect these candidates in the practice of bribery; for which purpose they produced a letter in their own hand-writing. They afterwards proceeded to disqualify particular voters, and summed up their evidence on the twenty-first day of January. Then the counsel for the other side began to refute the charge of partiality and corruption, and to answer the objections that had been made to particular voters. They produced evidence to prove that customary freeholders, or customary holdings, had voted at elections in the counties of Glamorgan, Monmouth, Gloucester, Wells, and Hereford; and that the customary tenants of the manor of Woodstock, in Oxfordshire, had been reputed capable of voting, and even voted at elections for that county. In a word, they continued to examine evidences, argue and refute, prove and disprove, until the twenty-third day of April, when, after some warm debates and divisions in the House, Lord Parker and Sir Edward Turner were declared duly elected; and the clerk of the crown was ordered to amend the return, by erasing the names of Lord Wenman and Sir James Dashwood. Many, who presumed to think for themselves, without recollecting the power and influence of the administration, were astonished at the issue of this dispute; which, however, might have easily been foreseen; inasmuch as, during the course of the proceedings, most, if not all, of the many questions debated in the House were determined by a great majority in favour of the new interest. A great number of copyholders had been admitted to vote at this election, and the sheriff incurred no censure for allowing them to take the oath appointed by law to be taken by freeholders; nevertheless, the Commons carefully avoided determining the question, whether copyholders possessed of the yearly value of forty-shillings, clear of all deductions, have not a right to vote for knights to represent the shire within which their copyhold estates are situated? This point being left doubtful by the legislature, puts it often in the power of the sheriff to return which of the candidates he pleases to support; for if the majority of the voting copyholders adheres to the interest of his favourites, he will admit their votes both on the poll and the scrutiny; whereas, should they be otherwise disposed, he will reject them as unqualified. What effect this practice may have upon the independency of Parliament, every person must perceive who reflects, that in almost all the counties of England the high sheriffs are annually appointed by the minister for the time being.

The attention of the legislature was chiefly turned upon the conduct of France, which preserved no medium, but seemed intent upon striking some important blow, that might serve as a declaration of war. At Brest, and other ports in that kingdom, the French were employed in equipping a powerful armament, and made no scruple to own it was intended for North America. Towards the latter end of March, Sir Thomas Robinson, secretary of state, brought a message from the king to the Parliament, intimating, that his majesty having, at the beginning of the session, declared his principal object was to preserve the public tranquillity, and at the same time to protect those possessions which constitute one great

*Message from the king to the House of Commons.*

source of the commerce and wealth of his kingdoms, he now found it necessary to acquaint the House of Commons, that the present situation of affairs made it requisite to augment his forces by sea and land, and to take such other measures as might best tend to preserve the general peace of Europe, and to secure the just rights and possessions of his crown in America, as well as to repel any attempts whatsoever that might be made to support or countenance any designs which should be formed against his majesty and his kingdoms; and his majesty doubted not but his faithful Commons, on whose affection and zeal he entirely relied, would enable him to make such augmentations, and to take such measures for supporting the honour of his crown and the true interest of his people, and for the security of his dominions in the present critical conjuncture, as the exigency of affairs might require; in doing which his majesty would have as much regard to the ease of his good subjects as should be consistent with their safety and welfare. In answer to this message a very warm and affectionate address was presented to his majesty; and it was on this occasion that the million was granted for augmenting his forces by sea and land.[1] The court of Versailles, notwithstanding the assiduity and despatch which they were exerting in equipping armaments, and embarking troops, for the support of their ambitious schemes in America, still continued to amuse the British ministry with general declarations, that no hostility was intended, nor the least infringement of the treaty.

*Court of Versailles amuses the English ministry.*

The Earl of Albemarle, the English ambassador at Paris, having lately died in that city, these assurances were communicated to the court of London by the Marquis de Mirepoix, who resided in England with the same character, which he had supported since his first arrival with equal honour and politeness. On this occasion he himself was so far imposed upon by the instructions he had received, that he believed the professions of his court were sincere, and seriously endeavoured to prevent a rupture

[1] The ministry having resolved to send a body of forces to America to act in conjunction with the provincial troops raised on that continent, it became necessary that the mutiny act should be rendered more clear and extensive. When this bill, therefore, fell under consideration, it was improved with a new clause, providing, "That all officers and soldiers of any troops being mustered and in pay, which are or shall be raised in any of the British provinces in America, by authority of the respective governors or governments thereof, shall, at all times, and in all places, when they happen to join or act in conjunction with his majesty's British forces, be liable to martial law and discipline, in like manner, to all intents and purposes, as the British forces are; and shall be subject to the same trial, penalties, and punishment."

between the two nations. At length, however, their preparations were so notorious that he began to suspect the consequence; and the English ministry produced such proofs of their insincerity and double dealing, that he seemed to be struck with astonishment and chagrin. He repaired to France, and upbraided the ministry of Versailles for having made him the tool of their dissimulation. They referred him to the king, who ordered him to return to London, with fresh assurances of his pacific intentions; but his practice agreed so ill with his professions, that the ambassador had scarce obtained an audience to communicate them, when undoubted intelligence arrived, that a powerful armament was ready to sail from Brest and Rochefort. The government of Great Britain, roused by this information, immediately took the most expeditious methods for equipping a squadron; and towards the latter end of April, Admiral Boscawen sailed with eleven ships of the line and one frigate, having on board a considerable number of land forces, to attend the motions of the enemy: but more certain and particular intelligence arriving soon after, touching the strength of the French fleet, which consisted of twenty-five ships of the line, besides frigates and transports, with a great quantity of warlike stores, and four thousand regular troops, commanded by the Baron Dieskau, Admiral Holbourne was detached with six ships of the line, and one frigate, to reinforce Mr. Boscawen; and a great number of capital ships were put in commission. In the beginning of May, the French fleet, commanded by Mr. Macnamara, an officer of Irish extraction, sailed from Brest, directing his course to North America; but, after having proceeded beyond the chops of the English Channel, he returned with nine of the capital ships, while the rest of the armament continued their course, under the direction of M. Bois de la Mothe.

On the twenty-fifth day of April, the king went to the House of Lords, where, after giving the royal assent to the bills then depending; for granting a certain sum out of the sinking-fund; for the relief of insolvent debtors; for the better regulation of the marine forces on shore; for the better raising of marines and seamen; and to several other public and private bills; his majesty put an end to the session of Parliament by a speech, in which he acquainted the two Houses, that the zeal they had shown for supporting the honour, rights, and possessions of his crown, had afforded him the greatest satisfaction: that his desire to preserve the public tranquillity had been sincere and uniform: that he had religiously adhered to the stipulations of the treaty of Aix-la-Chapelle, and made it his care not to injure or offend any power whatsoever; but that he never could entertain a thought of purchasing the name of peace at the expense of suffering encroachments upon, or of yielding up, what justly belonged to Great Britain, either by ancient possession or by solemn treaties: that the vigour and firmness of his Parliament, on this important occasion, had enabled him to be prepared for such contingencies as might happen: that, if reasonable and honourable terms of accommodation could be agreed upon, he would be satisfied, and, at all events, rely on the justice of his cause, the effectual support of his people, and the protection of Divine Providence. The Parliament was then prorogued to the twenty-seventh of May.

## CHAPTER XXIV.

PREPARATIONS FOR WAR.—EARL PAULET'S MOTION AGAINST THE KING'S GOING TO HANOVER. — REGENCY APPOINTED DURING HIS MAJESTY'S ABSENCE. — BOSCAWEN'S EXPEDITION. — THE ALCIDE AND LYS TAKEN.—FRENCH AMBASSADOR RECALLED.—THEIR TRADE GREATLY DISTRESSED. — AFFAIRS OF THE ENGLISH IN AMERICA. — COLONEL MONCKTON TAKES BEAU-SEJOUR. — GENERAL BRADDOCK'S UNFORTUNATE EXPEDITION. — HE FALLS INTO AN AMBUSCADE; IS DEFEATED AND KILLED. — DISAGREEMENT BETWEEN THE GOVERNOR AND ASSEMBLY OF PENNSYLVANIA. — EXPEDITION AGAINST CROWN-POINT AND NIAGARA RESOLVED ON. — GENERAL JOHNSON ENCAMPS AT LAKE GEORGE — WHERE HE IS ATTACKED BY THE FRENCH, WHO ARE ENTIRELY DEFEATED. — BRAVERY OF CAPTAIN M'GINNIS. — GENERAL JOHNSON CREATED A BARONET. — DESCRIPTION OF FORT OSWEGO AND LAKE ONTARIO. — NEGLECT OF THE ENGLISH IN NOT FORTIFYING IT. — EXPEDITION AGAINST NIAGARA. — GENERAL SHIRLEY RETURNS TO ALBANY. — END OF THE CAMPAIGN IN AMERICA. — FRUITLESS INTRIGUES OF THE FRENCH IN SPAIN AND GERMANY. — TREATY OF THE KING OF GREAT BRITAIN WITH THE LANDGRAVE OF HESSE-CASSEL. — NEWS OF THE CAPTURE OF THE ALCIDE AND LYS REACHES ENGLAND. — THE KING RETURNS FROM HANOVER, AND CONCLUDES A TREATY WITH RUSSIA. — DECLARATION OF THE FRENCH MINISTRY AT THE COURT OF VIENNA. — SPIRITED DECLARATION OF THE KING OF PRUSSIA. — THE FRENCH MAKE ANOTHER UNSUCCESSFUL ATTEMPT UPON THE COURT OF SPAIN. — THE IMPERIAL COURT REFUSES AUXILIARIES TO ENGLAND. — THE FRENCH TAKE THE BLANDFORD MAN OF WAR, BUT RETURN IT. — STATE OF THE ENGLISH AND FRENCH NAVIES. — SESSION OPENED. — REMARKABLE ADDRESSES OF THE LORDS AND COMMONS. — HIS MAJESTY'S ANSWER. — ALTERATIONS IN THE MINISTRY.— MR. FOX MADE SECRETARY OF STATE. — SUPPLIES VOTED. — EARTHQUAKE AT LISBON. — RELIEF VOTED BY PARLIAMENT TO THE PORTUGUESE. — TROOPS, &c., VOTED. — MUTINY BILL, MARINE, AND MARINERS' ACTS CONTINUED. — ACT FOR RAISING A REGIMENT OF FOOT IN NORTH AMERICA. — MARITIME LAWS OF ENGLAND EXTENDED TO AMERICA. — QUIET OF IRELAND RESTORED. — TREATY CONCLUDED WITH PRUSSIA. — NEW MILITIA BILL PASSED BY THE COMMONS, BUT REJECTED BY THE LORDS. — SESSION CLOSED.

WHILST all Europe was in suspense about the fate of the English and French squadrons, preparations for a vigorous sea war were going forward in England with an unparalleled spirit and success. Still the French court flattered itself that Great Britain, out of tenderness to his majesty's German dominions, would abstain from hostilities. Mirepoix continued to have frequent conferences with the British ministry, who made no secret that their admirals, particularly Boscawen, had orders to attack the French ships wherever they should meet them; on the other hand, Mons. de Mirepoix declared, that his master would consider the first gun fired at sea in an hostile manner as a declaration of war. This menace, far from intimidating the English, animated them to redouble their preparations for war. The 'press for seamen was carried on with extraordinary vigour in all parts of this kingdom, as well as in Ireland; and great premiums were given not only by the government, but also over and above his majesty's bounty, by almost all the considerable cities and towns in England, to such as should enlist voluntarily for sailors or soldiers. Other branches of the public service went on with equal alacrity; and such was the eagerness of the people to lend their money to the government, that instead of one million, which was to be raised by way of lottery, three millions eight hundred and eighty thousand pounds were subscribed immediately.

The situation of affairs requiring his majesty to go to Germany this summer, great apprehensions arose in the minds of many, lest the French should either intercept him in his journey, or prevent his return. Earl Paulet had made a motion in the House of Lords, humbly to represent to his majesty, " That it was an article in the original act of settlement by which the succession of these kingdoms devolved to his electoral house, that the king should not go to his foreign dominions without the consent of Parliament; and that this was a principal article in the compact between the crown and the people: that though this article was repealed in the late reign, yet, till of late, it had always been the custom for his majesty to acquaint the Parliament with his intended departure to his German dominions, both in regard to the true sense and spirit of the act that placed him on the throne, as well as for the paternal kindness of his royal heart, and the condescension he had been so good to show to his Parliament on all occasions; but that his majesty's declaration of his design to visit his electoral estates had always come on the last day of the session, when it was too late for the great constitutional council of the crown to offer such advice as might otherwise have been expedient and necessary: that his majesty's leaving his kingdoms in a conjuncture so pregnant with distress, so denunciative of danger, would not only give the greatest advantage to such as might be disposed to stir up disaffection and discontent, and to the constitutional and national enemies of England; but would also fill his loyal subjects with the most affecting concern, and most gloomy fears, as well for their own safety, as for that of their sovereign, whose invaluable life, at all times of the utmost consequence to his people, was then infinitely so, by

*Earl Paulet's motion against the king's going to Hanover.*

reason of his great experience, the affection of every one to his royal person, and the minority of the heir apparent." Such was the purport of this motion; but it was not seconded by any of the other lords.

The general uneasiness, on account of his majesty's departure, was greatly increased by an apprehension that there would, during his absence, be no good agreement amongst the regency, which consisted of the following persons: his royal highness William, Duke of Cumberland; Thomas, Lord Archbishop of Canterbury; Philip, Earl of Hardwicke, lord high chancellor; John, Earl of Granville, president of the council; Charles, Duke of Marlborough, lord privy-seal; John, Duke of Rutland, steward of the household; Charles, Duke of Grafton, lord chamberlain; Archibald, Duke of Argyle; the Duke of Newcastle, first commissioner of the treasury; the Duke of Dorset, master of the horse; the Earl of Holdernesse, one of the secretaries of State; the Earl of Rochford, groom of the stole; the Marquis of Hartington, lord lieutenant of Ireland; Lord Anson, first commissioner of the Admiralty; Sir Thomas Robinson, secretary of state; and Henry Fox, Esq., secretary at war. His majesty set out from St. James's on the twenty-eighth of April early in the morning, embarked at Harwich in the afternoon, landed the next day at Helvoetsluys, and arrived at Hanover on the second of May.

*Regency appointed during his majesty's absence.*

Admiral Boscawen, with eleven ships of the line and a frigate, having taken on board two regiments at Plymouth, sailed from thence on the twenty-seventh of April for the banks of Newfoundland, and in a few days after his arrival there, the French fleet from Brest came to the same station, under the command of M. Bois de la Mothe. But the thick fogs which prevail upon those coasts, especially at that time of the year, kept the two armaments from seeing each other; and part of the French squadron escaped up the river St. Lawrence, whilst another part of them went round and got into the same river, through the straits of Belleisle, by a way which was never known to be attempted before by ships of the line. However, whilst the English fleet lay off Cape Race, which is the southernmost point of Newfoundland, and was thought to be the most proper situation for intercepting the enemy, two French ships, the Alcide, of sixty-four guns, and four

*Boscawen's expedition. Alcide and Lys taken.*

hundred and eighty men, and the Lys, pierced for fifty-four guns, but mounting only twenty-two, having eight companies of land-forces on board, being separated from the rest of their fleet in the fog, fell in with the Dunkirk, Captain Howe, and the Defiance, Captain Andrews, two sixty gun ships of the English squadron; and after a smart engagement which lasted some hours, and in which Captain (afterwards Lord) Howe behaved with the greatest skill and intrepidity, were both taken, with several considerable officers and engineers, and about eight thousand pounds in money. Though the capture of these ships, from which the commencement of the war may in fact be dated, fell greatly short of what was hoped for from this expedition; yet, when the news of it reached England, it was of infinite service to the public credit of every kind, and animated the whole nation, who now saw plainly that the government was determined to keep no further measures with the French, but justly to repel force by force, and put a stop to their sending more men and arms to invade the property of the English in America, as they had hitherto done with impunity. The French, who for some time did not even attempt to make reprisals on our shipping, would gladly have chosen to avoid a war at that time, and to have continued extending their encroachments on our settlements till they had executed their grand plan of securing a communication from the Mississippi to Canada by a line of forts, many of which they had already erected.

Upon the arrival of the news of this action at Paris, the French ambassador, M. de Mirepoix, was recalled from London, and M. de Bussy from Hanover, where he had just arrived, to attend the King of England in a public character. They complained loudly of Boscawen's attacking the ships, as a breach of national faith; but it was justly retorted on the part of England, that their encroachments in America had rendered reprisals both justifiable and necessary. The resolution of making them was the effect of mature deliberation in the English council. The vast increase of the French marine of late years, which in all probability would soon be employed against Great Britain, occasioned an order for making reprisals general in Europe as well as in America; and that all French ships, whether outward or homeward bound, should be stopped, and brought into British ports. To give the greater weight to these orders, it was resolved to send out those admirals who had distinguished themselves most towards the end of the last war. Accordingly, on the twenty-first of July, Sir Edward Hawke sailed on a cruise to the westward, with eighteen ships of the line, a frigate, and a sloop; but not meeting with the French fleet, these ships returned to England about the latter end of September and the beginning of October; on the fourteenth of which last month another fleet, consisting of twenty-two ships of the line, two frigates, and two sloops, sailed again on a cruise to the westward, under Admiral Byng, in hopes of intercepting the French squadron under Duguay; and likewise that commanded by La Mothe, in case of its return from America. But this fleet likewise returned to Spithead on the twenty-second of November, without having been able to effect any thing, though it was allowed by all that the admiral had acted judiciously in the choice of his stations.

While these measures were pursued, for the general security of the British coasts and trade in Europe, several new ships of war were begun, and finished with the utmost expedition, in his majesty's docks: twelve frigates and sloops, contracted for in private yards, were completed by the month of August; and twenty-four ships and twelve colliers were then taken into the service of the government, to be fitted out as vessels of war, to carry twenty guns and one hundred and twenty men each. In the mean time the French trade was so annoyed by the English cruisers, that before the end of this year three hundred of their merchant ships, many of which, from St. Domingo and Martinico, were extremely rich, and eight thousand of their sailors, were brought into English ports. By these captures the British ministry answered many purposes: they deprived the French of a great body of seamen, and withheld from them a very large property, the want of which greatly distressed their people, and ruined many of their traders. Their outward-bound merchant ships were insured at the rate of thirty per cent., whilst the English paid no more than the common insurance. This intolerable burden was felt by all degrees of people amongst them: their ministry was publicly reviled, even by their Parliaments; and the French name, from being the terror, began to be the contempt of Europe. Their uneasiness was also

*Their trade greatly distressed.*

not a little heightened by new broils between their king and
the Parliament of Paris, occasioned by the obstinacy of the
clergy of that kingdom, who seemed determined to support
the church, in all events, against the secular tribunals,
and, as much as possible, to enforce the observance of the
bull Unigenitus, which had long been the occasion of so
many disputes among them. However, the Parliament continuing firm, and the French king approving of its conduct,
the ecclesiastics thought proper to submit for the present;
and in their general assembly this year granted him a free
gift of sixteen millions of livres, which he demanded of them
—a greater sum than they had ever given before, even in
time of war.

In the beginning of this year the assembly of Massachusett's Bay in New England passed an act, prohibiting
all correspondence with the French at Louisbourg;
and early in the spring they raised a body of troops,
which was transported to Nova Scotia, to assist
Lieutenant-Governor Laurence in driving the French
from the encroachments they had made upon that province.
Accordingly, towards the end of May, the governor sent a
large detachment of troops, under the command of Lieutenant-Colonel Monckton, upon this service; and three
frigates and a sloop were despatched up the bay of Fundy,
under the command of Captain Rous, to give their assistance
by sea. The troops, upon their arrival at the river Massa-
guash, found the passage stopped by a large number of
regular forces, rebel neutrals, or Acadians, and Indians,
four hundred and fifty of whom occupied a block-house, with
cannon mounted on their side of the river; and the rest were
posted within a strong breastwork of timber, thrown up by
way of outwork to the block-house. The English provincials attacked this place with such spirit, that the enemy
were obliged to fly, and leave them in possession of the
breastwork; then the garrison in the block-house deserted
it, and left the passage of the river free. From thence
Colonel Monckton advanced to the French fort of Beau-
sejour, which he invested, as far at least as the small number
of his troops would permit, on the twelfth of June; and
after four days' bombardment obliged it to surrender, though
the French had twenty-six pieces of cannon mounted, and
plenty of ammunition, and the English had not yet placed a
single cannon upon their batteries. The garrison was sent

to Louisbourg, on condition of not bearing arms in America for the space of six months; and the Acadians, who had joined the French, were pardoned, in consideration of their having been forced into that service. Colonel Monckton, after putting a garrison into this place, and changing its name to that of Cumberland, the next day attacked and reduced the other French fort upon the river Gaspereau, which runs into Bay Verte; where he likewise found a large quantity of provisions and stores of all kinds, that being the chief magazine for supplying the French Indians and Acadians with arms, ammunition, and other necessaries. He then disarmed these last, to the number of fifteen thousand; and in the mean time, Captain Rous with his ships sailed to the mouth of the river St. John, to attack the new fort the French had erected there; but they saved him that trouble, by abandoning it upon his appearance, after having burst their cannon, blown up their magazine, and destroyed, as far as they had time, all the works they had lately raised. The English had but twenty men killed, and about the same number wounded, in the whole of this expedition, the success of which secured the tranquillity of Nova Scotia.

While the New Englanders were thus employed in reducing the French in Nova Scotia, preparations were made in Virginia for attacking them upon the Ohio. A fort was built, which was likewise called Fort Cumberland, and a camp formed at Will's Creek. On the fourteenth of January of this year, Major-General Braddock, with Colonel Dunbar's and Colonel Halket's regiments of foot, sailed from Cork, in Ireland, for Virginia, where they all landed safe before the end of February. This general might consequently have entered upon action early in the spring, had he not been unfortunately delayed by the Virginian contractors for the army, who, when he was ready to march, had neither provided a sufficient quantity of provisions for his troops, nor a competent number of carriages for his army. This accident was foreseen by almost every person who knew anything of our plantations upon the continent of America; for the people of Virginia, who think of no produce but their tobacco, and do not raise corn enough even for their own subsistence, being by the nature of their country well provided with the conveniency of water conveyance, have but few wheel carriages, or beasts of burden; whereas Pennsylvania, which abounds in corn,

*General Braddock's unfortunate expedition.*

and most other sorts of provisions, has but little water carriage, especially in its western settlements, where its inhabitants have great numbers of carts, waggons, and horses. Mr. Braddock should, therefore, certainly in point of prudence have landed in Pennsylvania; the contract for supplying his troops should have been made with some of the chief planters there, who could easily have performed their engagements: and if his camp had been formed near Frank's-town, or somewhere upon the south-west borders of that province, he would not have had eighty miles to march from thence to Fort du Quesne, instead of a hundred and thirty miles that he had to advance from Will's Creek, where he did encamp, through roads neither better nor more practicable than the other would have been. This error in the very beginning of the expedition, whether owing to an injudicious preference fondly given to the Virginians in the lucrative job of supplying these troops, or to any other cause, delayed the march of the army for some weeks, during which it was in the utmost distress for necessaries of all kinds; and would probably have defeated the expedition entirely for that summer, had not the contractors found means to procure some assistance from the back settlements of Pennsylvania. But even when these supplies did arrive, they consisted of only fifteen waggons and a hundred draft horses, instead of a hundred and fifty waggons and three hundred horses, which the Virginian contractors had engaged to furnish, and the provisions were so bad that they could not be used. However, some gentlemen in Pennsylvania, being applied to in this exigency, amply made up for these deficiencies, and the troops were by this means supplied with every thing they wanted. Another and still more fatal error was committed, in the choice of the commander for this expedition. Major-General Braddock, who was appointed to it, was undoubtedly a man of courage, and expert in all the punctilios of a review, having been brought up in the English guards: but he was naturally very haughty, positive, and difficult of access; qualities ill suited to the temper of the people amongst whom he was to command. His extreme severity in matters of discipline had rendered him unpopular among the soldiers; and the strict military education in which he had been trained from his youth, and which he prided himself on scrupulously following, made him hold the American militia in great contempt, because they could not go through their exercise with the same dexterity and regularity as a regiment of guards in Hyde-Park; little knowing, or indeed being able to form any idea of the difference between the European manner of fighting, and an American expedition through woods, deserts, and morasses. Before he left England, he received, in the hand-writing of Colonel Napier, a set of instructions from the Duke of Cumberland. By these the attempt upon Niagara was, in a great measure, referred to him, and the reduction of Crown-Point was to be left chiefly to the provincial forces. But above all, his royal highness, both verbally and in this writing, frequently cautioned him carefully to beware of an ambush or surprise. Instead of regarding this salutary caution, his conceit of his own abilities made him disdain to ask the opinion of any under his command; and the Indians, who would have been his safest guards against this danger in particular, were so disgusted by the haughtiness of his behaviour, that most of them forsook his banners. Under these disadvantages he began his march from Fort Cumberland on the tenth of June, at the head of about two thousand two hundred men, for the meadows, where Colonel Washington was defeated the year before. Upon his arrival there, he was informed that the French at Fort du Quesne, which had lately been built on the same river, near its confluence with the Monangahela, expected a reinforcement of five hundred regular troops; therefore, that he might march with the greater despatch, he left Colonel Dunbar, with eight hundred men, to bring up the provisions, stores, and heavy baggage, as fast as the nature of the service would permit; and with the other twelve hundred, together with ten pieces of cannon, and the necessary ammunition and provisions, he marched on with so much expedition, that he seldom took any time to reconnoitre the woods or thickets he was to pass through; as if the nearer he approached the enemy, the farther he was removed from danger.

On the eighth of July he encamped within ten miles of Fort du Quesne. Though Colonel Dunbar was then near forty miles behind him, and his officers, particularly Sir Peter Halket, earnestly entreated him to proceed with caution, and to employ the friendly Indians who were with him, by way of advanced guard, in case of ambuscades; yet he resumed his march the next day, without so much as endeavouring to obtain

*He falls into an ambuscade; is defeated and killed.*

any intelligence of the situation or disposition of the enemy, or even sending out any scouts to visit the woods and thickets on both sides of him, as well as in front. With this carelessness he was advancing, when, about noon, he was saluted with a general fire upon his front, and all along his left flank, from an enemy so artfully concealed behind the trees and bushes, that not a man of them could be seen. The vanguard immediately fell back upon the main body, and in an instant the panic and confusion became general; so that most of the troops fled with great precipitation, notwithstanding all that their officers, some of whom behaved very gallantly, could do to stop their career. As to Braddock himself, instead of scouring the thickets and bushes from whence the fire came, with grape-shot from the ten pieces of cannon he had with him, or ordering flanking parties of the Indians to advance against the enemy, he obstinately remained upon the spot where he was, and gave orders for the few brave officers and men who stayed with him, to form regularly, and advance. Meanwhile his men fell thick about him, and almost all his officers were singled out, one after another, and killed or wounded; for the Indians, who always take aim when they fire, and aim chiefly at the officers, distinguished them by their dress. At last, the general, whose obstinacy seemed to increase with the danger, after having had some horses shot under him, received a musket shot through the right arm and lungs, of which he died in a few hours, having been carried off the field by the bravery of Lieutenant-Colonel Gage, and another of his officers. When he dropped, the confusion of the few that remained turned into a downright and very disorderly flight across a river which they had just passed, though no enemy appeared, or attempted to attack them. All the artillery, ammunition, and baggage of the army were left to the enemy, and, among the rest, the general's cabinet, with all his letters and instructions, which the French court afterwards made great use of in their printed memorials or manifestoes. The loss of the English in this unhappy affair amounted to seven hundred men. Their officers, in particular, suffered much more than in the ordinary proportion of battles in Europe. Sir Peter Halket fell by the very first fire, at the head of his regiment; and the general's secretary, son to Governor Shirley, was killed soon after. Neither the number of men which the enemy had in this engagement, nor the loss which they sustained, could be so much as guessed at: but the French afterwards gave out, that their number did not, in the whole, exceed four hundred men, mostly Indians; and that their loss was quite inconsiderable, as it probably was, because they lay concealed in such a manner that the English knew not whither to point their muskets. The panic of these last continued so long, that they never stopped till they met the rear division; and even then they infected those troops with their terrors; so that the army retreated without stopping, till they reached Fort Cumberland, though the enemy did not so much as attempt to pursue, nor even appeared in sight, either in the battle, or after the defeat. On the whole, this was perhaps the most extraordinary victory that ever was obtained, and the farthest flight that ever was made.

Had the shattered remains of this army continued at Fort Cumberland, and fortified themselves there, as they might easily have done, during the rest of the summer, they would have been such a check upon the French and their scalping Indians, as would have prevented many of those ravages that were committed in the ensuing winter upon the western borders of Virginia and Pennsylvania; but, instead of taking that prudent step, their commander left only the sick and wounded at that fort, under the protection of two companies of the provincial militia, posted there by way of garrison, and began his march on the second of August, with about sixteen hundred men from Philadelphia, where those troops could be of no immediate service. From thence they were ordered away to Albany, in New York, by General Shirley, on whom the chief command of the troops in America had devolved by the death of Major-General Braddock. Virginia, Maryland, and Pennsylvania, were by these means left entirely to take care of themselves, which they might have done effectually, had they been united in their councils; but the usual disputes between their governors and assemblies defeated every salutary plan that was proposed. Pennsylvania, the most powerful of the three, was rendered quite impotent, either for its own defence, or that of its neighbours, by these unhappy contests; though, at last, the assembly of that province, sensible of the danger to which they were exposed, and seeing the absolute necessity of providing a standing military force, and of erecting some forts to

*Disagreement between the Governor and Assembly of Pennsylvania.*

defend their western frontier, passed a bill for raising fifty thousand pounds. But even this sum, small as it was, even to a degree of ridicule, considering the richness of the province, and the extent of its frontier, could not be obtained; the governor positively refusing to give his assent to the act of the assembly, because they had taxed the proprietaries' estates equally with those of the inhabitants, which, he said, he was ordered by his instructions not to consent to, nor indeed any new tax upon the proprietaries; and the assembly, consisting chiefly of members whose estates lay in the eastern or interior parts of the province, as positively refusing to alter their bill. One would be apt to think that, in a case of such urgent necessity, the governor might have ventured to give his assent to the bill under a protest, that it should not prejudice the rights of the proprietaries upon any future occasion; but as he did not, the bill was dropped, and the province left defenceless; by which means it afterwards suffered severely, to the destruction of many of the poor inhabitants upon the western frontier, and to the impressing the Indians with a contemptible opinion of the English, and the highest esteem of the French.

*Expedition against Crown-Point and Niagara resolved on.* Our colonies to the north of Pennsylvania were more active and more successful in their preparations for war. New York, following the example of New England, passed an act to prohibit the sending of provisions to any French port or settlement on the continent of North America, or any of the adjacent islands; and also for raising forty-five thousand pounds, on estates real and personal, for the better defence of their colony, which lay more exposed than any other to a French invasion from Crown-Point. However, this sum, great as it might seem to them, was far from being sufficient; nor, indeed, could they have provided properly for their security, without the assistance of our other colonies to the east of them; but with their help, and the additional succour of the small body of regular troops expected under Colonel Dunbar, they boldly resolved upon offensive measures, which, when practicable, are always the safest; and two expeditions, one against the French fort at Crown-Point, and the other against their fort at Niagara, between the lakes Ontario and Erie, were set on foot at the same time. The former of these expeditions was appointed to be executed under the command of General Johnson, a native of

Ireland, who had long resided upon the Mohock river, in the western parts of New York, where he had acquired a considerable estate, and was universally beloved, not only by the inhabitants, but also by the neighbouring Indians, whose language he had learnt, and whose affections he had gained by his humanity towards them. The expedition against Niagara was commanded by General Shirley himself.

The rendezvous of the troops for both these expeditions was appointed to be at Albany, where most of them arrived before the end of June: but the artillery, batteaux, provisions, and other necessaries for the attempt upon Crown-Point, could not be prepared till the eighth of August, when General Johnson set out with them from Albany for the Carrying-place from Hudson's river to Lake George. There the troops had already arrived, under the command of Major-General Lyman, and consisted of between five and six thousand men, besides Indians, raised by the governments of Boston, Connecticut, New Hampshire, Rhode Island, and New York. Every thing was then prepared as fast as possible for a march; and towards the end of the month, General Johnson advanced about fourteen miles forward with his troops, and encamped in a very strong situation, covered on each side by a thick wooded swamp, by Lake George in his rear, and by a breastwork of trees, cut down for that purpose, in his front. Here he resolved to wait the arrival of his batteaux, and afterwards to proceed to Ticonderoga, at the other end of the lake, from whence it was about fifteen miles to the fort at the south end of Lake Corlaer, or Champlain, called Fort Frederick by the French, and by us Crown-Point. Whilst he was thus encamped, some of his Indian scouts, of which he took care to send out numbers along both sides, and to the farther end of Lake George, brought him intelligence that a considerable number of the enemy were then on their march from Ticonderoga, by the way of the south bay towards the fortified encampment, since called Fort Edward, which General Lyman had built at the Carrying-place; and in which four or five hundred of the New Hampshire and New York men had been left as a garrison. Upon this information General Johnson sent two expresses, one after the other, to Colonel Blanchard, their commander, with orders to call in all his out-parties, and to keep his whole force within the

*General Johnson encamps at Lake George.*

intrenchments. About twelve o'clock at night, those who had been sent upon the second express returned with an account of their having seen the enemy within four miles of the camp at the Carrying-place, which they scarcely doubted their having by that time attacked. Important as the defence of this place was for the safety of the whole army, and imminent as the danger seemed to be, it does not appear that the general then called any council of war, or resolved upon any thing for its relief; but early the next morning he called a council, wherein it was unadvisedly resolved to detach a thousand men, with a number of Indians, to intercept, or, as the general's expression was in his letter, to catch the enemy in their retreat, either as victors, or as defeated in their design. This expedient was resolved on, though no one knew the number of the enemy, nor could obtain any information in that respect from the Indian scouts, because the Indians have no words or signs for expressing any large number, which, when it exceeds their reckoning, they signify by pointing to the stars in the firmament, or to the hair of their head; and this they often do to denote a number less than a thousand, as well as to signify ten thousand, or any greater number.

Between eight and nine o'clock in the morning, a thousand men, with two hundred Indians, were detached under the command of Colonel Williams; but they had not been gone two hours, when those in the camp began to hear a close firing, at about three or four miles distance, as they judged; as it approached nearer and nearer, they rightly supposed that the detachment was overpowered, and retreating towards the camp; which was soon confirmed by some fugitives, and presently after by whole companies, who fled back in great confusion. In a very short time after, the enemy appeared marching in regular order up to the centre of the camp, where the consternation was so great, that, if they had attacked the breastwork directly, they might probably have thrown all into confusion, and obtained an easy victory; but, fortunately for the English, they halted for some time about a hundred and fifty yards' distance, and from thence began their attack with platoon firing, too far off to do much hurt, especially against troops who were defended by a strong breast-work. On the contrary, this ineffectual fire served only to raise the spirits of these last, who, having prepared their artillery

*[margin: Where he is attacked by the French, who are entirely defeated.]*

during the time that the French halted, began to play it so briskly upon the enemy, that the Canadians and Indians in their service fled immediately into the woods on each side of the camp, and there squatted under bushes, or skulked behind trees, from whence they continued firing with very little execution, most of their shot being intercepted by the brakes and thickets; for they never had the courage to advance to the verge of the wood. Baron Dieskau, who commanded the French, being thus left alone, with his regular troops, at the front of the camp, finding he could not make a close attack upon the centre with his small number of men, moved first to the left, and then to the right, at both which places he endeavoured to force a passage, but was repulsed, being unsupported by the irregulars. Instead of retreating, as he ought in prudence to have done, he still continued his platoon and bush-firing till four o'clock in the afternoon, during which time his regular troops suffered greatly by the fire from the camp, and were at last thrown into confusion; which was no sooner perceived by General Johnson's men, than they, without waiting for orders, leaped over their breast-work, attacked the enemy on all sides, and, after killing and taking a considerable number of them, entirely dispersed the rest. The French, whose numbers, at the beginning of this engagement, amounted to about two thousand men, including two hundred grenadiers, eight hundred Canadians, and the rest Indians of different nations, had between seven and eight hundred men killed and thirty taken prisoners: among the latter was Baron Dieskau himself, whom they found at a little distance from the field of battle, dangerously wounded, and leaning on the stump of a tree for his support. The English lost about two hundred men, and those chiefly of the detachment under Colonel Williams; for they had very few either killed or wounded in the attack upon their camp, and not any of distinction, except Colonel Titcomb killed, and the General himself and Major Nichols wounded. Among the slain of the detachment, which would probably have been entirely cut off, had not Lieutenant-Colonel Cole been sent out from the camp with three hundred men, with which he stopped the enemy's pursuit, and covered the retreat of his friends, were Colonel Williams, Major Ashley, six captains, and several subalterns, besides private men; and the Indians reckoned that they had lost forty men, besides the brave old Hendrick, the Mohock Sachem, or chief captain.

When Baron Dieskau set out from Ticonderoga, his design was only to surprise and cut of the intrenched camp, now called Fort Edward, at the Carrying-place, where there were but four or five hundred men. If he had executed this scheme, our army would have been thrown into great difficulties; for it could neither have proceeded farther, nor have subsisted where it was, and he might have found an opportunity to attack it with great advantage in its retreat. But when he was within four or five miles of that fort, his people were informed that there were several cannon there, and none at the camp; upon which they all desired to be led on to this last, which he the more readily consented to, as he himself had been told by an English prisoner, who had left this camp but a few days before, that it was quite defenceless, being without any lines, and destitute of cannon; which, in effect, was true at that time; for the cannon did not arrive, nor was the breast-work erected, till about two days before the engagement. To this misinformation, therefore, must be imputed this step, which would otherwise be inconsistent with the general character and abilities of Baron Dieskau. A less justifiable error seems to have been committed by General Johnson, in not detaching a party to pursue the enemy when they were defeated and fled. Perhaps he was prevented from so doing by the ill fate of the detachment he had sent out in the morning under Colonel Williams. However that may be, his neglect, in this respect, had like to have been fatal the next day to a detachment sent from Fort Edward, consisting of a hundred and twenty men of the New Hampshire regiment, under Captain M'Ginnes, as a reinforcement to the army at the camp. This party fell in with between three and four hundred men of Dieskau's troops, near the spot where Colonel Williams had been defeated the day before; but M'Ginnes, having timely notice, by his scouts, of the approach of an enemy, made such a disposition, that he not only repulsed the assailants, but defeated and entirely dispersed them, with the loss only of two men killed, eleven wounded, and five missing. He himself unfortunately died of the wounds he received in this engagement, a few days after he arrived at the camp with his party.

*Bravery of Captain M'Ginnes.*

It was now judged too late in the year to proceed to the attack of Crown-Point, as it would have been necessary, in that case, to build a strong fort in the place where the camp then was, in order to secure a communication with Albany, from whence only the troops could expect to be reinforced, or supplied with fresh stores of ammunition or provisions. They, therefore, set out upon their return soon after this engagement, having first erected a little stockaded fort, at the hither end of Lake George, in which they left a small garrison as a future prey for the enemy; a misfortune which might easily have been foreseen, because this whole army, being country militia, was to be disbanded, and return to their respective homes, as they actually did soon after their retreat to Albany. This was all the glory, this all the advantage, that the English nation acquired by such an expensive expedition. But so little had the English been accustomed of late to hear of victory, that they rejoiced at this advantage, as if it had been an action of the greatest consequence. The general was highly applauded for his conduct, and liberally rewarded; for he was created a baronet by his majesty, and presented with five thousand pounds by the Parliament. *General Johnson created a baronet.*

The preparations for General Shirley's expedition against Niagara were not only deficient, but shamefully slow; though it was well known that even the possibility of his success must, in a great measure, depend upon his setting out early in the year, as will appear to any person who considers the situation of our fort at Oswego, this being the only way by which he could proceed to Niagara. Oswego lies on the south-east side of the lake Ontario, near three hundred miles almost due west from Albany in New York. The way to it from thence, though long and tedious, is the more convenient, as the far greatest part of it admits of water carriage, by what the inhabitants call batteaux, which are a kind of light flat-bottomed boats, widest in the middle, and pointed at each end, of about fifteen hundred weight burden, and managed by two men, called batteaux men, with paddles and setting poles, the rivers being in many places too narrow to admit of oars. From Albany to the village of Shenectady, about sixteen miles, is a good waggon-road. From thence to the little Falls in the Mohock river, being sixty-five miles, the passage is by water-carriage up that *Description of fort Oswego and lake Ontario.*

river, and consequently against the stream, which, in many places, is somewhat rapid, and in others so shallow, that, when the river is low, the watermen are obliged to get out, and draw their batteaux over the rifts. At the little Falls is a postage, or land carriage, for about a mile over a ground so marshy, that it will not bear any wheel carriage; but a colony of Germans settled there attend with sledges, on which they draw the loaded batteaux to the next place of embarkation upon the same river. From thence they proceed by water up that river, for fifty miles, to the Carrying-place, near the head of it, where there is another postage, the length of which depends upon the dryness or wetness of the season, but is generally above six or eight miles over in the summer months. Here the batteaux are again carried upon sledges, till they come to a narrow river called Wood's Creek, down which they are wafted on a gentle stream, for about forty miles, into the lake Oneyada, which stretches from east to west about thirty miles, and is passed with great ease and safety in calm weather. At the western end of the lake is the river Onondaga, which, after a course of between twenty and thirty miles, unites with the river Cayuga, or Seneca, and their united streams run into the lake Ontario, at the place where Oswego fort is situated. But this river is so rapid as to be sometimes dangerous, besides its being full of rifts and rocks; and about twelve miles on this side of Oswego there is a fall of eleven feet perpendicular, where there is consequently a postage, which, however, does not exceed forty yards. From thence the passage is easy, quite to Oswego. The lake Ontario, on which this fort stands, is near two hundred and eighty leagues in circumference: its figure is oval, and its depth runs from twenty to twenty-five fathoms. On the north side of it are several little gulfs. There is a communication between this lake and that of the Hurons by the river Tanasuate, from whence it is a land carriage of six or eight leagues to the river Toronto, which falls into it. The French have two forts of consequence on this lake: Frontenac, which commands the river St. Lawrence, where the lake communicates with it; and Niagara, which commands the communication between the lake Ontario and the lake Erie. But of these forts, and this last lake, which is one of the finest in the world, we shall have occasion to speak hereafter.

Though we had long been in possession of fort Oswego, and though it lay greatly exposed to the French, particularly to those of Canada, upon any rupture between the two nations, we had never taken care to render it tolerably defensible, or even to build a single vessel fit for navigating the lake: nor was this strange neglect ever taken effectual notice of, till the beginning of this year, when, at a meeting which General Braddock had in April with the governors and chief gentlemen of several of our colonies at Alexandria, in Virginia, it was resolved to strengthen both the fort and garrison at Oswego, and to build some large vessels at that place. Accordingly a number of shipwrights and workmen were sent thither in May and June. At the same time, Captain Bradstreet marched thither with two companies of a hundred men each, to reinforce the hundred that were there before under Captain King, to which number the garrison had been increased since our contests with France began to grow serious. For a long time before, not above twenty-five men were left to defend this post, which, from its great importance, and the situation of affairs at this juncture, most certainly required a much stronger garrison than was put into it even at this period: but economy was the chief thing consulted in the beginning of this war, and to that, in a great measure, was owing its long duration.

*Neglect of the English in not fortifying it.*

From the above description of the passage from Albany to Oswego, it is plain how necessary it was, that the troops intended for this expedition should have set out early in the spring. But instead of that, the very first of them, Colonel Schuyler's New Jersey regiment, did not begin their march till after the beginning of July; and just as Shirley's and Pepperell's regiments were preparing to follow, the melancholy account of Braddock's disaster arrived at Albany, where it so damped the spirits of the people, and spread such a terror, that many of the troops deserted, and most of the batteaux men dispersed, and ran home, by which means even all the necessary stores could not be carried along with the troops. Notwithstanding this disappointment, General Shirley set out from Albany before the end of July, with as many of the troops and stores as he could procure a conveyance for, hoping to be joined in his route by great numbers of the Indians of the Six Nations, to whom he sent invitations to that effect as he passed by

*Expedition against Niagara.*

their settlements: but they, instead of complying with his desire, absolutely declared against all hostilities on that side of the country; and insisted that Oswego, being a place of traffic and peace, ought not to be disturbed either by the English or the French, as if they could have persuaded both parties to agree to such a local truce. Upon this refusal, Mr. Shirley proceeded forward, being joined by very few Indians, and arrived at Oswego on the seventeenth or eighteenth of August: but the rest of the troops and artillery did not arrive till the last day of that month; and even then their store of provisions was not sufficient to enable them to proceed against Niagara, though some tolerably good vessels had by this time been built and got ready for that purpose. The general now resolved to take but six hundred men with him for the attack of Niagara, and to leave the rest of his army, consisting of about fourteen hundred more, at Oswego, to defend that place, in case the French should attack it in his absence, which there was reason to apprehend they might, as they then had a considerable force at fort Frontenac, from whence they could easily cross over the lake Ontario to Oswego. However, he was still obliged to wait at Oswego for provisions, of which at length a small supply arrived on the twenty-sixth of September, barely sufficient to support his men during their intended expedition, and to allow twelve days' short subsistence for those he left behind. But by this time the rainy boisterous season had begun, on which account most of his Indians had already left him, and were returned home; and the few that remained with him declared that there was no crossing the lake Ontario in batteaux at that season, or any time before the next summer. In this perplexity he called a council of war, which, after weighing all circumstances, unanimously resolved to defer the attempt upon Niagara till the next year, and to employ the troops, whilst they remained at Oswego, in building barracks, and erecting, or at least beginning to erect, two new forts, one on the east side of the river Onondaga, four hundred and fifty yards distant from the old fort, which it was to command, as well as the entrance of the harbour, and to be called Ontario fort; and the other, four hundred and fifty yards west of the old fort, to be called Oswego new fort.

These things being agreed on, General Shirley, with the greatest part of the troops under his command, set out on his return to Albany on the twenty-fourth of October, leaving Colonel Mercer, with a garrison of about seven hundred men, at Oswego; though repeated advice had been received, that the French had then at least a thousand men at their fort of Frontenac, upon the same lake; and what was still worse, the new forts were not yet near completed; but left to be finished by the hard labour of Colonel Mercer and his little garrison, with the addition of this melancholy circumstance, that, if besieged by the enemy in the winter, it would not be possible for his friends to come to his assistance. Thus ended this year's unfortunate campaign, during which the French, with the assistance of their Indian allies, continued their murders, scalping, captivating, and laying waste the western frontiers of Virginia and Pennsylvania, during the whole winter.

*General Shirley returns to Albany. End of the campaign in America.*

The ministers of the two jarring powers were very busily employed this year at most of the courts of Europe; but their transactions were kept extremely secret. The French endeavoured to inspire the Spaniards with a jealousy of the strength of the English by sea, especially in America; and the Spanish court seemed inclined to accept of the office of mediator: but Mr. Wall, who was perfectly well acquainted with the state of affairs between England and France, seconded the representations of the British ministry, which demonstrated, that, however willing Great Britain might be to accept of the mediation of Spain, she could not agree to any suspension of arms in America, which France insisted on as a preliminary condition, without hazarding the whole of her interest there; and that the captures which had been made by the English were the necessary consequences of the encroachments and injustice of the French, particularly in that country. Upon this remonstrance, all further talk of the mediation of Spain was dropped, and the ministry of Versailles had recourse to the princes of Germany; amongst whom the Elector of Cologn was soon brought over to their party, so as to consent to their forming magazines in his territories in Westphalia. This was a plain indication of their design against Hanover, which they soon after made his Britannic majesty, who was then at Hanover, an offer of sparing, if he would agree to certain conditions of neutrality for that electorate, which he rejected with disdain. Then

*Fruitless intrigues of the French in Spain and Germany.*

the Count d'Aubeterre, envoy extraordinary from France at the court of Vienna, proposed a secret negotiation with the ministers of the empress-queen. The secret articles of the treaty of Petersburgh, between the two empresses, had stipulated a kind of partition of the Prussian territories, in case that prince should infringe the treaty of Dresden; but his Britannic majesty, though often invited, had always refused to agree to any such stipulation;' and the King of Poland, howsoever he might be inclined to favour the scheme, did not dare to avow it formally, till matters should be more ripe for carrying it into execution. The court of Vienna, whose favourite measure this was, began to listen to D'Aubeterre's insinuations, and by degrees entered into negotiations with him, which, in the end, were productive of that unnatural confederacy between the empress-queen and the King of France, of which further notice will be taken in the occurrences of the next year, when the treaty between them, into which they afterwards found means secretly to bring the Empress of Russia, was concluded at Versailles.

*Treaty of the King of Great Britain with the Landgrave of Hesse-Cassel.*
The King of England, taking it for granted that the French would invade Hanover, in consequence of their rupture with Great Britain, which seemed to be near at hand, began to take measures for the defence of that electorate. To this end, during his stay at Hanover, he concluded, on the eighteenth of June, a treaty with the Landgrave of Hesse-Cassel, by which his serene highness engaged to hold in readiness, during four years, for his majesty's service, a body of eight thousand men, to be employed, if required, upon the continent, or in Britain or Ireland; but not on board the fleet or beyond the seas; and also, if his Britannic majesty should judge it necessary or advantageous for his service, to furnish and join to this body of eight thousand men, within six months after they should be demanded, four thousand more, of which seven hundred were to be horse or dragoons, and each regiment of infantry to have two field pieces of cannon.* Another treaty was begun with Russia

* The king, on his side, promised to pay to the landgrave for these succours, eight crowns banco, by way of levy-money, for every trooper or dragoon duly armed and mounted, and thirty crowns banco for every foot soldier; the crown to be reckoned at fifty-three sols of Holland, or at four shillings and ninepence three farthings English money; and also to pay to his serene highness, for the eight thousand men, an annual subsidy of a hundred and fifty thousand crowns banco, during the four years, to commence from the day of signing the treaty; which subsidy was to be increased to three hundred

about the same time; but this did not take effect during his majesty's residence at Hanover: that others were not concluded was the more surprising, as our subsidy treaty with Saxony had then expired, and that with Bavaria was near expiring, and as the securing of these two princes in our interest was at least as necessary towards forming a sufficient confederacy upon the continent for the defence of Hanover, as it was to secure the Landgrave of Hesse-Cassel. If the reason of their not being engaged, and no other seems so probable, was, that they refused to renew their treaties with England upon any terms, all that can be said is, that they were guilty of flagrant ingratitude, as they had both received a subsidy from this kingdom for many years in time of peace, when they neither were nor could be of any service to the interest of Great Britain.

On the fifteenth of July an express arrived from Admiral Boscawen, with an account of his having taken the two French ships of war, the Alcide and the Lys. This was certainly contrary to the expectation of the court of France; for had they apprehended any such attack, they would not have ordered Mr. M'Namara to return to Brest with the chief part of their squadron; nor was it, perhaps, less contrary to the expectation of some of our own ministry; but as matters had been carried so far, it was then too late to retreat; and, therefore, orders were soon after given to all our ships of war to make reprisals upon the French, by taking their ships wherever they should meet them. Sir Edward Hawke sailed from Portsmouth on the twenty-first of July, with eighteen ships of war, to watch the return of the French fleet from America, which, however, escaped him, and arrived at Brest on the third day of September. Commodore Frankland sailed from Spithead for the West Indies on the thirteenth of August with four ships of war, furnished with orders to commit hostilities, as well as to protect our trade and sugar islands from any insult that the French might offer; and the Duke de Mirepoix, their ambassador at the

*News of the capture of the Alcide and Lys reaches England.*

thousand crowns yearly, from the time of requiring the troops, to the time of their entering into British pay; and in case of their being dismissed, the said subsidy of three hundred thousand crowns was then to revive and be continued during the residue of the term: but if twelve thousand men were demanded and furnished, the subsidy was then to be increased in proportion; and in case the King of Great Britain should at any time think fit to send back their troops before the expiration of the treaty, notice thereof was to be given to his serene highness three months beforehand; one month's pay was to be allowed them for their return, and they were to be furnished gratis with the necessary transport vessels.

court of London, set out for Paris on the twenty-second of July without taking leave.

*The king returns from Hanover, and concludes a treaty with Russia.*
A war being thus in some measure begun, his majesty thought proper, perhaps for that reason, to return to his British dominions sooner than usual; for he left Hanover on the eighth of September, and arrived on the fifteenth at Kensington, where the treaty of alliance between him and the Empress of Russia, which he had begun during his absence, was concluded on the thirtieth of the same month. By this treaty her Russian majesty engaged to hold in readiness in Livonia, upon the frontiers of Lithuania, a body of troops consisting of forty thousand infantry, with the necessary artillery, and fifteen thousand cavalry; and also on the coast of the same province, forty or fifty galleys, with the necessary crews; to be ready to act, upon the first order, in his majesty's service, in case, said the fifth article, which was the most remarkable, that the dominions of his Britannic majesty in Germany should be invaded on account of the interests or disputes which regard his kingdoms; her imperial majesty declaring that she would look upon such an invasion as a case of the alliance of the year one thousand seven hundred and forty-two; and that the said dominions should be therein comprised in this respect; but neither these troops nor galleys were to be put in motion, unless his Britannic majesty, or his allies, should be somewhere attacked; in which case the Russian general should march, as soon as possible after requisition, to make a diversion with thirty thousand infantry and fifteen thousand cavalry; and should embark on board the galleys the other ten thousand infantry, to make a descent according to the exigency of the affair. On the other side, his Britannic majesty engaged to pay to her Russian majesty an annual subsidy of a hundred thousand pounds sterling a year, each year to be paid in advance, and to be reckoned from the day of the exchange of the ratifications, to the day that these troops should upon requisition march out of Russia: from which day the annual subsidy to her imperial majesty was to be five hundred thousand pounds sterling, to be paid always four months in advance, until the troops should return into the Russian dominions, and for three months after their return. His Britannic majesty, who was to be at liberty to send once every year into the said province of Livonia a commissary, to see and examine

the number and condition of the said troops, further engaged, that in case her Russian majesty should be disturbed in this diversion, or attacked herself, he would furnish immediately the succour stipulated in the treaty of one thousand seven hundred and forty-two; and that in case a war should break out, he would send into the Baltic a squadron of his ships, of a force suitable to the circumstances. This was the chief substance of the treaty which, by agreement of both parties, was to subsist for four years from the exchange of the ratifications; but in the seventh article these words were unluckily inserted: "Considering also the proximity of the countries wherein the diversion in question will probably be made, and the facility her troops will probably have of subsisting immediately in an enemy's country, she takes upon herself alone, during such a diversion, the subsistence and treatment of the said troops by sea and land." And in the eleventh article it was stipulated, that all the plunder the Russian army should take from the enemy should belong to them. That his Britannic majesty, who now knew enough of the court of Vienna to be sensible that he could expect no assistance from thence, in case his German dominions were invaded, should enter into this convention with the Empress of Russia, in order to strengthen his defence upon the continent, was extremely natural; especially as he had lately lived in great friendship with her, and her transactions with the court of France had been so secret, by passing through only that of Vienna, that he had not yet been informed of them; neither had the project of the treaty of Versailles then come to his knowledge, or that of the King of Prussia, nor had either of these princes yet made any formal advances to the other.

The first intimation that appeared publicly of the negotiations of France with the Empress of Germany, was, when the French minister, Count d'Aubeterre, declared at Vienna, "That the warlike designs with which the king his master was charged were sufficiently confuted by his great moderation, of which all Europe had manifold proofs; that his majesty was persuaded this groundless charge had given as much indignation to their imperial majesties as to himself; that he was firmly resolved to preserve to Christendom that tranquillity which it enjoyed through his good faith, in religiously observing the treaty of Aix-la-Chapelle; but that if his

*Declaration of the French ministry at the court of Vienna.*

Britannic majesty's allies should take part in the war which was kindled in America, by furnishing succours to the English, his majesty would be authorized to consider and treat them as principals in it." France likewise made the same declaration to other courts.

The words and stipulation in the above recited clause, in the seventh article of the treaty of Great Britain with Russia, were looked on as a menace levelled at the King of Prussia, who, having some time found means to procure a copy of this treaty, and seeing it in that light, boldly declared, by his ministers at all the courts of Europe, that he would oppose, with his utmost force, the entrance of any foreign troops into the empire, under any pretence whatever. This declaration was particularly displeasing to the French, who had already marched large bodies of troops towards the frontiers of the empire, and erected several great magazines in Westphalia, with the permission of the Elector of Cologn, for which the English minister at his court was, in August, ordered to withdraw from thence without taking leave. However, as soon as this declaration of the King of Prussia was notified to the court of Versailles, they sent an ambassador extraordinary, the Duke de Nivernois, to Berlin, to try to persuade his majesty to retract his declaration, and enter into a new alliance with them. His Prussian majesty received this ambassador in such a manner as seemed to denote a disposition to agree to every thing he had to propose. This awakened in England a jealousy that his declaration alone was not to be relied on, but that it was necessary to bring him under some solemn engagement; especially as the French had by this time a numerous army near the Lower Rhine, with magazines provided for their march all the way to Hanover; and if the King of Prussia suffered them to pass through his dominions, that electorate must be swallowed up before the Russian auxiliaries could possibly be brought thither, or any army be formed for protecting it.[b] For this reason a negotiation was set on foot by Great Britain at Berlin; but as it was not concluded before the beginning of the next year, we shall defer entering into the particulars of it till we come to that period.

Meanwhile the French made another attempt upon the

---

[b] Perhaps the Elector of Hanover was more afraid of the Prussian monarch than of the most Christian king, knowing with what ease and rapidity this enterprising neighbour could, in a few days, subdue the whole electorate.

*Spirited declaration of the King of Prussia.*

court of Madrid, loudly complaining of the taking of their two men of war by Boscawen's squadron, before any declaration of war was made, representing it as a most unjustifiable proceeding, which threatened a dissolution of all faith amongst nations. This produced a strong memorial from Sir Benjamin Keene, our minister at that court, importing, "That it was well known that the French fleet carried troops, ammunition, and every thing necessary for defending the countries which the French had unjustly usurped in America, and of which the English claimed the property; that the rules of self-defence authorize every nation to render fruitless any attempt that may tend to its prejudice; that this right had been made use of only in taking the two French ships of war; and that the distinction of place might be interpreted in favour of the English, seeing the two ships were taken on the coast of the countries where the contest arose." In answer to this observation, the French minister represented the vast number of ships that had been taken in the European seas; for in fact the English ports soon began to be filled with them, in consequence of the general orders for making reprisals. But the court of Madrid was so far from being persuaded by any thing he could say, that it gave his Britannic majesty the strongest assurances of its friendship, and of its intention to take no part in the differences between him and France, but such as should be conciliatory, and tending to restore the public tranquillity.

*The French make another unsuccessful attempt upon the court of Spain.*

On the other hand, his Britannic majesty required, as King of Great Britain, the auxiliaries stipulated to him by treaty from the empress-queen. But these were refused, under pretence, that as the contest between him and France related to America only, it was not a case of the alliance; though at the same time the French made no scruple of owning, that they intended to make a powerful descent on Great Britain early in the spring. When, a little while after, France being employed in making great preparations for a land war in Europe, the King of England required her to defend her own possessions, the barrier in the Low Countries, with the number of men stipulated by treaty, which countries, acquired by English blood and English treasure, had been given to her on that express condition, she declared that she could not spare troops for that purpose, on account of her dangerous enemy the King

*The imperial court refuses auxiliaries to England.*

of Prussia; and afterwards, when he was secured by his treaty with England, she urged that as a reason for her alliance with France. It must be owned, however, for the sake of historical truth, that this was no bad reason, considering the power, the genius, and the character of that prince, who hovered over her dominions with an army of one hundred and fifty thousand veterans. It must likewise be owned, that she undertook to procure the French king's consent to a neutrality for Hanover, which would have effectually secured that electorate from the invasion of every other power but Prussia itself; and it is no strained conjecture to suppose, that the dread of this very power was the true source of those connections in Germany, which entailed such a ruinous continental war upon Great Britain.

Though the English continued to make reprisals upon the French, not only in the seas of America, but also in those of Europe, by taking every ship they could meet with, and detaining them, their cargoes, and crews; yet the French, whether from a consciousness of their want of power by sea, or that they might have a more plausible plea to represent England as the aggressor, were so far from returning these hostilities, that their fleet, which escaped Sir Edward Hawke, having, on the thirteenth of August, taken the Blandford ship of war with Governor Lyttelton on board, going to Carolina, they set the governor at liberty, as soon as the court was informed of the ship's being brought into Nantes, and shortly after released both the ship and crew. However, at the same time, their preparations for a land war still went on with great diligence, and their utmost arts and efforts were fruitlessly exerted to persuade the Spaniards and Dutch to join with them against Great Britain.

*The French take the Blandford man of war, but return it.*

In England the preparations by sea became greater than ever; several new ships of war were put in commission, and many others taken into the service of the government; the exportation of gunpowder was forbid; the bounties to seamen were continued, and the number of those that either entered voluntarily or were pressed increased daily, as did also the captures from the French, among which was the Esperance, of seventy guns, taken as she was going from Rochefort to Brest to be manned. The land forces of Great Britain were likewise ordered to be augmented; several new regiments were raised, and all half-

*State of the English and French navies.*

pay officers, and the out-pensioners belonging to Chelsea-hospital, were directed to send in their names, ages, and time of service, in order that such of them as were yet able to serve might be employed again if wanted. The English navy, so early as in the month of September of this year, consisted of one ship of a hundred and ten guns, five of a hundred guns each, thirteen of ninety, eight of eighty, five of seventy-four, twenty-nine of seventy, four of sixty-six, one of sixty-four, thirty-three of sixty, three of fifty-four, twenty-eight of fifty, four of forty-four, thirty-five of forty, and forty-two of twenty, four sloops of war of eighteen guns each, two of sixteen, eleven of fourteen, thirteen of twelve, and one of ten, besides a great number of bomb-ketches, fire-ships, and tenders; a force sufficient to oppose the united maritime strength of all the powers in Europe; whilst that of the French, even at the end of this year, and including the ships then upon the stocks, amounted to no more than six ships of eighty guns, twenty-one of seventy-four, one of seventy-two, four of seventy, thirty-one of sixty-four, two of sixty, six of fifty, and thirty-two frigates.

Such was the situation of the two kingdoms when, on the thirteenth of November, the Parliament met, and his majesty opened the session with a speech from the throne, in which he acquainted them—"That the most proper measures had been taken to protect our possessions in America, and to regain such parts thereof as had been encroached upon, or invaded; that to preserve his people from the calamities of war, as well as to prevent a general war from being lighted up in Europe, he had been always ready to accept reasonable and honourable terms of accommodation, but that none such had been proposed by France; that he had also confined his views and operations to hinder France from making new encroachments, or supporting those already made; to exert his people's right to a satisfaction for hostilities committed in a time of profound peace, and to disappoint such designs as, from various appearances and preparations, there was reason to think had been formed against his kingdoms and dominions; that the King of Spain earnestly wished the preservation of the public tranquillity, and had given assurances of his intention to continue in the same pacific sentiments; that he himself had greatly increased his naval armaments, and augmented his land forces in such a manner as might be least burdensome; and, finally, that he

*Session opened.*

had concluded a treaty with the Empress of Russia, and another with the Landgrave of Hesse-Cassel, which should be laid before them."

In answer to this speech, both Houses voted most loyal addresses, but not without a warm opposition, in each, to some of the particular expressions; for it having been proposed in the House of Lords, to insert in their address the words following, viz.—" That they looked upon themselves as obliged, by the strongest ties of duty, gratitude, and honour, to stand by and support his majesty in all such wise and necessary measures and engagements as his majesty might have taken in vindication of the rights of his crown, or to defeat any attempts which might be made by France, in resentment for such measures, and to assist his majesty in disappointing or repelling all such enterprises as might be formed, not only against his kingdoms, but also against any other of his dominions, (though not belonging to the crown of Great Britain,) in case they should be attacked on account of the part which his majesty had taken for maintaining the essential interests of his kingdoms;" the inserting of these words in their address was opposed by Earl Temple, and several other lords; because, by the first part of them, they engaged to approve of the treaties with Russia and Hesse-Cassel, neither of which they had ever seen; nor could it be supposed that either of them could be of any advantage to this nation; and by the second part of these words it seemed to be resolved, to engage this nation in a continental connexion for the defence of Hanover, which it was impossible for England to support, and which would be so far from being of any advantage to it at sea, or in America, that it might at last disable the nation from defending itself in either of those parts of the world. But upon putting the question, the inserting of these words was agreed to by a great majority, and accordingly they stand as part of the address of the House upon that occasion.

*Remarkable addresses of the Lords and Commons.*

To this remarkable address his majesty returned the following as remarkable answer: "My lords, I give you my hearty thanks for this dutiful and affectionate address. I see, with the greatest satisfaction, the zeal you express for my person and government, and for the true interest of your country, which I am determined to adhere to. The assurances which you give me for the defence

*His majesty's answer.*

of my territories abroad are a strong proof of your affection for me, and regard for my honour. Nothing shall divert me from pursuing those measures which will effectually maintain the possessions and rights of my kingdoms, and procure reasonable and honourable terms of accommodation."
—The address of the House of Commons breathed the same spirit of zeal and gratitude, and was full of the warmest assurances of a ready support of his majesty, and of his foreign dominions, if attacked in resentment of his maintaining the rights of his crown and kingdom; and his majesty's answer to it was to the same effect as that.to the House of Lords. The same, or nearly the same words, relating to the treaties concluded by his majesty, and to the defence of his foreign dominions, were proposed to be inserted in this address, which was opposed by William Pitt, Esq., then paymaster of his majesty's forces; the Right Hon. Henry Legge, Esq., then chancellor and under-treasurer of his majesty's exchequer, and one of the commissioners of the treasury; and by several other gentlemen in high posts under the government, as well as by many others; but upon putting the question, it was by a considerable majority agreed to insert the words objected to; and very soon after, Mr. Pitt, Mr. Legge, and most, if not all, of the gentlemen who had appeared in the opposition, were dismissed from their employments. In the mean time, a draft came over from Russia for part of the new subsidy stipulated to that crown; but some of the ministry, who were then at the head of the finances, refused to pay it, at least before the treaty should be approved of by Parliament.

Sir Thomas Robinson had not been long in possession of the office of secretary of state, before it was generally perceived, that, though an honest, well-meaning man, and a favourite with the king, his abilities were not equal to the functions of that post. Much less were they so at this juncture, when the nation was on the point of being engaged in a difficult and expensive war, and plunged into foreign measures and connexions, which would require the utmost skill of an able politician to render them palatable to the people. Mr. Pitt and Mr. Fox, though they scarce ever agreed in any other particular, had generally united in opposing his measures, and their superior influence in the House of Commons, and universally acknowledged abilities, though of very different kinds, had always prevailed,

*Alterations in the ministry. Mr. Fox made secretary of state.*

uncommon as it was to see two persons who held considerable places under the government, one of them being paymaster-general, and the other secretary at war, oppose, upon almost every occasion, a secretary of state, who was supposed to know and speak the sentiments of his master. Sir Thomas himself soon grew sensible of his want of sufficient weight in the senate of the nation; and, therefore, of his own accord, on the tenth of November, wisely and dutifully resigned the seals of his office to his majesty, who delivered them to Mr. Fox, and appointed Sir Thomas master of the wardrobe, with a pension to him during his life, and after his death to his sons. Lord Barrington succeeded Mr. Fox as secretary at war; and soon after Sir George Lyttelton was made chancellor of the exchequer, and a lord of the treasury, in the room of Mr. Legge, who had declared himself against the new continental system. However, notwithstanding these changes in the ministry, very warm debates arose in both Houses, when the treaties of Russia and Hesse-Cassel came to be considered by them: some of the members were for referring them to a committee; but this motion was overruled, in consideration of his majesty's having engaged in them to guard against a storm that seemed ready to break upon his electoral dominions, merely on account of our quarrel with the French. They were at length approved of by a majority of three hundred and eighteen against one hundred and twenty-six, in the House of Commons; and by eighty-four against eleven, in the House of Lords.

The House of Commons then proceeded to provide for the service of the ensuing year, and for the deficiencies of the provisions for the former. Fifty thousand seamen, including nine thousand one hundred and thirty-eight marines, were voted, on the twenty-fourth of November, for the service of the year one thousand seven hundred and fifty-six, together with two millions six hundred thousand pounds for their maintenance, and thirty-four thousand two hundred and sixty-three land soldiers, with nine hundred and thirty thousand six hundred and three pounds, six shillings, and ninepence for their support. A hundred thousand pounds were voted as a subsidy to the Empress of Russia; fifty-four thousand one hundred and forty pounds, twelve shillings, and sixpence, to the Landgrave of Hesse-Cassel; and ten thousand pounds to the Elector of Bavaria.

*Supplies voted.*

During these transactions, the public was overwhelmed with consternation by the tidings of a dreadful earthquake, which, on the first of November, shook all Spain, Portugal, and many other places in Europe, and laid the city of Lisbon in ruins. When the news of this great calamity first reached England, it was feared the consequences of it might affect our public credit, considering the vast interest which the English merchants had in the Portuguese trade; but fortunately, it afterwards proved inconsiderable, in comparison of what had been apprehended: the quarter in which the English chiefly lived, and where they had their warehouses, having suffered the least of any part of the city; and most of the English merchants then residing there, together with their families, being at their country houses, to avoid the insults to which they might have been exposed from the Portuguese populace, during the celebration of their *auto-da-fe*, which was kept that very day. The two first shocks of this dreadful visitation continued near a quarter of an hour, after which the water of the river Tagus rose perpendicularly above twenty feet, and subsided to its natural bed in less than a minute. Great numbers of houses, of which this city then contained about thirty-six thousand, extending in length near six miles, in form of a crescent, on the ascent of a hill, upon the north shore of the mouth of the river Tagus, within nine miles from the ocean, were thrown down by the repeated commotions of the earth, together with several magnificent churches, monasteries, and public buildings. But what entirely completed the ruin of this then most opulent capital of the Portuguese dominions, was a devouring conflagration, partly fortuitous or natural, but chiefly occasioned by a set of impious villains, who, unawed by the tremendous scene at that very instant passing before their eyes, with a wickedness scarcely to be credited, set fire even to the falling edifices in different parts of the city, to increase the general confusion, that they might have the better opportunity to rob and plunder their already desolated fellow-citizens. Out of three hundred and fifty thousand inhabitants which Lisbon was then supposed to contain, about ten thousand perished by this calamity; and the survivors, deprived of their habitations, and destitute even of the necessaries of life, were forced to seek for shelter in the open fields.

As soon as his majesty received an account of this

deplorable event from his ambassador at the court of Madrid, he sent a message to both Houses of Parliament, on the twenty-eighth of November, acquainting them therewith, and desiring their concurrence and assistance towards speedily relieving the unhappy sufferers; and the Parliament thereupon, to the honour of British humanity, unanimously voted, on the eighth of December, a gift of a hundred thousand pounds for the distressed people of Portugal. A circumstance which enhances the merit of this action is, that though the English themselves were, at that very time, in great want of grain, a considerable part of the sum was sent in corn, flour, rice, and a large quantity of beef from Ireland; supplies which came very seasonably for the poor Portuguese, who were in actual want of the necessaries of life. Their king was so affected by this instance of British generosity, that, to show his gratitude for the timely relief, he ordered Mr. Castres, the British resident at his court, to give the preference, in the distribution of these supplies, to the British subjects who had suffered by the earthquake; accordingly, about a thirtieth part of the provisions, and two thousand pounds in money, were set apart for that purpose; and his Portuguese majesty returned his thanks, in very warm terms, to the British crown and nation.

*Relief voted by Parliament to the Portuguese.*

The report of an intended invasion of these kingdoms by the French increasing daily, on the twenty-second day of January Lord Barrington, as secretary at war, laid before the House an estimate for defraying the charge of ten new regiments of foot, over and above the thirty-four thousand two hundred and sixty-three land soldiers before ordered to be raised; and a sum of ninety-one thousand nine hundred and nineteen pounds, ten shillings, was voted for these additional forces: upon another estimate presented a little after by the same lord, and founded upon the same reasons, for raising, for the further defence of the kingdom, eleven troops of light dragoons, forty-nine thousand six hundred and twenty-eight pounds, eleven shillings, and three pence, were voted for the ensuing year; together with eighty-one thousand one hundred and seventy-eight pounds, sixteen shillings, for a regiment of foot to be raised in North America; two hundred and ninety-eight thousand five hundred and thirty-four pounds, seventeen shillings, and ten pence halfpenny, for the maintenance of

*Troops, &c., voted.*

our forces already established in our American colonies; and seventy-nine thousand nine hundred and fifteen pounds, six shillings, for six regiments of foot from Ireland, to serve in North America and the East Indies. Besides all these supplies, Mr. Fox, on the twenty-eighth of January, presented to the House a message from the king, desiring them to take into consideration the faithful services of the people of New England, and of some other parts of North America: upon which one hundred and fifteen thousand pounds more were voted, and five thousand pounds as a reward to Sir William Johnson in particular. In short, including several other sums, as well for defraying the expense of the army and navy, as for a subsidy of twenty thousand pounds to the King of Prussia, and one hundred and twenty-one thousand four hundred and forty-seven pounds, two shillings, and sixpence, for Hanoverian troops, of which two last articles further notice will be taken hereafter, the whole of the supplies granted by Parliament in this session amounted to seven millions two hundred and twenty-nine thousand one hundred and seventeen pounds, four shillings and sixpence three farthings. For raising this sum, besides the malt-tax, and the land-tax of four shillings in the pound, the whole produce of the sinking fund, from the fifth of January one thousand seven hundred and fifty-six, till it should amount to one million five hundred and fifty-five thousand nine hundred and fifty-five pounds, eleven shillings, and eleven pence halfpenny, was ordered to be applied thereunto; together with a million to be raised by loans or exchequer-bills, at three per cent. interest: one million five hundred thousand pounds to be raised by the sale of redeemable annuities, at three and a half per cent., and five hundred thousand pounds to be raised by a lottery, at three per cent. All which sums, with eighty-three thousand four hundred and twelve pounds, two shillings, and five pence halfpenny, then remaining in the exchequer, amounted to seven millions four hundred and twenty-seven thousand two hundred and sixty-one pounds, five shillings, and seven pence.

The clause inserted in the mutiny bill last year, subjecting all officers and soldiers raised in America, by authority of the respective governors or governments there, to the same rules and articles of war, and the same penalties and punishments as the British forces were liable to; the act passed at the same time for regulating

Mutiny bill, marine, and mariners' acts continued.

the marine forces while on shore; and that for the more speedy and effectual manning of his majesty's navy; were not only confirmed now, but it was further enacted, with respect to this last, as well as for the more speedy and effectual recruiting of his majesty's land forces, that the commissioners appointed by the present act should be empowered to raise and levy, within their respective jurisdictions, such able-bodied men as did not follow any lawful calling or employment, or had not some other lawful and sufficient support; and might order, wherever and whenever they pleased, a general search to be made for such persons, in order to their being brought before them to be examined; nay, that the parish or town officers might, without any such order, search for and secure such persons, in order to convey them before the said commissioners to be examined; that if any three commissioners should find any person, so brought before them, to be within the above description, and if the recruiting officer attending should judge him to be a man fit for his majesty's service, they should cause him to be delivered to such officer, who might secure him in any place of safety provided by the justices of peace for that purpose, or even in any public prison; and that every such man was from that time to be deemed a listed soldier, and not to be taken out of his majesty's service by any process, other than for some criminal matter. Nothing could more plainly show either the zeal of the Parliament for a vigorous prosecution of the war, or their confidence in the justice and moderation of our ministry, than their agreeing to this act, which was to continue in force till the end of the next session; and which, in the hands of a wicked and enterprising administration, might have been made such a use of, as would have been inconsistent with that security which is provided by our happy constitution for the liberty of the subject.

The next object of the immediate attention of Parliament in this session was the raising of a new regiment of foot in North America; for which purpose the sum of eighty-one thousand one hundred and seventy-eight pounds, sixteen shillings, to which the estimate thereof amounted, was voted. This regiment, which was to consist of four battalions of a thousand men each, was intended to be raised chiefly out of the Germans and Swiss, who, for many years past, had annually transported them-

*Act for raising a regiment of foot in North America.*

selves in great numbers to the British plantations in America, where waste lands had been assigned them upon the frontiers of the provinces; but, very injudiciously, no care had been taken to intermix them with the English inhabitants of the place. To this circumstance it is owing, that they have continued to correspond and converse only with one another; so that very few of them, even of those who have been born there, have yet learned to speak or understand the English tongue. However, as they were all zealous Protestants, and in general strong hardy men, and accustomed to the climate, it was judged that a regiment of good and faithful soldiers might be raised out of them, particularly proper to oppose the French; but to this end it was necessary to appoint some officers, especially subalterns, who understood military discipline, and could speak the German language; and as a sufficient number of such could not be found among the English officers, it was necessary to bring over and grant commissions to several German and Swiss officers and engineers; but as this step, by the act of settlement, could not be taken without the authority of Parliament, an act was now passed for enabling his majesty to grant commissions to a certain number of foreign Protestants, who had served abroad as officers or engineers, to act and rank as officers or engineers in America only. An act was likewise passed in this session, strictly forbidding, under pain of death, any of his majesty's subjects to serve as officers under the French king, or to enlist as soldiers in his service, without his majesty's previous licence; and also for obliging such of his majesty's subjects as should, in time to come, accept of commissions in the Scotch brigade in the Dutch service, to take the oaths of allegiance and abjuration, on pain of forfeiting five hundred pounds.

As it had been resolved, in the beginning of the preceding summer, to build vessels of force upon the lake Ontario, an act was now passed for extending the maritime laws of England, relating to the government of his majesty's ships and forces by sea, to such officers, seamen, and others, as should serve on board his majesty's ships or vessels employed upon the lakes, great waters, or rivers in North America; and also, but not without opposition to this last, for the better recruiting of his majesty's forces upon the continent of America; to which end, by a new clause now added to a former act, a recruiting officer was empowered to enlist and detain an indented servant, even though his master should reclaim him, upon paying to the master such a sum as two justices of peace, within the precinct, should adjudge to be a reasonable equivalent for the original purchase-money, and the remaining time such servant might have to serve.

<small>Quiet of Ireland restored.</small> The intestine broils of Ireland were happily composed this year by the prudent management of the Marquis of Hartington, lord-lieutenant of that kingdom. By his steady and disinterested conduct, his candour and humanity, the Irish were not only brought to a much better temper, even among themselves, than they were before their late outrageous riots and dangerous dissensions happened; but also prevailed upon to acquiesce in the measures of England, without this last being obliged to give up any one point of her superiority. The leading men in the Parliament of Ireland were the first that conformed; and though the ferment continued very high for some time after, among the middling and lower ranks of people, it was at length entirely allayed by the wisdom of the lord-lieutenant, and the excellent law which he encouraged and passed for the benefit of that nation.* The P―――― of Ireland, who had been very busy in fomenting many of the late disturbances, was, by his majesty's command, struck off the list of privy-counsellors; and the greatest part of those patriots, whom faction had turned out of their employments there, were reinstated with honour.

<small>Treaty concluded with Prussia. 1756.</small> The Parliament of England, which had adjourned on the twenty-third of December, met again: the House of Commons on the thirteenth of January, and the Lords on the nineteenth. On the sixteenth of the same month, the treaty between his Britannic majesty and the King of Prussia was signed, importing that, for the defence of their common country, Germany, and in order to preserve her peace and tranquillity, which it was feared was in danger of being disturbed, on account of the disputes in America, the two kings, for that end only, entered into a

<small>* Among other objects of the attention of the legislature of that country, ten thousand pounds were granted for making the river Nore navigable from the city of Kilkenny to the town of Innestalge; twenty thousand pounds towards carrying on an inland navigation from the city of Dublin to the river Shannon; four thousand pounds for making the river Newry navigable; a thousand pounds a year for two years, for the encouragement of English Protestant schools; several sums, to be distributed in premiums, for the encouragement of the cambric, hempen, and flaxen manufactures; and three hundred thousand pounds to his majesty, towards supporting the several branches of the establishment, and for defraying the expenses of the government for two years.</small>

convention of neutrality, by which they reciprocally bound themselves not to suffer foreign troops of any nation whatsoever to enter into Germany, or pass through it during the troubles aforesaid, and the consequences that might result from them; but to oppose the same with their utmost might, in order to secure Germany from the calamities of war, maintain her fundamental laws and constitutions, and preserve her peace uninterrupted. Thus, the late treaty with Russia was virtually renounced. Their majesties, moreover, seized this favourable opportunity to adjust the differences that had subsisted between them, in relation to the remainder of the Silesia loan, due to the subjects of his Britannic majesty, and the indemnification claimed by the subjects of his Prussian majesty for their losses by sea during the late war; so that the attachment laid on the said debt was agreed to be taken off, as soon as the ratification of this treaty should be exchanged.

On the twenty-first of January the House took into consideration the laws then in being relating to the militia of this kingdom; and finding them insufficient, ordered a new bill to be prepared and brought in, for the better regulating of the militia forces in the several counties of England. A bill was accordingly prepared to that effect, and presented to the House on the twelfth of March by the Hon. Charles Townshend, Esq., who, to his honour, was one of the chief promoters of it. After receiving many amendments in the House of Commons, it was on the tenth of May passed, and sent to the Lords; but several objections being made to it by some of the peers, and it seeming to them that some further amendments were still necessary, which they thought they could not in that session spare time to consider so maturely as the importance of the subject required, a negative of fifty-nine against twenty-three was put upon the motion for passing the bill; though every one must have been sensible, not only of the propriety, but even of the absolute necessity of such a law, which was ardently desired by the whole nation. *New militia bill passed by the Commons, but rejected by the Lords.*

On the twenty-seventh of May his majesty went to the House of Peers, and after having given the royal assent to the bills then depending, thanked his Parliament, in a speech from the throne, for their vigorous and effectual support. He acquainted them, that the injuries *Session closed.*

and hostilities which had been for some time committed by the French against his dominions and subjects were then followed by the actual invasion of the island of Minorca, though guaranteed to him by all the great powers of Europe, and particularly by the French king; that he had, therefore, found himself obliged, in vindication of the honour of his crown, and of the rights of his people, to declare war in form against France; and that he relied on the Divine protection, and the vigorous assistance of his faithful subjects, in so just a cause. The Parliament was then adjourned to the eighteenth of June, and from thence afterwards to the eighteenth of July, and then it was prorogued.

## CHAPTER XXV.

LETTER FROM M. ROUILLÉ TO THE SECRETARY OF STATE. — THE TWO NATIONS RECRIMINATE ON EACH OTHER. — THE FRENCH THREATEN GREAT BRITAIN WITH AN INVASION. — REQUISITION OF SIX THOUSAND DUTCH TROOPS ACCORDING TO TREATY. — MESSAGE FROM THE KING TO THE PARLIAMENT. — A BODY OF HESSIANS AND HANOVERIANS TRANSPORTED INTO ENGLAND. — FRENCH PREPARATIONS AT TOULON. — ADMIRAL BYNG SAILS FOR THE MEDITERRANEAN. — HE ARRIVES AT GIBRALTAR. — ENGAGES M. DE LA GALISSONNIÈRE OFF MINORCA — AND RETURNS TO GIBRALTAR. — FERMENT OF THE PEOPLE AT HOME. — ADMIRAL BYNG SUPERSEDED AND SENT HOME PRISONER. — ACCOUNT OF THE SIEGE OF ST. PHILIP'S FORT, IN MINORCA. — PRECAUTIONS TAKEN BY GENERAL BLAKENEY. — SIEGE COMMENCED. — ENGLISH SQUADRON APPEARS. — GENERAL ATTACK OF THE WORKS. — THE GARRISON CAPITULATES. — SIR EDWARD HAWKE SAILS TO MINORCA. — REJOICINGS IN FRANCE, AND CLAMOURS IN ENGLAND. — GALLANTRY OF FORTUNATUS WRIGHT. — GENERAL BLAKENEY CREATED A BARON. — MEASURES TAKEN FOR THE DEFENCE OF GREAT BRITAIN. — PROCLAMATION. — EARL OF LOUDOUN APPOINTED COMMANDER-IN-CHIEF IN AMERICA. — HIS BRITANNIC MAJESTY'S DECLARATION OF WAR. — SUBSTANCE OF THE FRENCH KING'S DECLARATION. — ADDRESS OF THE CITY OF LONDON. — TRIAL OF GENERAL FOWKE. — AFFAIRS OF AMERICA. — COLONEL BRADSTREET DEFEATS A BODY OF FRENCH ON THE RIVER ONONDAGA. — EARL OF LOUDOUN ARRIVES AT NEW YORK. — OSWEGO REDUCED BY THE ENEMY. — FURTHER PROCEEDINGS IN AMERICA. — NAVAL OPERATIONS IN THAT COUNTRY. — TRANSACTIONS IN THE EAST INDIES. — CALCUTTA BESIEGED BY THE VICEROY OF BENGAL. — DEPLORABLE FATE OF THOSE WHO PERISHED IN THE DUNGEON THERE. — ADDITIONAL CRUELTIES EXERCISED ON MR. HOLWELL. — RESOLUTION AGAINST ANGRIA. — FORT OF GERIA TAKEN BY ADMIRAL WATSON AND MR. CLIVE. — THEIR SUBSEQUENT PROCEEDINGS IN THE RIVER GANGES.

IN the month of January Mr. Fox, lately appointed secretary of state, received a letter from M. Rouillé, minister and secretary of state for foreign affairs to the King of France, expostulating in the name of his sovereign upon the orders and instructions for committing hostilities, which his Britannic majesty had given to General Braddock and Admiral Boscawen, in diametrical opposition to the most solemn assurances so often repeated by word of mouth as well as in writing. He complained of the insult which had been offered to his master's flag in attacking and taking two of his ships in the open sea, without any previous declaration of war; as also by committing depredations on the commerce of his most Christian majesty's subjects, in contempt of the law of nations, the faith of treaties, and the usages established among civilized nations. He said, the sentiments and character of his Britannic majesty gave the king his master room to expect that at his

*1756. Letter from M. Rouillé to the secretary of state.*

return to London he would disavow the conduct of his Admiralty; but seeing that, instead of punishing, he rather encouraged those who had been guilty of such depredations, his most Christian majesty would be deemed deficient in what he owed to his own glory, the dignity of his crown, and the defence of his people, if he deferred any longer demanding a signal reparation for the outrage done to the French flag, and the damage sustained by his subjects. He, therefore, demanded immediate and full restitution of all the French ships which, contrary to law and decorum, had been taken by the English navy, together with all the officers, soldiers, mariners, guns, stores, and merchandise. He declared, that should this restitution be made, he should be willing to engage in a negotiation for what further satisfaction he might claim, and continue desirous to see the differences relating to America determined by a solid and equitable accommodation; but if, contrary to all hopes, these demands should be rejected, he would consider such a denial of justice as the most authentic declaration of war, and as a formed design in the court of London to disturb the peace of Europe. To this peremptory remonstrance the British secretary was directed to answer, that though the King of England would readily consent to an equitable and solid accommodation, he would not comply with the demand of immediate and full restitution as a preliminary condition; for his majesty had taken no steps but such as were rendered just and indispensable by the hostilities which the French began in time of profound peace, and a proper regard for his own honour, the rights and possessions of his crown, and the security of his kingdoms.

*The two nations recriminate on each other.* Without all doubt the late transactions had afforded specious arguments for both nations to impeach the conduct of each other. The French court, conscious of their encroachments in Nova Scotia, affected to draw a shade over these, as particulars belonging to a disputed territory, and to divert the attention to the banks of the Ohio, where Jamonville and his detachment had been attacked and massacred by the English, without the least provocation. They likewise inveighed against the capture of their ships before any declaration of war, as flagrant acts of piracy; and some neutral powers of Europe seemed to consider them in the same point of view. It was certainly high time to check the insolence of the French by force of arms, and surely this might have been as effectually and expeditiously exerted under the usual sanction of a formal declaration; the omission of which exposed the administration to the censure of our neighbours, and fixed the imputation of fraud and free-booting on the beginning of the war. The ministry was said to have delayed the ceremony of denouncing war from political considerations, supposing that, should the French be provoked into the first declaration of this kind, the powers of Europe would consider his most Christian majesty as the aggressor, and Great Britain would reap all the fruits of the defensive alliances in which she had engaged. But nothing could be more weak and frivolous than such a conjecture. The aggressor is he who first violates the peace; and every ally will interpret the aggression according to his own interest and convenience. The administration maintained the appearance of candour in the midst of their hostilities. The merchant ships, of which a great number had been taken from the French, were not sold and divided among the captors, according to the practice of war; but carefully sequestered, with all their cargoes and effects, in order to be restored to their right owners, in case the disputes between the two nations should not be productive of an open rupture. In this particular, however, it was pity that a little common sense had not been blended with their honourable intention. Great part of the cargoes consisted of fish, and other perishable commodities, which were left to rot and putrefy, and afterwards thrown overboard to prevent contagion, so that the owners and captors were equally disappointed, and the value of them lost to both nations.

The court of Versailles, while they presented remonstrances which they knew would prove ineffectual, and exclaimed against the conduct of Great Britain with all the arts of calumny and exaggeration at every court in Christendom, continued nevertheless to make such preparations as denoted a design to prosecute the war with uncommon vigour. They began to repair and fortify Dunkirk: orders were published that all British subjects should quit the dominions of France: many English vessels were seized in the different ports of that kingdom, and their crews sent to prison. At the same time an edict was issued, inviting the French subjects to equip privateers, offering a premium of forty livres for every gun, and as much

*The French threaten Great Britain with an invasion.*

for every man they should take from the enemy; and promising that, in case a peace should be speedily concluded, the king would purchase the privateers at prime cost. They employed great numbers of artificers and seamen in equipping a formidable squadron of ships at Brest; and assembling a strong body of land forces, as well as a considerable number of transports, threatened the island of Great Britain with a dangerous invasion.

The English people were seized with consternation: the ministry were alarmed and perplexed. Colonel Yorke, the British resident at the Hague, was ordered by his majesty to make a requisition of the six thousand men whom the States-General are obliged by treaty to furnish, when Great Britain shall be threatened with an invasion; and in February he presented a memorial for this purpose. Monsieur d'Affry, the French king's minister at the Hague, having received intimation of this demand, produced a counter-memorial from his master, charging the English as the aggressors, and giving the States-General plainly to understand, that, should they grant the succours demanded by Great Britain, he would consider their compliance as an act of hostility against himself. The Dutch, though divided among themselves by faction, were unanimously averse to any measure that might involve them in the approaching war. Their commerce was in a great measure decayed, and their finances were too much exhausted to admit of an immediate augmentation of their forces, which for many reasons they strove to avoid. They foresaw a great increase of trade in their adhering to a punctual neutrality: they were afraid of the French by land, and jealous of the English by sea; and, perhaps, enjoyed the prospect of seeing these two proud and powerful nations humble and impoverish each other. Certain it is, the States-General protracted their answer to Mr. Yorke's memorial by such affected delays, that the court of London perceived their intention, and, in order to avoid the mortification of a flat denial, the king ordered his resident to acquaint the princess regent that he would not insist upon his demand. The states, thus freed from their perplexity, at length delivered an answer to Mr. Yorke, in which they expatiated on the difficulties they were laid under, and thanked his Britannic majesty for having freed them by his declaration from that embarrassment into which

*Requisition of six thousand Dutch troops according to treaty.*

they were thrown by his first demand and the counter-memorial of the French minister. The real sentiments of those people, however, more plainly appeared in the previous resolution delivered to the states of Holland by the towns of Amsterdam, Dort, Haerlem, Gouda, Rotterdam, and Enckhuysen, declaring flatly that England was incontrovertibly the aggressor in Europe, by seizing a considerable number of French vessels; that the threatened invasion of Great Britain did not affect the republic's guarantee of the Protestant succession, inasmuch as it was only intended to obtain reparation for the injury sustained by the subjects of his most Christian majesty; finally, that the succours demanded could be of no advantage to the King of England; as it appeared by the declaration of his most Christian majesty, that their granting these succours would immediately lay them under the necessity of demanding, in their turn, assistance from Great Britain. From this way of arguing, the English may perceive what they have to expect in cases of emergency from the friendship of their nearest allies, who must always be furnished with the same excuse, whenever they find it convenient or necessary to their own interest. Such a consideration, joined to other concurring motives, ought to induce the British legislature to withdraw its dependence from all foreign connexions, and provide such a constitutional force within itself, as will be fully sufficient to baffle all the efforts of an external enemy. The apprehensions and distraction of the people at this juncture plainly evinced the expediency of such a national force; but different parties were divided in their opinions about the nature of such a provision. Some of the warmest friends of their country proposed a well-regulated militia, as an institution that would effectually answer the purpose of defending a wide extended sea-coast from invasion; while, on the other hand, this proposal was ridiculed and refuted as impracticable or useless by all the retainers to the court, and all the officers of the standing army. In the mean time, as the experiment could not be immediately tried, and the present juncture demanded some instant determination, recourse was had to a foreign remedy.

Towards the latter end of March, the king sent a written message to Parliament, intimating, that he had received repeated advices, from different persons and places, that a design had been formed by the French *Message from the king to the Parliament.*

court to invade Great Britain or Ireland; and the great preparations of forces, ships, artillery, and warlike stores, then notoriously making in the ports of France opposite to the British coasts, together with the language of the French ministers in some foreign courts, left little room to doubt the reality of such a design: that his majesty had augmented his forces both by sea and land, and taken proper measures and precautions for putting his kingdom in a posture of defence: that, in order further to strengthen himself, he had made a requisition of a body of Hessian troops, pursuant to the late treaty, to be forthwith brought over, and for that purpose ordered transports to be prepared; that he doubted not of being enabled and supported by his Parliament in taking such measures as might be conducive to an end so essential to the honour of his crown, the preservation of the Protestant religion, and the laws and liberties of these kingdoms. This message was no sooner received, than both Houses voted, composed, and presented, very warm and affectionate addresses, in which his majesty was thanked for the requisition he had made of the Hessian troops; a measure which, at any other time, would have been stigmatized with all the satire and rhetoric of the opposition.

*A body of Hessians and Hanoverians transported into England.* Even this precaution was not thought sufficient to secure the island, and quiet the terrors of the people. In a few days Mr. Fox, the new minister, encouraged by the unanimity which had appeared so conspicuous in the motions for the late addresses, ventured to move again, in the House of Commons, that another address should be presented to the king, beseeching his majesty, that for the more effectual defence of this island, and for the better security of the religion and liberties of his subjects, against the threatened attack by a foreign enemy, he would be graciously pleased to order twelve battalions of his electoral troops, together with the usual detachment of artillery, to be forthwith brought into this kingdom. There was a considerable party in the House to whom such a motion was odious and detestable; but, considering the critical situation of affairs, they were afraid that, a direct opposition might expose them to a more odious suspicion; they, therefore, moved for the order of the day, and insisted on the question's being put upon that motion; but it was carried in the negative by a considerable majority, which also agreed to the other proposal. The resolution of the House was communicated to the Lords, who unanimously concurred; and their joint address being presented, his majesty assured them he would immediately comply with their request. Accordingly, such expedition was used, that in the course of the next month both Hanoverians and Hessians arrived in England, and encamped in different parts of the kingdom.—As the fears of an invasion subsided in the minds of the people, their antipathy to these foreign auxiliaries emerged. They were beheld with the eyes of jealousy, suspicion, and disdain. They were treated with contempt, reserve, and rigour. The ministry was execrated for having reduced the nation to such a low circumstance of disgrace, as that they should owe their security to German mercenaries. There were not wanting some incendiaries, who circulated hints and insinuations, that the kingdom had been purposely left unprovided; and that the natives of South Britain had been formerly subdued and expelled by a body of Saxon auxiliaries, whom they had hired for their preservation. In a word, the doubts and suspicions of a people naturally blunt and jealous were inflamed to such a degree of animosity, that nothing would have restrained them from violent acts of outrage, but the most orderly, modest, and inoffensive behaviour by which both the Hanoverians and Hessians were distinguished.

Under the cloak of an invading armament, which engrossed the attention of the British nation, the French were actually employed in preparations for an expedition, which succeeded according to their wish. *French preparations at Toulon.* In the beginning of the year, advice was received that a French squadron would soon be in a condition to sail from Toulon: this was afterwards confirmed by repeated intelligence, not only from foreign gazettes, but also from English ministers and consuls residing in Spain and Italy. They affirmed that the Toulon squadron consisted of twelve or fifteen ships of the line, with a great number of transports; that they were supplied with provisions for two months only, consequently could not be intended for America; and that strong bodies of troops were on their march from different parts of the French dominions to Dauphiné and Provence in order to be embarked. Notwithstanding these particulars of information, which plainly pointed out Minorca as the object of their expedition; notwithstanding the extensive and important commerce carried on by the subjects of Great Britain in the Mediterranean; no care was taken to send thither a squadron of ships capable to protect the trade, and frustrate the designs of the enemy. That great province was left to a few inconsiderable ships and frigates, which could serve no other purpose than that of carrying intelligence from port to port, and enriching their commanders by making prize of merchant vessels. Nay, the ministry seemed to pay little or no regard to the remonstrance of General Blakeney, deputy-governor of Minorca, who, in repeated advices, represented the weakness of the garrison which he commanded in St. Philip's castle, the chief fortress on the island. Far from strengthening the garrison with a proper reinforcement, they did not even send thither the officers belonging to it who were in England upon leave of absence, nor give directions for any vessel to transport them, until the French armament was ready to make a descent upon that island.*

At length, the destination of the enemy's fleet being universally known, the ministry seemed to rouse from their lethargy, and, like persons suddenly waking, acted with hurry and precipitation. Instead of detaching a squadron that in all respects should be superior to the French fleet in the Mediterranean, and bestowing the command of it upon an officer of approved courage and activity, they allotted no more than ten ships of the line for this service, vesting the command of them in Admiral Byng, who had never met with any occasion to signalize his

*Admiral Byng sails for the Mediterranean.*

---

* It is with pleasure we seize this opportunity of recording an instance of gallantry and patriotism in a British officer, which would have done honour to the character of a Roman tribune. Captain Cunningham, an accomplished young gentleman, who acted as engineer en second at Minorca, being preferred to a majority at home, and recalled to his regiment by an express order, had repaired with his family to Nice, in Italy, where he waited for the opportunity of a ship bound for England, when he received certain intelligence that the French armament was destined for the place he had quitted. His lady, whom he tenderly loved, was just delivered, and two of his children were dangerously ill of the small-pox. He recollected that the chief engineer at Minorca was infirm, and indeed disabled by the gout, and that many things were wanting for the defence of the fortress. His zeal for the honour and service of his country immediately triumphed over the calls of tenderness and of nature. He expended a considerable sum of money in purchasing timber for the platforms, and other necessaries for the garrison; hired a ship for transporting them thither; and tearing himself from his wife and children, thus left among strangers in a foreign country, embarked again for Minorca, where he knew he should be, in a peculiar manner, exposed to all the dangers of a furious siege. In the course of this desperate service he acquitted himself with that vigilance, skill, and active courage, which he had on divers former occasions displayed, until the assault was given to the Queen's bastion: when mixing with the enemy, sword in hand, he was disabled in his right arm by the shot of a musket and the thrust of a bayonet. His behaviour was so acceptable to his sovereign, that when he returned to England he was preferred to the rank of colonel in the guards. He afterwards acted as chief engineer in the attempts and descents which were made on the French coast. Though grievously maimed, he accepted of the same office in the expedition to Guadaloupe, where he died universally regretted.

courage, and whose character was not very popular in the navy: but Mr. West, the second in command, was a gentleman universally respected for his probity, ability, and resolution. The ten ships destined for this expedition were but in very indifferent order, poorly manned, and unprovided with either hospital or fire-ship. They sailed from Spithead on the seventh day of April, having on board, as part of their complement, a regiment of soldiers to be landed at Gibraltar, with Major-General Stuart, Lord Effingham, and Colonel Cornwallis, whose regiments were in garrison at Minorca; about forty inferior officers, and near one hundred recruits, as a reinforcement to St. Philip's fortress.

After all the intelligence which had been received, one would imagine the government of England was still ignorant of the enemy's force and destination; for the instructions delivered to Admiral Byng imported, that on his arrival at Gibraltar, he should inquire whether any French squadron had passed through the straits; and that, being certified in the affirmative, as it was probably designed for North America, he should immediately detach Rear-Admiral West to Louisbourg, on the island of Cape-Breton, with such a number of ships as, when joined with those at Halifax, would constitute a force superior to the armament of the enemy. On the second day of May, Admiral Byng arrived at Gibraltar, where he found Captain Edgecumbe, with the Princess Louisa ship of war, and a sloop, who informed him that the French armament, commanded by M. de la Galissonnière, consisting of thirteen ships of the line, with a great number of transports, having on board a body of fifteen thousand land forces, had sailed from Toulon on the tenth day of April, and made a descent upon the island of Minorca, from whence he (Captain Edgecumbe) had been obliged to retire at their approach. General Fowke, who commanded at Gibraltar, had received two successive orders from the secretary at war, with respect to his sparing a battalion of troops to be transported by Mr. Byng, as a reinforcement to Minorca; but as the two orders appeared inconsistent or equivocal, a council of war was consulted, and the majority were of opinion that no troops should be sent from thence to Minorca, except a detachment to supply the deficiency in the little squadron of Captain Edgecumbe, who had left a good number of his seamen and marines under the command of Captain Scroop, to assist in the defence of Fort St. Philip's. These articles of intelligence the admiral despatched by an express to the lords of the Admiralty, and in his letter made use of some impolitic expressions, which, in all probability, it would have been well for him had he omitted. He said, if he had been so happy as to have arrived at Mahon before the French had landed, he flattered himself he should have been able to prevent their getting a footing on that island. He complained, that there were no magazines in Gibraltar for supplying the squadron with necessaries; that the careening wharfs, pits, and store-houses were entirely decayed, so that he should find the greatest difficulty in cleaning the ships that were foul; and this was the case with some of those he carried out from England, as well as with those which had been for some time cruising in the Mediterranean. He signified his opinion, that, even if it should be found practicable, it would be very impolitic to throw any men into St. Philip's castle, which could not be saved without a land force sufficient to raise the siege; therefore, a small reinforcement would only add so many men to the number which must fall into the hands of the enemy. He observed, that such engineers and artillery-men in Gibraltar as had been at Minorca, were of opinion, that it would be impossible to throw any number of men into St. Philip's, if the French had erected batteries on the two shores near the entrance of the harbour, so as to bar all passage up to the sally-port of the fortress; and with this opinion he signified the concurrence of his own sentiments. The first part of this letter was a downright impeachment of the ministry, for having delayed the expedition, for having sent out ships unfit for service, and for having neglected the magazines and wharfs at Gibraltar. In the latter part he seemed to prepare them for the subsequent account of his misconduct and miscarriage. It cannot be supposed that they underwent this accusation without apprehension and resentment; and as they foresaw the loss of Minorca, which would not fail to excite a national clamour, perhaps they now began to take measures for gratifying their resentment, and transferring the blame from themselves to the person who had presumed to hint a disapprobation of their conduct; for this purpose they could not have found a fairer opportunity than Mr. Byng's subsequent behaviour afforded.

The admiral being strengthened by Mr. Edgecumbe, and reinforced by a detachment from the garrison, set sail from Gibraltar on the eighth day of May, and was joined off Majorca by his majesty's ship the Phœnix, under the command of Captain Hervey, who confirmed the intelligence he had already received, touching the strength and destination of the French squadron. When he approached Minorca, he descried the British colours still flying at the castle of St. Philip's, and several bomb batteries playing upon it from different quarters where the French banners were displayed. Thus informed, he detached three ships a-head, with Captain Hervey, to reconnoitre the harbour's mouth, and land, if possible, a letter for General Blakeney, giving him to understand the fleet was come to his assistance. Before this attempt could be made, the French fleet appearing to the south-east, and the wind blowing strong off shore, he recalled his ships, and formed the line of battle. About six o'clock in the evening, the enemy, to the number of seventeen ships, thirteen of which appeared to be very large, advanced in order; but about seven tacked, with a view to gain the weather-gage. Mr. Byng, in order to preserve that advantage, as well as to make sure of the land wind, in the morning, followed their example, being then about five leagues from Cape Mola. At daylight the enemy could not be descried; but two tartanes appearing close to the rear of the English squadron, they were immediately chased by signal. One escaped, and the other being taken, was found to have on board two French captains, two lieutenants, and about one hundred private soldiers, part of six hundred who had been sent out in tartanes the preceding day, to reinforce the enemy's squadron. This soon re-appearing, the line of battle was formed on each side, and about two o'clock Admiral Byng threw out a signal to bear away two points from the wind and engage. At this time his distance from the enemy was so great, that Rear-Admiral West, perceiving it impossible to comply with both orders, bore away with his division seven points from the wind, and closing down upon the enemy, attacked them with such impetuosity, that the ships which opposed him were in a little time driven out of the line. Had he been properly sustained by the van, in all probability the British fleet would have obtained a complete victory; but the other division did not bear down, and the enemy's centre keeping that station, Rear-Admiral West could not pursue his advantage without running the risk of seeing his communication with the rest of the line entirely cut off. In the beginning of the action, the Intrepid, in Mr. Byng's division, was so disabled in her rigging, that she could not be managed, and drove on the ship that was next in position; a circumstance which obliged several others to throw all a-back, in order to avoid confusion, and for some time retarded the action. Certain it is, that Mr. Byng, though accommodated with a noble ship of ninety guns, made little or no use of his artillery, but kept aloof, either from an overstrained observance of discipline, or timidity. When his captain exhorted him to bear down upon the enemy, he very coolly replied, that he would avoid the error of Admiral Matthews, who, in his engagement with the French and Spanish squadrons off Toulon, during the preceding war, had broke the line by his own precipitation, and exposed himself singly to a fire that he could not sustain. Mr. Byng, on the contrary, was determined against acting, except with the line entire; and, on pretence of rectifying the disorder, which had happened among some of the ships, hesitated so long, and kept at such a wary distance, that he never was properly engaged, though he received some few shots in his hull. M. de la Galissonnière seemed equally averse to the continuance of the battle; part of his squadron had been fairly obliged to quit the line; and though he was rather superior to the English in number of men and weight of metal, he did not choose to abide the consequence of a closer fight with an enemy so expert in naval operations: he, therefore, took advantage of Mr. Byng's hesitation, and edged away with an easy sail to join his van, which had been discomfited. The English admiral gave chase; but the French ships being clean, he could not come up and close them again; so they retired at their leisure. Then he put his squadron on the other tack, in order to keep the wind of the enemy; and next morning they were altogether out of sight.

While he lay-to with the rest of his fleet, at the distance of ten leagues from Mahon, he detached cruisers to look for some missing ships, which joined him accordingly, and made an inquiry into the condition of the squadron. The number of killed amounted to forty-two, including Captain Andrews, of the Defiance; and

*And returns to Gibraltar.*

about one hundred and sixty-eight were wounded. Three of the capital ships were so damaged in their masts, that they could not keep the sea, with any regard to their safety; a great number of the seamen were ill, and there was no vessel which could be converted into an hospital for the sick and wounded. In this situation Mr. Byng called a council of war, at which the land officers were present. He represented to them, that he was much inferior to the enemy in weight of metal and number of men; that they had the advantage of sending their wounded to Minorca, from whence at the same time they were refreshed and reinforced occasionally; that, in his opinion, it was impracticable to relieve St. Philip's fort, and, therefore, they ought to make the best of their way back to Gibraltar, which might require immediate protection. They unanimously concurred with his sentiments, and thither he directed his course accordingly. How he came to be so well acquainted with the impracticability of relieving General Blakeney, it is not easy to determine, as no experiment was made for that purpose. Indeed, the neglect of such a trial seems to have been the least excusable part of his conduct; for it afterwards appeared, that the officers and soldiers belonging to the garrison might have been landed at the sally-port, without running any great risk; and a gentleman, then in the fort, actually passed and repassed in a boat, unhurt by any of the enemy's batteries.

Mr. Byng's letter to the Admiralty, containing a detail of the action, is said to have arrived some days before it was made public; and when it appeared, was curtailed of divers expressions, and whole paragraphs, which either tended to his own justification, or implied a censure on the conduct of his superiors. Whatever use might have been made of his letter while it remained a secret to the public, we shall not pretend to explain: but sure it is, that on the sixteenth day of June, Sir Edward Hawke and Admiral Saunders sailed from Spithead to Gibraltar, to supersede the Admirals Byng and West, in their commands of the Mediterranean squadron; and Mr. Byng's letter was not published till the twenty-sixth day of the same month, when it produced all the effect which that gentleman's bitterest enemies could have desired. The populace took fire like a train of the most hasty combustibles, and broke out into such a clamour of rage and indig-

*Ferment of the people at home.*

nation against the devoted admiral, as could not have been exceeded if he had lost the whole navy of England, and left the coasts of the kingdom naked to invasion. This animosity was carefully fomented and maintained by artful emissaries, who mingled with all public assemblies, from the drawing-room at St. James's to the mob at Charing-cross. They expatiated upon the insolence, the folly, the cowardice, and misconduct of the unhappy admiral. They even presumed to make their sovereign in some measure an instrument of their calumny, by suggesting, that his majesty had prognosticated Byng's misbehaviour from the contents of his first letter, dated at Gibraltar. They ridiculed and refuted the reasons he had given for returning to that fortress, after his scandalous rencounter with the French squadron; and in order to exasperate them to the most implacable resentment, they exaggerated the terrible consequences of losing Minorca, which must now be subdued through his treachery or want of resolution. In a word, he was devoted as the scapegoat of the ministry, to whose supine negligence, ignorance, and misconduct, the loss of that important fortress was undoubtedly owing. Byng's miscarriage was thrown out like a barrel to the whale, in order to engage the attention of the people, that it might not be attracted by the real cause of the national misfortune. In order to keep up the flame which had been kindled against the admiral, recourse was had to the lowest artifices. Agents were employed to vilify his person in all public places of vulgar resort; and mobs were hired at different parts of the capital to hang and burn him in effigy.

The two officers who succeeded to the command in the
*Admiral Byng superseded, and sent home prisoner.* Mediterranean were accompanied by Lord Tyrawley, whom his majesty had appointed to supersede General Fowke in the government of Gibraltar, that gentleman having incurred the displeasure of the ministry for not having understood an order which was unintelligible. By the same conveyance, a letter from the secretary to the Admiralty was transmitted to Mr. Byng, giving him notice that he was recalled. To this intimation he replied in such a manner as denoted a consciousness of having done his duty, and a laudable desire to vindicate his own conduct. His answer contained a further account of the engagement in which he was supposed to have misbehaved, intermixed with some puerile calculations

of the enemy's superiority in weight of metal, which served no other purpose than that of exposing his character still more to ridicule and abuse; and he was again so impolitic as to hazard certain expressions, which added fresh fuel to the resentment of his enemies. Directions were immediately despatched to Sir Edward Hawke, that Byng should be sent home in arrest; and an order to the same purpose was lodged at every port in the kingdom: precautions which, however unnecessary to secure the person of a man who longed ardently to justify his character by a public trial, were yet productive of considerable effect in augmenting the popular odium. Admiral Byng immediately embarked in the ship which had carried out his successor, and was accompanied by Mr. West, General Fowke, and several other officers of that garrison, who were also recalled, in consequence of having subscribed to the result of the council of war, which we have mentioned above. When they arrived in England, Mr. West met with such a gracious reception from his majesty as was thought due to his extraordinary merit; but Mr. Byng was committed close prisoner in an apartment of Greenwich hospital.

In the mean time, the siege of St. Philip's fort in Minorca was prosecuted with unremitting vigour. The armament of Toulon, consisting of the fleet commanded by M. de la Galissonnière, and the troops under the Duke de Richelieu, arrived on the eighteenth day of April at the port of Ciudadella and that part of the island opposite to Mahon, or St. Philip's, and immediately began to disembark their forces. Two days before they reached the island, General Blakeney had, by a packet-boat, received certain intelligence of their approach, and began to make preparations for the defence of the castle. The fort which he commanded was very extensive, surrounded with numerous redoubts, ravelins, and other outworks; and provided with subterranean galleries, mines, and traverses, cut out of the solid rock with incredible labour. Upon the whole, this was one of the best fortified places in Europe, well supplied with artillery, ammunition, and provision; and, without all doubt, might have sustained the most desperate siege, had it been defended by a numerous garrison, conducted by able engineers, under the eye and auspices of an active and skilful commander. All these advantages, however, did not concur, on this occa-

*Account of the siege of St. Philip's fort in Minorca.*

sion. The number of troops in Minorca did not exceed four regiments, whereas the nature of the works required at least double the number; and, even of these, above forty officers were absent. The chief engineer was rendered lame by the gout, and the general himself oppressed with the infirmities of old age. The natives of the island might have been serviceable as pioneers, or day labourers, but, from their hatred to the Protestant religion, they were generally averse to the English government, although they had lived happily and grown wealthy under its influence.

The governor ordered his officers to beat up for volunteers in the adjacent town of St. Philip's; but few or none would enlist under his banners, and it seems he would not venture to compel them into the service. He recalled all his advanced parties; and, in particular, a company posted at Fornelles, where a small redoubt had been raised, and five companies at Ciudadella, a post fortified with two pieces of cannon, which were now withdrawn as soon as the enemy began to disembark their forces. At the same time Major Cunningham was detached with a party to break down the bridges, and break up the roads between that place and St. Philip's; but the task of destroying the roads could not be performed in such a hurry, on account of the hard rock which runs along the surface of the ground through this whole island; nor was there time to demolish the town of St. Philip's, which stood so near the fort, that the enemy could not fail to take advantage of its neighbourhood. The streets served them for trenches, which otherwise could not have been dug through the solid rock. Here they made a lodgment close to the works; here they found convenient barracks and quarters of refreshment, masks for their batteries, and an effectual cover for their mortars and bombardiers. The general has been blamed for leaving the town standing; but if we consider his uncertainty concerning the destination of the French armament, the odious nature of such a precaution, which could not fail to exasperate the inhabitants, and the impossibility of executing such a scheme after the first appearance of the enemy, he will be found excusable, if not altogether blameless. Some houses and windmills were actually demolished, so as to clear the esplanade and the approaches. All the wine in the cellars of St. Philip's town was destroyed, and the butts were carried into the castle, where they might serve for gabions and traverses. Five and twenty Minorquin bakers were hired, and a large number of cattle brought into the fort, for the benefit of the garrison. The ports were walled up, the posts assigned, the sentinels placed, and all the different guards appointed. Commodore Edgecumbe, who then anchored in the harbour of Mahon, close under the walls of the castle, sailed away with his little squadron, consisting of the Chesterfield, Princess Louisa, Portland, and Dolphin, after having left all his marines, a detachment from Gibraltar, the whole crew of the Porcupine sloop, and the greater part of the Dolphin's, as a reinforcement to the fort, under the immediate direction and command of Captain Scroop, of the Dolphin, who, with great gallantry, offered himself for this severe duty, and bravely signalized himself during the whole siege. The French admiral might certainly have blocked up this harbour in such a manner as would have prevented the escape of these ships, and divers other rich merchant vessels which happened then to be at Mahon; but in all probability, they purposely allowed them to abandon the place, which, on any emergency or assault, their crews and officers would have considerably reinforced. The enemy were perfectly acquainted with the great extent of the works, and the weakness of the garrison, from which circumstances they derived the most sanguine hopes that the place might be suddenly taken without the trouble of a regular siege. After Mr. Edgecumbe had sailed for Gibraltar, and General Blakeney had ordered a sloop to be sunk in the channel that leads to the harbour, the French squadron made its appearance at this part of the island; but, without having attempted any thing against the fort, fell to leeward of Cape Mola. Next day they came in sight again, but soon bore away, and never afterwards, during the whole course of the siege, approached so near as to give the garrison the least disturbance.

On the twenty-second day of April, the governor sent a drummer to the French general with a letter desiring to know his reasons for invading the island. To this an answer was returned by the Duke de Richelieu, declaring he was come with intention to reduce the island under the dominion of his most Christian majesty, by way of retaliation for the conduct of his master, who had seized and detained the ships belonging to the King of France and his subjects. If we may judge from the first operations of this nobleman, he was but indifferently provided with engineers; for, instead of beginning his approaches on the side of St. Philip's town, close by the outworks, where he might have been screened from the fire of the garrison, his batteries were erected at Cape Mola, on the other side of the harbour, where they were more exposed, their fire much less effectual, and indeed at too great a distance to be of any service. The fire of St. Philip's was so severe, and the cannon so well served on this quarter, that in a little time the enemy thought proper to change their plan of attack, and advance on the side of St. Philip's town, which ought to have been the first object of their consideration, especially as they could find little or no earth to fill their gabions, and open their trenches in the usual form. On the twelfth of May, about nine at night, they opened two bomb batteries near the place where the windmills had been destroyed; and from that period an incessant fire was kept up on both sides, from mortars and cannon, the French continuing to raise new batteries in every situation from whence they could annoy the besieged.

On the seventeenth day of the month, the garrison were

*English squadron appears.*

transported with joy at sight of the British squadron, commanded by Admiral Byng; and Mr. Boyd, commissary of the stores, ventured to embark in a small boat with six oars, which passed from St. Stephen's Cove, a creek on the west side of the fortification, through a shower of cannon and musketry from the enemy's post on the other side, and actually reached the open sea, his design being to join the squadron; but this being at a great distance, stretching away to the southward, and Mr. Boyd perceiving himself chased by two of the enemy's light vessels, he returned by the same route to the garrison, without having sustained the least damage: a circumstance which plainly confutes the notion of Mr. Byng, that it was impracticable to open a communication with the garrison of St. Philip's. Next day the hopes of the besieged, which had prognosticated a naval victory to the British squadron, a speedy relief to themselves, and no less than captivity to the assailants, were considerably damped by the appearance of the French fleet, which quietly returned to their station off the harbour of Mahon. That same evening they were told by a deserter that the English fleet had been worsted in an engagement by M. de la Galissonnière; and this information was soon confirmed by a general discharge, or *feu de joie*, through the whole

French camp, to celebrate the victory they pretended to have obtained. How little soever they had reason to boast of any advantage in the action, the retreat of the English squadron was undoubtedly equivalent to a victory; for had Mr. Byng acquired and maintained the superiority at sea, the French forces, which had been disembarked in Minorca, would, in all probability, have been obliged to surrender prisoners of war to his Britannic majesty. The case was now much altered in their favour: their squadron cruised about the island without molestation: and they daily received, by means of their transports, reinforcements of men and ammunition, as well as constant supplies of provisions.

The English garrison, however mortified at finding themselves thus abandoned, resolved to acquit themselves with gallantry in the defence of the place, not without some remaining hope that the English squadron would be reinforced, and return to their relief. In the mean time, they sustained and retorted the enemy's fire with undaunted resolution. They remounted cannon, the carriages of which had been disabled: they removed them occasionally to places from whence it was judged they could do the greatest execution: they repaired breaches, restored merlons, and laboured with surprising alacrity, even when they were surrounded by the numerous batteries of the foe; when their embrasures, and even the parapets, were demolished, and they stood exposed not only to the cannon and mortars, but also to the musketry, which fired upon them, without ceasing, from the windows of the houses in the town of St. Philip's. By this time they were invested with an army of twenty thousand men, and plied incessantly from sixty-two battering cannon, twenty-one mortars, and four howitzers, besides the small arms; nevertheless, the loss of men within the fortress was very inconsiderable, the garrison being mostly secured in the subterranean works, which were impenetrable to shells or shot. By the twenty-seventh day of June they had made a practicable breach in one of the ravelins, and damaged the other outworks to such a degree, that they determined this night to give a general assault. Accordingly, between the hours of ten and eleven, they advanced to the attack from all quarters on the land side. At the same time a strong detachment, in armed boats, attempted to force the harbour, and penetrated into the creek, called St. Stephen's Cove, to storm Fort Charles, and second

*General attack of the works.*

the attack upon Fort Marlborough, on the farther side of the creek, the most detached of all the outworks. The enemy advanced with great intrepidity, and their commander, the Duke de Richelieu, is said to have led them up to the works in person. Such an assault could not but be attended with great slaughter; they were mowed down, as they approached, with grape-shot and musketry; and several mines were sprung with great effect, so that the glacis was almost covered with the dying and the dead. Nevertheless, they persevered with uncommon resolution; and though repulsed on every other side, at length made a lodgment in the Queen's redoubt, which had been greatly damaged by their cannon. Whether their success in this quarter was owing to the weakness of the place, or to the timidity of the defender, certain it is, the enemy were in possession before it was known to the officers of the garrison; for Lieutenant-Colonel Jeffries, the second in command, who had acquitted himself since the beginning of the siege with equal courage, skill, and activity, in his visitation of this post, was suddenly surrounded and taken by a file of French grenadiers, at a time when he never dreamed they had made a lodgment. Major Cunningham, who accompanied him, met with a severer fate, though he escaped captivity: he was run through the arm with a bayonet, and the piece being discharged at the same time, shattered the bones of his hand in such a manner, that he was maimed for life. In this shocking condition he retired behind a traverse, and was carried home to his quarters. Thus the governor was deprived of his two principal assistants, one being taken, and the other disabled.

*The garrison capitulates.* The enemy having made themselves masters of Anstruther's and the Queen's redoubts, from which perhaps they might have been dislodged, had a vigorous effort been made for that purpose, before they had leisure to secure themselves, the Duke de Richelieu ordered a parley to be beat, in order to obtain permission to bury the dead and remove the wounded. This request was granted with more humanity than discretion, inasmuch as the enemy took this opportunity to throw a reinforcement of men privately into the places where the lodgments had been made, and these penetrated into the gallery of the mines which communicated with all the other outworks. During this short cessation, General Blakeney summoned a council of war to deliberate upon the state of the fort and garrison; and the majority declared for a capitulation. The works were in many places ruined; the body of the castle was shattered; many guns were dismounted, the embrasures and parapets demolished, the palisadoes broke in pieces, the garrison exhausted with hard duty and incessant watching, and the enemy in possession of the subterranean communications. Besides, the governor had received information from prisoners, that the Duke de Richelieu was alarmed by a report that the Marshal Duke de Belleisle would be sent to supersede him in the command, and for that reason would hazard another desperate assault, which it was the opinion of the majority the garrison could not sustain. These considerations, added to the despair of being relieved, induced him to demand a capitulation. But this measure was not taken with the unanimous consent of the council. Some officers observed, that the garrison was very little diminished, and still in good spirits: that no breach was made in the body of the castle, nor a single cannon erected to batter in breach: that the loss of an outwork was never deemed a sufficient reason for surrendering such a fortress: that the counterscarp was not yet taken, nor, on account of the rocky soil, could be taken, except by assault, which would cost the enemy a greater number than they had lost in their late attempt: that they could not attack the ditch, or batter in breach, before the counterscarp should be taken, and even then they must have recourse to galleries, before they could pass the fossé, which was furnished with mines and countermines: finally, they suggested, that in all probability the British squadron would be reinforced, and sail back to their relief: or, if it should not return, it was the duty of the governor to defend the place to extremity, without having any regard to the consequences. These remarks being overruled, the chamade was beat, a conference ensued, and very honourable conditions were granted to the garrison, in consideration of the gallant defence they had made. This, it must be owned, was vigorous while it lasted, as the French general was said to have lost five thousand men in the siege; whereas the loss of the garrison, which at first fell short of three thousand men, did not exceed one hundred. The capitulation imported, that the garrison should march out with all the honours of war, and be conveyed by sea to Gibraltar. The French were put in possession of one gate as well as Fort Charles and

Marlborough redoubt; but the English troops remained in the other works till the seventh day of July, when they embarked. In the mean time reciprocal civilities passed between the commanders and officers of both nations.

<small>Sir Edward Hawke sails to Minorca.</small> The articles of capitulation were no sooner executed, than Monsieur de la Galissonnière sailed back to Toulon with all the prizes which had lain at anchor in the harbour of Mahon, since the fort of St. Philip was first invested. In all probability, the safety of himself and his whole squadron was owing to this expeditious retreat; for, in a few days after the surrender of the fort, Sir Edward Hawke's fleet, augmented by five ships of the line, which had been sent from England, when the first tidings arrived of Minorca's being invaded, now made its appearance off the island; but by this time Galissonnière was retired, and the English admiral had the mortification to see the French colours flying upon St. Philip's castle. What, perhaps, chagrined this gallant officer still more, he was not provided with frigates, sloops, and small craft to cruise round the island, and intercept the supplies which were daily sent to the enemy. Had he reached Minorca sooner, he might have discomfited the French squadron: but he could not have raised the siege of St. Philip's, because the Duke de Richelieu had received his reinforcements, and such a train of artillery as no fortification could long withstand. Indeed, if the garrison had been considerably reinforced, and the communication with it opened by sea, the defence would have been protracted, and so many vigorous sallies might have been made, that the assailants would have had cause to repent of their enterprise.

<small>Rejoicings in France, and clamours in England.</small> When the news of this conquest was brought to Versailles by the Count of Egmont, whom the Duke de Richelieu had despatched for that purpose, the people of France were transported with the most extravagant joy. Nothing was seen but triumphs and processions; nothing heard but anthems, congratulations, and hyperbolical encomiums upon the conqueror of Minorca, who was celebrated in a thousand poems and studied orations; while the conduct of the English was vilified and ridiculed in ballads, farces, and pasquinades. Nothing more argues the degeneracy of a warlike nation than the pride of such mean triumph for an advantage, which, in more vigorous times, would scarce have been distinguished by the ceremony

of a *Te Deum laudamus*. Nor is this childish exultation, that disgraces the laurels of victory, confined to the kingdom of France. Truth obliges us to own, that even the subjects of Great Britain are apt to be elevated by success into an illiberal insolence of self-applause and contemptuous comparison. This must be condemned, as a proof of unmanly arrogance and absurd self-conceit, by all those who coolly reflect, that the events of war generally, if not always, depend upon the genius or misconduct of one individual. The loss of Minorca was severely felt in England as a national disgrace; but, instead of producing dejection and despondence, it excited an universal clamour of rage and resentment, not only against Mr. Byng, who had retreated from the French squadron, but also in reproach of the administration, which was taxed with having neglected the security of Minorca. Nay, some politicians were inflamed into a suspicion, that this important place had been negatively betrayed into the hands of the enemy, that, in case the arms of Great Britain should prosper in other parts of the world, the French king might have some sort of equivalent to restore for the conquests which should be abandoned at the peace. This notion, however, seems to have been conceived from prejudice and party, which now began to appear with the most acrimonious aspect, not only throughout the united kingdoms in general, but even in the sovereign's councils.

Sir Edward Hawke, being disappointed in his hope of encountering La Galissonnière, and relieving the English garrison of St. Philip's, at least asserted the empire of Great Britain in the Mediterranean, by annoying the commerce of the enemy, and blocking up their squadron in the harbour of Toulon. Understanding that the Austrian government at Leghorn had detained an English privateer, and imprisoned the captain, on pretence that he had violated the neutrality of the port, he detached two ships of war, to insist, in a peremptory manner, on the release of the ship, effects, crew, and captain; and they thought proper to comply with his demand, even without waiting for orders from the court of Vienna. The person in whose behalf the admiral thus interposed was one Fortunatus Wright, a native of Liverpool, who, though a stranger to a sea-life, had, in the last war, equipped a privateer, and distinguished himself in such a manner, by his uncommon vigilance and valour, that, if he had been indulged

*Gallantry of Fortunatus Wright.*

with a command suitable to his genius, he would have deserved as honourable a place in the annals of the navy, as that which the French have bestowed upon their boasted Guai Trouin, Du Bart, and Thurot. An uncommon exertion of spirit was the occasion of his being detained at this juncture. While he lay at anchor in the harbour of Leghorn, commander of the St. George privateer of Liverpool, a small ship of twelve guns and eighty men, a large French xebeque, mounted with sixteen cannon, and nearly three times the number of his complement, chose her station in view of the harbour, in order to interrupt the British commerce. The gallant Wright could not endure this insult: notwithstanding the enemy's superiority in metal and number of men, he weighed anchor, hoisted his sails, engaged him within sight of the shore, and after a very obstinate dispute, in which the captain, lieutenant, and above threescore of the men belonging to the xebeque were killed on the spot, he obliged them to sheer off, and returned to the harbour in triumph. This brave corsair would, no doubt, have signalized himself by many other exploits, had he not, in the sequel, been overtaken in the midst of his career by a dreadful storm, in which the ship foundering, he and all his crew perished.

Sir Edward Hawke, having scoured the Mediterranean, and insulted the enemy's ports, returned with the homeward-bound trade to Gibraltar; from whence, about the latter end of the year, he set sail for England with part of his squadron, leaving the rest in that bay for the protection of our commerce, which, in those parts, soon began to suffer extremely from French privateers that now swarmed in the Mediterranean. General Blakeney had arrived with the garrison of Minorca, at Portsmouth, in the month of November, and been received with expressions of tumultuous joy: every place through which he passed celebrated his return with bonfires, illuminations, bell-ringing, and acclamations: every mouth was opened in his praise, extolling him for the gallant defence he had made in the castle of St. Philip. In a word, the people's veneration for Blakeney increased in proportion to their abhorrence of Byng: the first was lifted into an idol of admiration, while the other sunk into an object of reproach; and they were viewed at different ends of a false perspective, through the medium of prejudice and passion; of a perspective artfully contrived, and applied by certain ministers for the purposes of self-interest and deceit. The sovereign is said to have been influenced by the prepossession of the s——t. Mr. Blakeney met with a gracious reception from his majesty, who raised him to the rank of an Irish baron, in consideration of his faithful services; while some malecontents murmured at this mark of favour, as an unreasonable sacrifice to popular misapprehension.

In the beginning of the year, the measures taken by the government in England seem to have been chiefly dictated by the dread of an invasion, from which the ministers did not think themselves secured by the guardships and cruisers on different parts of the coast, or the standing army of the kingdom, though reinforced by the two bodies of German auxiliaries. A considerable number of new troops was levied; the success in recruiting was not only promoted by the landholders throughout the kingdom, who thought their estates were at stake, and for that reason encouraged their dependents to engage in the service; but also in a great measure owing to a dearth of corn, which reduced the lower class of labourers to such distress, that some insurrections were raised, and many enlisted with a view to obtain a livelihood, which otherwise they could not earn. New ships of war were built, and daily put in commission; but it was found impracticable to man them without having recourse to the odious and illegal practice of impressing sailors, which must always be a reproach to every free people. Notwithstanding large bounties granted by the government to volunteers, it was found necessary to lay an embargo upon all shipping, and impress all the seamen that could be found, without any regard to former protections: so that all the merchant ships were stripped of their hands, and foreign commerce for some time wholly suspended. Nay, the expedient of compelling men into the service was carried to an unusual degree of oppression; for rewards were publicly offered to those who should discover where any seamen lay concealed: so that those unhappy people were in some respects treated like felons, dragged from their families and connexions to confinement, mutilation, and death, and totally cut off from the enjoyment of that liberty which, perhaps, at the expense

*Measures taken for the defence of Great Britain.*

of their lives, their own arms had helped to preserve, in favour of their ungrateful country.[b]

*Proclamation.* About eighty ships of the line and threescore frigates were already equipped, and considerable bodies of land forces assembled, when, on the third day of February, a proclamation was issued, requiring all officers, civil and military, upon the first appearance of any hostile attempt to land upon the coasts of the kingdom, immediately to cause all horses, oxen, or cattle, which might be fit for draught or burden, and not actually employed in the king's service, or in the defence of the country, and also (so far as might be practicable) all other cattle and provisions, to be driven and removed twenty miles at least from the place where such hostile attempt should be made, and to secure the same, so as that they might not fall into the hands or power of those who should make such attempt; regard being had, however, that the respective owners should suffer as little damage as might be consistent with the public safety.

*Earl of Loudoun appointed commander-in-chief in America.* As the ministry were determined to make their chief efforts against the enemy in North America, where the first hostilities had been committed, and where the strongest impression could be made, a detachment of two regiments was sent thither, under the conduct of General Abercrombie, appointed as successor to General Shirley, whom they recalled, as a person nowise qualified to conduct military operations; nor, indeed, could any success in war be expected from a man who had not been trained to arms, nor ever acted but in a civil capacity. But the command in chief of all the forces in America was conferred upon the Earl of Loudoun, a nobleman of an amiable character, who had already distinguished himself in the service of his country. Over and above this command, he was now appointed governor of Virginia, and colonel of a royal American regiment, consisting of four battalions, to be raised in that country, and disciplined by officers of experience, invited from foreign service. Mr. Abercrombie set sail for America in March; but the Earl

[b] At this juncture, a number of public-spirited merchants of the city of London, and others, formed themselves into a very laudable association, under the name of the Marine Society, and contributed considerable sums of money for equipping such orphans, friendless and forlorn boys, as were willing to engage in the service of the navy. In consequence of this excellent plan, which was executed with equal zeal and discretion, many thousands were rescued from misery, and rendered useful members of that society, of which they must have been the bane and reproach, without this humane interposition.

of Loudoun, who directed in chief the plan of operations, and was vested with power and authority little inferior to those of a viceroy, did not embark till the latter end of May.

All these previous measures being taken, his majesty, in the course of the same month, thought proper to publish a declaration of war[*] against the French king, importing, that since the treaty of Aix-la-Chapelle, the usurpations and encroachments made upon the British territories in America had been notorious; that his Britannic majesty had, in divers serious representations to the court of Versailles, complained of these repeated acts of violence, and demanded satisfaction; but notwithstanding the repeated assurances given by the French king, that every thing should be settled agreeably to the treaties subsisting between the two crowns, and particularly that the evacuation of the four neutral islands in the West Indies should be effected, the execution of these assurances, and of the treaties on which they were founded, had been evaded under the most frivolous pretences: that the unjustifiable practices of the French governors, and officers acting under

*His Britannic majesty's declaration of war.*

[*] When the French ambassador returned to London, he proposed that orders should be immediately despatched to the English governors in America, with express orders to desist from any new undertaking, and all acts of hostility; but with regard to the lands on the Ohio, to put, without delay, matters on the same footing in which they stood before the late war, that the respective claims of both nations might be amicably referred to the commissaries at Paris. The British court agreed to the cessation of hostilities, and the discussion of the disputes by the ministers of the two crowns, on condition that all the possessions in America should be previously put in the situation prescribed by the treaty of Utrecht, confirmed by that of Aix-la-Chapelle. The French ministry, instead of complying with this condition, produced an evasive draft of a preliminary convention, and this was answered by a counter proposal. At length the ambassador of France demanded, as preliminary conditions, that Great Britain would renounce all claim to the south coast of the river St. Lawrence, and the lakes that discharge themselves into that river; cede to the French twenty leagues of country lying along the bay of Fundy, which divides Acadia, or Nova Scotia; and all the land between the rivers Ohio and Ouabache. A memorial was afterwards presented on the same subject, including the affair of the neutral islands in the West Indies; but this was amply refuted in another piece, in which the British ministry observed, that even at the very opening of the commission established at Paris for terminating amicably the disputes in North America, the French invaded Nova Scotia, erected three forts in the heart of that province, and would have destroyed the English settlements at Halifax, had they not been prevented: that the like hostilities were committed upon his Britannic majesty's subjects on the Ohio and Indian lakes, where the governors appointed by the French king, without any shadow of right, prohibited the English from trading; seized their traders by force, and sent them prisoners to France; invaded the territories of Virginia, attacked a fort that covered its frontier, and, to secure their usurpations, erected, with an armed force, a chain of forts on the lands which they had invaded: that his Britannic majesty had complained of these hostilities to the court of Versailles, but without effect; so that he found himself obliged to provide for the security of his subjects; and as the encroachments made by France were hostile, it could never be unlawful, or irreconcilable with the assurances of his majesty's peaceable disposition, to repel an aggressor: and that the same motives of self-defence had forced him to seize the French ships and sailors, in order to deprive that court of the means of making an invasion, with which their ministers in all the courts of Europe had menaced England.

their authority, were still continued, until they broke out in open acts of hostility in the year one thousand seven hundred and fifty-four; when, in time of profound peace, without any declaration of war, without any previous notice given, or application made, a body of French troops, commanded by an officer bearing the French king's commission, attacked in a hostile manner, and took possession of an English fort on the river Ohio, in North America: that great naval armaments were prepared in the ports of France, and a considerable body of French troops embarked for that country: that although the French ambassador was sent back to England with specious professions of a desire to accommodate those differences, it appeared their real design was only to amuse and gain time for the passage of these supplies and reinforcements, which they hoped would secure the superiority of the French forces in America, and enable them to carry their ambitious and oppressive projects into execution: that in consequence of the just and necessary measures taken by the King of Great Britain for preventing the success of such a dangerous design, the French ambassador was immediately recalled from England, the fortifications of Dunkirk were enlarged, great bodies of troops marched down to the sea-coasts of France, and the British dominions threatened with an invasion: that though the King of England, in order to frustrate such intentions, had given orders for seizing at sea the ships of the French king and his subjects, yet he had hitherto contented himself with detaining those ships which had been taken, and preserving their cargoes entire, without proceeding to confiscation; but it being at last evident, from the hostile invasion of Minorca, that the court of Versailles was determined to reject all proposals of accommodation, and carry on the war with the utmost violence, his Britannic majesty could no longer, consistently with the honour of his crown, and the welfare of his subjects, remain within those bounds which from a desire of peace he had hitherto observed. A denunciation of war followed in the usual form, and was concluded with an assurance, that all the French subjects residing in Great Britain and Ireland, who should demean themselves dutifully to the government, might depend upon its protection, and be safe in their persons and effects.

In the beginning of June the French king declared war in his turn against his Britannic majesty; and his declaration was couched in terms of uncommon asperity. He artfully threw a shade over the beginning of hostilities in North America, referring to a memorial which had been delivered to the several courts of Europe, containing a summary of those facts which related to the present war, and the negotiations by which it had been preceded. He insisted on the attack made by the King of England, in the year one thousand seven hundred and fifty-four, on the French possessions in North America; and afterwards by the English navy on the navigation and commerce of the French subjects, in contempt of the law of nations, and direct violation of treaties. He complained, that the French soldiers and sailors underwent the harshest treatment in the British isles, exceeding those bounds which are prescribed to the most rigorous rights of war, by the law of nature, and common humanity. He affirmed, that while the English ministry, under the appearance of sincerity, imposed upon the French ambassador with false protestations, orders diametrically opposite to these deceitful assurances of a speedy accommodation were actually carrying into execution in North America: that while the court of London employed every caballing art, and squandered away the subsidies of England, to instigate other powers against France, his most Christian majesty did not even ask of these powers the succours which guarantees and defensive treaties authorized him to demand, but recommended to them such measures only as tended to their own peace and security; that while the English navy, by the most odious violences, and sometimes by the vilest artifices, made captures of French vessels, navigating in full security under the safeguard of public faith, his most Christian majesty released an English frigate taken by a French squadron; and British vessels traded to the ports of France without molestation: that the striking contrast formed by these different methods of proceeding would convince all Europe, that one court was guided by motives of jealousy, ambition, and avarice, and that the conduct of the other was founded on principles of honour, justice, and moderation: that the vague imputations contained in the King of England's declaration had in reality no foundation; and the very manner in which they were set forth would prove their futility and falsehood: that the mention made of the works at Dunkirk, and the troops assembled on the coasts of the

*Substance of the French king's declaration.*

ocean, implied the most gross attempts to deceive mankind into a belief that these were the points which determined the King of England to issue orders for seizing the French vessels; whereas the works at Dunkirk were not begun till after two French ships of war had been taken by an English squadron; and depredations had been committed six months upon the subjects of France before the first battalions began their march for the sea-side. In a word, the most Christian king, laying aside that politeness and decorum on which his people value themselves above all the nations upon the face of the earth, very roundly taxes his brother monarch's administration with piracy, perfidy, inhumanity, and deceit. A charge conveyed in such reproachful terms, against one of the most respectable crowned heads in Europe, will appear the more extraordinary and injurious, if we consider that the accusers were well acquainted with the falsity of their own imputations, and, at the same time, conscious of having practised those very arts which they affected so much to decry. For, after all, it must be allowed, that nothing could be justly urged against the English government, with respect to France, except the omission of a mere form, which other nations might interpret into an irregularity, but could not construe into perfidious dealing, as the French had previously violated the peace by their insolence and encroachments.

Whatever might have been the opinion of other nations, certain it is, the subjects of Great Britain heartily approved of the hostilities committed and intended against a people whom they have always considered as their natural enemies, and the incendiaries of Europe. They cheerfully contributed to the expense of armaments,[a] and seemed to approve of their destination, in hopes of being able to wipe off the disgraces they had sustained in the defeat of Braddock, and the loss of Minorca. The last event made a deep impression upon the minds of the community. An address was presented to the king by the lord mayor, aldermen, and common council of London, containing strong hints to the disadvantage of the ministry. They expressed their apprehension that the loss of the important fortress of St. Philip and island of Minorca, possessions of the utmost consequence to the commerce and naval

*Address of the city of London.*

---

[a] Immediately after the declaration of war, the French ships and cargoes which had been taken were tried, and condemned as legal prizes, exposed to public sale, and their produce lodged in the Bank; but in what manner this money, amounting to a large sum, was distributed or employed, we have not been able to discover.

strength of Great Britain, without any attempt by timely and effectual succours to prevent or defeat an attack, after such early notice of the enemy's intentions, and when his majesty's navy was so evidently superior to theirs, would be an indelible reproach on the honour of the British nation. They expatiated upon the imminent danger to which the British possessions in America were exposed, by the mismanagement and delays which had attended the defence of those invaluable colonies, the object of the present war, the principal source of the wealth and strength of these kingdoms. They lamented the want of a constitutional well-regulated militia, the most natural and certain defence against all invaders whatsoever. They signified their hope, that the authors of the late losses and disappointments would be detected, and brought to condign punishment: that his majesty's known intentions of protecting and defending his subjects in their rights and possessions might be faithfully and vigorously carried into execution; and the large supplies so necessarily demanded, and so cheerfully granted, might be religiously applied to the defence of these kingdoms, their colonies, and their commerce, as well as to the annoyance of their inveterate and perfidious enemies, the only sure means of obtaining a lasting and honourable peace. In answer to this address, the king assured them that he would not fail to do justice upon any persons who should have been wanting in their duty to him and their country; to enforce obedience and discipline in his fleets and armies; and to support the authority and respect due to his government. Remonstrances of the same kind were presented by different counties and corporations; and the populace clamoured aloud for inquiry and justice.

The first victim offered to the enraged multitude was the unfortunate General Fowke, who had been deputy-governor of Gibraltar, and behaved with remarkable conduct and integrity in the exercise of that important office till that period, when he fell under the displeasure of the government. He was now brought to trial before a board of general officers, and accused of having disobeyed the orders he had received from the secretary at war, in three successive letters,* touching the relief of Minorca.

*Trial of General Fowke.*

---
\* *To Lieut.-Gen. Fowke, or, in his absence, to the commander-in-chief in his majesty's garrison at Gibraltar.*

SIR, *War-office, March 21, 1756.*
I am commanded to acquaint you, that it is his majesty's pleasure that you receive into your garrison Lord Robert Bertie's regiment, to do duty there; and in case you should

Mr. Fowke alleged in his own defence, that the orders were confused and contradictory, and implied a discretionary power: that the whole number of his garrison did not exceed two thousand six hundred men, after he had spared two hundred and seventy-five to the ships commanded by Mr. Edgecumbe: that the ordinary duty of the garrison requiring eight hundred men, the whole number was not sufficient for three reliefs: that, if he had detached a battalion on board the fleet, he should not have had above two reliefs, at a time when he believed the place was in danger of being attacked, for good reasons, which he did not think himself at liberty to mention; that his orders being doubtful, he held a council of war, which was of opinion, that as undoubted intelligence was received of the French army's being landed at Minorca, to the number of between thirteen and sixteen thousand men, and that a French squadron of sixteen ships was stationed off the harbour, the sending a detachment equal to a battalion from Gibraltar would be an

apprehend that the French intend to make any attempt upon his majesty's island of Minorca, it is his majesty's pleasure, that you make a detachment out of the troops in your garrison equal to a battalion, to be commanded by a lieutenant-colonel and major; such lieutenant-colonel and major to be the eldest in your garrison, to be put on board the fleet for the relief of Minorca, as the admiral shall think expedient, who is to carry them to the said island.

I am,
Your humble servant, B.

*To Lieut.-Gen. Fowke, or, in his absence, to the commander-in-chief at Gibraltar.*
SIR,                                                            *War-office, March 26, 1756.*
I am commanded to acquaint you, that it is his majesty's pleasure, in case the island of Minorca should be in any likelihood of being attacked, that you make a detachment from the troops in your garrison equal to a battalion, commanded by a lieutenant-colonel and major, for the relief of that place, to be put on board the fleet, at the disposition of the admiral; such lieutenant-colonel and major to be the eldest in your garrison.

*To Lieut.-Gen. Fowke, or, in his absence, to the commander-in-chief in his majesty's garrison at Gibraltar.*
SIR,                                                            *War-office, April 1, 1756.*
It is his majesty's pleasure, that you receive into your garrison the women and children belonging to Lord Robert Bertie's regiment.

*To Lieut.-Gen. Fowke, or the commander-in-chief at Gibraltar.*
SIR,                                                            *War-office, May 12, 1756.*
I wrote to you by General Stoward: if that order is not complied with, then you are now to make a detachment of seven hundred men out of your own regiment and Guise's; and also another detachment out of Pulteney's and Panmure's regiments, and send them on board the fleet for the relief of Mahon. But if that order has been complied with, then you are to make only one detachment of seven hundred men, to be commanded by another lieutenant-colonel and major, and to send it to Mahon; and you are also to detain all such empty vessels as shall come into your harbour, and to keep them in readiness for any further transportation of troops. I have also his royal highness the Duke of Cumberland's commands, to desire that you will keep your garrison as alert as possible during this critical time, and give such other assistance as may be in your power for the relief of Minorca; taking care, however, not to fatigue or endanger your own garrison.

ineffectual supply for the relief of the place, and a weakening of the garrison from which they must be sent. He observed, that supposing the orders to have been positive, and seven hundred men detached to Minorca, the number remaining at Gibraltar would not have exceeded one thousand five hundred and fifty-six : a deduction of seven hundred more, according to the order of May the twelfth, would have left a remainder of eight hundred and fifty-six : that the men daily on duty in the garrison, including artificers and labourers in the king's works, amounted to eight hundred and thirty-nine ; so that if he had complied with the orders as they arrived, he would not have had more than seventeen men over and above the number necessary for the daily work of the garrison : thus the important fortress of Gibraltar must, at this critical conjuncture, have been left almost naked and defenceless to the attempts of the enemy; and had those detachments been actually sent abroad, it afterwards appeared that they could not have been landed on the island of Minorca. The order transmitted to General Fowke to detain all empty vessels, for a further transportation of troops, seems to have been superfluous; for it can hardly be supposed he could have occasion for them, unless to embark the whole garrison and abandon the place. It seems likewise to have been unnecessary to exhort the general to keep his garrison as alert as possible, during that critical time ; inasmuch as it would have been impossible for the men to have enjoyed the least repose or intermission of duty, had the orders been punctually and literally obeyed. What other assistance it might have been in the governor's power to give for the relief of Minorca, or in what manner he could avoid fatiguing his garrison, while there was an impossibility of relieving the guards, it is not easy to comprehend. Be that as it may, when the trial was finished, and the question put to acquit or suspend for one year, the court was equally divided; and in such cases the casting vote being vested in the president, he threw it into the scale against the prisoner, whom his majesty thought fit to dismiss from his service.

The expectation of the public was now eagerly turned towards America, the chief, if not the sole scene of our military operations. On the twenty-fifth day of June, Mr. Abercrombie arrived at Albany, the frontier of New York, and assumed the command of the forces there

*Affairs of America.*

assembled, consisting of two regiments which had served under Braddock, two battalions raised in America, two regiments now transported from England, four independent companies which had been many years maintained in New York, the New Jersey regiment, four companies levied in North Carolina, and a body of provincial forces raised by the government of New England. Those to the southward, including Pennsylvania, Maryland, and Virginia, had not yet determined on any regular plan of operation, and were moreover hard pressed in defending their western frontiers from the French and Indians, who, in skulking parties, made sudden irruptions upon their unguarded settlements, burning, plundering, and massacring with the most savage inhumanity. As for South Carolina, the proportion of negro slaves to the number of white inhabitants was so great in that colony, that the government could not, with any regard to the safety of the province, spare any reinforcement for the general enterprise. The plan of this undertaking had been settled in the preceding year in a council of war, held at New York. There it was resolved to attack the fort of Niagara, situated between the lakes Ontario and Erie, in order to cut off the communication between Canada and Louisiana, and prevent the French from supporting their new fortresses on the Ohio: to reduce Ticonderoga, and Crown Point, so that the frontier of New York might be delivered from the danger of an invasion, and Great Britain become master of the lake Champlain, over which the forces might be transported in any future attempt: to besiege fort Du Quesne, upon the Ohio; and to detach a body of troops by the river Kennebec, to alarm the capital of Canada. This plan was too extensive for the number of troops which had been prepared: the season was too far advanced before the regiments arrived from England, the different colonies were divided in their opinions, and Mr. Abercrombie postponed the execution of any important scheme till the arrival of Lord Loudoun, who was daily expected. The reasons that delayed the reinforcement, and detained his lordship so long, we do not pretend to explain; though we may be allowed to observe, that many fair opportunities have been lost by the neglect and procrastination of an English ministry. Certain it is, the unaccountable delay of this armament rendered it useless for a whole year, afforded time and leisure to the enemy to take their precautions against any subsequent attack, and, in the mean time, to proceed unmolested in distressing the British settlements. Even before this period, they had attacked and reduced a small post in the country of the Five Nations, occupied by twenty-five Englishmen, who were cruelly butchered to a man, in the midst of those Indians whom Great Britain had long numbered among their allies.

Soon after this expedition, having received intelligence that a considerable convoy of provisions and stores for the garrison of Oswego would in a little time set out for Schenectady, and be conveyed in batteaux up the river Onondago, they formed an ambuscade among the woods and thickets on the north side of that river; but understanding the convoy had passed before they reached the place, they resolved to wait the return of the detachment. Their design, however, was frustrated by the vigilance and valour of Colonel Bradstreet, who expected such an attempt, and had taken his measures accordingly. On the third day of July, while he stemmed the stream of the river, with his batteaux formed in three divisions, they were saluted with the Indian war-whoop, and a general discharge of musketry from the north shore. Bradstreet immediately ordered his men to land on the opposite bank; and with a few of the foremost took possession of a small island, where he was forthwith attacked by a party of the enemy, who had forded the river for that purpose; but these were soon repulsed. Another body having passed a mile higher, he advanced to them at the head of two hundred men, and fell upon them, sword in hand, with such vigour, that many were killed on the spot, and the rest driven into the river with such precipitation, that a considerable number of them were drowned. Having received information that a third body of them had passed at a ford still higher, he marched thither without hesitation, and pursued them to the other side, where they were entirely routed and dispersed. In this action, which lasted near three hours, about seventy of the batteaux-men were killed or wounded; but the enemy lost double the number killed, and above seventy taken prisoners. In all probability the whole detachment of the French, amounting to seven hundred men, would have been cut off, had not a heavy rain interposed, and disabled Colonel Bradstreet from following his blow; for that same night he was joined by Captain Patten with his grenadiers,

*Colonel Bradstreet defeats a body of French on the river Onondago.*

in his march from Oneida to Oswego, and next morning reinforced with two hundred men, detached to his assistance from the garrison of Oswego; but by this time the rivulets were so swelled by the rain, that it was found impracticable to pursue the enemy through the woods and thickets. Patten and his grenadiers accompanied the detachment to Oswego, while Bradstreet pursued his voyage to Schenectady, from whence he repaired to Albany, and communicated to General Abercrombie the intelligence he had received from the prisoners, that a large body of the enemy were encamped on the eastern side of the lake Ontario, provided with artillery, and all other implements to besiege the fort of Oswego.

In consequence of this information, Major-General Webb was ordered to hold himself in readiness to march with one regiment to the relief of that garrison: but, before they could be provided with necessaries, the Earl of Loudoun arrived at the head-quarters at Albany, on the twenty-ninth day of July. The army at this time is said to have consisted of regular troops to the number of two thousand six hundred, about seven thousand provincials, supposed to be in readiness to march from fort William Henry, under the command of General Winslow, over and above a considerable number of batteaux-men at Albany and Schenectady. The garrison at Oswego amounted to fourteen hundred soldiers, besides three hundred workmen and sailors, either in the fort, or posted in small parties between the fort and place called Burnet's Field, to secure a safe passage through the country of the Six Nations, upon whose friendship there was no longer any reliance. By the best accounts received of the enemy's force, they had about three thousand men at Crown Point and Ticonderoga, upon the lake Champlain; but their chief strength was collected upon the banks of the lake Ontario, where their purpose undoubtedly was to reduce the English fort at Oswego. The immediate object, therefore, of Lord Loudoun's attention was the relief of this place; but his design was strenuously opposed by the province of New York, and other northern governments, who were much more intent upon the reduction of Crown Point, and the security of their own frontiers, which they apprehended was connected with this conquest. They insisted upon Winslow's being joined by some regiments of regular troops before he should march against this fortress; and stipulated that a body of reserve should be detained at Albany, for the defence of that frontier, in case Winslow should fail in his enterprise, and be defeated. At length they agreed, that the regiment which Mr. Abercrombie had destined for that purpose should be detached for the relief of Oswego; and on the twelfth day of August, Major-General Webb began his march with it from Albany; but on his arrival at the Carrying-place, between the Mohock's river and Wood's creek, he received the disagreeable news that Oswego was taken, and the garrison made prisoners of war. Mr. Webb, apprehending himself in danger of being attacked by the besieging army, began immediately to render the creek impassable, even to canoes, by felling trees, and throwing them into the stream; while the enemy, ignorant of his numbers, and apprehensive of a like visitation from him, took the very same method of preventing his approach: in consequence of this apprehension, he was permitted to retire unmolested.

The loss of the two small forts, called Ontario and Oswego, was a considerable national misfortune. *Oswego reduced by the enemy.* They were erected on the south side of the great lake Ontario, standing on the opposite sides, at the mouth of the Onondago river, that discharges itself into the lake, and constituted a post of great importance, where vessels had been built to cruise upon the lake, which is a kind of inland sea, and interrupt the commerce as well as the motions and designs of the enemy. The garrison, as we have already observed, consisted of fourteen hundred men, chiefly militia and new-raised recruits, under the command of Lieutenant-Colonel Mercer, an officer of courage and experience; but the situation of the forts was very ill chosen; the materials mostly timber or logs of wood; the defences wretchedly contrived and unfinished; and in a word, the place altogether untenable against any regular approach. Such were the forts which the enemy wisely resolved to reduce. Being under no apprehension for Crown Point, they assembled a body of troops, consisting of thirteen hundred regulars, seventeen hundred Canadians, and a considerable number of Indian auxiliaries, under the command of the Marquis de Montcalm, a vigilant and enterprising officer, to whom the conduct of the siege was intrusted by the Marquis de Vaudreuil, governor and lieutenant-general of New France. The first step taken by Montcalm was to block up Oswego by water, with two large armed vessels, and post a strong body of Canadians on the road between Albany and the forts, to cut off all communication of succour and intelligence. In the mean time, he embarked his artillery and stores upon the lake, and landed them in the bay of Nixouri, the place of general rendezvous. At another creek, within half a league of Oswego, he erected a battery for the protection of his vessels; and on the twelfth day of August, at midnight, after his dispositions had been made, he opened the trenches before fort Ontario. The garrison, having fired away all their shells and ammunition, spiked up the cannon, and, deserting the fort, retired next day across the river into Oswego, which was even more exposed than the other, especially when the enemy had taken possession of Ontario, from whence they immediately began to fire without intermission. Colonel Mercer being, on the thirteenth, killed by a cannon ball, the fort destitute of all cover, the officers divided in opinion, and the garrison in confusion, they next day demanded a capitulation, and surrendered prisoners of war, on condition that they should be exempted from plunder, conducted to Montreal, and treated with humanity. These conditions, however, the marquis did not punctually observe. The British officers and soldiers were insulted by the savage Indians, who robbed them of their clothes and baggage, massacred several men as they stood defenceless on the parade, assassinated Lieutenant De la Court, as he lay wounded in his tent, under the protection of a French officer, and barbarously scalped all the sick people in the hospital: finally, Montcalm, in direct violation of the articles, as well as in contempt of common humanity, delivered up above twenty men of the garrison to the Indians, in lieu of the same number they had lost during the siege; and, in all probability, these miserable captives were put to death by those barbarians with the most excruciating tortures, according to the execrable custom of the country. Those who countenance the perpetration of cruelties at which human nature shudders with horror, ought to be branded as infamous to all posterity. Such, however, were the trophies that, in the course of the American war, distinguished the operations of a people who pique themselves upon politeness and the virtues of humanity. The prisoners taken at Oswego, after having been thus barbarously treated, were conveyed in batteaux to Montreal, where they had no reason to complain of their reception; and before the end of the year they were exchanged. The victors immediately demolished the two forts, (if they deserved that denomination,) in which they found one hundred and twenty-one pieces of artillery, fourteen mortars, with a great quantity of ammunition, warlike stores, and provisions, besides two sloops, and two hundred batteaux, which likewise fell into their hands. Such an important magazine, deposited in a place altogether indefensible, and without the reach of immediate succour, was a flagrant proof of egregious folly, temerity, and misconduct.

The Earl of Loudoun, finding the season too far advanced to admit of any enterprise against the enemy, exerted all his endeavours in making preparations for an early campaign in the spring, in securing the frontiers of the English colonies, in forming an uniform plan of action, and promoting a spirit of harmony among the different governments, which had been long divided by jarring interests, and other sources of dissension. Meanwhile, the forts Edward and William Henry were put in a proper posture of defence, and secured with numerous garrisons; and the forces put into winter quarters at Albany, where comfortable barracks were built for that purpose. Fort Granville, on the confines of Pennsylvania, an inconsiderable block-house, was surprised by a party of French and Indians, who made the garrison prisoners, consisting of two-and-twenty soldiers, with a few women and children. These they loaded with flour and provision, and drove them into captivity; but the fort they reduced to ashes. Many shocking murders were perpetrated upon defenceless people, without distinction of age or sex, in different parts of the frontiers; but these outrages were, in some measure, balanced by the advantages resulting from a treaty of peace, which the governor of Pennsylvania concluded with the Delaware Indians, a powerful tribe that dwell upon the river Sasquehanna, forming, as it were, a line along the southern skirts of the province. At the same time the governor of Virginia secured the friendship and alliance of the Cherokees and Catawbas, two powerful nations adjoining to that colony, who were able to bring three thousand fighting men into the field. All these circumstances considered, Great Britain had reason to expect that the ensuing campaign would be vigorously prosecuted in America,

*Further proceedings in America.*

especially as a fresh reinforcement of troops, with a great supply of warlike stores, were sent to that country in fourteen transports, under convoy of two ships of war, which sailed from Cork, in Ireland, about the beginning of November.

<small>Naval operations in that country.</small> No action of great importance distinguished the naval transactions of this year on the side of America. In the beginning of June, Captain Spry, who commanded a small squadron, cruising off Louisbourg, in the island of Cape Breton, took the Arc-en-Ciel, a French ship of fifty guns, having on board near six hundred men, with a large quantity of stores and provisions for the garrison. He likewise made prize of another French ship with seventy soldiers, two hundred barrels of powder, two large brass mortars, and other stores for the like destination. On the twenty-seventh day of July, Commodore Holmes, being in the same latitude, with two large ships and a couple of sloops, engaged two French ships of the line and four frigates, and obliged them to sheer off after an obstinate dispute. A great number of privateers were equipped in this country, as well as in the West India islands belonging to the crown of Great Britain; and as those seas swarmed with French vessels, their cruises proved very advantageous to the adventurers.

<small>Transactions in the East Indies.</small> Scenes of higher import were this year acted by the British arms in the East Indies. The cessation of hostilities between the English and French companies on the peninsula of Indus, though it encouraged Mr. Clive to visit his native country, was not of long duration; for in a few months both sides recommenced their operations, no longer as auxiliaries to the princes of the country, but as principals and rivals, both in arms and commerce. Major Lawrence, who now enjoyed the chief command of the English forces, obtained divers advantages over the enemy; and prosecuted his success with such vigour as, in all probability, would, in a little time, have terminated the war according to his own wish, when the progress of his arms was interrupted and suspended by an unfortunate event at Calcutta, the cause of which is not easily explained; for extraordinary pains have been taken to throw a veil over some transactions, from whence this calamity was immediately or remotely derived.

The old Suba, or Viceroy of Bengal, Bahar, and Orixa,

dying in the month of April, in the year one thousand seven hundred and fifty-six, was succeeded by his adopted son, Sur Raja al Dowlat, a young man of violent passions, without principle, fortitude, or good faith, who began his administration with acts of perfidy and violence. In all probability, his design against the English settlements was suggested by his rapacious disposition, on a belief that they abounded with treasure; as the pretences which he used for commencing hostilities were altogether inconsistent, false, and frivolous. In the month of May, he caused the English factory at Cassimbuzzar to be invested, and inviting Mr. Watts, the chief of the factory, to a conference, under the sanction of a safe-conduct, detained him as prisoner; then, by means of fraud and force intermingled, made himself master of the factory. This exploit being achieved, he made no secret of his design to deprive the English of all their settlements. With this view he marched to Calcutta, at the head of a numerous army, and invested the place, which was then in no posture of defence.

*Calcutta besieged by the Viceroy of Bengal.*

The governor, intimidated by the number and power of the enemy, abandoned the fort, and, with some principal persons residing in the settlement, took refuge on board a ship in the river, carrying along with them their most valuable effects, and the books of the company. Thus the defence of the place devolved to Mr. Holwell, the second in command, who, with the assistance of a few gallant officers, and a very feeble garrison, maintained it with uncommon courage and resolution against several attacks, until he was overpowered by numbers, and the enemy had forced their way into the castle. Then he was obliged to submit; and the suba, or viceroy, promised, on the word of a soldier, that no injury should be done to him or his garrison. Nevertheless, they were all driven, to the number of one hundred and forty-six persons of both sexes, into a place called the Black Hole prison, a cube of about eighteen feet, walled up to the eastward and southward, the only quarters from which they could expect the least refreshing air, and open to the westward by two windows strongly barred with iron, through which there was no perceptible circulation. The humane reader will conceive with horror the miserable situation to which they must have been reduced, when thus stewed up in a close sultry night under such a climate as that of Bengal, especially when he

*Deplorable fate of those who perished in the dungeon there.*

reflects that many of them were wounded, and all of them fatigued with hard duty. Transported with rage to find themselves thus barbarously cooped up in a place where they must be exposed to suffocation, those hapless victims endeavoured to force open the door, that they might rush upon the swords of the barbarians by whom they were surrounded; but all their efforts were ineffectual: the door was made to open inwards, and being once shut upon them, the crowd pressed upon it so strongly as to render all their endeavours abortive: then they were overwhelmed with distraction and despair. Mr. Holwell, who had placed himself at one of the windows, accosted a Jemmautdaar, or serjeant of the Indian guard, and having endeavoured to excite his compassion, by drawing a pathetic picture of their sufferings, promised to gratify him with a thousand rupees in the morning, if he could find means to remove one-half of them into a separate apartment. The soldier, allured by the promise of such a reward, assured him he would do his endeavour for their relief, and retired for that purpose; but in a few minutes returned, and told them that the suba, by whose order alone such a step could be taken, was asleep, and no person durst disturb his repose. By this time a profuse sweat had broken out on every individual, and this was attended with an insatiable thirst, which became the more intolerable as the body was drained of its moisture. In vain those miserable objects stripped themselves of their clothes, squatted down on their hams, and fanned the air with their hats, to produce a refreshing undulation. Many were unable to rise again from this posture, but falling down were trod to death, or suffocated. The dreadful symptom of thirst was now accompanied with a difficulty of respiration, and every individual gasped for breath. Their despair became outrageous: again they attempted to force the door, and provoke the guard to fire upon them by execration and abuse. The cry of "Water! water!" issued from every mouth. Even the Jemmautdaar was moved to compassion at their distress. He ordered his soldiers to bring some skins of water, which served only to enrage the appetite, and increase the general agitation. There was no other way of conveying it through the windows but by hats, and this was rendered ineffectual by the eagerness and transports of the wretched prisoners, who, at sight of it, struggled and raved even in fits of delirium. In consequence of these contests, very little reached those who stood nearest the windows, while the rest, at the farther end of the prison, were totally excluded from all relief, and continued calling upon their friends for assistance, and conjuring them by all the tender ties of pity and affection. To those who were indulged, it proved pernicious; for, instead of allaying their thirst, it enraged their impatience for more. The confusion became general and horrid; all was clamour and contest: those who were at a distance endeavoured to force their passage to the window, and the weak were pressed down to the ground, never to rise again. The inhuman ruffians without derived entertainment from their misery: they supplied the prisoners with more water, and held up lights close to the bars, that they might enjoy the inhuman pleasure of seeing them fight for the baneful indulgence. Mr. Holwell seeing all his particular friends lying dead around him, and trampled upon by the living, finding himself wedged up so close as to be deprived of all motion, begged, as the last instance of their regard, that they would remove the pressure, and allow him to retire from the window, that he might die in quiet. Even in those dreadful circumstances, which might be supposed to have levelled all distinction, the poor delirious wretches manifested a respect for his rank and character: they forthwith gave way, and he forced his passage into the centre of the place, which was not crowded so much; because, by this time, about one-third of the number had perished, and lay in little compass on the floor, while the rest still crowded to both windows. He retired to a platform at the farther end of the room, and lying down upon some of his dead friends, recommended his soul to heaven. Here his thirst grew insupportable; his difficulty in breathing increased, and he was seized with a strong palpitation. These violent symptoms, which he could not bear, urged him to make another effort: he forced his way back to the window, and cried aloud, "Water! for God's sake!" He had been supposed already dead by his wretched companions, but finding him still alive, they exhibited another extraordinary proof of tenderness and regard to his person: "Give him water," they cried; nor would any of them attempt to touch it until he had drunk. He now breathed more freely, and the palpitation ceased; but finding himself still more thirsty after drinking, he abstained from water, and moistened his mouth from time to time, by sucking the perspiration from his shirt sleeves.¹ The miserable prisoners, perceiving that water rather aggravated than relieved their distress, grew clamorous for air, and repeated their insults to the guard, loading the suba and his governor with the most virulent reproach. From railing they had recourse to prayer, beseeching Heaven to put an end to their misery. They now began to drop on all hands; but then a steam arose from the living and the dead, as pungent and volatile as spirit of hartshorn; so that all who could not approach the windows were suffocated. Mr. Holwell, being weary of life, retired once more to the platform, and stretched himself by the Rev. Mr. Jervis Bellamy, who, together with his son, a lieutenant, lay dead in each other's embrace. In this situation he was soon deprived of sense, and lay to all appearance dead till day broke, when his body was discovered, and removed by his surviving friends to one of the windows, where the fresh air revived him, and he was restored to his sight and senses. The suba, at last, being informed that the greater part of the prisoners were suffocated, inquired if the chief was alive; and being answered in the affirmative, sent an order for their immediate release, when no more than twenty-three survived of a hundred and forty-six who had entered alive.

Nor was the late deliverance, even of these few, owing to any sentiment of compassion in the viceroy. He had received intimation that there was a considerable treasure secreted in the fort, and that Mr. Holwell knew the place where it was deposited. That gentleman, who, with his surviving companions, had been seized with a putrid fever, immediately upon their release, was dragged in that condition before the inhuman suba, who questioned him about the treasure, which existed no where but in his own imagination; and would give no credit to his protestations, when he solemnly declared he knew of no such deposit. Mr. Holwell and three of his friends were loaded with fetters, and conveyed three miles to the Indian camp, where they lay all night exposed to a severe rain: next morning they were brought back to town, still manacled, under the scorching beams of a sun intensely hot; and must infallibly have expired, had not nature

*Additional cruelties exercised on Mr. Holwell.*

---

¹ In his despair of obtaining water, this unhappy gentleman had attempted to drink his own urine, but found it intolerably bitter; whereas the moisture that flowed from the pores of his body was soft, pleasant, and refreshing.

expelled the fever in large painful boils, that covered almost the whole body. In this piteous condition they were embarked in an open boat for Muxadavad, the capital of Bengal, and underwent such cruel treatment and misery in their passage, as would shock the humane reader, should he peruse the particulars. At Muxadavad they were led through the city in chains, as a spectacle to the inhabitants, lodged in an open stable, and treated for some days as the worst of criminals. At length, the suba's grandmother interposed her mediation in their behalf; and as that prince was by this time convinced that there was no treasure concealed at Calcutta, he ordered them to be set at liberty. When some of his sycophants opposed this indulgence, representing that Mr. Holwell had still enough left to pay a considerable ransom, he replied, with some marks of compunction and generosity, "If he has any thing left, let him keep it; his sufferings have been great: he shall have his liberty." Mr. Holwell and his friends were no sooner unfettered than they took water for the Dutch tanksall or mint, in the neighbourhood of that city, where they were received with great tenderness and humanity. The reader, we hope, will excuse us for having thus particularized a transaction so interesting and extraordinary in all its circumstances. The suba having destroyed Calcutta, and dispersed the inhabitants, extorted large sums from the French and Dutch factories, that he might display a spirit of impartiality against all the Europeans, even in his oppression, and returned to his city of Muxadavad in triumph. By the reduction of Calcutta, the English East India Company's affairs were so much embroiled in that part of the world, that perhaps nothing could have retrieved them but the interposition of a national force, and the good fortune of a Clive, whose enterprises were always crowned with success.

As the English East India Company had, for a whole century, been at a considerable expense in maintaining a marine force at Bombay, to protect their ships from the piracies of the Angrias, who had rendered themselves independent princes, and fortified Geriah in that neighbourhood; many unsuccessful attempts had been made to destroy their naval power, and reduce the fortress, under which they always took shelter. In the year one thousand seven hundred and fifty-four, the fleet of Tul-

*Resolution against Angria.*

lagee Angria, the reigning prince, attacked three Dutch
ships of force, which they either took or destroyed. Elated
with this success, he boasted that he should, in a little time,
sweep the seas of the Europeans, and began to build some
large ships, to reinforce his grabs and gallivats, which were
the vessels on which he had formerly depended. Next year
his neighbours, the Mahrattas, having signified to the presi-
dency at Bombay that they were disposed to join in the
necessary service of humbling this common enemy, so formidable to the whole Malabar coast, Commodore James was
detached with some ships of force to attack Angria, in conjunction with those allies. They accordingly joined him
with seven grabs and sixty gallivats. They proceeded to
the harbour of Severndroog, where Angria's fleet lay at
anchor: but they no sooner received intelligence of his
approach than they slipped their cables, and stood out to
sea. He chased them with all the canvass he could carry;
but their vessels being lighter than his, they escaped; and he
returned to Severndroog, which is a fortress situated on an
island within musket-shot of the main land, strongly but
irregularly fortified, and mounted with fifty-four pieces of
cannon. There were three other small forts on the continent, the largest of which was called Goa. On the second
day of April, the commodore began to batter and bombard
the island, fort, and fort Goa, at the same time. That of
Severndroog was set on fire: one of the magazines blew up;
a general conflagration ensued; the garrison were overwhelmed with fire and confusion; the English seamen
landed under cover of the fire from the ships, and took the
place by storm with very little loss. The other forts were
immediately surrendered, and all of these, by treaty, delivered to the Mahrattas. On the eighth of April, the commodore anchored off Bancote, now called Fort Victoria, one
of the most northern parts of Angria's dominions, which
surrendered without opposition, and still remains in the
hands of the English East India Company, by the consent
of the Mahrattas. The harbour is good, and here is a
great trade for salt and other commodities sent hither from
Bombay.

It was in November following, that the squadron under
Admiral Watson arrived at Bombay, where it was resolved
to give Angria the finishing stroke, still in conjunction with
the Mahrattas. Meanwhile, Commodore James was sent to

reconnoitre Geriah, the capital of his dominions, and to sound the depth of the harbour; a service which he successfully performed. The admiral being joined by a division of ships, fitted out at the company's expense, having on board a body of troops commanded by Colonel Clive, sailed on the seventh day of February, and found in the neighbourhood of Geriah the Mahratta fleet, consisting of four grabs, and forty smaller vessels, called gallivats, lying to the northward of the place, in a creek called Rajipore; and a land army of horse and foot, amounting to seven or eight thousand men, the whole commanded by Rhamagee Punt, who had already taken one small fort, and was actually treating about the surrender of Geriah. Angria himself had quitted the place, but his wife and family remained under the protection of his brother-in-law; who, being summoned to surrender by a message from the admiral, replied that he would defend the place to the last extremity. In consequence of this refusal, the whole English fleet, in two divisions, sailed on the twelfth day of February into the harbour, and sustained a warm fire from the enemy's batteries as they passed, as well as from the grabs posted in the harbour for that purpose; this, however, was soon silenced after the ships were brought to their stations, so as to return their salutation. Between the hours of four and five in the afternoon, a shell being thrown into one of Angria's armed vessels set her on fire; and the flames communicating to the rest, they were all destroyed; between six and seven the fort was set on fire by another shell; and soon after the firing ceased on both sides. The admiral, suspecting that the governor of the place would surrender it to the Mahrattas rather than to the English, disembarked all the troops under Mr. Clive, that he might be at hand, in case of emergency, to take possession. In the mean time, the fort was bombarded; the line-of-battle ships were warped near enough to batter in breach; and then the admiral sent an officer, with a flag of truce, to the governor, requiring him to surrender. His proposal being again rejected, the English ships renewed their fire next day with redoubled vigour. About one o'clock the magazine of the fort blew up, and at four the garrison hung out a white flag for capitulation. The parley that ensued proving ineffectual, the engagement began again, and continued till fifteen minutes after five; when the white flag was again dis-

*Fort of Geriah taken by Admiral Watson and Mr. Clive.*

played, and now the governor submitted to the terms which were imposed. Angria's flag was immediately hauled down; and two English captains, taking possession of the fort with a detachment, forthwith hoisted the British ensign. To these captains, whose names were Buchannan and Forbes, the Mahrattas offered a bribe of fifty thousand rupees, if they would allow them to pass their guards, that they might take possession of the fort for themselves; but this offer was rejected with disdain, and immediately disclosed to Colonel Clive, who took effectual measures to frustrate their design. In this place, which was reduced with very inconsiderable loss, the conquerors found above two hundred cannon, six brass mortars, a large quantity of amunition, with money and effects to the value of one hundred and thirty thousand pounds. The fleet which was destroyed consisted of eight grabs, one ship finished, two upon the stocks, and a good number of gallivats. Among the prisoners, the admiral found Angria's wife, children, and mother, towards whom he demeaned himself with great humanity. Three hundred European soldiers, and as many sepoys, were left to guard the fort; and four of the company's armed vessels remained in the harbour for the defence of the place, which was extremely well situated for commerce.[s]

*Their subsequent proceedings in the river Ganges.* The admiral and Mr. Clive sailed back to Madras in triumph; and there another plan was formed for restoring the company's affairs upon the Ganges, recovering Calcutta, and taking vengeance on the cruel Viceroy of Bengal. In October they set sail again for the bottom of the bay; and about the beginning of December arrived at Balasore, in the kingdom of Bengal. Having crossed the braces, they proceeded up the river Ganges as far as Falta; where they found Governor Drake, and the other persons who had escaped on board of the ships when Calcutta was invested. Colonel Clive was disembarked with his forces to attack the fort of Busbudgia by land, while the admiral battered it by sea; but the place being ill provided with cannon, did not hold out above an

---

[s] When the admiral entered their apartment, the whole family, shedding floods of tears, fell with their faces to the ground; from which being raised, the mother of Angria told him, in a piteous tone, the people had no king, she no son, her daughter no husband, their children no father. The admiral replying, "they must look upon him as their father and their friend;" the youngest boy, about six years of age, seized him by the hand, and sobbing, exclaimed, "Then you shall be my father." Mr. Watson was so affected with this pathetic address, that the tears trickled down his cheeks, while he assured them they might depend upon his protection and friendship.

hour after the firing began. This conquest being achieved at a very easy purchase, two of the greater ships anchored between Tanny Fort and a battery on the other side of the river, which were abandoned before one shot was discharged against either; thus the passage was laid open to Calcutta, the reduction of which we shall record among the transactions of the ensuing year.

## CHAPTER XXVI.

MOTIVES OF THE WAR IN GERMANY.— CONSPIRACY IN SWEDEN.— MEASURES TAKEN BY THE KING OF PRUSSIA AND ELECTOR OF HANOVER.— ENDEAVOURS OF THE COURT OF VIENNA TO FRUSTRATE THEM.— HIS PRUSSIAN MAJESTY DEMANDS AN EXPLANATION FROM THE EMPRESS-QUEEN.— HER ANSWER.— THE PRUSSIAN ARMY ENTERS SAXONY, AND PUBLISHES A MANIFESTO.— PRINCE FERDINAND TAKES LEIPSIC.— KING OF PRUSSIA TAKES POSSESSION OF DRESDEN, AND BLOCKS UP THE KING OF POLAND AT PIRNA.— PRUSSIAN ARMY PENETRATES INTO BOHEMIA, AND FIGHTS THE BATTLE OF LOWOSCHUTZ. — SAXON ARMY SURRENDERS.— KING OF POLAND'S MEMORIAL TO THE STATES-GENERAL. — IMPERIAL DECREES PUBLISHED AGAINST THE KING OF PRUSSIA.— DECLARATIONS OF DIFFERENT POWERS.— HIS PRUSSIAN MAJESTY'S ANSWER TO THE SAXON MEMORIAL— AND JUSTIFICATION OF HIS CONDUCT.— REMARKS ON BOTH THOSE PIECES.— DISPUTES BETWEEN THE PARLIAMENT OF PARIS AND THE CLERGY.— DEARTH OF CORN IN ENGLAND.— HANOVERIAN AUXILIARIES SENT BACK.— SESSION OPENED.— DEBATES ON THE ADDRESS.— BILL PASSED FOR PROHIBITING THE EXPORTATION OF CORN.— MESSAGE TO THE HOUSE CONCERNING ADMIRAL BYNG.— SUPPLIES GRANTED.— REFLECTIONS ON THE CONTINENTAL WAR.— MESSAGES FROM THE KING TO THE PARLIAMENT.— MEASURES TAKEN TO REMOVE THE SCARCITY OF CORN.— MILITIA BILL.— PETITIONS FOR AND AGAINST IT.— ALTERED BY THE LORDS.— BILL FOR QUATERING THE FOREIGN TROOPS, AND FOR REGULATING THE MARINES WHILE ON SHORE.— BILL FOR THE MORE SPEEDY RECRUITING THE LAND FORCES AND MARINES.— ACT RELATING TO PAWNBROKERS AND GAMING-HOUSES.— LAWS RELATING TO THE WAGES OF WEAVERS, AND TO THE IMPROVEMENT OF THE BRITISH FISHERY. — ACT FOR IMPORTING AMERICAN IRON, DUTY FREE.— REGULATIONS WITH RESPECT TO THE IMPORTATION OF SILK.— SMUGGLERS ENCOURAGED TO ENTER INTO HIS MAJESTY'S SERVICE.— INQUIRY INTO THE SCARCITY OF CORN.— INVESTIGATION OF THE LOSS OF MINORCA.— EXAMINATION OF THE AMERICAN CONTRACT.— INQUIRY INTO THE CONDUCT OF ADMIRAL KNOWLES, AS GOVERNOR OF JAMAICA.— RESOLUTIONS CONCERNING MILFORD-HAVEN.— SESSION CLOSED.— TRIAL OF ADMIRAL BYNG.— RECOMMENDED TO MERCY.— MESSAGE FROM THE KING TO THE PARLIAMENT RESPECTING THE SENTENCE.— BILL TO RELEASE THE MEMBERS OF THE COURT MARTIAL FROM THEIR OATH OF SECRECY.— EXECUTION OF ADMIRAL BYNG.— PAPER DELIVERED BY HIM TO THE MARSHAL OF THE ADMIRALTY.— REMARKS ON HIS FATE.

HAVING thus, to the best of our power, given a faithful and exact detail of every material event in which Great Britain was concerned, either at home or in her settlements abroad, during the greatest part of the year one thousand seven hundred and fifty-six, we shall now return to Europe, and endeavour to explain the beginning of a bloody war in Germany, which then seemed to have become the chief object of the British counsels. On the eve of a rupture between France and England, it was natural for his Britannic majesty to provide for the safety of his electoral dominions, the only quarter by which he was at all accessible to the efforts of the enemy, who he foresaw would

*1756. Motives of the war in Germany.*

not fail to annoy him through that avenue. He, at that time, stood upon indifferent terms with the King of Prussia, who was considered as a partisan and ally of France; and he knew that the House of Austria alone would not be sufficient to support him against two such powerful antagonists. In this emergency, he had recourse to the Empress of Russia, who, in consequence of a large subsidy granted by England, engaged to furnish a strong body of forces for the defence of Hanover. His Prussian majesty, startled at the conditions of this treaty, took an opportunity to declare that he would not suffer foreign forces of any nation to enter the empire, either as principals or auxiliaries; a declaration which probably flowed from a jealousy and aversion he had conceived to the court of Petersburgh, as well as from a resolution he had formed of striking some great stroke in Germany, without any risk of being restricted or controlled. He knew he should give umbrage to the French king, who had already made preparations for penetrating into Westphalia; but he took it for granted he should be able to exchange his connexions with France for an alliance with Great Britain, which would be much less troublesome, and much more productive of advantage; indeed, such an alliance was the necessary consequence of his declaration. Had his Britannic majesty made a requisition of the Russian auxiliaries, he must have exposed himself to the resentment of a warlike monarch, who hovered on the skirts of his electorate at the head of one hundred and forty thousand men, and could have subdued the whole country in one week; and if he forebore to avail himself of the treaty with the czarina, he did not know how soon the King of Prussia might be reconciled to his most Christian majesty's design of invasion. As for the empress-queen, her attention was engrossed by schemes for her interest or preservation; and her hands so full, that she either could not, or would not, fulfil the engagements she had contracted with her former and firmest allies. In these circumstances the King of England sought and obtained the alliance of Prussia, which, to the best of our comprehension, entailed upon Great Britain the enormous burden of extravagant subsidies, together with the intolerable expense of a continental war, without being productive of one advantage, either positive or negative, to England or Hanover. On the contrary, this connexion threw the empress-queen into the arms of France, whose friendship she bought at the expense of the barrier in the Netherlands, acquired with infinite labour, by the blood and treasure of the maritime powers: it gave birth to a confederacy of despotic princes; sufficient, if their joint force was fully exerted, to overthrow the liberties of all the free states in Europe; and, after all, Hanover has been overrun and subdued by the enemy; and the King of Prussia put to the ban of the empire. All these consequences are, we apprehend, fairly deducible from the resolution which his Prussian majesty took at this juncture, to precipitate a war with the house of Austria. The apparent motives that prompted him to this measure we shall presently explain. In the mean time, the defensive treaty between the empress-queen and France was no sooner ratified, than the czarina was invited to accede to the alliance, and a private minister sent from Paris to Petersburgh, to negotiate the conditions of this accession, which the Empress of Russia accordingly embraced: a circumstance so agreeable to the court of Versailles, that the Marquis de l'Hopital was immediately appointed ambassador extraordinary and plenipotentiary to the court of Russia. Applications were likewise made to the courts of Madrid and Turin, soliciting their concurrence; but their Catholic and Sardinian majesties wisely resolved to observe a neutrality. At the same time, intrigues were begun by the French emissaries in the senate of Sweden, in order to kindle up a war between that nation and Prussia; and their endeavours succeeded in the sequel, even contrary to the inclination of their sovereign. At present, a plot was discovered for altering the form of government, by increasing the power of the crown; and several persons of rank being convicted upon trial, were beheaded as principals in this conspiracy. Although it did not appear that the king or queen were at all concerned in the scheme, his Swedish majesty thought himself so hardly treated by the diet, that he threatened to resign his royalty, and retire into his own hereditary dominions. This design was extremely disagreeable to the people in general, who espoused his cause in opposition to the diet, by whom they conceived themselves more oppressed than they should have been under an unlimited monarchy.

*Conspiracy in Sweden.*

The King of Prussia, alarmed at these formidable alliances, ordered all his forces to be completed, and held in readiness to march at the first notice; and a report was industriously circulated, that, by a secret article in the late treaty between France and the house of Austria, these two powers had obliged themselves to destroy the Protestant religion, and overturn the freedom of the empire, by a forced election of a king of the Romans. The cry of religion was no impolitic measure: but it no longer produced the same effect as in times past. Religion was made a pretence on both sides; for the partisans of the empress-queen insinuated, on all occasions, that the ruin of the Catholic faith in Germany was the principal object of the new alliance between the Kings of Great Britain and Prussia. It was in consequence of such suggestions, that his Britannic majesty ordered his electorial minister at the diet to deliver a memorial to all the ministers at Ratisbon, expressing his surprise to find the treaty he had concluded with the King of Prussia industriously represented as a ground of apprehension and umbrage, especially for religion. He observed, that as France had made open dispositions for invading the electorate of Hanover, and disturbing the peace of the empire; that as he had been denied, by the empress-queen, the succours stipulated in treaties of alliance; and as he was refused assistance by certain states of the empire, who even seemed disposed to favour such a diversion; he had, in order to provide for the security of his own dominions, to establish peace and tranquillity in the empire, and maintain its system and privileges, without any prejudice to religion, concluded a defensive treaty with the King of Prussia: that, by this instance of patriotic zeal for the welfare of Germany, he had done an essential service to the empress-queen, and performed the part which the head of the empire, in dignity and duty, ought to have acted; that time would demonstrate how little it was the interest of the empress-queen to engage in a strict alliance with a foreign power, which, for upwards of two centuries, had ravaged the principal provinces of the empire, maintained repeated wars against the archducal house of Austria, and always endeavoured, as it suited her views, to excite distrust and dissension among the princes and states that compose the Germanic body.

The court of Vienna formed two considerable armies in Bohemia and Moravia; yet pretended that they had nothing in view but self-preservation, and solemnly disclaimed both the secret article, and the design which had been laid to their charge. His most Christian majesty declared, by his minister at Berlin, that he had no other intention but to maintain the public tranquillity of Europe; and this being the sole end of all his measures, he beheld, with surprise, the preparations and armaments of certain potentates: that, whatever might be the view with which they were made, he was disposed to make use of the power which God had put into his hands, not only to maintain the public peace of Europe against all who should attempt to disturb it, but also to employ all his forces, agreeably to his engagements, for the assistance of his ally, in case her dominions should be attacked; finally, that he would act in the same manner in behalf of all the other powers with whom he was in alliance. This intimation made very little impression upon the King of Prussia, who had already formed his plan, and was determined to execute his purpose. What his original plan might have been, we shall not pretend to disclose; nor do we believe he imparted it to any confidant or ally. It must be confessed, however, that the intrigues of the court of Vienna furnished him with a specious pretence for drawing the sword, and commencing hostilities. The empress-queen had some reason to be jealous of such a formidable neighbour. She remembered his irruption into Bohemia, in the year one thousand seven hundred and forty-four, at a time when she thought that country, and all her other dominions, secure from his invasion, by the treaty of Breslau, which she had in no particular contravened. She caballed against him in different courts of Europe: she concluded a treaty with the czarina, which, though seemingly defensive, implied an intention of making conquests upon this monarch: she endeavoured to engage the King of Poland, Elector of Saxony, as a contracting power in this confederacy; and, if he had not been afraid of a sudden visit from his neighbour of Prussia, it cannot be supposed but he would have been pleased to contribute to the humiliation of a prince, who had once before, without the least provocation, driven him from his dominions, taken possession of his capital, routed his troops, and obliged him to pay a million of crowns to indemnify him for the expense of this expedition; but he carefully avoided taking such a step as might expose him to another invasion, and even refused to accede to the treaty of Petersburgh, though it was expressly defensive; the *casus fœderis* being his Prussian majesty's attacking either of the contracting parties. It appears, however, that Count de Bruhl, prime minister and favourite of the King of Poland, had, in conjunction with some of the Austrian ministers, carried on certain scandalous intrigues, in order to embroil the King of Prussia with the Empress of Russia, between whom a misunderstanding had long subsisted.

His Prussian majesty, perceiving the military preparations of the court of Vienna, and having obtained intelligence of their secret negotiations with different powers of Europe, ordered M. de Klingraafe, his minister at the imperial court, to demand whether all those preparations for war, on the frontiers of Silesia, were designed against him, and what were the intentions of her imperial majesty? To this demand the empress replied, that in the present juncture she had found it necessary to make armaments, as well for her own defence as for that of her allies; but that they did not tend to the prejudice of any person or state whatever. The king, far from being satisfied with this general answer, sent fresh orders to Klingraafe, to represent that, after the king had dissembled as long as he thought consistent with his safety and honour, the bad designs imputed to the empress would not suffer him longer to disguise his sentiments; that he was acquainted with the offensive projects which the two courts had formed at Petersburgh; that he knew they had engaged to attack him suddenly with an army of two hundred thousand men; a design which would have been executed in the spring of the year, had not the Russian forces wanted recruits, their fleet mariners, and Livonia a sufficient quantity of corn for their support; that he constituted the empress arbiter of peace or war: if she desired the former, he required a clear and formal declaration, or positive assurance, that she had no intention to attack him, either this year or the next; but he should look upon an ambiguous answer as a declaration of war; and he called Heaven to witness, that the empress alone would be guilty of the innocent blood that should be spilt, and all the dismal consequences that would attend the commission of hostilities.

*His Prussian majesty demands an explanation from the empress-queen.*

A declaration of this nature might have provoked a less haughty court than that of Vienna, and, indeed, seems to have been calculated on purpose to exaspe-

*Her answer.*

rate the pride of her imperial majesty, whose answer he soon received to this effect: that his majesty the King of Prussia had already been employed, for some time, in all kinds of the most considerable preparations of war, and the most disquieting with regard to the public tranquillity, when he thought fit to demand explanations of her majesty, touching the military dispositions that were making in her dominions; dispositions on which she had not resolved till after the preparations of his Prussian majesty had been made; that though her majesty might have declined explaining herself on those subjects, which required no explanation, she had been pleased to declare, with her own mouth, to M. de Klingraafe, that the critical state of public affairs rendered the measures she had taken absolutely necessary for her own safety, and that of her allies; but that, in other respects, they tended to the prejudice of no person whatsoever; that her imperial majesty had undoubtedly a right to form what judgment she pleased on the circumstances of the times; and likewise, that it belonged to none but herself to estimate her own danger; that her declaration was so clear, she never imagined it could be thought otherwise; that being accustomed to receive, as well as to practise, the decorums which sovereigns owe to each other, she could not hear without astonishment and sensibility the contents of the memorial now presented by M. de Klingraafe; so extraordinary both in the matter and expressions, that she would find herself under the necessity of transgressing the bounds of that moderation which she had prescribed to herself, were she to answer the whole of its contents; nevertheless, she thought proper to declare, that the information communicated to his Prussian majesty, of an offensive alliance against him, subsisting between herself and the Empress of Russia, together with the circumstances and pretended stipulations of that alliance, was absolutely false and forged; for no such treaty did exist, or ever had existed. She concluded with observing, that this declaration would enable all Europe to judge of what weight and quality those dreadful events were which Klingraafe's memorial announced; and to perceive that, in any case, they could not be imputed to her imperial majesty. This answer, though seemingly explicit, was not deemed sufficiently categorical, or, at least, not suitable to the purposes of the King of Prussia, who, by his resident at Vienna, once more declared, that if the empress-queen would sign a positive assurance that she would not attack his Prussian majesty, either this year or the next, he would directly withdraw his troops, and let things be restored to their former footing. This demand was evaded, on pretence that such an assurance could not be more binding than the solemn treaty by which he was already secured; a treaty which the empress-queen had no intention to violate. But, before an answer could be delivered, the king had actually invaded Saxony, and published his declaration against the court of Vienna. The court of Vienna, believing that the King of Prussia was bent upon employing his arms somewhere; being piqued at the dictatorial manner in which his demands were conveyed; unwilling to lay themselves under further restrictions; apprehensive of giving umbrage to their allies; and confident of having provided for their own security, resolved to run the risk of his resentment, not without hopes of being indemnified, in the course of the war, for that part of Silesia which the queen had been obliged to cede in the treaty of Breslau.

Both sides being thus prepared, and perhaps equally eager for action, the King of Prussia would no longer suspend his operations, and the storm fell first upon Saxony. He resolved to penetrate through that country into Bohemia, and even to take possession of it as a frontier, as well as for the convenience of ingress and egress to and from the Austrian dominions. Besides, he had reason to believe the King of Poland, Elector of Saxony, was connected with the czarina and the empress-queen; therefore, he thought it would be impolitic to leave that prince in any condition to give him the least disturbance. His army entered the Saxon territory towards the latter end of August, when he published a declaration, importing that the unjust conduct and dangerous views of the court of Vienna against his majesty's dominions laid him under the necessity of taking proper measures for protecting his territories and subjects; that for this purpose he could not forbear taking the disagreeable resolution to enter with his troops the hereditary dominions of his majesty the King of Poland, Elector of Saxony: but he protested, before God and man, that, on account of his personal esteem and friendship for that prince, he would not have proceeded to this extremity, had he not been forced to it by the laws of war, the fatality of the present conjuncture, and the necessity of providing for the defence and security of his subjects. He reminded the public of the tenderness with which he had treated the Elector of Saxony, during the campaign of the year one thousand seven hundred and forty-four, and of the bad consequences resulting to that monarch from his engagements with the enemies of Prussia. He declared that the apprehensions of being exposed again to such enterprises had obliged him to take those precautions which prudence dictated: but he protested, in the most solemn manner, that he had no hostile views against his Polish majesty, or his dominions; that his troops did not enter Saxony as enemies, and he had taken care that they should observe the best order and the most exact discipline; that he desired nothing more ardently than the happy minute that should procure to him the satisfaction of restoring to his Polish majesty his hereditary dominions, which he had seized only as a sacred depositum. By his minister at Dresden, he had demanded a free passage for his forces through the Saxon dominions; and this the King of Poland was ready to grant, with reasonable limitations, to be settled by commissiaries appointed for that purpose. But these were formalities which did not at all suit with his Prussian majesty's disposition or design. Even before this requisition was made, a body of his troops, amounting to fifteen thousand, under the command of Prince Ferdinand, brother to the Duke of Brunswick, took possession of Leipsic, on the twentieth day of September. Here he published a declaration, signifying that it was his Prussian majesty's intention to consider and defend the inhabitants of that electorate as if they were his own subjects; and that he had given precise orders to his troops to observe the most exact discipline. As the first mark of his affection, he ordered them to provide the army with all sorts of provisions, according to a certain rate, on pain of military execution. That same evening notice was given to the corporation of merchants that their deputies should pay all taxes and customs to the King of Prussia; then he took possession of the custom-house and excise-office, and ordered the magazines of corn and meal to be opened for the use of his soldiers.

The King of Poland, apprehensive of such a visitation, had ordered all the troops of his electorate to leave their quarters, and assemble in a strong camp marked out for them, between Pirna and Konigstein, which was intrenched, and provided with a numerous train of artillery. Thither the King of Poland repaired, with his two sons, Xaverius and Charles; but the queen and the rest of the royal family remained at Dresden. Of his capital, his Prussian majesty, with the bulk of the army, took possession on the eighth day of September, when he was visited by Lord Stormont, the English ambassador at that court, accompanied by Count Salmour, a Saxon minister, who, in his master's name, proposed a neutrality. The King of Prussia professed himself extremely well pleased with the proposal; and, as the most convincing proof of his neutrality, desired the King of Poland would separate his army, by ordering his troops to return to their former quarters. His Polish majesty did not like to be so tutored in his own dominions: he depended for his own safety more upon the valour and attachment of his troops thus assembled, than upon the friendship of a prince who had invaded his dominions and sequestered his revenue without provocation; and he trusted too much to the situation of his camp at Pirna, which was deemed impregnable. In the mean time, the King of Prussia fixed his head-quarters at Seidlitz, about half a German league distant from Pirna, and posted his army in such a manner as to be able to intercept all convoys of provisions designed for the Saxon camp: his forces extended on the right towards the frontiers of Bohemia, and the vanguard actually seized the passes that lead to the circles of Satzer and Leumeritz, in that kingdom; while Prince Ferdinand of Brunswick marched with a body of troops along the Elbe, and took post at this last place without opposition. At the same time, the king covered his own dominions, by assembling two considerable bodies in Upper and Lower Silesia, which occupied the passes that communicated with the circles of Buntzlau and Koningsgratz. Hostilities were commenced on the thirteenth day of September, by a detachment of Prussian hussars, who attacked an Austrian escort to a convoy of provisions, designed for the Saxon camp; and having routed them, carried off a considerable number of loaded waggons. The magazines at Dresden were filled with an immense quantity of provisions and forage for the Prussian army, and the bakers were ordered to prepare a vast quantity of bread, for which purpose thirty new ovens were erected. When the King of Prussia first arrived at Dresden, he lodged at the house of the

Countess Moczinska, and gave orders that the queen and royal family of Poland should be treated with all due veneration and respect:[a] even while the Saxon camp was blocked up on every side, he sometimes permitted a waggon loaded with fresh provisions and game, to pass unmolested, for the use of his Polish majesty.

During these transactions, the greatest part of the Prussian army advanced into Bohemia, under the command of Veldt-Mareschal Keith,[b] who reduced the town and palace of Tetchen, took possession of all the passes, and encamped near Aussig, a small town in Bohemia, at no great distance from the imperial army, amounting to fifty thousand men, commanded by Count Brown, an officer of Irish extract, who had often distinguished himself in the field by his courage, vigilance, and conduct. His Prussian majesty, having left a considerable body of troops for the blockade of Pirna, assumed in person the command of Mareschal Keith's corps, and advanced to give battle to the enemy. On the twenty-ninth day of September he formed his troops in two columns, and in the evening arrived with his van at Welmina; from whence he saw the Austrian army posted with its right at Lowoschutz, and its left towards the Egra. Having occupied with six battalions a hollow way, and some rising grounds, which commanded the town of Lowoschutz, he remained all night under arms at Welmina; and on the first day of

*Prussian army penetrates into Bohemia, and fights the battle of Lowoschutz.*

---

[a] His majesty seems to have abated of this respect in the sequel, if we may believe the assertions of his Polish majesty's queen, and the court of Vienna, who affirmed, that sentinels were posted within the palace where the queen and royal family resided; as also at the door of the secret cabinet, where the papers relating to foreign transactions were deposited. The keys of this cabinet were seized, and all the writings demanded. The whole Saxon ministry were discharged from their respective employments, and a new commission was established by the King of Prussia for the administration of affairs in general. When the queen entreated this prince to remove the sentinels posted within the palace and contiguous passages, agreeably to his assurances that all due respect should be observed towards the royal family, the king ordered the guards to be doubled, and sent an officer to demand of her majesty the keys of the secret cabinet. The queen obtained the officer's consent that the doors should be sealed up; but afterwards he returned with orders to break them open: then her majesty placing herself before the door, said, she trusted so much to the promise of the King of Prussia, that she could not believe he had given such orders. The officer declaring that his orders were positive, and that he durst not disobey them, she continued in the same place, declaring that if violence was to be used he must begin with her. The officer returning to acquaint the king with what had passed, her majesty conjured the ministers of Prussia and England to remind his majesty of his promise; but her representations had no effect; the officer returned with fresh orders to use force, in spite of the opposition she might make against it in person. The queen, finding herself in danger of her life, at length withdrew; the doors were forced, the chest broken open, and all the papers seized.

[b] Brother to the Earl Mareschal of Scotland, a gentleman who had signalized himself as a general in the Russian army, and was accounted one of the best officers of the time; not more admired for his warlike genius than amiable in his disposition.

October, early in the morning, formed his whole army in order of battle: the first line, consisting of the infantry, occupying two hills, and a bottom betwixt them; the second line, being formed of some battalions, and the third composed of the whole cavalry. The Austrian general had taken possession of Lowoschutz, with a great body of infantry, and placed a battery of cannon in front of the town: he had formed his cavalry chequerwise, in a line between Lowoschutz, and the village of Sanschitz; and posted about two thousand Croats and irregulars in the vineyards and avenues on his right. The morning was darkened with a thick fog, which vanished about seven: then the Prussian cavalry advanced to attack the enemy's horse; but received such a fire from the irregulars, posted in vineyards and ditches, as well as from a numerous artillery, that they were obliged to retire for protection to the rear of the Prussian infantry and cannon. There being formed and led back to the charge, they made an impression on the Austrian cavalry, and drove the irregulars, and other bodies of infantry, from the ditches, defiles, and vineyards which they possessed; but they suffered so severely in this dangerous service, that the king ordered them to reascend the hill, and take post again behind the infantry, from whence they no more advanced. In the mean time, a furious cannonading was maintained on both sides with considerable effect. At length the left of the Prussian infantry was ordered to attack the town of Lowoschutz in flank; but met with a very warm reception, and in all likelihood would have miscarried, had not Veldt-Mareschal Keith headed them in person; when he drew his sword, and told them he would lead them on, he was given to understand, that all their powder and shot were exhausted; he turned immediately to them with a cheerful countenance, said he was very glad they had no more ammunition, being well assured the enemy could not withstand them at push of bayonet; so saying, he advanced at their head, and, driving the Austrians from Lowoschutz, set the suburbs on fire. The infantry had been already obliged to quit the eminence on the right; and now their whole army retired to Budin, on the other side of the Egra. Some prisoners, colours, and pieces of cannon, were taken on both sides; and the loss of each might amount to two thousand five hundred killed and wounded: so that on the whole, it was a drawn battle, though both generals claimed the victory. The detail of the action, published at

Berlin, declares, that the King of Prussia not only gained the battle, but that same day established his head-quarters at Lowoschutz: whereas the Austrian gazette affirms, that the Mareschal Count Brown obliged his Prussian majesty to retire, and remained all night on the field of battle; but next day, finding his troops in want of water, he repaired to the camp at Budin. If the battle was at all decisive, the advantage certainly fell to the Austrians; for his Prussian majesty, who, in all probability, had hoped to winter at Prague, was obliged, by the opposition he met with, to resign his plan, and retreat before winter into the electorate of Saxony.

The Prussian army having rejoined that body which had been left to block up the Saxons at Pirna, his Polish majesty and his troops were reduced to such extremity of want, that it became indispensably necessary either to attempt an escape, or surrender to the King of Prussia. The former part of the alternative was chosen, and the plan concerted with Count Brown, the Austrian general, who, in order to facilitate the execution, advanced privately with a body of troops, to Lichtendorf, near Schandenau; but the junction could not be effected. On the fourteenth day of October the Saxons threw a bridge of boats over the Elbe, near Konigstein, to which castle they removed all their artillery; then striking their tents in the night, passed the river undiscovered by the enemy. They continued to retreat with all possible expedition; but the roads were so bad, they made little progress. Next day, when part of them had advanced about half way up a hill opposite to Konigstein, and the rest were entangled in a narrow plain, where there was no room to act, they perceived that the Prussians were in possession of all the passes, and found themselves surrounded on every side, fainting with hunger and fatigue, and destitute of every convenience. In this deplorable condition they remained, when the King of Poland, from the fortress of Konigstein, sent a letter to his general, the Veldt-Mareschal Count Rutowski, vesting him with full and discretionary power to surrender, or take such other measures as he should judge most conducive to the preservation of the officers and soldiers.° By this time Count Brown had retired to Budin,

*Saxon army surrenders.*

---

° The letter was to the following effect:
" Veldt-Mareschal Count Rutowski,
" It is not without extreme sorrow I understand the deplorable situation, which a chain of misfortunes has reserved for you, the rest of my generals, and my whole army; but we

so that there was no choice left. A capitulation was demanded: but, in effect, the whole Saxon army was obliged to surrender at discretion; and the soldiers were afterwards, by compulsion, incorporated with the troops of Prussia. The King of Poland, being thus deprived of his electoral dominions, his troops, arms, artillery, and ammunition, thought it high time to provide for his own safety, and retire with all expedition to Poland. His Prussian majesty cantoned his forces in the neighbourhood of Seidlitz and along the Elbe towards Dresden. His other army, which had entered Bohemia, under the command of the Count de Schwerin, retired to the confines of the county of Glatz, where they were distributed in quarters of cantonment; so that this short campaign was finished by the beginning of November.

The King of Poland, in his distress, did not fail to implore the assistance and mediation of neutral powers. His minister at the Hague presented a memorial to the States-General, complaining, that the invasion of Saxony was one of those attacks against the law of nations, which, from the great respect due to this law, demanded the assistance of every power interested in the preservation of its own liberty and independence. He observed that, from the first glimpse of misunderstanding between the courts of Vienna and Berlin, he had expressly enjoined his ministers at all the courts of Europe to declare, that it was his firm resolution, in the present conjuncture of affairs, to observe the strictest neutrality. He represented that a free and neutral state had been, in the midst of peace, invaded by an enemy, who disguised himself under the mask of friendship, without alleging the least complaint, or any pretension whatsoever; but, founding himself solely on his own convenience, made himself master, by armed force, of all the cities and towns of the electorate,

*King of Poland's memorial to the States-General.*

---

must acquiesce in the dispensations of Providence, and console ourselves with the rectitude of our sentiments and intentions. They would force me, it seems, as you give me to understand by Major-General the Baron de Dyherrn, to submit to conditions the more severe, in proportion as the circumstances become more necessitous. I cannot hear them mentioned. I am a free monarch; such I will live: such I will die; and I will both live and die with honour. The fate of my army I leave wholly to your discretion. Let your council of war determine whether you must surrender prisoners of war, fall by the sword, or die by famine. May your resolutions, if possible, be conducted by humanity; whatever they may be, I have no longer any share in them: and I declare you shall not be answerable for aught but one thing, namely, not to carry arms against me or my allies. I pray God may have you, Mr. Mareschal, in his holy keeping. Given at Konigstein, the 14th of October, 1756.

"AUGUSTUS, Rex."

" To the Veldt-Mareschal the Count Rutowski."

dismantling some, and fortifying others: that he had disarmed the burghers; carried off the magistrates as hostages for the payment of unjust and enormous contributions of provisions and forage; seized the coffers and confiscated the revenues of the electorate, broke open the arsenals, and transported the arms and artillery to his own town of Magdeburgh; abolished the privy-council, and, instead of the lawful government, established a directory, which acknowledged no other law but his own arbitrary will. He gave them to understand, that all these proceedings were no other than preliminaries to the unheard-of treatment which was reserved for a queen, whose virtues ought to have commanded respect, even from her enemies: that from the hands of that august princess, the archives of the states were forced away by menaces and violences, notwithstanding the security which her majesty had promised herself under the protection of all laws, human and divine; and notwithstanding the repeated assurances given by the King of Prussia, that not only her person, and the place of her residence, should be absolutely safe, but that even the Prussian garrison should be under her direction. He observed, that a prince who declared himself protector of the Protestant religion had begun the war by crushing the very state to which that religion owes its establishment, and the preservation of its most invaluable rights: that he had broken through the most respectable laws which constitute the union of the Germanic body, under colour of a defence which the empire stood in no need of except against himself: that the King of Prussia, while he insists on having entered Saxony as a friend, demands his army, the administration of his dominions, and, in a word, the sacrifice of his whole electorate; and that the Prussian directory, in the declaration of motives, published under the nose of a prince to whom friendship was pretended, thought it superfluous to allege even any pretext, to colour the usurpation of his territories and revenues.—Though this was certainly the case in his Prussian majesty's first exposition of motives, the omission was afterwards supplied, in a subsequent memorial to the States-General; in which he charged the King of Poland, as an accomplice in, if not an accessary to, the treaty of Petersburgh; and even taxed him with having agreed to a partition of some Prussian territories, when they should be conquered. This treaty of partition, however, appears to have been made in time of actual war, before all cause of dispute was removed by the peace of Dresden.

While the Austrian and Prussian armies were in the field, their respective ministers were not idle at Ratisbon, where three imperial decrees were published against his Prussian majesty: the first summoning that prince to withdraw his troops from the electorate of Saxony; the second commanding all the vassals of the empire employed by the King of Prussia to quit that service immediately; and the third forbidding the members of the empire to suffer any levies of soldiers, for the Prussian service, to be raised within their respective jurisdictions. The French minister declared to the diet, that the proceedings of his Prussian majesty having disclosed to the world the project concerted between that prince and the King of England, to excite in the empire a religious war, which might be favourable to their particular views, his most Christian majesty, in consequence of his engagement with the empress-queen, and many other princes of the empire, being resolved to succour them in the most efficacious manner, would forthwith send such a number of troops to their aid, as might be thought necessary to preserve the liberty of the Germanic body. On the other hand, the Prussian minister assured the diet, that his master would very soon produce the proofs that were come to his hands of the plan concerted by the courts of Vienna and Dresden, for the subversion of his electoral house, and for imposing upon him a yoke, which seemed to threaten the whole empire.

*Imperial decrees published against the King of Prussia.*

About the same time, the Russian resident at the Hague communicated to the States-General a declaration from his mistress, importing that her imperial majesty having seen a memorial presented at the court of Vienna, by the King of Prussia's envoy extraordinary, was thereby convinced that his Prussian majesty's intention was to attack the territories of the empress-queen; in which case, she (the czarina) was inevitably obliged to succour her ally with all her forces; for which end she had ordered all her troops in Livonia to be forthwith assembled on the frontiers, and hold themselves in readiness to march: that, moreover, the Russian Admiralty had been enjoined to provide immediately a sufficient number of galleys for transporting a large body of troops to Lubeck. The minis-

*Declarations of different powers.*

ters of the empress-queen, both at the Hague and at London, delivered memorials to the States-General and his Britannic majesty, demanding the succours which these two powers were bound to afford the house of Austria by the treaty of Aix-la-Chapelle; but their high mightinesses kept warily aloof, by dint of evasion, and the King of Great Britain was far otherwise engaged. The invasion of Saxony had well nigh produced tragedies in the royal family of France. The dauphiness, who was far advanced in her pregnancy, no sooner learned the distressful circumstances of her parents, the King and Queen of Poland, than she was seized with violent fits, which occasioned a miscarriage, and brought her life into the most imminent danger. The Prussian minister was immediately ordered to quit Versailles;' and directions were despatched to the French minister at Berlin, to retire from that court without taking leave. Finally, the Emperor of Germany concluded a new convention with the French king, regulating the succours to be derived from that quarter: he claimed, in all the usual forms, the assistance of the Germanic body, as guarantee of the pragmatic sanction and treaty of Dresden; and Sweden was also addressed on the same subject.

The King of Prussia did not passively bear all the imputations that were fixed upon his conduct. His minister at the Hague presented a memorial, in answer to that of the Saxon resident, in which he accused the court of Dresden of having adopted every part of the scheme which his enemies had formed for his destruction. He affirmed that the Saxon ministers had, in all the courts of Europe, played off every engine of unwarrantable politics, in order to pave the way for the execution of their project: that they had endeavoured to give an odious turn to his most innocent actions: that they had spared neither malicious insinuations, nor even the most atrocious calumnies, to alienate all the world from his majesty, and raise up enemies against him everywhere. He said he had received information that the court of Saxony intended to let his troops pass freely, and afterwards wait for events of which they might avail themselves, either by joining his enemies, or making a diversion in his dominions: that in such a situation he could not avoid having recourse to the only means which were left him for preventing his inevitable ruin, by putting it out of the

*His Prussian majesty's answer to the Saxon memorial.*

power of Saxony to increase the number of his enemies. He asserted, that all the measures he had pursued in that electorate were but the necessary consequences of the first resolution he was forced to take for his own preservation: that he had done nothing but deprived the court of Saxony of the means of hurting him : and this had been done with all possible moderation : that the country enjoyed all the security and all the quiet which could be expected in the very midst of peace, the Prussian troops observing the most exact discipline : that all due respect was shown to the Queen of Poland, who had been prevailed upon, by the most suitable representations, to suffer some papers to be taken from the paper-office, of which his Prussian majesty already had copies; and thought it necessary to ascertain the dangerous design of the Saxon ministry against him, to secure the originals; the existence and reality of which might otherwise have been denied. He observed, that every man has a right to prevent the mischief with which he is threatened, and to retort it upon its author; and that neither the constitutions nor the laws of the empire could obstruct the exertion of a right so superior to all others as that of self-preservation and self-defence; especially when the depositary of these laws is so closely united to the enemy, as manifestly to abuse his power in her favour.

But the most important step which his Prussian majesty took in his own justification was that of publishing another memorial, specifying the conduct of the courts of Vienna and Saxony, and their dangerous designs against his person and interest, together with the original documents adduced as proofs of these sinister intentions. As a knowledge of these pieces is requisite to form a distinct idea of the motives which produced the dreadful war upon the continent, it will not be amiss to usher the substance of them to the reader's acquaintance. His Prussian majesty affirms, that to arrive at the source of the vast plan upon which the courts of Vienna and Saxony had been employed against him ever since the peace of Dresden, we must trace it as far back as the war which preceded this peace; that the fond hopes which the two allied courts had conceived upon the success of the campaign in the year one thousand seven hundred and forty-four, gave occasion to a treaty of eventual partition, stipulating that the court of Vienna should possess the duchy of Silesia and the county

*And justification of his conduct.*

of Glatz; while the King of Poland, Elector of Saxony, should share the duchies of Magdeburgh and Croissen; the circles of Zullichow and Swibus, together with the Prussian part of Lusatia: that after the peace of Dresden, concluded in the year one thousand seven hundred and forty-five, there was no further room for a treaty of this nature: yet the court of Vienna proposed to that of Saxony a new alliance, in which the treaty of eventual partition should be renewed: but this last thought it necessary, in the first place, to give a greater consistency to their plan, by grounding it upon an alliance between the empress-queen and the czarina. Accordingly, these two powers did, in fact, conclude a defensive alliance at Petersburgh in the course of the ensuing year; but the body, or ostensible part of this treaty, was composed merely with a view to conceal from the knowledge of the public six secret articles, the fourth of which was levelled singly against Prussia, according to the exact copy of it, which appeared among the documents. In this article, the Empress-Queen of Hungary and Bohemia sets out with a protestation that she will religiously observe the treaty of Dresden; but explains her real way of thinking upon the subject, a little lower, in the following terms: "If the King of Prussia should be the first to depart from the peace, by attacking either her majesty the Empress-Queen of Hungary and Bohemia, or her majesty the Empress of Russia, or even the republic of Poland: in all these cases, the rights of the empress-queen to Silesia and the county of Glatz would again take place, and recover their full effect: the two contracting parties should mutually assist each other with sixty thousand men to achieve these conquests." The king observes upon this article, that every war which can arise between him and Russia, or the republic of Poland, would be looked upon as a manifest infraction of the peace of Dresden, and a revival of the rights of the house of Austria to Silesia; though neither Russia nor the republic of Poland is at all concerned in the treaty of Dresden: and though the latter, with which the king lived in the most intimate friendship, was not even in alliance with the court of Vienna: that according to the principles of the law of nature, received among all civilized nations, the most the court of Vienna could be authorized to do in such cases, would be to send those succours to her allies which are due to them by treaties, without her having the least pretence, on that account, to free herself from the particular engagements subsisting between her and the king: he appealed, therefore, to the judgment of the impartial world, whether in this secret article the contracting powers had kept within the bounds of a defensive alliance; or whether this article did not rather contain a plan of an offensive alliance against the King of Prussia. He affirmed it was obvious, from this article, that the court of Vienna had prepared three pretences for the recovery of Silesia; and that she thought to attain her end, either by provoking the king to commence hostilities against her, or to kindle a war between his majesty and Russia, by her secret intrigues and machinations: he alleged that the court of Saxony, being invited to accede to this alliance, eagerly accepted the invitation; furnished its ministers at Petersburgh with full powers for that purpose; and ordered them to declare that their master was not only ready to accede to the treaty itself, but also to the secret article against Prussia; and to join in the regulations made by the two courts, provided effectual measures should be taken, as well for the security of Saxony, as for its indemnification and recompense, in proportion to the efforts and progress that might be made: that the court of Dresden declared, if upon any fresh attack from the King of Prussia, the empress-queen should, by their assistance, not only reconquer Silesia, and the county of Glatz, but also reduce him within narrower bounds, the King of Poland, as Elector of Saxony, would abide by the partition formerly stipulated between him and the empress-queen. He also declared that Count Loss, the Saxon minister at Vienna, was charged to open a private negotiation for settling an eventual partition of the conquest which might be made on Prussia, by laying down, as the basis of it, the treaty of Leipsic, signed on the eighteenth day of May, in the year one thousand seven hundred and forty-five, as would appear by the documents affixed. He owned it had been supposed, through the whole of this negotiation, that the King of Prussia should be the aggressor against the court of Vienna; but he insisted, that even in this case the King of Poland could have no right to make conquests on his Prussian majesty. He likewise acknowledged, that the court of Saxony had not yet acceded in form to the treaty of Petersburgh; but he observed, its allies were given to understand again and again that it was ready to accede without restriction, whenever this could be done without risk, and the advantages to be gained should be secured in its favour; circumstances proved by divers authentic documents, particularly by a letter from Count Fleming to Count de Bruhl, informing him that Count Uhlefield had charged him to represent afresh to his court, that they could not take too secure measures against the ambitious views of the King of Prussia; that Saxony in particular ought to be cautious, as being the most exposed; that it was of the highest importance to strengthen their old engagements, upon the footing proposed by the late Count de Harrach, in the year one thousand seven hundred and forty-five; a step which might be taken on occasion of his Polish majesty's accession to the treaty of Petersburgh. The answer of Count Bruhl to this despatch imported, that the King of Poland was not averse to treat in the utmost secrecy with the court of Vienna about succours, by private and confidential declarations relating to the fourth secret article of the treaty of Petersburgh, on condition of reasonable terms and advantages, which in this case ought to be granted to his majesty. He quoted other despatches to prove the unwillingness of his Polish majesty to declare himself, until the King of Prussia should be attacked, and his forces divided; and that this scruple was admitted by the allies of Saxony. From these premises he deduced this inference, that the court of Dresden, without having acceded in form to the treaty of Petersburgh, was not less an accomplice in the dangerous designs which the court of Vienna had grounded upon this treaty; and that having been dispensed with from a formal concurrence, it had only waited for that moment when it might, without running any great risk, conquer in effect, and share the spoils of its neighbour. In expectation of this period, he said, the Austrian and Saxon ministers laboured in concert and underhand with the more ardour, to bring the *casus fœderis* into existence: for it being laid down as a principle in the treaty, that any war whatever between him and Russia would authorize the empress-queen to take Silesia, there was nothing more to be done but to kindle such a war: for which purpose no method was found more proper than that of embroiling the king with the Empress of Russia; and to provoke that princess with all sorts of false insinuations, impostures, and the most atrocious calumnies, in laying to his majesty's charge a variety of designs, sometimes against Russia, and even the person of the czarina; sometimes views upon Poland, and sometimes intrigues in Sweden. By these and other such contrivances, he affirmed they had kindled the animosity of the empress to such a degree, that in a council held in the month of October, in the year one thousand seven hundred and fifty-three, she had resolved to attack the King of Prussia, without any further discussion, whether he should fall upon any of the allies of Russia, or one of them should begin with him; a resolution which for that time was frustrated by their want of seamen and magazines; but the preparations were continued under pretence of keeping themselves in a condition to fulfil their engagements, contracted in the last subsidiary convention with England; and when all were finished, the storm would fall on the King of Prussia.

This is the substance of that famous memorial published by his Prussian majesty, to which the justifying pieces or authentic documents were annexed; and to which a circumstantial answer was exhibited by the partisans of her imperial majesty. *Remarks on both those pieces.* Specious reasons may, doubtless, be adduced on either side of almost any dispute, by writers of ingenuity; but, in examining this contest, it must be allowed that both sides adopted illicit practices. The empress-queen and the Elector of Saxony had certainly a right to form defensive treaties for their own preservation; and, without all doubt, it was their interest and their duty to secure themselves from the enterprises of such a formidable neighbour; but, at the same time, the contracting parties seem to have carried their views much farther than defensive measures. Perhaps the court of Vienna considered the cession of Silesia as a circumstance altogether compulsive, and, therefore, not binding against the rights of natural equity. She did not at all doubt that the King of Prussia would be tempted, by his ambition and great warlike power, to take some step which might be justly interpreted into an infraction of the treaty of Dresden; and in that case she was determined to avail herself of the confederacy she had formed, that she might retrieve the countries she had lost by the unfortunate events of the last war, as well as bridle the dangerous power and disposition of the Prussian monarch; and, in all probability, the King of Poland, over and above the same consideration, was desirous of some indemnification for the last irruption into his electoral dominions, and the great sums he had paid for the subsequent peace. Whether they were authorized by the law of nature and nations to make reprisals by an actual partition of the countries they might conquer, supposing him to be the aggressor, we shall not pretend to determine; but it does not at all appear that his Prussian majesty's danger was such as entitled him to take those violent steps which he now attempted to justify. By this time the flame of war was kindled up to a blaze that soon filled the empire with ruin and desolation; and the King of Prussia had drawn upon himself the resentment of the three greatest powers in Europe, who laid aside their former animosities, and every consideration of that balance which it had cost such blood and treasure to preserve, in order to conspire his destruction. The king himself could not but foresee this confederacy, and know the power it might exert; but probably he confided so much in the number, the valour, and discipline of his troops, in the skill of his officers, in his own conduct and activity, that he hoped to crush the house of Austria by one rapid endeavour at the latter end of the season, or at least establish himself in Bohemia, before her allies could move to her assistance. In this hope, however, he was disappointed by the vigilance of the Austrian councils. He found the empress-queen in a condition to make head against him in every avenue to her dominions; and in a fair way of being assisted by the circles of the empire. He saw himself threatened with the vengeance of the Russian empress, and the sword of France gleaming over his head, without any prospect of assistance but that which he might derive from his alliance with Great Britain. Thus the King of England exchanged the alliance of Russia, who was his subsidiary, and the friendship of the empress-queen, his old and natural ally, for a new connexion with his Prussian majesty, who could neither act as an auxiliary to Great Britain, nor as a protector to Hanover: and for this connexion, the advantage of which was merely negative, such a price was paid by England as had never been given by any other potentate of Europe, even for services of the greatest importance.

About the latter end of November, the Saxon minister at Ratisbon delivered to the diet a new and ample memorial, explaining the lamentable state of that electorate, and imploring afresh the assistance of the empire. The King of

Prussia had also addressed a letter to the diet, demanding succour of the several states, agreeably to their guarantees of the treaties of Westphalia and Dresden; but the minister of Mentz, as director of the diet, having refused to lay it before that assembly, the minister of Brandenburgh ordered it to be printed, and sent to his court for further instructions. In the mean time his Prussian majesty thought proper to intimate to the King and senate of Poland, that should the Russian troops be permitted to march through that kingdom, they might expect to see their country made a scene of war and desolation. In France, the prospect of a general and sanguinary war did not at all allay the disturbance which sprang from the dissension between the clergy and Parliament, touching the bull Unigenitus. The king being again brought over to the ecclesiastical side of the dispute, received a brief from the pope, laying it down as a fundamental article, that whosoever refuses to submit to the bull Unigenitus is in the way to damnation; and certain cases are specified, in which the sacraments are to be denied. The Parliament of Paris, considering this brief or bull as a direct attack upon the rights of the Gallican church, issued an arrêt or decree, suppressing the said bull; reserving to themselves the right of providing against the inconveniences with which it might be attended: as well as the privilege to maintain in their full force the prerogatives of the crown, the power and jurisdiction of the bishops, the liberties of the Gallican church, and the customs of the realm. The king, dissatisfied with their interposition, declared his design to hold a bed of justice in person at the palace. Accordingly, on the twelfth day of November, the whole body of his guards, amounting to ten thousand men, took post in the city of Paris; and next day the king repaired with the usual ceremony to the palace, where the bed of justice was held: among other regulations, an edict was issued for suppressing the fourth and fifth chambers of inquests, the members of which had remarkably distinguished themselves by their opposition to the bull Unigenitus.

In England, the dearth of corn, arising in a great measure from the iniquitous practice of engrossing, was so severely felt by the common people, that insurrections were raised in Shropshire and Warwickshire by the populace, in conjunction with the colliers, who seized by violence all the provisions they could find; pillaging without distinction the millers, farmers, grocers, and butchers, until they were dispersed by the gentlemen of the country, at the head of their tenants and dependents. Disorders of the same nature were excited by the colliers on the forest of Dean, and those employed in the works in Cumberland. The corporations, noblemen, and gentlemen, in different parts of the kingdom, exerted themselves for the relief of the poor, who were greatly distressed; and a grand council being assembled at St. James's on the same subject, a proclamation was published for putting the laws in speedy and effectual execution against the forestallers and engrossers of corn.

The fear of an invasion having now subsided, and Hanover being supposed in greater danger than Great Britain, the auxiliaries of that electorate were transported from England to their own country. At the latter end of the season, when the weather became severe, the innkeepers of England refused to admit the Hessian soldiers into winter quarters, as no provision had been made for that purpose by act of Parliament; so that they were obliged to hut their camp, and remain in the open fields till January; but the rigour of this uncomfortable situation was softened by the hand of generous charity, which liberally supplied them with all manner of refreshment, and other conveniences; an humane interposition, which rescued the national character from the imputation of cruelty and ingratitude.

*Hanoverian auxiliaries sent back.*

On the second day of December, his majesty opened the session of Parliament with a speech that seemed to be dictated by the genius of England. He expressed his confidence, that, under the guidance of Divine Providence, the union, fortitude, and affection of his people would enable him to surmount all difficulties, and vindicate the dignity of his crown against the ancient enemy of Great Britain. He declared, that the succour and preservation of America constituted a main object of his attention and solicitude; and observed, that the growing dangers to which the British colonies might stand exposed, from late losses in that country, demanded resolutions of vigour and despatch. He said, an adequate and firm defence at home should maintain the chief place in his thoughts; and in this great view he had nothing so much at heart as to remove

*Session opened.*

all grounds of dissatisfaction from his people: for this end, he recommended to the care and diligence of the Parliament the framing of a national militia, planned and regulated with equal regard to the just rights of his crown and people; an institution which might become one good resource in time of general danger. He took notice that the unnatural union of councils abroad, the calamities which, in consequence of this unhappy conjunction, might, by irruptions of foreign armies into the empire, shake its constitution, overturn its system, and threaten oppression to the protestant interest on the continent, were events which must sensibly affect the minds of the British nation, and had fixed the eyes of Europe on this new and dangerous crisis. He gave them to understand that the body of his electoral troops, which were brought hither at the desire of his Parliament, he had now directed to return to his dominions in Germany, relying with pleasure on the spirit and zeal of his people in defence of his person and realm. He told the Commons that he confided in their wisdom for preferring more vigorous efforts, though more expensive, to a less effectual and therefore less frugal plan of war; that he had placed before them the dangers and necessities of the public; and it was their duty to lay the burdens they should judge unavoidable in such a manner as would least disturb and exhaust his people. He expressed his concern for the sufferings of the poor, arising from the present dearth of corn, and for the disturbances to which it had given rise; and exhorted his Parliament to consider of proper provisions for preventing the like mischiefs hereafter. He concluded with remarking, that unprosperous events of war in the Mediterranean had drawn from his subjects signal proofs how dearly they tendered the honour of his crown; therefore they could not, on his part, fail to meet with just returns of unwearied care, and unceasing endeavours for the glory, prosperity, and happiness of his people.

The king having retired from the House of Peers, the speech was read by Lord Sandys, appointed to act as speaker to that house; then Earl Gower moved for an address, which, however, was not carried without objection. In one part of it his majesty was thanked for having caused a body of electoral troops to come into England at the request of his Parliament; and this article was disagreeable to those who had disapproved of the request in the last session. They said they wished to see the present address unanimously agreed to by the Lords; a satisfaction they could not have if such a paragraph should be inserted; for they still thought the bringing over Hanoverian troops a preposterous measure; because it had not only loaded the nation with an enormous expense, but also furnished the court of France with a plausible pretence for invading the electorate, which otherwise it would have no shadow of reason to attack; besides, the expedient was held in reprobation by the subjects in general, and such a paragraph might be considered as an insult on the people. Notwithstanding these exceptions, which did not seem to be very important, the address, including this paragraph, was approved by a great majority.

In the address of the Commons no such paragraph was inserted. As soon as the speaker had recited his majesty's speech, Mr. C. Townshend proposed the heads of an address, to which the House unanimously agreed; and it was presented accordingly. This necessary form was no sooner discussed, than the House, with a warmth of humanity and benevolence suitable to such an assembly, resolved itself into a committee, to deliberate on that part of his majesty's speech which related to the dearth of corn, that so much distressed the poorer class of people. A bill was immediately framed to prohibit, for a time limited, the exportation of corn, malt, meal, flour, bread, biscuit, and starch; and a resolution unanimously taken to address the sovereign, that an embargo might be forthwith laid upon all ships laden or to be laden with these commodities to be exported from the ports of Great Britain and Ireland. At the same time, Vice-Admiral Boscawen, from the board of Admiralty, informed the House, that the king and the board having been dissatisfied with the conduct of Admiral Byng, in a late action with the French fleet in the Mediterranean, and for the appearance of his not having acted agreeably to his instructions for the relief of Minorca, he was then in custody of the marshal of the Admiralty, in order to be tried by a court-martial: that although this was no more than what was usual in like cases, yet as Admiral Byng was then a member of the House, and as his confinement might detain him some time from his duty there, the board of

*Bill passed for prohibiting the exportation of corn.*

*Message to the House concerning Admiral Byng.*

Admiralty thought it a respect due to the House to inform them of the commitment and detainer of the said admiral. This message being delivered, the journal of the House in relation to Rear-Admiral Knowles[a] was read, and what Mr. Boscawen now communicated was also inserted.

The committees of supply, and of ways and means, being appointed, took into consideration the necessities of the state, and made very ample provision for enabling his majesty to maintain the war with vigour. They granted fifty-five thousand men for the sea-service, including eleven thousand four hundred and nineteen marines; and for the land service forty-nine thousand seven hundred and forty-nine effective men, comprehending four thousand and eight invalids. The supply was granted for the maintenance of these forces, as well as for the troops of Hesse and Hanover; for the ordnance; the levy of new regiments; for assisting his majesty in forming and maintaining an army of observation, for the just and necessary defence and preservation of his electoral dominions, and those of his allies, and towards enabling him to fulfil his engagements with the King of Prussia; for the security of the empire against the irruption of foreign[*] armies, as well as for the support of the common cause; for building and repairs of ships, hiring transports, payment of half-pay officers, and the pensions of widows; for enabling his majesty to discharge the like sum, raised in pursuance of an act passed in the last session of Parliament, and charged

*Marginal note: Supplies granted.*

---

[a] Rear-Admiral Knowles being, in the month of December, one thousand seven hundred and forty-nine, tried at Deptford, before a court-martial, for his behaviour in and relating to an action which happened on the first day of October in the preceding year, between a British squadron under his command and a squadron of Spain, the court was unanimously of opinion, that the said Knowles, while he was standing for the enemy, might, by a different disposition of his squadron, have begun the attack with six ships as early in the day as four of them were engaged, and that therefore, by neglecting so to do, he gave the enemy a manifest advantage; that the said Knowles remained on board the ship Cornwall with his flag; after she was disabled from continuing the action, though he might, upon her being disabled, have shifted his flag on board another ship; and the court were unanimously of opinion, he ought to have done so, in order to have conducted and directed, during the whole action, the motions of the squadron entrusted to his care and conduct. Upon consideration of the whole conduct of the said Knowles, relating to that action, the court did unanimously agree that he fell under part of the fourteenth article of the articles of war, namely, the word Negligence, and no other; and also under the twenty-third article.—The court, therefore, unanimously adjudged, that he should be reprimanded for not bringing up the squadron in closer order than he did, and not beginning the attack with as great force as he might have done; and also for not shifting his flag, upon the Cornwall's being disabled.

[*] Nothing could more gloriously evince the generosity of a British Parliament than this interposition for defending the liberties of Germany, in conjunction with two electors only, against the sense of the other seven, and in direct opposition to the measures taken by the head of the empire, who, in the sequel, stigmatized these two princes as rebels, and treated one of them as an outlaw.

upon the first aids or supplies to be granted in this session; for enabling the governors and guardians of the hospital for the maintenance and education of exposed and deserted young children to receive all such children, under a certain age, as should be brought to the said hospital within the compass of one year;[f] for maintaining and supporting the new settlement of Nova Scotia; for repairing and finishing military roads; for making good his majesty's engagements with the Landgrave of Hesse-Cassel; for the expense of marching, recruiting, and remounting German troops in the pay of Great Britain; for empowering his majesty to defray any extraordinary expenses of the war, incurred or to be incurred for the service of the ensuing year, and to take all such measures as might be necessary to disappoint or defeat any enterprises or designs of his enemies, as the exigency of affairs should require; for the payment of such persons, in such a manner as his majesty should direct, for the use and relief of his subjects in the several provinces of North and South Carolina and Virginia, in recompense for such services as, with the approbation of his majesty's commander-in-chief in America, they respectively had performed, or should perform, either by putting these provinces in a state of defence, or by acting with vigour against the enemy; for enabling the East India Company to defray the expense of a military force in their settlements, to be maintained in them in lieu of a battalion of his majesty's forces withdrawn from those forts and factories; for the maintenance and support of the forts on the coast of Africa; for widening the avenues, and rendering more safe and commodious, the streets and passages leading from Charing-cross to the two Houses of Parliament, the courts of justice, and the new bridge at Westminster.[g] Such were the articles

---

[f] This charity, established by voluntary contribution, might, under proper restrictions, prove beneficial to the commonwealth, by rescuing deserted children from misery and death, and qualifying them for being serviceable members of the community; but since the liberality of Parliament hath enabled the governors and corporation to receive all the children that are presented, without question or limitation, the yearly expense hath swelled into a national grievance, and the humane purposes of the original institution are, in a great measure, defeated. Instead of an asylum for poor forlorn orphans and abandoned foundlings, it is become a general receptacle for the offspring of the dissolute, who care not to work for the maintenance of their families. The hospital itself is a plain edifice, well contrived for economy and convenience, standing on the north side of the city, and a little detached from it, in an agreeable and salubrious situation. The hall is adorned with some good paintings; the chapel is elegant; and the regulations are admirable.

[g] The bridge at Westminster may be considered as a national ornament. It was built at the public expense, from the neighbourhood of Westminster Hall to the opposite side of the river, and consists of thirteen arches, constructed with equal elegance and simplicity.

under which we may specify the supplies of this year, on the whole amounting to eight millions three hundred fifty thousand three hundred and twenty-five pounds, nine shillings, and three pence. It must be acknowledged, for the honour of the administration, that the House of Commons could not have exhibited stronger marks of their attachment to the crown and person of their sovereign, as well as of their desire to see the force of the nation exerted with becoming spirit. The sums granted by the committee of supply did not exceed eight millions three hundred fifty thousand three hundred twenty-five pounds, nine shillings, and three pence; the funds established amounted to eight millions six hundred eighty-nine thousand fifty-one pounds, nineteen shillings, and seven-pence; so that there was an overplus of three hundred thirty-eight thousand seven hundred and twenty-six pounds, ten shillings, and four pence; an excess which was thought necessary, in case the lottery, which was founded on a new plan, should not succeed.

Some of these impositions were deemed grievous hardships by those upon whom they immediately fell; and many friends of their country exclaimed against the projected army of observation in Germany, as the commencement of a ruinous continental war, which it was neither the interest of the nation to undertake, nor in their power to maintain, without starving the operations by sea, and in America, founded on British principles; without contracting such an additional load of debts and taxes, as could not fail to terminate in bankruptcy and distress. To those dependants of the ministry who observed that, as Hanover was threatened by France for its connexion with Great Britain, it ought, in common gratitude, to be protected, they replied, that every state, in assisting any ally, ought to have a regard to its own preservation: that, if the King of England enjoyed by inheritance, or succession, a province in the heart of France, it would be equally absurd and unjust, in case of a rupture with that kingdom, to exhaust the treasures of Great Britain in the defence of such a province; and yet the inhabitants of it would have the same right to complain, that they suffered for their connexion with England. They observed, that other dominions, electorates, and principalities in Germany were secured by the constitutions of the empire, as well as by fair and equal alliances with their co-estates; whereas Hanover

*Reflections on the continental war.*

stood solitary, like a hunted deer avoided by the herd, and had no other shelter but that of shrinking under the extended shield of Great Britain: that the reluctance expressed by the German princes to undertake the defence of those dominions flowed from a firm persuasion, founded on experience, that England would interpose as a principal, and not only draw her sword against the enemies of the electorate, but concentrate her chief strength in that object, and waste her treasures in purchasing their concurrence: that exclusive of an ample revenue drained from the sweat of the people, great part of which had been expended in continental efforts, the whole national debt incurred, since the accession of the late king, had been contracted in pursuance of measures totally foreign to the interest of these kingdoms: that, since Hanover was the favourite object, England would save money, and great quantities of British blood, by allowing France to take possession of the electorate, paying its ransom at the peace, and indemnifying the inhabitants for the damage they might sustain; an expedient that would be productive of another good consequence; it would rouse the German princes from their affected indifference, and oblige them to exert themselves with vigour, in order to avoid the detested neighbourhood of such an enterprising invader.

The article of the supply relating to the army of observation took rise from a message signed by his majesty, and presented by Mr. Pitt, now promoted to the office of principal secretary of state; a gentleman who had, upon sundry occasions, combated the gigantic plan of continental connexions with all the strength of reason, and all the powers of eloquence. He now imparted to the House an intimation, importing, it was always with reluctance that his majesty asked extraordinary supplies of his people; but as the united councils and formidable preparations of France and her allies threatened Europe in general with the most alarming consequences; and as these unjust and vindictive designs were particularly and immediately bent against his majesty's electoral dominions, and those of his good ally, the King of Prussia, his majesty confided in the experienced zeal and affection of his faithful Commons, that they would cheerfully assist him in forming and maintaining an army of observation, for the just and necessary defence and preservation of those territories,

*Messages from the king to the Parliament.*

and enable him to fulfil his engagements with his Prussian majesty, for the security of the empire against the irruption of foreign armies, and for the support of the common cause. Posterity will hardly believe, that the emperor and all the princes of Germany were in a conspiracy against their country, except the King of Prussia, the Elector of Hanover, and the Landgrave of Hesse-Cassel; and they will, no doubt, be surprised, that Great Britain, after all the treaties she had made, and the numberless subsidies she had granted, should not have an ally left, except one prince, so embarrassed in his own affairs, that he could grant her no succour, whatever assistance he might demand. The king's message met with as favourable a reception as he could have desired. It was read in the House of Commons, together with a copy of the treaty between his majesty and the King of Prussia, including the secret and separate article, and the declaration signed on each side by the plenipotentiaries at Westminster: the request was granted, and the convention approved. With equal readiness did they gratify his majesty's inclination, signified in another message, delivered on the seventeenth day of May, by Lord Bateman, intimating, that in this critical juncture, emergencies might arise of the utmost importance, and be attended with the most pernicious consequences, if proper means should not be immediately applied to prevent or defeat them; his majesty was therefore desirous that the House would enable him to defray any extraordinary expenses of the war, incurred or to be incurred for the service of the current year; and to take all such measures as might be necessary to disappoint or defeat any enterprises or designs of his enemies, as the exigency of affairs might require. The committee of supply forthwith granted a very large sum for these purposes, including the charge of German mercenaries. A like message being at the same time communicated to the Upper House, their lordships voted a very loyal address upon the occasion; and when the article of supply, which it produced among the Commons, fell under their inspection, they unanimously agreed to it, by way of a clause of appropriation.

We have already observed, that the first bill which the Commons passed in this session was for the relief of the poor, by prohibiting the exportation of corn; but this remedy not being judged adequate to the evil, another bill was framed, removing, for a limited time, the duty then payable upon foreign corn and flour imported: as also permitting, for a certain time, all such foreign corn, grain, meal, bread, biscuit, and flour, as had been or should be taken from the enemy, to be landed and expended in the kingdom, duty free. In order still more to reduce the high price of corn, and to prevent any supply of provisions from being sent to our enemies in America, a third bill was brought in, prohibiting, for a time therein limited, the exportation of corn, grain, meal, malt, flour, bread, biscuit, starch, beef, pork, bacon, or other victual, from any of the British plantations, unless to Great Britain or Ireland, or from one colony to another. To this act two clauses were added, for allowing those necessaries, mentioned above, to be imported in foreign-built ships, and from any state in amity with his majesty, either into Great Britain or Ireland; and for exporting from Southampton or Exeter to the Isle of Man, for the use of the inhabitants, a quantity of wheat, barley, oats, meal, or flour, not exceeding two thousand five hundred quarters. The Commons would have still improved their humanity, had they contrived and established some effectual method to punish those unfeeling villains, who, by engrossing and hoarding up great quantities of grain, had created this artificial scarcity, and deprived their fellow-creatures of bread, with a view to their own private advantage. Upon a subsequent report of the committee, the House resolved, that, to prevent the high price of wheat and bread, no spirits should be distilled from wheat for a limited time. While the bill formed on this resolution was in embryo, a petition was presented to the House by the brewers of London, Westminter, Southwark, and parts adjacent, representing, that, when the resolution passed, the price of malt, which was before too high, immediately rose to such a degree, that the petitioners found themselves utterly incapable of carrying on business at the price malt then bore, occasioned, as they conceived, from an apprehension of the necessity the distillers would be under to make use of the best pale malt, and substitute the best barley in lieu of wheat; that, in such a case, the markets would not be able to supply a sufficient quantity of barley for the demands of both professions, besides other necessary uses; they therefore prayed, that in regard to the public revenue, to which the trade of the petitioners so largely contributed, proper measures might be taken for preventing the public loss, and relieving their particular distress. The House would not lend a deaf ear to a remonstrance in which the revenue was concerned. The members appointed to prepare the bill immediately received instructions to make provision in it to restrain, for a limited time, the distilling of barley, malt, and all grain whatsoever. The bill was framed accordingly, but did not pass without strenuous opposition. To this prohibition it was objected, that there are always large quantities of wheat and barley in the kingdom so much damaged as to be unfit for any use but the distillery; consequently a restriction of this nature would ruin many farmers, and others employed in the trade of malting. Particular interests, however, must often be sacrificed to the welfare of the community; and the present distress prevailed over the prospect of this disadvantage. If they had allowed any sort of grain to be distilled, it would have been impossible to prevent the distilling of every kind. The prohibition was limited to two months; but, at the expiration of that term, the scarcity still continuing, it was protracted by a new bill to the eleventh day of December, with a proviso, empowering his majesty to put an end to it at any time after the eleventh day of May, if such a step should be judged for the advantage of the kingdom.

The next bill that engaged the attention of the Commons was a measure of the utmost national importance; though secretly disliked by many individuals of the legislature, who, nevertheless, did not venture to avow their disapprobation. *Militia bill.* The establishment of a militia was a very popular and desirable object, but attended with numberless difficulties, and a competition of interests which it was impossible to reconcile. It had formerly been an inexhaustible source of contention between the crown and the Commons; but now both apparently concurred in rendering it serviceable to the commonwealth, though some acquiesced in the scheme who were not at all hearty in its favour. On the fourth day of December, a motion was made for the bill, by Colonel George Townshend, eldest son of Lord Viscount Townshend, a gentleman of courage, sense, and probity; endued with penetration to discern, and honesty to pursue, the real interest of his country, in defiance of power, in contempt of private advantages. Leave being given to bring in a bill for the better ordering of the militia forces in the several counties of England, the task of preparing it was allotted to Mr. Townshend, and a considerable number of the most able members in the House, comprehending his own brother, Mr. Charles Townshend, whose genius shone with distinguished lustre: he was keen, discerning, eloquent, and accurate; possessed of a remarkable vivacity of parts, with a surprising solidity of understanding; was a wit without arrogance, a patriot without prejudice, and a courtier without dependence.

While the militia-bill remained under consideration in the House, a petition for a constitutional and well-regulated militia was presented by the mayor, jurats, and commonalty of the king's town and parish of Maidstone, in Kent, in common-council assembled. At the same time remonstrances were offered by the protestant dissenting ministers of the three denominations in and about the cities of London and Westminster; by the protestant dissenters of Shrewsbury; the dissenting ministers of Devonshire; the protestant dissenters, being freeholders and burgesses of the town and county of the town of Nottingham, joined with other inhabitants of the church of England, expressing their apprehension, that, in the bill then depending, it might be proposed to enact, that the said militia should be exercised on the Lord's day, commonly called Sunday, and praying that no clause for such purpose might pass into a law. Though nothing could be more ridiculously fanatic and impertinent than a declaration of such a scruple against a practice so laudable and necessary, in a country where that day of the week is generally spent in merry-making, riot, and debauchery, the House paid so much regard to the squeamish consciences of those puritanical petitioners, that Monday was pitched upon for the day of exercise to the militia, though on such working-days they might be much more profitably employed, both for themselves and their country; and that no religious pretence should be left for opposing the progress and execution of the bill, proper clauses were inserted for the relief of the quakers. Another petition and counter-petition were delivered by the magistrates, freeholders, and burgesses of the town of Nottingham, in relation to their particular franchise, which were accordingly considered in framing the bill.

*Petitions for and against it.*

After mature deliberation, and divers alterations, it passed the Lower House, and was sent to the Lords for their concurrence: here it underwent several amendments, one of which was the reduction of the number of militia-men to one half of what the Commons had proposed; namely, to thirty-two thousand three hundred and forty men for the whole kingdom of England and Wales. The amendments, being canvassed in the Lower House, met with some opposition, and divers conferences with their lordships ensued: at length, however, the two Houses agreed to every article, and the bill soon received the royal sanction. No provision, however, was made for clothes, arms, accoutrements, and pay; had regulations been made for these purposes, the act would have become a money-bill, in which the Lords could have made no amendment: in order, therefore, to prevent any difference between the two Houses, on a dispute of privileges not yet determined, and that the House of Peers might make what amendments they should think expedient, the Commons left the expense of the militia to be regulated in a subsequent bill, during the following session, when they could, with more certainty, compute what sum would be necessary for these purposes. After all, the bill seemed to be crude, imperfect, and ineffectual; and the promoters of it were well aware of its defects; but they were apprehensive that it would have been dropped altogether, had they insisted upon the scheme's being executed in its full extent. They were eager to seize this opportunity of trying an experiment, which might afterwards be improved to a greater national advantage; and therefore they acquiesced in many restrictions and alterations which otherwise would not have been adopted.

*Altered by the Lords.*

The next measure that fell under the consideration of the House was rendered necessary by the inhospitable perseverance of the publicans and innholders, who conceived themselves not obliged by law to receive or give quarters in their houses to any foreign troops, and accordingly refused admittance to the Hessian auxiliaries, who began to be dreadfully incommoded by the severity of the weather. This objection, implying an attack upon the prerogative, the government did not think fit, at this juncture, to dispute any other way, than by procuring a new law in favour of those foreigners. It was entitled, "A bill to make provision for quartering the foreign troops now in this kingdom;" prepared by Lord Barrington, the chancellor of the

*Bill for quartering the foreign troops, and for regulating the marines while on shore.*

exchequer, and the solicitor-general, and immediately passed without opposition. This step being taken, another bill was brought in, for the regulation of the marine forces while on shore. This was almost a transcript of the mutiny act, with this material difference: it empowered the Admiralty to grant commissions for holding general courts-martial, and to do every thing, and in the same manner as his majesty is empowered to do by the usual mutiny-bill; consequently, every clause was adopted without question.

The same favourable reception was given to a bill for the more speedy and effectual recruiting his majesty's land-forces and marines; a law which threw into the hands of many worthless magistrates an additional power of oppressing their fellow-creatures: all justices of the peace, commissioners for the land-tax, magistrates of corporations and boroughs, were empowered to meet by direction of the secretary at war, communicated in precepts issued by the high sheriffs, or their deputies, within their respective divisions, and at their usual places of meeting, to qualify themselves for the execution of the act: then they were required to appoint the times and places for their succeeding meetings; to issue precepts to the proper officers for these succeeding meetings; and to give notice of the time and place of every meeting to such military officers, as, by notice from the secretary-at-war, should be directed to attend that service. The annual bill for preventing mutiny and desertion met with no objections, and indeed contained nothing essentially different from that which had passed in the last session. The next law enacted was, for the further preventing embezzlement of goods and apparel, by those with whom they are entrusted, and putting a stop to the practice of gaming in public-houses. By this bill a penalty was inflicted on pawnbrokers, in a summary way, for receiving goods, knowing them not to be the property of the pledger, and pawned without the authority of the owner.[b] With respect to gaming, the act ordained, that

<small>[b] It was enacted, that persons pawning, exchanging, or disposing of goods, without leave of the owner, should suffer in the penalty of twenty shillings; and on nonpayment be committed for fourteen days to hard labour; afterwards, if the money could not then be paid, to be whipped publicly in the House of Correction, or such other place as the justice of the peace should appoint, on application of the prosecutor: that every pawnbroker should make entry of the person's name and place of abode who pledges any goods with him; and the pledger, if he required it, should have a duplicate of that entry; that a pawnbroker, receiving linen or apparel entrusted to others to be washed or mended,</small>

CHAP. XXVI. 1757.   GEORGE II.   637

all publicans suffering journeymen, labourers, servants, or apprentices, to game with cards, dice, shuffle-boards, Mississippi, or billiard-tables, skittles, nine-pins, &c., should forfeit forty shillings for the first offence, and for every subsequent offence ten pounds should be levied by distress.

Divers inconveniences having resulted from the interposition of justices, who, in pursuance of an act of Parliament passed in the present reign, assumed the right of establishing rates for the payment of wages to weavers, several petitions were offered to the House of Commons, representing the evil consequences of such an establishment; and although these arguments were answered and opposed in counter-petitions, the Commons, actuated by a laudable concern for the interest of the woollen manufacture, after due deliberation removed the grievance by a new bill, repealing so much of the former act as empowered justices of the peace to make rates for the payment of wages.[1] The Commons were not more forward to provide supplies for prosecuting the war with vigour, than ready to adopt regulations for the advantage of trade and manufactures. The society of the free British fishery presented a petition, alleging, that they had employed the sum of one hundred thirty thousand three hundred and five pounds, eight shillings, and six pence, together with the entire produce of their fish, and all the monies arising from the several branches allowed on the tonnage of their shipping, and on the exportation of their fish, in carrying on the said fishery: and that, from their being obliged, in the infancy of the undertaking, to incur a much larger expense than was at that time foreseen, they now found themselves so far reduced in their capital as to be utterly incapable of further

*Laws relating to the wages of weavers, and to the improvement of the British fishery.*

---

should forfeit double the sum lent upon it and restore the goods: that upon oath of any person whose goods are unlawfully pawned or exchanged, the justice shall issue a warrant to search the suspected person's house; and upon refusal of admittance the officer might break open the door: that goods pawned for any sum not exceeding ten pounds might be recovered within two years, the owner making oath of the pawning, and tendering the principal, interest, and charges; that goods remaining unredeemed for two years should be forfeited and sold, the overplus to be accounted for to the owner on demand.

[1] It likewise imported, that all contracts or agreements made between clothiers and weavers, in respect to wages, should, from and after the first of May, in the year one thousand seven hundred and fifty-seven, be valid, notwithstanding any rate established, or to be established; but that these contracts or agreements should extend only to the actual prices or rates of workmanship or wages, and not to the payment thereof in any other manner than in money; and that if any clothier should refuse or neglect to pay the weaver the wages or price agreed on, in money, within two days after the work should be performed and delivered, the same being demanded, he should forfeit forty shillings for every such offence.

prosecuting the fisheries with any hope of success, unless indulged with the further assistance of Parliament. They prayed, therefore, that towards enabling them to carry on the said fisheries, they might have liberty to make use of such nets as they should find best adapted to the said fisheries; each buss, nevertheless, carrying to sea the same quantity and depth of netting, which by the fishery-acts they were then bound to carry: that the bounty of thirty shillings per ton, allowed by the said acts on the vessels employed in the fishery, might be increased; and forasmuch as many of the stock-proprietors were unable to advance any further sum for prosecuting this branch of commerce; and others unwilling in the present situation, and under the present restraints, to risk any further sum in the undertaking; that the stock of the society, by the said acts made unalienable, except in case of death or bankruptcy, for a term of years, might forthwith be made transferable; and that the petitioners might be at liberty, between the intervals of the fishing-seasons, to employ the busses in such a manner as they should find for the advantage of the society. While the committee was employed in deliberating on the particulars of this remonstrance, another was delivered from the free British fishery-chamber of Whitehaven in Cumberland, representing, that as the law then stood, they went to Shetland and returned at a great expense and loss of time; and while the war continued, durst not stay there to fish, besides being obliged to run the most imminent risks, by going and returning without convoy: that ever since the institution of the present fishery, experience had fully shown the fishery of Shetland not worth following, as thereby the petitioners had lost two months of a much better fishery in St. George's channel, within one day's sail of Whitehaven: they took notice, that the free British fishery society had applied to the House for further assistance and relief; and prayed that Campbeltown, in Argyleshire, might be appointed the place of rendezvous for the busses belonging to Whitehaven, for the summer as well as the winter fishery, that they might be enabled to fish with greater advantage. The committee, having considered the matter of both petitions, were of opinion that the petitioners should be at liberty to use such nets as they should find best adapted to the white herring fishery: that the bounty of thirty shillings per ton should be augmented to fifty: that the petitioners should be allowed, during the intervals of the fishing-seasons, to employ their vessels in other lawful business, provided they should have been employed in the herring fishery during the proper seasons: that they might use such barrels for packing the fish as they then used, or might hereafter find best adapted for that purpose: that they should have liberty to make use of any waste or uncultivated land, one hundred yards at the least above highwater mark, for the purpose of drying their nets; and that Cambeltown would be the most proper and convenient place for the rendezvous of the busses belonging to Whitehaven. This last resolution, however, was not inserted in the bill which contained the other five; and in a little time received the royal assent.

Such are the connexions, dependencies, and relations subsisting between the mechanical arts, agriculture, and manufactures of Great Britain, that it requires study, deliberation, and inquiry in the legislature to discern and distinguish the whole scope and consequences of many projects offered for the benefit of the commonwealth. *Act for importing American iron, duty free.* The society of merchant-adventurers in the city of Bristol alleged, in a petition to the House of Commons, that great quantities of bar-iron were imported into Great Britain from Sweden, Russia, and other parts, chiefly purchased with ready money, some of which iron was exported again to Africa and other places, and the rest wrought up by the manufacturers. They affirmed that bar-iron imported from North America, would answer the same purposes; and the importation of it tend not only to the great advantage of the kingdom, by increasing its shipping and navigation, but also to the benefit of the British colonies: that by an act passed in the twenty-third year of his present majesty's reign, the importation of bar-iron from America into the port of London, duty free, was permitted; but its being carried coastways, or farther by land than ten miles, had been prohibited; so that several very considerable manufacturing towns were deprived of the use of American iron, and the outports prevented from employing it in their export commerce: they requested, therefore, that bar-iron might be imported from North America into Great Britain, duty free, by all his majesty's subjects. This request being reinforced by many other petitions from different parts of the kingdom, other classes of men, who thought several interests would be affected by such a measure, took the alarm; and, in divers counter-petitions, specified many ill consequences which they alleged would arise from its being enacted into a law. Pamphlets were published on both sides of the question, and violent disputes were kindled upon the subject, which was justly deemed a matter of national importance. The opposers of the bill observed, that large quantities of iron were yearly produced at home, and employed multitudes of poor people, there being no less than one hundred and nine forges in England and Wales, besides those erected in Scotland, the whole producing eighteen thousand tons of iron: that as the mines in Great Britain are inexhaustible, the produce would of late years have been considerably increased, had not the people been kept under continual apprehension of seeing American iron admitted duty-free; a supposition which had prevented the traders from extending their works, and discouraged many from engaging in this branch of traffic: they alleged that the iron-works already carried on in England, occasioned a consumption of one hundred and ninety-eight thousand cords of wood, produced in coppices that grow upon barren lands, which could not otherwise be turned to any good account; that as the coppices afford shade, and preserve a moisture in the ground, the pasture is more valuable with the wood, than it would be if the coppices were grubbed up; consequently all the estates where these now grow would sink in their yearly value: that these coppices, now cultivated and preserved for the use of the iron-works, are likewise absolutely necessary for the manufacture of leather, as they furnish bark for the tanners; and that, according to the management of these coppices, they produced a great number of timber trees, so necessary for the purposes of building. They asserted, that neither the American iron, nor any that had yet been found in Great Britain, was so proper for converting into steel as that which comes from Sweden, particularly that sort called Oregrund; but as there are mines in the northern parts of Britain, nearly in the same latitude with those of Sweden, furnished with sufficient quantities of wood, and rivers for mills and engines, it was hardly to be doubted but that people would find metal of the same quality, and, in a few years, be able to prevent the necessity of importing iron either from Sweden or Russia. They inferred that American iron could never interfere with that which Great Britain imported from Sweden; because it was not fit for edged tools, anchors, chain-plates, and other particulars necessary in ship-building; nor diminish the importation of Russian iron, which was not only harder than the American and British, but also could be afforded cheaper than that brought from our own plantations, even though the duty of this last should be removed. The importation of American iron, therefore, duty free, could interfere with no other sort but that produced in Britain, with which, by means of this advantage, it would clash so much, as to put a stop in a little time to all the iron-works now carried on in the kingdom, and reduce to beggary a great number of families whom they support. To these objections the favourers of the bill solicited replied, that when a manufacture is much more valuable than the rough materials, and these cannot be produced at home in sufficient quantities, and at such a price as is consistent with the preservation of the manufacture, it is the interest of the legislature to admit a free importation of these materials, even from foreign countries, although it should put an end to the production of that material in this island: that as the neighbours of Great Britain are now more attentive than ever to their commercial interests, and endeavouring to manufacture their rough materials at home, this nation must take every method for lowering the price of materials, otherwise in a few years it will lose the manufacture; and, instead of supplying other countries, be furnished by them with all the fine toys and utensils made of steel and iron: that being in danger of losing not only the manufacture but the produce of iron, unless it can be procured at a cheaper rate than that for which it is sold at present,—the only way of attaining this end is by diminishing the duty payable upon the importation of foreign iron; or by rendering it necessary for the undertakers of the iron mines in Great Britain to sell their produce cheaper than it has been for some years afforded: that the most effectual method for this purpose is to raise up a rival, by permitting a free importation of all sorts of iron from the American plantations: that American iron can never be sold so cheap as that of Britain can be afforded; for, in the colonies, labour of all kinds is much dearer than in England: if a man employs his own slaves, he must reckon in his charge a great deal more than the common interest of their purchase money; because, when one of them dies, or escapes from his master, he loses both interest and principal: that the common interest of money in the plantations is considerably higher than in England, consequently no man in that country will employ his money in any branch of trade by which he cannot gain considerably more per cent. than is expected in Great Britain, where the interest is low, and profit moderate; a circumstance which will always give a great advantage to the British miner, who likewise enjoys an exemption from freight and insurance, which lie heavy upon the American adventurer, especially in time of war. With respect to the apprehension of the leather-tanners, they observed, that as the coppices generally grew on barren lands, not fit for tillage, and improved the pasturage, no proprietor would be at the expense of grubbing up the wood to spoil the pasture, as he could make no other use of the land on which it was produced. The wood must be always worth something, especially in counties where there is not plenty of coal, and the timber trees would produce considerable advantage: therefore, if there was not one iron mine in Great Britain, no coppice would be grubbed up, unless it grew on a rich soil, which would produce corn instead of cord-wood; consequently, the tanners have nothing to fear; especially as planting hath become a prevailing taste among the landholders of the island. The committee appointed to prepare the bill seriously weighed and canvassed these arguments, examined disputed facts, and inspected papers and accounts relating to the produce, importation, and manufactory of iron. At length Mr. John Pitt reported to the House their opinion, implying that the liberty granted by an act passed in the twenty-third year of his majesty's reign, of importing bar-iron from the British colonies in America into the port of London, should be extended to all the other ports of Great Britain; and that so much of that act as related to this clause should be repealed. The House having agreed to these resolutions, and the bill being brought in accordingly, another petition was presented by several noblemen, gentlemen, freeholders, and other proprietors, owners, and possessors of coppices and woodlands, in the west riding of Yorkshire, alleging, that a permission to import American bar-iron, duty free, would be attended with numberless ill consequences both of a public and private nature; specifying 'certain hardships to which they in particular would be exposed; and praying that, if the bill should pass, they might be relieved from the pressure of an act passed in the reign of Henry VIII., obliging the owners of coppice-woods to preserve them, under severe penalties; and be permitted to fell and grub up their coppice-woods, in order to a more proper cultivation of the soil, without being restrained by the fear of malicious and interested prosecutions. In consequence of this remonstrance, a clause was added to the bill, repealing so much of the act of Henry VIII. as prohibited the conversion of coppice or underwoods into pasture or tillage; then it passed through both Houses, and received the royal sanction. As there was not time, after this affair came upon the carpet, to obtain any new accounts from America, and as it was thought necessary to know the quantities of iron made in that country, the House presented an address to his majesty, desiring he would be pleased to give directions that there should be laid before them, in the next session of Parliament, an account of the quantity of iron made in the American colonies, from Christmas, in the year one thousand seven hundred and forty-nine, to the fifth day of January, in the year one thousand seven hundred and fifty-six, each year being distinguished.

From this important object, the Parliament converted its attention to a regulation of a much more private nature. In consequence of a petition by the lord mayor, aldermen, and commons of the city of London, a bill was brought in, and passed into a law without opposition, for the more effectual preservation and improvement of the fry and spawn of fish in the river Thames, and waters of the Medway, and for the better regulating the fishery in those rivers. The two next measures taken for the benefit of the public were, first a bill to render more effectual the several laws then in being, for the amendment and preservation of the highways and turnpike roads of the kingdom; the other for the more effectually preventing the spreading of the contagious distemper which, at that time, raged among the horned cattle. A third arose from the distress of poor silk manufacturers, who were destitute of employment, and deprived of all means of subsisting, through the interruption of the Levant trade, occasioned by war, and the delay of the merchant-ships from Italy. In order to remedy this inconvenience, a bill was prepared,

*Regulations with respect to the importation of silk.*

enacting, that any persons might import from any place, in any ship or vessel whatsoever, till the first day of December, one thousand seven hundred and fifty-seven, organzine thrown silk of the growth or production of Italy, to be brought to the custom-house of London, wheresoever landed; but that no Italian thrown silk, coarser than Bologna, nor any tram of the growth of Italy, nor any other thrown silk of the growth or production of Turkey, Persia, East India, or China, should be imported by this act, under the penalty of the forfeiture thereof. Notwithstanding several petitions, presented by the merchants, owners, and commanders of ships, and others trading to Leghorn, and other ports of Italy, as well as by the importers and manufacturers of raw silks, representing the evil consequences that would probably attend the passing of such a bill, the Parliament agreed to this temporary deviation from the famous act of navigation, for a present supply to the poor manufacturers.

The next civil regulation established in this session of Parliament was in itself judicious, and, had it been more eagerly suggested, might have been much more beneficial to the public. In order to discourage the practice of smuggling, and prevent the desperadoes concerned therein from enlisting in the service of the enemy, a law was passed, enacting, that every person who had been, before the first of May in the present year, guilty of illegal running, concealing, receiving, or carrying any wool, or prohibited goods, or any foreign commodities liable to duties, the same not having been paid or secured; or of aiding therein, or had been found with fire-arms or weapons, in order to be aiding to such offenders; or had been guilty of receiving such goods after seizure; or of any act whatsoever, whereby persons might be deemed runners of foreign goods; or of hindering, wounding, or beating any officer in the execution of his duty, or assisting therein, should be indemnified from all such offences, concerning which no suit should then have been commenced, or composition made, on condition that he should, before being apprehended or prosecuted, and before the first day of December, enter himself with some commissioned officer of his majesty's fleet, to serve as a common sailor; and should, for three years from such entry, unless sooner fully discharged, actually serve and do duty in that station, and register his name, &c., with the clerk of the peace of the county where he

*Smugglers encouraged to enter into his majesty's service.*

resided, as the act prescribes. An attempt was made in favour of the seamen employed in the navy, who had been very irregularly paid, and subject to grievous hardships in consequence of this irregularity: Mr. Grenville, brother to Earl Temple, moved for leave to bring in a bill for the encouragement of seamen employed in his majesty's navy, and for establishing a regular method for the punctual, speedy, and certain payment of their wages, as well as for rescuing them from the arts of fraud and imposition. The proposal was corroborated by divers petitions; the bill was prepared, read, printed, and after it had undergone some amendment, passed into the House of Lords, where it was encountered with several objections, and dropped for this session of Parliament.

The House of Commons being desirous of preventing, for the future, such distresses as the poor had lately undergone, appointed a committee to consider of proper provisions to restrain the price of corn and bread within due bounds for the future. For this purpose they were empowered to send for persons, papers, and records; and it was resolved, that all who attended the committee should have voices. Having inquired into the causes of the late scarcity, they agreed to several resolutions, and a bill was brought in to explain and amend the laws against regraters, forestallers, and engrossers of corn. The committee also received instructions to inquire into the abuses of millers, mealmen, and bakers, with regard to bread, and to consider of proper methods to prevent them in the sequel; but no further progress was made in this important affair, which was the more interesting, as the lives of individuals, in a great measure, depended upon a speedy reformation; for the millers and bakers were said to have adulterated their flour with common whiting, lime, bone-ashes, alum, and other ingredients pernicious to the human constitution: a consummation of villany for which no adequate punishment could be inflicted. Among the measures proposed in Parliament which did not succeed, one of the most remarkable was a bill prepared by Mr. Rose Fuller, Mr. Charles Townshend, and Mr. Banks, to explain, amend, and render more effectual a law passed in the reign of King William the Third, entitled "An Act to punish Governors of Plantations, in this Kingdom, for Crimes committed by them in the Plantations." This bill was proposed in consequence of some complaints,

*Inquiry into the scarcity of corn.*

specifying acts of cruelty, folly, and oppression, by which some British governors had been lately distinguished; but before the bill could be brought in, the Parliament was prorogued.

But no step taken by the House of Commons in the course of this session was more interesting to the body of the people than the inquiry into the loss of Minorca, which had excited such loud and universal clamour. By addresses to the king, unanimously voted, the Commons requested that his majesty would give directions for laying before them copies of all the letters and papers containing any intelligence received by the secretaries of state, the commissioners of the Admiralty, or any other of his majesty's ministers, in relation to the equipment of the French fleet at Toulon, or the designs of the French on Minorca, or any other of his majesty's possessions in Europe, since the first day of January, in the year one thousand seven hundred and fifty-five, to the first day of August, one thousand seven hundred and fifty-six. They likewise desired to peruse a list of the ships of war that were equipped and made ready for sea, from the first of August, in the year one thousand seven hundred and fifty-five, to the thirtieth day of April, in the following year; with the copies of all sailing orders sent to the commanders during that period; as also the state and condition of his majesty's ships in the several ports of Great Britain at the time of Admiral Byng's departure, with the squadron under his command, for the relief of fort St. Philip, during the period of time above-mentioned, according to the monthly returns made by the Admiralty, with the number of seamen mustered and borne on board the respective ships. They demanded copies of all orders and instructions given to that admiral, and of letters written to and received from him, during his continuance in that command, either by the secretaries of state, or lords of the Admiralty, relating to the condition of his squadron, and to the execution of his orders. In a word, they required the inspection of all papers, which could in any manner tend to explain the loss of Minorca, and the miscarriage of Mr. Byng's squadron. His majesty complied with every article of their requests: the papers were presented to the House, ordered to lie upon the table for the perusal of the members, and finally referred to the consideration of a committee of the whole House. In the course of their deliberations they addressed his majesty for more information, till at length the truth seemed to be smothered under such an enormous burden of papers, as the efforts of a whole session could not have properly removed. Indeed, many discerning persons without doors began to despair of seeing the mystery unfolded, as soon as the inquiry was undertaken by a committee of the whole House. They observed, that an affair of such a dark, intricate, and suspicious nature, ought to have been referred to a select and secret committee, chosen by ballot, empowered to send for persons, papers, and records, and to examine witnesses in the most solemn and deliberate manner; that the names of the committee ought to have been published for the satisfaction of the people, who could have judged, with some certainty, whether the inquiry would be carried on with such impartiality as the national misfortune required. They suspected that this reference to a committee of the whole House was a malcontrivance, to prevent a regular and minute investigation, to introduce confusion and contest, to puzzle, perplex, and obumbrate; to tease, fatigue, and disgust the inquirers, that the examination might be hurried over in a superficial and perfunctory manner; and the ministry, from this anarchy and confusion of materials, half explored and undigested, derive a general parliamentary approbation, to which they might appeal from the accusations of the people. A select committee would have probably examined some of the clerks of the respective officers, that they might certainly know whether any letters or papers had been suppressed, whether the extracts had been faithfully made, and whether there might not be papers of intelligence, which, though proper to be submitted to a select and secret committee, could not, consistently with the honour of the nation, be communicated to a committee of the whole House. Indeed, it does not appear that the ministers had any foreign intelligence or correspondence that could be much depended upon in any matter of national importance, and no evidence was examined on the occasion; a circumstance the less to be regretted, as, in times past, evil ministers have generally found means to render such inquiries ineffectual; and the same arts would at any rate have operated with the same efficacy, had a secret committee been employed at this juncture. Be that as it may, several resolutions were reported from the committee, though some of them were not carried by the majority without violent dispute and severe altercation. The first and last of their resolutions require particular notice. By the former, it appeared to the committee, that his majesty, from the twenty-seventh day of August, in the year one thousand seven hundred and fifty-five, to the twentieth day of April in the succeeding year, received such repeated and concurrent intelligence, as gave just reason to believe that the French king intended to invade his dominions of Great Britain or Ireland. In the latter they declare their opinion, that no greater number of ships of war could be sent into the Mediterranean than were actually sent thither under the command of Admiral Byng; nor any greater reinforcement than the regiment which was sent, and the detachment, equal to a battalion, which was ordered to the relief of fort St. Philip, consistently with the state of the navy, and the various services essential to the safety of his majesty's dominions, and the interests of his subjects. It must have been something more powerful than ordinary conviction that suggested these opinions. Whatever reports might have been circulated by the French ministry, in order to amuse, intimidate, and detach the attention of the English government from America and the Mediterranean, where they really intended to exert themselves, yet, the circumstances of the two nations being considered, one would think there could have been no just grounds to fear an invasion of Great Britain or Ireland, especially when other intelligence seemed to point out much more probable scenes of action. But the last resolution is still more incomprehensible to those who know not exactly the basis on which it was raised. The number of ships of war in actual commission amounted to two hundred and fifty, having on board fifty thousand seamen and marines. Intelligence and repeated information of the French designs upon Minorca had been conveyed to the ministry of England, about six months before it was put in execution. Is it credible, that in all this time the nation could not equip or spare above eleven ships of the line and six frigates, to save the important island of Minorca? Is it easy to conceive, that from a standing army of fifty thousand men, one regiment of troops could not have been detached to reinforce a garrison, well known to be insufficient for the works it was destined to defend? To persons of common intellects it appeared, that intelligence of the armament at Toulon was conveyed to the Admiralty as early as the month of September, in the year one thousand seven hundred and fifty-five, with express notice that it would consist of twelve ships of the line; that the design against Minorca was communicated as early as the twenty-seventh day of August, by Consul Banks, of Carthagena; confirmed by letters from Consul Bertes, at Genoa, dated on the seventeenth and twenty-sixth of January, and received by Mr. Fox, secretary of state, on the fourth and eleventh of February, as well as by many subsequent intimations; that, notwithstanding these repeated advices, even after hostilities had commenced in Europe, when the garrison of Minorca amounted to no more than four incomplete regiments, and one company of artillery, forty-two officers being absent, and the place otherwise unprovided for a siege, when the Mediterranean squadron, commanded by Mr. Edgecumbe, consisted of two ships of the line, and five frigates; neither stores, ammunition, nor provision, the absent officers belonging to the garrison, recruits for the regiments, though ready raised, miners, nor any additional troops, were sent to the island, nor the squadron augmented, till Admiral Byng sailed from Spithead on the sixth day of April, with no more ships of the line than, by the most early and authentic intelligence, the government were informed would sail from Toulon, even when Mr. Byng should have been joined by Commodore Edgecumbe; a junction upon which no dependence ought to have been laid; that this squadron contained no troops but such as belonged to the four regiments in garrison, except one battalion to serve in the fleet as marines, unless we include the order for another to be embarked at Gibraltar; which order was neither obeyed nor understood; that, considering the danger to which Minorca was exposed, and the forwardness of the enemy's preparations at Toulon, Admiral Osborne, with thirteen ships of the line and one frigate, who returned on the sixteenth of February, after having convoyed a fleet of merchant-ships, might have been detached to Minorca, without hazarding the coast of Great Britain; for at that time, exclusive of this squadron, there were eight ships of the line and thirty-two frigates ready manned, and thirty-two ships of the line and five frigates almost equipped; that Admiral Hawke was sent with fourteen ships of the line and one frigate to cruise in the bay of Biscay, after repeated intelligence had been received that the French fleet had sailed for the West Indies, and the eleven ships remaining at Brest and Rochefort were in want of hands and cannon, so that they could never serve to cover any embarkation or descent; consequently, Mr. Hawke's squadron might have been spared for the relief of Minorca; that instead of attending to this important object, the Admiralty, on the eighth day of March, sent two ships of the line and three frigates to intercept a coasting convoy off Cape Barfleur; on the eleventh of the same month they detached two ships of the line to the West Indies, and on the nineteenth two more to North America, where they could be of little immediate service; on the twenty-third two of the line and three frigates a convoy-hunting off Cherbourg; and on the first of April five ships of the line, including three returned from this last service, to reinforce Sir Edward Hawke, already too strong for the French fleet bound to Canada; that all these ships might have been added to Mr. Byng's squadron, without exposing Great Britain or Ireland to any hazard of invasion; that at length Mr. Byng was detached with ten great ships only, and even denied a frigate to repeat signals, for which he petitioned; although at that very time there were in port, exclusive of his squadron, seventeen ships of the line and thirteen frigates ready for sea, besides eleven of the line and nineteen frigates almost equipped. From these and other circumstances, particularized and urged with great vivacity, many individuals inferred, that a greater number of ships might have been detached to the Mediterranean than were actually sent with Admiral Byng; that the not sending an earlier and stronger force was one great cause of Minorca's being lost, and co-operated with the delay of the ministry in sending thither reinforcements of troops, their neglect in suffering the officers of the garrison to continue absent from their duty, and their omitting to give orders for raising miners to serve in the fortress of Mahon.

*Examination of the American contract.* The next inquiry in which the House of Commons engaged related to the contracts for victualling the forces in America, which were supposed by some patriots to be fraudulent and unconscionable. This suspicion arose from an ambiguous expression, on which the contractor being interrogated by the committee appointed to examine the particulars, he prudently interpreted it in such a manner as to screen himself from the resentment of the legislature. The House, therefore, resolved that the contract entered into on the twenty-sixth day of March, in the year one thousand seven hundred and fifty-six, by the commissioners of the treasury, with William Baker, Christopher Kilby, and Richard Baker of London, merchants, for furnishing provisions to the forces under the command of the Earl of Loudoun, was prudent and necessary, and properly adapted to the securing a constant and effectual supply for those forces in America.

The preceding session an address had been presented to the king by the House of Commons, desiring his majesty would give orders for laying before them several papers relating to disputes which had lately happened between his excellency, Charles Knowles, Esq., and some of the principal inhabitants of the island of Jamaica. *Inquiry into the conduct of Admiral Knowles as governor of Jamaica.* This governor was accused of many illegal, cruel, and arbitrary acts, during the course of his administration: but these imputations he incurred by an exertion of power, which was in itself laudable, and well intended for the commercial interest of the island. This was his changing the seat of government, and procuring an act of assembly for removing the several laws, records, books, papers, and writings belonging to several offices in that island, from Spanish-town to Kingston; and for obliging the several officers to keep their offices, and hold a supreme court of judicature at this last place, to which he had moved the seat of government. Spanish-town, otherwise called St. Jago de la Vega, the old capital, was an inconsiderable inland place, of no security, trade, or importance; whereas Kingston was the centre of commerce, situated on the side of a fine harbour filled with ships, well secured from the insults of an enemy, large, wealthy, and flourishing. Here the merchants dwell, and ship the greatest part of the sugars that grow upon the island. They found it extremely inconvenient and expensive to take out their clearances at Spanish-town, which stands at a considerable distance; and the same inconvenience and expense being felt by the rest of the inhabitants, who had occasion to prosecute suits at law, or attend the assembly of the island, they joined in representations to the governor, requesting that, in consideration of these inconveniences, added to that of the weakness of Spanish-town and the importance of Kingston, the seat of government might be removed. He complied with their request, and in so doing entailed upon himself the hatred and resentment of certain powerful planters who possessed estates in and about the old town of St. Jago de la Vega, thus deserted. This seems to have been the real source of the animosity and clamour incurred by Mr. Knowles, against whom a petition, signed by nineteen members of the assembly, had been sent to England, and presented to his majesty. In the two sessions preceding this year the affair had been brought into the House of Commons, where this governor's character was painted in frightful colours, and divers papers relating to the dispute were examined. Mr. Knowles having by this time returned to England, the subject of his administration was revived, and referred to a committee of the whole House. In the mean time, petitions were presented by several merchants of London and Liverpool, concerned in the trade to Jamaica, alleging, that the removal of the public courts, offices, and records of the island of Jamaica to Kingston, and fixing the seat of government there, had been productive of many important advantages, by rendering the strength of the island more formidable, the property of the traders and inhabitants more secure, and the prosecution of all commercial business more expeditious and less expensive than formerly; therefore, praying that the purposes of the act passed in Jamaica for that end might be carried into effectual execution, in such manner as the House should think proper. The committee having examined a great number of papers, agreed to some resolutions, importing, that a certain resolution of the assembly of Jamaica, dated on the twenty-ninth day of October, in the year one thousand seven hundred and fifty-three, implying a claim of right in that assembly to raise and apply public money without the consent of the governor and council, was illegal, repugnant to the terms of his majesty's commission to his governor of the said island, and derogatory to the rights of the crown and people of Great Britain; that the last six resolutions taken in the assembly of Jamaica, on the twenty-ninth day of October, in the year one thousand seven hundred and fifty-three, proceeded on a manifest misapprehension of the king's instruction to his governor, requiring him not to give his assent to any bill of an unusual or extraordinary nature and importance, wherein his majesty's prerogative, or the property of his subjects, might be prejudiced, or the trade or shipping of the kingdom any ways affected, unless there should be a clause inserted, suspending the execution of such bill until his majesty's pleasure should be known; that such instruction was just and necessary, and no alteration of the constitution of the island, nor any way derogatory to the rights of the subjects in Jamaica. From these resolutions the reader may perceive the nature of the dispute which had arisen between the people of Jamaica and their governor, Vice-Admiral Knowles, whose conduct on this occasion seems to have been justified by the legislature. The Parliament, however, forbore to determine the question, whether the removal of the courts of judicature from Spanish-town to Kingston was a measure calculated for the interest of the island in general.

The last subject which we shall mention as having fallen under the cognizance of the Commons during this session of Parliament was the state of Milford-haven on the coast of Wales, one of the most capacious, safe, and commodious harbours in Great Britain. Here the country affords many conveniences for building ships of war, and erecting forts, docks, quays, and magazines. It might be fortified at a very small expense, so as to be quite secure from any attempts of the enemy, and rendered by far the most useful harbour in the kingdom for fleets, cruisers, trading-ships, and packet-boats, bound to and from the westward; for, from hence they may put to sea almost with any wind, and even at low water: they may weather Scilly and Cape Clear when no vessel can stir from the British channel, or out of the French ports of Brest and Rochefort; and as a post can travel from hence in three days to London, it might become the centre of very useful sea intelligence. A petition from several merchants in London was presented, and recommended to the House in a message from the king, specifying the advantages of this harbour, and the small expense at which it might be fortified, and praying that the House would take this important subject into consideration. Accordingly, a committee was appointed for this purpose, with power to send for persons, papers, and records; and every circumstance relating to it was examined with accuracy and deliberation. At length the report being made to the House by Mr. Charles Townshend, they unanimously agreed to an address, representing to his majesty, that many great losses had been sustained by the trade of the kingdom, in time of war, from the want of a safe harbour on the western coast of the island, for the reception and protection

*Resolutions concerning Milford-haven.*

of merchant-ships, and sending out cruisers; that the harbour of Milford-haven, in the county of Pembroke, is most advantageously situated, and, if properly defended and secured, in every respect adapted to the answering those important puposes; they, therefore, humbly besought his majesty that he would give immediate directions for erecting batteries, with proper cover, on the sides of the said harbour, in the most convenient places for guarding the entrance called Hubberstone-road, and also such other fortifications as might be necessary to secure the interior parts of the harbour; and that, until such batteries and fortifications could be completed, some temporary defence might be provided for the immediate protection of the ships and vessels lying in the said harbour; finally, they assured him the House would make good to his majesty all such expenses as should be incurred for these purposes. The address met with a gracious reception, and a promise that such directions should be given. The harbour was actually surveyed, the places were pitched upon for batteries, and the estimates prepared, but no further progress has since been made.

We have now finished the detail of all the material transactions of this session, except what relates to the fate of Admiral Byng, which now claims our attention. In the mean time we may observe, that on the fourth day of July the session was closed with his majesty's harangue; the most remarkable and pleasing paragraph of which turned upon his royal assurance, that the succour and preservation of his dominions in America had been his constant care, and, next to the security of his kingdoms, should continue to be his great and principal object. He told them he had taken such measures as, he trusted, by the blessing of God, might effectually disappoint the designs of the enemy in those parts; that he had no further view but to vindicate the just rights of his crown and subjects from the most injurious encroachments; to preserve tranquillity, as far as the circumstances of things might admit; to prevent the true friends of Britain, and the liberties of Europe, from being oppressed and endangered by any unprovoked and unnatural conjunction.

*Session closed.*

Of all the transactions that distinguished this year, the most extraordinary was the sentence executed on Admiral Byng, the son of that great officer who had acquired such honour by his naval exploits in

*Trial of Admiral Byng.*

the preceding reign, and was ennobled for his services by the title of Lord Viscount Torrington. His second son, John Byng, had from his earliest youth been trained to his father's profession; and was generally esteemed one of the best officers in the navy, when he embarked in that expedition to Minorca, which covered his character with disgrace, and even exposed him to all the horrors of an ignominious death. On the twenty-eighth day of December his trial began before a court-martial, held on board the ship St. George, in the harbour of Portsmouth, to which place Mr. Byng had been conveyed from Greenwich by a party of horse-guards, and insulted by the populace in every town and village through which he passed. The court having proceeded to examine the evidences for the crown and the prisoner, from day to day, in the course of a long sitting, agreed unanimously to thirty-seven resolutions, implying their opinion, that Admiral Byng, during the engagement between the British and French fleets, on the twentieth day of May last, did not do his utmost endeavour to take, seize, and destroy the ships of the French king, which it was his duty to have engaged, and to assist such of his majesty's ships as were engaged, which it was his duty to have assisted; and that he did not exert his utmost power for the relief of St. Philip's castle. They, therefore, unanimously agreed that he fell under part of the twelfth article of an act of Parliament passed in the twenty-second year of the present reign, for amending, explaining, and reducing into one act of parliament, the laws relating to the government of his majesty's ships, vessels, and forces by sea; and as that article positively prescribed death, without any alternative left to the discretion of the court under any variation of circumstances, they unanimously adjuged the said Admiral John Byng to be shot to death, at such time, and on board of such ship, as the lords commissioners of the Admiralty should please to direct. But as it appeared by the evidence of the officers who were near the admiral's person, that no backwardness was perceivable in him during the action, nor any mark of fear or confusion either in his countenance or behaviour; but that he delivered his orders coolly and distinctly, without seeming deficient in personal courage; and, from other circumstances, they believed his misconduct did not arise either from cowardice or disaffection, they unanimously and earnestly recommended him as a proper object of mercy. The admiral himself behaved through the whole trial with the most cheerful composure, seemingly the effect of conscious innocence, upon which, perhaps, he too much relied. Even after he had heard the evidence examined against him, and finished his own defence, he laid his account in being honourably acquitted; and ordered his coach to be ready for conveying him directly from the tribunal to London. A gentleman, his friend, by whom he was attended, having received intimation of the sentence to be pronounced, thought it his duty to prepare him for the occasion, that he might summon all his fortitude to his assistance, and accordingly made him acquainted with the information he had received. The admiral gave tokens of surprise and resentment, but betrayed no marks of fear or disorder, either then, or in the court when the sentence was pronounced. On the contrary, while divers members of the court-martial manifested grief, anxiety, and trepidation, shedding tears, and sighing with extraordinary emotion, he heard his doom denounced without undergoing the least alteration of feature, and made a low obeisance to the president and the other members of the court as he retired.

*Recommended to mercy.* The officers who composed this tribunal were so sensible of the law's severity, that they unanimously subscribed a letter to the board of Admiralty, containing this remarkable paragraph:—" We cannot help laying the distresses of our minds before your lordships on this occasion, in finding ourselves under necessity of condemning a man to death, from the great severity of the twelfth article of war, part of which he falls under, which admits of no mitigation if the crime should be committed by an error in judgment; and, therefore, for our own consciences' sake, as well as in justice to the prisoner, we pray your lordships, in the most earnest manner, to recommend him to his majesty's clemency." The lords of the Admiralty, instead of complying with the request of the court-martial, transmitted their letter to the king, with copies of their proceedings, and a letter from themselves to his majesty, specifying a doubt with regard to the legality of the sentence, as the crime of negligence, for which the admiral had been condemned, was not expressed in any part of the proceedings. At the same time, copies of two petitions from George, Lord Viscount Torrington, in behalf of his kinsman Admiral Byng, were submitted to his majesty's royal wisdom and determination.

All the friends and relations of the unhappy convict employed and exerted their influence and interest for his pardon; and as the circumstances had appeared so strong in his favour, it was supposed that the sceptre of royal mercy would be extended for his preservation; but infamous arts were used to whet the savage appetite of the populace for blood. The cry of vengeance was loud throughout the land; sullen clouds of suspicion and malevolence interposing were said to obstruct the genial beams of the best virtue that adorns the throne; and the sovereign was given to understand, that the execution of Admiral Byng was a sacrifice absolutely necessary to appease the fury of the people. His majesty, in consequence of the representation made by the lords of the Admiralty, referred the sentence to the consideration of the twelve judges, who were unanimously of opinion that the sentence was legal. This report being transmitted from the privy-council to the Admiralty, their lordships issued a warrant for executing the sentence of death on the twenty-eighth day of February. One gentleman at the board, however, refused to subscribe the warrant, assigning for his refusal the reasons which we have inserted by way of note, for the satisfaction of the reader.[k]

[k] Admiral F——e's reasons for not signing the warrant for Admiral Byng's execution:—

"It may be thought great presumption in me to differ from so great authority as that of the twelve judges; but when a man is called upon to sign his name to an act which is to give authority to the shedding of blood, he ought to be guided by his own conscience, and not by the opinions of other men.

"In the case before us, it is not the merit of Admiral Byng that I consider: whether he deserves death or not, is not a question for me to decide; but whether or not his life can be taken away by the sentence pronounced on him by the court-martial, and after having so clearly explained their motives for pronouncing such a sentence, is the point which alone has employed my serious consideration.

"The twelfth article of war, on which Admiral Byng's sentence is grounded, says, (according to my understanding of its meaning,) 'That every person, who, in the time of action, shall withdraw, keep back, or not come into fight, to do his utmost, &c., through motives of cowardice, negligence, or disaffection, shall suffer death.' The court-martial does, in express words, acquit Admiral Byng of cowardice and disaffection, and does not name the word negligence. Admiral Byng does not, as I conceive, fall under the letter or description of the twelfth article of war. It may be said, that negligence is implied, though the word is not mentioned, otherwise the court-martial would not have brought his offence under the twelfth article, having acquitted him of cowardice and disaffection. But it must be acknowledged that the negligence implied cannot be wilful negligence; for wilful negligence in Admiral Byng's situation must have proceeded either from cowardice or disaffection, and he is expressly acquitted of both these crimes; besides, these crimes, which are implied only, and not named, may indeed justify suspicion and private opinion, but cannot satisfy the conscience in case of blood.

"Admiral Byng's fate was referred to a court-martial; his life and death were left to their opinions. The court-martial condemn him to death, because, as they expressly say, they were under a necessity of doing so by reason of the letter of the law, the severity of which they complained of, because it admits of no mitigation. The court-martial expressly say, that for the sake of their consciences, as well as in justice to the prisoner, they most earnestly recommend him to his majesty for mercy: it is evident, then, that in the opinions and consciences of the judges he was not deserving of death. "The

Though mercy was denied to the criminal, the crown seemed determined to do nothing that should be thought inconsistent with law.—A member of Parliament, who had sat upon the court-martial at Portsmouth, rose up in his place, and made application to the House of Commons in behalf of himself and several other members of that tribunal, praying the aid of the legislature to be released from the oath of secrecy imposed on courts-martial, that they might disclose the grounds on which sentence of death had passed on Admiral Byng, and, perhaps, discover such circumstances as might show the sentence to be improper. Although this application produced no resolution in the House, the king, on the twenty-sixth day of February, sent a message to the Commons by Mr. Secretary Pitt, importing, that though he had determined to let the law take its course with relation to Admiral Byng, and resisted all solicitations to the contrary, yet, as a member of the House had expressed some scruples about the sentence, his majesty had thought fit to respite the execution of it, that there might be an opportunity of knowing, by the separate examination of the members of the court-martial, upon oath, what grounds there were for such scruples, and that his majesty was resolved still to let the sentence be carried into execution, unless it should appear from the said examination that Admiral Byng was unjustly condemned. The sentence might be strictly legal, and at the same time very severe, according to the maxim, *summum jus, summa injuria*. In such cases, and perhaps in such cases only, the rigour of the law ought to be softened by the lenient hand of the royal prerogative. That this

<sub>Message from the king to the Parliament respecting the sentence.</sub>

---

"The question then is, shall the opinions or necessities of the court-martial determine Admiral Byng's fate? If it should be the latter, he will be executed contrary to the intentions and meaning of his judges: if the former, his life is not forfeited. His judges declare him not deserving of death; but, mistaking either the meaning of the law, or the nature of his offence, they bring him under an article of war, which, according to their own description of his offence, he does not, I conceive, fall under; and then they condemn him to death because, as they say, the law admits of no mitigation. Can a man's life be taken away by such a sentence? I would not willingly be misunderstood, and have it believed that I judge of Admiral Byng's deserts; that was the business of a court-martial, and it is my duty only to act according to my conscience; which, after deliberate consideration, assisted by the best light a poor understanding can afford it, remains still in doubt; and therefore I cannot consent to sign a warrant whereby the sentence of the court-martial may be carried into execution; for I cannot help thinking, that however criminal Admiral Byng may be, his life is not forfeited by that sentence. I do not mean to find fault with other men's opinions: all I endeavour at is to give reasons for my own; and all I desire or wish is, that I may not be misunderstood; I do not pretend to judge Admiral Byng's deserts, nor to give any opinion on the propriety of the act.

"Signed, 6th Feb. 1757, at the Admiralty.

"J. F——S."

was the case of Admiral Byng appears from the warm and eager intercession of his jury; a species of intercession which hath generally, if not always, prevailed at the foot of the throne, when any thing favourable for the criminal had appeared in the course of the trial. How much more then might it have been expected to succeed, when earnestly urged as a case of conscience in behalf of a man whom his judges had expressly acquitted of cowardice and treachery, the only two imputations that rendered him criminal in the eyes of the nation! Such an interposition of the crown in parliamentary transactions was irregular, unnecessary, and at another juncture might have been productive of violent heats and declamation. At present, however, it passed without censure, as the effect of inattention rather than a design to encroach upon the privileges of the House.

The message being communicated, a bill was immediately brought in to release the members of the court-martial from the obligation of secrecy, and passed through the Lower House without opposition: but in the House of Lords it appeared to be destitute of a proper foundation. They sent a message to the Commons, desiring them to give leave that such of the members of the court-martial as were members of that House might attend their lordships, in order to be examined on the second reading of the bill; accordingly they, and the rest of the court-martial, attended, and answered all questions without hesitation. As they did not insist upon any excuse, nor produce any satisfactory reason for showing that the man they had condemned was a proper object of mercy, their lordships were of opinion that there was no occasion for passing any such bill, which, therefore, they almost unanimously rejected. It is not easy to conceive what stronger reason could be given for proving Mr. Byng an object of mercy than those mentioned in the letter sent to the board of Admiralty by the members of the court-martial, who were empowered to try the imputed offence, consequently must have been deemed well qualified to judge of his conduct. *Bill to release the members of the court-martial from their oath of secrecy.*

The unfortunate Admiral, being thus abandoned to the stroke of justice, prepared himself for death with resignation and tranquillity. He maintained a surprising cheerfulness to the last; nor did he, from his condemnation to his execution, exhibit the least sign *Execution of Admiral Byng.*

of impatience or apprehension. During that interval he had remained on board of the Monarque, a third-rate ship of war, anchored in the harbour of Portsmouth, under a strong guard, in custody of the Marshal of the Admiralty. On the fourteenth of March, the day fixed for his execution, the boats belonging to the squadron at Spithead being manned and armed, containing their captains and officers, with a detachment of marines, attended this solemnity in the harbour, which was also crowded with an infinite number of other boats and vessels filled with spectators. About noon, the admiral having taken leave of a clergyman, and two friends who accompanied him, walked out of the great cabin to the quarter-deck, where two files of marines were ready to execute the sentence. He advanced with a firm deliberate step, a composed and resolute countenance, and resolved to suffer with his face uncovered, until his friends representing that his looks would possibly intimidate the soldiers, and prevent their taking aim properly, he submitted to their request, threw his hat on the deck, kneeled on a cushion, tied one white handkerchief over his eyes, and dropped the other as a signal for his executioners, who fired a volley so decisive, that five balls passed through his body, and he dropped down dead in an instant. The time in which this tragedy was acted, from his walking out of the cabin to his being deposited in the coffin, did not exceed three minutes.

Thus fell, to the astonishment of all Europe, Admiral John Byng; who, whatever his errors and indiscretions might have been, seems to have been rashly condemned, meanly given up, and cruelly sacrificed to vile considerations. The sentiments of his own fate he avowed on the verge of eternity, when there was no longer any cause of dissimulation, in the following declaration, which, immediately before his death, he delivered to the Marshal of the Admiralty: "A few moments will now deliver me from the virulent persecution, and frustrate the further malice, of my enemies; nor need I envy them a life subject to the sensations my injuries, and the injustice done me, must create. Persuaded I am, that justice will be done to my reputation hereafter; the manner and cause of raising and keeping up the popular clamour and prejudice against me will be seen through. I shall be considered (as I now perceive myself) a victim destined to divert the in-

*Paper delivered by him to the Marshal of the Admiralty.*

dignation and resentment of an injured and deluded people from the proper objects. My enemies themselves must now think me innocent. Happy for me, at this my last moment, that I know my own innocence, and am conscious that no part of my country's misfortunes can be owing to me. I heartily wish the shedding of my blood may contribute to the happiness and service of my country; but cannot resign my just claim to a faithful discharge of my duty according to the best of my judgment, and the utmost exertion of my ability for his majesty's honour and my country's service. I am sorry that my endeavours were not attended with more success, and that the armament under my command proved too weak to succeed in an expedition of such moment. Truth has prevailed over calumny and falsehood, and justice has wiped off the ignominious stain of my supposed want of personal courage, and the charge of disaffection. My heart acquits me of these crimes: but who can be presumptuously sure of his own judgment? If my crime is an error in judgment, or differing in opinion from my judges, and if yet the error in judgment should be on their side, God forgive them, as I do; and may the distress of their minds, and uneasiness of their consciences, which in justice to me they have represented, be relieved, and subside as my resentment has done. The Supreme Judge sees all hearts and motives, and to him I must submit the justice of my cause."

Notwithstanding all that has been said in his favour, notwithstanding the infamous arts that were practised to keep up the cry against him, notwithstanding this solemn appeal to Heaven in his last moments, and even self-conviction of innocence, the character of Admiral Byng, in point of personal courage, will still, with many people, remain problematical. They will still be of opinion, that if the spirit of a British admiral had been properly exerted, the French fleet would have been defeated, and Minorca relieved. A man's opinion of danger varies at different times, in consequence of an irregular tide of animal spirits, and he is actuated by considerations which he dares not avow. After an officer, thus influenced, has hesitated or kept aloof in the hour of trial, the mind, eager for its own justification, assembles, with surprising industry, every favourable circumstance of excuse, and broods over them with parental partiality, until it becomes not only satisfied, but even enamoured of their beauty and complexion, like a doting mother, blind to the deformity of her own offspring. Whatever Mr. Byng's internal feelings might have been, whatever consequences might have attended his behaviour on that occasion, as the tribunal before which he was tried acquitted him expressly of cowardice and treachery, he was without doubt a proper object for royal clemency; and so impartial posterity will judge him, after all those dishonourable motives of faction and of fear, by which his fate was influenced, shall be lost in oblivion, or remembered with disdain. The people of Great Britain, naturally fierce, impatient, and clamorous, have been too much indulged, upon every petty miscarriage, with trials, courts-martial, and dismissions, which tend only to render their military commanders rash and precipitate, the populace more licentious and intractable, and to disgrace the national character in the opinion of mankind.

END OF VOL. II.

www.ingramcontent.com/pod-product-compliance
Lightning Source LLC
Chambersburg PA
CBHW021219300426
44111CB00007B/362